Essays on Aristotle's *Rhetoric*

PHILOSOPHICAL TRADITIONS
General Editor
Amélie Oksenberg Rorty

Essays on Aristotle's *Rhetoric*

EDITED BY

Amélie Oksenberg Rorty

UNIVERSITY OF CALIFORNIA PRESS
Berkeley   Los Angeles   London

PN173
.E87

Pages 439–440 constitute an extension of this copyright page.

University of California Press
Berkeley and Los Angeles, California

University of California Press
London, England

Library of Congress Cataloging-in-Publication Data
Essays on Aristotle's Rhetoric / edited by Amélie Oksenberg Rorty.
    p.   cm. — (Philosophical traditions ; 6)
Includes bibliographical references.
ISBN 0-520-20227-9 (cl : alk. paper). — ISBN 0-520-20228-7 (pbk. : alk. paper)
1. Aristotle. Rhetoric.   I. Rorty, Amélie.   II. Series.
PN173.E82   1996
808'.5—dc20   95-14304
                                                                  CIP

Printed in the United States of America
2   3   4   5   6   7   8   9

The paper used in this publication meets the minimum requirements of American
National Standard for Information Sciences—Permanence of Paper for Printed
Library Materials, ANSI Z39.48-1984. ∞

For Jay Rorty
and
Laura Fraser

CONTENTS

PREFACE

It is time to reclaim the *Rhetoric* as a philosophic work, to analyze its relation to Aristotle's ethics, politics, and poetics; his psychology and logic; his account of practical reasoning; his views on how styles of language affect persuasive arguments. Renewed philosophic interest in a work that had been left largely in the hands of literary critics comes from several quite different directions: from a concern about the ethical constraints on public discourse; from an interest in the varieties and techniques of persuasive argument; and from investigations of the relations between Aristotle's theoretical works and his "handbooks" on practical reasoning and productive skills. Properly understood, these investigations lead us directly to the connections between Aristotle's psychology and his logic: What are the instruments of reasonable persuasion? How do appeals to the imagination and the emotions vary with subject matter and audience? How do linguistic devices actually work in persuasion? Does Aristotle have an implicit philosophy of language? How do rhetorical and political skills serve one another?

The *Rhetoric* provides a superb example of Aristotle's strategy of combining an analysis of the ends and structure of a practice with normative advice to its practitioners. His description of successful rhetorical strategies gives guiding counsel to aspiring rhetoricians, whether or not they intend to speak truthfully on behalf of what is worthy. But since he agrees with Plato that the best rhetoric—and, over the long run, also the most successful rhetoric—is truthful, he wants to give the best rhetoricians advice about how to construct sound as well as effectively persuasive arguments. He can make the best case for his complex position by concentrating on deliberative rhetoric, rhetoric intended to affect action-decisions whose benefits and merits are, at least in principle, capable of independent evaluation. It is for this reason that he treats epideictic rhetoric—funeral speeches and *encomia* presenting actions or *ēthē* for public admiration or condemnation—as exhortations, rather than as the brilliant showpieces they had become in the hands of sophists.[1] And it is for this reason, too, that he introduces so much of his own ethical theory to provide premises for the kind of forensic rhetoric that had become a highly formalized and specialized legal oratory.

Just as maps provide the necessary background for following the strategies of successful battles, so exemplary rhetorical speeches illustrate Aristotle's account of successful rhetorical technique. Three examples of model rhetorical speeches introduce the essays in this volume. Demosthenes' (c. 384/5–322 B.C.) speech, "The Son of Teisias Against Callicles, Regarding Damage to a Piece of Property," is a stellar example of forensic rhetoric. Thucydides' (c. 460–400 B.C.) (reconstructed) debate between Cleon and Diodotus, held in the Athenian Assembly in the summer of 427 B.C. is an outstanding example of deliberative rhetoric. It may seem strange to use Abraham Lincoln's Gettysburg Address (19 November 1863) to demonstrate the work of epideictic rhetoric. But as Garry Wills has shown, the Gettysburg Address is a compressed, skillful adaptation of Pericles' Funeral Address, one which—like the debate presented by Thucydides—blends praise with exhortation. Both addresses are set within the frame of a highly politicized interpretation of the "genius" of a *polis*.[2]

The essays in this volume have been organized to follow the rough sequence of topics presented in the *Rhetoric*. After discussing the proper ends of rhetoric, "Structuring Rhetoric" examines the structures of persuasive arguments; it sketches an account of the role of *ēthos, pathē, phantasia,* and *lexis* in binding the outcome of rhetorical persuasion to the future actions of the audience. The papers by Brunschwig, Wardy, and Burnyeat analyze rhetorical argument: Brunschwig discusses the role of dialectic in rhetoric; Wardy presents an account of the role of truth in rhetorical arguments; Burnyeat's interpretation of the enthymeme suggests a comprehensive revision in Aristotle's account of persuasive, argumentative reasoning. Engberg-Pedersen and Irwin discuss the ethical character of the rhetorician; Halliwell and Reeve explore the interdependence of politics and rhetoric. Leighton, Cooper, Frede, Striker, and Nussbaum discuss the ways that Aristotle's psychology—his views about emotions and motives—affects his advice to rhetoricians. Ricoeur and Moran argue that Aristotle's account of metaphorical speech links his philosophical psychology to the "pragmatics of language." Cary shows how several classical speeches exemplify Aristotle's categories of persuasion. Finally, Kennedy sketches the history of the composition of the

Rhetoric and its influence on oratorical practice as well as on the theory of rhetoric.

Many people and many places have contributed to the making of this book. If it had not been for a long-standing, passionate desire to visit the Hermitage and to explore St. Petersburg, I might not have discovered the riches of Aristotle's *Rhetoric*. It is embarrassing to confess that I originally accepted an invitation from Martha Nussbaum and Juha Sihvola—organizers of the 1991 Helsinki conference on Aristotle's *Rhetoric*—largely because it offered an opportunity to take the train from Helsinki to the Finland Station. As it turned out, however, the stimulating papers and searching discussions by the participants in the Helsinki seminars awoke my interest in the work. The van Leer Institute in Jerusalem and the Woodrow Wilson Center provided ideal conditions for the preparation of "Structuring Rhetoric"; Maude Chaplin and the audience at the Boston Area Colloquium in Ancient Philosophy at Wellesley College gave me useful comments; Mount Holyoke College provided a generous Faculty Research Grant. I am grateful to Myles Burnyeat and Ruth Nevo for excellent advice and illuminating discussions. Mary Whitlock Blundell, David Furley, and Markus Woerner saw me through some textual problems; Scott Ruescher and Rita Bashaw provided cheerful and efficient help in constructing the bibliography.

A.O.R.

NOTES

1. 1368a6 ff.: "If you intend to praise, consider what you would have suggested; if you intend to suggest, consider what you would praise." See Gorgias, *Encomium of Helen*, trans. D. M. MacDowell (Bristol, 1982); Lysias, *Selected Speeches*, ed. C. Carey (Cambridge, 1989).

2. See G. Wills, *Lincoln at Gettysburg* (New York, 1992), especially pp. 41–62, 249–259. Wills argues that Lincoln must have been familiar with the tradition that drew directly from Gorgias and Thucydides. To show how closely Lincoln follows rhetorical *lexes*, Wills also sends us to Lysias's speech during the Corinthian War (80–81); Demosthenes' speech on the Battle of Chaeronea (32–34); and Aspasia's speech, recited by Socrates in Plato's *Menexenus*.

Demosthenes by Polyeuktos. Roman copy in marble of a bronze of 280 B.C. Height with plinth approximately 6′ 7½″. The hands are restored on the basis of other replicas and literary evidence. The nose and details of the feet are also restored. Photo © Jo Selsing. Courtesy Ny Carlsberg Glyptotek, Copenhagen.

EXEMPLARY
RHETORICAL SPEECHES

FORENSIC RHETORIC

Demosthenes (c. 384/5–322 B.C.), "The Son of Teisias Against Callicles, Regarding Damage to a Piece of Property"*

[Demosthenes' speech is a tightly argued defense of a farmer charged with property damage. Because the defendant would have had to plead his case in his own voice, Demosthenes had to devise a speech that the judges would gauge appropriate to such a person. It seems that the farmer had constructed a wall around his property, thereby rerouting a course of water in such a way as to cause his neighbor's fields to be flooded. Demosthenes' brilliant defense shows the wide scope of the detailed knowledge the forensic rhetorician requires: in this case, he must not only know the law governing the enclosure of land and the particular history of these farmers' previous disputes, but he must also be able to give a graphic explanation of how water drains along a roadway, and centrally—since he is writing a speech to be delivered by the defendant on his own behalf—he must capture and represent the character, motives, and speech of quarrelsome neighboring farmers.]

There is after all, men of Athens, nothing more vexatious than to have a neighbour who is base and covetous; the very thing which has fallen to my lot. For Callicles, having set his heart on my land, has pestered me with malicious and baseless litigation: in the first place he suborned his cousin to claim my property, but the claim was proved manifestly false, and I got the better of that intrigue; then, again, he secured two awards against me

*Reprinted by permission of the publishers and the Loeb Classical Library from Demosthenes, *Vol. 6: Private Orations L–VIII*, translated by A. T. Murray, Cambridge, Mass.: Harvard University Press, 1964. Selections from pp. 167–181, 187 (oration 56: 1–26, 35).

for default, one in an action brought in his own name for one thousand drachmae, and another in an action which he persuaded his brother Callicrates, who is here in court, to bring. I beg you all to listen to me, and to give me your attention, not because I am going to show myself an able speaker, but in order that you may learn from the facts themselves that I am manifestly the victim of a malicious and baseless suit.

. . . My father built the wall around this land almost before I was born. . . . In all these years no one ever came to object or make complaint (and yet of course it often rained then, just as it does now); no one made any opposition at the start, as he would have done, if my father by walling in his land had caused injury to anyone; nor did anyone forbid him, or protest against his action. And yet, Callicles, when you saw that the watercourse was being dammed, you people might, I suppose, have gone at once to my father and complained angrily, and said to him, "Teisias, what is this that you are doing? Are you damming the watercourse? Why, then the water will burst through on to our land." In that case, if he had seen fit to desist, you and I would be having no quarrel with one another; or, if he paid no heed, and any such mischief resulted, you would have been able to avail yourself of those who were present as witnesses. . . . [M]en of Athens, I adduce their own acts as the strongest evidence against them all; for how is it that not one of them ever protested, or lodged a complaint, or even uttered a word of censure, but they were content to submit to this injury?

Well, I think that what I have said is by itself a sufficient answer to their shameless claims; but that you may be assured, men of Athens, on other grounds as well, that my father committed no wrong in walling in the land, and that these men have uttered nothing but falsehoods, I shall try to explain to you even more clearly. That the land is our private property is admitted by these men themselves. . . . [T]he space between my property and theirs is a road, and as a hilly country encircles them, unluckily for the farms, the water that flows down runs, as it happens, partly into the road, and partly on to the farms. And in particular, that which pours into the road, whenever it has free course, flows down along the road, but when there is any stoppage, then it of necessity overflows upon the farms. Now this particular piece of land, as it happened, was inundated after a heavy downpour had occurred. As a result of neglect, when my father was not yet in possession of the land, . . . the water overflowed two or three times, wrought damage to the land, and was more and more making itself a path. For this reason my father, when he saw it (so I am informed by those acquainted with the circumstances), inasmuch as the neighbours also began to encroach upon the property and walk across it, built around it this enclosing wall. . . . Callicles says that I am doing him an injury by having walled off the watercourse. . . . If it were not admitted to be our

private property, we should perhaps be guilty of this wrongdoing, if we had fenced off a piece of public land; but as it is, they do not dispute this, and on the land there are trees planted, vines and figs. Yet who would think of planting these in a watercourse? Nobody, surely. Again, who would think of burying his own ancestors there? . . . Well, both these things have been done. For not only were the trees planted before my father built the wall, but the tombs are old, and were built before we acquired the property. Yet, since this is the case, what stronger argument could there be, men of Athens? The facts afford manifest proof. . . .
. . . [C]onsider whether any one of you has ever seen or heard of a watercourse existing by the side of a road. I think that in the whole country there is not a single one. For what could induce any man to make a channel through his private lands for water which would otherwise have gone rushing down a public road? And what one of you, whether in the country or the city would allow water passing along the highway to flow into his farm or his house? On the contrary, when it forces its way in, is it not our habit to dam or wall it off? . . . If, men of the jury, there had been a watercourse below me to receive the water, I should perhaps have been wrong in not letting it in on my land, just as on certain other farms there are recognized watercourses in which the first landowners let the water flow (as they do the gutter-drains from the houses), and others again receive it from them in like manner. But on the land in question no one gives the water over to me or receives it from me. How, then, can it be a watercourse? . . . But this is the thing that is most outrageous of all, that Callicles, when the water overflows on his land, brings up huge stones and walls it off, but has brought suit for damages against me on the ground that my father was guilty of wrongdoing, because when the same thing happend to his land, he built an enclosing wall. . . .
. . . [Callicles] is himself at fault, first in that he made the road narrower by extending his wall beyond the property line, in order to enclose the trees of the road, and, secondly, in that he threw the rubbish into it, from which actions it resulted that he made the road higher as well as narrower. . . . But I shall now endeavour to show you that he has brought a suit for such heavy damages against me without having suffered any loss or damage worthy of mention. Before they undertook this malicious action against me, my mother and theirs were intimate friends and used to visit one another, as was natural, since both lived in the country and were neighbours, and since, furthermore, their husbands had been friends while they lived. Well, my mother went to see theirs, and the latter told her with weeping what had happened, and showed her the effects; this, men of the jury, is the way in which I learned all the facts. And I am telling you just what I heard from my mother;—as I speak the truth, so may many blessings be mine; if I am lying, may the opposite befall me.

She averred that she saw, and heard from their mother, that some of the barley got wet (she saw them drying it), but not so much as three medimni, and about half a medimnus of wheat flour; also, she said, a jar of olive oil had tilted over, but had not been damaged. So trivial, men of the jury, was the loss that befell them, yet for this I am made defendant in a suit with damages fixed at a thousand drachmae! . . . But since in the beginning my father was within his rights in enclosing the land and these people never made any complaint during the lapse of so long a time, and the others who were severely damaged make no complaint any more than they; and since it is the custom of all of you to drain the water from your houses and lands into the road, and not, heaven knows, to let it flow in from the road, what need is there to say more? These facts of themselves make it clear that the suit against me is a baseless and malicious one, since I am guilty of no wrong, and they have not suffered the damage they allege. . . .

Do not, then, men of the jury, I beg you in the name of Zeus and the gods, leave me as the prey of these men, when I have done no wrong. I do not care so much about the penalty, hard as that is on persons of small means; but they are absolutely driving me out of the deme by their persecution and baseless charges. To prove that I have done no wrong, I was ready to submit the matter for settlement to fair and impartial men who knew the facts, and I was ready to swear the customary oath; for I thought that would be the strongest proof I could bring before you, who are yourselves upon oath. . . .

DELIBERATIVE RHETORIC

*Thucydides (c. 460–400 B.C.), "Cleon and Diodotus Debate
the Fate of Mytilene," 427 B.C.**

[The debate between Cleon and Diodotus was held in the Athenian Assembly in
the summer of 427 B.C., the day after a vote had been passed to kill all the men
of Mytilene as a punishment for their defiance of Athenian authority. A proposal
to reconsider that decision led to the debate. The ingenious arguments on both
sides exemplify some of the characteristics that Aristotle marks as central to
deliberative rhetoric: considerations of prudence and justice, the projected political and psychological consequences of the decision and the likelihood of encouraging—or entrenching—similar rebellious attitudes amongst allies.]

A meeting of the assembly was held . . . at which various opinions were
expressed by the several speakers. One of these was Cleon son of Claene-
tus, who had been successful in carrying the earlier motion to put the
Mytilenaeans to death. He was not only the most violent of the citizens,
but at that time had by far the greatest influence with the people. He now
came forward a second time and spoke as follows:

"On many other occasions in the past I have realized that a democracy
is incompetent to govern others, but more than ever to-day, when I
observe your change of heart concerning the Mytilenaeans. The fact is
that, because your daily life is unaffected by fear and intrigue in your
relations to each other, you have the same attitude towards your allies
also, and you forget that whenever you are led into error by their rep-
resentations or yield out of pity, your weakness involves you in danger
and does not win the gratitude of your allies. For you do not reflect that
the empire you hold as a despotism imposed upon subjects who, for their
part, do intrigue against you and submit to your rule against their will,
who render obedience, not because of any kindnesses you may do them
to your own hurt, but because of such superiority as you may have
established by reason of your strength rather than of their goodwill. But
quite the most alarming thing is, if nothing we have resolved upon shall
be settled once for all, and if we shall refuse to recognize that a state which
has inferior laws that are inviolable is stronger than one whose laws are
good but without authority; that ignorance combined with self-restraint
is more serviceable than cleverness combined with recklessness; and that
simpler people for the most part make better citizens than the more

*Reprinted by permission of the publishers and the Loeb Classical Library from Thucy-
dides, *Vol. 2: History of the Peloponnesian War, Books III and IV*, translated by Charles Forster
Smith, rev. ed., Cambridge, Mass.: Harvard University Press, [1930] 1988. Selections from
pp. 57–85 (3.36–3.48).

shrewd. The latter always want to show that they are wiser than the laws, and to dominate all public discussions, as if there could never be weightier questions on which to declare their opinions, and as a consequence of such conduct they generally bring their states to ruin; the former, on the contrary, mistrusting their own insight, are content to be less enlightened than the laws and less competent than others to criticise the words of an able speaker, but being impartial judges rather than interested contestants they generally prosper. Thus, then, we ought to act and not be so excited by eloquence and combat of wits as to advise the Athenian people contrary to our own judgment.

"As for me, I have not changed my opinion, and I wonder at those who propose to debate again the question of the Mytilenaeans and thus interpose delay, which is in the interest of those who have done the wrong; for thus the edge of the victim's wrath is duller when he proceeds against the offender, whereas the vengeance that follows upon the very heels of the outrage exacts a punishment that most nearly matches the offence. And I wonder, too, who will answer me and undertake to prove that the wrong-doings of the Mytilenaeans are beneficial to us but that our misfortunes prove injurious to our allies. Manifestly he must either have such confidence in his powers of speech as to undertake to show that what is universally accepted as true has not been established, or else, incited by gain, will by an elaborate display of specious oratory attempt to mislead you. . . .

". . . I can make allowance for men who resorted to revolt because they were unable to bear your rule or because they were compelled by your enemies to do so; but men who inhabited a fortified island and had no fear of our enemies except by sea, and even there were not without the protection of a force of their own triremes, who moreover were independent and were treated by us with the highest consideration, when these men have acted thus, what else is it but conspiracy and rebellion rather than revolt—for revolt is the work of those who suffer oppression—and a deliberate attempt by taking their stand on the side of our bitterest enemies to bring about our destruction? And yet this is assuredly a more heinous thing than if they had gone to war against us by themselves for the acquisition of power. . . . [T]he Mytilenaeans from the first ought never to have been treated by us with any more consideration than our other allies, and then they would not have broken out into such insolence; for it is human nature in any case to be contemptuous of those who pay court but to admire those who will not yield.

"Let them be punished, therefore, even now, in a manner befitting their crime, and do not put the blame upon the aristocrats and exonerate the common people. . . . Consider, moreover, your allies: if you inflict upon those who wilfully revolt no greater punishment than upon those who revolt under compulsion from our foes, which of them, think you, will not revolt on a slight pretext, when the alternatives are liberty if he succeeds or a fate not irreparable if he fails? We, on the other hand, shall have to risk our money and our lives against each separate state, and when we succeed we shall recover a ruined state and be deprived for the future of its revenue, the source of our strength, whereas if we fail we shall be adding fresh enemies to those we have already, and when we should be resisting our present foes we shall be fighting our own allies. . . .

"I can sum up what I have to say in a word. If you take my advice, you will do not only what is just to the Mytilenaeans but also at the same time what is expedient for us; but if you decide otherwise, you will not win their gratitude but will rather bring a just condemnation upon yourselves; for if these people had a right to secede, it would follow that you are wrong in exercising dominion. But if, right or wrong, you are still resolved to maintain it, then you must punish these people in defiance of equity as your interests require; or else you must give up your empire and in discreet safety practise the fine virtues you preach. Resolve also to punish them with the same penalty that has already been voted, and that those who have escaped the plot shall not appear to have less feeling than those who framed it, bearing in mind what they would probably have done to you had they won the victory, especially since they were the aggressors. Indeed it is generally those who wrong another without cause that follow him up to destroy him utterly, perceiving the danger that threatens from an enemy who is left alive; for one who has been needlessly injured is more dangerous if he escape than an avowed enemy who expects to give and take.

"Do not, then, be traitors to your own cause, but recalling as nearly as possible how you felt when they made you suffer and how you would then have given anything to crush them, now pay them back. Do not become tender-hearted at the sight of their present distress, nor unmindful of the danger that so lately hung over you, but chastise them as they deserve, and give to your other allies plain warning that whoever revolts shall be punished with death. For if they realise this, the less will you have to neglect your enemies and fight against your own allies."

Such was Cleon's speech. After him Diodotus son of Eucrates, who in the earlier meeting had been the principal speaker against putting the Mytilenaeans to death, came forward now also and spoke as follows:

"I have no fault to find with those who have proposed a reconsideration of the question of the Mytilenaeans, nor do I commend those who object to repeated deliberation on matters of the greatest moment; on the contrary, I believe the two things most opposed to good counsel are haste and passion, of which the one is wont to keep company with folly, the other with an undisciplined and shallow mind. . . .

". . . I have come forward neither as an advocate of the Mytilenaeans in opposition to Cleon nor as their accuser. For the question for us to consider, if we are sensible, is not what wrong they have done, but what is the wise course for us. For no matter how guilty I show them to be, I shall not on that account bid you to put them to death, unless it is to our advantage; and if I show that they have some claim for forgiveness, I shall not on that account advise you to spare their lives, if this should prove clearly not to be for the good of the state. In my opinion we are deliberating about the future rather than the present. And as for the point which Cleon especially maintains, that it will be to our future advantage to inflict the penalty of death, to the end that revolts may be less frequent, I also in the interest of our future prosperity emphatically maintain the contrary. And I beg you not to be led by the speciousness of his argument to reject the practical advantages in mine. For embittered as you are toward the Mytilenaeans, you may perhaps be attracted by his argument, based as it is on the more legal aspects of the case; we are, however, not engaged in a law-suit with them, so as to be concerned about the question of right and wrong; but we are deliberating about them, to determine what policy will make them useful to us.

"Now the death-penalty has been prescribed in various states for many offences which are not so serious as this is, nay, for minor ones; but nevertheless men are so inspired by hope as to take the risk; indeed, no one ever yet has entered upon a perilous enterprise with the conviction that this plot was condemned to failure. And as to states, what one that was meditating revolt ever took the decisive step in the belief that the resources at hand, whether its own or contributed by its allies, were inadequate for success? All men are by nature prone to err, both in private and in public life, and there is no law which will prevent them; in fact, mankind has run the whole gamut of penalties, making them more and more severe, in the hope that the transgressions of evil-doers might be abated. It is probable that in ancient times the penalties prescribed for the greatest offences were relatively mild, but as transgressions still occurred, in course of time the penalty was seldom less than death. But even so there is still transgression. Either, then, some terror more dreadful than death must be discovered, or we must own that death at least is no prevention. Nay, men are lured into hazardous enterprises by the constraint of poverty, which makes them bold, by the insolence and pride of affluence, which makes them greedy, and by the various passions engendered in the other conditions of human life as these are severally mastered by some mighty and irresistible impulse. Then, too, Hope and Desire are everywhere; Desire leads, Hope attends; Desire contrives the plan, Hope suggests the facility of fortune; the two passions are most baneful, and being unseen phantoms prevail over seen dangers. Besides these, fortune contributes in no less degree to urge men on; for she sometimes presents herself unexpectedly and thus tempts men to take risks even when their resources are inadequate, and states even more than men, inasmuch as the stake is the greatest of all—their own freedom or empire over others—and the individual, when supported by the whole people, unreasonably overestimates his own strength. In a word, it is impossible, and a mark of extreme simplicity, for anyone to imagine that when human nature is wholeheartedly bent on any undertaking it can be diverted from it by rigorous laws or by any other terror.

"We must not, therefore, so pin our faith on the penalty of death as a guarantee against revolt as to make the wrong decision, or lead our rebellious subjects to believe that there will be no chance for them to repent and in the briefest time possible put an end to their error. Consider now: according to your present policy if a city has revolted and then realizes that it will fail, it may come to terms while still able to pay the indemnity and to keep up its tribute in the future; but, in the other case, what city, think you, will not prepare itself more thoroughly than now, and hold out in siege to the last extremity, if it makes no difference whether it capitulates quickly or at its leisure? And as for us, how can we fail to suffer loss, incurring the expense of besieging a city because it will not surrender, and, if we capture it, recovering one that is ruined, and losing thereafter the revenue from it—the source of our strength against our enemies? We must not, therefore, be such rigorous judges of the delinquents as to suffer harm ourselves, but we must rather see how for the time to come, by punishing moderately, we may have at our service dependent cities that are strong in material resources; and we must deem it proper to protect ourselves against revolts, not by the terror of our laws, but rather by the vigilance of our administration. At present we do just the opposite: whenever a free people that is forced into subjection revolts, as it naturally will, in order to recover its independence, we think that, as soon as we have subdued it, we must punish it severely. We ought, on the contrary, instead of rigorously chastising free peoples when they revolt, to watch them rigorously before they revolt, and thus forestall their even thinking of such a thing; and when we have subdued a revolt, we ought to put the blame on as few as possible.

"And do you consider, too, how great a mistake you would make in another point also by following Cleon's advice. At the present time the populace of all the cities is well disposed to you, and either does not join with the aristocrats in revolting, or, if forced to do so, is hostile from the beginning to those who stirred up the revolt; and so, when you go to war, you have the populace of the rebellious city as your allies. If, however, you destroy the populace in Mytilene, which took no part in the revolt, and which voluntarily put the city into your hands as soon as it got hold of arms, in the first place you will be guilty of killing your benefactors, and, in the second place, you will bring about what the influential men most wish: the next time they instigate a revolt among our allies they will at once have the populace on their side, because you will have published it abroad that the same punishment is ordained for the innocent and for the guilty. Why, even if they were guilty you should pretend not to know it, to the end that the only class that is still friendly to us may not become hostile. And it is, I think, far more conducive to the maintenance of our dominion that we should willingly submit to be wronged, than that we should destroy, however justly, those whom we ought not to destroy. And whereas Cleon claims that this punishment combines justice and expediency, it appears that in such a policy the two cannot be combined.

"Do you, then, recognize that mine is the better course, and without being unduly swayed by either pity or clemency—for neither would I have you influenced by such motives—but simply weighing the considerations I have urged, accede to my proposal: pass sentence at your leisure upon the Mytilenaeans whom Paches sent here as guilty, but let the rest dwell in peace. Such a course will be best for the future, and will cause alarm among our enemies at once; for he who is wise in counsel is stronger against the foe than he who recklessly rushes on with brute force." . . .

EPIDEICTIC RHETORIC

Abraham Lincoln (1809–1865), "Gettysburg Address,"
19 November 1863

Four score and seven years ago our fathers brought forth on this continent, a new nation, conceived in Liberty, and dedicated to the proposition that all men are created equal.

Now we are engaged in a great civil war, testing whether that nation, or any nation so conceived and so dedicated, can long endure. We are met on a great battlefield of that war. We have come to dedicate a portion of that field, as a final resting place for those who here gave their lives that that nation might live. It is altogether fitting and proper that we should do this.

But, in a larger sense, we can not dedicate—we can not consecrate—we can not hallow—this ground. The brave men, living and dead, who struggled here, have consecrated it, far above our poor power to add or detract. The world will little note, nor long remember what we say here, but it can never forget what they did here. It is for us the living, rather, to be dedicated here to the unfinished work which they who fought here have thus far so nobly advanced. It is rather for us to be here dedicated to the great task remaining before us—that from these honored dead we take increased devotion to that cause for which they gave the last full measure of devotion—that we here highly resolve that these dead shall not have died in vain—that this nation, under God, shall have a new birth of freedom—and that government of the people, by the people, for the people, shall not perish from the earth.

Structuring Rhetoric

Amélie Oksenberg Rorty

Despite having been written at different times, patched together of different pieces, and being far from the most elegant or perspicuously organized of Aristotle's writings, the *Rhetoric* forms a relatively coherent and familiar structure. In preparing a handbook for the rhetorician, Aristotle proceeds as he does for a discussion of any craft. He articulates a theory of its practice by locating it in a field of related activities; he formulates the proper end of rhetoric and distinguishes its varieties; and he analyzes the materials and techniques of the craft, the forms and premises of persuasive arguments, the psychology of audiences, and the techniques of style. Because he thinks previous authors on rhetoric have misunderstood the scope and therefore the primary concerns of the craft, Aristotle uncharacteristically gives his predecessors short shrift: he announces he must start the subject afresh (1354a1–3 ff.).[1]

THE AIMS OF RHETORIC

The proper aim of rhetoric is that of finding the best available means of persuasion, whatever the subject may be (1355a4 ff., 1355b26 ff.). Since the most effective exercise of any craft or faculty is conceptually connected to fulfilling its norm-defined aims, Aristotle's counsel is directed to guiding the master craftsman who is responsive to the larger issues that surround the exercise of his skill: he is a rhetorician speaking about important matters to those authorized to affect them. Aristotle's advice to the rhetorician imports the results of this philosophic investigation: the *Rhetoric* presupposes and is implicitly informed by Aristotle's logical works, by his philosophy of mind and his theory of action; it is also strongly conjoined with his political and ethical theory. But while the rhetorician relies on these theories, he is not himself a philosopher, logician, statesman, or moralist.[2] In order to construct persuasive arguments, the skilled rhetorician must understand the beliefs and psychology of his audience; but the exemplary rhetorician is also directed by what is true and guided by a sound understanding of what is genuinely useful and right.[3] Ideally, the best oratory addresses the minds as well as the psychology of its audience.[4] Aristotle chides the authors of earlier handbooks on rhetoric for concentrating primarily on techniques for swaying the emotions of judges and legislators, instead of first and primarily considering the best modes of persuasion. Enthymemes and metaphors are most convincing when they are clear and plausible; and even maxim-ridden speeches are most persuasive when their assumptions and conclusions are reasonable (1355a4–1355b7). Aristotle wryly complains that addressing the emotions of a judge is like warping a ruler before using it. The best orator does not manipulate beliefs in order to make the worse appear to be the better course, but rather presents the best case in a way that is comprehensible and moving to each type of character (1113a30 ff.). In suiting his arguments to his audience—presenting a course of action as gloriously noble to the young and as prudent to the elderly—the rhetorician need not be lying.[5] Aristotle's ethical works are meant to show that the best life is—in principle, under ideal circumstances, and in the long run—also the most pleasant, the most expedient, and the noblest (1140a25–28, 1142a1–11, 1359a30–1363b4). As long as his rhetoric is also constrained by what is true and what is best, the rhetorician will not "warp the ruler."

But like all abilities and crafts, rhetoric can be used well or ill. As the existence of clever villains attests, sheer intelligence is not sufficient for virtue; so too, highly successful but canny and corrupt orators attest to the undeniable fact that not every billiant rhetorician is a *phronimos*. A clever huckster might be skilled at presenting himself as a trustworthy ally and wise advisor, without ever coming close to being a *phronimos*. Even if—in principle—the best way to seem wise and good is to be so, even if you can't fool all of the people all of the time, still you can fool plenty of people most of the time.

Nevertheless even the most debased forms of rhetoric presuppose some knowledge of logic and of ethics. The successfully perverse uses of a craft depend on the techniques and knowledge required by its exemplary exercise. The sophist must know the structure of sound arguments in order to mimic them; the huckster has to know the marks of virtue in order to parade it. Just as the concept of "belief" is essentially linked to that of "truth," so too the concept of "decision" is essentially linked to that of "good," and "persuasive" is essentially linked to "soundly argued." The opaque object of every decision is a genuine good; the opaque object of every belief is a genuine truth. Deciders and believers want the intentional objects of their decisions and desires to hit their real—and not merely their notional—objects.[6] Since even a debased audience aims at the opaque objects of its desires—at the real (and not merely the apparent) good—it implicitly wants its rhetoricians to be, and not merely to seem, good. It is for these functional normative reasons that the rhetorician must know how to present himself as substantively intelligent and virtuous, rather than merely as cleverly skilled at rhetoric. He must not only convince his audience that his arguments are sound, but also that, like the physician, he has their real interests—and not merely their surface desires—at heart (101b5 ff.).[7]

But this attempt to make the rhetorician seem ethically respectable is surely too easy; after all, rhetorical skills might be conceptually and normatively linked to knowledge of what is good and what is true, without the practice of rhetoric requiring such knowledge. The successful rhetorician might only need to know how to mimic what the various types of audiences—the young, the old, democrats, aristocrats—take to be indications of practical wisdom. Aristotle's point about the ethical directions of rhetoric is not the overly strong claim that every successful rhetorician must be a *phronimos;* but it is also not the relatively weak claim that, like all crafts, rhetoric is directed to its best and most successful exercise.

To see how Aristotle charts a middle ground—and how he links rhetoric and politics—we need to turn to the three types of rhetoric and their primary instruments of persuasion.

THE VARIETIES OF RHETORIC

The three types of rhetoric—ceremonial (*epideiktikon*), forensic (*dikanikon*), and deliberative (*sumbouleutikon*)—are distinguished by their aims and audiences. While many forms of argument (e.g., dialectic and the enthymeme) and some kinds of knowledge (e.g., psychology) are common to them all, these differences prescribe some specialized strategies of argumentation and some specialized knowledge (1358a36–1359a5).

Epideictic Rhetoric

Superficially at least, epideictic rhetoric is typically ceremonial. Addressed to a general audience, it is directed to praising honor and virtue, censuring vice and weakness. Because it is largely concerned with matters that are not under dispute, amplification (*auxesis*) provides its most suitable arguments. To persuade an audience to celebrate what is noble and to condemn what is shameful, the epideictic rhetorician must be familiar with what the audience takes as indications and signs (*sēmeia*) of those virtues which, like justice and courage, they find exceptionally useful (1366a28–1366b12). But because epideictic rhetoric also has a latent, important practical and educative function, Aristotle wants to bring at least some of its uses under the aegis of deliberative rhetoric. Since praise and blame motivate as well as indicate virtue, they are also implicitly intended to affect future action. The deliberative rhetorician can—by turning a phrase—use *encomia* to counsel a course of action. "If you intend to praise, consider what you would have suggested; if you intend to suggest (*hupothesthai*), consider what you would praise" (1368a6 ff.).

Aristotle's books on ethics provide some background psychology for epideictic oratory: in describing an admirable or despicable deed (*ergon*), the rhetorician relies on the criteria for voluntary action.[8] But since the ethical works are primarily focused on the character (*ēthos*) of the *phronimos*, they do not provide material for *encomia* of admirable deeds that may be performed out of character (1367b25–1368b). Nor does general discussion of *akrasia* in *Nicomachean Ethics* 7—introduced to solve an embarrassing philosophical problem about how a person can voluntarily act against his beliefs about what is best—help the epideictic rhetorician identify and describe vicious and contemptible deeds.

Forensic Rhetoric

Intended to establish individuals as guilty or innocent of specific actions, forensic rhetoric is directed to judges. To be persuasive, the rhetorician's arguments and descriptions must take into account the commonplace psychological opinions (*endoxa*) of typical judges, their beliefs about the motives of various types of characters and the occasions on which they might be tempted to break the law. Because "the past most admits of demonstration (*apodeixin*) and causal explanation (*aitiain*)," Aristotle says that the enthymeme is "best suited to forensic rhetoric" (1368a30 ff.).[9] He understands the persuasiveness of such arguments extremely broadly: an enthymeme can indicate what a reasonable person is entitled to infer about what happened and how it happened. So, for instance, a rhetorician might argue that if the suspect's footprints were at the scene of the crime, his fingerprints on the knife, and he had long harbored a murderous hatred for the victim, it is reasonable to conclude that he was guilty of murder.

The discussion of forensic rhetoric introduces psychological generalizations that Aristotle had not elsewhere treated in a more rigorous and philosophical manner. The ethical works are focused on character traits rather than on specific actions; and on virtue rather than vice and weakness. Like the epideictic rhetorician, the forensic rhetorician relies on a general theory of voluntary action. But to establish the guilt (or innocence) of the accused, he needs to represent that person's motives in some detail. The list of (what are commonly thought to be) the causes of action is surprisingly heterogeneous and long; chance, nature, compulsion, character, reasoning, energetic feistiness (*thumos*), and appetite (*epithumia*) (1369a5 ff.).[10] Aristotle's dismissal of chance, nature, and compulsion is quick: such causes remove the action from the sphere of what is "up to us." Equally casually, he says that the causes of voluntary actions— those that are formed by character-based habits, reasoning, and desire— appear to boil down to the desire for what is seen as good (*agathon*) or beneficial (*ta sumpheronta*) and for what seems pleasurable (1369b20 ff.). He has, as he says, already discussed the means by which a deliberative rhetorician can persuade an audience that a course of actions is beneficial (1.6–7.1362a15–1365b21). He therefore turns to a long and phenomenologically acute but unsystematic description of the many kinds of activities and situations whose pleasures might lure a person to injustice (*adikia*) (1.11).

The *endoxa* concerning pleasure are summarized in *Rhetoric* 1.11–12 (1369b32–1373a39): it is believed to be "a kind of motion (*kinēsis*) of the soul (*psychē*), a sudden, perceptible settling (*katastasis*) to its natural (*phusin*) condition." This view seems in direct conflict with the philosophical analysis presented in *Nicomachean Ethics* 10, where Aristotle denies that pleasure is a kind of motion (1173a32 ff., 1174a18 ff.), arguing that it is an activity in accordance with nature (*energeia kata phusin*) (1153a14 ff.).[11] The discrepancy between the two accounts should not be surprising: they play quite different explanatory roles. The discussion of pleasure in *Nicomachean Ethics* 7 and 10 is a direct continuation of a central theme of the *Ethics:* an examination of the connection between virtue and the goods that constitute *eudaimonia*.[12] Since pleasure is thought by many to be among those goods, if not actually the paramount good, it requires a thorough philosophic examination. But Aristotle is, in the *Rhetoric,* primarily concerned with typical *endoxa* about the role of pleasure in motivating unjust actions. Whatever the philosophic truth about pleasure may be, the rhetorician must—beyond the obvious issues of fact that arise in such cases—limit himself to considerations that roughly accord with judges' opinions. It is for this reason that the analysis of pleasure as a source of unlawful or unjust actions in *Rhetoric* 1.11–12 does not accord— and (oddly enough) should not accord—with what Aristotle thinks is the truth of the matter.

But since not even the lure of pleasure is by itself sufficient to cause action, Aristotle turns to a discussion of the psychology of various types of agents. To construct a plausible accusation or defense, the forensic rhetorician needs to represent the psychology of specific types of persons, as they might be young, powerless, and ambitious, or middle-aged, wealthy, and jealous. He can ignore the general differences between varieties of vice (*kakos*) and *akrasia:* in establishing guilt or innocence, it doesn't matter whether the accused is vicious or just weak. What matters is the likelihood of whether the accused—an impulsive young man, in debt, without resources, and disowned by his family—has voluntarily broken the law. The forensic rhetorician also needs to represent the circumstances under which it seems safe to be unlawful, common beliefs about the kinds of people who can be injured without risking retribution (1.12).

Deliberative Rhetoric

Deliberative rhetoric is directed to those who must decide on a course of action (members of the Assembly, for instance) and is typically concerned with what will turn out to be useful (*sumpheron*) or harmful (*blaberon*) as means to achieve specific ends in matters of defense, war and peace, trade and legislation. Since the advice of the deliberative rhetorician implies predictions about the outcomes of various policies, his conclusions are in principle testable. The deliberative rhetorician who wishes to retain his reputation as trustworthy must pay attention to what is, in fact, actually likely to happen. It is this feature of deliberative rhetoric—that it is more bound by reasonable expectations about the future than about current beliefs about responsibility—that marks the significant character of de- liberative rhetoric; it explains why Aristotle is so eager to distinguish its arguments from epideictic and forensic rhetoric.

This explains why Aristotle makes deliberative rhetoric the focus of his analysis: it most clearly reveals the primary importance of truth as it functions *within the craft of rhetoric itself.* Since the deliberative rhetorician persuades an audience to form decisive judgments (*kriseis*) that are ac- tually likely to affect their interests, he has the enormously difficult task of aligning his audience's conceptions of their *eudaimonia* with his own judgment about how various policies are actually likely to affect their welfare, whatever their beliefs may be. Vivid and well-known examples (*paradeigmata*) of similar events—events that are presumed to indicate what is likely to happen in the future—are the best sorts of arguments for deliberative rhetoric.

In the interest of preserving the distinctions among deliberative, fo- rensic, and epideictic rhetoric, Aristotle warns rhetoricians against con- fusing issues of benefit and harm with those of lawfulness (*to dikaion kai to adikon*) and honor (1358b23). Considerable disagreement continues about whether Aristotle thinks that issues of justice are (*a*) irrelevant to deliberative oratory or (*b*) relevant but subsidiary. Certainly Aristotle thinks that the virtues—and justice among them—constitute as well as serve *eudaimonia*.[13] Still, the general conceptual connection between what is just and what is fundamentally beneficial is compatible with the independence of the two sorts of arguments. As Thucydides' account of the Mytilenaean dialogue amply demonstrates, the kinds of considerations that demonstrate the benefits of a specific policy are markedly different from those that show it to be just.

Although the rhetorician ideally attempts to direct his audience to a course that would promote their real interests, not even the best rhetorician need intend to educate his audience, to structure their ends or interests, or to promote their *eudaimonia*, all things considered. To sustain his reputation as a trustworthy guide in political matters, the exemplary rhetorician need not be a philosopher or a *phronimos*. He needs rather to be able to take advice from a philosophically oriented *phronimos*, who counsels him on standard issue fears and desires, on conditions for responsibility, on how to construct sound arguments. Call that person "Aristotle." And call his advice, "*The Rhetoric*." We can now turn, as Aristotle himself does, to some of his advice about modes of persuasion that all rhetoricians share and the kinds of knowledge that they all require, independently of their specific aims and audiences.

DIALECTIC AND RHETORIC

As a technical skill, rhetoric is a counterpart (*antistrophos*) of dialectic (1354a1); Aristotle also calls it a part of dialectic (*morion*) similar to it (*homoiōma*) (1356a31–32).[14] A double connection ties dialectic and rhetoric. First, the *philosophic* analysis of the craft of rhetoric proceeds dialectically: it evaluates previous opinions on the subject, reflecting on the extent to which they save and explain the phenomena. Since he thinks his predecessors have misunderstood the subject, Aristotle cannot follow his usual courteous practice of reconstructing their rationale, attempting to systematize their views. But although he must start the subject afresh, Aristotle attempts as best he can, given the unscientific and problematic character of the subject matter, to integrate previous opinions into his own analysis. While he denies that forensic and epideictic oratory provide the primary models of rhetoric, he grants that they are important, independent species. And although he denies that rhetoricians are primarily concerned with swaying the emotions of their audiences, he manifestly thinks that this is an important feature of rhetorical argument. Second, the *rhetorician* himself relies on the results, the methods, and the skills of dialectic. Like the dialectician, the rhetorician does not have a distinctive, specific subject matter (1354a1–12, 1355b32 ff.). He depends on—and must skillfully use—a heterogeneous collection of accepted and often conflicting opinions for the details of his arguments: general *endoxa* about *eudaimonia*, the opinion of strategists about what is genuinely dangerous in battle, the views of philosophers about criteria for voluntary action, and the views of experienced legislators about what sorts of laws are enforceable. Like the dialectician and the sophist, the successful rhetorician must be able to construct contrary arguments: he must first represent and then refute the considerations that appear to weigh against his position.[15]

Although rhetoric absorbs the skills of logic, dialectic, and sophistical argument, it differs from them in some important respects (1359b9 ff.).[16] It differs from logic in that it addresses contingent particulars and from dialectic in having more specific aims. Dialectic encompasses both theoretical as well as practical inquiry: it can serve as "a process of criticism that provides a path to general principles" (101b3–4). Rhetoric is more narrowly practical: it attempts to bring an audience to a decisive judgment in such a way that they will not easily be swayed to a different course (104b1–4, 1356b32–1357a1, 1359b31–1396a2). It is for this reason that Aristotle remarks that "rhetoric is an offshoot (*paraphues*) of ethics (*tēs peri ta ēthē pragmateias*) that can justly be called politics" (1356a26). Offshoots carry nutriments in both directions; *phronimoi* and *politikoi* need to be able to persuade their fellows to cooperate. For his part, the rhetorician needs to understand what people want, in wanting happiness; he needs to be able to represent the motives of lawlessness; and he should know how various political systems shape the beliefs and desires of their citizens.[17]

THE PSYCHOLOGY OF RHETORICAL PERSUASION

Besides sharing certain forms of argumentation, all rhetoricians are served by an understanding of psychology. Rough empirical generalizations about the psychology of various types of audiences and the folk-psychological beliefs of his audience serve as instruments of persuasion; they also provide significant substantive premises for all sorts of arguments.[18]

Aristotle distinguishes three interconnected dimensions of persuasion (*pistis*): *ēthos*, *pathos*, and *logos*. Each of these interdependent avenues to persuasion explain the dominant place that Aristotle accords psychology in the *Rhetoric*.

First, the knowledge of psychology enables the orator to present himself as having a trustworthy *ēthos*. Second, it enables him to address the interests of his audience persuasively. Third, it provides some of the basic premises for his arguments.

Since we have already touched on the first point, we can, like Aristotle, be brief about it. The character of the speaker is manifest in his discourse—in what he says and how he says it.[19] It is implicit in the way he argues and in the way he addresses the character and emotions of his audience (1356a5 ff.). Particularly when he might seem to speak from his own interests or on his own behalf, the rhetorician must establish his credibility, his intelligence (*phronēsis* and *eunoia*), and character (*aretē*) as such traits might be perceived by his audience. Of course, land mines surround the phrase "perceived by his audience." The rhetorician must understand his audience's perspective: he shows himself to be trustworthy in their eyes by showing that he understands their interests. His success in urging a defensive military policy depends on his presenting himself as a reliable judge of what is worth fearing; and this in turn depends on his knowing what his audience considers dangerous. While it is possible to fake an honest manner, it is exceedingly difficult to maintain a reputation for *phronēsis* without actually giving a considerable amount of sound advice. A vulgar rhetorician might for a time succeed in dazzling an audience by playing to their preconceptions. But a few persuasive speeches do not make a successful rhetorician. Since a rhetorician's reputation is, over the course of time, at least in part measured by the consequences of the policies he recommends, it would be difficult for a vulgar rhetorician—one who has only pandered to immediate desires, without considering the real interests of his audience—to sustain a reputation for either good sense or virtue.

Still, Aristotle's solution allows for the possibility that a vulgar rhetorician might succeed in fooling the citizens of an extremely corrupt state for a long time. Such citizens systematically fail to understand their own well-being. They might, for instance, so deeply prefer wild luxury to a soundly continuing *paideia* that they would not recognize the harm of following the advice of a vulgar rhetorician who urged them on to ever greater luxury. Indeed it is one of the signs of a hopelessly bad polity that its citizens are no longer able to distinguish a vulgar rhetorician from a *phronimos*. The dark side of what is usually considered Aristotle's optimism is that a polity gets the rhetoricians it deserves; and the distress of a corrupt polity is deepened by the rhetoricians it favors.

The second reason for including an extensive discussion of psychology follows from the aim of rhetoric. Since the point of rhetoric is to influence the kind of judgment (*krisis*) that is effectively an evaluative decision, rhetorical arguments are presented in the form of practical deliberations (1357a1–2). Judicial decisions, legislative enactments, praise, and blame express decisions that are, as we would say, performative actions.[20] In contrast to the arguments of philosophical dialectic that form opinions (*doxa*), or in the *mimēseis* of dramatic action that produce *katharsis*, the judgments formed by rhetorical persuasion carry the weight of decisions (1355a5 ff.). They are not only true or false, soundly or wildly derived, but also appropriate or inappropriate, reasonable or silly, germane or irrelevant to the situation. But since choice requires the conjunction of thought (*dianoia*) and desire (*orexis*) (*DA* 3.10; *NE* 6.2), the rhetorician must influence the desires as well as the beliefs of his audience, even when there are *phronimoi* among them. It is entirely appropriate—and indeed necessary—for the rhetorician to address the character of his audience: he crystallizes their general ends into specific desires.[21] The orator's speech—what he says and how he says it—links the character and desires of his audience to the decisions and actions the orator wants them to take (1355a20 ff.).

The third reason for Aristotle's including a detailed discussion of *ēthē* and *pathē* among rhetorical *topoi* is that pretheoretical psychology provides useful information for practical deliberation.[22] Like the poet, the rhetorician needs rough generalizations to represent the thoughts and desires, speech and action of many different types of agents, as they would be perceived by his audience. In urging the Assembly to send a belligerent rather than conciliatory delegation to a rebellious colony, the rhetorician must give a plausible account of the probable psychological effects of both policies on that particular colony. Here again, the deliberative rhetorician faces the enormously difficult task of coordinating his best understanding of what is, in fact, likely to happen with the folk-psychological beliefs of his audience, and to do this in a way that persuades.

Aristotle can send readers to *De Anima,* the *Politics,* and the ethical works for general propositions about practical reason and the teleological structure of action. Like the pre-theoretical biology of which it is a branch, the psychology of the *Rhetoric* hardly qualifies as a theory, let alone as explanatory scientific knowledge. But descriptive psychology is even further from rigor than descriptive biology: our psychology—the formation of attitudes and motives—is "up to us" (*eph hēmin estin*) to an astonishing degree (*DA* 3.3.427b15–21). Indeed rhetoric, politics, and poetry would have virtually no place if this were not so. Since human psychology is also strongly affected by education and political circumstance, its generalizations are not only qualified by constitutional psychophysical factors but also by other complex subvariables: age, sex, and temperament in a democracy or in the members of a specific class in an aristocracy.

The psychology that is essential to the *Rhetoric* suffers from yet a further restriction. Unlike the analysis of *aisthēsis* and *phantasia* in *De Anima* and the characterization of *phronēsis* in the ethical works, the discussion of character and the emotions in the *Rhetoric* does not proceed by describing an ideal type. The rhetorician is concerned with the typical psychology of the ambitious youth or the power-hungry demagogue rather than with the idealized psychology of the *phronimos* or that of the relatively noble tragic protagonist.[23] Even the best deliberative rhetorician attempting to persuade his audience of significant benefits and dangers can only rely on rough generalizations about the psychology— the interests, motives, and habits—that might be typical of potential allies and enemies. He can only address the fears and hatreds that are typical of various audiences, presenting considerations that are, at best, only likely to move them to pity or emulation. Instead of resembling a quasi-scientific treatise on breeding the best, most fertile chickens, the *Rhetoric* is like a treatise telling farmers how to get ordinary chickens to lay good eggs. For all of that, Aristotle is not one to shy away from giving important advice based on rough generalizations where it can be usefully given.

ARISTOTLE'S THEORY OF CHARACTER (*ĒTHOS*)[24]

The Constituents of Character[25]

The dispositions and habits that constitute character are layered in a veritable archaeological site. Some traits—like being hot-tempered or slow-witted—are constitutionally based; other derive from a person's social condition (as those with power are said to be serious and dignified [2.16–17]); yet others are formed by an individual's polity (as citizens in a democracy are said to love liberty). Still others (the habits that constitute the virtues and vices, for example) derive from individual education and experience (1114b26 ff.).[26]

As described in the *Rhetoric,* a person's character combines relatively specific first-order traits with a variety of second-order dispositions. Among the first are the love of honor typical of the young, the love of liberty typical of citizens in a democracy, and the suspiciousness of the elderly. Some second-order traits are modifiers or modalities of first-order traits (as the intensity with which the young love and hate; the feebleness of the emotions of the elderly); others are dispositions to acquire specific first-order traits (because the elderly are fond of themselves [*philautoi*] they are disposed to being small-minded and primarily guided by considerations of utility). Many second-order dispositions (*hexeis*) govern or control first-order *hexeis*. However difficult it may be, a constitutionally irascible person can, in principle, be good-tempered; this requires that he control some of his first-order traits. Many *hexeis*—particularly the cognitive components of the virtues and vices—are actively magnetizing because they structure what is salient or dominant in an individual's perceptual and conceptual field: they can predispose him to specific emotions. (For instance, someone who habitually perceives situations as dangerous is especially liable to fear; someone preoccupied with honor or wealth is especially liable to envy or emulation; someone who habitually notices slights is disposed to anger.) Both first-order and second-order character traits typically appear along a continuum of paired contraries. The various *hexeis* that form an individual's character fall somewhere on a scale between affability and surliness, between extravagance and miserliness.

Can two individuals have roughly the same character, but one be virtuous, the other not? Not surprisingly, Aristotle's answer is: in one sense, no, and in another, yes, depending on the generality with which their traits are described. To the extent that a person's character includes habits and ends that arise from individual experience and circumstance, his character is as wholly individuated as anything within an Aristotelian frame can be. So described, an individual's character includes the specification of his virtues. But for other purposes—like those of the *Rhetoric* for example—individuals can be adequately characterized by their general features. To say of someone that he is a powerful young democrat or an old aristocrat is to locate a range of his general traits, a rough guide to his typical thoughts, habits, and desires. In this sense, two individuals of the same character type can differ in virtue, in the specific ways that their ends form their desires and actions.

Putting words in his mouth, we can now present a rough first approximation of Aristotle's account of character. A person's character consists of those long-standing actively dispositional qualities and traits—his natural capacities and habits—that (by setting the general direction of his desires and the range of his passions) direct his choices. It is his nature and his second nature.[27]

The Structure of Character

A person's character, particularly as it structures his evaluative judgments and choices, is not just a heap of heterogeneous qualities: natural capacities, habits, and desires. After all, the old as well as the young can be concerned with matters of honor; the young as well as the middle-aged can be concerned with matters of security; the citizens of a democracy can be concerned with matters of wealth as well as of liberty. Character is a stable and enduring configuration of these, structured in an order of relative strength and importance.[28]

But there are distinctive measures by which the ordering of strength and importance takes place. The distinction between *hexis* and *diathesis* is introduced as a distinction between relatively enduring qualities and those that are hard to change. A relatively enduring quality (like health) might be easy to change, while one of short duration, like recently acquired knowledge, might be difficult to change.[29] A habit that is strong by one measure might be relatively weak by another. And while reason certainly has priority over perception by most measures of importance, perception might well have priority over reason in strength.

The first approximation to Aristotle's account of character must, therefore, be modified: character is the configuration of hierarchically ordered, long-standing, actively dispositional qualities and traits—a person's capacities and habits—that (by setting the general direction of his desires and the range of his passions) direct but surely do not determine his choices. In one way, therefore, a person's character can be summarized by his ends: they form an organized system of ordered preferences, the structure of his practical reasoning. In *Nicomachean Ethics*, Aristotle puts the importance of this aspect of character very strongly. Choice (*prohairesis*), he says, involves reasoning toward an end; it requires the combination of thought (*dianoia*) and desire (*orexis*) (*NE* 1.1.1139a32 ff.). Since thought moves nothing, choices require a combination of thought and *ēthos*. The ultimate source (*archē*) of action is the person (*anthrōpos*), presumably conceived as a structured unity of his character traits. For the purpose of understanding deliberation and choice, a person's character is a structured unity of a special kind, the union of reason and desire.

Character and Dianoia

Are there two, perhaps even three conceptions of character, having no bearing on one another?[30] In the *Rhetoric*, character is described as constituted by those traits that are organized in archaeological layers of deep-seated dispositions, that are ordered by their relative persistence and strength, and that—like laziness or timidity—have no apparent bearing on the person's ends (1113a30 ff.). But in the ethical works, character is manifest in the hierarchy of ordered desires or preferences that—together with *dianoia*—determine choice and action (1139a32 ff.). In this sense, a person's character reveals his ethical standing as virtuous or vicious. How—if at all—is archaeological character (irascibility, impulsiveness, mistrustfulness) summarized or expressed in the preference rankings that affect *prohairesis* and that determine a person's ethical standing?

In one way, it would appear that there is—and should be—no relation between a person's character and his thought (*dianoia*). Because *nous* and thought are, by definition, truth-oriented, they are not—or at any rate should not be—affected by the archaeological aspects of a person's character. We can distinguish two levels of desire (*orexis*) and *dianoia*. The higher levels are best exemplified in the practical reasoning of the *phronimos:* his desire is right, his thought is true, and they coincide in such a way that the source of his deliberation can be indifferently called *oretikos nous* or *orexis dianoetikē* (desiring-thought or thought-defined desire) (1139b5–6). His archaeological character is compatible with his rational preferences. In one way, the thought of the *phronimos* is unaffected by any lower-level traits—age, wealth, or the specific features of the polity in which he lives. Indeed he would not qualify as a *phronimos* if they did affect his thought. But the relation between the *phronimos'* character-*hexeis* and his preferences can also be described in another way: his archaeological character is adequately expressed in desires that are entirely compatible with the truth-bound directions of his *dianoia*. His intellect (*nous*) permeates or guides those aspects of his reasoning that—like perception and imagination—might be affected by his archaeological character.

This way of characterizing the *ēthos* of the *phronimos* raises an extremely difficult question, one that Aristotle did not himself address directly. Are all *phronimoi* identical for practical purposes, despite their historical and political differences? On the one hand, the *phronimos'* desires are formed by what is good and what is true, rather than by the practices of his *polis*. On the other hand, the ends and practices of his *polis* not only set the frame of his deliberations, but also partially constitute his preferences. The *phronimos* is an historical and politically located person. Aristotle provides a reconciliation of these apparently conflicting conditions. The ends of his *polis* figure in the deliberations of the *phronimos* because they provide substantive objective directions and constraints on his practical reasoning, rather than because they formed his character. In a sense all *phronimoi* are alike, and in a sense they are not, depending on the level of generality with which their characters and preferences are described. All *phronimoi* are, for instance, committed to preserving the integrity of their *polis;* and all are committed to an objective inquiry into what integrity requires. Nevertheless, as their polities differ, one *phronimos* might reasonably favor the restriction of trade, while another might favor its expansion.

But this solution only allows for some differences between Athenian and Spartan *phronimoi*. Can two Athenian *phronimoi* differ on trade policy? Can their clusters of virtue differ? The *phronimoi* described in the *Nichomachean Ethics* would seem to be identical: there is no sign of Aristotle thinking that the virtues might be sufficiently in tension so that the balance of virtues of one *phronimos* might, for instance, tip toward courage rather than *sōphrosunē*, while that of another might tip in the opposite direction. But the description of the *phronimos* in *Nicomachean Ethics* is strongly idealized. Aristotle could acknowledge that in an ordinary polity, two trustworthy *phronimoi* might differ in the balance of their virtues, and in the balance of their advice.

So much for the *phronimos*. For the rest of us, matters are more complicated, the fit between our thoughts and desires is not so neat. Each type of character has its own perspective on what is desirable, seeing it as noble, or as expedient, or as pleasant (1113a30 ff.). The practical reasons of ordinary folk, however intelligent and astute they may be, is influenced by their character-*hexeis*, their age, social status, and polity.[31] Their desires are not only constrained by such character traits but also directed and strongly specified by them. This does not mean that their characters completely determine their desires. After all, many fortuitous circumstances, including, for instance, the speeches of rhetoricians, enter into the full specification of their desires.

We are now in a position to understand why the psychology of the *Rhetoric* does not include a separate discussion of desire. The descriptions of character have already specified the archaeologically based desires and *dianoia* of each character-type. They have specified the active habits and dispositions that focus attention, the characteristic patterns of salience and interpretation that elicit specific desires and emotions. Given a dangerous situation, the young are likely to be challenged, and to delight in being challenged; given the very same situation, the elderly are likely to foresee and to fear disaster.

EMOTIONS *(PATHĒ)*

The psychology of the *Rhetoric* forms a neat pairing of character and emotions as, respectively, the active and passive features that affect a person's judgment and choice. Aristotle stresses the active aspect of character: a person's *hexeis* form and direct patterns of salience in his perceptions, thoughts, and desires. Character sets a pattern of activity that does not necessarily require any external intervention for its exercise. By contrast, *pathē* derive from contingent and fortuitous changes brought about by external causes.[32] Aristotle's definition of the emotions in the *Rhetoric* ("those modifications [*metaballontes*] which bring about changes [*diapherousi*] in [a person's] judgments and are accompanied by pain and pleasure" [1378a21]) develops the central motif of his general definition in the *Metaphysics: pathē* are exogenous and contingent changes that affect a person's judgment and motivation.[33] For all of that, a person's character—his deep-seated dispositions—defines his relative susceptibility or immunity to a specific range of emotional responses: a proud man is susceptible to anger, a courageous man finds little to fear.[34] Since political systems influence character, freedom-loving democrats are more prone to be jealous of those better off than are the citizens of an aristocracy.

Psychological passions—passions narrowly conceived as emotions— are individuated by the way they affect us (*diakeimenoi*), by their typical causes, objects, and rationales (1378a22 ff.). But if emotions are themselves changes, of what are they changes? *Pathē* have double-entry bookkeeping: they are identified by a conjunction of physical and psychological changes that themselves generate further changes (*DA* 403a3– 403b18; *Motu* 701b12–13; *Sensu* 436a10b2). The division of labor in the study of the physiology and psychology of *pathē* does not limit the *physikos* to "purely material causes," as if there were such things.[35] The astute *physikos* should, for instance, be able to distinguish the physical changes that occur when the blood around the heart boils in anger from those that occur when the blood around the heart boils from a high fever. Similarly, the psychologically astute rhetorician can tell the difference between the psychological changes that attend the angry thought that one has been unjustifiably injured and the equally painful changes that occur with the self-pitying thought of such an injury. Presumably, the former, but not the latter, generates a desire for revenge, along with the pleasurable anticipation of revenge—presumably also involving calculative *phantasiai*.

Because Aristotle's discussion of the individual passions in *Rhetoric* Book 2 is limited to those features that are relevant to the rhetorician's craft, he does not raise the kinds of questions that might seem germane to a philosophic account. How can the temporally prior psychological causes of an emotion also be among its necessary individuating constituents? How can thinking oneself to have been unjustly injured be both an (efficient) cause of anger and also among its (formal) individuating constituents (one's blood boiling *at* the thought of an unjustified injury)? Aristotle's standard laconic answer to questions of this sort—general questions about the relation between some efficient and some formal causes—is: in one sense they are identical in being; in another, they are different in definition. If that answer seems unsatisfactory, or at any rate, tantalizingly incomplete, it presents a problem in Aristotle's general theory of explanation, rather than in his theory of psychology. Beyond saying that they often coincide (*Phys.* 2.7.198a24 ff.), Aristotle seems unconcerned about just how—if at all—efficient and formal causes are related to one another.[36] Indeed, he would regard that question as confused and regressive. The schema of causal explanations is basic. Asking for an explanation of the relation among its dimensions carries the air of (what we would call) a category mistake. It is like asking for an explanation of the relation between measurements of height and width, one that would also explain how it is possible that the height and the breadth of a point coincide.

Another apparently germane philosophical question also carries the weight of an unnecessary apprehension. We need not worry about whether Aristotle's account of the desires that typically attend *pathē* might, in the end, be susceptible to hedonistic reduction. Although *pathē* are accompanied by pleasure and pain, their motivational force is not always governed by them. We do not need a motive to set about reproducing, thinking, or participating in political life; we are set to engage in these activities when the appropriate occasions present themselves. Under proper conditions, we find them pleasurable, but we do not engage in them for the sake of the pleasure they bring (1175a22–1176a29).[37] When Aristotle says that anger at the pain of a supposed unjustified injury (*hepetai*) is accompanied by the pleasurable anticipation of revenge, he is not claiming that revenge is always motivated by a painful *phantasia*-based *pathos* (*Rhet.* 2.8.1378a).[38] A *phronimos* might deliberately, as a result of a calculated piece of practical reasoning, decide on a vengeful course without ever having suffered the pain of anger. While the rhetorician may well find it useful to elicit anger in order to persuade his audience to adopt a policy of revenge, a group of *politikoi* can, solely on the basis of cool-hearted rational deliberation, decide on a policy of calculated revenge.

We do not need to worry that Aristotle might be driven to accept a hedonic calculus to evaluate the relative merits of activities. Pleasures are intentionally individuated and differentiated: They are pleasures-of-a-certain-kind-in-an-activity-that-is-thought-of-in-a-certain-way (*NE* 10.5. 1175a22–1175b2). A person's character—his dispositional cognitive and motivational profile—defines his typical pleasures and pains (*NE* 1.8.1099a5–31). The pleasures that attend the unimpeded exercise of natural activities are hierarchically ordered by their relative importance in a well-lived human life.

PATHĒ AND THE PERSUASIVE FORCE OF PHANTASIAI

How can the rhetorician ensure that the attitudes he has successfully aroused will persist beyond the occasion to command the actions of the audience at the appropriate time? Because Aristotle sees no need to develop a general theory about how *pathē* affect evaluative decisions, we can only extrapolate what he might say from his discussion of the aftermath of specific emotions—anger tends to lead to revenge, envy to emulation, and so on. The rhetorician evokes a cluster of *pathē*-laden memories: "Would your fathers have tolerated the persistent pattern of your neighbors' provocations? Remember how our fathers' responses to such challenges brought us both honor and benefit." Having aroused the audience's indignation and emulation, the rhetorician can direct their *phantasiai* of revenge or competition to actions that appear to satisfy long-standing attitudes and desires (1385a21 ff., 1388a36 ff.). Even passions that are not immediately motivational—grief, for example—can be directed toward specific action-guiding *phantasiai:* for example, commissioning a memorial tribute of some kind (1384a24, 1385b16 ff., 1387b22 ff.).[39]

There are enormous difficulties in interpreting Aristotle's views on *phantasia*, *phantasmata*, and *phantastikon*.[40] To begin with, his discussions are brief, often introduced tangentially in the course of another investigation, and scattered in works that seem to have been initially drafted.

during different periods. The frequently cited etymological connections of these words to the cognates of *phainesthai* and even to *phaos* are tantalizing but unclear explanations. We know more about what *phantasia* is not, than what it is (427b15–429a9, 431b3–19, 433b28 ff., 458b10–460b28, and 701b34–702a22). We are told this much: while there is no *hupolēpsis* (taking something to be the case, as in opinion or thought) without *phantasia* (426b16), *phantasia* is neither opinion (*doxa*) nor perception (*aisthēsis*) or any combination of these (428a25 ff.). Although *to phantastikon* and *to aisthētikon* are the same faculties or capacities, they are different in being or essence (*einai*): a *phantasia* can occur in the absence of its *aisthesis* (*Enupiōn* 459a15 ff.).[41] Moreover, *phantasia* is distinguished from perception in being, to some extent at least, "up to us" (*eph hēmin estin*): we can, in principle, call up mental images (*eidōlopoiountēs*) at will (*DA* 3.427b15–21).[42]

The primary texts for understanding Aristotle's views on *phantasia* come from *De Anima* and *De Motu Animalium*. Since at least part of the cognitive component of an emotion is a *phantasia* associated with pleasure and pain, *pathē* are presumptively motivating. The effects of pleasure and pain in directing and specifying the motivational force of *phantasia* are announced in *De Anima:*

> To that part of the soul which thinks (*dianoetikē*), *phantasmata* take the place of perceptions (*aisthēmata*) (*DA* 431a14 ff.). . . . When the object [of perception] is pleasant or painful, the soul . . . pursues or avoids the object. To be pleased or pained is to act with the perceptual mean towards what is good and bad (*DA* 431a11–16). . . . If one regards *phantasia* as thinking of a kind (*noēsin tina*), then desire (*orexis*) and mind (*nous*) are capable of causing movement (*kinounta*) (*DA* 433a10).[43] . . . An animal is not capable of appetite (*orektikon*) without *phantasia;* and all *phantasia* is either calculative (*logistikē*) or sensory (*aisthetikē*) (433b29–30).

Other helpful passages—texts that combine Aristotle's physiological with his psychological account of the sources of motion—appear in *De Motu Animalium.*[44]

> Alteration [in the motion of animals] is caused by *phantasiai* and sense perceptions and thought (*ennoiai*) (701b16 ff.). . . . Such things as shuddering and being frightened are *pathē* and changes (*alloioseis*) (701b23). . . . The origin (*archē*) of motion (*kinēsis*) . . . is the object of pursuit and avoidance. . . . [The *pathē*] of confidence, fears, sexual arousal, and other painful or pleasant (*lupēra kai hēdea*) bodily conditions (*sōmatika*) are accompanied by heating or chilling (702a3 ff.). . . . *Pathē* prepare (*paraskeuazei epitēdeiōs*) the parts of organs [for motion], desire (*orexis*) [prepares] the *pathē;* and *phantasia* [prepares] desire (702a18 ff.).

In identifying a *phantasia* as the content of an *aisthēsis* and asserting that the soul uses *phantasmata* in thinking, Aristotle may be extrapolating from the practice of diagramming mathematical discussions with sketches of geometrical figures.[45] Although we use *phantasmata* in thinking, they are not always the proper objects of our thought. We can think of the sum of the interior angles of an equilateral triangle without any reference to its size, although we use a specific triangle of a determinate size in reflecting on the properties that are the proper objects of our thought (449b31–450a5). This does not imply that *phantasmata* are completely determinate; in using a *phantasia* of a triangle of a determinate size to think about the sum of the interior angles of an equilateral triangle, many of its other properties—its color, for instance—can remain indeterminate and unspecified.

This much at least seems clear: both sensory and calculative *phantasiai* are particular; they are the content of perceptions that—unlike the perceptions themselves—can remain in the mind to reappear in dreams, afterimages, and memories; they are what the mind uses to think with; unlike proper perceptions—perceptions of proper objects—they can be false; they give specific directions to desires in producing motion and action (*orektikon de ouk aneu phantasias*) (433b28).[46] Beyond this we must turn to speculation. I suggest that *phantasiai* are how things appear to us, *given who, what, and where we are*. Since we are virtually always in some condition of desire, our perceptions carry a set of associated (but not constitutive) *phantasiai*. If we take these *phantasiai* literally—if we confuse them with perceptions—they are, as Aristotle says, almost always false, just as a sketch of a triangle in the sand would, if taken at face value, give a misleading idea of its properties. *Phantasiai* do not necessarily or always have the force of opinions. Although we can easily be misled, we needn't be: what we make of *phantasia*—how we take them—is at least partially up to us. Situated as we are, at a great distance from the sun, the sun appears to us as an object with a small diameter without this perception necessarily determining or dictating our beliefs about its size. Similarly, a wax apple might look juicy and succulent to a hungry person without fixing his opinion about whether it is edible. If it did, he would, other things being equal, reach for it. In neither case does the *phantasia* always involve seeing *as if*, or seeing *under a cognitive description:* for animals—who do not think, and certainly do not think hypothetically—have *phantasiai* that guide their desires to appropriate movement. Happily and significantly, *phantasiai* can indicate properties that objects really have. The object of desire (*orekton*) is said to start a movement (*to orekton gar kinei*) (433a18–19); under appropriate conditions, the perceived qualities of a specific object elicit a specific desire.[47] Aristotle seems to think there is a pre-established harmony between (*a*) the proper object (*orekton*) of an animal's desires, (*b*) the way that those normatively proper objects appear to it, and (*c*) its normally having (under the best circumstances) well-formed desires. And so, for us as well: under the best circumstances, the way things seem to us bears a law-like relation (*a*) to our situations and desires, and (*b*) to the way things are. But we are not always in the best circumstances: our situations, desires and passions can skew our *phantasiai*, the way things appear to us. Still, our proper perceptions are by definition always true. To a hungry person, a wax apple *seems* edible, even succulent, even when he knows he is looking at a bowl of artificial fruit. But what he *sees*—as the proper objects of sight—are the proper qualities of that object, whatever they may be.

LEXIS, LOGOS, AND KRISEIS

What has all this to do with rhetoric? A skillful rhetorician can persuade an audience to accept a course of action by eliciting *pathē* that are typically associated with an appropriate desire. For instance, if he wants to provoke his audience to revenge, he tries to make them angry by trying to convince them that former allies have unjustly injured the *polis* (1382a18 ff.). Or, if he wants to persuade his audience to retreat from an exposed position, he elicits fear by evoking vivid *phantasiai* of imminent danger (1382a20 ff.). In order for the rhetorician to form just the right sort of action-guiding desire, rather than whirligig diffuse *pathē*, he must be quite precise about the implications of his speech. Because *phantasiai* specify the intentional content of their associated *pathē*, they affect its typical concomitant desires. The *phantasiai* that he elicits should be associated with highly specific desires: the pleasure of a specific sort of revenge in anger, for instance, rather than that of winning a race at the Olympics. But since the audience's *phantasiai* are affected by their general dispositional desires, and emotions, the rhetorician must bear in mind the character of his audience. Since the elderly and the young have different dispositional desires, the rhetorician must attempt to evoke the *phantasiai* appropriate to their respective preoccupations. To persuade the young to take revenge, the rhetorician must evoke *phantasiai* of injured honor; to persuade the elderly, he must evoke *phantasiai* of lost property. To persuade the young to take their revenge by going to war rather than by an act of betrayal, the rhetorician must evoke calculative *phantasiai* of specific strategies that would bring glory on the battlefield. To persuade the elderly of the same course, he must add a vivid description of the low-risk gains that war could bring.

Aristotle does not explicity address a central problem of the role of the passions in rhetorical persuasion. For deliberative persuasion to be successful, it must not only arouse, but also stabilize appropriate emotions, along with their attendant desires. It is not enough that the audience be moved at hearing the rhetorician's speech in the Assembly: their decisive judgments must be sufficiently stable to guide their actions, when the time comes to issue orders to the fleet, or to order the prison guard to administer hemlock to Socrates. It is, after all, a poor rhetorician indeed whose persuasive arguments—however strong they may have been on the occasion—are insufficiently binding. The Athenians, for instance, having decided to send a ship to Mytilene, are moved to recall it the following day. The conclusions of valid syllogisms can be, and are, detached from their premises: their reliability is assured by the necessity of the argument. But while rhetorical arguments can be soundly reasonable, they often take a nonsyllogistic route, working through *phantasiai* and their associated *pathē*, as well as through maxims, analogies, and metaphors. Their conclusions are correspondingly unstable: even when an audience has been reasonably persuaded—when the conclusions are detached from the rhetorician's *logos*, it can be swayed to an opposed decision by another set of rhetorical considerations. So how do the best rhetoricians succeed in binding and stabilizing as well as eliciting the audience's evaluative decisions?

Since Aristotle does not address the problem directly, there is little textual evidence to suggest his solution. He might have taken the view that *phantasiai* and the passions reinforce one another by what Hume rather mysteriously calls a "double relation between impressions and ideas": just as a particular *phantasia* evokes a typical emotion, so too specific emotion-types tend to evoke characteristic *phantasiai*. The mutually reinforcing cycle would presumably continue until another set of associations intervenes. The "double relation" introduced by rhetorically induced *phantasiai*—and that relation's motivating passions—is typically reestablished when an appropriately similar set of perceptions occur. While this answer has considerable attractions, it seems to make the formative force of rhetorical persuasion unnecessary. If a set of perceptions were sufficient to elicit a motivating passion when it is time to act, the rhetorician's speech would play little role in persuasion.

I propose what seems a more Aristotelian solution: a successful rhetorician structures his speech to elicit emotions that are connected with stable motivational structures. That is, after all, why he needs to understand the character of his audience. To bind their convictions, he must appeal to their strongly entrenched, as well as to their immediate, interests and desires. He evokes *phantasiai* associated with the sorts of dispositions that are readily activated whenever appropriate circumstances present themselves. This solution would require Aristotle to distinguish the *phantasiai* and *pathē* aroused by the poets from those aroused by the rhetorician. And this is just what he does in the *Poetics:* the structure of the tragic plot is designed to effect a *katharsis* of pity and fear, while the *lexis* of the rhetorician is designed to lead to an action-guiding decision.[48]

But while this solution helps to explain the importance of Book 2 of the *Rhetoric*, it does not yet explain the importance of Aristotle's lengthy discussion of *lexis* in Book 3. What does the style of rhetorical persuasion contribute to the persistence as well as the persuasiveness of the rhetorical argument? The (right degree of) vividness of his *lexis*—its eliciting *phantasiai* that bind the decisions of the audience to their dispositional motives—can help form the appropriate action in the right way in the right place at the right time. If the rhetorician's speech is too vivid, the project becomes fanciful; if it is insufficiently vivid, his audience might remain unmoved. The exemplary rhetorician has a sensitive mastery of the techniques of style and rhythm in speech, a sophisticated level of sprachgefühl that moves the audience in the right way at the right time. He can form their interpretations of a situation in such a way as to elicit their deepseated dispositional desires. The details of his speech—its phrases and the style (*lexis*) of his delivery—should affect their descriptions of the occasion for action. When the *stragēgos* sees that the neighboring *polis* is strengthening its walls and arming its guard, his *phantasia* will have the force inspired by the ringing style of the rhetorician's description: the enemy is preparing for war. Having been persuaded to prefer an offensive to a defensive strategy, he will prepare to attack. The eloquence of rhetorical speech is instrumental in carrying persuasion to action: describing the changing of the guard as a hostile act, the *stratēgos* evokes *phantasiai* associated with the specific decision formed in the Assembly.

A good deal of the rhetorician's character is conveyed by the clarity, power, and rhythm of his speech, and by what we misleadingly call "figurative speech." The expression is misleading because metaphors, similes, and the like are not always imagistic. They are often intended to be literal: they represent terms as (unexpectedly but genuinely) different varieties of the same general category.[49] In speaking of Alcibiades as having the intensity of a volcanic explosion, a rhetorician need not intend to evoke any particular image, or even to condense a simile; he may rather be classifying Alcibiades' intensity together with that of volcanoes, as varieties of unpredictable, dangerous energy.

As a didactic instrument, metaphor can be used to persuade those whose primary terms are awry. A truthful literal speech can be unpersuasive for those whose conceptual scheme—whose beliefs and desires— are malformed. But the rhetorician can present what he takes to be a literal turn of phrase to his audience, knowing that they will interpret it as figuratively metaphorical. All the instruments of rhetoric, including appeals to *pathē*-laden *phantasiai*, can, taken together, gradually bring an audience to a new, literal interpretation of what they had once thought of as metaphorical speech. True to their etymology, metaphors *carry* meaning: like a shifting wind (*tropaia*), a *trope* turns the audience around.

Tropes give an audience vivid directions for (re)interpreting the situations in which they should act as they had been persuaded. Having originally taken a rhetorician's reference to "brothers of Athens" as metaphorical, an audience can come to think of brotherhood in a new light, one that reveals the proper and broader (literal) significance of the phrase. So understood, it can command the civic attitudes and actions that might once have been reserved for biological brothers. So, for instance, Plato's readers might have thought that he spoke metaphorically in referring to the various classes of the city as brothers of the same mother. But Plato intended to persuade them of what he took to be a literal truth: properly understood, the civic relation of interdependence reveals the real significance of the biological relation.[50]

Aristotle moderates Plato's attack on the dangers of metaphors, analogies, and similes. While acknowledging that such tropes can elicit *phantasiai* rather than reason, that they can inflame the emotions and elude truth-oriented confrontation, he nevertheless thinks that metaphor and myth can serve as didactic instruments for those who cannot be persuaded by strictly logical argumentation. Metaphor is not intrinsically dangerous or even misleading; but it can be misused. The issue about the use and abuse of metaphor in rhetoric is, as it is with poetic metaphor: who formulates it, with what knowledge and purpose? Since Aristotle is providing a handbook for the exemplary rhetorician, he can assume that truth will direct and constrain the use of such (ana)logical speech.

RHETORIC AND POLITICS

Without rhetoric, politics is empty; without politics, rhetoric is blind. Without rhetorical skill, even the wisest *politikos* is pathetic and helpless; without political knowledge—knowledge of the city's constitution and laws, its commercial and military treaties, its economic and military strength—even a clever, well-intentioned rhetorician is a menace, a danger to the state.[51] Beyond cryptically remarking that rhetoric is an offshoot of ethics that can be justly called politics (1356a26) and taking most of his examples from the rhetoric of political deliberation, Aristotle did not explicitly elaborate the details of their mutual dependence, perhaps because it was a platitude of the time, too obvious to need saying.

Even in the best of states, where citizens debating rationally among themselves can bypass rhetorical persuasion, they must persuade the rest of the polity that a specific decision will serve (their conceptions of) their interests. Although the interests of *phronimoi* can be presumed to coincide, not all citizens have the same conception of those interests. In an ordinary state, the *politikos* must be capable of rhetorical persuasion, bearing in mind not only the best and most truthful considerations, but also the

diverse interests and temperaments of his fellows, who cannot be presumed to be *phronimoi.* Even in the worst of states, the tyrant cannot rule
solely by coercion and force.

Like the *politikos,* the ordinary *phronimos* depends on his rhetorical
skills to advance his projects. His success often requires the cooperation
of those with distinctive abilities and interests. Sometimes, to be sure,
nothing needs to be said. Oarsmen naturally adjust their rhythms to row
together. But for more complex tasks—typically those that involve the
meshing of different aims and skills—something does need to be said,
and needs to be said well and convincingly. The master builder must
know how to tell the stone masons what to do, the general must know
how to tell his officers when to advance or retreat. When they all agree—
when they are all of a single mind about the task at hand—the master
builder can forthwith tell the stone mason what to do, the general can
tell his officers when to advance or retreat. But often the workers and
the officers have their own ideas, their own perspective on the matter:
the *phronimos*—who has a larger, "all things considered" view—must
know how to bring them round. Sometimes it is sufficient to sketch the
larger picture, to remind them of their common task; but often it is not.
Non-*phronimoi* have a more limited perspective; they tend to act from
habits that are more entrenched than rational, more automatic than
discriminating.

Every *phronimos* is, wittingly or unwittingly, intentionally or unintentionally, engaged in moral education. Because his activity is typically
successful, because he achieves his ends and wins the prizes of a good life,
he is widely imitated. But the *phronimos* who understands political life also
knows that *paideia* is the life of the polity; it is the expression as well as
the assurance of the polity's specific form of life. He knows, too, that the
well-formed laws and institutions are the polity's most powerful instruments. His role as moral educator is best fulfilled "if he makes himself
capable of legislating" (*NE* 1180a33 ff.). To be sure, the philosophic study
of constitutions does not make a man a wise legislator, any more than the
philosophic study of handbooks of rhetoric makes a man a good rhetorician. Sound judgment, perhaps even practical wisdom itself, is necessary
for a discerning use of a craft.

Of course the *phronimos* need not be a professional rhetorician, need
not have studied with a master rhetorician, and still less need he be a
theoretician of the craft. It is enough that he has absorbed the subtle and
difficult art of suiting his speech to his audience, just as he has mastered
hitting the mean, suiting his desires to his situation. The arts of rhetoric
are second nature to the *phronimos,* they are part and parcel of what he
knows.

The situation of the *politikos* is slightly different. In one sense, as Aristotle says, *phronēsis* and *politikē* are the same (*NE* 1141b23 ff.). But their essential descriptions differ: not every *phronimos* is a *politikos* and many *politikoi* are manifestly not *phronimoi*. Still, in the best case, the *politikos* has the knowledge and the skills of the *phronimos*-rhetorician: he knows what considerations to advance and how to advance them—formally or informally; laconically or ornately; authoritatively or fraternally; ironically or lyrically. If the *politikos* lacks the knowledge or the gifts of rhetoric, he must enlist the cooperation of the rhetorician; he must have him at his side, ready to speak for him. This dependence of course makes him vulnerable. Because the rhetorician may have his own ideas, the *politikos* must at the very least be able to present his case to his intermediary rhetorician clearly and forcibly.

The dependence also goes in the other direction as well. The forensic rhetorician must know the laws of the polity, the rules of evidence, and exculpating conditions (1.2.21). If the deliberative rhetorician argues in the Assembly, he must understand the institutions of his *polis*, its history and customs, its expenditures and sources of revenue, its military and economic strengths and treaties (1359b20 ff.).[52] We might add: he must know whom to cite and whom to enlist, who is powerful and who is laughable. The details of his argument—the considerations he advances—must also take into account the specific aims and psychology of different types of states. For instance, the occasions for anger, the typical strategies of revenge take one form in an aristocracy, another in a democracy (1379a1 ff., 1390b35–1391a30).

THE ARISTOTELIAN LEGACY

Nowhere are contemporary parallels to Aristotelian theory more evident than in the unsolved, apparently intractable problems (*aporiai*) that we share with him. Indeed, it is, ironically, at just those places where we find ourselves dissatisfied with the incompleteness and even the evasiveness of Aristotle's account that we come upon the stubborn difficulties of our own theories. We find ourselves issuing promissory notes in roughly the same places where Aristotle tends either to change the subject or to resolve it contextually.

One of the most vexed of these problems is, of course, that of specifying the relation between the physiology and the psychology of character, perception, desire, and the emotions. Not surprisingly, the general problem of specifying the details of an intention-oriented, physicalistic psychology has ramifications for other areas and other disciplines. How, if at all, do character traits like impulsiveness or brashness affect the beliefs and desires that shape practical reasoning? Are modes of practical reasoning and practical wisdom culturally and politically invariant? Are the general ends of a sound polity sufficiently indeterminate to allow for disagreement among its wisest and best statesmen?

Some of the submerged problems of Aristotle's *Rhetoric* are mirrored in our own deliberations about public and political discourse. As it stands, Aristotle's *Rhetoric* does not address the problem implicit in the substantive connections that he draws among rhetoric, politics, and ethics. The connections set the larger frame for his insistence that the best rhetoric rests on true premises and reasonable arguments. Should the rhetorician educate his audience as well as persuade them? Should he attempt to improve their characters—to draw them as close to *phronēsis* as their natural capacities allow—or should he rest content with addressing their immediate concerns as best he can? Of course Aristotle—refined contextualist that he is—has several answers to this question. As a master craftsman, the rhetorician has no political or educative responsibility. But the true *politikos,* who has—for the sake of exercising his own craft—acquired rhetorical skills, bears the responsibility of educating his citizens as well as satisfying their needs and constructing sound political institutions. While the rhetorician qua *politikos* must engage in deliberation, the *politikos* qua rhetorician takes the outcome of that deliberation as fixed. However he himself may have reached it, the rhetorician qua rhetorician starts with the conclusion—starts, that is, with what he wants the audience to accept—and is concerned with constructing the arguments that will best bring his audience to the predetermined judgment. No general rule determines when the rhetorician should take on the responsibilities of a *politikos:* like all ethically and politically decisive matters, that must be left to the judgment of the *phronimos.*

Like Aristotle, we want it both ways: on the one hand, we view all forms of oratory—journalism, political negotiation, election strategies—pragmatically, as directed to finding the most efficacious argument to produce the most satisfactory results. But, like Aristotle, we also construe "the satisfactory result" morally: we hold our rhetoricians responsible not only for reasoning well but also for telling us the harsh truths we might need to hear, however they might jar with our characters or confound our desires.[53]

NOTES

I am indebted to Juha Sivohla and Martha Nussbaum—the organizers of the 1991 Helsinki conference on Aristotle's *Rhetoric*—for stimulating my interest in the *Rhetoric* and to the other participants in that conference for their illuminating papers. The van Leer Institute in Jerusalem provided ideal working conditions for study and writing. I am also grateful to Mary Whitlock Blundell, Myles Burnyeat, David Furley, Donald Morrison, Ruth Nevo, and Markus Woerner for helpful discussions and corrections. An earlier, much abbreviated section of this paper, "The Directions of Aristotle's *Rhetoric*," appeared in the *Review of Metaphysics* 46 (1992): 63–95; another version appeared under the title "The Psychology of Aristotle's *Rhetoric*," *Proceedings of the Boston Area Colloquium in Ancient Philosophy* 8 (1992): 39–79.

    1. As we shall see, Aristotle thought his predecessors mistakenly took forensic and epideictic, rather than deliberative, rhetoric as setting the models for all forms of rhetorical persuasion. Instead of presenting careful analyses of the relation between *phantasia* and *lexis*, they concentrated on the techniques of directing the emotions of the audience.

    2. Parallel: Aristotle relies on his theory of action, his ethics, and his philosophy of mind in advising the tragedian, who can use this material without himself becoming a philosopher.

    3. See J. Cooper, "Ethical-Political Theory in Aristotle's *Rhetoric*," *Aristotle's Rhetoric: Philosophical Essays*, ed. D. Furley and A. Nehamas (Princeton, 1994). Also S. Halliwell, "Popular Morality, Philosophical Ethics and the *Rhetoric*," *Aristotle's Rhetoric: Philosophical Essays*, ed. D. Furley and A. Nehamas (Princeton, 1994); E. Garver, "Making Discourse Ethical: The Lessons of Aristotle's *Rhetoric*," with a commentary by C. Griswold, *Proceedings of the Boston Area Colloquium in Ancient Philosophy* 5 (1991); and T. Engberg-Pedersen, "Is There an Ethical Dimension to Aristotelian Rhetoric?" this volume.

    4. Although there are subtle distinctions between oratory and rhetoric, I shall use the terms interchangeably.

    5. Aristotle uses the analogy to *skiagraphia* (3.12.5) that Plato had developed in the *Republic* 10. The proportions of a successfully mimetic painting must—like those of pediment sculptures—be adjusted to the perspective from which it will be seen. But in taking into account the perspective from which it will be seen, the painter—and, Aristotle might add, the rhetorician—does not necessarily misrepresent his subject. Only those who do not understand the laws of perspective will construe what he does as distortion. See J.-L. Labarrière, "L'Orateur politique face à ses contraintes," *Aristotle's Rhetoric: Philosophical Essays*, ed. D. Furley and A. Nehamas (Princeton, 1994).

    6. See T. Irwin, *Aristotle's First Principles* (Oxford, 1988), p. 332; H. Richardson, "Desire and the Good in *De Anima*," *Essays on Aristotle's De Anima*, ed. M. C. Nussbaum and A. O. Rorty (Oxford, 1992), p. 381.

    7. See *Topics* 101b5 ff.: "We shall be in perfect possession of the way to proceed when we are in a position like that which we occupy in regard to rhetoric and medicine . . . for it is not every method that the rhetorician will employ to persuade; or the doctor to heal."

    8. Although it moves far beyond *endoxa*, the *Nicomachean Ethics* presents a thoroughgoing comprehensive discussion of the accepted views about the aims and motives for action and about the primary virtues (*NE* 1.1–13). Since only what is voluntary can be praised or blamed, the epideictic rhetorician must also know what sorts of actions are thought voluntary.

    9. For a full discussion of the enthymeme, see M. F. Burnyeat, "Enthymeme: Aristotle on the Rationality of Rhetoric," this volume.

10. See E. M. Cope, *An Introduction to Aristotle's Rhetoric* (London, 1867), pp. 218–229. All future page references to Cope will be to this edition.

11. See J. Annas, "Aristotle on Pleasure and Goodness," *Essays on Aristotle's De Anima,* ed. M. C. Nussbaum and A. O. Rorty (Oxford, 1992); D. Frede, "Mixed Feelings in Aristotle's *Rhetoric,*" this volume; and my "The Place of Pleasure in Aristotle's Ethics," *Mind* 83 (1974):481–497. It should not be surprising that the *endoxa* concerning pleasure in the *Rhetoric* do not accord with the discussions of pleasure in *De Anima* (3.7.431a10) and *Physics* (3.8.247a ff.). The forensic rhetorician must sidestep a philosophically sound analysis, and stay within the limits of the audience's *endoxa.*

12. See my *"Akrasia* and Pleasure: *NE* Book 7," *Essays on Aristotle's Ethics,* ed. A. O. Rorty (Berkeley, 1980). The *Nicomachean Ethics* discussions are mandated by the necessities of theory construction. Aristotle must protect his intellectually oriented analysis of *phronēsis* from entailing a denial of the phenomena of *akrasia.* Since the motivating force of pleasure (and to some extent of anger) are introduced to help solve this problem, he must—if he is to classify *akrasia* as voluntary—give an account of pleasure that accords with his analysis of voluntary action. And since he also wants to say that the best life is both *eudaimōn* and pleasurable, he must show that pleasures are intentional, that they vary with the activities they accompany.

13. See *NE* 6.5, 6.9, 6.10. To be sure, the account of *eudaimonia* in the *Nicomachean Ethics* is narrower and stricter than that presented in the *Rhetoric* (1.5–6.1362a15–1362b9). But while the account of the ends of action in the *Rhetoric* is by no means a philosophically complete or refined analysis, it is, on the whole, correct as far as it goes: the range of things accounted good are genuinely good. The rhetorician is concerned with the kinds of arguments that can be appropriately used to establish the relative priority among goods, while the task of providing a rigorous account of their normative priority is assigned to ethical and political philosophers. See Halliwell, "Popular Morality"; and C. D. C. Reeve, "Philosophy, Politics, and Rhetoric in Aristotle," this volume.

14. The best treatment of this subject is J. Brunschwig's "Rhetorique et dialectique: *Rhetorique* et *Topiques,*" *Aristotle's Rhetoric: Philosophical Essays,* ed. D. Furley and A. Nehamas (Princeton, 1994). See also his discussion of dialectic in *Topiques,* vol. 1 [Books 1–4] (Paris, 1967), pp. xxii ff. and 113–114; and his "Aristotle's Rhetoric as a 'Counterpart' to Dialectic," this volume.

15. See Brunschwig, *Topiques,* pp. xcvi–civ. Although Aristotle sometimes uses the term *dialektikos* pejoratively, to refer to futile inquiries and disputes that are not capable of strict demonstration, he certainly never intends to denigrate its general utility, even in scientific contexts. There is no indication that he criticizes rhetoric because it depends upon, and uses, *endoxa:* the rhetorician doesn't become a sophist, in the pejorative sense of that term, simply because he constructs contrary arguments. It is the aim, rather than the structure of its dialectical arguments, that determines whether a particular speech is merely sophistical (1355b20 ff.).

16. The structures of logical arguments are given full dress discussion in the logical works, in the *Prior Analytics* and *Posterior Analytics, De Interpretatione,* and

Sophistical Refutations. The structures of dialectical arguments are developed primarily in the *Topics.*

17. For more on the relation between politics and rhetoric, see pp. 23–25; F. Miller and D. Keydt, eds., *A Companion to Aristotle's Politics* (Oxford, 1991); J. P. Euben, *The Tragedy of Political Theory* (Princeton, 1990); S. Salkever, *Finding the Mean* (Princeton, 1990); Reeve, "Philosophy, Politics, and Rhetoric"; Halliwell, "Popular Morality"; and C. Lord, *Education and Culture in the Political Thought of Aristotle* (Ithaca, 1982).

18. Philosophical psychology is an investigation into the most general features of psychological functioning and practical reasoning: it starts with a dialectical examination of accepted philosophical opinion, and attempts to move toward a scientific account. Empirical psychology consists of a set of rough generalizations derived from experience and observation. An empirical study of human psychology encompasses an investigation of variations in fundamental psychological activities and functions as they might be affected by age, sex, and political and social circumstances.

19. 2.1.5–7. See Cope, *An Introduction to Aristotle's Rhetoric,* pp. 244–245; and Cooper, "Ethical-Political Theory in Aristotle's *Rhetoric.*" See also R. Moran, "Artifice and Persuasion: The Work of Metaphor in the *Rhetoric,*" this volume.

20. Even when epideictic rhetoric is directed to ordinary people whose judgments are not, by virtue of any public office, constitutive of action, it is intended to form that sort of evaluative judgment which is intended to influence their future actions.

21. There is, however, an important difference between the idealized forms of deliberation described in the ethical works and the kind of deliberation presented by a rhetorician. The rhetorician urges his audience to act on a decision, to treat it as a detachable conclusion of a sound argument. But the rhetorician typically argues for a reasonable rather than a formally valid conclusion. I shall return to this issue later, when I discuss the role of *phantasia* and *lexis* in rhetorical persuasion.

22. The *Topics* is, Aristotle says, directed to finding "a line of inquiry whereby we shall be able to reason from reputable opinions about any subject presented to us, and also shall ourselves, when putting forth an argument, avoid saying anything contrary to it" (100a20 ff.). The *Topics* points to a heterogeneous set of useful places to find strategies for constructing persuasive arguments: whether an event is unlikely or virtually certain to occur, general background knowledge (e.g., evidentiary rules in forensic rhetoric), and the types of argumentative skills on which a successful rhetorician relies. See W. Grimaldi, "Studies in the Philosophy of Aristotle's Rhetoric," *Hermes* (Wiesbaden) 100 (1972):115–135; Cope, *An Introduction to Aristotle's Rhetoric,* pp. 249–253; Brunschwig, *Topiques,* pp. lxxxv, liv–lv, and "Aristotle's Rhetoric as a 'Counterpart' to Dialectic."

Some commentators (Cope, *An Introduction to Aristotle's Rhetoric,* pp. 249–253; G. Kennedy, *The Art of Persuasion in Ancient Greece* [Princeton, 1963], pp. 101–103, citing F. Solmsen, *Die Entwicklung der Aristotelischen Logik und Rhetorik* [Berlin, 1929], p. 100) have found it surprising that *ēthos* and *pathos* appear among the rhetorical *topoi*. Kennedy thinks that the interruption in the sequence of Aristotle's exposition is best explained by the fact that Aristotle happened to be working on these matters at the same time, late in the development of the *Rhetoric*. But since it provides basic premises for deliberative arguments, an extensive discussion of *ēthos* and *pathos* is properly placed at the heart of a treatise on the art of reasonable persuasion.

23. The difference between the treatment of character in the ethical works and its treatment in the *Rhetoric* affords a nice example of the difference between the analysis of an ideal type and the analysis of a stereotype.

24. For a fuller discussion of character and the emotions, see my "Aristotle on the Metaphysical Status of *Pathē*," *Review of Metaphysics* 38 (1984):521–546. I am indebted to M. W. Blundell for her careful study of the various senses of *ēthos* in her "*Ēthos* and *Dianoia* Reconsidered," *Essays on Aristotle's Poetics*, ed. A. O. Rorty (Princeton, 1992).

25. I shall use the term "traits" to refer to the varieties of the constituents of character: habits, dispositions, and natural capacities. To call *hexeis* "states," as John Ackrill does in his translation, is to suggest they are static rather than dynamic (*Categories and De Interpretatione* [Oxford, 1963]). But despite this infelicity, Ackrill's comments on 8b26–10a11 (pp. 104–107) are admirably helpful.

26. See 1145a15–1145b7 for distinctions between the *phronēsis* and weakness (*akrasia*), strength (*enkrateia*), brutishness (*theriotēs*), and heroic godlikeness (*aretē heroikē kai theia*). The analysis of the individual virtues and of the psychology of the *phronimos* (*NE* 3.6–5.11) is a continuation of that discussion: it is a zoom lens, close-up view of the character of the *agathos*.

A good deal of the *Politics* is devoted to an account of how different types of polities foster distinctive psychological types, with distinctive action-guiding ends. Aristotle analyzes the motives toward liberty in democratic states, toward wealth in oligarchic states, toward education (*paideia*) and lawfulness in aristocratic states, toward self-protection in tyrannies. Since each polity is susceptible to specific and distinctive sorts of disorder and instability, he discusses the motives for revolution (*metabolē*) and political strife (*stasis*) (1301a19–1307b25) that are typical of each state. Because the *Politics* is a normative as well as a descriptive work, it includes a discussion of the psychological qualifications for citizenship and of the education of the civic virtues (1328a18–20, 1327b19–20, 1332a41–1332b11).

27. How determinate is a person's "second nature"? The extent to which general ends not only direct but determine specific desires presents a vexed interpretive question. The answer to that question determines whether an individual's general ends can be specified in a number of distinctive ways, and whether two *phronimoi* might reasonably disagree about a policy.

28. See C. Kirwan, *Aristotle's Metaphysics: Books Gamma, Delta and Epsilon* (Oxford, 1971), p. 170.

29. See Ackrill, *Categories*, p. 104.

30. See Blundell, "*Ēthos* and *Dianoia* Reconsidered"; Cope, *An Introduction to Aristotle's Rhetoric*, vol. 3, p. 193.

31. There are land mines buried beneath the glossy reference to the influence of character traits on practical reasoning. Just *how* does character "affect" or

"influence" perception, desire, and *dianoia?* Are the features of an individual's character expressed *in* his ends and actions? Or do character traits in some unspecified way *cause* him to have those ends and perform those actions? Or do they provide a "thicker" description of desires and actions?

32. This explains why Aristotle thinks he must provide an independent discussion of *pathē*, despite his already having described the emotions that are typical of the various types of character. While a person's character is directly expressed in the range of his desires, it is indirectly expressed in his habits and dispositions concerning his emotions rather than in emotions that occur fortuitously (*NE* 2.6.1106b1 ff.).

33. The most comprehensive account of *pathē* appears in the *Metaphysics,* where they are characterized as (*a*) qualities in respect to which a thing can change (its color or mood, for instance), (*b*) the alteration itself (blushing or anger, for instance), (*c*) injurious or painful alterations (a wound, for instance), or (*d*) extreme misfortune like that suffered by Priam (1022b15 ff.). So described, the class of passions is very broad indeed: it includes physical as well as psychological reactions. By contrast to the active essential function (*ergon*) of a thing, its *pathē* are typically accidental, exogenous, and temporary conditions. For the role of *pathē* in other contexts, see: *Cat.* 9a28–10a11, 11b1–9; *Phys.* 202a22–202b29; *Gen. Cor.* 322b15–323a33, 324b25–326a28, 326b29–327a28; *DA* 429a10–429b10, 430a14–25, 431a1–431b20; *Motu* 701b20 ff.; *NE* 1104b4 ff., 1106b36–1107a6, 1108a30 ff. For a more extended discussion of the class of *pathē* as it encompasses physiological modifications as well as the kinds of cognitively individuated emotions that are in principle subject to voluntary control, see my "Aristotle on the Metaphysical Status of *Pathē.*"

34. But a belief or a desire formed by external manipulation can, for some purposes, be classified with *pathē*, even if the belief happens to be true and the desire happens to be right (*orthos*). On the other hand, there are individual cases of indignation—the wrath of Achilles, for example—that are fundamentally based in character. Since such conditions are long-standing dispositions rather than fortuitous reactions to contingent events, they are not strictly speaking *pathē*, even though indignation is typically a *pathos* (1369a6). See Cope, *An Introduction to Aristotle's Rhetoric,* pp. 113–118.

35. The division of labor in the analysis of the emotions is at best quite complex, at worst unclear. The physiology studied by the *physikos* is never purely material. It already contains a form-defined intentional selector: not *any* boiling of the blood around the heart, but the blood boiling *in anger* rather than, say, solely from fever. Nor is the psychologist's contribution purely conceptual. As J. Barnes observes ("Aristotle's Concept of Mind," *Articles on Aristotle,* vol. 4, ed. J. Barnes, M. Schofield, and R. Sorabji [London, 1979], p. 37), the dialectical definition of anger marks it as painful (*lupē*), which is, "with the body" (*kata tōn sōmatōn*) (*Sensu* 436a10–436b2). In *De Motu Animalium,* Aristotle combines the physiological with at least some psychological dimensions of movement and action: *phantasiai* change the size, shape, and temperature of the bodily parts (701b12–32).

36. I suspect, but cannot prove, that he would regard the question as making an odd and obvious category mistake.

37. See Annas, "Aristotle on Pleasure and Goodness"; J. Ackrill, "Aristotle's Distinction Between *Energeia* and *Kinēsis*," *New Essays on Plato and Aristotle*, ed. R. Bambrough (London, 1965); G. E. L. Owen, "Aristotelian Pleasures," *Articles on Aristotle: Ethics and Politics*, ed. J. Barnes, M. Schofield, and R. Sorabji (London, 1979); Rorty, "The Place of Pleasure in Aristotle's Ethics."

38. See Frede, "Mixed Feelings in Aristotle's *Rhetoric*."

39. See M. C. Nussbaum, "Aristotle on Emotions and Rational Persuasion," this volume, and her *Aristotle's De Motu Animalium* (Princeton, 1978), especially essay 5; M. Schofield, "Aristotle on the Imagination," *Essays on Aristotle's De Anima*, ed. M. C. Nussbaum and A. O. Rorty (Oxford, 1992); D. Frede, "The Cognitive Role of *Phantasia* in Aristotle," *Essays on Aristotle's De Anima*, ed. M. C. Nussbaum and A. O. Rorty (Oxford, 1992); and D. Charles, "Fear: Imagination and Belief" (unpublished manuscript of a talk, Helsinki conference, 1991), for an excellent discussion of the role of *phantasia* in producing and sustaining action-guiding fear.

40. Beyond the difficulties presented by the texts themselves, there are those that arise from our own associations, from the history of the philosophical derivatives and descendants of *phantasia:* seventeenth- and eighteenth-century theories of images and imagining; the role of imagination and the schematism in Kant's transcendental psychology; the pejorative post-Romantic distinction between fantasy and the imagination; recent discussions of the intentionality of mental activity. All of these give us glimpses of *phantasia,* glimpses that can mislead us.

41. This is compatible with Aristotle's saying that *phantasia* has the same objects as *aisthēsis,* and that it cannot arise without sensations (*ouk aneu aisthēsis gignesthai*). While no particular *phantasia* can arise without a specific sensation, and while its content is the same as "its" sensation, the *aisthēsis* is always true. But since *phantasia* is how the content of an *aisthēsis* appears to us, it can be either true or false (428b).

42. How can *phantasia* be "up to us"? Is there some connection between the latitude of *phantasia* (*DA* 427b15–21) and the way that we—or at any rate some of us—are responsible for our actions? See Schofield, "Aristotle on the Imagination"; J. McDowell, "The Role of *Eudaimonia* in Aristotle's Ethics," *Essays on Aristotle's Ethics,* ed. A. O. Rorty (Berkeley, 1980); M. C. Nussbaum, *The Fragility of Goodness* (Cambridge, 1986), pp. 277–279; Nussbaum, *Aristotle's De Motu Animalium,* essay 5; D. Charles, *Aristotle's Philosophy of Action* (Ithaca, 1984), and "Fear: Imagination and Belief"; D. Wiggins, "Deliberation and Practical Reason," *Essays on Aristotle's Ethics,* ed. A. O. Rorty (Berkeley, 1980); Frede, "The Cognitive Role of *Phantasia* in Aristotle."

43. Myles Burnyeat helped me to see that *phantasia* is thinking of a kind, rather than a type, of thought.

44. See Nussbaum, *Aristotle's De Motu Animalium,* pp. 233 ff.

45. See D. Gallop, "Animals in the *Poetics*," *Oxford Studies in Ancient Philosophy* 8 (1990):145–171. Aristotle has used this kind of explanatory strategy elsewhere: public debate—attempting to form an "all things considered" judgment by weighing the pros and cons advanced by different voices—provides the model for intrapsychic deliberation.

46. Useful discussions of the functions of *phantasia* are to be found in Schofield, "Aristotle on the Imagination"; Frede, "The Cognitive Role of *Phantasia*"; and Nussbaum, *Aristotle's De Motu Animalium,* especially essay 5, and her essay in this volume.

47. See Richardson, "Desire and the Good in *De Anima.*"

48. See my "The Psychology of Aristotle's Poetics," *Essays on Aristotle's Poetics,* ed. A. O. Rorty (Princeton, 1992).

49. See R. Padel, *In and Out of the Mind* (Princeton, 1993), for a brilliant account of how (what we consider) "merely metaphorical speech" was taken literally by ancient dramatists, poets, orators, and physicians. I am also grateful to Myles Burnyeat and Richard Moran for discussions about the ways that metaphor can be truthful and persuasive.

50. Rousseau makes a similar point when he says that metaphorical speech precedes literal speech. Jacques Derrida and Paul de Man might be making this sort of claim when they say that literal speech derives from poetic signifiers.

51. See Salkever, *Finding the Mean*; Euben, *The Tragedy of Political Theory.*

52. An astute deliberative rhetorician trying to persuade the *polis* of the danger of an enemy attack should indicate the probability of its occurrence (is it merely possible or virtually assured?), its timing (when is it most likely to occur?), its size (how large and well armed are the enemy forces?), its degree (how does it compare with other relevant risks and dangers?), and its trend (are the enemy forces being enlarged or diminished?) (2.19).

Aristotle's Rhetoric as a "Counterpart" to Dialectic

Jacques Brunschwig

The most famous sentence in Aristotle's *Rhetoric* is quite probably the first one, namely "Rhetoric is a counterpart (*antistrophos*) to dialectic." After delivering this sentence (likely to have shattered the walls of Plato's Academy),[1] Aristotle offers the rationale for his statement: both arts (*technai*) have many features in common, and most of these features belong to no other art. However, the two treatises he wrote in order to teach rhetoric and dialectic, respectively the *Rhetoric* and the *Topics*, do not look like each other much. Admittedly, we read a number of explicit references to the *Topics* in the *Rhetoric;* this last treatise makes abundant use of the very notion of *topos;* indeed, it is only in the *Rhetoric* (2.26.1403a16–17) that we find something that looks like a definition of *topos,* whereas such a definition is strangely missing in the *Topics* themselves, in spite of their title and of their usual generosity otherwise in the matter of definitions. Nevertheless, if we take a panoramic look at the two treatises, we can only be struck by their many contrasts from a number of such points of view as style, presentation, teaching method, expected readership, pedagogical results, and so on. Quite obviously, Aristotle did not think that there was only one way of teaching a *technē,* even when it was a matter of teaching two *technai* as closely connected as are the two main arts of discourse: rhetoric and dialectic.

My problem here may be stated quite simply. It will be to try to offer some suggestions about the history, the meaning, and the grounds of the following contrast: on the one hand, if we consider rhetoric and dialectic *qua* arts, Aristotle claims that they strongly resemble each other; on the other hand, if we consider rhetoric and dialectic *qua* works both written by Aristotle, they no less strongly differ from one another.

Let us first return to the initial sentence of the *Rhetoric.* Roughly speaking, the *antistrophic* relation thereby established between rhetoric and dialectic makes rhetoric a "counterpart" of dialectic (the image is of course taken from the theater: the *antistrophē* was the part of the song which the chorus sang when returning to the place where they had come from when first singing the *strophē*). This relation is immediately exploited by Aristotle, in the sense that Chapter 1.1 consistently describes rhetoric in reference to dialectic. The reader is assumed to know the main features of dialectic: the absence of determined subject matter, its elaboration on earlier empirical practice, the explication of its aims or ends, the type of utility or utilities, the definition of the proper function of the art in terms of method rather than in terms of performance, the existence of degenerate forms, and so on. These features can then easily be transposed to the analysis of rhetoric. Moreover, this chapter contains what is probably the most precise reference in the *Rhetoric* to the *Topics* (1355a28, which significantly refers to *Topics* 1.2.101a26–30, a description of this particular utility of dialectic that concerns "encounters" with "ordinary people").

However, Chapter 1.2 *prima facie* seems to dismantle this strict parallelism: for now a new component is introduced into the picture, namely the ethical-political component of rhetoric. Aristotle explicitly says (1356a25) that "it appears that rhetoric is as it were an offshoot (*paraphues ti*) of dialectic and of the science of ethics, which may be reasonably called politics." Is this new picture in contradiction with, or at least at variance with, the *antistrophic* picture of Chapter 1.1? Not necessarily so; and even, I think, necessarily not so. For a few lines after this sentence, Aristotle himself refers to "what was said at the outset" (1356a31), that is, to the *antistrophē* statement. True, this reference raises a problem, because it is designed to support a different statement about the relationship between the two arts, namely that "rhetoric is a sort of part or likeness (*morion ti* or *homoiōma*—variant reading *homoia*) of dialectic." Now Aristotle had precisely not said, "at the outset," that rhetoric was a part of dialectic. Perhaps the text here should be suspected.[2] In any case it is difficult to build anything solid on this rather enigmatic sentence. On the other hand, it seems perfectly possible to understand the ethical-political component of rhetoric as an elucidation, not as a rectification, of the *antistrophē* statement. An *antistrophē* (we can take it for sure if we remember the seminal passage of Plato's *Gorgias*, 464b ff.) has the logical structure of an analogy: it holds between *A* and *B* if and only if there are two items *C* and *D* such that what *A* is to *C*, *B* is to *D*. Now, if dialectic is *A* and rhetoric is *B*, what are *C* and *D*? They can be identified through Aristotle's descriptions of the common and spontaneous activities with which they are, according to him, continuous: "all men in a manner have a share of both, for all, up to a certain point, endeavour to criticise or uphold statements, and to defend themselves or to accuse" (1354a3–6). The first part of this sentence obviously refers to the activity for which dialectic provides the techniques; the second part, fairly clearly, designates by metonymy all the activities that rhetoric (in all its varieties) masters technically. Dialectic and rhetoric are antistrophic in the precise sense that what dialectic is to the private and conversational use of language (between two people alternatively speaking and hearing, asking questions and answering them), rhetoric is to the public use of language (political, in a broad sense), addressed by a single speaker to a collective audience.

If we now look at the actual contents of the *Rhetoric* and the *Topics*, the first and most dramatic breach in the *antistrophē* relation between rhetoric and dialectic is simply that, whereas the *Rhetoric* emphatically states this relation and builds a great deal on it, the *Topics* is completely silent on the matter. Whereas the *Rhetoric* often refers to the *Topics*, to dialectic and its typical concepts, the *Topics* contains no reference at all to the *Rhetoric*, and very few references to the art of rhetoric as such.[3] Whereas the reader of the *Rhetoric* cannot ignore that the author of the treatise had also written about dialectic, no reader of the *Topics* could be aware of the fact that Aristotle had written a treatise on rhetoric, or at least planned to do so, or even that he was interested in rhetoric. No reader of the *Topics* could imagine that the art he was learning actually had a "counterpart," that this counterpart was rhetoric, *a fortiori* that a study of rhetoric could be of any use to the reader.

These facts could help explain in a very simple way why Aristotle, although treating dialectic as a model for rhetoric, did not take his own work on dialectic, namely the *Topics*, as a model for his writing of the treatise he devotes to rhetoric. For the facts suggest that the *Topics* was written not only before the *Rhetoric*, but also, and more important, before Aristotle came to think that dialectic and rhetoric were counterparts. The *Topics*, composed with no idea whatsoever of the *antistrophē*, could thus not work as a model for composing a treatise about what Aristotle had eventually come to see as the "counterpart" of their subject matter.

Now, there are at least two objections to this simple chronological explanation, which I shall briefly summarize. The first objection is that, although it is probably true that the core of the *Topics* was written before the *Rhetoric*, some parts of the *Rhetoric* definitely seem to be earlier than the parts of the *Topics* that are close to them but do not refer to them. The most intriguing case is *Rhetoric* 1.7, which contains many common elements with *Topics* 3.1–3. Neither section mentions the other; nevertheless, it is obvious that one of them was already written when Aristotle composed the other; and the more likely hypothesis, it seems to me, is that *Rhetoric* 1.7 preceded *Topics* 3.1–3.[4]

The second objection is drawn from what is left of a lost work by Aristotle, quite probably an early one. In this work, boldly entitled *The Sophist* we are told, Aristotle had claimed that Empedocles had invented rhetoric, and Zeno dialectic.[5] Moreover, the testimony of Sextus Empiricus about this work makes clear that the idea of the *antistrophē* between the two arts was already present in it. The historical *antistrophē* between Zeno and Empedocles was thus reinforcing, and reinforced by, the theoretical *antistrophē* between the arts they were supposed to have invented.[6] If so, the point of departure of Aristotle's thoughts about the relationship between rhetoric and dialectic would be this strong, simple, and slightly naive view, according to which both arts are linked by this double *antistrophē*, simultaneously theoretical and historical. The problem is now to understand how and why, and through which steps, this initial structure came to be dismantled, so as to leave almost no trace in the treatises devoted to dialectic and to rhetoric.

One very important step in this story is the famous last chapter of the *Sophistical Refutations*. To put it in a nutshell, one could say that Aristotle here completely gives up the idea of a historical *antistrophē* between dialectic and rhetoric, while retaining some important elements of the idea of a theoretical *antistrophē* between them. The historical *antistrophē* disappears: Aristotle now acknowleges that rhetoric, at the time of his writing, already is a technical discipline, with a long, rich, and cumulative history, whereas in the field of dialectic he claims, quite abruptly, that before himself "nothing existed at all" (183b36). Moreover, he does not even try to find any theoretical explanation of this time lag, which he considers a mere accident (183b16–17, 27). He also gives up using the myth of the "first inventor" (*prōtos heuretēs*), which was dominant in the early *Sophist*.[7] However, he keeps a discontinuist view, according to which the birth of an art is a technological break, an absolute beginning (*archē*, 183b22) that coincides with the discovery of the principles (*archai*, 183b28) of the art. But this beginning is only a beginning: it has nothing dramatic in it (it is something very small, *mikron, mikrotaton*, 183b20–24, 29), and the art does not appear in its final form all of a sudden. Here the beginnings of rhetoric are significantly attributed to an anonymous group of *prōtoi*, followed by a succession (*diadochē*, 183b30) of individual technographers: Tisias, then Thrasymachus, then Theodorus.

Although rhetoric is mentioned here only as an example of "all the other discoveries" that are contrasted with dialectic, and not as the privileged *antistrophon* of dialectic, there are some important signs that Aristotle remembers their antistrophic relation. First, he makes use of it in order to reject a possible objection against his bold claim that in the field of dialectic "nothing existed at all" before him. Is it not the case, so the objection would run, that dialectic was not only practiced but also actually taught before the writing of the *Topics*? The answer (183b36–184a4) is that such transmission was no teaching properly speaking. Aristotle draws a parallel between the "training" (*paideusis*) given by "the paid masters of eristic arguments" and the "quick" but "atechnic" method of Gorgias, who used to give his pupils speeches to learn by heart: this was imparting to them "not an art, but the products of an art."[8] So, there is still an *antistrophē* of a sort at the pedagogical level; but it is a link between the fraudulent anticipations of technical teaching within the paired fields of dialectic and rhetoric.

The same *antistrophē* is also working in the passage (184a8–184b3) where Aristotle again describes the contrast between what is the case in rhetoric ("there already existed much material enunciated in the past") and what is the case "in the field of deductive reasoning," *peri tou sullogizesthai* ("we had absolutely no earlier work to quote, but were for a long time labouring at tentative researches"). Although this *sullogizesthai* has often been, and is still sometimes, taken as referring to the deductive reasoning as described in the *Prior Analytics*, it seems obvious that Aristotle is still speaking here of the same *pragmateia* that he had already contrasted with rhetoric as completely new (183b16–36); that is, the *Topics* (*Sophistical Refutations* included). All in all, the privileged theoretical relationship between dialectic and rhetoric is thus still operative in this final chapter of the *Sophistical Refutations*, even if there is no longer any mention of the historical *antistrophē*, any occurrence of the word *antistrophē* itself, or any use of the coarsest aspects of the myth of the "first inventor."

Now we are in a better position to understand why the *Rhetoric* looks so little like the *Topics*. I would like to ask the following question: if we only had the final chapter of the *Sophistical Refutations*, could we reconstruct the structure of Aristotle's treatise on the art of dialectic (of which this chapter is the conclusion) and the structure of the treatise on the rhetoric that he eventually composed (although he does not say anything about composing it in this chapter)? But, first of all, we must raise a more general question about the way (or the ways) open to Aristotle when undertaking to teach any *technē*, given his conception of what a *technē* is. This question remains open because of the nature and history of any given art.

In Aristotelian terms, a *technē*, *qua* productive disposition supported by rational and true foundations (*NE* 6.4.1140a11), could be taught in various ways. By its nature, a *technē* is a rational, discursive, and universal body of knowledge and skills. But it has not appeared *ex nihilo:* the specific needs a *technē* satisfies in a rational and methodical way existed and were satisfied in a rudimentary way, through lucky guesses, trials, and errors, before it appeared. Such procedures were eventually capitalized into an "experience" (*empeiria*), and this experience is the raw material on which the inventor of the *technē* works.[9] The "technological break" precisely corresponds to the discovery of the causes by virtue of which the empirical procedures succeed or fail (*Rhet.* 1.1.1354a9–11). Once these causes are identified and known, the technician can produce, in a rational and methodical way, the same effects that the experienced man produced without method or rationality; hence, he can now teach how to produce them in a methodical way.

The outcome of this situation is that there is more than one way, for Aristotle or for an Aristotelian, of writing a *Technē*, that is, a treatise designed for the teaching of a *technē*. The technographer can introduce his disciple, so to speak, into his own workshop: he shows him the raw material that he employed, he takes him through the same process by which he developed the rationale of his method. In the course of explicating the new *technē*, he will refer to the work of his predecessors, to make clear his own contribution. Another way of teaching a *technē* involves clearing the scaffolding away from his construction, so as to present the building with the purity and dryness of a rational and systematic method. Instead of turning backward, to the sources of the art, he turns forward, in the direction of its outcome. Let us call "historical" or "referential" the style of presentation that corresponds to the first choice, since it constantly refers to the historical accumulation of material on which the technographer has worked. And let us call "theoretical" or "unhistorical" the second choice, since the theorizing process is now kept in the dark, all the light being projected on the theoretical results of this process.

The choice between these two ways of writing a *Technē* is strongly influenced, if not entirely necessitated, by the personal position of the writer in the history of the art he is about to teach. If he is a pioneer in the field, or if he thinks he is, he will normally be tempted to adopt the unhistorical, theoretical approach, which adequately reflects his own importance as an innovator and the discontinuity between what was the case before him and what becomes possible thanks to him. On the other hand, if he is not the inventor of the *technē*, if he sees himself as a simple link within a long, continuous succession of technographers, then he is more likely to adopt the historical, referential approach, which more faithfully corresponds to his own historical position.

Let us notice, however, that there is nothing compelling about such a choice. A pioneer might well like to refer to the empirical material on which he worked; an heir might well prefer to present his legacy in a systematic fashion. The difference marked by Aristotle, in the final chapter of the *Sophistical Refutations*, between the history of dialectic and the history of rhetoric is not enough to determine, in a strictly necessary way, a difference between his way of writing, respectively, the *Topics* and the *Rhetoric*. Nothing prevented him from adopting the "referential" style in both treatises: in the *Topics*, he could have exhibited in detail the argumentative material out of which he had worked out the rules of the art of dialectic; in the *Rhetoric*, he could have used the many treatises already left by his predecessors. Nothing prevented him either from presenting both treatises in a nonreferential mode, leaving aside the whole of his preliminary working material. All that can be said is that the difference marked by the *Sophistical Refutations* could at least have inclined him to choose the theoretical mode for the writing of the *Topics*, and the referential one for the writing of the *Rhetoric*.

My claim here will be that these expectations are confirmed by the facts: such was indeed his choice, in full awareness of his own situation within the respective development of dialectic and rhetoric.

I shall be very brief on the *Topics*, and I shall only stress points that might be useful for comparison with the *Rhetoric*. Roughly speaking, I think that the presentation adopted by Aristotle in this treatise is of the "theoretical" type, as might be expected from his claim that "nothing of the kind existed before." In spite of some appearances to the contrary, this claim, properly understood, can be accepted. It is of course true that he worked on a rich argumentative material that gave him the empirical basis he needed in order to build his *Technē*. But the text of the *Topics* is certainly not the simple recording of the "tentative researches" on which he has been "labouring for a long time" (*Soph. El.* 34.184b2–3). From the beginning (*Top.* 1.1.100a18, 1.3.101b5, 1.4.101b11) to the end (*Soph. El.* 34.184b4, 7), he describes what he offers as a *methodos*, that is, something looking not backward but forward, and aiming at a systematic production of new objects (in this case, dialectical syllogisms).[10] This description of the work as a *methodos* is confirmed, I think, by the powerful structure given to the treatise as a whole by the use of the exhaustive quadripartite scheme of the so-called predicables (accident, genus, property, and definition).

One might object that the *Topics* is full of concrete examples that precisely seem to register Aristotle's "long and tentative researches." On this point, I would first note, however, that these examples are for the most part borrowed from a rather narrow circle, the circle of the problems usually discussed by Plato and the ancient Academy with their typical partners (philosophers, physicists, sophists, and so on).[11] No mention is made of any use of dialectical instruments by such nonphilosophers as poets, orators, historians, and the like, let alone by ordinary people (although one of the purposes of dialectic, according to *Topics* 1.2.101a27, 30–34, is to favor "conversations" or "encounters" with such people). But above all, I would like to stress an important, although little noticed feature of the examples in the *Topics*. As a matter of principle, one could imagine two very different ways of illustrating a given argumentative *topos*: one would be to quote a particular argument (real or fictitious) that brings or has brought this *topos* into play; the other would be to quote a particular claim that could be argued, either *pro* or *con*, with the help of this *topos*. Now, the examples in the *Topics* always belong to the second type. They are not, properly speaking, examples of dialectical reasonings; they are rather examples of dialectical situations in which a given type of dialectical reasoning might be put to work. Aristotle does not show his disciple how nontechnical practitioners of dialectic have reasoned before; he does not even show how he has himself victoriously discussed the theories of Plato or Xenocrates within the Academy debates. When he mentions the possible use of a given *topos* against "those who posit the existence of Ideas," he does not say "This is how I used to argue"; he says "This is how you should argue, if you happen, in the future, to be opposed to such people."

The conception of the *topos* itself, in the *Topics,* makes clear that Aristotle here consciously refrains from any referential point of view. Of course, the point is rather hard to prove, since, as we already noted, no definition of the *topos* is offered in the *Topics.* But we can at least draw on a negative fact, namely that nothing in the dialectic treatise answers to the definition given of the *topos* in the *Rhetoric* (2.26.1403a17): "It is the same thing which I call element (*stoicheion*) and *topos;* for element and *topos* are that under which many enthymemes fall (*eis ho polla enthumēmata empiptei*)." Of course, it is tempting to transpose this definition (antistrophically) to the dialectical *topos:* the easy way is to substitute "syllogisms" for "enthymemes." Many commentators,[12] naturally enough, yielded to the temptation, and believed they had thus gotten the definition of the *topos* that was missing in the *Topics.* But this was the wrong thing to do. The right thing to do was, on the contrary, to stress that Aristotle himself did not make this easy move and to suppose that he had good reasons for not doing so. The definition given in the *Rhetoric* is typically referential and empirical.[13] According to it, a *topos* can be identified on the basis of a given collection of rhetorical arguments, picked out of the oratory practice, which present a sort of family resemblance, and out of which a common structure can be brought to light. It is perfectly understandable that the equivalent of such a definition is not to be found in the *Topics.* In this work, the *topoi* are never presented as "that under which many syllogisms fall." They are not retrospectively related to a number of already produced syllogisms, but prospectively related to a number of syllogisms still to be produced out of them, as out of argumentative matrices. Their standard formulation is that of a rule, inviting the learner to examine (*skopein, skepteon*) whether such and such a condition holds; if it does, the production of the appropriate syllogism is possible.

This prospective conception of the *topos* is exactly expressed by the quite different definition offered by Theophrastus:[14] "The *topos* is a principle or element, out of which (*aph'hou*) we grasp the principles [i.e., the premises] concerning each thing [i.e., each problem]; it is determinate as far as its description is concerned, and indeterminate as far as its particular applications are concerned." This Theophrastean definition, far from being revisionary in respect to Aristotle, seems to me to capture the essence of the *topos* in the *Topics* much better than any antistrophic version we could extract from the definition given in the *Rhetoric*. Substituting *aph'hou* for *eis ho* is a highly significant change in the definition of *topos*: *aph'hou* suggests that the *topos* is essentially the source from which the premises of a syllogism are to be derived; *eis ho* suggests that the *topos* is derived by reflection on what is common to a collection of particular instances of arguments.

A comparison between two passages apparently quite close to each other (*Rhet.* 1.1.1354a3–11 and *Soph. El.* 34.172a23–36) confirms the point. In both passages, Aristotle is keen on showing that dialectical or rhetorical techniques follow an activity that everybody somehow practices without any method. But the *Rhetoric* passage, as we already saw, expresses the idea that the working out of the *technē* is conditioned by a reflection on the successes and failures of this preliminary, unmethodical practice that provides a diagnosis of the causes of these successes and failures. This typically referential idea is, so to speak, rubbed out in the parallel passage of the *Sophistical Refutations*. Speaking of the "peirastic" branch of dialectic (which puts to the test, Socrates-like, claims to knowledge), Aristotle tries to show why a questioner, although devoid of knowledge in the field in which his partner claims to possess knowledge, is quite legitimately able to debar him from his pretensions, because he is relying on "common" principles, of which even specialized branches of knowledge necessarily make use. He then says:

> Accordingly, everybody, including the laymen, makes some kind of use of dialectic and peirastic; indeed all, up to a certain point, attempt to test those who profess knowledge. Now this is where the common principles come in; for they know these themselves just as well, even though their expression of them seems to be very inaccurate. Thus they all practise refutation; for they perform unmethodically (*atechnōs*) the task which dialectic performs methodically (*entechnōs*).

Here Aristotle contents himself with juxtaposing the "atechnical" activity of laymen and the "technical" activity of the dialecticians, without saying or suggesting that the dialectical *technē* was born out of a reflection on the causes of the successes or failures of the spontaneous, pretechnical activity, let alone that its "function" (*ergon*) is to think about such causes (cf. *Rhet.* 1.1.1354a10–11). The general trend of the passage is not to explain the origins of the theory with experience, but rather to explain the experience with a theory: the theoretical conditions of *peira* make understandable the fact that everybody can put claims to knowlege to a critical test by the use of common principles, even in the absence of substantive knowledge.

The general approach of the *Topics* to their subject, and many details of their elaboration, witness to the systematically nonreferential style that Aristotle adopted in his writing of them, as could be expected on the basis of the final chapter of the *Refutations*.

Now, what about the *Rhetoric*? We have already seen, from this same chapter of the *Sophistical Refutations*, that Aristotle could not and did not see himself, in this field, as the first technographer. We have also seen that this position did not compel him to adopt a particular method, but that it inclined him to choose a referential mode of exposition, better fitted to the historical situation of the rhetorical discipline, to his own position in its history, and to his awareness of this position.

The actual contents of the *Rhetoric* seem to me for the most part to correspond to this expectation. As a whole, the mode of exposition of the treatise is basically referential, although some of the references to be found in it are not exactly those which might be expected.

Let us begin with the use of examples. Any reader of the *Rhetoric* can see that the general strategy of the treatise, in this respect, is quite different from what can be found in the *Topics*. First of all, from the point of view of quantity and diversity, the examples of the *Rhetoric* are much more numerous and various than those in the *Topics*. The *Rhetoric* is a very scholarly work: it has been a source of information and of problems. Aristotle here borrows his examples from vastly different sources: first of all, of course, the various branches (deliberative, forensic, epideictic) of the oratory of his time; but also poetry, written prose, drama, comedy, proverbs, and anecdotes of every kind. It is surprising to find numerous examples of philosophical arguments in a treatise which was, after all, designed for the training of orators. Aristotle often mentions or alludes to famous events and persons of his time; modern historians are generally able to identify his allusions, which provide a *terminus post quem* to the writing (or the insertion) of the passages that contain them. Moreover, and above all, in contrast with the examples in the *Topics*, the examples in the *Rhetoric* are, so to speak, first-order illustrations of the procedures recommended by Aristotle to the orator: once he has described the procedure in abstract terms, he quotes an argument that has already been used, and which actually puts to work the procedure in question.

The general preference of the author of the *Rhetoric* for a referential style can also be seen, on a lesser scale, in the definition or use of some important notions. I have already cited the lines at the beginning of the treatise where Aristotle says, strangely enough, that "all would at once admit that to examine the cause why some [untechnically] attain their end [i.e., to criticize or to uphold an argument, to defend themselves or to accuse] by familiarity, and others by chance, is the function (*ergon*) of an art." What is a bit strange here is that *prima facie* he seems to think that the proper function of the art is not, or at least is not primarily, to make it possible to produce objects of a given type (here speeches), but rather to think in a retrospective mood about the reasons why untechnical practitioners have already succeeded, either by chance or by mere experience, in producing objects of this type.

Of course, the *Rhetoric* does not ignore that the rhetorical *technē* is also a creative capacity, producing speeches and providing arguments (*dunamis tou porisai logous*, 1.2.1356a33). But it is remarkable that, even when he describes this aspect of the *technē*, Aristotle makes little use of the vocabulary of production or creation (*poiēsis*) of something which is not yet in existence. Without any apparent reason, he often uses the vocabulary of vision, as if the relevant object were already here, existing (*huparchon*), and just waiting to be brought into view (*idein*).[15] What has to be brought into view is sometimes described as "what the existing means of persuasion are (*ta huparchonta pithana*)," sometimes as "what the possible means of persuasion are (*to endechomenon pithanon*)"; but in both cases, rhetoric is described as an ability to "see" the relevant sort of *pithanon*.

Moreover, it should be stressed that the description of rhetoric as "a capacity for producing speeches [or arguments, *logoi*]" (1356a33) is supported by a comparison with dialectic and a reference to the initial statement about the *antistrophē* (1356a31), as if this aspect of rhetoric could not be brought out without such a reference. We may actually observe the slight modification occasioned by this new point of view by comparing the contexts of an apparently identical statement in both passages. In 1356a33, the idea that rhetoric and dialectic both are "capacities for producing arguments" is associated with a negative complement, namely that "neither of them is a science of any definite subject (*peri oudenos hōrismenou epistēmē*), [of which it would say] how it is." The basic opposition here is the contrast between theoretical science (which describes how things necessarily are) and a science of *technē* and *poiēsis* (which describes how to produce things that would not otherwise exist).[16] Mentioning the absence of a definite subject for both capacities is not strictly relevant to the formulation of this contrast. On the other hand, at the beginning of chapter 1.1, rhetoric and dialectic are antistrophically associated, in the sense that "both have to do with matters that are in a manner within the cognizance (*gnōrizein*) of all men and not confined to any special science" (1354a1–3). The basic contrast between these arts and other disciplines is not that between knowledge and production, but that between two types of knowledge: the knowledge of definite objects accessible through special sciences and the knowledge of objects commonly accessible to everybody. The relevant opposition has thus changed: in both passages, it is still said that rhetoric and dialectic are not sciences of any particular object; but that means, in the earlier passage, that they are sciences of universal objects, and in the later, that they are not sciences of any objects at all.

The *Rhetoric* is thus referential in this first and simple sense, that Aristotle here constantly refers to the widespread and variegated oratory experience out of which he tries to build his *technē*. It is also referential in a more complex sense, namely that the text itself contains the traces of the technicizing process that is applied to this raw material. In contrast with the *Topics*, which leaves in the dark the registering of the "tentative researches" preliminary to its elaboration, the *Rhetoric* introduces the reader to the corresponding "labors" to such an extent that the reader often faces serious problems of comprehension. I would like to examine two particular examples, both crucial for the structure of the treatise as a whole, namely the distinctions among three types of "proofs" (*pisteis*) and among three types of rhetorical speeches.[17]

Let us first take the three types of proofs (the *ēthos*, the *pathos*, and the so-called rational proof). Obviously, Aristotle borrowed this distinction from oratory practice in courts and political assemblies, as well as from the works of a number of contemporary *technologoi* (cf. 1.1.1354a12–16, 1354b16–29, 1355a19–20). As is well known, Aristotle offers in chapter 1.1 a strongly purist and intellectualist view of rhetoric, distancing himself from the *technologoi:* he seems to identify technical proofs with enthymemes, and accordingly to expel *ēthos* and *pathos* from the technical field proper. He shows in some detail that the *technologoi* he criticizes have neglected what he calls "the body of proof," that is, the enthymeme, in favor of "accessories" (*prosthēkai*) and of "matters outside the subject" (*ta exō tou pragmatos*), namely the means of influencing the audience or the jury by appealing to feelings and passions. He also shows why this exclusive concern with the accessories of rhetoric led the *technologoi* to concentrating upon forensic eloquence, where these aspects have pride of place.

Is there any contradiction between this position, as expressed in chapter 1.1, which is a sort of "false start,"[18] and chapter 1.2, where Aristotle admits *ēthos* and *pathos* as "entechnical" proofs, only designating as "atechnical" proofs such things as witnesses, avowals obtained under torture, quotations of written texts of laws or contracts, and the like, all of which preceded the elaboration of the speech (1355b35–39)? A careful examination of both chapters suggests that there is no contradiction between them, and that Aristotle kept them alongside each other because he wanted to show his reader the theorizing process that had led him from his starting point to a different but not incompatible position. Several clues might be found to make this point.

First of all, at the very moment where Aristotle deals with the *pathos*, not acknowledged as a fully fledged entechnical proof (1356a14–19), he feels inclined to refer to chapter 1 (*phamen*, 1356a17) in order to remind the reader that the *technologoi* criticized there were only interested in this aspect of rhetoric. If he had first condemned the appeal to passion as atechnical, and subsequently accepted it as entechnical, is it likely that he would have drawn the reader's attention to this contradiction, instead of leaving it in an unobtrusive darkness? It is much more likely that this backward reference is designed to show under which condition (a condition not satisfied by the *technologoi*, but satisfied in the Aristotelian rhetoric) the *pathos* can find its legitimate place in the overall repertory of available technical means.[19] This condition is precisely stated, in the description of the entechnical *pathos*, by the phrase *hupo tou logou* (1356a14): appealing to the passions is an entechnical practice when the *pathos* is raised in the audience "by the speech itself" (in contradistinction with nondiscursive means, like cries, tears, gesticulations, wry faces, or the production of moaning women or weeping children). Such is, in fact, the general criterion of "entechnicality": the atechnical proofs preexist the speech (*prohupērchen*, 1355b36), the speaker can only "make use of them" (*chrēsasthai*, 1355b39), whereas entechnical proofs are those that he brings out with his method, in and through his own speech (1355b35–39).[20]

Second, when Aristotle deals with *ēthos*, he uses the same general criterion in order to legitimate its place among entechnical proofs: the confidence inspired by the speaker must "be due to the speech itself, not to any preestablished reputation of the speaker" (1356a9–10). Aristotle goes so far as to qualify *ēthos*, although with some caution, as "so to say, the main proof" (1356a13). But the most remarkable feature of this passage, from the point of view that concerns us, is that Aristotle here mentions, in a polemic vein, "some of the *technologountes*" who put *ēthos* out of the art and claim that "the worth of the orator in no way contributes to his powers of persuasion." These purist (or cynical) technographers are probably not the same as those who were criticized in chapter 1, and who, on the contrary, were only concerned with "how to put the judge into a certain frame of mind" (1354b20). It is clear that Aristotle misses no occasion of referring to various and even opposite tendencies in the rhetoric of his time, so as better to distance himself from them, and to polish the description of his own position.

Thus, the entechnical versus atechnical distinction does not separate rational arguments from those that appeal to *ēthos* and *pathos:* it cuts through these last two classes, with the help of a precise criterion. This differentiating process is a nice illustration of how Aristotle, starting from various data picked out from rhetorical tradition and experience, proceeds to a theoretical filtering of such data, and does so right before the reader's eyes. In this way, he is able to determine to what extent some parts of these data (rejected as a whole in a somewhat simplified version of the antirhetorical Platonic tradition, and one-sidedly exploited, on the contrary, by some technographers) could be saved and incorporated within a new rhetoric, both philosophically respectable and practically efficient.

Still on the same topic of the three types of *pisteis*, it might be useful to look at the passages that seem to sketch a deduction of their number and nature. "Sketch" is the right word, I think, especially if one compares these attempts with the neat *sullogismos* of *Topics* 1.8, which establishes the rational and exhaustive character of the four predicables system.

I first quote the following passage (1.2.1356a1–4): "The proofs furnished by the speech are of three kinds. The first depends upon the moral character of the speaker, the second upon putting the hearer into a certain frame of mind, the third upon the speech itself, in so far as it proves or seems to prove." These lines contain, as if in suspension, all the elements of a rational justification of the tripartition of proofs: the speaker, the hearer, and the speech indeed delineate a sort of pragmatic triangle (emitting pole, receiving pole, transmitted message), which one would have good reason to consider as exhaustive and rationally necessary, and out of which it would be fairly easy to build a theoretical foundation for the tripartition of *pisteis*. But Aristotle does not push this logical move to its end: he describes the three kinds of proofs without justifying their determinate number or their particular nature, and he does not explicitly offer the pragmatic triangle as the basic *ratio essendi* of the tripartition of *pisteis*. It is difficult to say whether the force of *gar* in 1356a2 is deductive ("for") or inductive ("as a matter of fact"); nor is it said (as in *Top.* 1.8) that the system could be justified both deductively and inductively.

In a later summary (2.1.1377b20 ff.), Aristotle admittedly takes a step further in the direction of a genuine deduction of the tripartition of *pisteis*, using the word *anankē* (1377b22), which he had not used in chapter 1.2. But here, the rationalizing process is still to be seen *in statu nascendi:* the "necessity" is introduced only in order to add the whole *ēthos*-plus-*pathos* to the rational proof (22–24). The reason given for this double addition is unique (20–21), and Aristotle does not try to deduce separately the necessity of *ēthos* and the necessity of *pathos* (see the vague phrase in 27–28, *pros de toutois*).

Similar conclusions could be drawn from the examination of the second conceptual tripartition, which also plays such an important part in the whole structure of the *Rhetoric*, namely the tripartition of oratory kinds (deliberative, forensic, and epideictic). Here again, it is obvious that Aristotle could illuminate these three rhetorical genres just by observing the current practice of oratory. But we have to see whether and how he has tried to theoretically justify their number and nature.

The crucial text, in this respect, is chapter 1.3, which enumerates a number of arguments in this sense (the simple fact that there are so many already seems to show that neither, for Aristotle himself, is a rationally conclusive *sullogismos*). Let us look at the first argument (1356a36–1356b8):

> The kinds of Rhetoric are three in number, corresponding to the three kinds of hearers. For every speech is composed of three parts: the speaker (*tou legontos*), the subject of which he treats (*peri hou legei*), and the person to which it is addressed (*pros hon*); and the end (*telos*, i.e., of the speech) is addressed to this last one, I mean the hearer. Now the hearer must necessarily be either a spectator (*theōros*), or a judge (*kritēs*), and a judge either of things past or of things to come. A judge of things to come is for instance the member of the general assembly; [a judge] of things past is for example the member of the court; [a judge] of the ability [of the speaker] is the spectator. Therefore there are necessarily three kinds of rhetorical speeches, deliberative, forensic, and epideictic.

This passage is a bit perplexing. First, Aristotle offers a slightly modified version of his pragmatic triangle: the third element now is the subject of the speech, not the speech itself; and the phrases he uses seem to indicate, this time, that the analysis is considered as exhaustive. But although Aristotle inserts into the text these traces of a process of reflection, he does not actually make a full use of it: the new version of the pragmatic triangle is introduced only in order to concentrate the attention at once on one single summit of it, namely the hearer; and an extra tripartition, bearing now on the kinds of hearers, is designed to serve as a foundation for the tripartition of rhetorical kinds.

Moreover, the stress put on necessity (*anankē*, 1358b2; *ex anankēs*, 1358b6) does not conceal the difficulties of this move. According to the first dichotomy, the hearer of epideictic speeches should be a mere spectator, and not a judge. However, in the following lines, he turns out to be a judge of a sort, namely the judge of the ability of the speaker (*krinōn* is certainly to be understood at the beginning of the sentence that concerns him).[21]

The arguments that follow this one, in chapter 1.3, are still more devoid of any syllogistic pretensions. In 1358b8–13, Aristotle establishes a correspondence between the tripartition of oratory kinds and a tripartition of pairs of speech-acts (to exhort vs. to dissuade, to accuse vs. to defend, to praise vs. to blame); but he says nothing to the effect that this tripartition is exhaustive or systematic.[22] In 1358b13–20, the tripartition of kinds is put into correspondence with the tripartition of times (future, past, present), which might seem quite naturally complete, without any need to dwell on it. But now there is some awkwardness in the superposition of the two schemes, as Aristotle himself admits (1358b19–20). As a matter of principle, the specific times assigned to the epideictic kind should be the present; but as a matter of fact, the speakers "often" have recourse to evocations of the past and anticipations of the future (see the example in 1359a1–5). In 1358b20–29, at last, the three kinds are once again put into correspondence with three pairs of specific values (expedient vs. harmful, just vs. unjust, honorable vs. disgraceful); but nothing in the text suggests that these pairs form a system. Furthermore, Aristotle does not even try to present the correspondence as a justification of the tripartition of kinds, since, far from arguing from values to kinds, he actually argues from kinds to values (see 1358b22, 29–30).

So far, I hope to have pointed out some of the features that allow us to say that Aristotle has adopted, in his *Rhetoric,* a referential method of exposition, which means not only a constant reference to the material he has worked on when elaborating his treatise but also the registering and communication of the very work he has done on this material. The *Rhetoric* fits the expectations one might have on the basis of what is said about the situation of rhetoric in the final chapter of the *Sophistical Refutations:* Aristotle was by no means in a position to teach this discipline—already supplied with a long practical and theoretical history—as if he were the first teacher in the field.

Nevertheless, there are some remaining differences between the actual *Rhetoric* and the imaginary treatise that one might describe by sticking strictly to the lines of the *Sophistical Refutations.* In conclusion, I shall try to point to these differences and to account for them.

Let us suppose that the *Rhetoric* is lost, and that we are asked to describe an imaginary treatise on rhetoric written by the author of the *Sophistical Refutations.* We should probably say: Aristotle knows very well that he is not the inventor of the art of rhetoric; in this field, as in so many others, he has an acute awareness of his own historical situation; he is, and he knows he is, an heir. But he also knows that he still has to exploit, to develop, and to improve his inheritance. It is thus quite likely that he would begin with a critical review of the technical contributions of his predecessors, as he does in so many of his other works. In saying this, we would be both right and wrong. Right, since Aristotle has written a *Technōn sunagōgē,* a collection of rhetorical treatises earlier than his own, more or less summarized and rewritten by himself, a work that is lost to us, but that was so successful and so widely read in antiquity that we may suspect it is responsible for the loss of the works that it used as its raw material.[23] But we would also be wrong, since (strangely enough) nothing substantial in the actual *Rhetoric* seems to come from this work, and no mention of it or allusion to it is ever made there. The reader of the treatise is never referred to it for further information, and the reader could not even suspect that the author of the treatise ever gathered up such a collection. There is something quite enigmatic in this silence; perhaps it betrays Aristotle's hesitation in integrating his contributions to the art of rhetoric with those contributions of his predecessors.

Following this line of thought, we would probably suppose that after his critical examination of the work of his predecessors, Aristotle had presented his own contribution, showing how it enters into the development of the succession of technographers, either by extending it or by bringing it to its fulfillment. Here we would be completely wrong. The very notion of a succession of rhetorical masters, so far as I can see, is totally missing in the *Rhetoric*. Of course, the treatise is not silent about the authors of rhetorical *technai;* but the allusions made to them never refer to the idea of a *diadochē*. These allusions belong, roughly speaking, to two different classes. On the one hand, a number of authors are mentioned by name, some of them being also mentioned in the *Refutations* list, some not;[24] on the other hand, some *technologoi* are evoked, anonymously and collectively, in chapter 1.1. The historical and professional relationships among these various people are not clarified; but it is obvious that they are not dealt with in the same way. The people mentioned by name are not criticized, at least explicitly; Aristotle usually quotes them in order to indicate that such and such a form of rhetorical argument, which he is analyzing, constitutes "the whole of their *technē*"; this seems to imply that they certainly had a much too narrow view of rhetorical argumentation, and that they were only too ready to take the small part of the art they had discovered as its whole; but Aristotle does not insinuate that they were not genuine technicians. On the other hand, the *technologoi* attacked in chapter 1.1 are presented in an extremely polemical manner; Aristotle clearly does not see himself as their successor or debtor, but as their antagonist and rival.

Is this attitude inconsistent? Certainly not, since the people involved are not the same. The polemical sections of chapter 1.1 are entirely written in the present tense:[25] Aristotle here has in mind contemporary authors, not his predecessors. In contrast to the *Topics*, where he did not hesitate to mention by name persons who, like Plato or Xenocrates, were probably still alive, he seems to follow, in the *Rhetoric*, the general rule of not mentioning living people in a written work. This difference between the *Topics* and the *Rhetoric* could signify a difference in the audience: it was perhaps normal to follow the rule in a work designed for an audience at least partly independent of the school circle, and to dispense with it when the audience was strictly confined to this circle.

A last point is to be noticed. In spite of his criticisms toward the contemporary *technologoi*, who are only concerned with the accessories of the art and with "matters outside the subject," Aristotle allows them the status of *technologoi.* He would probably not have done so if the *diadochē* scheme had been dominant in his view of the history of rhetoric: in this case, he should have said that after the old masters, who contributed in a limited but genuine way to the investigation of "the body of the proof," all those contemporary traders of low vulgar recipes had nothing to do with the *technē.* Perhaps he had come to think, in contrast to what probably was his view at the time of the *Sophist,* and to what he had written in the *Sophistical Refutations,* that the history of rhetoric is not a cumulative and progressive history, but an utterly irregular and meaningless sequence of tiny and disconnected findings.

I suspect that it is the very nature of rhetoric—not its eternal nature, but the nature it had as practiced and reflected upon at Aristotle's time— which led Aristotle, as he worked on it more deeply and concretely, to give up bit by bit the various schematic conceptual structures he had tried to apply, starting from his own initial thesis in the *Sophist,* namely the historical and theoretical *antistrophē* between dialectic and rhetoric. This renunciation is understandable, and entirely to the credit of Aristotle's realism. In spite of its possible use in "encounters" with "ordinary people," dialectic is basically a greenhouse flower that grows and flourishes in the protected atmosphere of the school. The philosopher is able to keep it under intellectual control; and when he is Aristotle, he can even try to reinforce its intellectual purity and to clear it as far as possible from the influence of passions.[26] But rhetoric is a plant growing in the open air of the city and the public places. This is why it smashes abstract schemas into fragments; it offhandedly makes fun of the most respectable theoretical distinctions.[27] With it, contingency invades history, politics seize logic, passions rush into discourse. After all, Aristotle has never been a better Aristotelian than when he chooses not to be a formulaic Aristotelian and not to adopt the same method in the *Topics* as in the *Rhetoric.*

NOTES

This essay is an abridged and revised English version of "Rhétorique et dia- lectique, *Rhétorique* et *Topiques,*" my contribution to *Aristotle's Rhetoric: Philosophical Essays,* ed. D. J. Furley and A. Nehamas (Princeton, 1994). I have presented other versions in Paris (at Ecole Normale Supérieure in a seminar held by Francis Wolff) and Budapest (at Eötvös University, Department of History of Philosophy, in a class held by Professors Bodnar and Steiger). On all these occasions I took advantage of many acute observations from the audience. I am especially grateful to Amélie Rorty, who kindly insisted on including this essay in the present collection and found the words to overcome my hesitations. I also would like to thank her for taking the time to revise my English.

I usually quote from the Loeb translations (J. H. Freese for the *Rhetoric,* E. S. Forster for the *Topics* and *Sophistical Refutations*).

1. Chapter 1.1 has often been considered, either in part or in its entirety, as having been written earlier than the rest of the *Rhetoric*, which might itself have been written fairly early in Aristotle's career (see Kantelhardt 1911 and Solmsen 1929). However, I shall not dwell here on evolutionist hypotheses. The backward reference of 1.2.1356a31, to "what was said at the outset," shows (if genuine, of course) that Aristotle himself is responsible for the integration of chapter 1.1 into the whole of the treatise. If delivered by Aristotle during his stay in Plato's Academy, this first sentence could not fail to remind the audience of the famous passage in Plato's *Gorgias* (465e), where rhetoric was pictured as an *antistrophon* to cookery. Aristotle added a new provocation, by means of a strongly deflationist description of dialectic, as compared with the sublimity of the tasks assigned to it by Plato.

2. Instead of *morion ti,* Kassel (1971) suggests reading *homoron ti* (something neighboring) (p. 123).

3. See *Topics* 1.3.101b6–8 (pointing to a feature common to both arts, but also to others, like medicine, see *Rhet.* 1.1.1355b10–14); 6.12.149b25–30 (a definition of the orator, paralleled with the thief—a passage less closely related to *Rhet.* 1.2.1355b25–26, than appears from the text of the manuscripts: Alexander of Aphrodisias has preserved what I take to be the right text in his *In Topica* 484.17–18 Wallies); 8.14.164a5–6 (the only occurrence of the word *enthumēma* in the *Topics*). The *Sophistici Elenchi* (an appendix to the *Topics* proper, likely to have been written a little later than most of the *Top.* 1–8) are a bit more talkative about rhetoric (see 5.167b8–12, to compare with *Rhet.* 2.24.1401b23–24; 15.174b19–20; and of course the famous final chapter, on which more later).

4. In addition to some general points (greater mastery in the handling of comparative predicates in the *Topics* section), one can notice that in each case of punctual parallelism, the *Topics* version is clearer, subtler, or more elegant than the *Rhetoric* version. If Aristotle does not refer to the *Rhetoric* version in the *Topics* version, which I think came later, it may be precisely because he is correcting a model that he finds no longer satisfactory.

5. See Diogenes Laertius VIII 57, IX 25; and Sextus Empiricus, *Adv. Math.* 7.6–7.

6. Of course, sophistic could not be absent from the picture in a work called *Sophistēs.* One may surmise that the *antistrophē* between dialectic and rhetoric was still reduplicated by an *antistrophē* between their degenerate versions, namely sophistic (mimicking dialectic) and an anonymous mixture of rhetorical skill with fraudulent intentions (see *Rhet.* 1.1.1355b15–21).

7. On this subject in general, see Kleingünther 1933. Many fragments of the lost early works of Aristotle (*On Education, On Poets*) show a vivid interest in this sort of question.

8. Gorgias's name was significantly absent from the succession of (genuine) technographers mentioned earlier.

9. Traces of the *empeiria* are still to be found within the later *technē:* for instance, the universal propositions in which the latter is expressed keep the aorist tense of the singular propositions in which the former was expressed (see *Met.* 1.1.981a8, 11).

10. Note the frequency of verbs in the future tense (e.g., *Top.* 1.1.100a19, 21; 1.4.101b13; *Soph. El.* 34.183b5–6, 9–10), and of verbs in the first person plural. This last feature seems much less frequent in the *Rhetoric:* as a master of dialectic, Aristotle identifies himself with his pupils; as a master of rhetoric, he does not do so. He is a practitioner of his own teaching in the first case, not in the second.

11. See Düring 1968.

12. I made this mistake earlier myself (see Brunschwig 1967, pp. xxxix–xl).

13. Note that the vocabulary of this definition is strongly reminiscent of the description given by Aristotle of the *empirical* training dispensed by Gorgias in the *Sophistical Refutations* (*logous . . . eis hous pleistakis empiptein,* 183b38–39).

14. Quoted by Alexander of Aphrodisias, *In Topica* 5.21 and 126.14 Wallies.

15. See 1.1.1355b10, 15–16, 1.2.1355b25–26, 1.9.1367b9–11.

16. See also the opposition between "sciences of things" and "sciences of discourses" (1.4.1359b15–16), and of course the distinction between science and art in *NE* 6.4.1140a12–17.

17. There is another crucial distinction in Aristotle's *Rhetoric,* which would require a detailed comparison with the *Topics,* namely the "common" vs. "specific" contrast, which is connected with the notoriously thorny question of the *topoi* vs. *eidē* contrast. These distinctions occur in several important and difficult theoretical sections, like 1.2.1358a2–35 and 1.4.1359b12–18. For want of any completely satisfactory understanding of these sections, I have decided, to my regret, to leave them untouched here. I would like to refer the reader to the literature (in particular, Grimaldi 1972 and 1980, Ryan 1984).

18. See 1355b23–24. If genuine (as it seems likely to be), this transition seems to show that Aristotle wanted to keep chapter 1 in its present place, although he clearly intends to push it into a somewhat marginal position with regard to the "true start," chapter 2.

19. Notice that the word *atechnos* is not used in the critical passages of chapter 1. The phrases used in the polemic against the *technologoi* (*prosthēkai, ta exō tou pragmatos*) are not equivalent to it.

20. Remarkably enough, this criterion raises an awkward expository problem in describing the third of the entechnical proofs. Proofs of the third type must meet the general criterion of such proofs, namely their verbal or discursive character: they must be *dia tou logou.* But they must also differ from the two other kinds of entechnical proofs: the differentiating feature is their purely rational nature, for the description of which Aristotle also needs the word *logos* (see *en autōi tōi logōi,* 1356a3–4). His solution is to use the various constructions of the preposition *dia:* with the genitive, *dia tou logou,* it expresses the general criterion of entechnical proofs (see 1356a1); with the accusative, *dia ton logon,* it only characterizes the purely rational proof (see 1356a19, where the reading of the manuscript A, *dia ton logon,* should be kept against *dia tou logou,* suggested by Vahlen 1854, p. 555, and adopted by Spengel 1867 and Ross 1959).

21. A solution to this difficulty would be to suppress the last phrase of the sentence, *ho de peri tēs dunameōs ho theōros* (1358b5–6) as an interpolation inspired by 2.18.1391b16–17 (suggested by Kassel 1976, p. 125). But it is unlikely that Aristotle might conclude with such confidence (*hōst' ex anankēs*) without

having given more of an explanation about the spectator (briefly mentioned in 1358b2) and about the relation of the spectator to the epideictic speech. There are other traces of Aristotle's difficulties with this topic: see 2.1.1377b20–21, 2.18.1391b7–21.

22. Aristotle claims to demonstrate something in this paragraph (see *aei*, 1358b9; *anankē*, 1358b12); but he only shows that, in each of the discursive situations, the speaker has to choose between the two terms of each pair. The official *demonstrandum* of the passage, namely the tripartition of rhetorical kinds, is by no means affected by this necessity.

23. See Fortenbaugh 1989, p. 42. To my knowledge, there is no evidence for determining the order of the *Technai* in this "collection"; but the word *sunagōgē* clearly favors neither the hypothesis of a historical presentation nor the hypothesis of a theoretical exposition within a systematic global frame. Perhaps Aristotle thought that it was not possible to put the *Technai* introduced by his predecessors into an intelligible order.

24. Callippus, 2.23.1399a17; Pamphilus and Callippus, 2.23.1400a4; Theodorus, 2.23.1400b17; Corax, 2.24.1402a18.

25. The perfects in 1354a12–13 and 1355a20 are, of course, no exception. This observation, already made by Solmsen 1929, pp. 215 ff., cannot be supported by the *nun* of 1354a11, which marks a coming back to reality after the optative *homologēsaien*. But the *nun* of 1.2.1356a17 (*tous nun technologountas*), in the context of a backward reference to chapter 1 (*phamen*), undeniably has a temporal meaning.

26. The superficial indications I had given in Brunschwig 1986 have been remarkably strengthened and deepened by Dorion 1995.

27. This seems to be what Aristotle has in mind when he comments upon "the most important and least noticed difference" between two classes of enthymemes (1.2.1358a2), in one of the thorny passages I decided to ignore for the purposes of exposition (see note 17 of this essay).

REFERENCES

Brunschwig, J. "Aristotle on Arguments Without Winners or Losers." In *Wissenschaftskolleg Jahrbuch 1984/1985*, ed. P. Wapnewski. Berlin, 1986.

Brunschwig, J., ed. *Topiques*. Vol. 1 [Livres I–IV]. Paris, 1967.

Dorion, L.-A. *Les Réfutations Sophistiques d'Aristote. Introduction, traduction et commentaire*. Paris, 1995.

Düring, I. "Aristotle's Use of Examples in the *Topics*." In *Aristotle on Dialectic*, ed. G. E. L. Owen. Oxford, 1968.

Fortenbaugh, W. W. "Cicero's Knowledge of the Rhetorical Treatises of Aristotle and Theophrastus." In *Cicero's Knowledge of the Peripatos*, ed. W. W. Fortenbaugh and P. Steinmetz. London, 1989.

Grimaldi, W. M. A. *Studies in the Philosophy of Aristotle's Rhetoric*. Wiesbaden, 1972.

———. *Aristotle, Rhetoric 1: A Commentary*. New York, 1980.

Kantelhardt, A. *De Aristotelis Rhetoricis*. Dissertation. Göttingen, 1911. In *Rhetorika. Schriften zur aristotelischen und hellenistichen Rhetorik*, ed. R. Stark. Hildesheim, 1968.

Kassel, R. *Der Text der Aristotelischen Rhetorik*. Berlin, 1971.

Kassel, R., ed. *Aristotelis Ars Rhetorica*. Berlin, 1976.

Kleingünther, A. ΠΡΩΤΟΣ ΕΥΡΕΤΗΣ. *Untersuchungen zur Geschichte einer Fragestellung*. Leipzig, 1933.

Ross, W. D., ed. *Ars Rhetorica*. Oxford, 1959.

Ryan, E. E. *Aristotle's Theory of Rhetorical Argumentation*. Montreal, 1984.

Solmsen, F. *Die Entwicklung der Aristotelischen Logik und Rhetorik*. Berlin, 1929.

Spengel, L., ed. *Aristotelis Ars Rhetorica*. 2 vols. Leipzig, 1867.

Vahlen, J. "Zur Kritik der Rhetorik des Aristoteles." *Rheinisches Museum für Philologie* 9 (1854): 555–567. Reprinted in his *Gesammelte Philologische Schriften*, vol. 1 (Leipzig, 1911).

Mighty Is the Truth
and It Shall Prevail?

Robert Wardy

The *Rhetoric* is a deeply provocative, almost shocking text. Rhetoric's near total domination of both general and political culture in the West from the time of the Roman Republic down to at least the beginning of the nineteenth century has dulled our appreciation of the *Rhetoric's* polemical power, for it eventually achieved a position in the regiment of canonical handbooks equaling Cicero's and Quintilian's in influence. How can the *Rhetoric* shock, when it so perfectly exemplifies our most venerable educational tradition? Only—or, at least, most effectively—by the shattering of that same tradition. Nowadays the term "rhetoric" and its etymological kin in the Romance languages tend to suggest, in ordinary parlance, no more than the dissembling, manipulative abuse of linguistic resources for self-serving ends; outside certain antiquarian and literary critical coteries, the word is unfailingly pejorative. Not that the mere mention of "rhetoric" in fourth-century B.C. Athens would have failed to evoke a host of similar, and similarly sinister, associations: rather, Aristotle was the immediate inheritor of the violent controversy over the nature and power of persuasion initiated by Gorgias and given enduring form by Plato in his *Gorgias*.[1] The pronounced contemporary tendency (to put it no more strongly) to feel disquieted by the mere mention of "rhetoric" should help us to appreciate that if the *Rhetoric* was finally instrumental in forging the ruling cultural consensus on the legitimacy of persuasive training, no such consensus existed when it was constructed.

To appreciate the *Rhetoric's* significance, then, we must absorb Aristotle's reactions to Gorgias and the *Gorgias* as such. But to appreciate them we must first look to Gorgias's own predecessors. Much as the idea might appall at least philosophers of a Platonic disposition, Parmenides' goddess heralds the start of ancient rhetoric no less than of ancient philosophy. When she announces "you must hear everything, both the unmoved heart of persuasive truth and the opinions of mortals, wherein there is no true conviction" (fr. 1), the recurrence of "truth" and "true" might suggest that truth is *objectively* persuasive. Insofar as rational conviction acts in concert with what is and derives its persuasiveness from reality itself, the philosopher empowered to instill it would appear to possess complete control over our intellects. But of course this is not the case; and when she passes from truth to human delusion, the goddess acknowledges as much: "Now I put an end to persuasive *logos* and thought about truth, and from this point do you learn mortal opinions by listening to the deceptive arrangement of my words" (fr. 8). *Logos*—argument—here stands in stark, polar opposition to the mere "words" of the remainder of Parmenides' poem. Why should such deceitful falsehoods find utterance at all? "So that never shall any mortal outstrip you in judgement" (fr. 8).

Thus the master-persuader Parmenides can be seen as at once philosopher and rhetorician; philosopher, insofar as he has access to a *logos* whose logic should persuade us, if we are wise enough to follow the argument; rhetorician, insofar as his deception will be more effective than anyone else's, if we are foolish enough not to grasp the repercussions of the *logos*. But it is essential that we not import this conception of Parmenides' (claimed) status into his own self-conception. Explicit, contrastive definitions of philosophy and rhetoric first emerge in Parmenides' wake—indeed, I would argue, emerge by way of a contentious resolution of the unstable tension created by his attempt to combine what was to become philosophy with what was to become rhetoric within a single work of genius.[2]

In his *Encomium of Helen* one of Parmenides' intellectual children, Gorgias, extols the overwhelming potency of the word: "*Logos* is a great ruler, which accomplishes divine deeds with the smallest and least apparent of bodies; for it is able to stop fear, remove pain, implant joy and augment pity" (§8). Since its divine accomplishments are all, apparently, in the field of emotional rather than intellectual change, this *logos* cannot be the *logos* of Parmenides which was opposed to mere "words": Gorgias does not even mention the production of rational conviction. As further examples of *logos* "molding" the soul as it wishes, Gorgias adduces "contests through *logoi*, in which a single *logos* written with skill, not uttered in truth, pleases and persuades a great crowd; and the conflicts of philosophical *logoi*, in which swiftness of judgment is also shown to make the conviction of opinion readily changeable" (§13). In making philosophical argument just another species of *logos*, Gorgias is deliberately ignoring Parmenides' insistence that deductive *logos* is *sui generis*: all varieties of *logos* are alike displays of persuasive contention; despite its pretensions, philosophy does not establish secure, well-founded theses, but only demonstrates the mutability of passive belief as now one, now another participant in philosophical contests gains the upper hand.

Parmenides' philosophical offspring, Plato, responds to Gorgias in his dialogue the *Gorgias* with the most emphatic reaffirmation of that aspect of Parmenides' thought which is confident that *real* persuasion lies with truth and reality: a scheme of dialectic utterly distinct from and immeasurably superior to rhetoric, which is fiercely castigated as nakedly exploitative emotional manipulation. Socrates will not permit Gorgias in the dialogue to define rhetoric as "knowledge of *logoi*" (449e); he demands an explanation of what rhetoric is about in particular. Gorgias's comment that specifically rhetorical persuasion is aimed at "crowds" (454b), coupled with the admission that teaching also issues in persuasion, gives Socrates the premises he needs to reach the damning conclusion that rhetoric, as opposed to teaching, only persuades in the absence of knowledge. If a speaker is more persuasive in the rhetorical context, that is only because one who does not know has the advantage among those as ignorant as he is over one who does.

Even the most casual perusal of Aristotle's introductory case for the legitimacy and utility of rhetoric in the first chapter of the first book reveals that the *Gorgias*'s argument with Gorgias set the terms by which Aristotle wished to see his own project assessed. The famous first words of the treatise, "rhetoric is the counterpart of dialectic" (1354a1), flatly reject Socrates' uncompromising thesis that philosophical arguments are categorially distinct from rhetorical pleas. And while the Platonic Gorgias had, embarrassingly, a struggle to demonstrate what rhetoric is about in particular, here rhetoric's very generality in grasping what is persuasive (and what is not) is just the respect—topic neutrality—in which it so closely resembles dialectic; for dialectic is also of universal application in testing and sustaining argument (1354a4–6, 1355b8–9).

As for the utility of rhetoric, Aristotle contends that "even the most exact knowledge" would not make persuading certain people any easier. Such knowledge is characteristic of teaching, which—apparently because of the orator's typical audience (a multitude, not a select gathering)—is impossible in the rhetorical situation (1355a24–29). Precisely that impossibility had, in the *Gorgias,* led to the lethal inference that rhetoric can be effective only to the extent that it trades on ignorance. Aristotle, in contrast, concludes that it proceeds on the basis of "common" assumptions and beliefs, and so feels able to convert what, in Plato, had been a devastating criticism of rhetoric into a point in its favor. The effectiveness of Aristotle's maneuver depends on the intrinsic interest and plausibility of his anti-Platonic presumption that the nonphilosophical multitude is far from ignorant, if also far below the heights of penetration, accuracy, and learning that only those who know achieve ("*easy* learning is naturally pleasant for all," 1410b10–11).

But by far the most audacious of all Aristotle's claims on behalf of rhetoric is the very first ground he alleges for its utility: "Rhetoric is useful because what is true and what is just are naturally stronger than their opposites, so that if legal judgments do not turn out correctly, truth and justice are necessarily defeated by their opposites, and this deserves censure" (1355a24).[3] If losers are blameworthy—obviously, only those with justice on their side are to be considered here—that must be due to their stupidly squandering the advantage conferred on them by the rightness of their cause. It is rather as if the facts automatically communicate themselves, so that if the wiles of our (unjust) opponents interfere with the true message, our rhetorical expertise comes into play, but only to serve the strictly ancillary function of countering the other side's dissembling interference. Not that what Aristotle sees as the advantage that the truth enjoys is abundantly clear at this point. He might mean that people tend, at least in normal circumstances, to recognize the truth, and that the reason for this tendency is something to do with their psychology. Or—and the possibilities are not necessarily exclusive—he might mean that the truth is *intrinsically* more plausible, although people are cognitively neutral with regard to their reactions to truth and untruth. (One might compare having a test for gold, as distinct from gold's being of such a sort that it is very hard to make something which looks just like it, but isn't.)

Nothing could be further removed than this benign vision from Gorgias's proclamation that "a *logos* written with skill, not uttered in truth, pleases and persuades a great crowd." At this juncture Aristotle approximates much more closely to Plato's reassuringly moralistic Gorgias, who insists that rhetoric *properly* deployed will never abet injustice (*Gorgias* 456e ff.). But Aristotle's position is actually even more extreme: the Platonic Gorgias merely asserts that rhetoric *should* not go wrong, not that it *could* not, whereas Aristotle insists that the defeat of justice is blameworthy—and that must be because he supposes that, other things being equal, truth and justice will prove victorious, where "other things" are the comparative levels of verbal skill of the contestants. Defeat of justice is to be deplored because victory is—"naturally"—easy. So, although for the Platonic Gorgias rhetoric is an ethically neutral tool or weapon, and much the same holds for Aristotle, he makes the significant addition that circumstances "naturally"—and so routinely—favor the morally upright use, not the corrupt abuse, of the instruments of persuasion. Thus, for Aristotle, rhetoric *could* indeed go wrong—after all, what are our opponents up to?—but not very wrong, since the nature of things itself militates against persistent persuasive malpractice.

Aristotle's confidence that truth prevails readily accounts for the equanimity with which he deliberately concedes to the *Gorgias* that rhetorical "teaching" is an impossibility. If truth is naturally more powerful than untruth, then presumably even people unfitted for full-scale knowledge both intrinsically and as a consequence of their situation in an arena of public debate might nevertheless "naturally" incline toward correct verdicts, naturally attain a state of true (if unjustified and perhaps unarticulated) belief. So Aristotle's confidence that rhetoric defeats the accusation leveled in the *Gorgias*, that it succeeds only at the cost of pandering to ignorance, stems from an assurance that truth and justice are natural victors. But what are the precise implications of such epistemological optimism?[4]

This view that grasping the truth is a natural achievement is expressed elsewhere in the *Rhetoric*: "To speak without qualification, what is true and what is better are always naturally easier to argue for and more persuasive" (1355a37–38). *Physics* 2.8 teaches us that what is natural occurs "always or for the most part." Disputes in which truth is worsted by falsehood must, therefore, be somehow "unnatural." Two ways for truth to be defeated suggest themselves: our just cause may be defeated because we are ourselves "unnaturally" puny in disputation, so that our audience falls prey to malicious rhetoric despite the persuasive edge truth lends us; or our political arrangements may themselves go against nature, in that they lessen the advantage those in the right ought to enjoy, and usually do. In either case, such aberrations cannot be plentiful. Again, the contrast with Gorgias's triumphant "*logos* is a great ruler"—over *both* right and wrong—could not be greater.

One final, crucial quotation on this topic from the *Rhetoric*: "To see both the truth and what is similar to it belongs to the same capacity, and at the same time people have a sufficient natural disposition towards truth, and in most cases they reach it; that is why someone likely to hit on reputable opinions is also someone likely to hit on the truth" (1355a14–18). The notion that people are naturally disposed toward truth calls to mind perhaps the most celebrated declaration in Aristotle, the opening words of the *Metaphysics*: "All men naturally desire to know" (989a21). This striking parallel forces us to look for light to throw on the epistemological optimism of the *Rhetoric* outside as well as within the *Rhetoric* itself. In fact, the optimistic pronouncements of the *Rhetoric* are obviously continuous with Aristotle's descriptions of his dialectical method, which are of such consuming interest to students of philosophical methodology: witness the *Rhetoric*'s mention of the capacity to hit on "reputable opinions," the raw material from which Aristotle ultimately refines his finished theories.[5] The proper approach must be to explore his portrayal of people as trackers of the truth both philosophically *and* rhetorically.

We should also carefully register the connection between Aristotle's rehabilitation of rhetoric on the basis of the remarkable prevalence of truth and Parmenides' original assurance that truth is in itself persuasive. Gorgias's reaction was to deny the distinctiveness of philosophical reasoning; his is a monolithic conception of *logos,* according to which would-be persuaders evidently differ only in the skill with which they attempt to manipulate their audiences. Plato's reaction to Gorgias was to reinstate the Parmenidean antithesis between *logos* as argument and "mere" words. Finally, Aristotle's reaction to Plato's reaction hardly endorses the rejected Gorgianic extreme—persuading the many is *not* teaching them, rhetoric is *not* philosophy—but does perhaps speak of an ambition to reach a new conceptual unity: one which, unlike Parmenides' volatile combination, might survive the strains generated by the conflict between competing images of what persuasion is, and of how it might best be achieved.

The issue we should now address can be formulated more sharply: a reader of the *Rhetoric,* properly impressed by its introductory expressions of epistemological optimism, would reasonably become troubled on discovering that more than a few of the persuasive techniques outlined in the sequel are at best neutral with regard to the truth, and on occasion downright misleading.[6] In parallel, a reader of the *Topics,* encouraged by the impression that this work offers instruction in the positive philosophical task of the construction and inspection of definitions, might very well be brought up short with a rude shock on coming to Book 8 and the *Sophistici Elenchi:* what has this intimidating catalog of tricky procedure and fallacies to do with authentic philosophical dialectic? There are, of course, standard, dismissive responses to both problems: in the case of dialectic, that Aristotle's intention is purely prophylactic; in the case of rhetoric, that his refreshingly anti-Platonic realism induces him to grapple with political realities, including the murkier ones, even if this means that his hands get dirty while the detached philosopher's hands stay clean.

My purpose is to resist such pat reactions. I shall investigate some of the evidence for Aristotle's tolerating, or even conniving at, invalid persuasion. By "invalid" I intend something much less formal and more flexible than strictly logical invalidity, taking in whatever might properly strike us as we go along as at least veering toward argumentative impropriety, and "impropriety" here applies to any feature of debate designed to occlude or suppress the truth for the sake of victory. Then I shall try to square my conclusions with Aristotle's commitment to the persuasive force of truth, always comparing and contrasting the rhetorical and dialectical material.

In addition to the issue of consistency, I shall also examine that of triviality—although in the nature of the case my results here are bound to prove inconclusive. It would be grotesque to suppose that the *Metaphysics'* description of *Homo philosophicus* entails that everyone aspires to be, or has the capacity to become, a full-fledged philosopher. The evidence Aristotle cites in support of his contention that the desire to know is universal is that we all take pleasure in the exercise of our senses (980a21–22); and presumably the proto-intellectual aspirations of some simple people never get beyond the satisfaction they take in perception. By the same token, in the rhetorical context our natural intellectualism means only that "easy learning is naturally pleasant" (1410b10–11), not that abstruse, demanding argument will delight a mass audience. The examples of devices for captivating auditors in 3.10, such as metaphor, come with the warning that, although we must avoid the flatly obvious, we should also not make things too difficult: "quick learning" (1410b21) is the goal of "smart" rhetorical language (cf. "the function of rhetoric . . . lies among such listeners as are not able to see many things at once or to reason from a distant starting-point" [1357a1–4][7]).

The issue of triviality is thus the worry that, despite its lofty Parmenidean associations, our natural appetite for the truth might be too easily sated. Gorgias excused his passing over the events leading up to Helen's departure for Troy because "to tell those who know what they know carries conviction, but conveys no pleasure" (*Encomium of Helen*, §5). Although novelty is of course not incompatible with truth, his commitment to the principle that the criterion of pleasure governs (at least partially) what will be said makes Gorgias's other commitment, to truth (§1), look shaky, since only a philosopher would even pretend to take pleasure in the truth alone. So Aristotle's deployment of the idea that we all desire to know can perhaps be seen as yet another prime but unrecognized component of his reaction to "the Gorgias/*Gorgias* problematic." But again, if Aristotle, unlike Gorgias, escapes the suspicion that hedonistic and epistemic drives conflict rather than combine, that might only be because the truth we all desire to know has been surreptitiously devalued, is a truth so mediocre that his response to the *Gorgias'* separation of rhetoric from teaching comes to ring hollow.

Still within the first chapter of Book 1, Aristotle deprecates rhetorical appeals to the *pathē:* "Slander and pity and anger and such emotions of the soul have no bearing on the issue, but are directed at the juryman" (1354a16–18). Since Gorgias's *logos* had bragged that *logos* is "able to stop fear, remove pain, implant joy and augment pity" (*Encomium of Helen*, §8), one might be tempted to conclude that here Aristotle, by sternly and absolutely forbidding the orator to touch the emotions of his audience, unqualifiedly abjures Gorgianic rhetoric in favor of Platonic philosophy. Were that so, his enterprise of mediating between Gorgias and Plato would be doomed from the outset, since the modes of persuasion ostensibly rejected in 1.1 are clearly detailed later in the *Rhetoric* and most certainly do not conform to a program of exclusively rationalistic persuasion.[8] The temptation should be resisted: one of the crowning virtues of Aristotelian philosophy of mind is precisely that it permits us to drive a wedge between the concepts of emotional appeal and of emotional manipulation. Thought and desire combine in the act of deliberation to constitute the choices that are the precondition for fully rational human behavior. Philosophical analysis detects intellectual and affective aspects in deliberation, but this analytical distinction is just that, it does not reflect a difference in kind between reason and passion in the soul.

The consequences for rhetorical theory could not be more radical. Whatever version of the Platonic soul one chooses, Platonic emotions are irrational, not in the sense that they are reducible to, for example, simple tastes or tactile feelings, but rather because they are, by definition, unmotivated and unmodified by the full-blown, active rationality most evident in philosophical *logos*. In complete contrast, Aristotelian emotions are permeated by reason. When I, for instance, unhappily perceive a state of affairs as unfortunate and react accordingly, I do indeed perceive it *as* unfortunate: cognitive, evaluative, and affective responses are, apart from pathological cases, typically indissoluble. This is not, of course, to pretend that misperception (along any of these dimensions—cognitive, evaluative, affective) does not occur; but it *is* to insist that emotion as such must not be prised apart from *logos* and then, inevitably, disparaged.

"There are three sorts of credibility furnished by the *logos:* those in the character of the speaker, those in the disposition of the hearer, and those in the *logos* itself, through its demonstrating or seeming to demonstrate" (1356a1–4). Aristotle here not only acknowledges that rhetoric includes aspects irreducible to argument (that is, *ostensible* argument), but also that those aspects enjoy a certain (limited) independence. Explicating the second, emotive means of persuasion, he says that "the orator persuades through his hearers, when they are led into *pathos* by his *logos;* for when pained or loving we do not render judgment similarly to when in joy or hating" (1356a14–16). The possibility is thus left open that the *proper* use of rhetorical skill will indeed speak to our emotions, but only when the *pathē* so formed enhance our receptivity to truthful *logos,* rather than setting our feelings at odds with our reasoning. Aristotle's simile likening rhetoric to an "offshoot" of dialectic and politics (1356a25–27) indicates a refusal either to assimilate or to rip asunder reasoning and affective motivation: this intricate scheme is intended at once to divide and to unify. Although rhetoric is a "part and likeness" of dialectic (1356a30–31), in general its arguments, even when valid, do not meet the high (and inappropriate) standards of theoretical investigation; but they are *real* arguments for all that.

If so, then perhaps the first chapter's comment that the arousal of emotion is "directed at the juryman" without any "bearing on the issue" might be restricted to abusive emotional manipulation; after all, Aristotle insists a little later that "one must not *warp* the juryman by leading him into anger or envy or pity; that would be like making the rule one were about to use crooked" (1354a24–26). Were this injunction not limited to *improper* emotional manipulation, then it would, say, permit an orator condemning an act of flagrant injustice to encourage his listeners to use their practical reason to infer that what he condemns is wrong, but prohibit him from further urging them to react angrily to real wrongdoing: in that case, "warping" would be caused by any emotional addition whatsoever to reason. But Aristotelian philosophy of mind forces us to realize that the good orator in arguing and in influencing our feelings need not be precariously engaged in disparate activities. Just as the perception of something *as* unfortunate is a unitary state, so my persuading you to see it as such is a single, if highly complex, act of rhetoric. I conclude that what Aristotle rejects is not emotional appeal per se, but rather emotional appeals that have no "bearing on the issue," in that the *pathē* they stimulate lack, or at any rate are not shown to possess, any intrinsic connection with the point at issue—as if an advocate were to try to whip an anti-Semitic audience into a fury because the accused is Jewish; or as if another in drumming up support for a politician were to exploit his listeners's reverential feelings for the politician's ancestors. The difficulty of harmonizing the rational and the emotive features of rhetoric does not, after all, give good reason for fearing that Aristotle's attempt to reconcile Gorgias and Plato must founder at the outset; whether the *Rhetoric*'s later prescriptions for shaping *logos* with *pathos* can be similarly justified, however, remains to be seen.

> Further, one must be able to persuade people of opposite cases, just as in syllogisms too, not in order to do both—for one must not persuade people to what is wrong[9]—but so that the state of things should not escape us, and so that if someone else uses *logoi* unjustly we shall be able to refute them. None of the other arts argues for opposites; dialectic and rhetoric alone do this, because they are both similarly about opposites. (1355a29–36)

The standard conservative reaction to the sophistical rhetorician was (and is) the claim that he is able to make the worse case appear better.[10] Aristotle does not, unlike the Platonic Gorgias, suggest that it is up to rhetorical expertise itself to ensure that the verbal dexterity it imparts is never used to further evil ends; but he does share the idea that when rhetoric functions as a weapon rather than a tool, it is only for defense (*Gorgias* 456e).

How is it that the capacity to speak persuasively on both sides enables the rhetorician to recognize "the state of things"? When philosophers engage in dialectic for the sake of investigation, that is because the truth is not yet known, or at any rate not yet understood and explained according to the high epistemic standards appropriate to philosophy; thus, if they are uncertain about the (im)mortality of the soul, for example, the ability to argue both *pro* and *contra* might very well strengthen comprehension on both sides of the potential argumentative resources available for resolution of the point at issue. But it is hard to see how an analogous ability might help the upright rhetorician. Surely he should never seek to persuade unless he is certain of the rightness of his cause; and so no need or occasion for rhetoric would ever seem to arise comparable to the need or occasion for investigative dialectic wherever the truth is unknown or not fully clear (in the relaxed sense in which one might be said to have or lack knowledge of such issues as fall within the scope of rhetorical debate).

In asserting that the certainty of having justice on one's side is a prerequisite for legitimate rhetorical activity I do not mean to imply that the competent rhetorician of integrity must approximate to the condition of the *phronimos*, always reliably reaching and abiding by correct decisions for the right reasons; by Aristotle's lights, one could be expert in persuasion and never misapply one's skills while nevertheless being something less than a moral exemplar. What I have in mind is rather that if, say, the rhetorician were to elect to pursue someone in the courts on a charge of *hubris* in the belief that that person had assaulted the rhetorician's father in the *agora,* both the factual belief that the assault had occurred and the ethical supposition that the attack is an outrage warranting retribution would be as well founded as such beliefs can be. Again, if acting as a *logographos*, the rhetorician would not write a speech for another unless justifiably convinced of his client's bona fides.

It might be supposed that the analogy with investigative dialectic would look more promising were we to switch rhetorical genres. Judicial rhetoric concerns only past fact and the application of uncontentious moral principles, so that it affords the ideal Aristotelian orator no grounds for uncertainty. But perhaps deliberative rhetoric, since it concerns future contingencies and the more or less likely outcomes of alternative policies, is a better prospect for comparison with dialectic. Just as philosophers are not sure about the soul, so, one might argue, rhetoricians participating in political debate are not sure about whether, say, the Athenians ought to dispatch a hostile fleet to Sicily. But once more the analogy does not survive inspection. Since Aristotle believes that ethics and politics are fully integrated, his orator should be in no more doubt, at the level of principle, that imperial expansionism is (presumably) wrong than he is about the culpability of *hubris*.[11] At the factual level, he should also know, as well as such things can be known, what the most likely consequence of the expedition might be.[12]

Any linkage between the rhetorical capacity to speak persuasively on both sides and improved insight into "the state of things" thus remains obscure. The conclusion that suggests itself is that Aristotle is reacting to a perennial misgiving: since rhetoric is an amoral power, nothing prevents its immoral operation. I have argued that the natural prevalence of truth, its persuasive superiority, is intended to offset mistrust of rhetoric. Perhaps the seemingly fruitless attempt to associate rhetoric's undeniable, and undeniably suspicious, two-sidedness with improvement in knowledge is a further facet of Aristotle's defensive reaction to that misgiving.[13] My procedure up to this point has been to make us doubt that characterizations of investigative dialectic can be transferred to (proper) rhetoric. But the problem becomes considerably more interesting, if not necessarily any more tractable, if we entertain some skepticism about the positive role straightforwardly attributed to dialectic hitherto. Only investigative dialectic has been under discussion; but there are other varieties, and any reader of Plato's *Euthydemus* will have learned that distinguishing between them, and correspondingly between the dialectician/philosopher and eristic/sophist, is an ambiguous affair.

Since for Aristotle the classic dialectical encounter involves a respondent attempting to avoid refutation in answering questions on his set topic put to him by the questioner, one of the first issues broached in his disquisition on the theory and practice of dialectic is how such questions are best formulated. In *Topics* 8.1 he distinguishes between "necessary" premises (that is, as warranting the questioner's inferences [155b29]), and those that one must get the respondent to concede (155b19). Among this latter class of propositions are those used "to conceal the conclusion" (155b23): these are "for the sake of the contest; but since all such business is directed against someone else, it is necessary to employ these too" (155b26–28; cf. 155b10).

One might have thought that use of these camouflaging premises would count as a flagrant breach of dialectical propriety; if not an instance of invalidity in the narrow sense, its purpose is still the deliberate confusion of the respondent (cf. 156a7–13).[14] But Aristotle is not dissecting some shady sophistical dodge: "all such business" refers to dialectic in its entirety, of whatever kind. Nor is this problem limited to premises to be sought from the respondent; "necessary" ones "should not be laid out immediately" (155b29–30), again just to make things as difficult as possible. Aristotle sums up: "to speak generally, one putting questions stealthily must enquire in this way: so that when the *logos* in its entirety has been presented in question-and-answer form, and he has uttered the conclusion, one [presumably the respondent, and everyone but the questioner?] searches for the reason why" (156a13–15). According to Aristotle's own theory of demonstration,[15] we understand something when we are in possession of its explanation; and explanation *is* "the reason why." So the dialectical questioner succeeds when he bewilders the respondent, when he *deprives* him of the understanding Aristotle himself insists is constitutive of the philosophical enterprise.[16] If this reminds us of anything in Plato, it is Dionysodorus's odious boast that "everything we ask is similarly inescapable" (*Euthydemus* 276e5).

To reformulate and exacerbate the puzzle, if all dialectic is "directed *against* someone else"—is a "contest"—how ever can it serve as even a fallible guide to the truth? The point of contests is, after all, winning; if the dialectician invariably competes to win, then will he not fight, and fight dirtily, against an opponent who happens to be defending a true thesis, or attacking a false one? Surely competitive dialectic and rhetoric alike are vivid manifestations of the ruthless, agonistic tenor of Athenian civilization which tore its fabric so violently that it more than occasionally threatened to dissolve into anarchy.

Once more help is to be sought from the *Gorgias*. When he insists on more clarification of the true nature of rhetoric from Gorgias, Socrates explains that his motive in applying dialectical pressure is not personal, as it were "directed *against*" Gorgias: ". . . not for your sake, but for the *logos*, so that it will advance in the fashion best able to render what is under discussion clear to us" (453c). Gorgias had represented rhetoric as an asymmetric, exploitative relation: the active individual uses *his own logos* to enslave the passive multitude. Socrates counters that the dialectical *logos* does not fall within the scope of a personal pronoun, it progresses through the phases of argumentative development to the intellectual benefit of questioner and answerer together. Socratic dialectic is ultimately for the sake of knowledge. If it appears either to attack or to spare the interlocutor, that is a mere appearance. The *logos* itself is not only our chief but our sole concern: we interact with the other participant in the investigation only because and insofar as he contributes to it. By the same token we do not care about our own dialectical fate as such, that is, whether whatever fragment or figment of truth or victory emerging from the discussion is "ours." This model of (investigative) dialectic opens the paradoxical possibility that opponents might, at a deeper level, be partners in the search for truth.[17] The dialectical encounter remains a contest in which questioner and respondent strive to win (within certain, perhaps indeterminate, limits). But, on the crucial condition that their motive is philosophical and impersonal, their discussion might track the truth despite its agonistic structure; in fact, it is that very structure that improves dialectic's efficacy as a tool for philosophical research, since its combativeness constantly guards against arguments passing muster too easily.

This Socratic precedent certainly enables us to begin to understand how the *Topics* might justifiably offer advice about concealed questioning on the grounds that "all such business is directed against someone else," without thereby disastrously collapsing the distinction between edifying dialectic and repulsive eristic. But the *Euthydemus* issues a sharp reminder. Only a thoroughly naive reader of that dialogue would conclude, complacently, that the difference between Socrates and the sophistical brothers is palpably obvious: a large part of the deftness of Plato's denunciation of sophistry lies in the care with which he makes it clear how unclear the gulf separating Socrates from Euthydemus and Dionysodorus might be. If huge, it will nevertheless remain invisible to onlookers unaware of the spirit in which they debate. Socrates' dialectical moves may be "for the *logos*," not for self-aggrandizement at the cost of humiliating others; but that of itself will not help an observer of his dialectical behavior to discriminate his philosophical aspirations from the brothers' sordid ambitions.[18]

One might protest that the *Topics* does not really attribute such aggressive tactics to the philosopher. Immediately after the manifesto that dialectic "is directed against someone else," Aristotle seems to say that, in complete contrast to the dialectician, the philosopher does *not* argue combatively.

> It is of no concern to the philosopher and the individual enquirer, if the propositions constituting his argument are true and familiar, and the respondent does not accept them because they are closely linked to the starting-point of his argument, and because he anticipates what will follow. Rather, the philosopher might even be keen for axioms as familiar and close as possible, since scientific arguments are constructed from them. (155b10–16)

But so far from being complete, the contrast is superficial. First, although Aristotle does intend us to mark the difference between dialectic, which is *essentially* relational, and "individual enquiry," this means, not that philosophical investigation cannot proceed dialectically, but that it need not. Second, and crucially, the passage does not say that when the philosopher works dialectically, he does not care about winning (for the sake of the truth) without qualification. Rather, the implication is that if he is thwarted in some particular dialectical match for the reasons stated, he goes away happy because, in this instance, the respondent's refusal to concede the argument—and so *formally* to concede victory to the questioner—is, if anything, a sign that he is philosophically on the right track. One might usefully compare those occasions in Platonic dialogues when

Socrates' interlocutors dig their heels in; usually (if not always—consider Protagoras in the *Protagoras*) their refusal to cooperate signifies that Socrates is pursuing a telling line of argument, although his opponent/ partner's stalling tactics mean that an explicit *elenchos* cannot happen.

The relevance of all this ambiguity and potential confusion in the sphere of dialectic to the viability of Aristotle's conception of rhetoric should be readily apparent. The natural prevalence of truth dictates that in rhetoric we are prone to be persuaded of the truth (or at the very least are not actually inclined to be taken in by falsehood), while in dialectic we are likely to draw nearer to philosophical understanding of the way things are (and not take each other in with a packet of fallacies). Our point of departure was the *aporia* of how Aristotle's epistemological optimism might be reconciled with his unembarrassed recommendation of what look to be some extremely dodgy argumentative tactics. If a general, Socratic strategy is available for vindicating agonistic debate in dialectic (that is, interlocutors can come that much closer to the truth by virtue of impersonally motivated competition), then we might try to transfer that strategy to rhetoric, to vindicate *its* exploitation of some less than scrupulously fair combative techniques. Of course, how successful we would be might vary from case to case; but in large measure it will hinge on one vital issue that has not yet been settled. I have maintained that "anything goes" is not a rule in dialectic: but I have still to fix even the rough location of the bounds within which dialectical competitors must operate. So, before we can judge the success of something like a Socratic strategy in justifying epistemological optimism in rhetoric, we must first consider just how unscrupulous Aristotle is prepared to imagine the *non*-sophistical disputant in dialectic might be.

First, Aristotle recommends that the crafty questioner should occasionally resort to self-objection: "For respondents are not disposed to be suspicious of those who *seem* to be arguing fairly" (156b18–20); if this does not entail that skillful dialectical argument wears only the semblance of fairness, it also does nothing to exclude it.[19]

Second, note Aristotle's advice with regard to popular beliefs: "And it is useful to say as well that 'this sort of thing is habitual and widely said'; for if they have no objection, they hesitate to unsettle what is customary. At the same time, they also guard against it because they themselves are making use of such things" (156b20–23). Now, in his confrontation with Callicles, Socrates bitingly dismissed from consideration arguments constructed from premises that may be popularly endorsed, but to which he has not committed himself. The only witness to the truth of interest to him at this point is Callicles, since, by Socrates' own rules, his interlocutor is *committed* to his dialectical assertions (*Gorgias* 471e2–472d4). But since the *endoxa* (reputable opinions) to which the Aristotelian dialectician must attend are beliefs that commend themselves either to everyone, or to the majority, or to the wise (*Top.* 100b21–23), his admirers might contend that the stated goal of paying heed to collections of *endoxa* as comprehensive as possible is a good index of the superiority of Aristotle's method over Socrates': while Socrates gathers dialectical results piecemeal, satisfied with the all too typically inconclusive implications of his one-on-one encounters, Aristotle's sensitive catholicity promises far more substantive results. But throwing in "this sort of thing is habitual and widely said" in the hope that the respondent cannot find any objection seems expressly designed to cow him, to intimidate, precisely to make him bow to the popular consensus[20] of which Socrates was so scornful. And if the respondent himself also derives his ammunition from *endoxa*, Aristotelian disputants would seem to be in danger of succumbing to a degree of dialectical conformism inimical to genuine philosophical endeavor.[21]

Aristotle now turns (*Top.* 8.4) from prescriptions for the questioner to recommendations for the respondent. The remarks he makes about the different species of dialectic go some distance toward countering the unfavorable impression of his method that his readers have perhaps begun to form. This text is of such seminal importance that it deserves quotation *in extenso:* "People teaching or learning do not have the same targets as people competing, and the latter do not have the same targets as people who spend their time with one another in order to carry out an investigation. This is because the learner must always state what he believes, since no one so much as attempts to teach something false. In contrast, when they are competing, the questioner must at all costs appear to be having an effect, while the respondent must appear not to be affected at all. And in dialectical gatherings, when people propound arguments not to compete, but to test someone and to carry out an investigation, the respondent's goal, and what sort of thing he should grant and what he should not, with a view to the proper or improper defense of his position, have not yet been articulated" (159a26–36).

One might argue that this passage puts paid to my effort to establish that Aristotle's epistemological optimism is fraught with ambiguities, since it so emphatically separates benign varieties of dialectic from malign ones. Take, in particular, my earlier claim that 155b26–28 is to be construed as indicating that cutthroat competition is a generic characteristic of dialectic: the present text suggests to the contrary that only one type of dialectic is brutally agonistic, and that employment of propositions "to conceal the conclusion" and other such unseemliness go no further than nastily competitive dialectic. Therefore, the complaint runs, my rendering of 155b26–28 and 155b10 as saying that dialectic is "directed *against* someone else" is a tendentious overtranslation: while the Greek could bear such a construction, we can now see that it only means that dialectic is an essentially *relational* activity.[22]

Is this really so? First, that the targets of the different species of dialectic are different need not entail that their procedures are also (entirely) distinct: one moral of the *Euthydemus,* as we have seen, is that sophistry is so readily confused with philosophy because the difference between their respective motivations, while fundamental, might nevertheless remain invisible. All that can be *seen* is aggressive argumentation. Second, perhaps what singles out "competitive" dialectic as a species is not competition per se, but rather the necessity of appearing[23] to strike or avoid a blow "*at all costs*" (159a31). Third, the statement that dialectical gatherings are "not to compete, but to get experience and to carry out an investigation" should be construed (in the light of all the passages in which a relatively unbridled, global, agonistic tendency in dialectic is made clear) as meaning not that dialectic proper is not a contest, but that its raison d'être is not winning, as it is of eristic (*Soph. El.* 171b22 ff.).[24] In a manner reminiscent of the doctrine of double effect, such a stance could be intended[25] as fully consistent with the view that the philosophical disputant sets out to win. In this larger context, therefore, 155b26–28 and 155b10 do speak of genuinely adversarial activity: to translate as if dialectic were only neutrally relational would be weak and misleading. Finally, the quotation ends with Aristotle's explanation that he has rehearsed these purported dialectical *differentiae* because how the respondent in a gymnastic and investigative exercise should best conduct himself has not yet received clarification; in Aristotle's opinion, his predecessors as teachers of dialectic have neglected this issue (159a36–37). So we should inspect what he supposes will fill this gap before reaching any decision on how clean a cut can realistically be made between dialectic and eristic.

One of the most revealing suggestions of the *Sophistici Elenchi* for coping with fallacies is that sometimes one does better to confront their propounders with "apparent," rather than "real," solutions:

> Just as we say that one must occasionally elect to argue plausibly rather than truthfully, so too on occasion one should resolve fallacies plausibly rather than in truth. For in general one should fight against eristics not as if they were refuting us, but as if they were appearing to do so; for at any rate we deny that they argue, so that one must set things right with a view to not seeming to have been refuted. (175a31–36)

The *Sophistici Elenchi* is supposed to teach us how to avoid sophistical victimization; and surely it is reasonable to assume that one should *not* do this by stooping to their level, as Ctesippus does in the *Euthydemus.* But now we are told that even if we are not sophists—but philosophers, presumably?—there are occasions when truth must be sacrificed to appearance. An element of the dialectical situation in ancient Greece whose influence it is almost impossible to exaggerate is its aspect of display. Just as athletic—and rhetorical—competitions are decided by more or less formally constituted bodies of judges, so dialectical encounters too take place in (semi-)public venues that accommodate an audience, perhaps a partisan one, in whose eyes the debate is lost or won. Aristotle recommends that when a genuine refutation would seem to the dialectical audience not to hit the mark, one should instead use a counterargument that, while itself spurious, will nevertheless appear convincing. Thus arguing or refuting "plausibly" in my translation must be read as *merely* plausible, in the light of the contrast with arguing or refuting "in truth." Furthermore, the Greek original of "plausibly" is an adverb cognate with *endoxa,* the key word of constructive philosophical dialectic; the troubling suggestiveness of this semantic connection must not be pressed too hard, but the realization that under sophistical assault the Aristotelian philosopher might, at least for the nonce, renounce his allegiance to truth and validity—for appearances' sake—should give us pause. It becomes increasingly difficult to resist the conclusion that in practice, as opposed to the occasional pious injunction, there is no hard-and-fast distinction between "pure" dialectic and "impure" eristic.

But it is not only when facing up to agonistic sophistry that Aristotle advocates what, in my terms, are "invalid" tactics:

> Since such *logoi* take place for the purpose of exercise and of testing someone, not of teaching someone, it is clear that one must argue not only for truths, but also for falsehoods; and not only using truths, but also occasionally using falsehoods. For frequently, when a truth has been posited, the dialectician must eliminate it, with the consequence that he must advance falsehoods. And sometimes, too, when a falsehood has been posited, it must be eliminated by means of falsehoods; for nothing prevents someone believing what is not rather than truths,[26] so that as the *logos* proceeds from what he believes, he will be persuaded rather than benefited. (161a25–33)

Here Aristotle asserts that the exigencies of the dialectical encounter—that is, the obligation to argue *against* one's opponent/partner—can involve the philosophical dialectician in both asserting falsehoods and propounding invalid arguments (or at least in deliberately taking advantage of the respondent's falsehoods and invalidity).

As in the case of the other examples we have canvassed, a purist might protest that this text is of only limited application because it concerns gymmastic and peirastic *logoi,* not ones developed for the sake of investigation. The authentic philosopher might train himself and his co-workers in this flexible and uncommitted fashion, but would never argue other than validly, for anything but truth, once his serious business was under way. But this objection fails. Admittedly, Aristotle does maintain a loose distinction between gymnastic/peirastic and investigative dialectic. For example, in 159a26–36, quoted above, he slips easily between "for the sake of investigation" and "for exercise and investigation." However, that is explained by the context (the distinction is between agonistic dialectic and other types—didactic, peirastic, investigative) and clearly at 161a30 ff. arguing falsely is only used by the *echt* dialectician for testing.[27] But, much more important, if what we are about *is* really investigative, then neither of us can know at present where the truth lies; and so neither of us has any choice but to attack and defend to the best of our ability, impersonally, so that our chances of attaining truth might increase. Or if, as previously mentioned, we know what the truth is, but do not comprehend "the reasons why," then deliberate exploitation of "invalidity" might serve to enhance our theoretical understanding.

True, the occasional necessity for combating adherence to falsehood with falsehood described in the final sentence of the quotation must be strictly peirastic (for, were it genuinely investigative, how would the questioner be certain that the beliefs turned against the respondent were false?); but it is only in such circumstances that one's knowing and deliberate indulgence in invalidity could be neatly circumscribed. Moreover, Aristotle betrays anxiety lest this *ad hominem* approach to correction through dialectic should lead one to refute invalidly *and* eristically, for in the immediate sequel he urges: "But one converting another properly must convert him dialectically and not eristically, just as a geometrician would do so geometrically, whether the conclusion were false or true" (161a33–36). The comparison is more than a trifle puzzling: if, say, I were to rid you of your false belief that 156 is prime by reminding you that you believe no even number is prime, should that count as mathematical rather than sophistical conversion?[28]

It is time to take stock before returning to the *Rhetoric*. We have hardly exhausted the (maddening) riches of the dialectical component of the *Organon,* but we have gathered more than enough material for our comparative purposes. We set out from the conviction that the right way to try to deal with the epistemological optimism enunciated in *Rhetoric* 1.1 is not to shrug it off as something special for dialecticians, a Platonic *apologia* to be reverently set aside before the grimy, pragmatic business of rhetorical chicanery is up and running. That would be a viable option only were dialectic itself manifestly, always, innocent of playing fast-and-loose with the truth. But even in the course of our very limited survey of the *Topics* we have discovered quite impressive evidence of dialectic's being a thoroughly agonistic, occasionally coercive activity—in fact, a sort of intellectual spectator sport. We have also had repeatedly to take account of texts declaring that there are distinctions to be made between varieties of dialectic; but time and again we have found that such distinctions, if not trifling, do not credibly amount to systematic grounds for the isolation of good dialectical procedure from bad.

Aristotle is undoubtedly committed to a version of what I have called "the Socratic strategy" to excuse dialectical competitiveness: "Since in business someone who obstructs the common task is a bad partner, it is clear that this also holds for *logos;* because here, too, some common project has been proposed, except in the case of those who compete" (161a37–39; cf. 161a20–21). Opponents *are* partners in the search for truth—because they argue, that is, precisely because they are opposed. So what are the prospects for a quasi-Socratic vindication of rhetorical combat? I put it so circumspectly because it should be obvious that justifications for ostensibly sharp practice in dialectic and rhetoric must respect the disanalogy between them in just the respect I have been dwelling on: namely, that whatever implausibility may attach to Aristotle's attempt to show that a good dialectical opponent is at once and thereby a partner, such an attempt cannot even be made for rhetorical opponents (not that Aristotle ever pretends otherwise). There is no rhetorical parallel to peirastic or investigative dialectic, where competitive partnership might flourish; there is only the upright rhetorician fighting witting or unwitting evil, analogous to the philosophical dialectician confronting competitive sophists—whom one must occasionally show up by foul means, as well as fair.[29]

The first item in our catalog of fishy persuasive techniques comes from *Rhetoric* 1.7, where Aristotle is giving instruction in how to concoct arguments in situations where both sides agree on what is advantageous, but differ over how much benefit might accrue from the policy in question (1363b5–6): "The same things divided into their parts seem greater; for more things seem to exceed" (1365a10–11). Just as with the *Topics'* less scrupulous recommendations, one suspects that the "seeming" here must be specious appearance, intended to hoodwink the gullible assembly. Is the tactic any better than the merest subterfuge, as if one were to console an infant disappointed with a ten-pence piece by exchanging it for ten pennies?[30] Perhaps there is an answer, but it is at best a partial mitigation. By dividing something into its parts and dwelling over them, my rhetoric might get you to perceive and assess concealed benefits you would otherwise be likely to ignore; this technique thus teaches us to divide up whatever it is we are advocating, not so it might appear greater than it actually is, but rather in order to help the assembly appreciate its real magnitude. (One might even try to forge a further, advantageous link with the issue of the triviality of the rhetorician's didactic role: if the intention of dividing into parts is benignly informative, then the rhetorician employing this device is doing something to educate ignorance rather than taking advantage of it, albeit in the humble manner appropriate to the proto-intellectualism characteristic of a crowd of ordinary citizens.) The problem with this attempt at justification is that the reference to apparent "excess" does seem to indicate that the rhetorician should trade on the adult remnant of the childish delusion about the coins, the common cognitive defect that fools us into automatically correlating having more parts with an increase in magnitude.[31]

The next, surefire candidate for recognition as an instance of licensed invalid persuasion is this prescription for epideictic oratory: "One should take features [of character] close to the actual ones to be the same with regard to both praise and blame . . . and [when praising] always put the best construction on each of the accompanying qualities . . . and describe those in states of excess as being in states of virtue . . . for it will seem so to the many" (1367a33–1367b3). In the *Symposium* Socrates insists that he will inevitably suffer humiliation on taking his turn to praise *eros* after what he describes as Agathon's consummately Gorgianic performance (*Symposium* 198c1–5):

> On account of my stupidity I had imagined that one must speak the truth about each subject being praised, and once that has been established, make a selection of the fairest of the actual characteristics and arrange them as attractively as possible. . . . But, so it seems, it has turned out that this is not the way to go about praising any subject properly: rather, one should heap up the greatest and fairest attributes possible, whether it is so or not; and if this is false, no matter. (198d3–198e2)

So far from being an example of more or less oblique Socratic irony, this is surely an expression of absolutely direct, withering sarcasm. Socrates is not outlawing speech in praise or blame as such; but he is implying that the virtuously philosophical man trying his hand at rhetoric should tolerate no deviation from the truth. The function of legitimate epideictic oratory is indeed to present its subject in as attractive (or unattractive) a light as possible, but for Socrates truth sets unassailable limits on the possibilities, the illumination must be veridical, there must be nothing factitiously cosmetic in it.[32]

Aristotle's advice places him squarely in the company of Agathon et al.: he recommends, say, that we display sensible prudence as icy calculation, substitute "generous" for "spendthrift," or represent the excessive timidity of the coward as the moderate caution that belongs only to the brave. "For it will seem so to the many": the simpletons will fail to notice the distortion, so long as the cunning rhetorician masks his subject's actual features with close, but to them utterly deceptive, *simulacra*. Aristotle says explicitly not only that "it will seem so to the many," but also that they will "reason falsely about the motive." And this is by no means a freakish, if lamentable, exception: "Since praise rests on actions, and one must attempt to display [the subject of praise] as acting in accordance with choice; useful too is his appearing to have so acted frequently. This is why one must take coincidences and chance events as if they resulted from choice; for if many similar instances are advanced, they will seem to be a sign of virtue and choice" (1367b23–27). What has become of the "natural" prevalence of truth?

Nor is such disturbing material to be found only in the chapters devoted to epideictic rhetoric. Students of the *Euthydemus* and the *Sophistici Elenchi*[33] require no reminder that perhaps the chief weapon in the sophistical armory is the deliberate propagation of amphibolies: in whichever of its multiple senses the hapless interlocutor takes some ambiguous term or construction, the merciless eristic will trip him up by then responding as if some other sense had been intended. But Aristotle's tip for the aspiring rhetorician seems to be to turn legal amphiboly to his advantage, rather than to take measures to avoid it or minimize its influence. If a law is ambiguous, one should "turn it around and see with which construction either justice or the advantageous will harmonize, and then employ it" (1375b11–13). Admittedly, Aristotle is not urging the orator to interpret an ambiguously formulated law in one sense, when he knows perfectly well that those who proposed and enacted it intended another. Nonetheless, the encouragement to "turn it around" with an eye to finding and exploiting a partisan interpretation sounds like good advice for a brilliant shyster, not the competent but upright rhetorician delineated in the first chapter of Book 1.

A case can be made that Aristotle's recommendations may not be as blatantly opportunistic as the juxtaposition of "justice" and "the advantageous" might suggest. *Rhetoric* 1.15, while associating "nontechnical proofs," such as laws and other documents, with forensic oratory in particular (1375a23 ff.), does not exclude them from consideration by the deliberative orator as well (cf. 1375a26 ff.), which is just as we would anyway expect. So perhaps the forensic orator looks to what is just, the deliberative orator to what is advantageous, in choosing which interpretation of a disputed document to adopt, rather than one and the same rhetorical professional being prepared to sacrifice justice to expediency when the occasion demands. But, still, there is no suggestion that a single *correct* meaning be teased out and adhered to regardless of whatever motives, noble or base, may have guided the authors of the law, or should guide us in our interpretation of it. The orator's attention is wholly on the purpose to which he wishes to put the document in question and, so, on which meaning best suits his purpose.[34]

Chapter 19 of Book 2 contains a thesaurus of schemata for arguments about past or future events. Aristotle suggests that it is possible to argue from antecedents to consequents, or vice versa, where they are related *naturally*:

> And if what naturally precedes or happens for the sake of a thing has happened [then that thing has also happened]: *e.g.*, if lightning has struck, then there has also been a thunderclap, and if he tried, he also did it. And if what naturally succeeds a thing, or for the sake of which that thing happens has happened, then the prior event and the event which happens for the sake of the later event have occurred too: *e.g.*, if there has been a thunderclap, then lightning has also struck, and if he did it, he also tried. Of all these cases, some are so of necessity, others for the most part.
> (1392b26–32)

Now of course the most salient feature of the sublunary world in Aristotle's natural philosophy is that by far the greater proportion of the events that occur there are contingent. Nature expresses itself in complex, stable proclivities, but such tendencies can and often do fail to come to fruition, especially when coincidence intervenes. It is only to be expected, therefore, that reasoning about animals, including the human animal, will generally lack apodeictic necessity: "The enthymeme and the paradigm must in many cases concern matters which can be otherwise" (1357a13–15; cf. 1396a2–3).

But there is nevertheless something worthy of note in Aristotle's exposition. He illustrates mere natural precedence and consequence with the sequence lightning-thunder, the natural teleological relation with the sequence attempt-action. If, for Aristotle, thunder and lightning are meteorological, rather than celestial, phenomena, and so are not bound by adamantine superlunary necessity, it is still startling to find them grouped together with the example of human intentional action. If we cannot be as sure of the sequence lightning-thunder as that the sun will rise tomorrow, we also cannot entertain any real, even vanishingly small, doubt about the matter. But when we come to the sequence "he tried, so he did it," our perfectly reasonable doubt is anything but infinitesimal (the reverse inference from action to attempt, if less treacherous, remains outrageously fallible).

One might be mildly inclined to associate the Aristotelian principle that truth naturally prevails with the crude motto "if it seems so, then chances are it is so," with the particular consequence, when combined with faulty reasoning about motive and opportunity, that it would be safe to argue that if the generals failed to rescue the crews from capsized triremes who were left floating in the water, then they meant to let them drown. But the motto would seem to have less to do with epistemological optimism as I have defined it than with the reasoning from plausibility so characteristic of Greek rhetorical practice. *Eikos,* perhaps the most important word in Greek rhetoric, can be rendered as "likely," "plausible," "probable," often with the positive normative connotation of "reasonable." It is *reasonable*—at any rate, reasonable enough, one hopes, for the purpose of swaying the judges—to assume that if they did so, then they meant to do so. A commonplace of subsequent rhetorical theory would have it that the orator's task of instilling confidence in the likelihood of his case depends on achieving verisimilitude that might—but need not—coincide with the facts; his occupancy of the ambiguous space *between* the likely and the (necessarily) true enables him to serve ably *pro* or *contra.* We should therefore acknowledge the possibility that the schema of 2.19 for moving from what has really happened to something else that has—as likely as not?—occurred at least skirts the edges of persuasive invalidity.

By the same token, the schema might erode our confidence in how well Aristotle copes with the issue of triviality: if our common appetite for knowledge can be glutted by such idle speculations as this, then the Socrates of the *Gorgias* need not waver in his dismissal of rhetorical persuasion as the befuddlement of the ignorant by the ignorant.[35] Indeed, in an unmistakable reminiscence of the Platonic dialogue, Aristotle *concedes* that "the uneducated are more persuasive than the educated *among mobs*" (1395b27–28).[36] The words I have italicized are crucial, for the Platonic Gorgias asserts that specifically rhetorical persuasion is aimed at "mobs" (454b). The original Greek word *ochlos* most definitely carries pejorative connotations; Plato puts in Gorgias's mouth an expression intended to exacerbate any democrat's suspicions of his indispensable but dubious ally, the orator. "Democracy" means "rule of the *dēmos*," and *dēmos* neutrally means "the common people," as opposed to the affluent and aristocratic few. Only an enemy of the people would designate them "the mob," a term of opprobrium at home in oligarchic polemics.

So does Aristotle disconcertingly give Plato everything he could want? Not necessarily, and for the most important of reasons. To the Platonically inspired cognitive elitist, any and every gathering of the common people might very well constitute a "mob." But the Aristotelian epistemological optimist might have every reason to protest that only degenerate collections of humanity deserve to be called "mobs"—the assembly, the courts, are reassuringly often much better than that. On this reading, therefore, the concession of 1395b27–28 to the *Gorgias* is not fatal: one could paraphrase the text by saying "the Platonic Socrates has a point, but it is vastly exaggerated; intellectual standards are not universally so demeaned." And that finally is why—or so my Aristotelian apologist would claim—the triviality issue need not affect him radically.

From a Platonic perspective, the crowds of lovers of sights and sounds flocking to the festivals may be no better than an ignorant rabble; but, from the vantage of moderate Aristotelianism, they are more realistically viewed as typical groups of *Homo philosophicus,* an animal enamored of a truth it is equipped to see, but not with any great precision, nor to any great depth.

Earlier I tried to lay to rest the fear that Aristotle's warning against emotional manipulation in 1.1 cannot mesh with his attitude toward the Gorgias/*Gorgias* problematic, but I left hanging how far his later prescriptions for arousing emotion can be justified. *Rhetoric* 3.7 establishes a particular connection between effective word choice and oratorical working on the *pathē* of the auditors: "Appropriate phrasing also enhances plausibility; for the soul reasons as if the truth were being spoken, because people's attitude to things like this is such that they think that things are as the speaker says, even if they are not; and the listener always sympathizes with [literally, "shares the *pathos* of"] someone who speaks with *pathos,* even if what he says amounts to nothing" (1408a19–24). This is almost undiluted Gorgias, whose rhetorical psychology is nothing but psychopathology, the theory of the dominance of the passive *psychē* by the active *logos.* Its mention of cognitive error induced by emotional distortion confirms that the passage is prescribing full-scale emotional manipulation, not mere appeal to emotions that might *complement* a true *logos.* If his auditors are reasoning faultily,[37] that must be because their supposition that this orator speaks the truth is false; his "appropriate" phrasing—appropriate for deception—has cozened them. This orator is a sophistical rhetorician pure and simple, a rampant instance of Plato's worst nightmare (and the persuasive paragon of *The Encomium of Helen*) come to life. And consider Aristotle's last, deflationary, remark: most orators really are "full of sound and fury, signifying nothing." Listening to them is like being hit over the head.

Elsewhere (1418a12–17) Aristotle goes so far as to proscribe the use of enthymemes when arousing the feelings, on the grounds that *logos* and *pathos* are like impulses whose simultaneous impact on the soul must either wipe out or, at best, diminish the force they would otherwise have had. This may be a rogue text; nowhere else in the *Rhetoric* does Aristotle give signs of sharing the limiting preconceptions in the philosophy of mind, allegiance to which leads both Gorgias and Plato in the *Gorgias* to assume that persuasion either addresses *logos* to the exclusion of *pathos* or molds *pathos* by scanting *logos.* Yet even if we are willing to set it aside as an ignorable exception, we must still conclude that the advice given in Book 3 on the stimulation and management of emotion carries ominous implications; were they to be generalized, epistemological pessimism, not optimism, ought to be the order of the day.

The time for final stocktaking has arrived, although we have come no closer than we did in the case of the *Topics* to measuring the full scope for vexing, and commensurately fascinating, argumentative invalidity left open by the *Rhetoric*. Can rhetorical combat be vindicated from within the constraints imposed by epistemological optimism? At the beginning I set aside the question of identifying the ultimate metaphysical rationale for such optimism; our puzzle has rather been whether, given such optimism, the range of persuasive techniques that Aristotle apparently tolerates makes good sense. Assessment of this puzzle must be tentative, and calls for nice judgment. It should be clear that, in principle, toleration of almost any mode of persuasion—possibly even the most violent compulsion, not to mention gentle attempts at manipulation—may be purchased at the price of inflating the doctrine that the truth naturally prevails. Were its prevalence so strong that people almost could not help believing the truth, no matter how powerful the inducements to endorse falsehood, then anything might as well go in rhetoric, since deceit would "naturally" prove so massively unpersuasive; the defeat of truth and justice would not only "deserve censure," it would be an unforgivable disgrace. Needless to say, this would be an all but worthless victory at an exorbitant cost: Aristotle's epistemological optimism is so endlessly provocative a philosophical thesis because it mysteriously contends that, *with effort,* the truth is there to be found—it doesn't hit one in the face.

So what have we found? Our partial sample has revealed that Aristotle apparently countenances dividing something into parts so as to make it look bigger; wanton falsification in epideictic oratory; turning ambiguities in legal phraseology to one's advantage; inferences from one member of a contingent natural sequence to the other; and a distressing version of Gorgianic psychopathology. Exploitation of ambiguity and bad inferences could perhaps be artfully reconciled with substantial, serious epistemological optimism, and just possibly misleading subdivision might be so accommodated as well. No reconciliation with either epideictic falsification or emotional manipulation is remotely plausible. How does this compare with our study of "invalidity" in the *Organon?* There Aristotle seemed to accept the technique of "concealing the conclusion"; duplicitous self-objection; conformist intimidation; proffering apparent, rather than real, solutions for sophisms; and deliberate exploitation of falsehood and invalidity in the narrow, logical sense. Concealment, self-objection, and use of falsehood might or might not be susceptible to vindication along the lines suggested by "the Socratic strategy"; conformism seems to reveal the dark side of Aristotle's methodological dependence on the *endoxa,* and endoxic refutation shows that Aristotle knows that for spectator sports, even intellectual ones, the appearances are sometimes all-important.

If for no other reason, the pains I have taken to emphasize that our coverage has been anything but comprehensive (although I do maintain that it is representative) should stop us from doing a simple sum and comparing the results—such a decision procedure would be simple-minded, in any event. I originally insisted that we should struggle against the lazy inclination to break the theoretical back of the *Rhetoric* by relegating 1.1 to the status of a sop to the Platonists; but reasonable readers might well feel by this point that I have had my opportunity to persuade them that an ambitious conceptual unity informs the work—and failed. Why should the list of improprieties I have culled from the *Rhetoric* be taken as evidence for tensions, tolerable or otherwise, in Aristotle's project, rather than as (regrettable, but real) evidence against 1.1's forming an organic unity with the main structure of the work? The corresponding list of improprieties drawn from the *Topics* is, I hope, a persuasive rejoinder: any skepticism we may experience about Aristotle's awareness of, and responsiveness toward, the Gorgias/*Gorgias* problematic in the *Rhetoric,* actually feeds off no more than an unreflective assumption—the assumption that in any comparison between dialectical and rhetorical methodology, rhetoric must inevitably come off worse. The *Topics* material has suggested otherwise.

Does Aristotle pay lip service to the *Gorgias,* while actually in cahoots with Gorgias? This survey of invalid persuasion in the *Rhetoric* and beyond his yielded no firm answer. My purpose has not been to advance the depressing, reductionist proposal that if the *Rhetoric* can be dismayingly unethical, at least the *Topics* fares no better. Rather, we should now be clear that the sometimes dubious validity of the persuasive and argumentative techniques Aristotle is willing to consider might well undermine his commitment to epistemological optimism. Since that optimism itself underpins both a major part of his defense of rhetoric against the onslaught of the *Gorgias,* and his reliance on *endoxa* for the development of philosophical theory, the tenability of his neo-Parmenidean conviction that truth prevails in persuasion remains both intensely problematic and profoundly important. But that, of course, is what makes the *Rhetoric* and the *Topics* so intensely interesting—to the dialectically minded. It comes as no surprise, when the rhetorician, like the eristic, sets out to win, that truth should go to the wall; nor even that Aristotle expects the truth to prevail nonetheless: the surprising thing is that his own handbook, time and again, subordinates truth to victory.[38]

NOTES

1. I am not questioning the universal presumption that the *Rhetoric* takes serious note of the *Phaedrus;* to mention only what is perhaps the most obvious

and generally recognized influence, Aristotle's various schemata for organizing emotional proclivities within a typology of character surely take their original impetus from the notion of "scientific" psychology advanced in that dialogue. My concern is not to exclude the *Phaedrus* from consideration, but rather to ensure that the vital contribution of the *Gorgias* to the formulation of Aristotle's views receives the attention it deserves.

2. Of course, the sense in which Parmenides supposes his false cosmology to be superior to the competition, not to mention what right he might have to present it, remain unresolved, hotly contested questions: his deception is clearly presented as better in the sense of "better at taking us in," but is it also better in the sense of deviating as little as possible from the truth? And if so, is that why it is better in the first sense? But, if anything, this lack of clarity supports, rather than scotches, the claim that Parmenides was the source from which flowed the two diverse streams, rhetorical and philosophical.

3. The correct translation of this passage is a matter of debate; for defense of my construal, see Grimaldi 1980, p. 27. The alternative (defended by, for example, Cope 1877, pp. 22–23) is to translate the passage as "necessarily they (viz. the losing parties) are defeated through their own fault." But since only Aristotle's claim that truth and justice enjoy a natural superiority has a bearing on my argument, I can accept either rendering of the latter part of the sentence.

4. Recent Aristotelian scholarship abounds with alternative explanations of what sort of argument might sustain his confidence in the (eventual) accessibility of truth to human inquirers; Jonathan Lear's idealistic and T. H. Irwin's Kantian interpretations (Lear 1988, Irwin 1988) have proved particularly fertile. My own explanation, which attributes to his philosophical biology Aristotle's faith in the utility of his dialectical method as an instrument for discovering absolute truth, is to be found in the chapter "Aristotle and His Predecessors on Mixture" (Wardy 1990).

5. The *locus classicus* for discussion of Aristotle's dialectical method remains "*Tithenai ta phainomena*" (Owen 1986); the most important subsequent modifications to Owen's reading mostly involve enlarging the range of data coming within the scope of the method (see Nussbaum's chapter "Saving Aristotle's Appearances," 1986). The scholarship is voluminous, but Denyer is noteworthy for putting together material from the *Rhetoric* with the standard "philosophical" passages that constantly recur in the literature (see Denyer 1991, pp. 183–185).

6. It might be objected that since the first chapter of the first book is so manifestly at odds with the remainder of the *Rhetoric*, my issue is merely a pseudo-problem; there is no consistency, but none should be sought, since the lack of theoretical cohesion is the consequence of imperfect textual integration:

> What is now regarded as the first chapter of Book 1 was apparently originally addressed to students who had completed a study of dialectic (such as is found in the *Topics*) and who had little knowledge of rhetoric, though they may have been aware of the existence of handbooks on the subject. For them Aristotle explains the similarities between dialectic as they know it and rhetoric as he understands it but does not comment on the differences. The chapter as a whole is very Platonic and contains echoes of several of Plato's dialogues. (Kennedy 1991, p. 26)

Of course I agree that the Platonic cast of *Rhetoric* 1.1 is very marked; but I attribute that character to Aristotle's earnest engagement in what we might label "the Gorgias/*Gorgias* problematic," rather than to any genetic hypothesis. Kennedy is right that "chapter 1 creates acute problems for the unity of the treatise" (p. 27); but his conclusion that "despite other possible interpretations, it is probably better to acknowledge frankly that chapter 1 is inconsistent with what follows, that it is far more austere in tone than Aristotle's general view of rhetoric, and that the difference results from addressing different audiences and from the attempt to link the study of dialectic with that of rhetoric" (p. 28) is far too hasty. If I am right that the Gorgias/*Gorgias* problematic is at the heart of the matter, then "the attempt to link the study of dialectic with that of rhetoric" must be much more than a passing fancy: in which case the degree of incoherence into which Aristotle (supposedly) lapses might well be an index of the pressure to which he submits in order to maintain his distinctive position with regard to that problematic, rather than just the upshot of untidiness.

7. Indeed, in the *Sophistici Elenchi,* Aristotle lists this very limitation, among other weaknesses, as useful for refuting someone: lengthy argument is a good thing "since it is hard to see many things at once" (174a17–18).

8. But the Stoa did endorse something like such a program, advocating, for the most part, an extreme, Socratic renunciation of anything but a rigorously "informative" variety of rhetoric (see Atherton 1988).

9. Kennedy comments that "this principle, important as a response to the criticisms of Plato, appears only in a parenthetical remark and is not repeated in the prescriptive parts of the treatise" (Kennedy 1991, p. 34). This is not quite right. Although his translation follows modern editions of the text in placing the Greek original of the words "for one must not persuade people to what is wrong" within parentheses, the paratactic construction of that original does not make it some sort of minor aside. Furthermore, its not being repeated is of no significance unless one supposes that *Rhetoric* 1.1 is *not* prescriptive.

10. The best-known exposition of this conservatism is the contest between the Just and Unjust *Logoi* in Aristophanes' *Clouds.*

11. This claim might seem much less plausible in its application to state policy than to interpersonal ethics; but the *Politics* betrays no more doubt about the validity of Aristotle's political science than does the *Nicomachean Ethics* about the correctness of his moral theory. His delineation of the ideal *polis* would seem to ensure that in his view the rhetorician in politics *must* eschew imperialism.

12. Of course, his knowing as much as can be known about the "probabilities" (to be understood in an unsophisticated, prestatistical manner, to avoid anachronism) is fully compatible with their being so distributed that even the best-placed predictor is radically uncertain about what will really happen; but such uncertainty does nothing to support the idea that an ability to promote conflicting policies persuasively aids us in seeing "how things are" (or "how they might be").

13. Grimaldi supposes that the statement "it is characteristic of one and the same art to see both what is plausible and what is apparently plausible, just as it is up to dialectic to see both the syllogism and the apparent syllogism" (1355b15–17) is yet another Aristotelian response to worry about the ethical status of rhetoric: "Aristotle's reference to dialectic and the apparent syllogism is clearly

to the *Sophistici Elenchi*. . . . And so our passage asserts: the art of rhetoric enables one to see that which persuades to the truth as well as that which persuades to what is not true, although its object is the truth as far as that is possible" (Grimaldi 1980, p. 33). But his own reference to the *Sophistici Elenchi* shows that his interpretation is unsound: if an "apparent syllogism" is a piece of reasoning that is only speciously valid, then the apparently plausible must be a piece of discourse that appears to be persuasive, but is not. This specious plausibility must of course strike the inexpert speaker, not his potential audience, since if *they* found it plausible, and so were persuaded, it really would be plausible. Now given Aristotle's epistemological optimism, from his perspective it might indeed happen, even frequently, that a falling away from the truth is responsible for some rhetoric's *merely* apparent plausibility; but that does not alter the fact that what Aristotle is here talking about is what persuades or what seems to persuade *tout court*, not "that which persuades to the truth" or to its opposite.

14. And cf. *Soph. El.* 12: people say they are "just asking questions because they want to learn"—and so avoid setting out explicitly what they want to (seem to) prove/refute (172b21–24).

15. It makes no odds to my argument whether one conceives of this theory as recommending that explanations be cast in the terms of the *Posterior Analytics'* apodeictic syllogisms, or simply that one acquire accounts of the reason why expressed nonsyllogistically.

16. There is another passage that might initially take us aback at *Soph. El.* 33: "The strong *logos* is the one which has us most at a loss" (182b32 ff.); but a distinction is made here between genuine syllogisms that leave unclear which reputable opinion is to be rejected, and eristical ones that just have us asking "how shall I answer that?" and "how did I get into *this* mess?" (cf. also 171b10 ff.).

17. But the typical Socratic personal *elenchos* is reduced at *Soph. El.* 172b35 ff. to getting someone to contradict his own *superficial* beliefs and desires.

18. I am not arguing that there is nothing to choose between the sophists' fallacies and (some of) Socrates' arguments in the *Euthydemus*, only that there is not everything, and that it would not just be such dimwits as Isocrates, if he is to be identified with the anonymous carping critic at the end of the dialogue, who might be prone to confuse dialectic and eristic. The constant refrain of the *Euthydemus* is that the sophists' victims are "thunderstruck" by their fallacies (e.g., 276d3); but the famous image of the *Meno* ascribes a numbing effect to Socrates' dialectic that is just as easy, and as understandable, for his victims to resent.

19. There is a partial parallel at *Rhet.* 3.7: one reprimands oneself for exaggerated language—because then people *think* one is in earnest (1408b2 ff.). Aristotle similarly advocates resorting to the artifice of "natural" language at 3.2 (1404b18 ff.), and says that we must not "overact" (3.7.1408b4 ff.).

20. This consensus cannot always be complete, since otherwise the *aporiai* generated by the appearance or reality of conflict between *endoxa* to which the Aristotelian philosopher reacts would never arise; but the threat remains that his consensual method is readily open to conformist abuse.

21. Implicit, perhaps, in *Top.* 1.2.101a30–34; cf. *Rhet.* 3.7.1408a34–36. Fi-

nally, there is an explicit comparison between rhetorical and elenctic procedures at *Soph. El.* 174b19 ff.

22. Cf. *Soph. El.* 170a12 ff. for a purely relational *pros tina:* the sophistical refutation is *only* a relational refutation, if at all.

23. The emphasis at 156b18–20 on producing an appearance of argumentative fairness was said to do nothing to dispel the worry that this appearance is merely specious. If competitiveness at all costs is the *proprium* of agonistic dialectic, then it may be that samples of the other species of dialectic cannot indulge in *completely* untrammeled argumentative unfairness concealed beneath a judicious gloss of equitability; but that is not a very reassuring concession. (The label "agonistic" does not imply that the other species of dialectic are *not* agonistic, on the common understanding that a genus and one of its subordinate species might share a designation, justified in this instance by the hypothesis that specifically "agonistic" dialectic is so to the exclusion of all else.)

24. Note that Aristotle is careful to make preserving one's reputation a third, but definitely *non*-philosophical motive for engaging in sophistic (175a12–16).

25. I hedge my claim with this qualification because, just as the doctrine of double effect is notoriously problematic, so my running theme is that we might decide that the boundaries between dialectical species are considerably more porous than Aristotle is always prepared to admit (not that at other times he is not perfectly ready to concede quite casually that real dialectical situations are very fluid, for example: "Those practicing are incapable of abstaining from agonistic dialectic" [164b13–15]).

26. At first blush, this denial might seem flatly incompatible with epistemological optimism. But, on reflection, it emerges that Aristotle must mean that this or that *individual* bucks the optimistic trend. And this solution finds support in the context, which is describing explicitly peirastic argument, that is, the sort of argument conducted with immature, ignorant individuals.

27. And note the careful distinctions at *Soph. El.* 171b3 ff., 172a21 ff.

28. The parallel makes (some) sense in the light of Aristotle's careful comparison between eristic arguments and cases of faulty scientific reasoning at *Soph. El.* 171b3 ff. The geometer arguing *qua* geometer does so "in accordance with his subject matter," even if he gets it wrong; that is, he stays inside his expertise. The dialectician does so too, although he has no special subject matter. In consequence, the faulty scientific reasoner is comparable, in some ways, to the eristic— although not in all. Aristotle still has grave problems because he has to make the dialectician's field "the common things," and that is too vague a specification to establish a firm distinction between being "in accordance with his subject-matter" and not in the case of dialectic—which puts the rhetorician in the same boat.

29. Note the comparison with rhetoric at *Soph. El.* 174b19 ff.—there is no cooperation.

30. There is a counterpart in modern special offers, guarantees, and so on: a guarantee is for twelve months (all those months), not one (measly) year. But you can get fit in twenty-eight days (not a whole month).

31. The quotation from Meleager immediately after this passage might suggest that Aristotle is thinking of qualitative rather than quantitative division—

Meleager specifies what *sort* of evils there are, not how many. It thus appears that Aristotle has not sufficiently distinguished between quantitative and qualitative components; nonetheless, his abstract description of the case is resolutely quantitative.

32. Furthermore, the potentially explosive implications of Aristotle's "cosmetic" recommendations are not restricted to the epideictic genre, damaging as that in itself might be, for he says that victory in general goes to the man who *seems* wise, virtuous, and benign (1378a6 ff.)—so the speaker is always conducting his own encomium, as it were.

33. Aristotle refers us to the *Topics* for how to deal with ambiguities (1419a20 ff.).

34. In later rhetorical treatments of ambiguity as a cause of legal dispute, the two approaches, by appeal to honorable or dishonorable motives and by appeal to ordinary linguistic usage, tend to be combined: see, for example, *Ad Herennium* 3.16; Cicero, *De Inventione* 2.116–118.

35. Cf. 3.14 on the sorts of things people tend to pay attention to (1415b1 ff.)—with not a word about truth.

36. But note Aristotle's *reasons:* he quotes Euripides approvingly ("they speak in a more cultured way") because the mob speaks of what it knows, of what is close to home, whereas the educated waffle on about generalities and principles. *That* determines what sort of reputable opinions—including ones that are only "true as a rule"—are to be used. Note too that deliberative oratory is less "ill-willed" than forensic, precisely because it deals with such generalities (1354b ff.).

37. At 1404a1 ff. Aristotle blames the need to use a fancy delivery on the wickedness of the audience; at 1415b4 ff., a fancy proemium is "irrelevant to the argument" and "directed at a vulgar listener." So, is the rhetorician's excuse the moral degeneracy and stupidity of his audience? One must also take account of Aristotle's advice that the narrative in a speech for the defense should be very selective about mentioning past events—only such as if they had *not* occurred, they would stimulate "pity or indignation" in the auditors (1417a8 ff.). Again, at 1419b24 ff., part of the purpose of the epilogue is to whip up feeling; this task is separate from, and subsequent to, the relation of what the facts were and how important they were, as if intellect and emotion were separate—or separable by the devious orator (1377b31 ff. is also open to this disturbing interpretation).

38. I have benefited considerably from the advice and criticism of Catherine Atherton and Myles Burnyeat—neither of whom is completely persuaded.

REFERENCES

Atherton C. "Hand over Fist: The Failure of Stoic Rhetoric." *Classical Quarterly* 38 (1988): 392–427.

Cope, E. M. *The Rhetoric of Aristotle, with a Commentary*, rev. and ed. J. E. Sandys. 3 vols. Cambridge, 1877.

Denyer, N. *Language, Thought and Falsehood in Ancient Greek Philosophy*. London, 1991.

Grimaldi, W. M. A. *Aristotle, Rhetoric I: A Commentary*. New York, 1980.

Irwin, T. H. *Aristotle's First Principles.* Oxford, 1988.

Kennedy, G. A. *On Rhetoric: A Theory of Civic Discourse.* Oxford, 1991.

Lear, J. *Aristotle, The Desire to Understand.* Cambridge, 1988.

Nussbaum, M. C. *The Fragility of Goodness, Luck and Ethics in Greek Tragedy and Philosophy.* Cambridge, 1986.

Owen, G. E. L. *Logic, Science and Dialectic: Collected Papers in Greek Philosophy,* ed. M. C. Nussbaum. London, 1986.

Wardy, R. *The Chain of Change: A Study of Aristotle's Physics VII.* Cambridge, 1990.

Enthymeme: Aristotle on the Rationality of Rhetoric

M. F. Burnyeat

ZENO'S CHALLENGE

Against the person who said, "Don't give your verdict until you have heard both sides," Zeno argued as follows: The second speaker is not to be heard whether the first speaker proved their case (for then the inquiry is at an end), or they did not prove it (for this is tantamount to their not having appeared when summoned, or to their having responded to the summons with mere prattle). But either they proved their case or they did not. Therefore, the second speaker is not to be heard. (Plutarch, *On Stoic Self-Contradictions*, 1034e)

Zeno's argument is shocking. He would be disappointed if we did not find it shocking. The shock depends on our understanding of what it is to prove something.

Imagine we are sitting in court or a political assembly, listening to opposed arguments on whether the accused is guilty of rape, or whether it is time to raise taxes. It cannot be that both speakers *prove* their case, the one that the accused is guilty, the other that he is not, or the one that it is time to raise taxes, the other that it is not. That cannot be, at any rate, if by "prove" Zeno means at least the following: to derive a conclusion by valid argument from true premises that are known to be true.

The reason it is impossible to derive opposite conclusions by valid argument from true premises is simple. If the conclusions are opposite, that means they cannot be true together, and if the arguments are valid, that means the truth of their conclusion is guaranteed by the truth of the premises. So if both speakers proved their case, in the above sense of "prove," the net result would be a guarantee of the joint truth of two propositions that cannot be true together. Which is self-contradictory and impossible.

This confirms the first arm of Zeno's disjunctive argument. If one speaker has proved their conclusion by valid argument from true premises that are known to be true, the opposite conclusion cannot be correct and cannot be shown to be correct. It may be impolite, or impolitic, not to stay on to hear the second speaker, but no cognitive purpose is served by doing so. The second speaker can tell us nothing we need to know about the issue before us, can offer no arguments we need to consider. For the issue is now settled. It has been *proved* that the accused is (not) guilty, that taxes should (not) be raised. We can all go home.

But we don't. We stay on, usually, and not just to be polite or fair or because it is required by our rules of procedure. Very seldom in courts and assemblies can such conclusive proof be achieved. We stay on, therefore, precisely because the first speaker has not proved their case with finality and there will be cognitive gains from listening to the second. Hearing both sides is a prerequisite for a properly informed judgment on the issue. That indeed is the rationale for the procedural rules, ancient and modern, which insist that both sides are to be heard. The issues that come before courts and assemblies are typically ones where conclusive proof is not available to either side.

Yet according to the second arm of Zeno's argument, a speaker who fails to prove their case has effectively said nothing to support it at all. They may have spoken words, perhaps many eloquent words. But these words have no cognitive value. Their contribution to the speaker's cause, and to our deliberations about it, is zero. Zeno's claim, in short, is that an argument that is not a proper proof is no argument at all; evidence that is not conclusive is simply not evidence of anything; and a speech without argument or evidence is mere prattle.

Such is Zeno's challenge to the rationality of proceedings in court and assembly. If there is no good reason to uphold the procedural rule "Don't give your verdict until you have heard both sides," there is no good reason to continue with courts or assemblies as we know them. Either they should be abolished (in Zeno's own *Republic* law courts were abolished[1]), or we stop pretending that what goes on in them has any claim to rationality. On such complex issues as they typically have to consider, neither proof nor conclusive evidence is available; so by Zeno's standards there is no argument at all, nor evidence, to supply the basis for an informed, reasonable judgment on whether the accused is guilty or taxes should be raised. We might as well give in to Gorgias's contention that what goes on in court and assembly is nothing but persuasion, and persuasion nothing but the manipulation of subjective opinion—an exercise not of reason but of power.

Gorgias would be as disappointed as Zeno if we did not find that shocking. However cynical we may be about politics these days, indignation is quickly roused at the thought of someone not receiving a fair trial. I have not done jury service, but I regularly sit on committees and examination boards. How could anyone do such things with a clear conscience unless their deliberations can be put in a kinder light than Zeno and Gorgias allow?

What seems to be needed is a less demanding notion of proof such that the first arm of Zeno's argument fails, because one speaker's proving their case does not settle the issue with finality, and the second arm becomes less offensive, because the speaker's not proving their case amounts to their falling short of a lesser standard; in a modern court the judge will on occasion halt the proceedings and send everyone home on the grounds that the opening speaker has not offered enough of a case for the other side to be required to answer. The difficulty is to see how a specification less demanding than the one I used in expounding Zeno, viz. "valid argument from true premises that are known to be true," can still claim to define a notion of *proof*. How could an invalid argument or false premises prove anything? The proposal sounds as shocking as the rival claims of Gorgias and Zeno.

As for the epistemic requirement that the premises be known to be true, that too is already quite weak. It allows the following to count as a proof:

258 + 258 = 516.
When equals are divided by equals (in this case, 129 on either side of the equation), the remainders are equal.
Therefore, 2 + 2 = 4.

To which most people would object that you cannot prove that 2 + 2 = 4 from premises that no one could know if they did not already know the conclusion to be proved from them.

Both Aristotle in the *Organon* and Zeno agree with this objection. Both require that the premises of a proof should be better known than the conclusion derived from them. A proof should be an argument that affords knowledge of something we did not know before. And this notion of proof is more stringent than the one I have been working with, not less.

But Aristotle has more respect than Zeno for the well-tried, established institutions of legal and political decision making. In the *Rhetoric*, therefore, he needs a *via media* between Zeno and Gorgias. As the founding father of the study of logic, Aristotle was not only the first person to define basic logical notions like valid argument and proof. He was also, precisely because he knew what a valid argument or a proof is, the first person to appreciate that and why there are many arguments which are not logically valid, hence not strict proofs in the sense defined in the *Organon* or by Zeno later, but which nonetheless are not mere prattle and not just manipulative moves in a struggle for power.[2] They are respectable arguments that have a rightful claim on our minds. They give good reasons for deciding one way or the other. When such arguments occur in speeches to a court or assembly, they are called "enthymemes." Aristotle's doctrine of the enthymeme embodies the claim that the clash of opposing arguments in deliberative and forensic gatherings is a positive expression of human reasonableness in a world where issues are complex and deciding them is difficult, because there really is something to be said on either side. As such, Aristotle's doctrine of the enthymeme is one of his greatest and most original achievements.

This high praise for Aristotle will of course sound strange, in its own way even shocking, to those who have been brought up to think of an enthymeme as an abbreviated syllogism. Logic books since the Middle Ages have discussed abbreviated syllogisms under the heading "enthymeme," usually with the idea that they have Aristotelian authority for doing so. But that, as I have shown elsewhere, is a total misunderstanding of what an enthymeme is for Aristotle.[3] The misunderstanding came about through the confluence of Stoic and Aristotelian logic in the commentaries of late antiquity, so it is not surprising that its chief and most damaging effect was to leave people with the impression that Aristotle's attitude to rhetorical argument is as severe as Zeno's: if, when the missing premise is supplied, an enthymeme does not meet the standards of syllogistic validity, it has no probative value at all.

That impression is still very much alive in the scholarly literature on Aristotle. To dispel it, I aim here to show, as clearly and carefully as I can, how Aristotle escapes between the horns of Zeno's dilemma. Aristotle's account of the enthymeme does, I believe, define the less demanding notion of proof that is needed to defend, against Zeno and Gorgias, the rationality of the rule "Don't give your verdict until you have heard both sides."[4]

ENTHUMĒMA: WORD AND CONTEXT

Let us open Aristotle's *Rhetoric* and try to read it with an eye untrammeled by the erroneous, Stoic-influenced idea that an enthymeme is an abbreviated syllogism. We are, let us imagine, students at the afternoon lectures where Aristotle is said to have taught easier and more popular subjects like rhetoric. We may know little about logic and even less about the syllogism, but Aristotle apparently expects us to be familiar with the term *enthumēma*, or at least to have a rough idea of its meaning, for he offers no explanation or elucidation when he first uses the word at 1.1.3.1354a11–16. He is complaining that current handbooks on rhetoric say nothing about enthymemes. Why is this a fault? Because *pistis*, proof, is what the art of rhetoric, qua art, is all about, and enthymemes are the body of proof (*sōma tēs pisteōs*).

The metaphor is not luminously clear and has been much discussed. But there is no doubt that we are being told that enthymemes are the main or the most important part of *pistis*. And this, to repeat, is a message that Aristotle expects his afternoon students to understand, without further explanation or elucidation, at the very beginning of the course. So what would the word *enthumēma* mean to an audience of Aristotle's time, innocent of subsequent history (because it has not yet happened), innocent of any previous technical treatment of the subject (because according to Aristotle there has been no previous technical treatment of this subject), and as yet uninstructed in Aristotle's own rhetorical theory?

Enthumēmata (plural) occurs five times in Isocrates, a dozen times in a short work by his contemporary Alcidamas, *On the Writers of Written Speeches or on Sophists,* and on every single one of these occasions it refers to the ideas expressed in a speech as contrasted with the language (*lexis* or *onomata*) by which they are conveyed. One example will suffice for them all:

> The *enthumēmata* in speeches are few and important, the words and expressions many and insignificant and little different from each other; and each of the *enthumēmata* is displayed once, whereas with the words we are forced to use the same ones many times. (Alcidamas §19)[5]

The cognate verb *enthumeisthai* means to think about something, consider it. The ideas in a speech are thoughts or considerations that the speaker wishes to communicate to the audience. And this is precisely the sense of *enthumēmata* in its earliest extant occurrence.

After Oedipus's famous plea for sanctuary at Athens, the Chorus, who had previously demanded that he go away, replies:

> The thoughts (*enthumēmata*) urged on thy part, old man, must needs move awe; they have been set forth in words not light; but I am content that the rulers of our country should judge in this cause. (Sophocles, *Oedipus Coloneus,* 292–295, Jebb's translation; cf. 1199)

Another instructive example is Xenophon pondering the captains' request that he take command of the army. The considerations (*enthumēmata*) that make him want to do so are such things as the greater honor he will have among his friends and the greater name he will achieve when he finally reaches the city. On the other hand, he reflects (*enthumeisthai*) that the future is always uncertain and he may lose the reputation he has already won. Unable to decide either way, he consults the gods (*Anabasis* 6.1.19–22).

These *enthumēmata* are considerations one is swayed by when reflecting on an issue where conclusive argument is not to be had. Such considerations can well be seen as the body, or, if you prefer a modern metaphor, the nuts and bolts of *pistis*. You prove your case, to the best of your ability, by advancing considerations for the audience to think about. Aristotle's remarks now make good sense. Previous handbooks have said a lot about accessory means of persuasion such as the arousing of emotions, but no one has got down to the hard work of analyzing the ways in which the considerations constitutive of *pistis* can be devised and assembled together to make a satisfactory case. In other words, the argumentative side of rhetoric still awaits its Aristotle.

Fortunately, the afternoon students have not long to wait. In *Rhetoric* 1.1.11 Aristotle offers a more specific, although still very general approach to enthymeme, starting as before from the notion of *pistis*. He says that *pistis* is a sort of demonstration (*apodeixis tis*), and that rhetorical demonstration is enthymeme (1355a4–7).

These two claims are neither weighty nor technical. They amount to the following. The task of a speaker is to prove a case to the satisfaction of an audience (*pistis*). That is above all a matter of demonstrating various things (*apodeixis tis*), and a speech that sets out to demonstrate various things (*apodeixis rhētorikē*) does it by presenting considerations for the audience to think about (*enthumēma*). At this level of generality there is little more that Aristotle's students could expect him to say, unless it be to make explicit, what is already obviously implied, that presenting considerations to an audience is a matter of advancing arguments. And that, I submit, is why Aristotle adds, finally, that the enthymeme is *sullogismos tis*, a kind of *sullogismos* (repeated at 2.24.1.1400b37). He means neither more nor less than that an enthymeme, a consideration, is a sort of argument.

This is the moment at which enthymeme is first focused as an object of logical study. Aristotle insists that the thought content of a speech, which Isocrates and Alcidamas contrasted with its verbal expression, is fundamentally argument. More often than not, it is argument in a context where certainty and conclusive proof are not to be had (1.2.4.1356a7–8, 1.2.12.1357a1–2), yet a judgment must be made (1.3.1–3.1358a36–1358b8, 2.1.2–3.1377b21–1378a6, 2.18.1.1391b8–20, 3.19.6.1420b2–3). Hence it is argument that aims to secure the right judgment when, as Xenophon and the Sophoclean Chorus were acutely aware, there are things to be said on either side (2.25.2.1402a31–34). The challenge for a logician is to find the terms and techniques to make this sort of argument amenable to systematic study (see 1.1.1–2.1354a1–11).

The challenge, it should be noted, is self-imposed. It was imposed when Aristotle glossed *pistis* as *apodeixis tis* (1355a4–6). *Pistis* is the orators' own word for what they do when, as I put it, they have to prove a case to the satisfaction of an audience. Aristotle from the outset contrasts *pistis* with the accessory means of persuasion discussed by the handbooks (1354a12–18). So he is taking it that *pistis* really does mean proof, not (mere) persuasion as discussed in the handbooks.[6] Consequently, I need a different English word for *apodeixis*, even though it is the noun from the verb *apodeiknumi*, which was Zeno's word for "prove" in the text I began from. For the remainder of this essay I follow standard practice among translators of Aristotle in rendering *apodeixis* as "demonstration." The difference to be marked is this: both *pistis* and *apodeixis* occur in the orators, but when used by Aristotle and Zeno, *apodeixis* is the term that suggests logical stringency.

Aristotle's self-imposed challenge may now be formulated more clearly. Given his more respectful attitude toward the proceedings of courts and assemblies, he believes that what the orators do does deserve to be called proof. Hence a logician ought to be able to account for what they call *pistis* as some kind of demonstration: *apodeixis tis*.

THE AMBIGUITY OF *TIS*

Both *apodeixis* and *sullogismos* are words of ordinary language with which an educated student would be familiar. They are also technical terms of Aristotle's logic. To complicate matters further, in the present passage they are accompanied by the qualification *tis*, which might mean either of two things. It might mean that enthymeme is a species of *apodeixis* and hence also of *sullogismos*, distinguished from other species by its own mark of difference.[7] Or it might be an *alienans* qualification, meaning that an enthymeme is only a sort of *apodeixis*, only a sort of *sullogismos*, not as it were your full-blooded specimen, not something from which you can expect everything that you would normally expect from an *apodeixis* or a *sullogismos*.[8] In English the difference is the difference between "a kind of demonstration," on the one hand, and "a demonstration of a kind," on the other. So there is a double problem: Do the words *apodeixis* and *sullogismos* carry a technical or a nontechnical sense, and what kind of qualification is imported by *tis*?

It will be easier to tackle *apodeixis* first. Aristotle has a lot to say about *apodeixis* in the *Posterior Analytics*. He imposes notoriously stringent conditions on what is to count as an *apodeixis*. It is a *sullogismos* that proceeds from premises that are true and primary and immediate and better known than, prior to and explanatory of, the conclusion demonstrated from them. More briefly, it is an explanatory demonstration in which a necessary truth is shown to follow necessarily from necessary and self-explanatory axioms. This is very far from being an analysis of the ordinary educated speaker's notion of *apodeixis*. It should be seen as a systematic characterization of the best possible case of *apodeixis*, an explication (to use the philosopher's jargon) of the kind of demonstration which, as Aristotle believes, you need to have if you are to achieve full *epistēmē*, scientific understanding, of something. Lesser cases of *apodeixis* are admitted even within the *Posterior Analytics* (*apodeixis* that proves a fact without explaining it, *reductio ad absurdum*),[9] and elsewhere Aristotle is ready to concede that some demonstrations proceed in a "more relaxed" (*malakōteron*) manner than others (*Gen. Cor.* 2.6.333b25–26; *Met.* 6.1.1025b13). So the least we can suppose about the qualification *tis* is that it restores *apodeixis* closer to its ordinary nontechnical meaning, warning us not to expect an orator's *apodeixis* to meet the stringent conditions laid down for scientific demonstration.

That, as I say, is the least we can suppose. Whether it is enough must depend on a corresponding inquiry into *sullogismos tis*. Aristotle defines *sullogismos* in several places, including the *Rhetoric*. The earliest formulation is probably the one at *Topics* 1.1.100a25–27:

A *sullogismos* is a discourse [or: argument] in which, certain things being posited, something different from the things laid down necessarily results through the things laid down.

Prior Analytics 1.1.24b18–22 says the same exept that, instead of "through the things laid down" (*dia tōn keimenōn*), it has "by virtue of these things being the case" (*tōi tauta einai*), plus a gloss on what this is supposed to mean. It means that the conclusion results because of the premises (*dia tauta*) in the sense that the premises on their own are sufficient to necessitate the conclusion; no extra term (*exōthen horos*) is needed. We will not pause for an exhaustive examination of this definition. It is enough for present purposes that a *sullogismos* as Aristotle defines it is at least the following: a valid deductive argument in which the premises (note the plural) provide a logically sufficient justification for a conclusion distinct from them. The notion of *apodeixis* can then be defined by adding further conditions on the premises. For *apodeixis*—and here the *Topics* is both less detailed and therefore less stringent than the *Posterior Analytics*—the premises must be true and primary, or known on the basis of other premises that are themselves true and primary; by contrast, a dialectical *sullogismos* is specified as one that proceeds from premises that are reputable (100a27–30).

It should be obvious that these definitions come nowhere near to defining either *sullogismos* or *apodeixis* as a syllogism. Nothing is said about a *sullogismos* having exactly two premises, only that it has more than one.[10] Nothing is said about its involving exactly three terms—major, minor, and middle. Nothing is said about its constituent propositions all having one of the four syllogistic forms "All *A* is *B*," "No *A* is *B*," "Some *A* is *B*," "Some *A* is not *B*." Nothing is said about the syllogistic moods and figures. The entire technical apparatus of syllogistic is absent, for two very good but quite distinct reasons. First, because when Aristotle wrote down the definition in the *Topics* he probably had not yet discovered syllogistic. Second, because when he did discover it, he thought of it not as a further contribution to the definition of *sullogismos*, which the *Prior Analytics* repeats from the *Topics*, but as a way of testing when an argument is valid in the sense thereby defined and when it is not. He did not suppose that people ordinarily present their arguments in strict syllogistic form, but that the arguments they present are valid, that is, their conclusion results necessarily from their premises, if and only if they can be recast in one or a combination of the formally valid syllogistic moods.

Thus the term *sullogismos*, as used by Aristotle in his logical works, refers to a valid argument, and should never be translated "syllogism."[11] An enthymeme is *sullogismos tis*, but it is not thereby a syllogism; *a fortiori* it is not an abbreviated syllogism.

It has emerged that the relation between *sullogismos* as a technical term of Aristotle's logic and *sullogismos* in ordinary educated discourse is somewhat different from the corresponding relation in the case of *apodeixis*. The definition of *sullogismos* is a rather precise characterization of what one ordinarily expects from a valid argument, where the *Posterior Analytics* account of *apodeixis* is the stipulation of a very unordinary, especially favored case. It is therefore much easier to see how there can be "more relaxed" cases of *apodeixis* than to understand what would be meant by a "more relaxed" case of *sullogismos*. Surely, as Zeno will urge, an argument that does not meet all the conditions required for a valid argument is simply an invalid argument, no better than prattling. Accordingly, one is inclined to suppose that *sullogismos tis* means "a kind of *sullogismos*," not "a *sullogismos* of a kind," and that the notion of rhetorical *sullogismos* is to be reached in the same way as the notion of dialectical *sullogismos* is reached in the *Topics*, by adding to the standard notion of *sullogismos* some further condition on the premises. That inclination, I want to argue, is mistaken.

RELAXED ARGUMENTS

First, let me highlight a passage of the *Rhetoric* that acknowledges the possibility of a more relaxed *sullogizesthai*. Aristotle has been illustrating the point that one demonstrates something by drawing inferences from the facts, or presumed facts, about whatever the subject of discourse happens to be (2.22.4–9.1396a3–33). He now sums it up by saying that this is obvious from any demonstration, whether the speakers argue in a more precise or in a more relaxed way, *ean te akribesteron ean te malakōteron sullogizoneai* (1396a34–1396b1). I infer that the notion of a more relaxed *sullogismos* is not to be ruled out of court.

Second, when we look to see how the notion of rhetorical *sullogismos* is in fact reached in the *Rhetoric* (1.2.8.1356a35 ff.), we find that it is not defined as a species of *sullogismos*. It is defined as *sullogismos*. The pronouncement "For I call enthymeme rhetorical *sullogismos*, example rhetorical *epagōgē*" (1356b4–5) equates enthymeme with *sullogismos* and example with *epagōgē*, when, and only when, these occur in a rhetorical speech rather than in a dialectical discussion. This is clear both from the preceding sentence (1356a35–1356b4) and from the more detailed elaboration in the sequel.

The framework for the account is a logical claim that, of necessity, there are two and only two ways to show something. *Sullogismos* and *epagōgē* (roughly and for the moment: deduction and induction) are an exhaustive division of proof to which, consequently, rhetorical proofs must correspond (1356b7–9). Aristotle has independently observed that two and only two ways of showing something are used in rhetorical speechs, viz. enthymeme and example (1356b5–7; cf. 1.2.10.1356b18–24). So he concludes that enthymeme and *sullogismos* must be the same, and likewise example and *epagōgē* are the same (1356b9–10). And by "the same" he means "same in definition." For when he continues, "the difference between example and enthymeme is clear from the *Topics*" (1.2.9.1356b10–12), he is not referring to the *Topics* for definitions of example and enthymeme, but for his definitions of *epagōgē* (quoted later) and *sullogismos* (quoted earlier).[12] What is clear from the *Topics* is that

(i) *showing that something is so on the basis of many like cases* is there (*sc.* in dialectic) *epagōgē*, here example; and
(ii) *when, certain things being the case, something different results in addition to them by virtue of their being the case, either universally or for the most part*, there it is called *sullogismos*, here enthymeme.

The *Rhetoric's* official definition of enthymeme is its definition of *sullogismos*.

This is enough to show that *sullogismos tis* does not mean "a kind of *sullogismos*." But to help make it plausible that the phrase means "a *sullogismos* of a kind" we must turn briefly to the parallel case of example and *epagōgē*. According to *Prior Analytics* 2.24.69a16–19, *epagōgē* and example differ in both premises and conclusion: *epagōgē* reasons from all the particulars to a covering generalization, while example reasons from one or two of the particulars to a conclusion about a new particular. Quite a difference for two things that are supposed to be the same. But it would be a pity to find the *Prior Analytics* and the *Rhetoric* at variance with each other, for the *Prior Analytics* analysis of differences between example and *epagōgē* is broadly true of the arguments by example and *epagōgē* cited within the *Rhetoric* itself.[13] A better resolution of the problem lies to hand. If example and *epagōgē* are different in the *Rhetoric's* practice, but their definition is still the same, the differences may indicate a deviation or falling off from the conditions specified in their common *definiens*. Example carries the function of *epagōgē* but it takes a narrower evidential base and does not formulate the covering generalization it works through.[14] It is *epagōgē tis,* induction of a kind. Not that Aristotle calls it that. But he calls it similar to *epagōgē* and says that it is more suitable than *epagōgē* for rhetorical speeches (2.20.2.1393a26; 2.20.9.1394a11). The best way to reconcile such statements with the statement in 1.2 that example and *epagōgē* are in fact the same is to treat example as degenerate *epagōgē:* an induction indeed, but one from which you cannot expect everything you would normally expect from *epagōgē*.

The next point to notice is that the definition of example/*epagōgē* in 1.2 is slightly different from the corresponding definition in the *Topics* (1.12.105a13–14), which reads:

> *Epagōgē* is a passage from particulars to universals.

The definition is inapplicable to example, which has a singular not a universal conclusion. The vaguer phrase at *Rhetoric* 1356b14, "that something is so" (*hoti houtōs echei*), fits either type of conclusion. Has Aristotle deliberately relaxed the conditions in order to make it easier for example and *epagōgē* to share a common definition? One way to find an answer is to go back to enthymeme and *sullogismos* to see whether their definition shows signs of a parallel relaxation.[15]

The *Rhetoric's* definition of *sullogismos*/enthymeme certainly is different from the *Topics* definition I quoted earlier. It is different in at least two respects.[16]

First, instead of "certain things being posited" (*tethentōn tinōn*), we find "certain things being the case" (*tinōn ontōn*). The most natural interpretation of this is that it caters for the point mentioned just now, that rhetorical argument is a matter of drawing inferences from the *facts* about something. Dialectical reasoning typically proceeds from premises which are merely posited, for argument's sake or because they are acceptable to one's respondent. Rhetorical reasoning is more assertive: one's premises either state the facts of the case or at least they purport to do so, and this assertiveness is a condition of the argument's being an *apodeixis* as well as a *sullogismos*. *Apodeixis* aims to prove a conclusion from premises that are true.

The second divergence from the *Topics* is the omission of "necessarily" (*ex anankēs*) and the substitution of "either always or for the most part" (*ē katholou ē hōs epi to polu*). On the face of it,[17] the effect of this substitution is to weaken the requirement that the premises must provide a logically sufficient justification for the conclusion. There must still be a conclusion distinct from the premises (note that the enthymeme by definition has more than one premise!), and it must result by virtue of these premises being the case (*tōi tauta einai*, the *Prior Analytics* variant on *dia tōn keimenōn*). But the connection that provides the justification may not be absolutely exceptionless. It may hold for the most part, but not universally.

Here, then, is my suggestion. Given the apparent relaxation in the accompanying definition of *epagōgē*, it is a reasonable inference that the apparent relaxation in the definition of *sullogismos* is a deliberate attempt by Aristotle to fashion a concept of degenerate deduction that can be applied to contexts where conclusive proof is not to be had. More positively, it is a reasonable inference that "reasonable inference" is the notion Aristotle aims to develop for the study of rhetorical argumentation.

I make the suggestion in this self-referential fashion because I want to acknowledge that there are things to be said on either side. A strict deductivist who dislikes the suggestion can defend the Zenonian stance over much of the relevant text. My case for relaxation will be made gradually. My aim is to show that the relaxed party has the most reasonable, as well as the most interesting, overall account of Aristotle's project.[18]

BREVITY

This much, however, is already firm: an enthymeme is an argument (*sullogismos tis*) in a rhetorical speech, and whereas the difference between a dialectical *sullogismos* and scientific *apodeixis* is defined by the character of their premises (see earlier), the difference between a dialectical and a rhetorical *sullogismos* is defined rather by the context in which they occur. Both take their premises from *endoxa*, propositions that enjoy good repute, in the one case with people who require reasoned discussion, in the other with people who are accustomed to deliberation.[19] Accordingly, if the standards of validity do need to be relaxed somewhat to accommodate rhetorical *sullogismoi* under the same definition as dialectical ones, then it is to the context that we should look to understand why and how.

The relevant features of the rhetorical context are described at 1.2.12–13.1357a1–22. First, the variable subject matter: rhetoric's function is to speak on issues where we deliberate because (*a*) we have no specialist expertise (*technē*) to guide us,[20] and (*b*) we believe that the outcome is open and can be affected by our decision. Second, the simple audience: not only is the speaker no specialist on the question to be decided, but he is addressing an audience of people who cannot easily follow a long train of reasoning. This too is part of the function of rhetoric, to adjust a speech to the limitations of its audience.[21] The consequence Aristotle draws for the enthymeme is correspondingly twofold. First, the enthymeme must be argument (*sullogismos*) about things which, in the main, are capable of being otherwise than they are—few of them are invariable necessities.[22] Second, it must restrict itself to a small number of premises—often fewer than the primary (that is, normal) *sullogismos*.[23]

It is by these two marks of difference, both of them consequential on the difference in context, that Aristotle distinguishes rhetorical from dialectical *sullogismoi* (cf. the recapitulation at 2.22.2–3.1395b22–1396a3). Do either of them affect the question of validity?

The remark about minimizing the number of premises is claimed by Cope as support for the traditional logic book doctrine that an enthymeme is an abbreviated syllogism.[24] But if *sullogismos* meant "syllogism," the plural phrase *ex oligōn te kai pollakis elattonōn* would be baffling, for the only way an argument can have fewer premises than the normal syllogism is by having just one premise. It would be equally odd to describe a normal two-premise syllogism as reasoning too lengthy (*porrōthen*) for the audience to follow. The truth is that neither here nor anywhere else does Aristotle say that an enthymeme *must* have a premise omitted, on pain of not being an enthymeme at all.

Certainly, an enthymeme must be brief, if it is to fulfill its function. But this can be achieved by a suitable choice of premises rather than by their suppression. It is a good enthymeme, not an enthymeme as such, which omits to formulate premises that the audience can supply for themselves, where a "good" enthymeme is to be understood, again by reference to the function of rhetoric, as one that is effective with an audience of limited mental capacity.[25]

Instructive in this connection is a passage at 2.21.2 where Aristotle illustrates the difference between an enthymeme and a maxim (*gnōmē*). The saying "There is no man who is really free" taken by itself is a maxim, but when you add the next verse "for he is the slave either of wealth or of fortune" you have an enthymeme (1394b3–6, from Euripides, *Hecuba* 864–865). This is as compressed as one could wish. Like many of Aristotle's examples of enthymeme, on the surface it is simply a claim backed by a reason. But logically it is quite complex, involving a disjunctive predicate, which syllogistic cannot represent. The preceding example is more complex still. "No man who is sensible ought to have his children taught to be excessively clever" is the maxim. Add the reason, says Aristotle, and you get an enthymeme: "No man who is sensible ought to have his children taught to be excessively clever, for, quite apart from becoming idle, they earn jealous hostility from the citizens" (1394a26–34, from Euripides, *Medea* 294–297). It is simply impossible to represent this argument as a syllogism, even if one sets aside the clause "quite apart from becoming idle." It is impossible because the children have to appear both as the subjects who earn hostility and as the objects of the verb "to teach" inside the predicate of the maxim, and this is something that syllogistic cannot represent.[26]

But the fact that brevity is a virtue in enthymemes tells us nothing about the standards of validity to be expected of a rhetorical speech, nor does Aristotle ever suggest that it does. A premise suppressed is still a premise of the argument. What we are interested in is the relation of premises to conclusion. More important than the fact that the premises are few is that few of them are invariable necessities.

NECESSITY AND LIKELIHOOD

The necessity in question is not the necessity of apodeictic propositions, which state, truly or falsely, that something is necessary. It is the necessity that Aristotle associates with invariable exceptionless truth and contrasts with being true "for the most part." A good place to study both the association and the contrast is 2.19 on proof projects common to all branches of rhetoric.[27]

Among the patterns of inference that Aristotle adduces to illustrate how to prove a point about the past are the following (2.19.18–19.1392b18–23):

(A) If X was able and wished (*ebouleto*) to φ, X φed.
(B) If X wished (*ebouleto*) to φ and there was no external obstacle, X φed.[28]

In support of (A), Aristotle states that everyone does a thing when they have the wish and are able to carry it out, for nothing hinders them. In support of (B) (and of two more inferences to the same conclusion with subtly varied antecedents), he states merely that people do for the most part do what they want (*oregontai*), provided they are able to. (The exceptions envisaged here are presumably due to some internal obstacle or incapacity, but we must not be sidetracked into moral psychology.) So when he sums up the whole series of illustrations by saying, "Of all these some are so of necessity, others for the most part" (2.19.21.1392b31–32), it is evident that inference (A) goes with the category "of necessity," inference (B) with that of "being so for the most part." Inference (A) exploits a necessary (because invariable) connection, inference (B) one that holds only for the most part.

Now let us envisage, as Aristotle does not, a syllogistic reconstruction of the two inferences in which the supporting principles appear as major premises. Inference (A) is straightforward: the conclusion follows validly

from the singular premise in conjunction with the universal generalization "All those who are able and wish to φ do φ." But inference (B) is
invalid if the major premise is "For the most part those who wish to φ and
are not hindered by an external obstacle do φ." For its conclusion is the
unqualified assertion "X φed," not "X is likely to have φed."

Alternatively, if the major is taken as "All those who wish to φ and are
not hindered by an external obstacle do φ," (B) is valid but unsound, for
the universal premise is false. The only way to turn these materials into
an argument one might present as both valid and sound is to qualify the
conclusion as a likelihood.

Sometimes Aristotle does mention a qualified conclusion:

(C) If the sky is clouded over, it is likely to rain (2.19.24.1393a6–7).

But more commonly his sample conclusions are unqualified, for the good
reason that they are quotations (real or imaginary) from speeches, and the
makers of speeches are not fussy about the difference between "*p*" and
"probably *p*."

Orators are equally unfussy about the difference between generalizations that are necessary in the sense that they hold in all cases without
exception and those that hold only for the most part. The sample generalizations in the *Rhetoric* are typically unquantified assertions like:

Other practitioners of an art are not contemptible (2.23.5.1397b23).
The dissolute are not satisfied with the enjoyment of one body only
(2.23.8.1398a23–24).
The true friend should love as if he were going to be a friend for ever
(2.21.14.1395a30–31).
Foolish is he who, having slain the father, allows the children to live
(2.21.11.1395a16–17; cf. 1.15.14.1376a6–7).

There are of course exceptions, both affirmative (e.g., 2.23.10.1398a29–
30) and negative (e.g., 2.21.2 and 2.21.5.1394b2, 4, 16). But it is significant that the unquantified form is treated as canonical for the generalizations under scrutiny in Aristotle's syllogistic analysis of rhetorical
reasoning at *Prior Analytics* 2.27 (70a5–6, 16, 20–21, 26–27; cf. *Rhet.*
1.2.18.1357b12). For if the reasoning in a speech is full of unquantified
generalizations and unqualified conclusions, it will often be *indeterminate*
whether a given enthymeme—the argumentation seen on the page or
heard in the Assembly on the Pnyx—is sound or not. The logician must
first ask how the speaker intends these generalizations and conclusions
and how they are received by the audience.

So far as rhetorical generalizations are concerned, Aristotle both asks
the question and answers it. Most of the generalizations are likelihoods,
where a likelihood is defined as a "for the most part" regularity *which*

people know or believe to be one.[29] So the orators are not necessarily being unscrupulous when they use unquantified forms of expression. Nobody need be deceived about the scope of their generalizations, almost everybody recognizes the possibility of exceptions to the rule.[30]

But what about conclusions based on such generalizations? How are they intended and received? The logician who wrote the *Analytics* maintains that for the argument to be valid they should be qualified as true only for the most part (*Post. Anal.* 1.30.87b24–25). He says nothing about the validity of arguments to a singular conclusion, where the qualification "for the most part" makes no sense. It does make sense to qualify a singular conclusion as a likelihood—but the careful observer of persuasive practices who compiled the *Rhetoric* knows that frequently this is left undone. Inference (B) is accompanied in 2.19 by many other instances of the same format, as well as some in the style of inference (C); the chapter proceeds as if the qualifying of conclusions was optional. Is there a tension between Aristotle's logic and his sense of reality? Or is it a dastardly lack of scruple that leads orators to prefer "*p*" to "probably *p*"?[31]

Both parties can be cleared by a single defense. Take the prefix "It is likely to" in (C) as qualifying the inference, not the conclusion inferred. Let it express *probabilitas consequentiae*, not *probabilitas consequentis*.[32] Then the difference between (B) and (C) is indeed a difference of style, not substance. It is comparable to the difference between (A) and

(A)′ If *X* was able and wished to φ, *X* must have φed,

where the "must" makes explicit, what (A) leaves to be understood, that "*X* φed" is asserted on the strength of a necessary connection.[33] Just so, (C) makes explicit, while (B) leaves it to be understood, that its conclusion "It will rain" is asserted on the strength of a connection that holds only for the most part.

This reading of 2.19 makes honest sense of rhetorical practice. It would also win the approval of those modern logicians who urge that the very concept of *probabilitas consequentis* leads to paradox, as follows.[34] Let inference (C) be pitted against a rival argument,

(C)′ If the barometer is high, it is likely not to rain.

The conclusions of (C) and (C)′ contradict each other if "It is likely to" is understood as a modal operator comparable to "It is necessary that." Yet it may well happen that both conclusions are inferred from a true "for the most part" generalization. One could never demonstrate both "It is necessary that *p*" and "It is necessary that not-*p*" from true premises. The solution is to accept that "It is likely to" is not a modal operator but an inferential connective. No inconsistency arises if the assertion "It will rain" is warranted by one piece of evidence and the assertion "It will not rain" by another. That is what it is to confront an issue where there are things to be said on either side. As Aristotle himself puts it,

[Argument and] counter-argument can be derived from the same topics. For the *sullogismoi* proceed from reputable propositions and many of these are contrary to one another. (2.25.2.1402a31–34; cf. 2.26.3.1403a25–29)

But can Aristotle's own logic accommodate this insight? Is there room in his theory for a concept of *probabilitas consequentiae*? The answer is "Yes," but the place to look for such a concept is not the place where a modern logician would expect to find it.

Aristotle's study of rhetorical reasoning is constrained by a firm commitment to the claim that the division of proofs into *sullogismos* and *epagōgē* is necessarily exhaustive (p. 97).[35] Viewing these terms through their conventional translations as "deduction" (or even "syllogism") and "induction" respectively, one expects inferences (B) and (C) to be classified on the inductive side of the division by anyone who would construe them in terms of *probabilitas consequentiae*. One expects this just because so construing (B) and (C) means denying that their premises are presented as necessitating their conclusions. But Aristotle never associates *epagōgē* with probability, and he does not define *epagōgē*, in the way moderns sometimes define inductive argument, as any argument that does not purport to be deductively valid. He specifically requires the conclusion of an *epagōgē* to be inferred from a number of like cases (p. 97). No such reference to like cases is involved in inferences (B) and (C). Therefore they cannot be examples of *epagōgē*.

But any proof which is not an *epagōgē* is a *sullogismos*. The division is exhaustive. Unless the notion of *epagōgē* is revised to include inferences (B) and (C)—this would be the modern preference[36]—the notion of *sullogismos* must be stretched to include some arguments in which the premises do not purport to necessitate their conclusions. That is how inferences (A), (B), and (C) can be grouped together in the way they are, without regard to the differences between them. All are enthymemes, rhetorical *sullogismoi*.[37] *Sullogismos* in the *Rhetoric* must therefore cover *probabilitas consequentiae* as well as *necessitas consequentiae*.

No doubt a strict deductivist will continue to insist that the only conclusion that can result by virtue of a generalization being the case for the most part is one that is qualified (explicitly or implicitly) as a likelihood. But out there on the Pnyx it is not enough to determine what the likelihoods are. On the basis (balance) of those likelihoods an unqualified judgment must be reached: "He is guilty," "We should go to war." And now that we have seen how to make the *Rhetoric*'s official definition of enthymeme consistent with all the patterns of inference collected in 2.19, nothing stands in the way of a verdict affirming that Aristotle's logic can do justice to the realities of rhetorical practice. There is no need to fault either the speakers' reasoning or his analysis of it.

INTERIM CONCLUSION

I conclude that an excellent case can be made for the view that the *tis* in *sullogismos tis* is an *alienans* qualification. An enthymeme is not a kind of *sullogismos*, still less a kind of syllogism. It is a *sullogismos* of a kind and a demonstration of a kind, a deduction from which you cannot expect everything you would normally expect from a valid deductive argument.

An excellent case for something is not a conclusive proof. It is *apodeixis tis*, which leaves room for objections. But objections, if we go by Aristotle's own account of objection in 2.25, must do more than show that a strict deductivist reading of the relevant texts can keep going. They must show that the relaxed interpretation is not likely—or better, that it is less likely than its Zenonian rival (2.25.8–11.1402b21–1403a2; cf. 2.25.13.1403a5– 10). The same applies to 2.25 itself. Is it about objections to relaxed arguments in which the premises make likely an unqualified conclusion, or about objections to strict arguments in which the premises necessitate a likelihood? On first perusal the chapter could be taken either way. I recommend the relaxed interpretation here as elsewhere, on the grounds that it gives the most reasonable overall account of how Aristotle adapts his logical theory to rationalize the phenomena of rhetorical practice.

But the toughest challenge for strict deductivism lies ahead. There is more relaxing to do.

THE LOGIC OF SIGN ARGUMENTS

The logic of the *Rhetoric* is the informal dialectic of the *Topics*, to which Aristotle often refers. On the one hand, not all of the patterns of argument he illustrates can be fitted into the syllogistic mold; on the other, much of the interest of the *Rhetoric* lies in the highly professional way that Aristotle handles informally patterns of argument that were not to be formalized until later.[38] There are, however, two sections of the *Rhetoric* (1.2.14–19.1357a22–1358a2, and the passage just cited for its remarks on refutation, 2.25.8–14.1402b13–1403a16) which refer to *Prior Analytics* 2.27 for its syllogistic demonstration of the invalidity of two out of three forms of sign argument. These two sections contain all but one of the *Rhetoric*'s five references to the *Analytics*,[39] and there are grounds for believing them to be later insertions, written by Aristotle after, and in the light of, his discovery of syllogistic.[40] But what interests me here is their logical, not their chronological significance. Sign arguments (*sullogismoi ek sēmeiōn*) are a distinct type of enthymeme added to the arguments from likelihood (*sullogismoi ex eikotōn*) on which we have concentrated so far. *Prior Analytics* 2.27 is where the distinction is clarified and its consequences considered.

The chapter is the last of a series of chapters which fulfill a promise made earlier in 2.23 to show that syllogistic is a universally applicable test of validity:

> We must now explain that not only are dialectical and demonstrative *sullogismoi* effected by way of the aforesaid figures [i.e., are reducible to syllogisms in the narrow sense defined by the figures], but so also are rhetorical ones and in general any proof (*pistis*),[41] whatever its procedure. For all our convictions come either through *sullogismos* or from *epagōgē*. (68b9–14)

Rhetorical proof (*pistis*) is a central but not the sole concern of this passage. *Apagōgē*, discussed in 2.25, is important in mathematics, and 2.27 will in fact examine sign arguments in physiognomonics (70b7–38) as well as in rhetoric. Likewise enthymeme is the central but not the sole topic of 2.27. Not all sign arguments are enthymemes.[42] Nor are all arguments from likelihood.[43] The distinctive logical features of enthymeme are due to its reliance on likelihoods and signs, but in themselves likelihood and sign are of much broader scope. It is when they are used to prove something in public discourse—in a speech to court or assembly—that they become premises of enthymemes (*Rhet.* 1.2.4.1357a31–34, 2.25.8.1402b14; see earlier).

What follows in 2.27 is a group of one-premise sign inferences for which a second premise is supplied to complete a syllogism. This yields a form of argument the validity or invalidity of which is already known from syllogistic theory. It is not that Aristotle has relaxed the requirement that a *sullogismos*, hence an enthymeme, must have at least two premises: 70a25 is sufficient evidence to the contrary. But he promised to show how syllogistic can test the logical validity of rhetorical proofs, where singular terms abound and familiar premises are suppressed (cf. 70a19–20, 24–28). It is syllogistic that limits him to examples in which one premise is expressed and one is supplied.

Let us look at the examples. The fact that a woman has milk in her breasts is a sign that she is pregnant; the fact that Pittacus is good is a sign that wise men generally are good; the fact that a woman is of sallow complexion is a sign that she is pregnant. The last two inferences are shown to be invalid when the extra premise is supplied. The milk example is pronounced valid on the strength of a first figure reconstruction as a sylllogism in *Barbara*. "She has milk" thus exemplifies the first disjunct in Aristotle's explication of a sign as a premise, either necessary or reputable, for demonstrating something (*protasis apodeiktikē ē anankaia ē endoxos*,

70a6–7). It is a necessary sign in the sense that it necessitates the conclusion "She is pregnant," by virtue of the (allegedly) exceptionless universal generalization "All who have milk are pregnant," which appears as the major premise in the syllogistic reconstruction.[44] Similarly in the *Rhetoric*, "I call those signs necessary from which a *sullogismos* can be constructed" (1.2.17.1357b5–6).[45] That leaves the second disjunct to cover the other two signs: "Pittacus is good" and "She is sallow" are premises that merely make the inferred conclusion a respectable thing to believe.

This is a remarkable enlargement of the scope of enthymeme. It is one thing to endorse the kind of *probabilitas consequentiae* exhibited by inferences (B) and (C), quite another to accept that deductively invalid sign arguments can be respectable too. It is neither universally nor for the most part true that women of sallow complexion are pregnant, and in any case Aristotle is quite clear that the generalization that (anyone propounding) the sign inference actually relies on its "Pregnant women are sallow."[46] Hence even the relaxed interpretation of the *Rhetoric*'s definition of enthymeme/*sullogismos* does not cover "She is pregnant because she is sallow." How are we to understand this wider category of arguments that make their conclusion a respectable thing to believe?

The *probabilitas consequentiae* of (B) and (C) is apparently subsumed under the wider category when Aristotle states that a likelihood is a reputable premise (*protasis endoxos*, 70a3–4). For given that at 70a7 both "necessary" (*anankaia*) and "reputable" (*endoxos*) characterize the inferential power, in the first case of a necessitating, in the second of a non-necessitating sign premise, it becomes probable that "reputable premise" at 70a3–4 should be taken the same way.[47] The alternative is to accept that Aristotle, having distinguished likelihood from sign, has nothing of logical import to tell us about it. Yet he can hardly fulfill the promise of 2.23 if one huge class of rhetorical *sullogismoi*, those from likelihoods, are left out of account.

If the suggested interpretation of likelihood is correct, then at least in *Prior Analytics* 2.27, where he has the benefit of syllogistic, Aristotle sides with the relaxed interpretation of inferences (B) and (C). To make a conclusion likely is to make it a respectable thing to believe, where that contrasts with necessitating a conclusion (70a7) and making it secure for knowledge (70b1–2). Similarly in the *Rhetoric* (1.2.15.1357a34–1357b1),[48] likelihood is defined functionally, in terms of its inferential power: when applied to the variable subject matter of rhetoric, it makes a singular conclusion likely in a manner analogous to that in which a properly universal premise makes a singular conclusion necessary.[49]

But sign arguments are a distinct way of conferring respectability on a conclusion, as Aristotle emphasizes in the first words of the chapter:

"Likelihood and sign are not the same" (70a2–3). If they are not the same, the logical resources devised for handling likelihood will not suffice for sign arguments. The logic of inferences like the milk example, which exploit a necessary connection, is well enough understood. But Aristotle accepts many sign inferences that are not conclusive, and so do we.[50] Some new resource is needed.

The new resource is the idea that respectability comes in degrees. There is truth in each of the three patterns of sign argument; that is, each is capable of leading from a true premise to a true conclusion (70a37–38), but the first figure pattern of necessary sign arguments is the most true, that is, the most productive of true conclusions. It is also the most respectable (70b4–6). Aristotle surely means that it is the most respectable because it is the most productive of true conclusions.[51]

Now the degrees Aristotle is talking about here are degrees of acceptability to the nonspecialist audience of rhetorical speeches.[52] This comes out in connection with the sign argument "She is pregnant because she is sallow," which we nowadays might describe as an example of "inference to the best explanation." What Aristotle says is: "Since sallowness is a concomitant of pregnancy, and she is sallow, people *think* it has been shown (*oiontai dedeichthai*) that she is pregnant" (70a20–23). This is not a dismissive comment. The *Rhetoric* is founded on the axiom (1.1.11.1355a14–18) that human beings have a natural aptitude for discerning truth which is simultaneously an aptitude for discerning what is like the truth (verisimilitude). But it does mean we should be cautious about the idea that degrees of respectability can be translated into our language as degrees of probability.

If our language was Latin, the translation would be fine. But *endoxos* does not go over straightforwardly into any contemporary sense of "probable."[53] Nor does *eikos*, the word I have rendered "likelihood." A rhetorician contemporary with Aristotle goes so far as to say, "It is *eikos* when one's hearers have examples in their minds of what is said,"[54] which amounts to: when what is said is common sense. And what counts as common sense is culture-relative in a way contemporary ideas of probability aspire not to be.

But no caution is needed, and we avoid getting caught up in the nuances of the history of probability, if we translate degrees of respectability into degrees of reasonableness. Aristotle uses the man on the Pnyx, as English law uses the man on the Clapham omnibus, as a rough and ready, informal test of reasonableness. He has not started out on the road to the probability calculus or canons of inductive logic; signs are still on the *sullogismos* side of the dichotomous division of proofs. But he does have the essential insight that an argument that is formally invalid is not necessarily to be condemned as totally useless or irrational. It may not provide a logically sufficient justification for its conclusion, but for all that it may offer a consideration (*enthumēma*)—a consideration, if I may adapt a famous phrase of John Stuart Mill's, which is capable of determining the intellect either to give or withhold its assent. And that, as Mill also said, is equivalent to proof, that is, to *apodeixis* in the everyday sense of the word.

CONCLUSION

It is a mark of Aristotle's wisdom that he did include nonnecessary signs among the premises of enthymemes, contrary to the strict deductivist's advice and contrary to his own official account of what an enthymeme is. But neither syllogistic nor the concept of *sullogismos tis* can take the analysis further. We would like to know under what conditions it is appropriate for a speaker to advance, and for the audience to accept, a sign argument that is deductively invalid. The only answer we get from the *Rhetoric* is: when it is convincing.[55]

A contemporary reader is bound to regret Aristotle's unwillingness to extend the range of *epagōgē*. In our world inductive logic has the use of subtle techniques of probabilistic reasoning. But this is a comparatively recent development. For a long time people made do with an older, less rigorous thing called "probable reasoning." Aristotle was its first theorist. John Locke in the seventeenth century can still write,

> As Demonstration is the shewing the Agreement, or Disagreement of two *Ideas*, by the intervention of one or more Proofs, which have a constant, immutable, and visible connection one with another: so *Probability* is nothing but the appearance of such an Agreement, or Disagreement, by the intervention of Proofs, whose connection is not constant and immutable, or at least is not perceived to be so, but is, or appears for the most part to be so, and is enough to induce the Mind to *judge* the Proposition to be true, or false, rather than the contrary. (Locke, *An Essay Concerning Human Understanding* IV.15.1)

Like Aristotle, Locke distinguishes probable from demonstrative reasoning by a weakening of the inferential connection on which the proof relies. The result is that opposite conclusions can both be proved. Our task, when we sit on a jury or committee, is not to decide which speaker proved his case and which was merely prattling, but to listen to both sides, weighing "the Arguments and Proofs, *pro* and *con*" (IV.16.9), and then allow our assent "to be determined by the preponderancy, after a due weighing of all the Proofs, with all Circumstances on both sides" (IV.17.5).[56]

Philosophical readers may feel uncomfortable with Locke's relaxed use of the word "proof." Translate it back into the Greek *pistis*, if you prefer.

Or you may like to imagine that Locke capitalized the initial letter of "Proof" for the same reason as Aristotle added *tis* to *apodeixis tis:* to signal that this is not a kind of proof but a proof of a kind, a proof from which you cannot expect everything you would expect from a valid argument with true premises that are known to be true. The important issue is not whether Locke's English (or Zeno's Greek) is correct, but the reasonableness of maintaining the procedural rule "Don't give your verdict until you have heard both sides."

NOTES

This essay is a re-presentation, with additional material, of selections from "Enthymeme: Aristotle on the Logic of Persuasion," *Aristotle's Rhetoric: Philosophical Essays*, ed. D. J. Furley and A. Nehamas (Princeton, 1994).

1. Diogenes Laertius, *Lives of the Philosophers* VII 33. Zeno's opponent speaks of giving verdicts (δικάζειν), which implies a law court setting. I have extended the argument to assemblies, on my own responsibility, because in normal political life, outside the ideal Stoic city of wise men and women, the same logic applies. By "assembly" I mean any deliberative body, large or small.

2. As so often, there are anticipations in Plato: *Phaedo* 92d, *Theaetetus* 162e, and, with a more positive attitude to unstrict arguments, *Timaeus* 40e and passim. But the difference made by Aristotle's understanding of "the why" is profound.

3. See my article "Enthymeme: Aristotle on the Logic of Persuasion," 1994. This study will be referred to hereafter by the abbreviation ALP.

4. What follows is in substance a re-presentation, with additional material, of those portions of ALP that bear directly on the interpretation of Aristotle's account of enthymeme. The extra material is to explain or emphasize the important points for a less specialist audience than ALP was written for. Correspondingly, I keep scholarly controversy to a curt minimum, and leave out some of the twists and turns of the fuller exposition; for textual matters I rely on Kassel's magisterial 1976 edition. If the result strikes you at any point as overly dogmatic, turn to ALP for a more dialectical treatment.

5. For Isocrates, see *Against the Sophists* 16; *Evagoras* 10 (*bis*); *Antidosis* 47; *Panathenaicus* 2. The first passage, at least, was written well before Aristotle reached Athens.

6. In the Oxford Translation (both revised and unrevised) πίστις is rendered " mode of persuasion": the Greek word could mean this, but Aristotle doesn't. Cf. note 41 of this essay.

7. Thus "species of" is most certainly the meaning of τις in συλλογισμός τις when Aristotle says at *Pr. Anal.* 1.4.25b30 that ἀπόδειξις is συλλογισμός τις.

8. Compare Plato, *Apology* 20d7 σοφίαν τινά; *Euthydemus* 285b1 φθόρον τινά; *DA* 3.10.433a10 ε ἴ τις τὴν φαντασίαν τιθείη ὡς νόησίν τινα; *Mem.* 2.453a11–12 τὸ ἀναμιμνήσκεσθαί ἐστιν οἷον συλλογισμός τις; cf. *DA* 3.12.434b18; 1.1. 403a8–9.

9. See Lloyd 1990.

10. συλλογισμοί with more than two premises are mentioned at *Pr. Anal.* 1.23.41a17–20; 1.27.43b35; 2.18.66a17–18. Two notable examples are *DA* 3.1.424b22–425a13; *NE* 9.9.1170a25–1170b19.

11. In the Revised Oxford Translation, Barnes uses "deduction," for which see Barnes 1981, p. 23.

12. 1356b12–13 ἐκεῖ γάρ . . . πρότερον in Vahlen's parentheses, without a stop after τοπικῶν.

13. For ἐπαγωγή, see 2.23.11.1398a32–1398b19; for example, see 1.2.19. 1357b25–36, 2.20.2–3.1393a27–1393b3, 2.25.8.1402b16–18, 2.25.13.1403a5–10. Another difference is that example can reason from fictitious particulars: 2.20.2–3 and 5–8.1393a27–30 and 1393b8–1394a9.

14. The role of the covering generalization is well discussed by Ryan 1984, pp. 119–129 (cf. pp. 136–137).

15. An affirmative answer to both questions was urged long ago by Vahlen 1867, pp. 108–110.

16. Noticed by Wörner 1982, pp. 82–85, and 1990, pp. 352–357. Cf. also Ryan 1984, pp. 92–93.

17. Certain complications of text and translation are dealt with in ALP, pp. 19–21. I have accepted Kassel's deletion of διὰ ταῦτα at 1356b16, but it is not essential to my argument.

18. By "the relaxed party" I refer to a coalition of previous scholars who, while differing in the details of their interpretation, agree that deductive validity has to go. Recent representatives include Raphael 1974, Ryan 1984, and Wörner 1982, 1990, preceded by McBurney 1974. The deductivist side is represented with exemplary strictness by Sprute. Deductivism is common among commentators on *Pr. Anal.* 2.27 (Philoponus, Pacius 1597, Smith 1989), but I enlist Ross as an ally in note 47 of this essay.

19. 1.2.11.1356b32–1357a1 with Maier's δεομένων . . . εἰωθόσιν; cf. 2.22. 3.1395b31–1396a2, which confirms that the rhetorician has to work with a much narrower range of ἔνδοξα than the dialectician.

20. Cf. *Phys.* 2.8.199b28; *NE* 3.3.1112a34–1112b9.

21. I wish I could write a footnote explaining that Aristotle is not as snobbish as he sounds, merely realistic about communication with a nonspecialist audience.

22. This is implied already by ὡς τὰ πολλά (1357a15), before being elaborated in the next section at 1.2.14.1357a23–27.

23. On the meaning of πρῶτος here, which has nothing to do with the first figure of syllogistic, see ALP, p. 22 n. 58.

24. Cope 1877, vol. 2, p. 209. So too Anonymus, *In Aristotelis Artem Rhetoricam* 2.25–27. Pacius's objection (1597, p. 265) that "often fewer" excludes "always" remains unanswered.

25. This is confirmed by the recapitulation at 2.22.2–3.1395b22–26, and even more clearly at 3.18.4.1419a18–19: enthymemes should be compressed as much as possible because of the weakness of the hearers of rhetorical speeches. Likewise in the pseudo-Aristotelian *Rhetorica ad Alexandrum*, brevity is not a condition for

being an enthymeme at all, but a recommendation for a good one, especially when the audience is interrupting: 11(10).1430a35–39, 12(11).1430b4–6, 19(18). 1432b24–26, 1433a24–26.

26. One can of course construct a syllogism in *Barbara* by taking *A* = children who are taught to be excessively clever, *B* = children who earn hostility from the citizens, *C* = children whose father is not sensible. But this conspicuously fails to conclude with a recommendation to fathers about how they should bring up their children.

27. See also 2.25.8 and 2.25.10.1302b19 (with Vahlen's ἀεί), 30; *Top.* 2.6. 112b1–20; *Phys.* 2.5.196b10–13.

28. On these forms as expressing *inference*, not just the assertion of a conditional proposition, see Brunschwig 1967, pp. xxxii–xxxiv. On the "variables en blanc" for which I have supplied "*X*" and "φ," ibid., pp. lxxxix and 138 n. 2.

29. Nowhere, despite frequent assertions to the contrary (e.g., Solmsen 1929, p. 139 n. 1, Kneale 1946, p. 150, Madden 1957, p. 167, Sprute 1982, p. 74), is εἰκός simply equated by Aristotle with τὸ ὡς ἐπὶ τὸ πολύ. *Rhet.* 1.2.15.1357a34–35, explicitly rejects the idea: cf. p. 107 with n. 49). The nontechnical definition at *Pr. Anal.* 2.27.70a2–3 restricts εἰκός to "for the most part" truths that are generally known, while *Rhet.* 2.25.8.1302b14–16 enlarges it to include what people believe to be true for the most part.

30. I write "almost" to signal the fact that the unquantified ἴσασι at *Pr. Anal.* 2.27.70a3 allows for the occasional idiot in the audience.

31. This would seem to be the imputation of Sprute's claim (1992, pp. 73, 78–79) that, while the speaker is aware that the conclusion is only a likelihood, the simpleminded hearer is not.

32. I use Latin here for two reasons. First, to create an analogue to the more familiar phrases *necessitas consequentiae* and *necessitas consequentis,* commonly used to tag the distinction between the necessity that connects premises and conclusion in a valid inference (*consequentia*); i.e., $\Box$ ($p \to q$), and the necessity of the conclusion itself (*consequens*) in such an inference; i.e., ($p \to \Box q$). Second, to avoid overly assimilating Aristotelian likelihood to modern notions of probability: see following.

33. For an example in the style of (A)′, see 2.23.8.1398a16–17.

34. See, most notably, Hempel 1965, pp. 53–67, 380–385; a simpler version of the same argument in Salmon 1963, pp. 60–63.

35. *Top.* 1.12.105a10–12; cf. *Pr. Anal.* 2.23.68b13–14 (quoted in the following); *Post. Anal.* 1.1.71a9–11; 1.18.81a40; *NE* 6.3.1139b26–28. For the purposes of this division "immediate inference" (as in the square of opposition) does not count as proof, being neither συλλογισμός nor ἐπαγωγή.

36. For a striking manifestation, see Raphael's statement (1974, p. 161) of what Aristotle ought to have said: "Both enthymemes and examples are forms of inductive argument, *except* in the case of necessary signs."

37. For what etymology is worth, συλλογισμός suggests putting things together to reckon up what they amount to (cf. Plato, *Gorgias* 479c5–6), while ἐπαγωγή suggests leading you on to something from a survey of cases: (B) and (C) do put things together to derive their conclusion.

38. Thus Stoic logic can analyze the argument "from division" at 2.23. 10.1398a30–32 in terms of the fifth indemonstrable, but the *Medea* example discussed earlier requires modern resources.

39. The fifth is 1.2.8.1356b9, on which see ALP, nn. 36 and 76.

40. Solmsen 1929, pp. 13–27, 28–31; Barnes 1981, n. 55; ALP, p. 31 with n. 76, p. 36–38.

41. The same translation choice as at note 6 of this essay, but this time in a context where the Oxford Translation's "any form of persuasion" (both revised and unrevised versions) would make Aristotle promise a syllogistic analysis even of the accessory means of persuasion!

42. From which it follows that the sentence "An enthymeme is a συλλογισμός from likelihoods or signs" (which should be read in its traditional place at 70a10, not transposed with Ross to the beginning of the chapter—see ALP, pp. 9, 32) does not give the definition of enthymeme; Sir William Hamilton's proposal (1860, Lecture XX) to read it as Aristotle's official definition of enthymeme has been the leading alternative to the traditional logic book interpretation in terms of abbreviated syllogisms. See ALP, pp. 8 ff.

43. Thus Bonitz 1870 s.v. εἰκός (an entry giving only a small proportion of the occurrences) lists several arguments from likelihood in the *Meteorology*.

44. For help toward tolerating "All who have milk are pregnant" as the exceptionless universal that 70a30 alleges it to be, see Burnyeat 1982, p. 204 n. 30.

45. From the first of the two sections that link with the *Prior Analytics*.

46. Any argument "$P_1, P_2, \ldots, P_n \vdash Q$" can be made valid by supplying as premise "If $P_1, P_2, \ldots, P_n$, then Q." Aristotle is not interested in such tricks.

47. Sprute 1982, pp. 88–109, is an important witness here. Because he understands very well that at 70a7 ἀναγκαῖα characterizes the inferential power of a τεκμήριον, as a strict deductivist he excises ἢ ἔνδοξος from Aristotle's text (p. 90 note)! Then, because he does not let πρότασις ἔνδοξος at 70a3–4 characterize the inferential power of εἰκός, he wonders at length why the chapter omits to consider signs with a "for the most part" connection to what they signify. The view I am proposing seems to have the support of Ross 1949, pp. 499–500, for both occurrences of ἔνδοξος.

48. Note 45 of this essay applies again.

49. The definition should be printed without the usual comma after ἔχειν at 57a36, so that οὕτως ἔχον κτλ is joined with τό in the previous line: see Kassel 1971, p. 124. Raphael 1974, p. 159, has the essential point that εἰκός is defined by its role in "probabilifying" a singular statement.

50. The Index Graecus in Kassel's edition lists numerous references to signs, and several nonconclusive sign inferences, outside the two sections we are discussing. More in Bonitz 1870 s.v. σημεῖον.

51. For advocacy of this reading of the truth contrast, see Burnyeat 1982, p. 195 note 4, pp. 199–202. With valid syllogisms the three figures are absolutely equal in their capacity to deliver true conclusions from true premises. A comparable distinction between σημεῖα that induce knowledge in the audience and those that induce only opinion is found in *Rhetorica ad Alexandrum* 13(12). 1430b35–38, 15(14).1431a39–42.

52. Recall note 19 of this essay.

53. Boethius made *probabile* the accepted translation of ἔνδοξον, see Barnes 1980, pp. 498–505. A glance through the wide range of things that Cicero in *De Inventione* 1.44–49 classifies as *probabile* on the grounds that they make a conclusion *probabile* (cf. 1.57) will confirm that the translation made good sense then. The *De Inventione* was an important influence in the Middle Ages (McBurney 1974, p. 134); yet wider vistas appear in Hacking 1975.

54. *Rhetorica ad Alexandrum* 8(7).1428a25–26.

55. The subsequent rhetorical tradition is for the most part no better. The exception is Quintilian, whose answer to our question is: when it is supported by other arguments of the same type (*Institutiones Oratoriae* 5.9.11).

56. The fact that this last quotation comes from Locke's notorious attack on the Aristotelian syllogism should not distract our attention. The second book of Aristotle's *Rhetoric* (from which the key evidence for my thesis has come) was the one work of the Stagirite that Locke recommended in *Some Thoughts Concerning Reading and Studying for a Gentleman*. Contemporary readers may turn to Cohen for an up-to-date version of the idea that degrees of probability are to be understood as degrees of provability or inferential soundness.

REFERENCES

Barnes, J. "Aristotle and the Methods of Ethics." *Revue Internationale de Philosophie* 133–134 (1980): 490–511.

———. "Proof and the Syllogism." In *Aristotle on Science: The Posterior Analytics*, ed. E. Berti. Padua, 1981.

Bonitz, H. *Index Aristotelicus*. In *Aristotelis Opera*, vol. 5, ed. I. Bekker. Berlin, 1870. Reprinted separately: Darmstadt: Wissenschaftliche Buchgesellschaft, 1960.

Brunschwig, J., ed. *Topiques*. Vol. 1 [Books I–IV]. Paris, 1967.

Burnyeat, M. F. "The Origins of Non-Deductive Inference." In *Science and Speculation: Studies in Hellenistic Theory and Practice*, ed. J. Barnes, J. Brunschwig, M. Burnyeat, and M. Schofield. Cambridge, 1982.

———. "Enthymeme: Aristotle on the Logic of Persuasion." In *Aristotle's Rhetoric: Philosophical Essays*, ed. D. Furley and A. Nehamas. Princeton, 1994.

Cohen, L. J. *The Probable and the Provable*. Oxford, 1977.

Cope, E. M. *The Rhetoric of Aristotle, with a Commentary*, rev. and ed. by J. E. Sandys. 3 vols. Cambridge, 1877.

Hacking, I. *The Emergence of Probability: A Philosophical Study of Early Ideas about Probability, Induction and Statistical Inference*. Cambridge, 1975.

Hamilton, W. *Lectures on Logic*, ed. H. L. Mansel and J. Veitch. Edinburgh, 1860.

Hempel, C. G. *Aspects of Scientific Explanation and Other Essays in the Philosophy of Science*. New York, 1965.

Kassel, R. *Der Text der aristotelischen Rhetorik: Prolegomena zu einer kritischen Ausgabe*. Berlin, 1971.

Kassel, R., ed. *Aristotelis Ars Rhetorica*. Berlin, 1976.

Kneale, W. *Probability and Induction*. Oxford, 1946.

Lloyd, G. E. R. "The Theories and Practices of Demonstration in Aristotle." *Proceedings of the Boston Area Colloquium in Ancient Philosophy* 6 (1990): 371–401.

Madden, E. H. "Aristotle's Treatment of Probability and Signs." *Philosophy of Science* 24 (1957): 167–172.

McBurney, J. H. "The Place of the Enthymeme in Rhetorical Theory." *Speech Monographs* 3 (1936): 49–74. Cited from *Aristotle: The Classical Heritage of Rhetoric*, ed. K. V. Erikson (Metuchen, N.J., 1974).

Pacius, J. *Aristotelis Organon cum commentario analytico*. 2d ed. Frankfurt, 1597.

Raphael, S. "Rhetoric, Dialectic and Syllogistic Argument: Aristotle's Position in *Rhetoric* I–II." *Phronesis* 19 (1974): 153–167.

Ross, W. D., ed. *Prior and Posterior Analytics*. Oxford, 1949.

Ryan, E. E. *Aristotle's Theory of Rhetorical Argumentation*. Montreal, 1984.

Salmon, W. *Logic*. Englewood Cliffs, 1963.

Smith, R., trans. *Prior Analytics*. Indianapolis, 1989.

Solmsen, F. *Die Entwicklung der aristotelischen Logik und Rhetorik*. Berlin, 1929.

Sprute, J. *Die Enthymemtheorie der aristotelischen Rhetorik*. Göttingen, 1982.

Vahlen, J. "Rhetorik und Topik. Ein Beitrag zu Aristoteles' Rhetorik." *Rheinisches Museum für Philologie* 22 (1867): 101–110. Reprinted as chapter 3 in his *Gesammelte Philologische Schriften* (Leipzig, 1911).

Wörner, M. "Enthymeme—Eine Rückgriff auf Aristoteles in systematischer Absicht." In *Rhetorische Rechtstheorie*, ed. O. Ballweg and T. M. Seibert. Freiburg, 1982.

———. *Das Ethische in der Rhetorik des Aristoteles*. Freiburg, 1990.

Is There an Ethical Dimension to Aristotelian Rhetoric?

Troels Engberg-Pedersen

For Johnny Christensen

Aristotle's overall conception of rhetoric continues to intrigue his interpreters. What is his view of the legitimacy of rhetoric in terms both of its cognitive and moral value? To one modern scholar, Whitney J. Oates, the *Rhetoric* is "a practical handbook for the instruction of public speakers in all the techniques and tricks of the trade," a book that moves into a "realm of amoralism, if not immoralism" (1963, 333, 351). How could that be so? In the *Gorgias* Aristotle's teacher Plato had denounced rhetoric as wholly illegitimate, cognitively as well as morally. He did rehabilitate it in the *Phaedrus,* but only in a completely reconstructed form identifying the genuinely accomplished orator with the philosopher who has full knowledge of ethical and political matters and who will also apply it in moral practice. Did Aristotle just neglect the Platonic challenge? In Aristotle's view, how, if at all, does the accomplished orator grasp ethical-political truth? And what is his moral character? Did Aristotle have a coherent conception of the art of rhetoric that answers these questions? And how does it fit with his views on other skills, in particular those of the dialectician, the *phronimos,* and the *politikos?*

Recently, Markus H. Wörner has argued extensively for a view that is almost exactly the opposite of that of Oates.[1] When Wörner speaks of *Das Ethische in der Rhetorik des Aristoteles,* he wishes to be taken quite seriously. According to Wörner, Aristotle requires that the accomplished orator be "an *epieikēs,* an *agathos,* a vir bonus," a man with moral insight capable of grasping what is proper and of expressing it in appropriate language (1990, 24). Wörner's view reminds one of that of the elder Cato, who characterized the accomplished orator as a *vir bonus dicendi peritus.* Is that Aristotle's very simple response to the Platonic challenge? Is Wörner right when he explicitly denies that Aristotelian rhetoric is a mere *Redetech-*

nologie (a technique of persuasive speaking; ibid., 281) and instead sees it as "an appropriate tool for finding the good, the noble, and the just in the hands of people who have the proper *prohairesis*," a rhetoric for "free, equal, and politically active citizens" who are also "auf sittlicher Höhe stehend" (ibid., 282–283), that is, morally responsible?

According to Wörner, not only must the accomplished orator be morally good. He must also have genuine knowledge of moral and political matters (ibid., 24, 193). Thus, speaking to what is in fact the cognitive side of the Platonic challenge, Wörner takes it that when Aristotle refers in the *Rhetoric* to the *Politics* for further precision on a certain topic (1366a21–22), he means to suggest that such precision is part of rhetoric itself—in spite of the fact that Aristotle seems rather to be deferring further analysis of the matter to a different *type* of investigation (ibid., 194). Wörner even claims that in giving "sensible advice" (ibid., 198 n. 15) an accomplished public speaker will have his eye on the best overall constitution of the city-state, not just on existing ones or the one favored by his hearers (ibid., 197–200).

So close a connection between Aristotelian rhetoric and ethical-political knowledge is rightly rejected in more recent papers by John M. Cooper and Stephen Halliwell. Although not directly addressing the issue of Aristotle's reaction to the Platonic challenge, indirectly the two papers have much to say that is relevant to the question.

Cooper correctly elucidates the famous statement of Aristotle's that rhetoric is an "offshoot of" (1356a25–27) or a "construction from" (1359b9–11) dialectic and ethics-politics. On the one hand, Cooper notes, "Aristotle does not mean that only someone who has a deep, philosophical knowledge of the truth about the nature of justice, etc. . . . can reliably know all about the *endoxa* needed to argue effectively as an orator" (1994, 203). The rhetorician is a dialectician. He will have some knowledge of valid reasoning and also of the ethical-political premises needed to argue validly (or apparently so) in the relevant contexts. But these premises are *endoxa* (reputable beliefs) as opposed to final scientific truths, and so "rhetoric, like dialectic, is limited to knowing about and speaking from *endoxa*, regarded strictly as such (or, at any rate, not as conclusions of ethical-political reasoning of any specialized sort)" (ibid., 206).

On the other hand, since Aristotle held that there is continuity between *endoxa* and truth, there also is a sense in which rhetoric is in fact an offshoot of ethics-politics. For "the expert dialectician (and, in the area of ethical-political questions, the rhetorician) is the person above all others who knows and has command over the *endoxa* on political matters" (ibid., 207), from which ethics and politics take their starting point. And so Cooper concludes, rightly, that rhetoric is an offshoot of ethical-political philosophy in the sense (and only in that sense) that "it has the *dialectician's* grasp of and control over the subjects dealt with in ethical-political science *from* which that science itself takes its *origin*" (ibid., 208, my italics).

Cooper's emphasis on the particularly close connection of rhetoric with dialectic is right on target. He is also, of course, right to tie rhetoric in with ethics and politics by seeing the expert rhetorician as an expert dialectician "in the area of ethical-political questions." But how, on his understanding, if at all, does Aristotle respond to the Platonic challenge? It is fair to put this question to Cooper since he does argue that an intriguing remark of Aristotle's in the first chapter of the book is a reversal of Socrates' claim in the *Phaedrus* that the orator must know the truth in order to see what is *like* the truth (ibid., 203–204, 206–208). Aristotle says (1355a14–18): "It belongs to the same capacity (*dynamis*) to see the truth and what is like the truth. Also, human beings are by nature well fitted to the truth and they most often reach it. Therefore, to be able to hit the *endoxa* belongs with the one who stands in the same relationship with the truth." On Cooper's reading of Aristotle, this means that "the dialectician/rhetorician has, as such, the ability to discern the truth itself," namely, by having good control over the sphere—that of reputable beliefs—from which the process of arriving at a full understanding of the final truth in ethics and politics must *begin*. "In that limited sense they have the capacity to see not only what is *like* the truth, but the truth itself, too" (ibid., 208).

However, will that remark of Aristotle's really supply an adequate response to the Platonic challenge? If the challenge is defined by Socrates' demand that one must know the full truth in order to see what is like the truth, it will hardly be sufficient to have "good control" over "reputable beliefs," that is, over beliefs that must presumably be reorganized and sometimes even corrected before they will express ethical and political truths. To have a grasp of the beginnings of the truth is not necessarily to be in possession of the whole truth. Nor is it likely that Aristotle would have claimed this even, as Cooper sees it, in a pointed reversal of Socrates' claim. In fact (see later), I believe Cooper has misconstrued the point of Aristotle's remark. Thus although he is on the right track, he has not provided a full Aristotelian response to the cognitive side of the Platonic challenge.

There is a parallel problem (not discussed by Cooper) about the orator's moral qualifications. Is rhetorical skill just a matter of seeing? And if so, how does one avoid its becoming a mere *Redetechnologie*, a knack of persuasive speaking? The Socratic claim that those who know the true good must also choose it applies to the orator too. Aristotle notoriously distinguished between seeing and willing. Is accomplished rhetorical skill, on his conception, merely about seeing? If so, might a skilled orator be a bad (or an indifferent) person who chooses not to let his grasp of the truth determine the direction of his performance?

Like Cooper, Halliwell is concerned with the relationship between popular morality as expressed in *endoxa* and the "values that a philosophically respectable *politikē* could avow as its own" (1994, 222). He thinks that "the *Rhetoric* remains open to the possibility that the orator's engagement with popular morality will sometimes, and non-accidentally, succeed in contributing to the realization of the human good" (ibid., 228). Like Cooper, however, he does not explicitly discuss Aristotle's response to the Platonic challenge, though he notes that Aristotle's views must be seen against "the inescapable background of Plato's critique of its nature and status" (ibid., 211). The outcome is that we must ascribe to Aristotle "an essentially ambiguous and inconclusive verdict on the potential involvement of the rhetorician in the tasks of a philosophically respectable *politikē*" (ibid., 229).

There is obviously need for further thought.[2] The basically clear and forthright but opposed interpretations of Oates and Wörner are likely to be false as they stand. The subtler ones by Cooper and Halliwell, which occupy the middle territory between those of Oates and Wörner, are only partially concerned with the Platonic challenge and in part so ambiguous as to suggest that Aristotle did not have a well thought out conception of rhetoric at all. Is that really so?

I

It will be helpful if I begin by setting out my thesis in some detail. I propose to reconcile a number of apparently conflicting interpretations of Aristotle's view of the ethical and political import of the *Rhetoric*. These interpretations may draw on different lines of thought in the *Rhetoric* itself. In sections I–III, I present these different lines and in section IV my proposed solution. Only later (sections V ff.) shall I look at the text itself for argument and support.

[1] The first line of thought in the *Rhetoric* presents rhetorical skill as a pure *Redetechnologie*. [i] Rhetoric is different from any science, in particular from ethical-political knowledge. It is so for two reasons. [a] It aims at finding what will produce *peithō* (which we may initially translate as "persuasion"), instead of truth (1355b10–11, 25–26). Thus rhetoric is essentially related to a specific audience (1356b28). [b] The typical audience of rhetoric consists of people who are (relatively) simpleminded (1357a3–4, 11–12) and morally *mochthēroi* or at least less than thoroughly good (1404a7–8, 1403b34–35). The accomplished orator must therefore

argue from beliefs that are "general" (*koina*) and/or already generally accepted (*endoxa*) by the many (*hoi polloi*, 1355a24–29). He must also be concerned with creating an emotional state (*pathos*) in his audience (1356a2–3, 14–17) and representing his own character (*ēthos*, 1356a2, 4–13) in such a way as to persuade the audience. (I shall call the two types of proof that reflect this concern *pathos*-proofs and *ēthos*-proofs respectively.)

[ii] Rhetoric is intrinsically morally neutral. It involves specific knowledge and the ability to find persuasive arguments on ethical-political issues. It does not presuppose any particular moral character or motivation. Rhetorical skill is formally identical with *deinotēs*, a morally neutral ability to find the proper means, which, if the aim is morally good, is praiseworthy, but if morally bad, is villainy (see *NE* 6.12.1144a23–28). Thus rhetoric is an ability to "prove opposites" (*tanantia sullogizesthai*, 1355a34) and to "see both what is persuasive and what only appears so" (*to pithanon kai to phainomenon pithanon idein*, 1355b15–16). Rhetoric may be used "well" or it may be used "badly" (1355b2–7)—if the speaker is himself *mochthēros*.

This first general conception of rhetoric construes it on the model of dialectic rather than as a special science. It is a conceptualization of rhetoric as it was typically understood and practiced in contemporary Athens. We may speak of it as the "normal conception" of rhetoric and schematize it as follows.

Rhetoric (and dialectic)	Science (*epistēmē*)
Persuasion (*peithō*)	Truth (*alētheia*)
koina/endoxa	*to akribes*
hoi polloi	*epistēmēn echontes*
tanantia sullogizesthai/to pithanon kai	
to phainomenon pithanon idein	*to alēthes deiknunai*
Concern about hearers	
(*pathos*- and *ēthos*-proofs)	

II

[2] Setting out the normal conception of rhetoric is, however, only the beginning of getting a full grasp of Aristotle's understanding of the art. I shall leave the normal conception intact as it stands, but suggest that it is transformed when it is inserted into a wider framework. Two ideas in particular point in this direction. But they do not by themselves supply an adequate response to Plato's challenge.

[i] The first is the intrinsic connection that Aristotle sees between *endoxa* and truth (see 1355a15–18, quoted earlier). This connection is of course reflected in the fact that the scientific truths stated in Aristotle's own

ethical and political treatises are developed out of the wider, generally accepted ethical and political beliefs that he catalogs in the *Rhetoric*. But we saw in connection with Cooper's view that, in spite of the connection, there remains a gap between the two sets of beliefs. When an accomplished orator manages to persuade his audience by expert manipulation of *endoxa*, there is no automatic guarantee that he will also be stating ethical and political truths. The intrinsic connection between *endoxa* and truth does not by itself provide an adequate response to the Platonic challenge on the cognitive issue.

[ii] There is another remark early in the book to the effect that one "must not" use one's rhetorical skill to persuade people of morally bad things (1355a31). Important as this remark no doubt is, it cannot be construed as a general requirement that the accomplished orator be a morally good man. First, it comes in far too tangentially. Second, it is impossible to combine such a view with the normal conception of rhetoric as stated above. For that was intrinsically morally neutral and only a matter of seeing and understanding, not of willing. This isolated remark of Aristotle's cannot, therefore, supply an adequate response to the Platonic challenge on the moral issue.

In spite of this the two ideas are obviously important. But they need to be developed. Here we should just note that the connection between *endoxa* and truth implies that we must make a simple addition at the end of the scheme given above.

Rhetoric (and dialectic)	Science (*epistēmē*)
Persuasion (*peithō*)	Truth (*alētheia*)
koina/endoxa	*to akribes*
hoi polloi	*epistēmēn echontes*
tanantia sullogizesthai/to pithanon kai to phainomenon pithanon idein	*to alēthes deiknunai*
Concern about hearers (*pathos*- and *ēthos*-proofs)	

———⟶

The point of the arrow is brought out well in the famous first chapter of the *Physics*, where Aristotle discusses the difference between things that are better known and clearer to us and those (the *archai*) that are so by nature. The former, so he says, are mixed-up (*synkechumena*) and general (*katholou*). The latter, the basic ingredients (*stoicheia* and *archai*, 184a23), become known when we divide up and draw distinctions within the former things and "proceed" (*proienai*, 184a24—as it were, along the line I have drawn) toward specifics (*ta kath' hekasta*). Rhetoric, according to Aristotle's conception of it, handles beliefs that are mixed-up, general, and unclear.

But it does, in general, lie on a single line with philosophy and science and so it is at least possible to move forward from one to the other.

III

[3] In addition to the normal conception of rhetoric, there is another, which shows that Aristotle was keenly concerned about its legitimacy. Here a proper rhetorical performance is one that will "fight the case with the facts of the matter themselves" (*autois tois pragmasin agōnizesthai*, 1404a5–6). The idea is specifically contrasted with the concern about the audience that is part of the normal conception. On the new conception, such a concern lies "outside the fact of the matter itself" (*exō tou pragmatos*, 1.1 passim), even in the form in which Aristotle does allow it in the normal conception, as a concern for effects on the audience created by the argument itself (1356a2–3, 14–17) and not by ways of influencing them that have no intrinsic connection with the case itself.

The new, "austere" conception of rhetoric is not one that is put to use in everyday rhetorical practice. Nor is it the one analyzed by Aristotle in his treatise. He does think of it as a form of rhetoric and not, for instance, a piece of scientific investigation—thus it is in principle directed to the many and aimed at generating persuasion in them. But its austere character almost makes it a form of rhetoric as nonrhetoric. In fact, it is best understood as an ideal, something rhetoric should, but cannot, be like because of the actual character of the audience.[3]

Aristotle introduces the austere conception from time to time throughout the book, even though he constantly bases his discussion on the normal conception.[4] This is evidence of his genuine concern about the legitimacy of rhetoric as normally practiced (and as captured by himself in the normal conception of it). It also shows that there is a vital tension within his general understanding of rhetoric between what appears to be rhetoric as a mere *Redetechnologie* and rhetoric as it should be. Introducing the austere conception does not settle the issue of legitimacy. On the contrary, it raises it.

We may schematize the tension by placing the austere conception on the line we already know. It should be placed between normal rhetoric and science. The difference between the two conceptions of rhetoric does not lie in their aim. Both aim at persuasion, not truth. But the idea of fighting the case with the facts of the matter points in the *direction* of science. This is clear from an important remark of Aristotle's early in the book. After he has summarized his view that rhetoric and dialectic are both equally concerned with opposites (1355a33–36), he states (1355a36–38): "But the underlying facts (*pragmata*) do not behave in the same way, but, speaking generally, what is true (*talēthē*) and what is better (*ta beltiō*) is by nature always easier to prove (*eusullogistotera*) and more convincing (*pithanōtera*)." In that case a speaker who is concerned only with the *pragmata* themselves would almost automatically be oriented toward what is by nature true and better and so, without necessarily wishing to, he would be appreciably closer to the perspective of a scientific investigation than a normally accomplished orator will be.

The new schema adds a column for austere rhetoric and looks like this:

Rhetoric (and dialectic)	Rhetoric as nonrhetoric	Science (*epistēmē*)
Persuasion (*peithō*)	Persuasion (*peithō*)	Truth (*alētheia*)
koina/endoxa	*koina/endoxa*	*to akribes*
hoi polloi	*hoi polloi*	*epistēmēn echontes*
tanantia sullogizesthai/	*tanantia sullogizesthai/*	
to pithanon kai	*to pithanon kai*	
to phainomenon	*to phainomenon*	
pithanon idein	*pithanon idein*	*to alēthes deiknunai*
Concern about	*autois tois*	
hearers (*pathos*-	*pragmasin*	
and *ēthos*-proofs)	*agōnizesthai*	

It may seem that the austere conception of rhetoric is the one best qualified to serve in a response to the Platonic challenge. If, however, it is only an ideal and moreover one that stands in tension with the normal conception, how would Aristotle defend this latter conception, which is the overall topic of the whole book, in response to the Platonic challenge?

IV

[4] We need to find a way that will make rhetoric, as normally practiced, legitimate without removing the properties that seemed to offend. We do not want to say that merely by having good command over the relevant *endoxa,* an accomplished orator is already one who sees truths. Instead, he is able to generate persuasion. This holds in spite of the fact that Aristotle does see a general connection between *endoxa* and truth (see [2.i]). Nor do we want to say that an accomplished orator will himself be a morally good man and so be personally concerned with persuading people of what is *best*. Instead, he is concerned with finding the best *means* of persuasion, irrespective of the moral quality of the belief he is trying to generate in his audience. This holds even though Aristotle also claims that one "ought not" persuade people of morally bad things (see [2.ii]). On the normal conception of rhetoric the accomplished orator need

neither have knowledge nor be a morally good man. And we must keep him like that.

But we must also account for Aristotle's view that there *is* a general connection between *endoxa* and truth and his claim that one "ought not" in fact persuade people of morally bad things. Moreover, we must find ways of allowing for the perspective on rhetoric encapsulated in Aristotle's austere conception of it and of dissolving the tension between the two conceptions.

The solution, I suggest, lies in diagnosing a misunderstanding in our own preconceived conception of rhetoric, the one with which we approach Aristotle's discussion without having made that highly distinctive conception clear to ourselves. Basically, I submit, we take it that if rhetoric is concerned with generating *peithō*, it is *not* concerned with *truth*. We therefore translate *peithō* as "persuasion" and focus exclusively on the element of causing the audience to have some belief or other. Moreover, the modern distrust of rhetoric will more or less automatically make us interpret this aim *in malam partem*. If rhetoric is concerned with persuasion, not only is it not concerned with truth, but also, quite likely, with *deflecting* the audience from the truth.

Suppose, however, that we translate *peithō* as "conviction." The accomplished orator will still be concerned with generating some belief in his audience, that is, with "persuading" them. At the same time, however, what he is trying to generate is a *belief about certain facts*. This holds no matter whether he is addressing a simple question of fact (whether something has happened or will happen) or the ethical or political—as we would partly say, evaluative—quality of a given event (whether it is right, good, beneficial, or what not).

We may generalize the point. Perhaps Aristotle presupposes throughout that rhetoric—understood as usual as an intrinsically neutral art of persuasion—will in fact be used within a *setting* that basically makes it a case of search for factual, ethical, or political truth, a case of *Wahrheitsfindung* (truth-discovery, a term I borrow from Wörner).[5] Perhaps Aristotle thought that it was part of the "language-game" of rhetoric as institutionalized in Athens before judges or the assembly, that the aim of the exercise as a whole was to arrive at judgments in ethical and political matters that were true. Perhaps he was even right in thinking so. In that case we may hold together a whole number of seemingly conflicting ideas.

We may, of course, keep the idea that rhetoric produces *peithō* (see [1.i.a]), but not now in the sense of "mere" persuasion as something that is intrinsically distinct from, and even opposed to, truth. Instead, rhetoric aims, as part of its setting, at generating convictions that answer the implicit question about the facts of the matter. Similarly, we may of course keep the two ideas (see [1.i.b]) that served to define the normal conception of rhetoric. Since he is addressing the many, the accomplished orator must argue from beliefs that are "general" (*koina*) and/or already generally accepted (*endoxa*) by the many. And he must also be concerned with creating an emotional state (*pathos*) in his audience and an image of his own character (*ēthos*) that will help him to persuade. There is nothing intrinsically obnoxious in this as long as one remembers that these various strategies are adopted within a general framework of *Wahrheitsfindung* but are also addressed to people who are like most human beings, with hardly more than a general understanding of the matter and with all the normal moral failings. The two strategies of the accomplished orator are, regrettably, necessary, but they do not in and by themselves change the whole direction of the rhetorical exercise.

In fact, we may take two Aristotelian remarks I quoted earlier (under [2.i] and [2.ii]) to refer to his general presupposition that the framework of rhetorical exercise is *Wahrheitsfindung*. The reference will be somewhat oblique, but that is precisely the point. When Aristotle claims that there is a general connection between *endoxa* and truth and that one "must not" persuade people of something morally bad, one may understand this as a reflection, in Aristotle's conceptualization of the institutionalized language-game he is analyzing, of something that is presupposed in that language-game itself. If these two points did not hold, the institutionalized language-game of rhetoric as practiced in contemporary Athens would not be what it was supposed to be. They are not just Aristotle's own, more or less private stipulations, but a reflection of how rhetoric was generally understood and practiced.

We may also keep the idea that rhetorical skill is intrinsically morally neutral (see [1.ii]). It *is* a skill like *deinotēs*, which may be employed either morally well or morally badly without itself undergoing any change. At the same time, if rhetoric was understood as part of a type of activity, the general purpose of which was *Wahrheitsfindung*, it also becomes possible to say that a morally bad use of rhetorical skill, one that attempts to deflect the audience from the truth, is a misuse of it. We cannot, however, conclude from this that the proper use of that skill requires the accomplished orator to be himself morally good. Even a morally bad man may, as the case may be and for reasons of his own, play the rhetorical game in the way in which it is meant to be played. What we see here is a fundamental asymmetry between the proper use of rhetorical skill and its misuse. The proper use does not require a *special* moral motivation on the part of the accomplished orator. The improper one does. The reason lies in the presupposed general character of the rhetorical exercise, which is definitely tilted toward *Wahrheitsfindung*. Working within the general setting of rhetoric, the accomplished orator will use his intrinsically morally neutral skill to generate beliefs in his audience that are true. And this holds no matter what his individual moral motivation is. If, by contrast, he does not use his skill in that way, then a *special* moral motivation is required.

The same asymmetry is reflected in the idea that underlies Aristotle's austere conception of rhetoric (see [3]), the idea that "speaking generally, what is true and what is better are by nature always easier to prove and more convincing" (1355a37–38). If those addressed in a rhetorical performance were not for the most part relatively simpleminded and with all the normal moral failings, it would be sufficient to employ a rhetoric that consisted in fighting the case with the facts of the matter alone. But since they are simple and immoral, there is a need for rhetoric as normally practiced. But then, what is the point of bringing in the austere conception if that is not, after all, relevant to rhetoric as normally practiced? The answer is that the austere conception and the idea that underlies it make explicit the general presupposition behind rhetoric even as normally practiced. Basically, rhetoric, which is concerned with generating conviction in certain people, is *Wahrheitsfindung* and in this task it is dependent on the asymmetry in appearances that Aristotle formulates in the idea quoted earlier. If the true and the good were not by nature more convincing, the whole enterprise of addressing the many, with their various deficiencies in relation to truth, in an exercise that is intrinsically concerned with discovering the truth, would be seriously jeopardized.

We may conclude that all the seemingly conflicting ideas may be kept in place as soon as we bring in the following vital premise: Aristotle presupposes all through that rhetoric, on any conception of it, is institutionally a matter of *Wahrheitsfindung*, and in this it is vitally helped by the asymmetry in appearances just noted. I have not yet argued directly for this suggestion, only indirectly by showing how it may dissolve a tension that may otherwise appear unsolvable. I shall turn later to more direct argumentation. Here, by way of summary, it will be helpful to consider my proposal in terms of the notion of a retreat from the level of insight and the direction of argumentation that belong to a genuine science (even in ethics-politics), in other words from the right-hand end of the continuum depicted in my schema.

In a first retreat, a rhetorical performance as austerely conceived would address the many and do it in terms of generally accepted beliefs, which may or may not be scientifically correct—the *endoxa*. It would also be concerned with generating conviction in its audience, instead of merely proving the truth irrespective of whether one is being understood by an audience. (But it would not try to "sell" itself by attending to the emotional state of the hearers and their perception of the speaker.) Still, since the audience is being convinced of something as being *true;* since *endoxa* are *generally* true; and since in addressing only the facts of the matter the speaker's performance will reflect the fact that "speaking generally, what is true and what is better are by nature always easier to prove and more convincing," a rhetorical performance of this kind would continue to be concerned with truth in the following two senses (and no matter what the orator's individual moral motivation may be). First, the rhetoric will, if only ostensibly, be concerned with the truth of the matter. For that is what the language-game is generally taken to be all about. Second, it is more likely than not that the truth about the given issue will in fact "shine through." For even though somebody may be good at misrepresenting the issues, his opponent will be *better* placed in regard to making his case convincing.

In a second retreat, a rhetorical performance of the normal type will also attend to the aspect of "selling" itself. But even this kind of rhetorical performance will remain dedicated to discovering the truth and for the two reasons we just noted. First, it is part of a language-game whose basic purpose, implicitly recognized by all, is to discover, to have presented to one, and to be convinced of the true view on some factual, ethical, or political issue. Only now that we are talking of rhetoric as actually practiced, the accomplished orator needs not only to argue in terms of *endoxa* (in recognition of the fact that his audience is in principle simpleminded and incapable of following a long train of thought); he must also attend to the emotional state of his listeners since in terms of motivation they are no more than human. Second, even with such people it is more likely than not that the truth of the matter will "shine through" and the true representation of it will win.

By understanding Aristotle's two conceptions of rhetoric in terms of a retreat from the level of insight and the direction of argumentation that go into a genuine science, we become able to see why Aristotle formulates these two conceptions and why in spite of being intrinsically opposed to one another they do not in fact conflict. Indeed, we become able to see why they are rightly placed on a single line with science. What underlies the notion of a retreat (or conversely the idea that the two conceptions do lie on a single line with science, a line that goes in the direction of it, but does not reach it) is the conception of rhetoric as part of a language-game of *Wahrheitsfindung* where arguing for the truth is more likely than not to be successful. This conception, so I have contended, is presupposed by Aristotle all through. Together with the fact that Aristotle insists, very sensibly, that rhetoric is directed to the many, that conception *explains* the many things he says about rhetoric.

Again it must be emphasized (against Wörner) that seeing rhetoric as *Wahrheitsfindung* does not in any way imply that the participants in a rhetorical performance are themselves either morally good or ethically and politically insightful. On the contrary, the various features that characterize rhetoric on the normal conception precisely reflect the fact that they cannot be taken to be that. There is room, therefore, for all the features that make it look as if rhetorical skill is a mere *Redetechnologie*. What saves rhetoric, in the end, from being this is the general institutionalized framework of rhetorical performances that sees them as engaged in *Wahrheitsfindung* and the further presupposition in this that, speaking generally, the true and the better are by nature more convincing. The aim of rhetoric is to present considerations that will convince the audience by making them take a given understanding of the matter to be the true one. In seeking to reach this aim, rhetorical performances will be under an obligation to the principle that the true account is *more* likely to convince.

V

I have presented my proposal as fully as seemed required before providing any textual argument for it. Here I wish only to identify the main textual support, to show how I read the texts, and to ward off the most obvious objections. I shall concentrate on those passages where my reading is controversial.

[1.i] The point that rhetoric is different from any science, in particular from ethical-political knowledge, is made recurrently throughout the first four chapters of Book 1, where Aristotle sets out the basic elements in his conception of rhetoric. This is the main claim underlying his constant effort to connect rhetoric with dialectic. One idea is that rhetoric, like dialectic, has no definite subject matter; instead, both are abilities for procuring arguments (1356a32–33, also 1355b31–34). The formulation is perhaps not the most happy one. It ties in well with the idea that rhetoric, like dialectic, uses premises that are "common" (*koina*, 1355a24–29) in the sense of shared by several areas of discipline (1358a10–21). But in fact, as Aristotle also notes (1358a26–28), most rhetorical enthymemes make use of premises that are not in fact "common," but rather specific to a certain subject matter. It is better, therefore, to take him to be saying that the connection of rhetoric with dialectic shows itself in two forms, both when an orator makes use of premises that are genuinely common to many different types of subject matter (1358a9–17) and also when he uses premises that are directly about a specific subject matter—but in the nonscientific form of endoxic knowledge. The difference between rhetoric (and dialectic) and science (in this case, ethical-political knowledge) is not so much one of subject matter as of the degree of precision in the premises.

On such an understanding the basic contrast between rhetoric and ethics-politics lies in the attitude of the person involved toward the premises he uses. The scientist will go for the "first principles" (*archai*), the orator for what is convincing to his audience. Indeed, as Aristotle says (1358a23–26), the better the orator selects his premises, the more he will unconsciously produce a different form of knowledge than dialectic and rhetoric. For if he happens to hit upon first principles, he will no longer be engaged in dialectic or rhetoric but in the science whose principles he now possesses. We may speak of a potential "category mistake" if the orator forgets what it is his task to do: find ideas that he may make convincing to the many.

The insistence on Aristotle's part that rhetoric is different from science also lies behind the special way in which he relates rhetoric to dialectic and to the "discipline of ethics, which may be reasonably called politics" (1356a26–27), namely, as an "offshoot" of either (1356a25). Aristotle does not in fact wish to say that rhetorical skill presupposes ethical-political knowledge. For he goes immediately on to say (1355a27–30) that rhetoric and those who claim to possess it *falsely* "assume the character of politics." By contrast, as he continues,[6] rhetoric is a sort of division (*morion ti*) or likeness (*homoiōma*) of *dialectic* (1356a30–33).

How, then, should we understand the relationship of rhetoric with ethics-politics? In light of the above discussion of the subject matter of rhetoric, the answer is clear. Rhetoric "resembles" dialectic in its general character, but its subject matter is the same as that handled by ethical-political knowledge and for the premises of its arguments it mostly (but not always) draws on that specific subject matter. Thus rhetoric is in fact a kind of offshoot of ethical-political knowledge, but not viewed specifically as knowledge.[7]

Exactly the same picture comes out of the second passage in which Aristotle formally compares rhetoric with dialectic and ethics-politics: 1359b8–12. On the one hand (Greek *men*), rhetoric is said to be a combination of (*sunkeitai ek*) dialectic and ethics-politics. On the other hand (*de*), it is "similar to" dialectic. But in order to ward off a possible misunderstanding of the relationship between rhetoric and ethics-politics, Aristotle immediately adds his earlier caveat (from 1358a2–35): "But in proportion as anyone endeavors to make of dialectic or rhetoric, not what they are, faculties (*dunameis*), but sciences (*epistēmai*), to that extent he will, without knowing it (*lēsetai*, 1358a3, 24), destroy their real nature, in thus altering their character, by attempting to make them cross over into the domain of sciences (*epistēmai*), whose subjects are certain definite things, not merely words." Here the notion of crossing over (*metabainein*) implies that of a "category mistake."

[1.ii] The intrinsic moral neutrality of rhetoric is brought out in certain passages in 1.1 (1355a29–36, 1355b2–7), in which Aristotle is arguing for the usefulness of rhetoric. It is important to notice, however, that even though rhetoric is intrinsically, as he says (1355b3–4), a "capacity for arguments," it is also implied to be an intrinsic *good*, like bodily strength, health, wealth, and the like (1355b4–7). Is that because it is intrinsically better to be able to persuade people of what one wishes merely as that and without paying any attention to the objective goodness or badness of one's aim? Hardly. For the things with which rhetorical skill is here compared are genuine human goods (*agatha*, 1355b4), indeed the "most useful" goods (*chrēsimōtata*, 1355b5). It is therefore likely that we should see here a reflex of the asymmetry involved in rhetorical skill: even though it is an ability to prove opposites (and "equally" so, 1355a35–36, that is, the bad one no less than the good one), still, as part of the general institutionalized framework within which it is put to use, it is also loaded toward proving the true and the good—those things which, speaking generally, are by nature always easier to prove and more convincing (1355a37–38). Taken by itself rhetorical skill is morally neutral, in the way *deinotēs* is. It does not presuppose moral goodness in the accomplished orator. And it can be used morally badly without detriment to its intrinsic character. But it is also a genuine good alongside many others. For when it is used in a way that reflects the general framework within which it has its place, it helps to find the true and the good.

The idea of the intrinsic moral neutrality of rhetoric also lies behind a point on rhetoric, dialectic, and sophistic that Aristotle makes twice in the initial chapters of Book 1: 1355b17–21 and 1359b11–12. Consider the first passage. In the case of dialectic, says Aristotle, one must distinguish between the ability (*dunamis*) and the moral purpose, the *prohairesis*. A person is called a dialectician in terms not of his *prohairesis*, but of his ability. It is the task of dialectic to be able to diagnose both real (that is, true and valid) syllogisms and also those that are only apparent. Sophistic, by contrast, lies not in the ability, but in the *prohairesis*. The same is true of rhetoric, only here one person is called a rhetorician with reference to his knowledge (*epistēmē*, used here as another word for "ability," *dunamis*) and another with respect to his *prohairesis*.

In this passage Aristotle acknowledges the existence of a perception of rhetoric that accounts for Plato's negative construal of it. There is a rhetorician who is comparable (in the area of rhetoric) to the sophist (in the area of dialectic). However, that person is characterized in a certain way in *addition* to having a certain knowledge and ability, namely in terms of his *prohairesis*, obviously meaning his morally bad *prohairesis*. The rhetorician proper, by contrast, is not thought of in terms of his *prohairesis*, but exclusively in terms of his cognitive ability. Thus rhetoric is intrinsically morally neutral.

[2.i] In 1355a15–18 Aristotle claims that there is an intrinsic connection between *endoxa* and truth. I argued earlier against Cooper that this claim is insufficient by itself to meet the Platonic challenge. It corresponds with this that the connection is only introduced in a curiously lopsided manner. In fact, Aristotle uses his point to make an argument that goes in the opposite direction from the way it would go as a response to the Platonic challenge. What he is concerned to show is that because of the connection the expert dialectician, who is *already* capable of seeing the *true* syllogism, will *also* be able to see the rhetorical, endoxic one (the enthymeme), the one that is *like* the true one—and so it is the *expert* dialectician who is that master of enthymemes (*enthymēmatikos*) that the accomplished rhetorician is.[8]

Aristotle does not, therefore, bring in the connection between *endoxa* and truth in order directly to defend normal rhetoric vis-à-vis the Platonic challenge. And quite sensibly so. For he will not wish to say that all the *endoxa* that an accomplished orator may rightly canvass are *eo ipso* true. Still, when generalized the point does help Aristotle to meet the Platonic challenge since its general validity corresponds with the idea that rhetoric is as such part of a general process that both aims to discover the truth and is generally successful in doing this.

VI

The notion of an austere conception of rhetoric needs extensive defense, not least on the background of recent discussions of some of the relevant texts.[9]

A classic issue in the discussion of the *Rhetoric* concerns the relationship between Aristotle's conception of the art as expressed in 1.1 and 1.2. Friedrich Solmsen claimed that there is a discrepancy between the two chapters. Whereas 1.1 reflects a purely dialectical conception of rhetoric based on *endoxa*, 1.2 is completely oriented toward Aristotle's fully developed analytics in such a way that rhetorical practice has become a matter of full-fledged *didaxis* (Solmsen 1929, 223, 225). Solmsen then attempted to explain the change by chronological considerations. More recent scholarship has seen a different discrepancy between the two chapters. In chapter 1 Aristotle wished to restrict the subject matter of rhetoric to nothing but proofs, and here primarily enthymemes. In chapter 2, by contrast, he included *ēthos*- and *pathos*-proofs alongside proofs proper. Against this latter view, Cooper has recently claimed that in the crucial lines in chapter 1 (1354a11–18), Aristotle does not in fact deny the legitimacy of *ēthos*- or (even) *pathos*-proofs; he only insists that if they are not provided *through* the argument itself, they fall "outside the subject matter" (of the speech) and so should be curtailed.[10] I shall argue that a different conception of rhetoric is in fact involved in chapter 1, and that there is no discrepancy with the later one of the kind suggested by either Solmsen or Cooper.

The relevant section in chapter 1 is 1354a11–1355a18, in which Aristotle argues that his predecessors have all been concerned with "what is outside the subject matter" (ta exō tou pragmatos, 1355a19). In the first sentences of this section (1354a11–18) the claim is that the predecessors have provided or worked out only a small part of the art (or alternatively virtually no part of it).[11] For proofs are the only thing that come within the art of rhetoric's province, the rest being mere "additions" (prosthēkai, 1354a14). The predecessors, however, have said nothing about enthymemes, which is the body of proof, but have chiefly devoted their attention to things outside the subject. For arousing prejudice, compassion, anger, and similar emotions in the soul is not concerned with the matter in hand, but directed at the judge or members of the jury—those "hearers" who must decide on the matter.

On a natural reading, Aristotle is here saying that although the art of rhetoric may be broadly defined as being made up of two elements, proofs and the arousing of emotions, the two parts are of unequal status. Proofs constitute the main element; indeed, proofs are the only thing that really falls within the province of the art, while the other element has the status of "additions" only. Within proofs fall enthymemes, which are the body or heart of proof. (So, is there another part of proof as distinct from the "additions," for instance rhetorical examples, paradeigmata? Aristotle does not say—but see 1356a35–1356b11.) The predecessors said nothing whatever (ouden) about enthymemes. Instead, they spent most of their time on things outside the subject, that is, outside the direct subject matter of the speech and, correspondingly, outside the main element of the art, the proofs. (Did the predecessors then spend a little time on a part of the genuine proofs that is not enthymemes and so not the heart of proof, for instance on rhetorical examples, paradeigmata? Again Aristotle does not explicitly say.) But in that case, it is fair to say that they have mistaken the art.

It looks, then, as if Aristotle wishes to push the traditional concern about the pathē of the judge if not completely outside the province of rhetoric, at least as far away from its center as possible. At the center are the enthymemes. Then there may be other kinds of proof proper, which are not quite so central, but of which Aristotle's predecessors may, or may not, have said a little. And then, as mere additions, though still, perhaps, within the province of rhetoric as broadly construed, there is the traditional concern about the pathē of the judge. However, since this concern is a mere "addition," and since Aristotle's predecessors have concentrated on that, they have been basically mistaken about the art.

This general picture of rhetoric is supported by the rest of this section of chapter 1. Aristotle repeatedly dissociates himself from the phenomenon of speaking "outside the subject matter" (1354a15–16, 22–23, 1354b17, 27, 1355a2, 19). It is clear that he understands this as trying to influence the mental attitude of the judge in terms of anger, prejudice, or compassion (1354a24–25, 1354b20, cf. 1354b8–11). That is wrong because it is like making crooked the rule that one intends to use (1354a25–26)—that is, the jury. In fact, in a lawsuit there is no other legitimate task for the litigant than proving, about the matter itself (*to pragma*), that it either is or is not the case or has or has not happened. The rest, for instance deciding on its importance or its moral quality, should be left to the jury (1354a26–31). The same is true with regard to speeches held before the assembly. Here too a person who recommends a given measure has no other task than proving that the matter is as stated by him (1354b29–31).

On this austere conception of rhetoric, its task is simply to prove the facts of the matter (*deixai to pragma*, 1354a27–28, cf. *apodeixai* in 1354b30). Correspondingly, speaking "outside the *pragma*" means speaking to things other than the facts of the matter—for instance, the feelings of the jury. It is for this very reason that enthymemes constitute the body of proof (1354a15), with proofs being the only thing that falls genuinely under the art (1354a13, also, for both points, 1354b21–22). Indeed, the whole purpose of Aristotle's criticism of his predecessors in 1354a11–1355a18–19 is to introduce the "master of enthymemes" (the *enthymēmatikos*, 1354b22, 1355a11–12) as the truly accomplished rhetorician.

The general direction of Aristotle's argument in the whole section is therefore clear. What counts in an accomplished rhetorical performance is the argument, and the argument is about the facts of the matter, the *pragma*.

Aristotle draws exactly the same picture much later in the work, in 3.13–14, when he discusses the parts of a speech. In fact, his discussion there is prefigured in 1.1.1354b16–22, where he uses the accounts given by his predecessors of the content of an exordium or a narrative to show that they have been exclusively concerned about how to put the jury into a certain frame of mind.

In 3.13.1414a31–32, he states that there are two and only two parts of a speech. For it is necessary first to state the *pragma* (subject) that one is speaking about and then to prove it (*apodeixai*). Thus the two parts are "statement of the case" (*prothesis*) and "proof" (*pistis*) (1414a35–36). The rest, for instance narrative (1414a37) and exordium (1414b2), are not necessary parts of any speech, only *prothesis* and *pistis* are (they are *idia*, intrinsic to any speech, 1414b7–8)—but still, most speeches have *four* parts, exordium, *prothesis, pistis,* and epilogue (1414b8–9). Here Aristotle obviously starts out from exactly the same austere conception of rhetoric as in 1.1, but goes on to extend the range of the art in conformity with the way it is traditionally conceived—as he does too in 1.2.

In 3.14 Aristotle analyzes the exordium. Here too he begins from an austere conception. The most essential function of the exordium, its special function (*idion*), is to make clear the end for the sake of which the speech is made (1415a22–24). All the other things that people say in exordia are only remedies (*iatreumata*) and "common" (*koina,* 1415a25–26), presumably to the other parts of the speech as well. Still, Aristotle goes on to discuss them, concentrating on the speaker's concern about his audience (1415a26 ff.). Suddenly, however, he breaks off his exposition to make the following statement (1415b4–9):

> But we must not lose sight of the fact that all such things are outside the argument (*exō tou logou*); for they are only addressed to a hearer who is (morally) bad (*phaulos*) and who is ready to listen to what is outside the facts of the matter (*exō tou pragmatos*). For if he is not a man of this kind, there is no need at all of an exordium, except just to make a summary statement of the subject (*pragma*), so that, like a body, it may have a head.

A third example of the austere conception is found in chapter 1 of Book 3, where Aristotle introduces the new theme of *lexis* (style). He first reminds his listeners that he has now treated the proofs. From this he intends to turn to style and, as the third general topic, delivery (*ta peri tēn hupokrisin*). The latter topic he intends to treat only briefly since, in spite of its immense effectiveness, it has hardly been taken up by anybody (1403b20–22). However, it is very important. Thus those who use the various means of delivery properly nearly always carry off the prizes in dramatic contests. At present, actors too have greater influence on the stage than the poets themselves and it is the same in political contests (before the public assembly) because of the bad moral character (*mochthēria*) of the citizens (1403b31–35). However, no *technē* has been written about these matters (1403b35), partly because it is, rightly, considered vulgar (*phortikon,* 1403b36–1404a1).

Then comes one of the comments that display the austere conception of rhetoric (1404a1–8). In spite of its vulgarity, one must still (*all'*, 1404a1) pay attention to the topic of delivery, not because it is right, but necessary. For the whole discussion of rhetoric has to do with appearance (it is *pros doxan,* 1404a1). If one went by what is just, one would seek no more in an argument than to cause neither pain nor pleasure. For it would be just to fight with the facts alone (*autois . . . tois pragmasin,* 1404a5–6), so that all the rest, which is outside proving (*exō tou apodeixai,* 1404a6), would be superfluous. Still, it matters greatly because of the bad moral character (*mochthēria*) of the hearer. And the same is true of matters of style: all such things are mere outward show (*phantasia*) and directed to the hearer (1404a11).

Nothing could be more Platonic in sentiment. It shows incontrovertibly that there is a conception of rhetoric in Aristotle, or an attitude toward it, which is so pure that it is difficult to square it, initially, with rhetoric as traditionally conceived. This austere attitude will only allow fighting with the facts. In particular, it takes all considerations that pertain to the emotions of the hearers to be superfluous. At most it will be concerned *not* to cause pain or pleasure! And the reason is that such things are directed to the hearer (they are *pros ton akroatēn*, 1404a11) as opposed to being about the facts of the matter.

VII

Finally, I need to give specific arguments in direct support of my main contention: that Aristotle presupposed throughout that, institutionally, rhetoric belongs within a language-game of *Wahrheitsfindung*.

One argument is an extension of the point made earlier about how to translate and understand the notion of *peithein/peithō*. In 1.1.1355b15–16 Aristotle states that it is the task of rhetoric to "see both what is convincing (*to pithanon*) and what appears convincing (*to phainomenon pithanon*)." The notion of something *appearing* convincing seems to prove that what is "convincing" (*pithanon*) is something that presents itself as *true*. Thus Aristotle's contrast is between what presents itself as true and is true (in that case the presentation is right) and what presents itself as true without being it (in that case the presentation is only apparent). To be concerned with the genuine or apparent *pithanon* is therefore to be concerned with truth.

A second set of arguments turns on the implications of certain things Aristotle himself says about the way he, at least, took rhetoric to be perceived by its actual addressees in contemporary Athens. For instance, by using the phrase *exō tou pragmatos*, he aligns himself, as he himself notes (1354a22–25), with a perspective actually adopted by certain cities. Since this particular perspective must reflect a concern about truth and the facts of the matter, and since Aristotle explicitly aligns himself with it, we are entitled to conclude that he himself did presuppose that rhetoric (as actually practiced and as analyzed by himself in the book) was concerned with *Wahrheitsfindung*.

There is another line of thought that makes its appearance several times in the book and belongs under this second group of arguments. It revolves around the role played by the speaker's own character (*ēthos*) in the rhetorical performance, *ēthos*-proofs. Why is the speaker's character so important? Obviously, as Aristotle himself says (1356a4–6), because a given character of the speech (and by implication of the speaker) will make the speaker *axiopistos* (trustworthy). Now this might of course be used as a mere stratagem, for instance if a competent speaker chose to address old people "in character." Even then, however, it would probably be significant for showing that people are convinced by speakers who are like them because they then think that they are speaking the truth. (They are saying what the hearers *already* believe.)

More important, however, is the way Aristotle continues (1356a6–8): "For we feel confidence to a greater degree and more readily in persons who are (morally) good[12] in regard to everything in general, but where there is no certainty and there is room for doubt [and this, of course, holds precisely for the subject matter of ethics and politics], there our confidence [namely in good people] is absolute." Aristotle concludes that "moral character (*ēthos*), so to say, constitutes the most effective means of persuasion (*pistis*)" (1356a13). Similarly, in 1366a25–28 he states that through *ēthos*-proofs we may make ourselves trustworthy (again *axiopistos*)—*pros aretēn*, that is, with a view to good moral character. So, that is what will gain credence for a speaker. But why? What is it that makes a good moral character so effective for convincing other people?

Chapter 1 of Book 2 (1378a6–19) provides the answer. Aristotle says: "Three things are responsible for making the speakers themselves convincing (*pistoi*). For, besides demonstrations, there are three things on account of which we form beliefs—*phronēsis, aretē, eunoia* (goodwill). For speakers are wrong (*diapseudontai*) about what they speak or advise about either through all of these or through one of them" (1378a6–10). The point is this. A speaker must know what he is talking about (by possessing *phronēsis*), he must tell us frankly what he himself thinks (through his *aretē*), and he must not withhold any of his knowledge, rather he must give us his best advice (through his *eunoia*).

We should conclude that there is a fundamental presupposition here to the effect that in a rhetorical situation the hearers are concerned about the facts of the matter, the truth about it, whether factual, prudential, moral, or political. The hearers want to know. That is why they believe in a speaker whom they take to be a good man—and why a competent speaker will construct (see 1378a18) a *persona* of goodness in himself. (For as we know, Aristotle never says that the speaker must himself *be* good.)

Certain other ideas support this view. Thus in 3.2, in one of his remarks about *to prepon* (due proportion), Aristotle states that people who practice a certain artifice must "conceal it and avoid the appearance of speaking artificially (*peplasmenōs*) instead of naturally (*pephukotōs*); for the latter is convincing (*pithanon*), whereas the former is not. For men become suspicious of one whom they think to be laying a trap for them, as they are of mixed wines" (1404b18–21). The implication is clear: the hearers do not want to be deceived; they want the truth.

Again, in a later passage (3.7) Aristotle states that the style will have due proportion (*to prepon*) "if it is emotional (*pathētikē*) and in character (*ēthikē*) and corresponds to the underlying *pragmata* (the subject matter)" (1408a10–11). The reason why it should be emotional is that in general

> the appropriate style (*hē oikeia lexis*) also makes the fact (*to pragma*) appear credible (it *pithanoi* it). For the mind (of the hearer) draws a wrong conclusion (*paralogizetai*) *under the impression that the speaker is speaking the truth* (*hōs alēthōs legontos*), because in such circumstances his feelings are the same so that he thinks the things are as the speaker represents them even if they are not (in fact) as the speaker says; and the hearer always sympathizes (*sunomopathei*) with one who speaks emotionally (1408a19–24).

Here too, Aristotle obviously presupposes that in the rhetorical situation the hearers are fundamentally trying to find out the truth about the given issue.

Finally, there is a passage in 3.16 in which Aristotle discusses narrative (*diēgēsis*) and claims that it should be "of moral character" (*ēthikē*, 1417a16–36). It may be this in several ways, for instance if the speaker appears to be speaking not *apo dianoias* (from premeditation) but *apo prohaireseōs* (from a moral purpose) so as to express either *phronēsis* or *aretē* (1417a24–28). Further, if one says something that appears unconvincing, one must give a reason for it or at least admit one's awareness that it is incredible—while adding that it is just one's nature to think like that. And this is necessary: "For no-one believes that a man ever does anything of his own free will except from motives of self-interest" (1417a28–36). Now if that is the normal understanding, then why should a competent speaker care to make his narrative reflect a morally good character, which Aristotle has himself just implied (in 1417a26) will be unconcerned about self-interest? I can see only one answer: because if a speaker manages to convince the hearer of his moral virtue, then he will have made himself *axiopistos* to the highest degree. For then the hearer will believe everything he says, taking him now to be concerned only about what the whole thing is about: the truth of the matter.

We should conclude that Aristotle's handling of *ēthos*-proofs shows him to have presupposed that rhetoric was part of a language-game concerned with *Wahrheitsfindung*.

A third argument for the same conclusion turns on the fact that Aristotle seems to have thought of the subject matter of ethics and politics as being just as factual as, for instance, that of medicine. Moreover, in spite of whatever disagreement on moral matters one may come across (and it *is* an area "where there is no certainty, but rather room for doubt,"

1356a7–8), and in spite of the difference in cognitive capacity and insight of the many and the educated, Aristotle did not in the least reckon with what we would call radical conflict of values. Basically (as he says in yet another revealingly parenthetical remark, 1371a20), all men desire to be good—at least all *hoi aisthanomenoi* (no matter what that means). Basically, they all also know sufficiently what it means to be good. At least, one gets the firm impression from the first page of Aristotle's discussion of the motives for injustice (1.10) that if one asks people what injustice is, one will find that there is general agreement on the matter. Thus the subject matter of rhetoric is intrinsically suited to *Wahrheitsfindung*. That, then, so Aristotle will have thought, is what went on in the language-game of rhetoric.

VIII

It all adds up. The subject matter of rhetoric is intrinsically suited to *Wahrheitsfindung*. The hearers are concerned with the same, as is shown by the effectiveness of *ēthos*-proofs. And rhetoric is about producing conviction in the hearers, that is, making them have beliefs that they at least take to be true ones. What all this shows is not necessarily more than that the concept of truth is central in the description of rhetoric: the rhetorical language-game is taken by those involved to be *about* truth. Add to this, however, Aristotle's idea that generally speaking the true and the better are in fact more convincing. We saw that this idea is directly presupposed in his austere claim that ideally cases ought to be fought in terms of the subject matter alone—but also that this idea apparently remains valid in connection with rhetoric on its normal conception. We may then combine the two sets of ideas. The rhetorical language-game is taken to be about truth and what is in fact the true account of a given issue is intrinsically more likely to convince. The result of the combination is a comprehensive, real defense of the legitimacy of rhetoric, even in its normal, nonaustere form.

So, is there an ethical dimension to Aristotelian rhetoric? Both yes and no. In one way no. To be accomplished, an orator need not be morally good. Nor indeed need he have full ethical and political knowledge. But also yes. For in spite of the moral and epistemic conditions of its individual practitioners and addressees, rhetoric was conceived of by Aristotle as part of a comprehensive language-game that was directed toward discovering truth. Moreover, in this enterprise it could rely on an epistemologically based asymmetry—with regard to what produces conviction—that favors the success of the enterprise. Generally speaking, the true and the better are more likely to convince. Thus even though the accomplished orator need not himself be morally good, it remains the case that whenever he puts to use his intrinsically morally neutral rhetorical skill, it is more likely than not that he will generate convictions in his hearers about factual, moral, or political questions that are in fact true. The ethical dimension of rhetoric is not maintained by any features that pertain to the moral motivation or willing of the individuals involved. What does give a clear ethical dimension to rhetoric are instead certain facts about human seeing—the way human beings are related to truth—concerning ethical and political matters no less than any other. Human beings seek the truth and they are generally better placed for reaching it than for being deluded.

Then there also is a comprehensive Aristotelian response to the Platonic challenge. Indeed, this response is situated exactly where it should be in view of the general philosophical relationship between the two philosophers. Aristotle's defense of the legitimacy of rhetoric does not lie in considerations that he had himself thought out in order to provide solid criteria for its legitimacy. Rather, it lies in pointing to the way "we" (standing for Aristotle's contemporaries) actually act, speak, and think. Aristotle was firmly against any kind of philosophizing that ended up rejecting the whole area of actual ways of acting, speaking, and thinking that it was intended to reflect upon, and indeed to reflect, philosophically. The essence of his response to Plato's challenge about rhetoric therefore lies simply in pointing to the facts—that is, to the actual practices. Simple as it is in itself, this gesture may be anything but simple when seen precisely as a response to the Platonic challenge.

One corollary may be explicitly drawn. If we ask about the interest to us of Aristotle's construal of rhetoric, the answer should be that what is interesting about it is not so much the construal itself as the actual shape of the practice in contemporary Athens reflected in it—if, that is, we give credence to Aristotle's account. Apparently, in spite of all the contemporary talk of rhetorical sophistry and all the handbooks directed to help people make the worse case win, rhetoric in contemporary Athens was generally understood as functioning, and indeed successfully functioning, as part of a general social institution whose aim was *Wahrheitsfindung*. That is interesting.

NOTES

I am grateful for comments on a predecessor of this essay (cited in note 2, below) to the organizers and participants of the Helsinki 1991 conference on the *Rhetoric*, among whom were David Charles, John M. Cooper, Stephen Halliwell, Jaakko Hintikka, Paavo Hohti, Simo Knuuttila, Martha Craven Nussbaum, Amélie Rorty, and Juha Sihvola. A later version was read to the Copenhagen Aristotelian Group, where Johnny Christensen, Finn Collin, Sten Ebbesen, Karsten

Friis Johansen, Poul Lübcke, and, last but not least, David Sachs helped me to clarify the issue. John Ackrill kindly provided me with written comments. At a later stage I was much helped by Lesley Brown.

1. My critical remarks are not meant to detract from the value of Wörner's book (1990) which is both solid and perceptive. I just do not think that Wörner has got Aristotle's general conception of rhetoric right.

2. The basic idea that I shall present in this essay was first worked out in a paper entitled "In What Way Is Aristotelian Rhetoric an Offshoot of Ethics?" read at an international conference on Aristotle's *Rhetoric* in Helsinki, August 1991, organized by the Philosophical Society of Finland. I am particularly grateful to John M. Cooper and Stephen Halliwell for sharing with me their papers from the Symposium Aristotelicum on the *Rhetoric* held at Princeton in 1990, both in their August 1991 forms and in their final, prepublication form. Other works I have consulted include Grimaldi 1972 (especially pp. 18–52), Ryan 1972, Hellwig 1973 (especially pp. 24–63), Sprute 1977, Lord 1981, Lossau 1981, and Sprute 1982 (especially pp. 32–67).

3. Wörner 1990, pp. 66–71, is on the right track when he understands 1354a16 ff. as a "thought experiment of isolating what is rhetorically central *under ideal conditions*" (p. 70, my italics).

4. See the passages discussed in section VI.

5. Wörner 1990, p. 70. Wörner, of course, thinks that in Aristotle's view the term is directly applicable to the accomplished rhetorical performance. I argue that it is only indirectly applicable.

6. Note the emphatic *ésti gar* in 1356a30.

7. This is also essentially Cooper's solution (1994).

8. Cooper 1994, p. 203, finds that Aristotle's argument in 1355a14–18, and its connection to what precedes, is "not perfectly clear." In fact, it is sufficiently clear if one does not expect it to be intended to meet the Platonic challenge.

9. Cooper 1994, pp. 194–198. Wörner 1990, pp. 66–82.

10. Cooper 1994, pp. 194–195. Wörner 1990, pp. 66–67, agrees. Cooper also claims that his discussion undermines "a good part of Solmsen's influential discussion, pp. 208–229, of alleged differences between Aristotle's" 1.1 program "for rhetoric and the program from 1.2 onward." This is a little strange since Solmsen was not really concerned with the supposed discrepancy with regard to the inclusion or exclusion of what in 1.2 becomes *pathos*- and *ēthos*-proofs.

11. Depending on the text. Ross 1959: "provided" (*peporikasin*) and "virtually no" (*ouden hōs eipein . . . morion*). Kassel 1976: "worked out" (*peponēkasin*) and "a small (part)" (*oligon . . . morion*).

12. *Tois epieikesi*, not "persons of worth," as J. H. Freese 1926 has it. In general, Freese's translation is quite good and I have borrowed freely from it.

REFERENCES

Cooper, J. M. "Ethical-Political Theory in Aristotle's *Rhetoric*." In *Aristotle's Rhetoric: Philosophical Essays*, ed. D. J. Furley and A. Nehamas. Princeton, 1994.

Erickson, K. V., ed. *Aristotle: The Classical Heritage of Rhetoric.* Metuchen, 1974.

Freese, J. H. *Aristotle: The "Art" of Rhetoric.* London, 1926.

Furley, D., and A. Nehamas, eds. *Aristotle's Rhetoric: Philosophical Essays.* Princeton, 1994.

Grimaldi, W. M. A. *Studies in the Philosophy of Aristotle's Rhetoric.* Hermes Einzelschriften, vol. 25. Wiesbaden, 1972.

Halliwell, S. "Popular Morality, Philosophical Ethics, and the *Rhetoric.*" In *Aristotle's Rhetoric: Philosophical Essays,* ed. D. Furley and A. Nehamas. Princeton, 1994.

Hellwig, A. *Untersuchungen zur Theorie der Rhetorik bei Platon und Aristoteles.* Hypomnemata, vol. 38. Göttingen, 1973.

Kassel, R. *Aristotelis Ars Rhetorica.* Berlin, 1976.

Lord, C. "The Intention of Aristotle's *Rhetoric.*" *Hermes* 109 (1981): 326–339.

Lossau, M. J. *Pros Krisin Tina Politikēn. Untersuchungen zur aristotelischen Rhetorik.* Wiesbaden, 1981.

Oates, W. J. "Evidence from the *Rhetoric.*" In *Aristotle and the Problem of Value.* Princeton, 1963. Reprinted in Erickson 1974.

Ross, W. D., ed. *Ars Rhetorica.* Oxford, 1959.

Ryan, E. E. "Aristotle's *Rhetoric* and *Ethics* and the Ethos of Society." *Greek, Roman and Byzantine Studies* 13 (1972): 291–308.

Solmsen, F. *Die Entwicklung der aristotelischen Logik und Rhetorik.* Neue Philologische Untersuchungen, vol. 4. Berlin, 1929.

Sprute, J. "Der Zweck der aristotelischen Rhetorik." In *Logik, Ethik, Theorie der Geisteswissenschaften, XI. Deutscher Kongress für Philosophie Göttingen,* ed. G Patzig, E. Scheibe, and W. Wieland. Hamburg, 1977.

———. *Die Enthymemtheorie der aristotelischen Rhetorik.* Abhandlungen der Akademie der Wissenschaften in Göttingen, Philologisch-Historische Klasse, Dritte Folge, no. 124. Göttingen, 1982.

Wörner, M. H. *Das Ethische in der Rhetorik des Aristoteles.* Freiburg, 1990.

Ethics in the *Rhetoric* and in the Ethics

T. H. Irwin

THE USE OF THE *RHETORIC*

Students of Aristotle's Ethics[1] naturally turn to the *Rhetoric* for information and evidence; for it discusses some topics that are relevant to the Ethics, and on some of these topics its treatment is fuller and more informative than anything we find in the Ethics themselves. But what sorts of information can we gain from the *Rhetoric,* and how ought we to use it? We need to understand what Aristotle is trying to do in the *Rhetoric,* and how his aims in the *Rhetoric* affect its relevance to the Ethics.

The *Rhetoric* is not a work of ethical theory. It is about making speeches to persuade audiences of ordinary people; though it obviously appeals to ethical beliefs and assumptions, the purpose of the treatise apparently gives us no reason to suppose that these must be Aristotle's own beliefs and assumptions. Indeed, we might expect persuasive arguments to rely quite often on ethical beliefs and assumptions that Aristotle himself rejects; why should we suppose that the only ethical views he regards as persuasive are views that he accepts?[2]

If this is the right view of the *Rhetoric,* then it may still be important for understanding the Ethics. For the Ethics claim to begin from the "common beliefs" (*endoxa;* 1145a2–7; cf. 1095a28–30);[3] and if the *Rhetoric* is indeed a work on persuasive argument, we might expect it to give us some idea of some of the common beliefs held on ethics, since Aristotle claims that they are a source of persuasive arguments (1355a17–18, 1356b33–34). We will not, therefore, suppose that the ethical views reported in the *Rhetoric* are bound to reflect Aristotle's views, but we may, and indeed should, use the *Rhetoric* as a useful catalog of common beliefs.

This view of the *Rhetoric,* however, is oversimplified. For even if Aristotle discusses persuasion rather than truth, it does not follow that he must be completely undiscriminating in his attitude to persuasive arguments; we cannot assume, therefore, that he appeals to all common beliefs that might be used effectively in a persuasive argument. If he is selective in his appeal to common beliefs, any comparison of the *Rhetoric* with the Ethics ought to take account of his principle of selection. To see how discriminating he is in his attitude to persuasive arguments, we must examine his account of what he says he is doing, and we must compare this account with his actual practice in the body of the treatise.

To answer our question about the *Rhetoric* and the Ethics, then, we must first go back to the beginning of the *Rhetoric* and remind ourselves of what Aristotle says he is doing. In the light of what he says, we can see what we might reasonably expect from the remarks about ethics in the *Rhetoric;* and then we can see whether we get what we expect. I will confine my discussion to two topics that are treated at length in both works: happiness and virtue.

THE PROPER FUNCTION OF RHETORIC

Aristotle asserts that rhetoric is about producing convincing arguments (*pisteis*) and that it aims at persuasive rather than true conclusions. Still, a student of rhetorical argument should also be a student of dialectic and logic, not because rhetorical arguments aim at truth, but because a study of arguments that aim at the truth will be a good basis for study of arguments that aim at capturing common beliefs, since people's views tend in general to be fairly close to the truth (1355a14–18). This explanation of why the study of arguments aiming at the truth is relevant to rhetoric makes it clear that the relevance is indirect, and that rhetorical argument itself does not aim at the truth.

Some of Aristotle's reasons for claiming that rhetoric is useful also imply that it does not aim at the truth. It is more useful for some purposes than scientific knowledge would be, because the audiences persuaded by rhetoric would not be persuaded by scientific argument (1355a24–29). Since rhetoric is concerned with persuasion rather than truth, it is not concerned with any specific subject matter (1355b25–34). Nor is it concerned with persuading every sort of audience, but with "the sorts of audiences who cannot keep many steps in mind at once or keep track of a long argument" (1357a1–4). If we begin to give more rationally compelling arguments, and argue from premises that belong more properly to scientific knowledge in a given area, we depart from properly rhetorical arguments (1358a21–26). Accurate knowledge of a particular question does not necessarily supply suitable material for rhetorical argument, given the character of the audience (1359b2–18).

These passages suggest that since rhetoric aims at persuasion, we must expect Aristotle to choose all and only those premises and arguments that he regards as most likely to be persuasive on different occasions. In fact, however, he is more selective. He believes that on the whole people have some tendency to accept true assertions and legitimate arguments, and so he urges the orator to study these. Moreover, he warns the orator against resorting indiscriminately to any argument that seems likely to be persuasive (1355a29–38). We should focus on what is true and what is better, because these are more persuasive "to speak without qualification" (1355a38).

By adding "to speak without qualification" Aristotle warns us that what is true and what is better may not invariably be more persuasive in fact, in face of an especially ignorant or especially prejudiced audience. In this case Aristotle does not suggest that the orator ought to use whatever tricks are necessary to sway such an audience; the task of the orator is to see what is properly persuasive (*ta huparchonta pithana*) on a given subject, just as the task of the doctor is to see what is appropriate for healing (1355b10–14). It is not the doctor's business to bribe or intimidate patients into taking their medicine, and it is not the orator's business to use illegitimate means to convince an audience.

By drawing these distinctions Aristotle seeks to answer some of Plato's charges against rhetoric in the *Gorgias*.[4] He agrees that rhetoric is liable to misuse (1355b1–7), and that the students of rhetoric must learn about illegitimate as well as legitimate types of argument, so that they can recognize crooked arguments when their opponents use them. But he insists that orators must not use their skills unjustly. The sophistical, deceptive orator has the same skills, but makes the wrong decision (*prohairesis*) (1355b17–21).[5] Aristotle implies that there are some limits, apart from considerations of persuasiveness, on the choice of premises and arguments; he does not allow the orator to resort to every device that will persuade a particular audience. How are the limits to be settled?

RHETORIC AND POLITICAL SCIENCE

Aristotle argues that rhetoric relies not only on the nature of the argument itself but also on the audience's views about the character of the speaker and on the feelings (*pathē*) that the speech arouses in the audiences (1356a1–20). Orators must know enough about the audience's ethical convictions to understand what the audience regards as a good character, and they must know enough about psychology to grasp what different emotions are and how they can be aroused. Aristotle infers that rhetoric is a sort of appendage both of dialectic and of political science (1356a20–33).

The references to character and feelings do not fully explain why rhetoric is an appendage of political science.[6] For someone could become familiar with the aspects of ethics needed for knowing about characters and feelings, while remaining largely ignorant of political science as a whole and of its ethical aspects. When Aristotle suggests that the pretensions of some rhetoricians to knowledge of political science are unjustified, he surely does not mean simply that they are ignorant about what their audience esteems and admires, or that they are ignorant about ways of influencing emotions. In the *Nicomachean Ethics* he refers to the pretensions of sophists who treat political science as identical or inferior to rhetoric, and he says that these people do not even know what political science is or what it is about (1181a12–15). Since political science is about the ultimate ends and first principles of individual and social action, we would expect that rhetoricians who falsely claim knowledge of political science would claim that the arguments they are offering are appropriate and that the conclusions they reach express a correct view about what is good and just. Aristotle believes that rhetoricians uninformed by political science are not entitled to these claims. In claiming that rhetoric is properly an appendage of political science, Aristotle claims that something more than persuasive skill is needed if rhetoric is to carry out its proper function.

Ethical knowledge is relevant if an orator is to reject illegitimate means of persuasion. Aristotle argues that it is not the orator's task to deliberate about whether to persuade or not; he has already undertaken the aim of persuading in deciding to become an orator (1112b11–15). But he does not mean that once we have laid down this aim, the only question is about the most effective means of persuading this or that audience. The deliberator faced with several means that would apparently achieve the end must consider which means will achieve it "most easily and most finely (*kallista*)" (1112b16–17); if we can find only one effective means, we must consider whether that is possible. We cease to pursue this means if we come across something impossible, "for instance, if money is needed, and it cannot be supplied" (1112b24–26). Aristotle probably does not mean that if we can achieve our end only by stabbing and robbing an innocent person on the street, then that is what we must do. If considerations of what is fine enter into a choice between one means and another, why should they be excluded from our judgment about whether, for instance, money "can" or "cannot" be supplied?

The view that considerations of what is "fine" and morally right enter into deliberation about means fits Aristotle's claim about rhetoric. When he says that the orator must not try to persuade every audience and must not be unscrupulous in the choice of means to secure persuasion, he implies that moral considerations should influence the orator's decisions. Since moral considerations belong to political science, the relevance of these considerations may explain why Aristotle regards rhetoric as an appendage of political science.

This explanation is not completely satisfactory, however. Surely we could avoid illegitimate means of persuasion even if we had only the ordinary person's grasp of justice. Why should we need the deeper knowledge that we gain from ethical and political science? Would it not be unrealistic, in any case, to expect an orator to be an expert in political science?[7]

Aristotle might reasonably answer that a commonsense grasp of ethical questions is inadequate for the sorts of issues that confront an orator. Commonsense beliefs may be an adequate guide in ordinary circumstances, but oratory is needed in circumstances that are not ordinary, and therefore cannot be simply resolved by appeal to commonsense beliefs. Aristotle insists in the Ethics that common beliefs lead to puzzles that need to be resolved by philosophical reflection. The questions appropriate for rhetoric include many questions that raise puzzles for common beliefs, and so common beliefs will not be a reliable guide all by themselves.

This does not imply that practicing orators themselves must be experts in ethical and political science. They will be able to improve on common sense as long as they are guided by political science. If, for instance, they learn from political science what premises are the appropriate ones to use, what sorts of arguments are relevant to ethical questions, what ways are legitimate ways of presenting oneself, and what appeals to the emotions are permissible, they will be better off than they would be if they approached these practical questions with the benefit of nothing more than unaided common sense.

If political science guides the orator to this extent, it still does not guarantee that either the premises or the conclusions of the orator's argument will be true. For if the true principles are too far removed from common beliefs, or if the true conclusions can be reached from the true premises only by a rather complicated argument, neither the true premises nor the true conclusions are appropriate for rhetorical argument, given the limitations that Aristotle has mentioned. But not all false premises and conclusions are equally objectionable; if guidance from political science helps the orator to pick the least misleading premises and to argue to the least misleading conclusions, it is more reliable than unaided common sense would be.

RHETORIC, ETHICS, AND COMMON BELIEFS

If we have correctly understood these general remarks about the relation of rhetoric to political science, we have some idea of what to expect from the ethical claims presented in the *Rhetoric*. We will not assume that they state Aristotle's own views. Nor, however, will we assume that they are simply a record of common beliefs. Aristotle is concerned with a subset of commonly held views: those that are best for leading the audience, by the appropriate rhetorical arguments, to the best conclusions that are open to them, given their starting point.

In that case we will not turn to the *Rhetoric* for a completely impartial survey of common beliefs, but we will expect Aristotle to focus on a reasonable range of common beliefs. If the beliefs he appeals to are in obvious conflict with more fundamental common beliefs, they will not serve the purpose that he intends them to serve; and so we will expect him to give us a fair impression of the variety of views included in common beliefs—whether they are present in the outlook of a single person or they are distributed among different members of an audience.

What sorts of criticisms of Aristotle's presentation of common beliefs would be appropriate? It would be irrelevant to object that Aristotle leaves out some widely shared ethical beliefs, or that his view about the importance of one or another belief is not generally shared; for part of the point of the orator's selection is to focus people's attention on those beliefs that help the orator's case, and if orators are guided by political science, they will focus on those ordinary beliefs that help them to convince people of the best available conclusions. It would be quite fair, however, to criticize Aristotle if he appealed to some assumption that most of his audience would be likely to reject, or if he overlooked an objection that would immediately occur to most people.

How might we expect this selection from ordinary moral attitudes to differ from the ethical views that Aristotle presents in the Ethics? Aristotle tells us that he begins with the common beliefs and that he tries as far as is reasonable to show that they are true (1145b2–7); to this extent, then, we might expect the Ethics to agree with the *Rhetoric*. He warns us, however, of an important difference in his approach to common beliefs. In pointing out that rhetoric has to rely on common beliefs Aristotle refers to the *Topics:* "We must use the things commonly believed, . . . as we also said in the *Topics,* when we discussed the way to encounter the many" (1355a27–29). In the passage cited from the *Topics* Aristotle mentions that dialectic is useful for encounters with the many: "It is useful for encounters, because once we have cataloged the beliefs of the many, our approach to them will begin from their own views, not from other people's, and we will redirect them whenever they appear to us to be wrong" (*Top.* 101a30–34).[8] The *Rhetoric*, like the *Topics*, is meant to equip us for "encounters with the many," but, unlike the *Topics*, says nothing about "redirecting" (*metabibazein*) the views of the many.

The aim of redirecting the views of the many is part of Aristotle's conception of ethical argument. In the *Eudemian Ethics* he states his approach to the views of the many:

> [We should] use the appearances (*phainomena*) as testimonies and examples. For it is best if all human beings are shown to agree with what we are going to say, or at least that they all agree in a way. They will do this when they are redirected (*hoper metabibazomenoi poiēsousin*). (1216b27–30)

The *Nicomachean Ethics* describes the same critical attitude to common beliefs when it sets out to examine (*exetazein*) them: "Presumably, then, it is rather futile to examine all these beliefs, and it is enough to examine those that are most current or seem to have some argument for them" (1095a28–30).

In selecting the beliefs that are most current, the Ethics agree with the advice in the *Rhetoric* that we should not bother ourselves with views that simply happen to strike this or that individual (1356b35–1357a1); but its principle of selection is different from the one assumed in the *Rhetoric*. The difference is particularly important when Aristotle says we should set out not only from current views but also from views that "seem to have some argument for them." For we might well decide that some unpopular view is unlikely to be put forward or assumed in a public discussion and deliberation, and hence is not a proper concern of rhetoric, but nonetheless has something to be said for it and deserves discussion in ethics.

This is why Aristotle considers views that are not widely shared, and are not *endoxa* at all, but "philosophers' paradoxes" (*theseis;* cf. 1096a2, *Top.* 104b19–28, 159b25–35). In the Ethics the views of Socrates are discussed for this reason, not because they count as *endoxa*. These views are not suitable for rhetoric; for we are inclined to dismiss them (as Socrates' interlocutors sometimes do) until we see the arguments that can be given for them. Orators do not have time to persuade their audiences to take such views seriously by reflecting on the arguments that can be given for them.

One way to see that paradoxical views have something to be said for them is to notice that "ordinary" views are not as straightforward as they seem, but actually raise puzzles (*aporiai*); the puzzles that arise from the beliefs of the many make us more inclined to take the paradoxical claims of the philosophers more seriously. Aristotle describes a puzzle as the result of "equality of contrary reasonings" (*Top.* 145b16–18). In order to see that the arguments for contrary conclusions seem to be equally cogent, we have to carry out the exercise that Aristotle calls "expounding the puzzles" (*diaporein;* see, for example, *Met.* 995a27–33). The *Rhetoric* is concerned with situations that may raise moral doubts and puzzles, but it is not concerned to expound these puzzles; it does not even use *aporein* and its cognates in the technical sense familiar from Aristotle's dialectical inquiries.[9]

An exposition of the puzzles requires us to go through the arguments on each side; but the orator cannot normally expect an audience to do this. The orator's task is to persuade the audience of the correctness of some course of action, by arguing from moral beliefs they already share; an orator who called the audience's initial beliefs into question would be making the task of persuasion more difficult, for no obvious practical benefit. Often the orator wants to "redirect" his audience insofar as he wants to turn them from their prejudices against the course of action that he favors. But this limited redirection does not involve the broader redirection that Aristotle aims at in the Ethics; indeed, it would be self-defeating to attempt this broader redirection in a rhetorical argument (as Socrates recognizes in *Apology* 37a5–7, *Crito* 49d2–5).

These limits on rhetorical argument do not imply that it must be dishonest or sophistical.[10] The orator need not claim that he is teaching his audience moral philosophy, and the audience do not expect to learn moral philosophy from him. They expect him to argue according to his honest moral convictions about what it is best to do or about what the just decision is, and if they are to be persuaded by his honest convictions, they must suppose that these convictions are the closest approximation to the truth that is available. If the orator is entitled to expect his audience to suppose this about him, then his moral convictions must be more reliable than those of uninstructed common sense, and he must argue in accordance with his honest convictions. It does not follow, however, that the orator has to state all his honest convictions on every ethical question that is raised by the issue being discussed, or that he must try to persuade his audience to share all these convictions. Though he must be guided by the conclusions of political science, including moral philosophy, he need not fully grasp the principles of political science, and he need not, indeed should not, instruct his audience in moral philosophy.

If, then, we have the right expectations about how the ethical views in the *Rhetoric* will differ from those in the Ethics, a comparison of the two works should show us something about the status of the different beliefs that Aristotle accepts or examines in the Ethics. We ought to be able to see, for instance, which views are close enough to ordinary beliefs to serve as an appropriate starting point for rhetorical argument; which beliefs— his own or other people's—Aristotle regards as too controversial or complex to be used in rhetorical argument; which aspects of ordinary beliefs need to be corrected, for the purposes of the Ethics, in ways that are not described in the *Rhetoric;* and which puzzles about ordinary beliefs are noticed in the Ethics but not in the *Rhetoric.* I will consider these questions by comparing Aristotle's treatment of happiness and of virtue in the two works.

HAPPINESS

Aristotle begins his discussion of ethical questions and assumptions with happiness. He claims that we must find what happiness is, and what its parts are, because happiness is the ultimate end for all action and deliberation (1360b4–13). The rest of the chapter is devoted to the two tasks of saying what happiness is and what its parts are.

In his claim about happiness Aristotle agrees with Socrates. In the *Euthydemus* Socrates begins his discussion of ethics by asking whether we all want to "do well" (278e3–6), or to 'be happy' (Plato, *Euthydemus* 280b6). He assumes that this is our ultimate aim; indeed, he suggests that it is foolish to ask the question whether we want to do well, as though there could be any question about it. Socrates' next question concerns what we must do to be happy; this question leads him into a discussion of virtues and other goods.

Aristotle does not move quite as quickly as Socrates does; before asking what the parts of happiness are, he asks first what happiness is. The *Magna Moralia* and *Eudemian Ethics* do not ask this question in so many words, but the *Nicomachean Ethics* asks it, remarking that the many and the wise disagree about the answer to the question (1095a16–22). The *Nicomachean Ethics* makes it clear (as the *Eudemian Ethics* does) that although people generally agree that happiness is the ultimate good, they disagree about what it consists in. The *Rhetoric* does not mention any disagreement about what happiness is; it mentions several descriptions of happiness that we can take for granted in arguing about what promotes happiness.

Aristotle now presents several descriptions of what happiness is, without suggesting that they arouse disagreement, or that we have to choose among them:

> Let us, then, take happiness to be (1) doing well together with virtue, or (2) self-sufficiency of life, or (3) the pleasantest life together with safety, or (4) prosperity of possessions and slaves[11] together with the power to protect them and act with them; for practically everyone agrees that happiness is one or more of these things. (1360b14–18)

These accounts are supposed to tell us "by way of illustration" (*paradeigmatos charin*, 1360b7) what happiness is, "speaking without qualification" (*hōs haplōs eipein*). They provide illustrations, rather than exhaustive accounts.[12] They constitute a general statement, rather than an exact one that might tell us how far each of these descriptions is or is not an adequate account of happiness.[13] In saying "Let us take . . ." (*estō*) Aristotle takes the accounts for granted rather than arguing for them. It does not follow that he does not believe they are broadly correct; but he is not endorsing them as conclusions of his own argument.[14]

At first sight, it is by no means obvious that these accounts are equivalent. The fourth seems to be the narrowest; it seems as though we could satisfy it without possessing either virtue or pleasure. None of the accounts except the first makes it clear that virtue is required for happiness. Apparently, then, the accounts give us different answers if we ask whether virtue and pleasure are needed for happiness. But Aristotle does not draw attention to these apparent disagreements, and he does not explain how they might be resolved.

Why does he even bother giving all these accounts? Why should he not stick to the first two, which seem to be the most general? These questions seem especially relevant when we consider Aristotle's use of his accounts of happiness to support his list of the parts of happiness:

> If, then, happiness is this sort of thing, its parts must be good birth, many friends, good friends, wealth, good children, many children, prosperous old age. They must also include bodily excellences (e.g., health, beauty, strength, size, athletic ability), honor, good fortune, and virtue. For this is the way for someone to be most self-sufficient, by having both the goods internal to himself and the external goods, since there are no other goods besides these. The internal goods are those in the soul and body, and the external are good birth, friends, money, and honor; and we also think it suitable for him to have power and good fortune, since that makes life safest. (1360b19–30)

When Aristotle says "If, then, happiness is this sort of thing, its parts must be . . . ," we expect him to appeal to the accounts of happiness to support his claims about what the parts of happiness are. But in fact it looks as though only one of the accounts of happiness is being used to support the list of parts. In "For this is the way for someone to be most self-sufficient" Aristotle appeals to the account of happiness as the most self-sufficient life. He assumes that self-sufficiency is to be understood as the condition in which we need nothing added because we have all the goods. In speaking of power and good fortune, he also refers to the account of happiness as including safety; but it seems unnecessary for him to do this, since these goods could apparently be understood as aspects of, or means to, self-sufficiency.

Perhaps Aristotle agrees that the appeal to self-sufficiency will support all his claims about the parts of happiness, provided that the nature of self-sufficiency is correctly understood and provided that we have the correct view of what all the goods actually are. But if we are to meet these conditions, we may need to reflect further on self-sufficiency and goods. The *Nicomachean Ethics* suggests that an appeal to self-sufficiency by itself does not tell us what the final good actually is. After we have been told that the final good is complete and self-sufficient, Aristotle says: "But presumably the remark that the best good is happiness is apparently something agreed, and what we miss is a clearer statement of what the best good is" (1097b22–24). The next step in the *Nicomachean Ethics* is the argument about the human function, and the resulting account of happiness that describes it as activity of the soul in accordance with complete virtue in a complete life.

If Aristotle agrees, in writing the *Rhetoric,* with the suggestion in the *Nicomachean Ethics* that self-sufficiency gives an insufficiently definite account of happiness, it is easy to see why he does not choose to formulate a more definite account through the argument he uses in the *Nicomachean Ethics.* For the appeal to the human function needs to be understood by reference to Aristotle's account of the soul. Moreover, even when it is understood, the appeal to function does not provide a list of the virtues and other goods that constitute happiness; that list can be settled only after we have reflected on the account of virtue that fits the account of happiness. For these reasons, the account given in the *Nicomachean Ethics* is not suitable for the purposes of the *Rhetoric,* and so it is not surprising that Aristotle omits it.

We can now see why Aristotle adds the other accounts of happiness that might at first sight seem superfluous. If we are concerned to make our point readily comprehensible and acceptable, superfluity may be useful. Even if we could work out the same list of parts of happiness from just one of the accounts that Aristotle gives us, it is better to include the other descriptions if they make it easier to arrive at the list. For this purpose the apparently quite inadequate fourth account of happiness (referring to prosperity of possessions with the power to protect and use them) may be especially useful; for it is easier to apply to particular cases than the other three are, and so it is easier to see what it requires in a particular case.

Even if Aristotle can give this reason for accepting these different accounts of happiness, he faces a further objection. If he does not decide between them, and they may conflict in particular cases, is he not in danger of instructing the orator to give inconsistent advice? In some circumstances it will matter whether we think of happiness as consisting simply in material prosperity or as including nonmaterial goods as well. Even if one account does not exclude the parts of happiness recognized by other accounts, it may surely imply a different view about which parts are most important. If we face a choice between an action that promises power and security and one that is required by honor, we must apparently decide which part of happiness is more important.

Aristotle sees exactly this question in the *Eudemian Ethics* and *Nicomachean Ethics;* for he notices that different conceptions of happiness support the "three lives" of pleasure, honor, and contemplation. Aristotle makes it clear that people who identify happiness simply with a life of pleasure or a life of honor are mistaken (1095b14–30). In the *Rhetoric* he does not criticize the popular conceptions of happiness in this way. His uncritical attitude seems surprising, since *Rhetoric* 1.7 is devoted to disputes that arise when we recognize that two courses of action would both be expedient and we must choose the more expedient. In the course of discussing this question Aristotle appeals to his earlier remarks about happiness, pointing out that the more self-sufficient good is to be preferred over the less self-sufficient (1364a5–6), the more pleasant over the less pleasant (1364b23–26), and the finer over the less fine (1364b26–28). These grounds for preference might apparently lead to conflicting results for people with different conceptions of happiness. Why, then, does Aristotle not face these conflicts by bringing his initial discussion of happiness to a more definite conclusion favoring some more specific conception of happiness?

Perhaps we can see why Aristotle does not believe that this is the best way to resolve the kinds of disputes that are likely to arise about the more expedient course of action. We cannot form a conception of happiness without some intuitive views of which things are goods and which goods are better goods than others; for our conception of happiness requires the revision of these initial intuitive views. If other people do not share our view of happiness, then we need to examine their views about goods, and see how we can convince them both to trace the consequence of these views in forming a conception of happiness and to modify these views once they have formed a conception of happiness. This process requires reflection on one's views about goods in the light of other convictions that are relevant to questions about happiness. The process is complicated; it would be inappropriate for orators to believe that they could take their audience through it as a preliminary to convincing them to favor one course of action over another.

It would be reasonable for Aristotle to tell orators to appeal to the audience's conception of happiness, if the audience shared a conception that was determinate enough to tell them which goods are greater than which. He suggests, however, that people do not share a conception as determinate as this. If they share the sorts of convictions that are summed up in *Rhetoric* 1.5, then it is understandable that Aristotle does not recommend appealing to a conception of happiness in order to answer the questions about what is more and less expedient.

If orators forgo any argument about the content of happiness, then their advice about which course of action is more expedient may well be less securely grounded than it would be if they could rely on the conclusions of such an argument. In the Ethics Aristotle argues that reference to a final good has a practical use: once we know what it is, we will have a definite target to aim at (1094a22–25). In the *Rhetoric* Aristotle does not give this advice to the orator. Although the chapter on happiness aims to say what happiness is "for the sake of example" (1360b7–8), it does not give the general account that the Ethics look for, and it cannot appeal to a general account of happiness to answer practical questions.

This difference between the Ethics and the *Rhetoric* may be explained by a further difference that we noticed earlier. The Ethics suggest that we need to find a general account of happiness because people have different views about what happiness is, and we ought to see how far each of these views is right. We see a practical point in ethical theory once we see the extent and depth of ethical disagreement. The *Rhetoric*, by contrast, does not mention disagreement about the nature of happiness; it does not suggest, therefore, that recognition of disagreement should lead us into theory or that theory has a function in resolving disagreements.

Since orators do not even attempt to find a general account of the nature of the good, they must appeal to particular convictions about goods, and especially about the superiority of one good to another. These comparative convictions are especially liable to conflict; for instance, we may suppose that pleasure is better than honor if we consider some pleasures, but may change our view if we think more carefully about other sorts of pleasures. Aristotle suggests that some of people's comparative convictions are mistaken. He explains why people tend to believe that receiving a benefit is better than giving one, and that health is better than justice (1365a37–1365b8): the former are goods that we would choose even if no one knew about them, while the latter are not. People also tend to believe, however, that it is better to suffer injustice rather than do it, because it is what the better person would choose (1364b21–23). These beliefs might easily conflict; for the better person would choose to give a benefit rather than receive one, and would prefer justice over health.

Since widely shared beliefs might be used to support either of two incompatible conclusions, orators must be able to decide which beliefs they should appeal to on a particular occasion. This is why Aristotle believes they ought to rely on the conclusions of political science. They lack a reliable method for reaching the right conclusion if their own deliberation relies simply on the materials that Aristotle offers them for use in rhetorical arguments. Aristotle's exposition of shared beliefs about happiness shows us why the *Rhetoric* does not present the account of happiness that is offered in the Ethics, and why nonetheless we need that account if we are to make the right use of his exposition in the *Rhetoric*.[15]

HAPPINESS IN THE *RHETORIC* AND IN THE ETHICS

What, then, do we learn about common views of happiness from reading the *Rhetoric* that we would not learn if we confined ourselves to the Ethics?

First of all, we can see that some of Aristotle's criteria and conclusions are not very distant from popular views. In saying that happiness must be self-sufficient, he agrees with the common view that it is self-sufficiency of life. In saying that it must involve pleasure, he agrees with the view that it is the most pleasant life. In saying that it requires an adequate supply of external goods, he agrees with the common view that it must be "secure" or "safe" (*asphalēs*), since external goods help to make one's life more secure.[16] In *Nicomachean Ethics* 1.8 Aristotle claims that his account of happiness conforms with the common beliefs on these points; the description in the *Rhetoric* confirms his claim. Even the fourth view, referring to the possession and maintenance of external goods, although a clearly inadequate account of happiness, is intelligible once we understand the importance of external goods in happiness. Aristotle's list of popular views makes it easier to see how he might defend his own account of happiness.[17]

Even Aristotle's own account of happiness as activity of the soul in accordance with complete virtue in a complete life does not depart widely from common views. For one of the generally accepted views of happiness describes it as "doing well with virtue." The exact sense of this description is not completely clear, but we might take "doing well" to refer to the aspect of happiness that involves success, and therefore requires external goods; Aristotle's own account of happiness refers to external goods in the clause "in a complete life."

The most controversial feature of Aristotle's account of happiness, measured by the description in the *Rhetoric,* is his belief that happiness is primarily virtuous activity and secondarily external success. The *Nicomachean Ethics* is more careful than the other two ethical works are in recognizing and defending this controversial element in his account. Three chapters of *Nicomachean Ethics* 1 (9–11) are devoted to a discussion of the place of external goods and an affirmation of the primacy of virtuous action. This affirmation has no parallel in the *Rhetoric*. The different descriptions of happiness have, or may be thought to have, different implications for the role of virtue in happiness, and Aristotle abstains, for reasons we have considered, from any attempt to decide the relative merits of the different conceptions. The *Rhetoric* does not explain why virtue should be given a special place, contrasting it with other goods, in an account of happiness; this is the omission that Aristotle seeks to rectify in the *Nicomachean Ethics*, by deriving the requirement of virtuous action from the argument about the human function.

In claiming that virtuous action is primary in happiness, and to be preferred to other goods, Aristotle draws a distinction between goods, of which virtuous action is one, that are parts of happiness and goods that are simply instrumental to happiness. He does not state the distinction in exactly these terms in Book 1 of the *Nicomachean Ethics*, although he implicitly accepts it;[18] but in the discussions of happiness in the *Magna Moralia* (1184a15–38) and the *Eudemian Ethics* the distinction is prominent. The *Magna Moralia* takes it to be obvious that happiness is composed of many goods (*tēn d'eudaimonian ek pollōn agathōn suntithemen*, 1184a18–19),[19] but only the *Eudemian Ethics* explains why this is an important claim. Aristotle argues that we must raise questions about the nature of happiness so that we can decide "in which feature of us living well consists, and what the things are without which this [feature in which living well consists] cannot be present to us" (1214b12–14). He explains that people often do not attend properly to this distinction, and so they confuse the parts of happiness with its necessary conditions (1214b24–27). In Aristotle's view, the question about what happiness is will tell us which goods are parts of happiness, in contrast to the goods that are necessary conditions. Failure to draw the appropriate distinction is the cause of dispute (*amphisbētēsis*, 1214b24) about happiness.

If we approach the *Rhetoric* in the light of this comment in the *Eudemian Ethics*, its failure to draw the crucial distinction is rather glaring.[20] The list of "parts" of happiness includes some that seem to be simply means (wealth, bodily strength), and others that might plausibly be treated as ends (friendship, virtue, pleasure). We probably ought not to suppose that Aristotle is writing with his eye on the distinction drawn in the *Eudemian Ethics* and claiming that most people regard some or all of this long list of goods as ends in themselves, and hence as goods that are taken to meet the conditions laid down in the *Eudemian Ethics* for being parts of happiness. It is more reasonable to suppose that he is using "part" rather loosely, without reference to any distinction between parts and necessary conditions.

Aristotle is quite right to insist, as he does in the *Eudemian Ethics*, on the importance of the distinction, and he draws it throughout his ethical discussions. He relies on it again in the *Politics* in the summary of his account of happiness (*Polit.* 1325a5–7). Why, then, does he fail to draw the distinction in the *Rhetoric*? Failure to draw it seems to be an obvious source of confusion in our thought about ends and means, and hence of confusion in our reflections about happiness. Are the commonsense views described in the *Rhetoric* really subject to this confusion? If they are, ought not Aristotle to point it out?

Aristotle does not suggest that common sense is completely confused about means and ends. In the discussion of goods he distinguishes those that are used from those that are enjoyed (1361a16–19). One type of good is the type that is chosen for its own sake (1362b21–22), and Aristotle remarks that some of the parts of happiness are chosen for their own sakes, as well as for their results (1362b19–22, 26–27). In discussing comparisons he remarks that what is good for its own sake is more choiceworthy than what is good for the sake of something else (1363b38–1364a5). He does not suggest, however, that this distinction among goods is important for articulating our conception of happiness. Common sense, as presented by Aristotle, clearly has the resources needed for understanding the point made in the *Eudemian Ethics* about parts and necessary conditions. Still, Aristotle chooses not to apply this point to happiness. Why should he make this choice?

Perhaps the *Eudemian Ethics* itself answers this question. Aristotle says that the division between parts and necessary conditions of happiness is a source of controversy, because the goods that some people count as parts other people count as mere necessary conditions. Drawing the distinction is not simply a way of clarifying a point on which people might be confused; once it is drawn, there is still room for dispute about which goods fall into which class. This is the sort of dispute that the *Rhetoric* apparently seeks to avoid by using an undiscriminating notion of "part" and by lumping together (we might be inclined to say) means and ends in the list of parts of happiness. Aristotle suggests that it is relatively easy to agree that these goods belong in some way to happiness, but more difficult to decide what sort of place they have in happiness.

Standing aside from this dispute about parts and necessary conditions in our account of happiness cannot protect us entirely from facing the dispute; for we evidently must face it when we are facing a conflict between promoting one or another good. But Aristotle prefers to resolve such conflicts simply by appealing to our view that one good is noninstrumental and the other good is purely instrumental, rather than trying to support this view by appeal to a more discriminating conception of happiness. He seems to assume, then, that raising disputes about the constitution of happiness will divert us from the immediate practical task of rhetoric.

Once we see this, we have a clearer appreciation of what Aristotle needs to argue for in his ethical theory. He can rely on some intuitive view that the virtues are parts of happiness. But he cannot appeal to common sense in support of his view that they are parts in the strict sense specified in the *Eudemian Ethics,* or in support of his view that they are the most important parts. The specific connection that he sees between virtue and happiness is omitted from the discussion in the *Rhetoric.* Aristotle implies that we ought not to rely on it in ethical arguments appealing to common-sense beliefs.

VIRTUE AND PRAISE

The rather brief remarks about virtue in Aristotle's discussion of happiness do not give a complete picture of the importance of the virtues in Book 1 of the *Rhetoric.* Although virtues are mentioned only briefly in the chapters on happiness, goods, expediency, and comparative expediency, they also receive a whole chapter to themselves, since they are the subject of epideictic oratory. The chapter is also relevant to the deliberative oratory that Aristotle has been discussing: since virtues are fine, and fineness is a ground for recognizing something as a good, clarification of the fineness of virtue will also clarify the place of virtue among goods. This clarification is relevant to the weighing of goods that is necessary in deliberative oratory; for an orator will often argue that a particular course of action is unjust and shameful, and will urge this argument as at least one weighty consideration against pursuing the course of action.

Aristotle relies on some fairly general agreement about the sorts of qualities that deserve to be considered as the virtues. It is often remarked that "*aretē*" is often used for all sorts of good qualities, not necessarily qualities of character or moral qualities. Aristotle recognizes this general use of "*aretē*" by specifying the sort of excellence he has in mind (as in "bodily *aretai*" [plural], 1360b21). He also assumes, however, that his readers will have no difficulty in picking out a narrower use of the term, applying to traits of character in particular. He mentions certain traits of character without further specification as *aretē* (singular; 1360b23). A person who has these traits is properly called *agathos* (good) without further specification.

Aristotle describes a virtue as "a capacity that provides and preserves goods" (1366a37); but although health and strength satisfy this description, he does not include them in the list of virtues that are proper subjects of praise. He clearly intends his list to be confined to states of character. The virtues he lists are "justice, courage, temperance, magnificence, magnanimity, generosity, intelligence (*phronēsis*), wisdom (*sophia*)" (1366b1–3). These virtues are "fine" (*kala*), because they are both good in themselves and praiseworthy (1366a33–36); praise is "speech displaying the greatness of virtue" (1367b28). Virtue is praiseworthy because it is "a capacity (so it seems) that secures and preserves goods, and a capacity that benefits in many ways, and great ways, and in all sorts of ways on all sorts of matters" (1366a36–1366b1). The definitions of the virtues of character show how they satisfy this general condition. Moreover, the actions done for the sake of another are especially fine and characteristic of virtue because they are done less for the agent's own sake (1366b36–1367a4). Hence "the extreme degree of virtue is to benefit everyone" (1367b6–7); the context shows that by "everyone" Aristotle means "everyone else."

In praising someone, we do not consider whether he benefited himself; indeed we often praise him more if he benefited himself less:

> because he counted his own interest for little and did something fine, as they praise Achilles because he came to the aid of his companion Patroclus, knowing that he would have to die even though it was open to him to stay alive. For him such a death was finer, while being alive was expedient. (1359a1–5)

Achilles is praiseworthy because of his self-sacrifice, counting his own interest for less than the interest of another. His action is characteristic of the young, who tend to be magnanimous, and to choose fine actions over expedient: "for their lives are guided by their character rather than by reasoning, and reasoning is of [*sc.* aims at] the expedient, whereas virtue is of the fine" (1389a32–35). Older people, however, "live with a view to the expedient, not the fine, more than is right, because they are self-lovers; for the expedient is good for oneself, but the fine is good without qualification" (1389b36–1390a1).

THE *RHETORIC* AND THE ETHICS ON VIRTUE

How should we compare this discussion of virtue in the *Rhetoric* with those in the Ethics?

First, it is worth considering differences in the list of virtues that are mentioned in the *Rhetoric* and the list in the *Nicomachean Ethics* (which differs from the lists in the other two ethical works). The *Rhetoric* omits the nameless virtues that are considered in the Ethics.[21] In omitting them, it confirms Aristotle's suggestion in the *Nicomachean Ethics* that these virtues are not commonly recognized, and that some argument needs to be given for adding them to the list.[22] The *Rhetoric* does not give this argument. It is possible that the *Rhetoric* also omits theoretical wisdom (*sophia*) from its list;[23] at any rate, it does not give any description of wisdom in its brief descriptions of each of the virtues. The omission is comprehensible in the light of the general characterization of a virtue as a capacity to benefit others; for it does not seem plausible to describe wisdom, as the *Nicomachean Ethics* understands it, in this way.

The *Rhetoric* claims that the greatest virtues are those that are most useful to others, and that therefore bravery and justice, followed by generosity, are the greatest virtues (1366b3–9). These claims have no precise parallel in the Ethics. They have a partial parallel, however, in the claim that general justice, more than any other virtue, is complete virtue, because it is the complete use of complete virtue (1129b30–31),[24] and it is the complete use because it is the use of virtue for the benefit of others.[25]

The *Rhetoric* describes virtue as a capacity (*dunamis*), whereas the Ethics describe it as a state (*hexis*) in contrast to a capacity (*NE* 2.5). Aristotle is not satisfied with describing it as a capacity, because we cannot have a virtue as long as we do not use our capacities in the right way on the right occasion; to ensure the right use we have to add that virtue is a state involving decision (*hexis prohairetikē*). In the *Rhetoric* Aristotle does not mention these aspects of virtue, but he does not overlook them entirely. His division between the sophistical and the legitimate use of dialectic and rhetoric rests on the distinction between capacity and decision (1355b17–18),[26] and it is reasonable to suppose that he intends the same distinction to apply to his account of virtue. He surely does not mean that people are virtuous if they have these beneficial capacities, even if they use them wrongly.[27]

It is puzzling, then, that Aristotle prefers to speak of a capacity rather than a state (*hexis*) or condition (*diathesis*). It is certainly not because he wants to deny that virtue requires decision; far from denying it, the *Rhetoric* emphasizes this feature of virtue (1367b22–27). He also remarks that virtues and vices are states rather than feelings (1388b31–34), although he does not distinguish states from capacities, as the Ethics do. Perhaps it is best just to say that the *Rhetoric* uses "capacity" broadly; the fact that virtue is more than a capacity does not make it false to say that the virtuous person has the capacity to do virtuous actions, even if more needs to be said about how a mere capacity differs from a state of character. Indeed, a preference for using "*dunamis*" might be partly explained by the fact that a *dunamis* is an active power to perform a certain type of action, and he wants to emphasize the connection between virtue and beneficial action. In doing this, he chooses not to emphasize the distinction between a capacity and a state.

Our previous explanation of Aristotle's use of "parts of happiness" applies to the account of virtue also; Aristotle resists the drawing of a distinction that would clarify his position, and assigns a broad scope to a term that he uses in the Ethics with a narrower scope. Whether his preference is justified or unjustified, we ought not to suppose that in the *Rhetoric* he holds the view that he would be holding if he used the term with the narrow scope assigned to it in the Ethics.

It is perhaps more surprising that the rest of the account of a virtue of character in the Ethics lacks a parallel in the *Rhetoric;* for the *Rhetoric* says nothing about the doctrine of the mean, which underlies the account of virtues of character in the Ethics. Why should Aristotle omit this feature of the virtues? It does not seem especially abstruse or theoretical; the suggestion that virtuous people neither have uncontrolled emotions nor attempt to eliminate emotions altogether (1104b18–26) is easy to understand and fairly easy to accept, and we may be surprised that the *Rhetoric* omits it.

The omission in the *Rhetoric* is especially surprising if we accept one view of the doctrine of the mean that has been widely accepted, although often challenged. If Aristotle is offering some sort of counsel of moderation, urging the formation of moderate emotional reactions rather than violent ones, such a piece of rough-and-ready practical advice seems quite appropriate for a work like the *Rhetoric*. Aristotle is willing to use his doctrine of the mean in support of political moderation, when he advocates the rule of the "intermediate" element in a city (*Polit.* 1295a34–1295b5). Why, then, should Aristotle deny himself this sort of argument in the *Rhetoric*?

We might argue that in fact he does not deny himself this argument. At the end of his discussion of the emotions he considers the characters of the young and the old, and then claims that the characters of people in their prime (forty-nine years old) are "between" those of the young and the old and avoid their "excesses" and "deficiencies," so that they have reached the "measured" and best condition (1390a28–29, 1390b8–9). These expressions may easily remind us of the doctrine of the mean;[28] Aristotle, however, neither mentions nor clearly alludes to that doctrine. His discussion would be perfectly intelligible to someone who knew nothing of Aristotle's ethical theory. If we contrast this chapter with *Politics* 4.11 (on the mean in politics), we ought to be even more struck by the fact that the *Rhetoric* avoids any appeal to the distinctive doctrines of the Ethics.

Why should the *Rhetoric* be silent about the doctrine of the mean? We might seek an explanation in the context of the doctrine of the mean in the Ethics. It is mentioned first of all in the account of early moral education and habituation; and so we might think it is part of the genesis of virtue. When Aristotle uses it to give practical advice, he thinks of people trying to form their own character, and urges them, for instance, to aim at the opposite extreme to the one they are naturally prone to (1109a30–1109b7). Since *Rhetoric* 1.9 is about the praise of virtuous people, it is concerned with the character of people who are already virtuous, rather than with the means of making people more virtuous. For this reason, any mention of the doctrine of the mean might seem inappropriate in the immediate context.

This answer is not completely satisfactory. The mean is relevant to more than the genesis of the virtues. It is part of Aristotle's account of each of the virtues, and he is still concerned with it when he turns to his discussion of wisdom (*phronēsis*) in Book 6 of the *Nicomachean Ethics* (1138b18–25). It can hardly be excluded, then, simply on the ground that it is irrelevant to the assessment of someone's developed moral character. It would be readily intelligible at several points in the *Rhetoric*, and most obviously, as we have noticed, in the account of different characters in Book 2.

The connection between the doctrine of the mean and wisdom may help us to understand the omission in the *Rhetoric*. When Aristotle incorporates a reference to the mean in his account of virtue of character, he says that the mean is the one that is defined by reason, and by the reason by which the wise person would define it (1106b36–1107a2). This is the first step in Aristotle's argument to show that every virtue of character requires wisdom, and that the wise person's deliberation about what promotes happiness is necessary for the discovery of the mean that is characteristic of each virtue. A reference to the mean, then, is not a rule of thumb that enables us to do without the wise person's deliberation; quite the contrary, it points to the indeterminate element in the initial account of virtue that needs to be made determinate by the judgments of the wise person. If this is true, then an appeal to the mean is not likely to be much help by itself in telling us what a virtuous action is, or which people are virtuous people. Probably, then, the *Rhetoric* omits the doctrine of the mean because a proper understanding and application of it requires us to absorb some of the more complex aspects of Aristotle's theory.

Instead of the more complex account of virtue mentioning the mean, decision, and the judgment of the wise person, the *Rhetoric* describes the virtues as beneficial capacities. Is this a significant departure from the Ethics? It must be admitted that the Ethics say nothing about the benefit of others in their general account of the virtues, and do not include it, as the *Rhetoric* does, in the description of individual virtues. Still, before we conclude that the *Rhetoric* and the Ethics differ on this important point about the virtues, we should notice how the Ethics explain the doctrine of the mean. We hit the mean by doing a certain kind of action (standing firm against danger, for instance) in the various conditions (defined by times, places, people, and so on) in which we ought (*dein*) to do it. The conditions in which we ought to do a particular type of action are specified by correct reason, and Aristotle insists several times that correct reason aims at what is fine (1115b17–20, 1117a18, 1162b25, 1169a4–6, 1180a4–5, 10–12; *EE* 1229a1–9). This concern with the fine involves concern for the common good (1169a8–11). These aspects of the Ethics show that Aristotle does not overlook the reference to the good of others that is so prominent in the description of the virtues in the *Rhetoric*.[29]

We might argue, then, that the *Rhetoric* simply focuses on one aspect of the virtues whose various aspects are described in the Ethics; the fact that its focus is selective does not show that it says anything incompatible with Aristotle's general theory. Still, the selective focus makes a difference to what Aristotle takes to be essential to virtue in the *Rhetoric* and the Ethics. If we treat the descriptions in the *Rhetoric* as stating sufficient conditions for each of the virtues, some differences from the Ethics become clearer. Justice is described as the virtue "because of which each lot of people have their own, and as the law [prescribes]" (1366b9–10). The reference to the law might make us think of what the Ethics call general justice, but the scope assigned to justice limits it to what the Ethics call particular justice (1132b16–18). Not only justice, but also bravery and temperance are described as conforming to the prescriptions of the law (1366b11–15). The concern with securing conformity to the law is shared by the Ethics (1102a9–10), but it is not part of the account of each virtue.

This difference is important because someone could conform to the condition stated in the *Rhetoric* without having the virtues described in the Ethics. The conditions for bravery stated in the *Rhetoric* could be satisfied by someone who has what the Ethics call "citizen bravery." Aristotle describes this by saying that "citizens seem to stand firm against dangers with the aim of avoiding reproaches and legal penalties and of winning honors" (1116a18–19). This is close to being genuine bravery, "since it is caused by a virtue; for its cause is shame and desire for something fine—for honor—and aversion from reproach, which is disgraceful" (1116a27–29). Nonetheless, it falls short of bravery. The brave person is not moved primarily by considerations of honor and shame, but by the fact that brave action is itself fine, whether or not it wins him honor. While those who have the bravery of citizens are concerned for something that is fine, they do not choose brave action for its own sake and because it is fine. They therefore do not meet Aristotle's demand that the brave person should decide (*prohaireisthai*) on virtuous action for its own sake (1105a32). The crucial feature of real bravery is described both as "acquiring decision and the goal" (*proslabousa prohairesin kai to hou heneka*, 1117a4–5) and as acting "because of the fine" and "as reason [prescribes]" (1117a8).[30]

If this is right, and if the bravery of citizens counts as genuine bravery by the criterion used in the *Rhetoric*, it follows that the *Rhetoric* does not fully capture the demand in the Ethics that the virtuous person should act on the right decision. This does not mean that the *Rhetoric* is indifferent to the question of whether a virtuous person acts on the right decision. Aristotle recognizes this as an appropriate demand on virtue (1367b22–27), and suggests ways of arguing that someone has the decision characteristic of a virtuous person. He does not, however, specify exactly what the decision has to be like; and so he does not impose as precise a demand as he imposes in the Ethics.

In the Ethics, Aristotle gives no argument for his claim that the virtuous person must decide on the virtuous action for its own sake. Is he justified in assuming this? The *Rhetoric* implies that some sort of decision is needed, and that in some way the virtuous person must decide on the virtuous action for itself. Vice belongs to an agent's decision (1368b10–14, 1382a35–1382b1), so that an action of wanton aggression (*hubris*), for instance, is not just a certain kind of action, but must also be done for a particular reason (1374a9–17). Moral assessment is not directed simply to the gravity of the action, but to the attitude underlying it (1374b24–29); that is why evidence of premeditation warrants a harsher judgment (1375a7), and why we distinguish action on decision from action on emotion (1373b35–38).[31] We present our character in making our *prohairesis* clear (1395b13–14); since a *prohairesis* characterizes a person as a whole, a reference to a person's *prohairesis* draws attention to the broader context of his action, and therefore to his normal behavior, so that we do not confine ourselves to this particular action (1374b13–16).

Our *prohairesis* is important for the assessment of our character because it reveals the end we aim at; hence in making our *prohairesis* clear, we also make clear the end we are aiming at (1366a14–16), and we counter any suggestion that we are acting on some motive that might leave us open to suspicion (1395a27–33). In making a good action appear to proceed from our *prohairesis,* we suggest that it did not result from rational calculation of our own benefit, but from concern for the fine that is independent of our benefit; the virtuous person even says that if he loses by doing the fine thing, that is better (1417a24–28). This last remark especially suggests why Aristotle might reasonably expect the readers of the Ethics to agree that the virtuous person must decide on the virtuous action for its own sake.

If, then, the brave person recognized by the *Rhetoric* fails to meet the conditions laid down in the Ethics for deciding on the brave action for its own sake, this is not because the *Rhetoric* completely ignores the demand for the right sort of decision. It must be because the *Rhetoric* relies on a less demanding view of what the right sort of decision must be like. Aristotle seems to assume (without specifically raising the question) that if we are ready to choose the virtuous action when we do not gain the ordinary sorts of advantages—wealth, power, social status, and so on—from it, then we decide on the virtuous action for its own sake. In the Ethics Aristotle does not assume this; we must also see that the action is worth choosing precisely because it is fine and virtuous, irrespective of the motives that underlie the bravery of citizens.

The treatment of magnanimity in the *Rhetoric* reveals a further difference from the Ethics. It is said to be a virtue that produces benefits on a large scale (1366b17). We can see from the Ethics why these results may be expected from a magnanimous person: he is the one who takes the appropriate attitude to great honors, and since he deserves great honors, he ought to receive them for great services. He does not waste his efforts on small benefits, but waits until he can do something suitable for his abilities (1124b23–26); this is why the *Rhetoric* regards him as a source of great services. This is not the main emphasis, however, in the Ethics. Aristotle takes the virtue of magnanimity to consist in the right attitude to great honor, and to external goods more generally. Magnanimous people do not identify their good primarily with external success, and that is why the right attitude to misfortune is the magnanimous attitude (1100b30–33). This aspect of magnanimity—the virtuous person's attitude to himself and his happiness—is not represented directly in the description given in the *Rhetoric*.

It is perhaps not entirely absent, however. Aristotle probably suggests that people tend to make a "willful," "self-pleasing" (*authadēs*) person seem better than he is by describing him as magnanimous (1367a38–1367b1).[32] He also recognizes that a person is appropriately praised for being magnanimous in ill fortune (1367b15–16). These aspects of magnanimity are not immediately intelligible if we refer simply to the description given in this chapter of the *Rhetoric,* but they are intelligible if we keep in mind the features of the magnanimous person that are highlighted in the Ethics.

This example should warn us against supposing that the descriptions of the virtues at the beginning of *Rhetoric* 1.9 are meant to be definitions or accounts that will adequately capture or suggest the range of the virtues, even for the purposes of rhetoric; for in the case of magnanimity Aristotle goes on to allude to aspects of the virtue that are not evidently contained in, or even suggested by, his initial description. It is better to suppose that the descriptions are intended to suggest the aspects of the virtues that constitute the most obvious grounds for praising them. The relevant aspects are the ones that make virtues beneficial to others; and so these are the aspects that are emphasized in the initial descriptions. From the point of view of the Ethics, we can see why it is reasonable to pick out these features of the virtues. We ought not to infer either that Aristotle believes he is giving adequate accounts of them, or even that common sense would recognize these as adequate accounts capturing all the relevant common beliefs. These points may help us to avoid exaggerated contrasts and oppositions between the views expressed in the *Rhetoric* and those expressed in the Ethics.

VIRTUE AND HAPPINESS

Despite all this, however, one sharp and striking contrast remains unexplained. The Ethics claim that virtue promotes the happiness of the virtuous individual, and so they argue against the view that there is any conflict between self-love and the sort of concern for the common good and the good of others that is expected of the virtuous person. The

Rhetoric mentions the virtues among the "parts" of happiness; we have seen, however, that it does not say either that they are parts of happiness itself rather than simply means to it (to use the contrast drawn in the *Eudemian Ethics*) or that they are to be preferred over other parts of happiness. Even the bare claim that they are parts of happiness plays no role in the chapter on the virtues and praise. Indeed, the reverse seems to be true; the contrast between concern for one's own good and concern for virtue seems to be presupposed in Aristotle's grounds for regarding some cases of virtuous action as especially deserving of praise.

How are we to account for this difference between the *Rhetoric* and the Ethics? We might suggest that the connection between virtue and the agent's happiness is strictly irrelevant for the purposes of the *Rhetoric*. The chapter on the virtues is concerned with them as subjects for praise; we praise people for their concern with the fine and with the good of others, and we might think that if it turns out that they really did what they did for their own good, there is no reason to praise them. Self-love can be assumed to be present in everyone, and everyone can be expected to do what they take to be required by self-love; actions done for this reason are apparently not suitable objects of praise.

This would not be a good reason for refusing to praise virtuous people who recognize that their virtue is part of their happiness. We praise virtuous people because they have a genuine concern for the fine, and people who believe that virtue is part of their happiness have a genuine concern for the fine. Moreover, we might actually suppose that people deserve more praise if they care so much about virtue that they cannot conceive their happiness as something separable from virtue. If virtuous people do not regard virtue as involving genuine self-sacrifice, that is because they do not identify themselves as agents whose central aims can be defined independently of the virtues.

Aristotle himself makes this point in *Nicomachean Ethics* 9.8, when he argues that people who identify self-love with selfishness simply have the wrong conception of the self whose aims are in question.

> [The virtuous person] most of all is a self-lover, but a different kind from the self-lover who is reproached, differing from him as much as the life guided by reason differs from the life guided by feelings, and as much as the desire for what is fine differs from the desire for what seems advantageous. (1169a3–6)[33]

This passage should be contrasted with the comment in the *Rhetoric* on elderly people who are said to lack magnanimity insofar as they are self-lovers more than they should be:

> and they live with a view to the advantageous, not with a view to the fine, more than they ought to, because they are self-lovers; for the advantageous

is good for oneself, while the fine is good without qualification. (1389b35–1390a1)

The three ethical works differ on the relation of self-love to virtue. The *Eudemian Ethics* does not discuss the issue at all. Both the *Magna Moralia* and the *Nicomachean Ethics* discuss it in the account of friendship, but they draw different conclusions. The *Magna Moralia* concludes that the virtuous person is not a lover of himself, but a lover of the good, since he loves himself only insofar as he is good, whereas the vicious person really is a lover of himself (1212b18–23). The *Nicomachean Ethics*, however, is unwilling to concede the title of "self-lover" to the vicious person; Aristotle argues that since the virtuous person is concerned about himself as a rational agent, and hence as what he essentially is, he is the genuine lover of himself.

Both the discussions of self-love in the Ethics imply that the claims in the *Rhetoric* are mistaken. It would have been entirely appropriate to the topics of the *Rhetoric* if Aristotle had argued that virtuous people deserve praise because they have fully integrated their concern for virtue with their concern for their own happiness, and do not regard virtue as involving real self-sacrifice.

But even if this sort of argument would be relevant, it might nonetheless be difficult to make convincing. At the beginning of the chapter where he argues for the reconciliation of virtue and self-love, Aristotle recognizes that his view is not generally shared:

> There is also a puzzle about whether one ought to love oneself or someone else most of all; for those who like themselves most are criticized and denounced as self-lovers, as though this were something shameful. Indeed, the base person does seem to go to every length for his own sake, and all the more the more vicious he is; hence he is accused, for instance, of doing nothing of his own accord.[34] The decent person, on the contrary, acts for what is fine, all the more the better he is, and for his friend's sake, disregarding his own good. (1168a28–35)

The attitude that Aristotle describes here in order to explain what is wrong with it is just the attitude that he takes in the *Rhetoric* in his discussions of virtue and self-love.

We might find it puzzling that in the *Rhetoric* Aristotle does not challenge the attitude that he rejects in the Ethics. For we might suppose that he has already suggested how it might be challenged. He has already said in 1.5 that happiness is the ultimate aim that we refer to in what we choose and avoid (1360b4–7). Virtuous people choose to do virtuous actions; if we understand their choices in the light of Aristotle's remarks about happiness, must we not agree that they choose virtuous actions for the sake of their happiness? There is nothing surprising about this, given that he mentions the virtues among the parts of happiness. We can infer that the virtuous person regards virtues as more important than external goods in the constitution of happiness. Once we see this, we cannot accept the assumption of 1.9 that virtuous action involves a sacrifice of one's own good to the fine and to the good of others. Aristotle's eudaemonism and his acceptance of the virtues leaves him with no escape from the claim that he makes in *Nicomachean Ethics* 9.8.

It would not be too difficult to present this argument in the *Rhetoric* if Aristotle wanted to present it. Why does he not present it? The discussion of self-love suggests that if ordinary people were presented with it, they would not be convinced that virtue promotes happiness; they would simply be forced into a puzzle, because they would face apparently cogent arguments with conflicting conclusions. On the one hand, the eudae-monist argument is difficult to resist; on the other hand, the conviction that virtuous people sacrifice their own good is equally difficult to shake off. In order to undermine this conviction Aristotle has to argue that people who believe in a conflict between virtue and self-love have a mistaken conception of the self; but to see the mistake in the popular conception, we have to pay attention to the aspects of human nature that are emphasized in the function argument. The function argument is prominent in the Ethics, but entirely absent in the *Rhetoric*.

To accept Aristotle's conception of happiness is to deny that happiness is simply a secure collection of external goods enjoyed by the agent. If, then, Aristotle tries to persuade us of his views about correct self-love, he must raise controversies about happiness that he avoids in the *Rhetoric*. In taking his side in these controversies, we must become more sympathetic to the Socratic view that virtue is sufficient for happiness; our sympathy must not lead us to accept the Socratic view, however, since Aristotle believes common sense is right in taking external goods to be necessary for happiness. Instead of modifying the connected common views that happiness consists of external goods and that virtue benefits other people at the agent's expense, Aristotle in the *Rhetoric* chooses to leave these views unquestioned and to argue from them.

A QUESTION ABOUT ARISTOTLE'S STRATEGY

The divergence between the *Rhetoric* and the Ethics can be explained, therefore, by appeal to Aristotle's desire to prevent the *Rhetoric* from raising puzzles about common beliefs. Once we see the puzzles, we have to take up moral philosophy in order to solve them; and the *Rhetoric* steers clear of moral philosophy. If we raise the puzzles, but do not turn to moral philosophy, then—Aristotle believes—our puzzlement leaves us at the mercy of sophists, and we cannot resist all sorts of absurd conclusions that seem to follow from the beliefs that raise the unsolved puzzles (cf. *NE* 1145b21–27).

We might wonder whether Aristotle is not taking a bigger risk than he ought to. Since the conflict between the eudaemonism of 1.5 and the claims about self-sacrifice in 1.9 is quite easy to point out, does he not leave his arguments open to potentially devastating criticism? It seems that someone who had learned even a few of Gorgias's skills could argue that no one ever deserves praise for anything, and no one is ever genuinely virtuous, since everyone is always looking out for his own interest. Not only could the critic make this nihilist argument about virtue; he could apparently show that all the premises can be derived from Aristotle's own claims in the *Rhetoric*. The general form of argument has not lost its appeal to students taking their first course in moral philosophy.

The nihilist argument, indeed, illustrates very clearly why Aristotle is right to insist that one ought to examine the principles underlying one's ethical beliefs. He suggests that if we do not do this, we will find that sophists bring in inappropriate arguments (*EE* 1216b36–1217a10; cf. 1218b23–24). Some of them do this because of ignorance, others because of empty pretension (*alazoneia*), and we are vulnerable to their arguments if we suffer from "lack of education" (*apaideusia*), inability to distinguish appropriate from inappropriate forms of argument. These comments on sophists and their audiences are somewhat similar to those that the *Rhetoric* makes on rhetoricians who fancy themselves as experts in political science; some do this because of empty pretension, others from lack of education, and others from other human weaknesses (1356a27–30). A proper understanding of ethical theory allows us to see through sophistic arguments (cf. *NE* 1146a21–31).[35]

Is it not, therefore, rather unwise of Aristotle to leave his rhetorical arguments open to this line of nihilistic challenge? Experience shows that the challenge is not rhetorically ineffective; it is just the sort of apparently sophisticated argument that can easily impress people who have not thought enough about the assumptions that support the nihilistic argument.

Aristotle's decision not to question common sense may be explained by his conviction that the puzzle about virtue and self-love is more easily stated than resolved. Both the eudaemonist assumption and the belief that virtue involves self-sacrifice are easily accepted; but the views about virtue, happiness, human nature, and the self that resolve the apparent conflict between virtue and happiness are difficult to appreciate without the sort of reflection that we cannot reasonably expect from the audiences that an orator addresses. Aristotle, therefore, prefers to appeal to different commonsense convictions about happiness and virtue without trying to reconcile them.

From looking at these chapters in the *Rhetoric* we can form some idea of what Aristotle regards as controversial parts of his arguments about virtue in the Ethics. Some general eudaemonist assumption is intuitively acceptable; the claim that the virtues both aim at fine action benefiting others and promote the agent's happiness is not controversial; but the claim that virtuous action is the most important component of the agent's happiness, and that therefore it never involves a genuine sacrifice of one's happiness is so controversial that Aristotle keeps it completely out of the picture in the *Rhetoric*, even though an appeal to it would have allowed the orator to appeal to a more consistent set of ethical assumptions. If we understand what is said and what is omitted in the *Rhetoric*, we can see more clearly what Aristotle takes to be the most difficult aspects of his task in the Ethics.

NOTES

In revising the first draft of this essay, I have benefited from comments by the editor and by Carlo Natali, and from the papers by John M. Cooper (1993) and Carlo Natali (1990 and 1993).

1. For convenience I will use "Ethics" (in roman, with initial capital) to refer to the *Magna Moralia*, *Eudemian Ethics*, and *Nicomachean Ethics* collectively. I take this to be the probable chronological order. (While I do not assume that Aristotle actually wrote the *MM*, I take it to embody an early course of his on ethics.)

2. Such reflections on the *Rhetoric* tend to support the general attitude displayed throughout Cope's introduction and commentary (Cope 1867, 1877). Cope regularly insists on the "popular" character of the ethical views presented in the *Rhetoric*, and contrasts them with the "scientific" treatment of the same ethical issues in the Ethics. Cope's view is opposed by Grimaldi 1980 and 1988; the issue is discussed by Natali 1990.

3. I have defended "common beliefs" as a translation of *endoxa*, in Irwin 1988, p. 494 n. 42, and more fully in Irwin 1987, p. 132 n. 16.

4. The relation between the *Rhetoric* and the *Gorgias* is discussed by Natali 1993.

5. Cf. *Met.* 1004b22–26.

6. The relation between rhetoric and political science is discussed well by Cooper 1994, p. 200. See also Lord 1981.

7. On Plato's discussion of this issue in the *Phaedrus* see Cooper 1994, p. 202; Natali 1993, p. 143.

8. Brunschwig 1967 translates "quand nous voudrons les persuader de renoncer à des affirmations qui nous paraîtront manifestement inacceptables." He refers to 161a33–37, where Aristotle distinguishes dialectical from eristic methods of changing people's point of view.

9. On the different uses of *aporein*, see Irwin 1987, pp. 120–124. None of the occurrences in the *Rhetoric* (1372a36, 1376a26, 1418a30, 1419a16) refers to a dialectical *aporia*.

10. Lord 1981, p. 335, argues from 1355a21–22 that Aristotle believes there are circumstances in which the orator must be able "to make the weaker argument the stronger." I do not see any reason to believe (as Lord seems to) that, in Aristotle's view, the orator ought to use this ability in order to argue dishonestly.

11. Literally "bodies," *sōmatōn.*

12. Grimaldi 1980, p. 105, claims "What we are given in the *Rhetoric* is the explanation of *eudaimonia* as it is commonly understood by the people *together with* an incorporation of some of the philosophical ideas which appear in *EN.*" The basis for "together with . . ." is not clear.

13. For the contrast between *haplous* and *akribēs* see *Met.* 1030a16. For *hōs haplōs eipein* see Bonitz 1870, 77b15.

14. Cope ad loc. (following Brandis 1849, p. 28) takes *estō* to mark "the popular character of the definitions that follow—as if it were a matter of indifference whether they are right or not, provided that they are so generally acceptable as to be certain to satisfy the audience." This seems to me to go too far in attributing indifference to Aristotle. In Cope 1867, p. 12, he cites 1369b31–32, which also fails to justify his claim. In his discussion of the definitions in the *Rhetoric* Cope seems not to distinguish two points: (*a*) the definitions do not meet the criteria for definitions that Aristotle accepts in other works; (*b*) Aristotle is indifferent to their truth or approximate truth. While (*a*) is correct, (*b*) is by no means obvious, and certainly does not follow from (*a*). Grimaldi ad loc. rejects Cope's claim about the use of *estō,* claiming that "the evidence for such usage . . . is not really adequate." He mentions 1355b23, where the definition of rhetoric is "quite precise." Fortenbaugh 1970 discusses *estō* at length (pp. 136–141). He points out correctly that the use of *estō* does not by itself imply that the account to be given is false or unimportant; he seems to me to react too far against Brandis and Cope when he suggests (if I understand him correctly) that Aristotle himself usually (though not always; see p. 134) accepts the accounts introduced with *estō.*

Fortenbaugh rightly draws attention (p. 140) to the use of *estō* in deductive arguments in the *Analytics* (*Cael.* 269b23 and 278a25 are difficult to classify). In the *Eudemian Ethics* premises taken for granted are more often marked by *hupokeisthō.* At 1219a23 *estō* appears to be used for a premise that Aristotle evidently accepts (but the text has been suspected). See also Natali 1990, pp. 54–55.

15. Ryan 1972 argues that the account of happiness and its parts in the *Rhetoric* is acceptable from the point of view of the Ethics. He does not discuss the differences I have emphasized.

16. This is only one way of interpreting the demand for security. Another interpretation suggests that the happy person is independent, as far as possible, from external goods, since they expose us to fortune. These two interpretations of security are relevant to Epicurus's remarks about it; see Diogenes Laertius, *Lives of the Philosophers* X 141, 143. But the second is not suggested in the *Rhetoric.*

17. Are these really popular views? Burnet 1900, p. 1, followed by Fortenbaugh 1970, pp. 134 ff., claims that Aristotle intends to cover the views current in the Academy, rather than popular views. He finds some Platonic and Academic parallels for the content of the second account, but none for the content of the first (he shows only that the form has some parallels in the *Topics* and in the

pseudo-Platonic *Definitions*). He suggests that the third account "is possibly that of Eudoxus, while the fourth alludes to the *hupēretikē dunamis* of Xenocrates." Xenocrates' account, however, describes happiness as *ktēsin tēs oikeias aretēs kai tēs hupēretikēs autē(i) dunameōs* (Burnet 1900, p. 3). This is quite different from the account that refers to *euthenia ktēmatōn kai sōmatōn meta dunameōs phulaktikēs kai praktikēs toutōn*. While Burnet may be right to suggest that Academic debate has influenced Aristotle's formulation of the different views about happiness, his case for the claim that the views themselves are Academic views is quite weak. Since the audiences that orators must address are not members of the Academy, a list of Academic accounts of happiness would not necessarily be very useful for the tasks that an orator must face.

18. On Aristotle's silence about "parts" of happiness in the *Nicomachean Ethics*, see Ackrill 1974, p. 29.

19. This argument uses distinctions that we find in *Rhet.* 1363b18–21, *Top.* 117a16–24 (closing the parenthesis in 117a24, following Brunschwig, not in 117a21, where the OCT [ed. W. D. Ross] closes it). But neither of these passages uses the distinctions to make the point about happiness that is made in the *Magna Moralia* and in the *Nicomachean Ethics* (1097b16–20).

20. See Natali 1990, p. 58.

21. Most manuscripts add *praotēs* after *eleutheriotēs* in 1366b2, but no description of the virtue is given. Cope, Grimaldi (citing 1367a35, 1380a5–1380b1), and Kassel retain *praotēs* in the text. I follow the OCT in deleting it.

22. *MM* 1.22 and *EE* 3.3 do not say that *praotēs* is a nameless virtue.

23. Some editors suspect *sophia* in 1366b3, but the manuscripts all contain it. If we are entitled to be doubtful about *praotēs* in 1366b2, the case for suspecting *sophia* is strengthened.

24. Reading *tēs teleias aretēs [teleia] chrēsis estin*, with Stewart 1892.

25. *MM* 1193b1–18 recognizes a type of justice as *teleia aretē*, but, contrary to the *Eudemian Ethics* and *Nicomachean Ethics*, argues that this sort of justice is not essentially *pros heteron*. This view is sharply different from the *Rhetoric*.

26. Cf. *Top.* 126a30–126b6.

27. Cope is probably wrong, therefore, to say that "instead of a *hexis* it [*sc.* virtue] is a mere *dunamis*, an undeveloped feeling or power" (Cope 1877, ad loc.; contrast Grimaldi).

28. See Cope 1877, vol. 2, p. 160; Grimaldi 1988, p. 211. Some general influence of the doctrine of the mean on Aristotle's rhetorical theory is suggested by Rosenfield 1965. It is not clear to me that this "influence" involves anything more than the vague advice to avoid extremes (which does not require the specific doctrine in the Ethics).

29. I have discussed the fine in the Ethics in Irwin 1985.

30. I agree with Gauthier and Jolif 1970 that 1117a4–5 (*phusikōtatē . . . andreia einai*) should be transposed to 1117a9 (after *echousi ti*).

31. Premeditation is connected with *prohairesis* at *NE* 1135b25–27, *EE* 1226b36–1227a1 (cf. *MM* 1189b3–6).

32. The reference to magnanimity here depends on accepting Cope's emendation of *megaloprepē* to *megalopsuchon*. Grimaldi retains the manuscript text,

suggesting that Aristotle uses *megaloprepē* in a Platonic sense. (Kassel may have the same point in mind in suggesting "sed circumscriptam illam *megaloprepeias* notionem hic laxavit philosophus"). This suggestion is rather implausible, given that Aristotle has just been careful to distinguish the sense of *megaloprepēs* and *megalopsuchos*. But even if the manuscript text is retained, it is still true that Aristotle's remark about the virtue relies on features that are not covered by the initial description of the virtue.

33. I read *oregesthai tou kalou* rather than *oregesthai ē tou kalou* (read by the OCT) in 1169a4–5.

34. Or perhaps "doing nothing away from himself." This translation is defended by Engberg-Pedersen 1983, p. 38.

35. It is tempting to follow Burnet in reading *entuchōsin* in 1146a23, referring to *enteuxeis* (see Section "*Rhetoric*, Ethics, and Common Beliefs," above).

REFERENCES

Ackrill, J. L., "Aristotle on Eudaimonia." In *Essays on Aristotle's Ethics*, ed. A. O. Rorty. Berkeley, 1980. Reprinted from *Proceedings of the British Academy* 60 (1974): 339–359.

Bonitz, H. *Index Aristotelicus*. In *Aristotlis Opera*, vol. 5, ed. I. Bekker. Berlin, 1870.

Brandis, C. A. "Ueber Aristoteles' *Rhetorik* und die griechischen Ausleger derselben." *Philologus* 4 (1849): 1–47.

Brunschwig, J., ed. *Topiques*. Vol. 1 [Books I–IV]. Paris, 1967.

Burnet, J., ed. *Aristotle: Ethics*. London, 1900.

Cooper, J. M. "Rhetoric, Dialectic, and the Passions." *Oxford Studies in Ancient Philosophy* 11 (1993): 175–198.

———. "Ethical-Political Theory in Aristotle's *Rhetoric*." In *Aristotle's Rhetoric: Philosophical Essays*, ed. D. J. Furley and A. Nehamas. Princeton, 1994.

Cope, E. M. *An Introduction to Aristotle's Rhetoric*. London, 1867.

———. *The Rhetoric of Aristotle, with a Commentary*, rev. and ed. J. E. Sandys. 3 vols. Cambridge, 1877.

Engberg-Pedersen, T. *Aristotle's Theory of Moral Insight*. Oxford, 1983.

Fortenbaugh, W. W. "Aristotle's *Rhetoric* on Emotions." In *Articles on Aristotle*, vol. 4, ed. J. Barnes, M. Schofield, and R. Sorabji. London, 1979. Reprinted from *Archiv für Geschichte der Philosophie* 52 (1970): 40–70.

Gauthier, R. A., and J. Y. Jolif, eds. and trans. *L'Ethique à Nicomaque*. 2d ed. 4 vols. Louvain, 1970.

Grimaldi, W. M. A., ed. *Aristotle: Rhetoric I: A Commentary*. New York, 1980.

———. *Aristotle: Rhetoric II: A Commentary*. New York, 1988.

Irwin, T. H. "Aristotle's Concept of Morality." *Proceedings of the Boston Area Colloquium in Ancient Philosophy* 1 (1985): 115–143.

———. "Ways to First Principles." *Philosophical Topics* 15 (1987): 109–134.

———. *Aristotle's First Principles*. Oxford, 1988.

Kassel, R., ed. *Aristotelis Ars Rhetorica*. Berlin, 1976.

Lord, C. "The Intention of Aristotle's *Rhetoric*." *Hermes* 109 (1981): 326–339.

Natali, C. "Due modi di trattare le opinioni notevole. La nozione di felicità in Aristotele, *Retorica* I 5." *Methexis* 3 (1990): 51–63.

———. "Opinioni, verità, prassi in Aristotele e la recente rivaluazione della retorica." In *Dimonstrazione, argomentazione dialettica, e argomentazione retorica nel pensiero antico,* ed. A. M. Bategazzore. Genoa, 1993.

Rosenfield, L. W. "The Doctrine of the Mean in Aristotle's *Rhetoric.*" *Theoria* 31 (1965): 191–198.

Ryan, E. E. "Aristotle's *Rhetoric* and *Ethics* and the Ethos of Society." *Greek, Roman, and Byzantine Studies* 13 (1972): 291–308.

Stewart, J. A. *Notes on the Nicomachean Ethics of Aristotle.* 2 vols. Oxford, 1892.

The Challenge of Rhetoric to Political and Ethical Theory in Aristotle

Stephen Halliwell

Within the conceptual framework of Aristotelian thought there exists an apparently firm separation between the art of rhetoric, conceived as a general facility of persuasion, and the province of *politikē*, whose concern, on the philosopher's understanding, is the realization of the human good in the activity of both individual and communal lives. Aristotle had pressing reasons for requiring the subordination of rhetoric to *politikē*, and for insisting on a distinction that, in his view, had been dangerously compromised by the tendencies of Sophistic culture.[1] The *Rhetoric* itself borrows a theatrical metaphor from Plato's *Gorgias* (464c) in making this very point, when it alleges that rhetoric, in the sciolistic claims of certain proponents, sometimes illicitly masquerades as, or slips into the guise of, *politikē*.[2] Yet this negative remark occurs in the same passage where Aristotle employs another, more positive metaphor to acknowledge that rhetoric's necessary engagement with ethical and political matters makes it an "offshoot" of *politikē*. Already here we can discern a significant poise of considerations within the Aristotelian reappraisal of rhetoric against the inescapable background of Plato's critique of its nature and status. This aspect of the *Rhetoric* assumes special importance in the work of a thinker whose own philosophical contribution to *politikē* recognizes contact at various points with the domain of current morality in which the major forms of Greek rhetoric were actively and extensively implicated. Aristotle is not just an informative witness to popular morality;[3] he reckons with some of its content inside the processes of his own ethical thought. It should therefore prove worthwhile to attend to his handling of that demarcation between (philosophical) ethics and rhetoric, not only in order to refine our interpretation of his conception of rhetoric as such, but also in the hope that some indirect light may be shed on his enterprise in ethics as a whole.[4]

Aristotle acknowledges that, despite its lack of a circumscribable subject matter, most of the premises or propositions of rhetoric belong in practice to special domains of knowledge or expertise (1.2.22.58a26–28), and it is immediately apparent from the preliminary account of the "ends" of the three kinds of rhetoric, at 1.3.5.58b20–29, that each of them has a salient interest in ethical and political matters. With symbouleutic oratory in particular, this might give some plausibility to the thought that the better the rhetorician, the more of a true *politikos* he will be, uniting the two spheres within an indivisible understanding of souls and societies, and thereby, perhaps, providing one fulfillment for the ideal prescribed in Plato's *Phaedrus*. Rhetoric, on this admittedly normative reading, could be appropriately deemed a part of the exercise of political excellence that is needed, according to *Politics* 4.4.1291a40–1291b2, for the success both of civic deliberation and of judicial justice. But how far can the *Rhetoric* itself be said to envisage or endorse any such possibility?

The answer adumbrated by the explicit comments on the relation of rhetoric to *politikē* at 1.2.7.56a20–30 involves a balance of considerations, both sides of which reveal traces of Platonic influence. Aristotle first proposes what sounds close to a requirement for expertise, on the rhetorician's part, in moral psychology (a capacity for reasoning and reflective understanding about character, virtue, and emotion), only to follow this with his forceful aspersion on Sophistic pretensions to political wisdom. This combination of attitudes is clarified, and somewhat readjusted in tone at least, at 1.2.21.1358a23–28, where Aristotle explains that, in rhetoric as in dialectic, the more successful the choice of premises, the more the art will converge upon and turn into some other *epistēmē*. Here, and in a similar though more obviously paradoxical passage a little later (1.4.6–7.1359b12–18),[5] we do not seem to be far from an admission that rhetoric and *politikē* can be cogently combined, or, more precisely, that the practice of outwardly rhetorical art can become the locus of properly ethical and political reasoning. Strictly understood, however, what this yields is a model of rhetoric that allows it to aspire to something of the condition of *politikē*, yet leaves it apparently incapable of achieving that aspiration: since to do so, on Aristotle's terms, would be to relinquish its purely rhetorical status and to become something different. The point is further exemplified in a context where, after stressing the deliberative orator's need for political knowledge and a wide-ranging familiarity with laws, peoples, and history, Aristotle feels a pressure to reassert his fundamental partition: "But all this is the task of *politikē*, not of rhetoric."[6]

In these passages, and in the tenor of the treatise more generally, there is reason to identify a distinctive but somewhat elusive response to what we can broadly characterize as a tension between Platonic and Isocratean principles.[7] Aristotle has both conceptual and methodological reasons for maintaining a basic distinction between rhetoric and *politikē*. But he is faced—in part because of the dynamics of Greek political culture (the most intensely rhetorical culture, perhaps, of which we know),[8] in part because of his own sense of the way in which certain possibilities of ethical value depend upon the civic forms of life available within a community—with the problem of how far to recognize the potential of rhetoric to function as an activity or expression of *politikē* in the full sense of an ethico-political architectonic or master art. If 1.2.21.1358a23–28 represents a solution to this problem, it is one that apparently entails the conviction that rhetoric can be no more than an indirect medium for *politikē*: "For if he [the rhetorician or dialectician] encounters [comes face-to-face with *or* reaches][9] first principles, it will no longer be dialectic or rhetoric but the sphere whose first principles he grasps" (1.2.21. 1358a25–26). As part of a general reaffirmation of the idea that rhetoric is an art without an intrinsic subject matter of its own, and hence without any internally specifiable grasp of a particular body of ideas, this seems readily intelligible. But where issues of *politikē* are concerned, and *politikē* in an (for Aristotle) appropriately active rather than purely theoretical character, an emphasis on the extensively ethical and political interests of rhetoric, from the level of definition upward (1.3.5.1358b20–29), sits uneasily with his separation of the two realms. This separation could only be made secure, I suggest, if *politikē* were to be required to satisfy conditions of theoretical abstraction and systematization—the conditions, in short, of a science—to which Aristotle's own philosophical ethics does not in fact wholly or consistently aspire.

If, on the other hand, the "first principles" of *politikē* can be equated with the practical ends, the *archai tōn praktōn*, posited by the *Nicomachean Ethics*,[10] it remains far from clear why they should not, when appropriate, be encompassed by the persuasive aims of a suitably endowed and conscientious rhetorician; why arguments "from" and "to" such principles cannot sometimes be conveyed by the reasoning of well-grounded political oratory; and why, more especially, the procedures of symbouleutic oratory should not conform, on a civic scale, to the various types of practical reasoning, the *sullogismoi tōn praktōn*, which are postulated within the philosopher's own ethical thought.[11] These possibilities seem all the more plausible, and therefore all the more threatening to the clean separation between rhetoric and *politikē*, if we take into account what the *Rhetoric* itself, with its itemization and hence atomization of the resources of the art, tends to underestimate, namely the scope for substantial structures of oratorical thought (a point, incidentally, on which Aristotle's credibility might be thought to be reduced by some of our surviving evidence for actual Greek oratory).[12] Besides, some of the details and ramifications of Aristotle's treatise do themselves help to reveal, I wish to argue, the delicacy of a demarcation that the philosopher is yet so anxious to protect. I propose to elaborate this observation by attending to the place in the *Rhetoric* of two concepts—practical wisdom (*phronēsis*) and expediency (*to sumpheron*)—which can shed light on the boundary between the popular morality exploited by rhetoric, on the one hand, and the principles of Aristotelian *politikē*, on the other.

Rhetoric functions, and shows its effects, within processes of judgment. Those forms of rhetoric that are integral to the fabric of civic life[13] are typically directed to judgment of ethical particulars; as such, they are both virtually coextensive with the activity of judgment that partly defines citizenship (*Polit.* 3.1.1275a23) and convergent upon the concern with action that is basic to *politikē* itself (see *NE* 1.1.1095a5–6). These remarks are especially and tellingly applicable to symbouleutic oratory, for three reasons: its function instantiates the general ethical process of deliberation, *bouleuesthai* (1.2.12.1357a1–7; 1.4.3.1359a37–38), and hence bears precisely upon choices of action; its judges are directly involved with their own affairs;[14] and its issues or ends, virtually by definition, coincide with those of *politikē* itself.[15] If one were to take seriously Aristotle's allowance that persuasion may aim at a single judge, rhetoric—perhaps indistinguishable at this level from some exercises of dialectic—might seem to have a ubiquitous role to play in the lives of individuals as well as that of the community as a whole.[16] But since this last point is marginal to the work (see 3.12.5.1414a11–12), it is with the implications for symbouleutic rhetoric in its central political forms that we most need to engage.

The judgment occurrent in rhetorical contexts involves an interplay between audience and rhetorician; it is the entire institutional procedure, not the persuasive speech alone, which carries the processes of deliberation, decision, and action. Although final judgment as such is made by the auditors (they vote), Aristotle appears to assume that the main determinant of it will be the skill of the orator. At the same time, the material on which this skill is manipulatively exercised is, in large part, the substance of popular morality as embodied in the convictions presumed to be widely shared by a representative audience. As regards the possible activity of *politikē* generated by this interplay, it seems apt to adduce the distinction drawn at *NE* 6.11.1142b34–1143a24 between *phronēsis*, an excellence of active and "commanding" intelligence, and *sunesis*, a capacity to judge well in the same sphere as *phronēsis* but "when someone else speaks." *Sunesis* is of general political importance; it provides a broad ground of civic deliberation (see *Polit.* 4.4.1291a28). Although, on a normative view, *phronēsis* too is called for by the whole apparatus of political deliberation and judgment (*Polit.* 7.9.1329a2–9), a realistic appraisal of actual constitutions will presumably conclude that this is a virtue to be expected more in exceptional practitioners than in typical audiences of rhetoric.[17] What has already been said about Aristotle's attitudes to audiences of oratory indeed suggests some radical limitations on rhetoric's potential as a medium or locus of *politikē*. But it is necessary to ask at this point how much scope the treatise allows for an ethical or political expertise embodied in the *phronēsis* of the orator himself: can the good orator lift the rhetorical exercise above the level of a mechanical or uncritical popular morality?

Phronēsis is included, at 1.9.5.1366b3, in the list of virtues of which the rhetorician must have some grasp, and its definition in this context (1.9.13.1366b20–22) approximates to what we are given at, for example, *Nicomachean Ethics* 6.5.1140a25–31. The implication of this ought to be that the conception of *phronēsis* as a virtue is itself some kind of *endoxon*, since such is the declared status of all the propositions that Aristotle records as serviceable to the rhetorician.[18] But it is a significant feature of the work's discourse as a whole that its account of popularly acceptable premises is subtly colored, even to some degree overlaid, by views that are identifiably Aristotle's own. This is not to say that Aristotle in any obvious sense selects *endoxa* that favor his own ethical views; but rather that his formulation of certain common principles and values allows us to discern a convergence between them and the philosopher's commitments. The result is that the text seems sometimes suspended, as it were, between the exposition and endorsement of *endoxa,* and this in itself reflects and exemplifies the intricate relation of Aristotelian ethics to popular morality. The terms in which *phronēsis* is defined in 1.9.13 thus supply a particular instance of a more or less pervasive problem in the interpretation of Aristotle's stance toward the material he collects and categorizes in this treatise. We are inside the domain of popular morality with which the rhetorician needs to negotiate, yet we are simultaneously moving over ground that has recognizable and revealing affinities with the stricter arguments of the ethical treatises: the result is that we may feel we can hear Aristotle's own voice, so to speak, in or through some of the *endoxa* which he records.

If *phronēsis* is an excellence of deliberative reasoning, so that *phronimos* and *euboulos* are virtually synonymous,[19] we should expect symbouleutic oratory to give special opportunities for it. *Phronēsis* in this context will be the markedly political variety that in the ethical works is actually called *politikē* and attributed to figures such as Pericles; it will, moreover, be an asset peculiarly appropriate to leaders, not to the mass of ordinary citizens, and hence, in the rhetorical context, to speakers not audiences.[20] The *Rhetoric*'s main acknowledgment of the possibility of such *phronēsis* on the part of the orator comes in Book 2, where it is specified as one cause, alongside virtue and goodwill, of the impression of conviction or trust-worthiness that can be carried by a speaker's character (2.1.5–7.1378a6–19). But what is immediately striking here is the seemingly sharp sepa-ration of *phronēsis* and *aretē:* it is clearly implied, quite contrary to the main conception of *phronēsis* elaborated in the ethical works, that a speaker may possess the first without the second.[21] *Phronēsis* in the orator is understood to be a calculative and rational capacity that need not be directed to ethically laudable ends, and this makes it coincide with what in the ethical writings is called "cleverness" (*deinotēs*) in distinction to *phronēsis*.[22] If we can take Aristotle to be relying here on a popular not a philosophical conception (note the nature of the first-person plural at 2.1.5.1378a8), there has now emerged a gap between these two (and hence an issue about the axis between philosophy and popular morality) that was not visible in the definition of *phronēsis* as a "part" of virtue in Book 1.

A similar fluctuation in emphasis seems also to occur in those passages in which *phronēsis*, or the *phronimos*, is cited as an authority to which the orator's audience is likely to respond and to which he can therefore appeal (see *Top.* 3.1.116a14, 6.6.145a26). In the fullest of these, 1.7.21.1364b11–19, the judgments of *phronēsis* are clearly proffered as a criterion of "good" or value, as indeed they earlier were at 1.7.3.1363b14–15 (coupled with *nous*). The last two of these passages contain some characteristic Aristotelian formulations (especially the notion of the good as "what everything aims at," 1.6.2.1362a23), but these are used to enforce the principle that *phronēsis* can be popularly exploited as an authority in rhetorical persuasion. When the same point is made at 1.6.25.1363a16–19, the reference to mythological exempla and to poetry underlines the nonphilosophical tenor of the observations, and the same is true of the attribution of *phronēsis* to the elderly and the educated at 2.6.17.1384a33–34. But in neither of these cases is there any necessary incompatibility with the stricter understanding of *phronēsis* that *Nicomachean Ethics* 6 offers.[23]

What, then, can these brief references to *phronēsis* in the *Rhetoric* tell us?[24] If nothing else, they provide illustration of some common ground between the *endoxa* of popular morality and the stricter definitions of Aristotle's own thought, and by the same token they intimate that the standards of practical wisdom and insight that *phronēsis* represents do have a purchase on the general audiences of rhetoric: in this sense, they suggest a real possibility that deliberations conducted by means of rhet-oric may conform with values that a philosophically respectable *politikē* could avow as its own. At the same time, the treatise cannot be said to leave the impression that it attaches great weight to this possibility, whose implications are limited in at least two ways: first, the extent to which Aristotle believes that *phronēsis* prevails over other forces (such as vulgar prejudices not shared by any *phronimos*) in actual rhetorical situations remains uncertain; second, insofar as rhetoricians are assumed to be skilled exponents of *phronēsis*, this attribute is regarded principally as a type of calculative acuteness, akin to the *deinotēs* of the ethical works, which need not carry any deeper ethical or political wisdom with it.[25] The *phronēsis* of the *Rhetoric* seems, therefore, to illustrate an equivocal Aristotelian view of the functioning of popular morality in the context of civic deliberations.

In the hope of characterizing this view more fully, I want now to consider the place of *to sumpheron*—"advantage," "utility," "benefit," "expediency," "self-interest" (none of these translations being singly adequate for all occurrences of the term)—in the scheme of the *Rhetoric*. A link between *phronēsis* and advantage is indicated by one further passage in which the former is mentioned. At 3.16.9.1417a23–27, Aristotle states that the *phronimos* typically pursues what is beneficial (*ōphelimon*, a term near-synonymous with *sumpheron*), while the good man pursues what is noble (*kalon*).[26] This may appear only to reinforce the impression that *phronēsis* in the *Rhetoric* is a more amorally calculative faculty than its namesake in the ethical works. But a qualification is at once necessitated by the fact that an alignment of *phronēsis* with *sumpheron* is equally affirmed in the ethical treatises too, and in a way that helps to intimate that *sumpheron* is itself of basic, although problematic, ethical significance: "We take it to be the part of a *phronimos* to be able to deliberate well about what is good and advantageous for him, not in some partial way . . . but with a view to living well."[27] If the requirements of advantage properly belong to the deliberations of *phronēsis* even in the refined sense of the term used in the ethical treatises, this encourages us to look to the *Rhetoric*'s treatment of *sumpheron* for a sharper sense of how Aristotle takes popular morality to function within the most "political" branch of the art (1.1.10.1354b24). For advantage is, of course, stated to be the supreme concern of deliberative oratory (1.3.5–6.1358b20–36, 1.6.1.1362a17–18), and in view of the observation that it is a standard by which "all men are persuaded" (1.8.2.1365b25), it has a claim to be regarded as paradigmatic of the content and workings of popular morality.

I have already cited two passages (2.1.5–7.1378a6–19, 3.16.9.1417 a23–27) that prompt the reflection that *sumpheron* is a criterion of value detachable from ethical virtue. The *Rhetoric* seems more pervasively to sustain such a view by both general and particular contrasts between utility and either justice or nobility: thus, for instance, a man may be praised for the nobility of voluntarily facing a certain kind of death in preference to the inglorious expediency of saving his life (1.3.6.1359a1–6; cf. *NE* 9.8.1169a19–26); and choosing between such values is more broadly referred to as a factor in moral behavior (e.g., 2.12.12.1389a34–36, 2.13.9.89b36–90a1). The practitioners of symbouleutic oratory are said to be prepared to sacrifice, on occasion, all consideration of justice, but they would never admit that their proposals were deficient in expediency (1.3.6.1358b33–37). Moreover, *sumpheron* seems, on the face of it, to be an intrinsically selfish or self-regarding criterion: by definition, it refers always to the advantage or benefit of an "interested party," whereas nobility offers an express contrast to this (1.9.17–19.1366b36–1367a61, 2.13.9.1390a1), and virtue in general is held by Aristotle, in the *Rhetoric* at any rate, to involve behavior that benefits others (*euergetein*).[28] Twice, indeed, the *Rhetoric* cites the idea—as a commonplace, and hence rhetorically serviceable, prejudice—that human beings are, in harsh reality, incorrigibly committed to pursuing self-interest, however much their public professions might suggest otherwise.[29] All this appears to fit well with the thesis, shared by some modern scholars with Plato, that it was rhetoric itself, and its exploitation by hard-headed Sophistic "realism" or *realpolitik,* which had established and disseminated the notion of expediency as a dominant mechanism of human behavior, especially in struggles for political power.[30]

But it would be premature to attribute to Aristotle any such unqualified view of the place of *sumpheron* in either rhetorical arguments or the popular morality on which they rest. Two points are fundamental here, and their combined import justifies a reappraisal of the idea that *sumpheron* exists in essential and necessary detachment from, or conflict with, justice and nobility. The first, assumed in the pairing of "good and advantageous" at *Nicomachean Ethics* 6.5.1140a25–28 (quoted earlier), and extensively elaborated in *Rhetoric* 1.4–6.1359a30–1363b4, is that expediency falls unequivocally within the sphere of ethically pertinent values or "goods" (*agatha*).[31] The second is that expediency is not a single or invariable criterion, but a mode of construing or applying the notion of value ("good") in relation to the interests of particular agents: as such it requires, but does not presuppose in a given form, a notion of just what counts as being in the interests of an agent. The diversity of considerations that can be embraced by the description of *sumpheron* is conveniently illustrated in passing (although by a quite deliberate juxtaposition) at *Rhetoric* 1.1.7. 1354b4–9, where the concept is first coupled with justice as the appropriate object of judicial judgments, but also appears, qua private or personal advantage (*to idion sumpheron*), as something that can jeopardize the very jurisprudential standards that those judgments ought to sustain.[32]

The distinction between private and public in this last passage is crucial to an understanding of the role of *sumpheron* in symbouleutic oratory. It is the public world of politics, not that of private morality, to which such oratory belongs, whereas many of the passages in the *Rhetoric* which emphasize the limited scope of expediency as narrow self-interest refer directly to the personal behavior of individuals. The political dimension of *sumpheron* means that what is perceived as advantageous or expedient for a society or a state depends on the larger character of its constitution, and it is expressly in this connection that the remark "all men are persuaded by advantage" occurs (1.8.2.1365b25).[33] As the immediate continuation indicates ("and what is to a state's advantage is that which preserves it"), this principle does not mark a general tendency to amoral calculations, but one of the essential conditions of a civic community's existence:[34] *sumpheron* here is not a narrow or optional value, but a systematically (and therefore legally) necessary requisite for a political society; it is assuredly something with which the true *politikos*, whether as a leader of deliberations or in the role of lawgiver, would have to reckon. This view is given a strongly Aristotelian cast by his frequent endorsement of the idea—which of course has Platonic antecedents, but is presented at 1.15.7.1375b3–4, as a popular *endoxon* too—that justice itself is a shared benefit or communal *sumpheron, to koinē sumpheron*.[35] The positive import of the thought behind this position appears in passages such as *Politics* 3.6.1278b21–23 and *Nicomachean Ethics* 8.11.1160a8–25, where it is contended that the common advantage embodied in justice is something that generates possibilities of good life, *kalōs zēn*, for those who participate in the civic order (who will of course need, for the fullest realization of this principle, to be "citizens" in the stronger Aristotelian sense of the term). The common advantage is not to be perceived solely in terms of a distribution of material goods, or equality of protection from material harm; it resides, as a principle and a potential, in the enabling conditions that justice provides for certain kinds of purposive and therefore moral living: from this perspective, we could say, it is as though self-interest is politically sublimated and transformed into a social precondition of human excellence. Here, then, is one important strand in an Aristotelian view of the vexed relationship between morality and self-interest.[36]

This recognition of the close interrelation of *sumpheron* and justice on the political level can be complemented by attention to the *Rhetoric*'s exegesis of the former as a good. What needs to be appreciated here is that it is only in a partial or limited sense that *sumpheron* can be interpreted as instrumental or consequentialist in character. Symbouleutic oratory, as a medium of deliberation, is concerned with choices aimed at the final end (of *eudaimonia*, 1.5.2.1360b7–11); and Aristotle defines the content of such choices as a matter of practically realizable *sumpheron* (1.6.1. 1362a18–20). *Sumpheron*, being here virtually synonymous with considerations "conducive to the end" (*pros to telos*, 1.8.5.1366a2–8), represents no circumscribable group of objects or standards, and no restriction to the external aids or instruments of *eudaimonia*, but rather an evaluative mode of bringing conceptions of "good" to bear on the situation of an individual agent or group: to perceive the good, in other words, will sometimes involve, and be involved in, seeing what is advantageous for oneself or one's community. Aristotle's explanation in this context of what it is to be a good, which is intended to illuminate the nature of arguments from *sumpheron,* intertwines possibilities of instrumentality and finality, and thus lends confirmation to the independently arguable idea that the phrase "conducive to the end" (*pros to telos*) has a more complex scope than that of merely external means to an end.

On the *Rhetoric*'s account, the basic criterion of a good is that it be chosen for its own sake; yet the description "good" also applies to things that are expressly productive of, or conducive to, other goods (1.6.2.1362a21–29). The implication of this is specifically borne out by the remark at 1.10.16.1369b7–9 that considerations of *sumpheron* may be chosen either as a *telos* (see 2.19.26.1393a13–14) or "as conducive to the end" (*hōs pros to telos*). This analysis, being designed to suit the workings of rhetoric in relation to popular morality, matches the fact that the conception of *eudaimonia* in 1.5.1360b4–1362a14 is not a tightly unitary one, but a kind of pluralist cluster or congeries of values that cut across the instrumental/intrinsic distinction.[37] It seems, then, that the considerations of advantage or benefit that typically decide political deliberations may be conceived in particular cases either as directly satisfying a prevailing sense of a community's overriding well-being (so that utility would here be equated with the *telos*), or as contributing, whether instrumentally or as subordinate but constitutive components, to the further attainment of such prosperity. The difference might hinge, for example, on whether deliberative choices are seen within an immediate and relatively self-contained context, or viewed in the longer-term perspective of a city's continued existence and flourishing. In the latter case, arguments from *sumpheron* might, at the highest, be used not to advocate a particular action but in the framing of a law that would regulate many future actions;[38] and as such they would entail a concern with justice, or the common advantage, which we have already seen to be a crucial aspect of Aristotle's interpretation of *sumpheron* in a civic context.

Seen in this light, the relation of *sumpheron* to the just and the noble comes to appear as much less of a straightforward contrast or antithesis than certain passages might superficially lead us to suppose. This is not, of course, to ignore the thrust of those passages, for what they refer to remains entirely intelligible: that there are indeed ethical situations in which perceptions of the expedient and the just might conflict, producing a disjunctive choice between the two (see 1.3.6.1358b33–37 again). But this is wholly compatible with the larger tenet that the pursuit of what is deemed advantageous or beneficial to a certain party is a good in its own right, and need not fundamentally or persistently clash with other criteria of moral value. Expediency understood as crudely or brutally selfish action is a form of behavior that does not capture the essence or whole scope of *sumpheron*; there is no invariable equivalence, we might say, between *sumpheron* and the unjust excesses of *pleonexia*. The former always makes intrinsic reference to some interest of the person or community concerned (and thus differs from the ostensibly disinterested character of *to kalon*, though less clearly from justice),[39] but its function within processes of ethical reasoning is not thereby reduced to a mere calculation of material gain, for all depends on just what and how much the conception of "interest" is allowed to encompass. We can thus readily imagine contexts (say, political decisions regarding war and peace) in which a judgment of self-interest might be indivisible from an inclination to the exercise of courage and other virtues. Nothing in the *Rhetoric* suggests a confidence that this commonly occurred in actual Greek states, any more than in the lives of individuals: we are not dealing here with an unrealistically optimistic outlook. But it remains clear, I submit, that Aristotle did believe a harmonization of *sumpheron* with justice and nobility was ethically conceivable on the political (and indeed on the personal) plane of action.[40] It is an incidental but interesting reflection of this belief, I think, that the term *ta sumpheronta* is used at *Nicomachean Ethics* 2.2.1104a4 as though it characterized something of the subject matter of ethics as a whole.[41]

If this is right, the dominant place of expediency within the *Rhetoric*'s account of symbouleutic persuasion does not amount to an inherently or irredeemably unfavorable judgment on this major component in popular political morality. It yields, in fact, a position that is not only consistent with, but actually related to, my earlier conclusions about the status of *phronēsis* in the treatise. *Phronēsis* is the skill or excellence most called for in the rhetorician who works in the deliberative domain where *sumpheron* prevails; the *phronimos* orator will be the person best able to discern, calculate, and persuasively convey the advantage that has the most direct purchase on the minds of political audiences. How far the *phronēsis* of such an orator can incorporate, or his audience's sense of expediency be responsive to, a grasp of political and ethical principles fuller and richer than a narrowly amoral construal of self-interest would permit, is something on which Aristotle offers no simple or definitive finding. Neither the orator's skill nor the values on which he depends can guarantee ethico-political understanding or the virtues needed for its enactment; rhetorical art is compatible with *prohairesis* of very divergent kinds.[42] Yet the *Rhetoric* remains open to the possibility that the orator's engagement with popular morality will sometimes, and not accidentally, succeed in contributing to the realization of the human good, and will do so in ways that embrace legitimate appeals to the criteria both of *phronēsis* and of *to sumpheron*.

If this leaves us close to where we started, with an essentially ambiguous and inconclusive verdict on the potential involvement of the rhetorician in the tasks of a philosophically respectable *politikē*, we should by now, I think, be prepared to regard this very indeterminacy as an ineliminable and thoroughly significant feature of the work's interpretation of its subject. Despite intermittent affinities with the ideas of both thinkers, the *Rhetoric* largely eschews both the Platonic proposal for a philosophical revision of rhetoric and the Isocratean attempt to redefine the relation of rhetoric to philosophy by collapsing the distinction into a new model of *politikoi logoi* (13.21, 15.46, 15.260). Aristotle accepts the existence and the validity of a rhetoric unregenerated by philosophical means. He countenances the fact that the functions of persuasion can be independent of the grounding commitments on which his own conception of a philosophical ethics and politics is built, but he nonetheless concedes the capacity of rhetoric to serve as a vital expression of the forces and processes of civic morality.[43]

Yet this concession is underpinned by a finally uncompromised demarcation between rhetoric and *politikē;* and that this should be so is a reflection on Aristotle's conception of the latter as much as his attitude to the former. To the extent that *politikē* is an art of the practical, actively focused on given actualities and conditioned by the ethical *endoxa* of its culture, there are unavoidable difficulties in seeing how it can itself aspire to anything more than a form of "conviction," *pistis*.[44] But in this case, rhetoric (within Greek culture, but not there alone) can make a forceful claim to be accepted as a necessary, integral agency for the formation and operation of the principles of *politikē*. Aristotle's ultimate resistance to this inference is due, it seems to me, to the faith that the truest *politikē* must also make some room for theoretical procedures of abstraction, analysis and systematization, as well as a commitment to cohesion and depth of understanding (a grasp of first principles, a hierarchy of values), which only an enterprise deserving the name of philosophy can hope to supply.[45] Because of this, we ought to recognize that part of what is at issue within and behind the arguments of the *Rhetoric* is Aristotle's own project—Aristotle's ambition—for a philosophical ethics that can maintain itself on a level lying somewhere between the flawed compromises of popular morality and the final certainties of "science."

NOTES

This paper is an abbreviated version of my "Popular Morality, Philosophical Ethics, and the *Rhetoric*," *Aristotle's Rhetoric: Philosophical Essays*, ed. D. J. Furley and A. Nehamas (Princeton, 1994). The main difference is the removal of a stretch of preliminary argument that appeared on pp. 212–216. I am grateful to Amélie Rorty for her advice.

1. Subordination: *NE* 1.1.1094b3. Sophists: *NE* 10.10.1181a12–15, with context. Cf. Plato, *Sophist* 304b–e, which need not be earlier than *Rhet.* 1.2.7.1356 a27–28.

2. *Rhet.* 1.2.7.1356a27–28 (unfortunately mistranslated in the new version by H. C. Lawson-Tancred, *The Art of Rhetoric* [Harmondsworth, 1991], p. 75); resemblances to *Met.* 3.2.1004b17–26, *EE* 1.6.1216b40–1217a7, are pertinent.

3. Although I take him to be that too: see C. Taylor, "Popular Morality and Unpopular Philosophy," *"Owls to Athens": Essays on Classical Subjects Presented to Sir Kenneth Dover*, ed. E. Craik (Oxford, 1990).

4. My argument is independent of specific chronological hypotheses, although I make the conservative assumption that our *Rhetoric,* whatever its history of composition, received some attention from Aristotle in his second Athenian period. The recent treatment of dating in J. M. Rist, *The Mind of Aristotle: A Study in Philosophical Growth* (Toronto, 1989), pp. 85–86, 136–144, is unsatisfactory. Rist does not properly consider the idea that many of the *Rhetoric*'s propositions are "raw" *endoxa;* his detailed arguments also contain some blemishes, not least the contradiction between pp. 85 (with incorrect reference), 138, 141 and, on the other hand, p. 303 n. 19, in the interpretation of *Rhetoric* 1.8.7. 1366a22.

5. The paradox resides in the combination of *peiratai* with *lēsetai.* In fact, the earlier passage too contains the paradox, since it is hard to see how one can "unwittingly" (*lēsei,* 1.2.21.1358a24) engage in a form of knowledge whose first principles one "grasps" (*echei,* 1.2.21.1358a26, with note 9 of this essay).

6. *Rhet.* 1.4.12–13.1360a17–38; cf. 1.8.1.1365b22–25. Note also that the use of such "documentary" material could be of benefit only to those with an existing *hexis* and ability to judge: *NE* 10.10.1181b1–12.

7. Tensions in Aristotle's position are stressed by W. J. Oates, *Aristotle and the Problem of Value* (Princeton, 1963), pp. 333–351, and C. Lord, "The Intention of Aristotle's *Rhetoric,*" *Hermes* 109 (1981): 326–339, at 329–332; but both assume too severe a disjunction between popular and Aristotelian values, as does C. J. Classen, "Principi e Concetti Morali nella *Retorica* di Aristotele," *Elenchos* 10 (1989): 5–22. Closer to my position is E. E. Ryan, "Aristotle's *Rhetoric* and *Ethics* and the Ethos of Society," *Greek, Roman and Byzantine Studies* 13 (1972): 291–308, as also is Troels Engberg-Pedersen's contribution in this volume.

8. For Athens, note for example the force of Demosthenes 19.184, "our political life depends on speeches/arguments" (*en logois hē politeia*).

9. Although the verbs are sometimes semantically interchangeable, the present context, including the implication of *echein* (1.2.21.1358a26), suggests that *entunchanein* here stresses the accidental less than would *epitunchanein* (e.g., 2.21.15.1395b3). I have not found an Aristotelian parallel for this use of the former; for illustrative nonphilosophical occurrences, see for example Hyperides, *Euxenippus* 21; Menander, *Dyscolus* 73.

10. *NE* 6.5.1140b16–20; but see note 25 of this essay.

11. Symbouleutic rhetoric may well have need of three kinds of practical reasoning: (*a*) the *sullogismoi tōn praktōn* of *NE* 6.13.1144a31–33, where the "starting point" or first principle is reference to the *telos;* (*b*) the combination of universal and particular *doxai* of *NE* 7.4.1146b35 ff. (cf. *Rhet.* 2.21.1–16.1394a19 ff.,

where some *gnōmai* are universal *doxai* of this kind); (c) general deliberation regarding *ta pros to telos*.

12. Aristotle's remarks at 1.2.12–13.1357a3–12 seem inimical to the building of structures of argument; but the kinds of political oratory dramatized by Thucydides, and practiced by Demosthenes, pose a challenge to such a stance.

13. The exception is epideictic: 2.1.2.1377b21, 2.18.1.1391b8; cf. 1.3.2.1358 b2–5.

14. *Rhet.* 1.1.10.1354b29–30; cf. *NE* 1.1.1094b27–28 for one implication of this.

15. See *Rhet.* 1.4.1–13.1359a30 ff.; 1.1.10.1354b24. Insofar as *politikē* is concerned with *ēthos* (1.2.7.1356a20–27), deliberative oratory is again the most political of the three kinds, as 2.1.3.1377b25–26 suggests.

16. *Rhet.* 2.18.1.1391b9–13; cf. 1.1.1.1354a3–6, 1.3.3.1358b9: Aristotle may be thinking partly of such things as legal arbitration (see 1.13.19.1374b19–22), but the point is clearly wider. The further step of linking rhetoric with individual deliberation was taken by Isocrates 3.8 (also at 15.256); Aristotle's *Post. Anal.* 1.10. 76b24–25 could have mediated some such link, had Aristotle wanted to make it.

17. *Rhet.* 1.1.7.1354b1 suggests that *phronēsis* is required (although usually found wanting, hence the importance of law) in judges not speakers: this applies to forensic contexts, whereas my comments principally concern deliberative rhetoric, where speaker and audience are differently related. For convergence of *phronēsis* and *sunesis* see *NE* 6.12.1143a25–35; also 10.10.1181b10–12 distinguishes *krinein kalōs* (here an exercise of *politikē*) from *eusunetos einai*.

18. See especially *Rhet.* 2.1.1.1377b18, 2.18.2.1391b24 (*doxai*); *endoxon/-a* occurs at 1.1.11.1355a17, 1.2.11.1356b32, 1.2.13.1357a10–14, 2.25.2.1402a34. As regards *phronēsis*, note that *NE* 6.5.1140a25–28 itself implies a link with prevailing conceptions: the *dokei dē* is precisely of the same kind as 7.2.1145b8 (on *akrasia*), which explicitly represents *endoxa* (1145b2–7).

19. See for example *NE* 6.4–5.1140a9–14, 25–31, 6.10.1142b31–33. Larger problems about *phronēsis* in Aristotle lie outside my concern.

20. See *NE* 6.5.1140b7–11, 6.8.1141b23–33; leadership, *Polit.* 3.4.1277a14– 16, 1277b25–29.

21. I assume, as the context seems to warrant, that *doxazontes orthōs* at 2.1.6.1378a11–12 is here equivalent to *phronimoi;* the separation of *phronēsis* and *aretē* is anyway clear at 3.16.9.1417a26–27.

22. *NE* 6.13.1144a28–29, 1144b2–3, 7.2.1145b18–19, 7.11.1152a6–14; cf. *MM* 1.35.1197b17–27. *Rhet.* 1.12.13.1372b13–16 also, in context, implies a type of *phronēsis* independent of *aretē*. For the possible detachment of *phronēsis* and *aretē* in some passages of the *Nicomachean Ethics*. See W. F. R. Hardie, *Aristotle's Ethical Theory*, 2d ed. (Oxford, 1980), pp. 225–226.

23. *Phronēsis* and age: see for example *Top.* 3.2.117a28–30, *NE* 6.9.1142a11– 20, *Polit.* 7.9.1329a15–16.

24. A further passage, 1.11.16.1371a13–14, reveals nothing. For some recent remarks on *phronēsis* in the *Rhetoric*, see M. H. Wörner, *Das Ethische in der Rhetorik des Aristoteles* (Freiburg, 1990), pp. 180–189.

25. *Phronēsis* without *aretē* would entail a lack of ethical "first principles" (see *NE* 6.13.1144a29–36), and would presumably create the danger of the false *politikē* deprecated at 1.2.7.1356a27–30; cf. *EE* 1.5.1216a23–27.

26. The contrast here between *dianoia* and *prohairesis* should be compared to that between *rhētorikē* and *politikē* at *Poet.* 6.1450b4–8: in both cases the point is that rhetoric can be divorced from ethical commitment. Synonymity of *ōphelimon* and *sumpheron*: 1.3.6.1358b34–35; 1.6.19–20.1362b31–37; cf. 3.17.4.1417b36, and for example Thucydides 1.75.5–1.76.1, Isocrates 8.31–32, 35; but see note 41 of this essay on Plato.

27. *NE* 6.5.1140a25–28; cf. 6.5.1140b7–11, 6.9.1142a1–11, 6.10.1142b32–33, and pseudo-Plato, *Definitions* 413b11, where *politikē* is defined as "knowledge of what is noble and advantageous."

28. *Rhet.* 1.9.4–6.1366a36–1366b5; cf. 1.9.16–17.1366b36–38. This idea is not divergent from the doctrines of the *Nicomachean Ethics:* see the notion that justice—perfect *aretē*—functions "toward another" (*NE* 5.3.1129b25–1130a13); for a particular virtue, *eleutheriotēs*, note *NE* 4.1.1120a21–23 (matched by *Rhet.* 2.4.8.1381a21).

29. *Rhet.* 2.23.16.1399a28–32, 3.16.9.1417a35–36; cf. Isocrates 8.28.

30. For modern statements, see for example J. H. Finley, *Thucydides* (Cambridge, Mass., 1942), pp. 51–54; L. Pearson, *Popular Ethics in Ancient Greece* (Stanford, 1962), chapter 6.

31. See the interchangeability, where appropriate, of *sumpheron* and *beltion*: for example 1.3.5.1358b22–24, *Polit.* 1.6.1254b6–20.

32. See *Polit.* 3.6.1279a17–21. The complexity of *sumpheron*, as well as its interrelation with other goods, is implicit in the condensed remarks at pseudo-Aristotle, *Rhetorica ad Alexandrum* 2.1422a4–15; some kindred considerations occur in a Stoic context at Cicero, *De Finibus* 3.64. One recent approach to the subject is provided by Wörner, *Das Ethische*, pp. 168–192.

33. Contrast the allegation of universal *pleonexia* at Plato, *Republic* 2.359c5.

34. Oates, *Aristotle and the Problem of Value*, p. 340, finds "latent amoralism" and mechanical conventionalism here, as in other places. My own argument offers an alternative to this reductive reading of the passage.

35. *Rhet.* 1.6.16.1362b28, 1.15.7.1375b3; see for example *NE* 5.3.1129b12–19, *Polit.* 1.2.1253a14–15. This conception of justice applies to political and administrative arrangements: it might be supplemented by a notion of natural justice (*NE* 5.10.1134b35–1135a5, cf. *Rhet.* 1.15.25.1376b21–22). The popular familiarity of such ideas is suggested by for example Aeschines 1.178, where the close coupling ("justice and advantage," *to dikaion kai to sumpheron*) is a virtual hendiadys; for a variety of attitudes see Thucydides 3.40.4, 5.90, 98, 105.4, 107; pseudo-Xenophon, *Constitution of Athens* 1.13; Isocrates 8.28–35; Demosthenes 16.10; Hyperides, *Philippides* 13; with C. Macleod, *Collected Essays* (Oxford, 1983), pp. 55–56. After the rejection of the Thrasymachean definition of justice as the interest of the stronger, Plato's entire *Republic* seeks to preserve and elaborate the intuition (*Republic* 1.339b3–4) that justice is some kind of self-interest; 3.412d–e, 4.442c7, and cf. *Laws* 9.875a.

36. See D. P. Gauthier, ed., *Morality and Rational Self-Interest* (Englewood Cliffs, N.J., 1970), for a collection of philosophical views on this issue.

37. See R. Kraut, *Aristotle on the Human Good* (Princeton, 1989), pp. 290–291.

38. Lawmaking, more than any other context of symbouleutic oratory, calls for knowledge that belongs to *politikē*: *Rhet.* 1.4.12–13.1360a17–38; for the connection see especially *NE* 6.8.1141b24–33, 10.10.1180a32–1181b12 (with note

44 in this essay). Aristotle would not, of course, be sanguine about the prospects of lawmaking determined by rhetorical persuasion: contrast Isocrates 15.79–80.

39. See *Rhet.* 1.9.17–19.1366b36–1367a6, 2.12.12.1389a34–36, 2.13.9.1389 b36–1390a1.

40. Personal ethics: see *Rhet.* 2.14.2.1390a34–1390b1, *NE* 4.12.1126b28–1127a5, *EE* 7.15.1249a10–11; also *NE* 9.8.1168a28 ff. on the good man's true "self-love," with Hardie, *Aristotle's Ethical Theory*, pp. 327–331, Kraut, *Aristotle on the Human Good*, pp. 115–128: if ordinary self-love represents a dominance of expediency over nobility, as *NE* 1168a29–35 accepts (cf. *Rhet.* 2.13.9.1389b35–1390a1), the good man's superior variety can be seen as a kind of consummate synthesis of self-interest and nobility (i.e., a higher version of the more mundane reality referred to at *Rhet.* 2.14.2.1390a34–1390b1), as the phrases about his benefiting from the greater good imply (9.8.1169a12, 17, 28–29). Political morality: note especially the link between *sumpheron* and political *eudaimonia* at *NE* 5.3.1129b14–19; in addition to the passages considered in the text, *Rhet.* 1.3. 5.1358b24–25, 3.17.4.1417b36, do allow justice and nobility to be of concern to symbouleutic rhetoric, just as 3.17.3.1417b31 brings advantage (*ōphelimon:* note 26 in this essay) within the scope of epideictic.

41. It may be relevant here that Aristotle sometimes talks of even virtue as "useful": e.g., *Polit.* 7.1.1323b10–12, 7.8.1328a38. Cf. Plato's denotation of value in general as *ōpheleia* at *Theaetetus* 186c, which reflects his frequent equation of *agathos/kalos* and *ōphelimos* (e.g., *Theaetetus* 177d2–4, *Republic* 5.457b4–5, 10.608e3, with my notes on the last two passages); but he seems to avoid using *sumpheron* in this way (although see the cognate *sumphoron* at *Republic* 5.458b5): see *Theaetetus* 172a, and note 26 in this essay.

42. *Rhet.* 1.1.14.1355b18–20: Oates, *Aristotle and the Problem of Value*, pp. 335–336, misconstrues the sense of *sophistēs* in this passage.

43. See evidence for a medieval view of the *Rhetoric* as an adjunct to *politikē:* J. J. Murphy, *Rhetoric in the Middle Ages* (Berkeley, 1974), pp. 97–100.

44. For *pistis* in this context see *EE* 1.6.1216b26–28, *Polit.* 7.1.1323a40; see for example *DA* 1.1.402a11.

45. At *EE* 1.4.1215b1–4, and 1.6.1216b35–39, Aristotle allows for a distinction between philosophical and nonphilosophical *politikē*, but the full implications of this distinction are nowhere elaborated. At for example *NE* 10.10.1180a32–1181b12, we see a taut attempt to balance concern for "the universal," *to katholou* (necessary for *politikē* insofar as this aspires to the status of some degree of *epistēmē*), with the importance of experience for any *politikē* that properly realizes itself in action. Significant in this connection is the way in which Aristotle allows *politikē* to be variously associated with the concepts of *epistēmē, technē, dunamis, pragmateia,* and *hexis:* see *Rhet.* 1.2.7.1356a26–27, 1.4.7.1359b17 (with 1.4.4. 1359b6–7), *NE* 1.1.1094a26–1094b5, 6.4.1141b23–24, *EE* 1.6.1216b16–19, *Polit.* 2.8.1268b34–38, 3.12.1282b14–16. A. W. H. Adkins, "*Theoria* versus *Praxis* in the *Nicomachean Ethics* and the *Republic*," *Classical Philology* 73 (1978): 297–313, offers one view of the tension between theory and practice in Aristotelian ethics.

Philosophy, Politics, and Rhetoric in Aristotle

C. D. C. Reeve

Since the external disorder, and extravagant lies;
The baroque frontiers, the surrealist police;
What can truth treasure, or heart bless,
But a narrow strictness?

Of the many types of political systems (*politeia*) Aristotle recognizes, tyranny and extreme democracy are the worst, barely counting as genuine "political" systems at all (*Polit.* 1292a30–32, 1293b27–30). These bad systems—deviations from kingship on the one hand and from a polity or republic on the other—have their own characteristic rhetorics: flattery in the case of tyranny; demagoguery in the case of extreme democracy (*Polit.* 1292a2–30). It is this fact and its significance for our understanding of Aristotle's conceptions of the relations that hold among philosophy, politics, and rhetoric that I propose—all too schematically, I'm afraid—to explore. Any reader who has fished these waters to any extent will see that I have neither positively courted controversy nor tried to avoid it altogether.

In the opening chapters of the *Nicomachean Ethics,* politics (*politikē*) is characterized as an architectonic science[1] that controls rhetoric as well as all the other crafts and sciences, prescribing which of them "ought to be studied in cities, and which ones each class in the city should study and to what extent they should study it" (1094a1–1094b10). To prescribe effectively, its practitioner—the *politikos*—has to know what the goal of the enterprise is, he has to know the human good, *eudaimonia,* and how to bring it about for a city. But he also has to know quite a bit about the various crafts and sciences he is directing in order not to become hostage to the experts who practice them, and have politics lose its place as the science with the most control. If he needs to know just as much as the experts in every case, politics becomes unattractively encyclopedic—too much like omniscience to be of any practical significance. If he needs to know as much as some experts but less than others, we will need a credible explanation of why this is so, and of how possessing some lesser knowledge will prevent him from becoming controlled by those who have more.

Politics comprises ethics (*NE* 1094b10–11), household management, legislation, deliberative and judicial expertise (*NE* 1141b29–33), and the knowledge of political systems: what the best political system is, what system is appropriate for what people, how any political system whatsoever can come into existence and be preserved, and what system is appropriate for all cities (*Polit.* 1288b21–35). Just what else it comprises—in particular, whether it comprises the art or craft of rhetoric—remains to be seen. It is plain, however, that simply by virtue of having mastered politics, a *politikos* must know a lot. Nonetheless, there are things he ideally should not know. He must have theoretical knowledge of all of the practical aspects of the craft of wealth-acquisition, but "he will gain practical experience of them only if he has to" (*Polit.* 1258b10–11; see also 1258b33–35, 1277a33–35); "even in the case of some of the civilized sciences (*tōn eleutheriōn epistēmōn*), whereas it is not unfree to participate in them up to a point, to study them too assiduously or pedantically" is liable to debase the mind and deprive it of leisure (*Polit.* 1337b15–17). Thus some kinds of knowledge are positively off-limits (except perhaps in extreme situations) to the *politikos*, who must always be an *eleutherios*, a civilized person, a free man.

Moreover between ignorance and expert knowledge, there is a kind of knowledge that has, at least in some areas, just as much authority as expert knowledge. One might think that only an expert doctor "should judge whether or not someone has treated a disease correctly," but, in Aristotle's view, an educated person who has studied medicine "as part of his general education" is also capable of judging such questions (*Polit.* 1282a3–7). In the *De Partibus Animalium,* the scope of such judgment is shown to be extremely wide:

> In relation to every study and investigation, humbler or more valuable alike, there appear to be two kinds of proficiency. One can properly be called scientific knowledge of the subject, the other as it were a sort of educatedness. For it is the mark of an educated man to be able to judge successfully what is properly expounded and what is not. This in fact is the sort of person we take the generally educated man to be, and by being educated we mean being able to do just this—except that in his case we consider one and the same man capable of judging about practically everything, whereas we consider another capable in some limited field; for there may be another who is qualified in the same way as the former, but only in a restricted area. (*Part. An.* 639a1–6. See also *NE* 1094b27–1095a13, *Met.* 1006a5–9)

Thus, for example, an educated person is in a position to judge whether a treatise by someone purporting to be an expert biologist is "properly expounded," is indeed the product of genuine biological knowledge.

Aristotle does not have much to say in general terms about what general education is or just how it confers this very broad capacity to judge. But his scattered remarks suggest that it is philosophical knowledge and ability—dialectical acumen appropriately understood—that is largely responsible for making someone civilized and educated. Thus, for instance, errors that show lack of education (*apaideusia*) are all philosophical failures: not knowing that logic precedes metaphysics (*Met.* 1005b2–15), not knowing "what we should, and what we should not, seek to have demonstrated" (*Met.* 1006a5–11), "inability to judge which reasonings are appropriate to the subject and which foreign to it" (*EE* 1217a7–10), or thinking that rhetoric is the same as politics (*Rhet.* 1356a7–9). On the other hand, things that show that one is educated (*pepaideumenos*)—such as knowing whether a scientific exposition is properly expounded, or knowing what kind of precision to look for in any area (*NE* 1094a23–27)—clearly include being able to reveal the "ignorant pretender" to either knowledge or demonstration, an ability that dialectical training in particular bestows.[2] Indeed, the entire *De Partibus Animalium* is a contribution to general education, designed in part to enable one to judge whether expositions in biology are properly expounded (*Part. An.* 639a12 ff.). But it is also, of course, a sophisticated essay on the philosophy of biology that anyone other than a trained philosopher would have trouble absorbing and appreciating.

A *politikos* must know the human good, we said, in order to design a political system and introduce legislation that will help bring it about for his city. Where does he get this knowledge? Since politics is the same state (*hexis*) as practical wisdom (*NE* 1141b23–24), he must get it from the same sources as the practically wise man. And one of these is the sort of philosophical investigation into *eudaimonia* that we find in Aristotle's ethical writings.[3] A *politikos* might be able to acquire this knowledge secondhand by listening to expert philosophers, whose views he is himself able to evaluate because of the philosophical acumen he has acquired as part of his general education.[4] His own philosophical expertise will have to be a good deal deeper than that, however, for what Aristotle's investigation into *eudaimonia* reveals is that theorizing (*theōria*)—and in particular the kind of theorizing about god that alone exemplifies wisdom (*sophia*) and that is identified with first philosophy or metaphysics—is either *eudaimonia* or the most important component of it.[5] Consequently, since a *politikos*, as a practically wise person, achieves *eudaimonia* both for himself and for his city if anyone does, he must be a philosopher.

Philosophy, then, like ethics, legislation, and the rest, is a discipline of which the *politikos* has expert knowledge: in his own right he *is* a philosopher, an ethicist, a legislator, and so on. But there are many areas of expertise of which a *politikos* has only general knowledge and others of which he has no practical knowledge. This is how he achieves authority without omniscience.

The acquisition of practical wisdom (and hence of politics or political science) is a cognitive task, a matter of coming to know what the goal of life is, but it is also a conative one, a matter of acquiring the virtues of characters, of having feelings and appetites "at the right times, about the right things, towards the right people, for the right end, and in the right way" (*NE* 1106b16–24). These two tasks are inseparable, however, because we come to know the goal in part as a result of a reflective intellectual process whose raw materials are our own socialized appetites, emotions, and feelings. If we have been properly socialized and educated, the things we desire and enjoy, or that inspire our love and affection, will be the very things that promote *eudaimonia;* while those we avoid and find painful or abhorrent, or that make us angry, will be the very things that are impediments to it. When we ask what it is that makes life worth living and lacking in nothing, when we ask what *eudaimonia* is, we draw on our experience of what we find enjoyable and life enhancing. If we have been socialized to enjoy the right things, the things that really are life enhancing, the answer we arrive at will be correct. If we have been badly socialized, our answer will be mistaken. That is why "virtue makes the aim correct" (*NE* 1144a8–9, 29–36).[6]

Socialization is, of course, effected by many different means, but the most important of these is education—education that is inevitably tailored to the particular type of political system in which one is (or is eventually) to live as a citizen:

> But the most important of all of the ways that are mentioned of making a political system last is one that everyone in fact despises, namely, a system of education that is suited to the political system. The most beneficial laws, even when ratified by all the citizens, are no use if people are not habituated and educated by the political system—democratically if the laws are democratic, oligarchically if they are oligarchic. (*Polit.* 1310a12–18)

Just how one is socialized, then, is in large part a political matter. And because it is, a gap is opened up between the virtues of a good man and those of a good citizen. What is taken to be justice in an oligarchy or democracy, for example, is not unconditional justice, but conditional justice or justice of a sort (*Polit.* 3.9). Hence what someone acquires under the name justice, through being socialized in those systems, is not justice, but a conditional form of it. Thus—drawing the relevant one of a series of interesting conclusions—what in such a citizen occupies the place of practical wisdom (politics) is not unconditionally practical wisdom (politics), but practical wisdom (politics) *of a sort*. Only in the best political system do the virtues of a good man coincide with those of a good citizen, only there are citizens socialized into true practical wisdom, true politics.

The relativity of the virtues to political systems is explicitly recognized by Aristotle in the *Politics* (3.4 and elsewhere).[7] The corresponding relativity of conceptions of *eudaimonia* to types of life (and hence, although the inference is not explicitly drawn, to the political systems that see one life in particular as the good life for people to lead) is central to the *Nicomachean Ethics* (1.5). I do not know of any text, however, in which Aristotle recognizes his commitment not just to conditional virtues but to the conditional types of practical wisdom and politics to which they necessarily give rise. Nonetheless, committed to them he is. He does, of course, carefully distinguish practical wisdom, which has *eudaimonia* as its only goal or end, from the cleverness that enables one to choose good means to any end whatever (1144a28–36). But unlike cleverness conditional practical wisdom—practical wisdom of a sort—also has one specific end. It is just that the end in question is not *eudaimonia* but only *eudaimonia* of a sort.

We are now in a position to formulate three related questions about rhetoric in an appropriately rich and nuanced way. First, when a *politikos* is prescribing which of the various crafts and sciences "ought to be studied in cities, and which ones each class in the city should study and to what extent they should study them," what will he prescribe for himself in the case of the art or craft of rhetoric? Should he study it at all? If so, should he acquire the kind of expert knowledge of it that he has of politics itself, or just the kind of knowledge that an educated person has? (In answering these questions, we should bear in mind that in order to argue successfully that a *politikos* needs to have a certain kind of knowledge of rhetoric himself, we have to show that he cannot get what he needs simply by employing experts who have that level of knowledge already. In other words, we need to be able to show that the knowledge in question is somehow intrinsic to politics itself, so that the *politikos* must have it as part of his own repertoire.) Second, do the answers to these questions remain stable as we move from political system to political system? Will a home-grown *politikos* prescribe the same knowledge of rhetoric for himself in an aristocracy as in an oligarchy or democracy? Third, in the case of some arts or crafts, as we have seen, Aristotle allows the *politikos* to have some level of theoretical knowledge of them, but forbids him any practical knowledge. We will need to be clear in the case of rhetoric, too, whether we are discussing practical knowledge or theoretical knowledge.

In *Rhetoric* 1.1, Aristotle castigates the "framers of the current treatises on rhetoric" for ignoring the enthymeme,[8] which is its argumentative substance or body (*sōma*), while focusing exclusively on such supplementary matters as how to arouse prejudice, pity, anger, and similar emotions in audiences. Here he characterizes the enthymeme as "unconditionally speaking the most controlling of the *pisteis* or modes of persuasion (*hōs eipein haplōs kuriōtaton tōn pisteōn*)" (1355a7–8).[9] In 1.2, however, he recognizes three *pisteis:* persuasion "through character"—when the speech makes "the speaker worthy of credence"; persuasion "through the hearers"—when the audience is "led to feel emotion by the speech"; and persuasion "through the arguments"—when "we show the truth or apparent truth from whatever is persuasive in each case" (1356a1–20). Here he characterizes persuasion through character not enthymematic persuasion as "roughly speaking the most controlling factor in persuasion" (*schedon hōs eipein kuriōtatēn echei pistin*) (1356a13). Various attempts have been made to reduce the tension between these two views of rhetoric—which is epitomized though not reducible to the apparent conflict over which mode of persuasion has the most control—but none has met with much success. Indeed, a recent translator and commentator has concluded that "it is probably better to acknowledge frankly that chapter 1 is inconsistent with what follows."[10]

When we look more closely at *Rhetoric* 1.1, however, we see that Aristotle's highlighting of the enthymeme is in part justified by political arguments. In cities with good laws, as little as possible is left to the discretion of judges (*Rhet.* 1254a31–33). This is because the law is dispassionate, while judges are not:

> Someone who asks law to rule would seem to be asking god—that is to say, intellect[11] alone to rule—while one who asks a human being asks a wild beast as well. For passion is like a wild beast, and anger or spiritedness perverts rulers, even when they are the best men. That is why law is intellect without passion. (*Polit.* 1287a28–32; see also 1286a17–20)

So the ideal would be for the opponents in a trial to have "no function except to show that something is or is not true or has or has not happened" (*Rhet.* 1354a26–28), and for the judge to have no function except to decide, on the basis of the opposing arguments, "whether something has happened or has not happened" (*Rhet.* 1354a26–28).

Moreover, when we turn from the judicial or forensic oratory (*dikanikon*)—on which the traditional writers on rhetoric focused—to deliberative rhetoric (*sumbouleutikon*), we find Aristotle telling very much the same kind of story. In cities with good laws, where the citizens are educated in virtue, all a speaker addressing a deliberative body will have to do is "to show that circumstances are as the speaker says" (1354b30–31).[12]

Thus rhetoric is not only restricted to enthymemes in such cities, but enthymemes are restricted to the very narrow role of establishing the facts. The speaker is not even allowed to comment on whether what happened is "important or trivial, just or unjust" (1354a28–29). Let us say, then, that in well-ordered cities rhetoric—whether deliberative or judicial—is narrowly enthymematic. To be sure, this ideal is closely approximated only in cities with good laws, and fully achieved only in cities with the very best ones, but it remains the ideal nonetheless.

We have already had occasion to notice that Aristotle contrasts what is unconditionally just with what is just only in relation to a given political system. But, of course, this type of contrast is one he makes quite systematically. Moreover, he usually identifies what is unconditionally *F* with what is *F* in relation to a good thing of some sort. For example, what is unconditionally choiceworthy is what is choiceworthy to a good man (*NE* 1113a22–33); what is unconditionally pleasant is what is pleasant to the good man (*NE* 1176a15–19); what is unconditionally just is what is just in the best political system. In *Rhetoric* 3.1 this contrast is invoked to make a point about the importance of delivery in persuasion:

> Since the whole business of rhetoric is with opinion, one should pay attention to delivery, not because it is just to do so but because it is necessary, since justice, at any rate, seeks nothing more in a speech than that it neither pains nor pleases. For it is just to fight the case by appeal to the facts alone, so that everything except the demonstration is incidental. All the same, as has been said, because of the corruption of audiences delivery has great power. (1404a1–8)

It is surely reasonable to conclude that the apparently conflicting claims made in 1.1 and 1.2 about which of the *pisteis* has the most control are in fact consistent ones of this same kind. The enthymeme has the most control unconditionally speaking (or in good cities); persuasion through character has the most control conditionally speaking (or in cities generally). It matters, then, and it matters from the very outset of the *Rhetoric*, that we bear in mind that what holds true of rhetoric in one political system may not hold true of it in another, since otherwise we will find ourselves unable to read that work as a unified treatise.

It is evident from the foregoing discussion that even in the best city or political system, a *politikos* must have an educated person's nonspecialist knowledge of rhetoric in order to know what sort of legislation to pass regarding it, in order to know who in the city should study it and to what degree. Moreover, it is evident that this kind of nonspecialist knowledge is constitutive of politics, given its defining status as the science with the most control. It may also seem evident that in such a city or system a *politikos* will have to have practical knowledge of narrowly enthymematic—or bare fact or circumstance establishing—rhetoric. But, as we are about to find out, more is needed to secure even this weak conclusion.

In 1.2 and again in 1.4, Aristotle makes two important remarks about the relationship of rhetoric to the various sciences. The first of them is as follows:

> To the degree that someone makes a better choice of the premises, he will have created knowledge different from dialectic and rhetoric without its being recognized; for if he succeeds in hitting on first principles, the knowledge will no longer be dialectic or rhetoric but the science whose first principles he has got hold of. (*Rhet.* 1358a23–26)

The picture here is of a basket of premises available to the rhetorician to use in constructing his enthymemes. If he is very lucky in selecting his premises, so that those he hits are actually the first premises of a science, the conclusion he reaches will be a piece of knowledge that belongs, not to rhetoric, but to the relevant science itself. It follows that there are sciences—competitor sciences, as I shall call them from now on—whose first principles belong in the basket of premises from which rhetoric draws, and which must therefore deal with the same deliberative matters as rhetoric does. It is easy to confuse rhetoric with these sciences, but it should be kept carefully distinct from them.

It may seem, however, that this picture is inconsistent with the characterization of the contents of the basket as *endoxa*. But, in actual fact, it is the usual understanding of *endoxa* as "common beliefs" that is inconsistent with the passage. Some *endoxa* are indeed common beliefs, believed by pretty well everyone, but others are believed by scarcely anyone: "Some of these views are traditional, held by many, while others are held by a few reputable men (*endoxoi*)" (*NE* 1098b27–28). Plato's views about the good are certainly not commonplace, indeed they conflict with common views, but they are *endoxa* nonetheless because Plato is a notable and reputable philosopher, whose views are supported by argument as well as by the weight of his reputation as a thinker (*NE* 1095a26–28, 1096a11–1097a14). Socrates' view that *akrasia* or weakness of will is impossible is almost universally rejected, but it counts as an *endoxon* for similar reasons (*NE* 1145b21–31). Expert opinions, whether widely shared or not, are *endoxa* because experts have and are recognized as having superior knowledge.[13] That is why—to comment in passing on a matter that is often misrepresented or made to seem mysterious—Aristotle's own views as well as other less outré and more widely accepted ones are often lumped together as appropriate premises for enthymemes.

The second passage underwrites the message of the first, but now the focus is not on the rhetorician making his choice of premises, but on a theorist of rhetoric allocating those premises to various crafts and sciences:

> Insofar as someone tries to make dialectic or rhetoric not just practical faculties (*dunameis*) but sciences (*epistēmas*), he unwittingly obscures their nature by the change, reconstructing them as sciences that deal with certain underlying facts, rather than only with arguments (*logōn*). (1359b12–16)

The message is that the rhetorician knows something about persuasive arguments, but qua rhetorician he is not in the business of generating the premises of those arguments. He needs to know which of them various kinds of audiences find persuasive. Hence he needs to know which of them are true, because "true and better underlying facts are by nature always more productive of good arguments and are, in a word, more persuasive" (1355a37–38).[14] But he does not need to know, as the scientist does, *why* they are true. It is when someone fails to make this distinction that he dresses rhetoric up as a form of politics and rhetoricians as *politikoi* (1356a27–29). Throughout his lengthy discussion of the political data of which a deliberative orator needs to be aware Aristotle is careful to remind us on a number of occasions that this data properly belongs to politics not to rhetoric (see 1359b16–18, 1360a37).

In the best political system, all the citizens are men of practical wisdom, all of them are *politikoi*, experts in politics. Since political and judicial offices are open only to citizens, they alone hold such offices. Hence both in the law courts and the deliberative chambers, where political and judicial judgment take place, the audiences to be persuaded are expert audiences. To the degree that the various sciences constitutive of politics are competitors of rhetoric, then, they will obviate the need for it. After all, the function or job (*ergon*) of rhetoric is to deal with "matters that we deliberate about without arts or crafts to guide us, before an audience that is not able to see many things all together or to reason from a distant starting point" (1357a2–3). Hence, when experts are talking to experts, who are able to see many things together and reason from distant starting points, they will need only the appropriate competitor science not rhetoric. To the extent that this is true, to the extent that competitor sciences can do all of rhetoric's work, the *politikos* will not need practical knowledge even of narrowly enthymematic rhetoric.

It would be a long and difficult task, no doubt, to establish just what this extent is—in part because there is considerable disagreement about just how scientific or demonstrative politics and its constituents really are. I have argued elsewhere[15] that they are more closely analogous to the acknowledged sciences than they are usually represented as being, and that unconditional scientific knowledge (*epistēmē haplōs*) is available in them, but it is not my intention to presuppose that controversial view here. Instead I want simply to advertise the fact that these texts from the *Rhetoric* show Aristotle committed to the existence of competitor sciences that need to be carefully distinguished from rhetoric itself, and to point out that there is an open question about whether in the best political system a *politikos* needs even narrowly enthymematic rhetoric in order to carry out the central political tasks of deliberating and judging.

One factor we need to take into account, then, in determining whether a *politikos* needs to have some minimal practical knowledge of rhetoric in the best political system is the existence and scope of competitor sciences, "either those in existence or those not yet understood" (1358a7). But another factor is the type of enthymeme he will need to know. If he needs narrowly enthymematic rhetoric at all, it will be in order to construct deliberative enthymemes. But when we turn to judicial rhetoric and to epideictic rhetoric matters are somewhat less straightforward, although the constraints on acceptable answers are obvious enough. Judicial rhetoric addresses judges of past happenings in order to persuade them to judge someone as just or unjust; epideictic rhetoric addresses an audience of spectators acting as judges (*Rhet.* 1391b15–16) in order to persuade them to judge someone or something as fine or shameful. A *politikos* will need sufficient general theoretical knowledge of these, as of deliberative rhetoric, in order to know who in the city should study them and to what degree. But practical knowledge of how to prosecute others or defend himself in court is hardly constitutive of politics. Here, it seems, a *politikos*, who finds himself needing to do either of these things, might well hire an expert to help him, without in any way compromising his own claim to political expertise. (Presumably this is part of the reason deliberative rhetoric is said to be "more political" than its judicial counterpart at 1354b24.)

Epideictic rhetoric often acts as an aid to both deliberative and judicial rhetoric, since it is useful to any speaker who wishes to persuade his audience by arguing that he himself is a fine (*kalos*) fellow or that his opponent is a bad or unreliable (*aischros*) one. Among men of practical wisdom living in the best kind of city, which is of necessity small enough to allow the citizens to have good knowledge of one another's characters (*Polit.* 1326b14–25), it is unlikely to be often needed for these purposes. But, in any case, since judicial and deliberative rhetoric are restricted to a very narrow compass in good cities, the compass of epideictic rhetoric, too, whether acting as their assistants or in its own right (say, in delivering funeral orations) will be correspondingly restricted to establishing facts or circumstances. Thus, even if a *politikos* does need narrow expertise in deliberative enthymemes, he may not need a similar expertise in judicial or epideictic ones.

The third factor we need to consider is audience. When a *politikos* in the best system is talking to his fellow political experts, he may not need even narrowly enthymematic rhetoric. But surely he will sometimes have to talk to people who are not experts, such as the members of his household—wife, children, and slaves—as well as any other inhabitants of his city who are not citizens possessed of practical wisdom. Of course, he will. But the fact that he does may have little bearing on the question of how much practical knowledge of rhetoric he—at any rate qua *politikos*—needs to have. The fact is, after all, that women, children, slaves, and noncitizens are all nonparticipants in the ideal political system, and so are excluded from deliberative and judicial decisions. Hence a *politikos* in his role as a *politikos* will never find himself having to persuade them to judge or decide that someone or something is just or unjust, advantageous or disadvantageous, fine or shameful. He will, of course, talk to them, and it is even conceivable that he might explain to them on occasion why certain sorts of decisions have been made on their behalf by the citizens, but these communications, not being aimed at eliciting judgment, do not involve rhetoric as Aristotle—in contrast with contemporary thinkers who see rhetoric as having a place in all communication—understands it. (I add, more as a parenthetical moment of comic relief than anything else, that the difficulty we should feel in imagining the much-satirized *megalopsuchos*—or great-souled man—engaging in epideictic rhetoric should make us recognize just how unlikely it is that an ideal *politikos* would praise or blame anyone before any audience let alone an audience of farmers, tradesmen, and common laborers.)[16]

When we turn to the *politikos* in his role as ideal head of a household, matters are no doubt a lot less clear. They are certainly less clear to me. Nonetheless, it is hard to imagine a *politikos* (especially if he is a *megalopsuchos*) treating the members of his household as judges with the power to decide important questions. Surely, he decides for them and does not try to persuade them to decide for themselves. This does not mean, of course, that he simply issues orders to them. A *politikos* rules his wife and children "in a manner appropriate to free people" (*Polit.* 1259a39–40), and rules his wife in particular with precisely the kind of "political" rule that he exercises in a political system governed by himself and his peers.[17] Even where slaves are concerned, Aristotle is explicit that "those who tell us not to use reason with slaves but to give them orders exclusively are mistaken" (*Polit.* 1260b5–7). But reasoning with slaves, and talking with family members—even if it involves lots of discussion of what is fine or shameful, just or unjust, advantageous or disadvantageous, even if it is intended to educate some of them in practical wisdom or politics—is not for the purpose of eliciting their judgments or decisions. Hence, for the same reason as before, such communication does not seem to involve an exercise of Aristotelian rhetoric, strictly conceived.

When we look at the best political system, then, what we find are *politikoi* who are expert philosophers possessed of unconditional practical wisdom, who have general theoretical knowledge of rhetoric but either make no political use of it or only minimal use of that part of it that is narrowly enthymematic. Clearly, this is an extremely austere and Platonic view of rhetoric. But when we leave the best political system, a very different picture emerges.

Given the influence of law and education on character, a homegrown *politikos* will usually have the kinds of virtues, practical wisdom, and politics that are fitted or suited to his political system. But it is surely possible nonetheless for a mismatch to occur—for an unconditional *politikos*, possessed of unconditional practical wisdom, to be living in a less than ideal political system. In any case, by beginning with the latter situation, even if it is only a remote possibility, we shall be able to see just how rhetoric comes to infiltrate not just the political life of a city but the soul of the *politikos* himself. (Remember that Aristotle is as keen a student of psychopolitical symbiosis as Plato is.)

Since rhetoric aims at persuasion and "what is persuasive is always persuasive to someone" (1256b8), an artful or technically competent rhetorical argument is suited to the souls of its audience. Hence the further those souls are from practical wisdom—the further they are from having the right feelings and emotions "at the right times, about the right things, towards the right people, for the right end, and in the right way"—the more the orator or rhetorician will need to deal with their unruly emotions in order to gain conviction. If he is defending a "Laconizer" before a large jury of working-class veterans of the Peloponnesian wars, he will have to arouse emotions to counteract their antipathy. If he is prosecuting a popular leader, he will need to arouse their animosity to counteract their existing affection and approval. Thus even a good orator who is also a good man (1355b17–21) aiming to persuade his audience to do what is in fact just or advantageous will need to make use of *pisteis* beyond the enthymeme to persuade audiences whose own characters are less than good (see 1404a1–8, quoted earlier). Like the fact that Aristotle is no deontologist, this too is something that needs to be taken into account in assessing the apparent amoralism or immoralism that some readers have detected in his advice to speakers. Persuading the bad to pursue the good involves corrective deception, "noble lies," full-blown rhetoric.

So much, no doubt, is pretty obvious. A *politikos*—even one possessed of practical wisdom and all the virtues of character—will need rhetoric to achieve moral political purposes before corrupt audiences. But in a less than ideal political system, a homegrown *politikos* will, of course, be tinged with some of the same corruption as the audience, corruption that, as we have seen, consists very largely in a defect of feeling or emotion. Like a lover or a coward (see *Parva* 460b3–11), he will register the facts at less or more than their true weight. He will be made furious by a trivial slight or left indifferent by the grossest insults. In metaphorical but illuminating terms, it is as if his appetites, desires, and emotions are always being either inappropriately stimulated or quieted by a less than narrowly enthymematic rhetoric. As a result, his virtues will be no more than the conditional virtues that are suited to his political system, and what he pursues as *eudaimonia* will not be true happiness, but what living in that system has caused to look like happiness to him, honor (say) or pleasure and gratification (*NE* 1.5). In other words, the goals of what in him is practical wisdom or politics are, as it were, shaped and controlled by a concealed rhetoric. But when the goals a *politikos* pursues, whether for himself or the city he controls, are themselves shaped and controlled in this way, rhetoric has in effect begun to infiltrate politics and philosophy. For, as we have seen, it is philosophy that yields the truth about *eudaimonia* to those who have been properly socialized, and only politics informed by philosophy can socialize a city to live in the light of that truth.

Just how extensive the infiltration is depends on just how far from being narrowly enthymematic the inner rhetoric is. But when we reach extreme democracy or tyranny, where those in control are themselves controlled by their appetites, and live a life suitable for cattle (*NE* 1095b19–22, 1176b9–17), it is perhaps intelligible without further argument that both in the soul of the *politikos* and in his city a narrowly enthymematic rhetoric will have been all but replaced by demagoguery and flattery. The infiltration of philosophy and politics by rhetoric will then be so complete that rhetoric will have dressed itself up as politics in earnest and taken control of the city.

In an ideal city rhetoric has a minimal role to play; in a very corrupt one it has dressed itself up as politics and taken control. But most cities lie somewhere in between. And in them rhetoric, in the right political hands, can be a powerful force for good, counteracting distorting feelings and emotions to move a city toward genuine *eudaimonia*. Of course, there is always a danger, as there is with any powerful weapon, that giving it houseroom will result in its taking over. Certainly, any *politikos* who uses all of rhetoric's resources, even for good ends, risks having his own soul infiltrated by it: In the face of external disorder and extravagant lies it is difficult for truth to treasure or heart to bless an inner narrow strictness.

But in Aristotle's view, this, in an imperfect world, is simply the challenge rhetoric poses to practical wisdom and politics.[18]

NOTES

1. I use the term "science" to translate Aristotle's *epistēmē*. But I do so, as lawyers say, without prejudice—in other words, without intending to prejudge the vexed question (briefly referred to below) of whether all the various disciplines Aristotle classifies as *epistēmai* are to be thought of as canonical Aristotelian sciences, as systems of syllogistic demonstrations from necessary first principles.

2. See *Pr. Anal.* 24a22–24b15, *Post. Anal.* 72a8–11, 77a31–32, 81b18–23, *Top.* 161a24–33, 162a27–28, *Soph. El.* 169b25–29.

3. See my *Practices of Reason: Aristotle's Nicomachean Ethics* (Oxford, 1992), pp. 22–66.

4. In a fragment of *Peri Basileas*, Aristotle suggests that it would be disadvantageous for a king actually to be a philosopher, but that he "should be attentive and obedient to true philosophers." But not all kings are *politikoi*, and, besides, if the kings should be obedient to the philosophers, one might well ask, as Aristotle himself does in a similar context (see *Polit.* 1269b32–34), what the difference is between having philosopher-kings and having kings who are obedient to philosophers.

5. See *Practices of Reason*, pp. 139–159.

6. See *Practices of Reason*, pp. 48–61.

7. This is one of the many reasons that it is so important to read the *Politics* and the *Nicomachean Ethics* together.

8. Enthymemes are authoritatively discussed in M. Burnyeat, "Enthymeme: Aristotle on the Logic of Persuasion," *Aristotle's Rhetoric: Philosophical Essays*, ed. D. J. Furley and A. Nehamas (Princeton, 1994). See also his "Enthymeme: Aristotle on the Rationality of Rhetoric," this volume.

9. This sentence is excised by R. Kassel—in his book *Aristotelis Ars Rhetorica* (Berlin, 1976)—but retained by most editors.

10. G. A. Kennedy, *On Rhetoric: A Theory of Civil Discourse* (Oxford, 1991), p. 28.

11. *Ho theos kai ho nous.* The same phrase occurs at *NE* 1096a24–25, where *kai* is widely agreed to be epexegetic or explanatory. *Ho theos* is used to refer to intellect at *EE* 1249b9–23 (cf. *NE* 1177b27–28).

12. No author as aware as Aristotle is of the role of demagoguery in extreme democracies could possibly make this claim about cities with bad or mediocre laws, whose citizens have correspondingly bad characters.

13. See *Practices of Reason*, pp. 31–45.

14. See *Met.* 993a30–993b11, *Parva* 436b10–437a3, *Rhet.* 1355a15–17, and *Practices of Reason*, pp. 45–48.

15. See *Practices of Reason*, especially pp. 7–56.

16. The *megalopsuchos* is described in *NE* 4.3.

17. This suggests that there will be a fair amount of give-and-take in their

relationship. But then Aristotle also claims that the deliberative part of a woman's soul is *akuron* or lacking in authority or control, which suggests that her views never prevail over her husband's. See *Polit.* 1260a13, 1328a6–7, 1327b23–38.

18. I am grateful to Amélie Rorty for suggesting that I write on this topic and for some very helpful discussions and criticisms.

Aristotle and the Emotions

Stephen R. Leighton

Since the object of rhetoric is judgment (*Rhet.* 1377b21) and since what appears does vary with the emotions (1378a1), a concern for rhetoric provided Aristotle with the opportunity to develop his most sustained thoughts on emotions; not only does he define, explicate, compare, and contrast various emotions, but also he characterizes emotions themselves. His observation is quite striking.

> Emotions are the things on account of which the ones altered differ with respect to their judgments, and are accompanied by pleasure and pain: such are anger, pity, fear, and all similar emotions and their contraries. (*Rhet.* 1378a20–23)

Here a number of things provoke thought. First, how did Aristotle take the altering of judgments to occur? Second, what does Aristotle mean by speaking of the "accompaniment" of pleasure and pain? Last, and best resolved only after the above questions are answered, is the conception of emotion like our own?[1] These questions are worth answering not only for their value in understanding Aristotle but also insofar as they shed light on our understanding of emotion. Let us begin with the matter of altering judgment.

I

We would agree that emotions may alter our judgments. Love's flame flaring, we view a beloved, and sometimes the whole world, through rose-colored glasses; our blood boiling, these same things are viewed quite differently.

> For it does not seem the same according as men love or hate, are wrathful or mild, but things appear altogether different, or different in degree; for

when a man loves one on whom he is passing judgment, he either thinks that the accused has committed no wrong at all or that his offense is trifling; but if he hates him, the reverse is the case. And if a man desires anything and has good hopes of getting it, if what is to come is pleasant, it seems to him that it is sure to come to pass and will be good; but if a man is unemotional or in a bad humor, it is quite the reverse. (*Rhet.* 1377b30–1378a4, based on Freese's translation)

From this and the previous quotation we can infer that emotions may move one to a particular judgment, may alter the severity of a judgment, or may change a judgment entirely. The field in which emotion operates is not restricted. Although the judgments altered that are foremost in Aristotle's mind are formal verdicts given at the end of proceedings, there is no reason to doubt emotion's effect on judgments on the way to a formal verdict, or on any other judgment for that matter. Moreover, so far, there is no requirement of belief in the judgment. Yet, as the passage immediately above suggests, belief and changes in belief may well be involved. Again, the relevant judgments are not restricted to stated judgment, or even terminating judgment of any sort. Also, the sorts of changes Aristotle seems to envisage can be quite dramatic. For example, concerning the exhaustion of anger that results in growing mild, Aristotle observes:

For although the Athenians were more indignant with him [Ergophilus] than with Callisthenes, they acquitted him, because they had condemned Callisthenes to death on the previous day. (*Rhet.* 1380b11–14, Freese's translation)

Thus the range of things to be included under affected judgment forms quite a diverse grouping. Nevertheless, that such changes occur sits rather well with our own intuitions on the matter.

What, then, explains changes of judgment involving emotion? Aristotle nowhere explicitly reports on this matter. However, he does provide for a number of solutions.

1

A good place to begin is with the definitions of each of the emotions. The aim or end of an emotion could explain a change of judgments. In anger's definition Aristotle speaks of seeking revenge (1378a31–34). It is easy to see that one way of seeking revenge in a courtroom would be to return an unfavorable verdict. (Indeed, Aristotle's thoughts on growing mild and angry, quoted earlier, suggest this sort of thing.) In more pedestrian settings one could achieve the same end by, say, slandering the person. Similarly, in love's definition, Aristotle speaks of seeking the beloved's good for the beloved's own sake (1380b35–1381a2). Again, it is easy to see that one way of seeking the beloved's good in a courtroom would be by bringing down a favorable verdict. In more pedestrian settings the lover could sing the beloved's praises (although not really deserved) and thereby alter her or his judgments.

Similar considerations apply to other emotions Aristotle examines. Pity and indignation require a sense of justice. We are moved to pity because the misfortune suffered is undeserved (1386b11); we are roused to indignation because the good fortune enjoyed is undeserved (1386b10). Thus we can suppose that our judgments concerning those we pity would be lenient and generous, while our judgments concerning those with whom we are indignant would be severe and mean-spirited. In both cases one would be compensating for the injustice that roused the emotion. This compensation takes the form of an alteration in judgment.[2]

One may be well aware of what one is doing in such cases. We make certain judgments in public that are at odds with what we really believe.[3] We are like persons who form the right opinion, but through viciousness or lack of goodwill do not say what they really think (1378a12–15). Just how this works is fairly transparent. One holds view *A,* but because one wants to do well or poorly by another, says *B.* This, then, is our first explanation of emotions altering judgments.

It is most unlikely that Aristotle intends this sort of insincerity to bear much of the burden of explaining how emotions alter judgments. For although this insincerity can explain why one's pronouncements vary and to that extent how judgments are altered, it does not help explain Aristotle's remark that things appear differently through emotion (1377b30). Moreover, unless we suppose Aristotle to hold a wild and unacknowledged theory of self-deception, his theory has not yet begun to account for the interesting cases of emotions altering judgment: cases in which one is more like the person who lacks good sense than like those who are vicious or without goodwill (1378a8–16); cases in which the change of judgment has to be a matter of belief. Thus we must seek a further explanation of emotion's effect.

2

A different sort of explanation is implicit in Aristotle's remark about the speaker who rouses the judges' indignation toward those pleading for forgiveness.

> If then the speech puts the judges into such a frame of mind [indignation] and proves that those who claim our pity (and the reasons why they do so) are unworthy to obtain it and deserve that it should be refused them, then pity will be impossible. (1387b17–21, based on Freese's translation)

The same sort of explanation is implicit in Aristotle's remarks concerning one made envious.

> So that if the judges are brought into that frame of mind [envy], and those who claim their pity or any other boon are such as we stated, it is plain that they will not obtain pity from those with whom the decision rests. (1388a26–29, Freese's translation)

The defendant vainly struggles to move the judges to one emotion while they are in the grips of another. The point seems to be that emotions have certain judgments connected with them such that certain other emotions, their judgments, and other judgments too are excluded. For example, John's indignation with Mary involves John making a judgment of Mary's unmerited good fortune (1386b10). So judging precludes John from making the judgment of Mary's undeserved misfortune (1385b14) that he would have made were he roused to pity her. Again, Mary's envy of John involves, for example, Mary making a judgment of self-reproach through John's successes (1388a17). So judging precludes Mary making a judgment of John's undeserved misfortune that she would have made were she roused to pity him (1385b14). This is not a matter of insincerity on John's or Mary's part. Rather, being moved to one emotion with its judgments rules out being moved to another emotion with its judgments. Those judgments obtain that are connected with the emotion one is moved to. Thus insofar as one moves to a given emotion one thereby alters one's judgments; and this may exclude other emotions and their judgments.[4]

We can see the same sort of alteration with other emotions as well. Should one be moved to anger, one thereby views the object of anger as having insulted one (1378a31–33). Becoming ashamed of a person involves being brought to view the person as involved in misdeeds that bring dishonor (1383b15–16). Again, to the extent that one is moved to these emotions, one's judgments are thereby altered; other emotions and their judgments may, in turn, be excluded. Similar points can be made for all the emotions Aristotle here discusses.

How this works is transparent also. To be moved to emotion *A* involves making judgments of *A*; to be moved to emotion *B* involves making judgments of *B*; and so on. Thus "things do not seem the same" as one finds oneself in one emotional state as opposed to another, or none at all. Moreover, the judgments in any given complex may logically exclude those of another complex, or any other judgments.

The most obvious contrast between the two cases considered is that while the former tends to be a matter of insincerity, the latter is not. An equally striking contrast is that while the former is an example of emotion altering judgments, the latter concerns emotion being an alteration of judgments. In the second case, emotions are complexes involving judgments, each complex excluding certain other emotion complexes, their judgments, and certain other judgments as well. It is not that envy brings about a change of judgments such that one does not show or feel pity; rather, to be moved to envy involves being moved to a particular set of judgments that excludes those of pity. Similarly, it is not that being angry makes us view the object of emotion as insulting, but being angry involves viewing the object as insulting.

This sophisticated thesis sits very well with many modern analyses of emotion in which changes of emotion are, in part at least, changes in judgments. Although this is not what we began searching for—given the passages quoted earlier and Aristotle's understanding of indignation, envy, shame, anger, and so on, and given how well this suits his claim that things do not seem the same when one is in different emotional states (1377b30)—we have no reason to doubt that the thesis is Aristotle's. It should also mean that we have not exhausted Aristotle's thoughts on emotions and changes of judgments. For the characterization of emotion quoted at the outset of this essay describes emotions as that on account of which judgments change, not emotions themselves as changes of judgments. Since, as we have seen, the initial case of insincerity cannot be the whole of the explanation, there should be more to the account. Thus we must search for further explanations of emotions altering our judgments.

So far, our study has revealed two kinds of changes of judgment involving emotion: (1) change of judgment as a consequence of emotion; (2) change of judgment as a constituent of emotion. The latter we have just considered. It will not be further subdivided; it works by means of emotions involving particular sets of judgments, judgments that exclude the judgments constitutive of certain other emotions. The former will subdivide into four species, one of which is the matter of insincerity.

3

Another way in which emotion might affect judgment is like our first explanation (1) insofar as it depends upon the aim or end of the emotion, but is like the second (2) insofar as it is not disingenuous, but rather a seduction by emotion. Consider again the angry person. We have seen that the person seeks revenge. A change of judgment may result here because the aim of revenge disposes one to give an unfavorable interpretation where the case is ambiguous. One never grants the benefit of the doubt, quite the opposite. In this way one would not only say that the person acted vilely, but would have come to believe it: one's anger having seduced one's judgment. Again, in love's seeking the benefit of a beloved, where circumstances are unclear, one would be inclined to give the beloved a favorable interpretation because love, by seeking to benefit favorably, disposes one to the beloved. One thereby arrives at a far more charitable judgment than one would have had one been more rigorous and less passionate when considering the matter.

As with the previous explanations, how this favor/disfavor method works is fairly transparent. Of a certain case, which otherwise we would be unsure how to evaluate, the emotion disposes us and makes us desire to favor or disfavor the person to whom the emotion relates. Since we do need to form some opinion of the case, we correspondingly judge the case harshly or favorably. Thus emotion alters judgment.[5] Should there be a number of related cases, one's judgment not just of each particular case, but of the person will be likewise swayed. For example, we shall tend to be charitable about the motives of a beloved, judging ambiguous cases in this light. Should we be faced with a number of such cases, this will strengthen our charitable interpretation not only of the person's role in particular cases but also of the person. This, then, is a third (and twofold) way in which emotion changes judgment.

It should be noted that there are some limitations on the application of this explanation. For the explanation does not seem helpful in the cases of fear, shame, and shamelessness, given Aristotle's definitions of these. For these emotions have no announced aim toward the realization of which our judgments might be bent.

This may lead us to think that the *Rhetoric*'s characterization of these emotions is inadequate. They too should have an aim in their definitions, or at least the general characterization of these emotions should include an aim. For example, it would be plausible to say that fear aims at flight. Moreover, given Aristotle's teleological views, it would be a very plausible understanding. If this sort of suggestion could be made for all emotions, then we could say that all emotions could affect judgment in each of the three ways discussed so far.

However, to the extent that we are trying to discern the position of the *Rhetoric*, we cannot conclude that the third explanation applies to all *ta pathē*. Moreover, even if we want to suggest an aim for fear, shame, and shamelessness, and so apply the third explanation, it is not clear that we should do the same for all emotions. What does sadness or joy aim at? Because, on our own behalf as well as Aristotle's, we should leave open the possibility that some emotions have no aim, the present explanation is limited in its field of application.

While we are increasing our ability to understand emotions involving changes of judgment, still there are cases that so far elude our grasp. Consider Aristotle's example of the hopeful person (1378a1, quoted earlier). It is plausible that one could explain, in the favorable interpretation manner, the person who hopes for something good, and thus supposes it will come to pass. The person desires its occurrence; it is likely that she or he would give her- or himself the benefit of the doubt concerning the many hurdles she or he has to face, but does not really know whether she or he can leap or not. Likewise, ones without hope would be disposed to underestimate their prospects. So one can see how the third explanation will apply. However, if the case is unambiguous, if the hurdles to be faced are insurmountable, then any seduction of judgment seems inadequately explained in terms of a favorable interpretation. Because of this, and because certain emotions lack an aim, we must hope that there are further explanations of emotion altering judgment in Aristotle's work.

4

The *Nicomachean Ethics* is helpful.

> Anger seems to listen to argument to some extent, but to mishear it, as do hasty servants who run out before they have heard the whole of what one says, and then muddle the order, or as dogs bark if there is a knock at the door, before looking to see if it is a friend. So anger, by reason of the warmth and hastiness of its nature, when it hears, though not hearing an order, springs to take revenge. (1149a24–31, Ackrill's revision of Ross's translation)[6]

The position here is not that there is something particularly ambiguous; it is not that one would not otherwise be sure how to take something, but does take it in a particular way through the aim of one's emotion. Neither is it a matter of conniving, nor of anger itself being a change in judgments. Rather, through the emotion one mishears, that is, does not hear the order given. The seduction arises from a mishearing, a misperception of what may be very clear evidence. This misperception in its turn affects judgment.

This seems quite insightful, covering certain cases quite plausibly. For emotion can alter perception and consequently the judgments based on these perceptions. Excited supporters of opposing tennis players often see rather different things. Their judgments based on these perceptions are accordingly influenced. Thus the seduction of the hopeful person facing nearly insurmountable hurdles can be explained by the misperception of those hurdles and consequent misjudgment.

Although we might like to agree that something along these lines is surely right, the account needs to be developed. For the precise operation of emotion, especially upon perception, is not yet clear. Until it is clear, we do not know if Aristotle has adequately provided an additional way in which emotion alters judgment.

To see how Aristotle can suppose this to work, we need to begin with a passage in *De Somniis* and then reflect upon the theory of objects of perception in *De Anima*.

> With regard to our original inquiry, one fact, which is clear from what we have said, may be laid down—that the percept still remains perceptible even after the external object perceived is gone, and moreover that we are easily deceived about our perceptions when we are in emotional states, some in one state and others in another; e.g. the coward in his fear, the lover in his love; so that even from a very faint resemblance the coward expects to see his enemy, and the lover his loved one; and the more one is under the influence of emotion, the less similarity is required to give these impressions. Similarly, in fits of anger and in all forms of desire all are easily deceived, and the more easily, the more they are under the influence of emotions. So to those in a fever, animals sometimes appear on the wall from a slight resemblance of lines put together. Sometimes the illusion corresponds to the degree of emotion so that those who are not very ill are aware that the impression is false, but if the malady is more severe, they actually move in accordance with appearances. (460b1–16, based on Hett's translation)

Like the passage from the *Nicomachean Ethics* and unlike the first three explanations, this concerns the perceptual level of emotions affecting perceptions rather than the epistemic level of emotions affecting beliefs and knowledge. Aristotle claims that deception occurs readily when we are excited by the emotions—cowards by their fear, lovers by their love. With little basis cowards will see their foes; lovers, their beloved. Moreover, the more deeply the emotion is felt, the more remote a resemblance may be that gives rise to illusory impressions. However, this is not to hold that we always get it wrong when in an emotional state: Aristotle suggests that we may recognize the illusion if the emotion is slight.

In addition to concurring with the view of the *Nicomachean Ethics*, this provides part of the explanation we seek. Emotion is meant to alter perception through the expectation of emotion and the "putting together" (*suntithemenōn*) of things accordingly. If this occurs, then, having the wrong perceptions, we go on to make poorly founded and likely inadequate judgments. Still, how emotion can operate in this way on what we perceive is unclear, even if we grant, say, that the fearful would expect and put things together differently from the amorous.

If we recall the distinction between objects of perception *per se* and objects of perception *per accidens* in *De Anima* 2.6, we can make good sense of putting together through the expectation of emotion. An object of perception *per se* is a white thing; *per accidens*, Socrates. We are meant to perceive both sorts of objects.[7] And what is noteworthy for us is that while the former object has little or no room for misperception or difference in perception, the latter object has a good deal of room. Thus with this latter object error can occur; emotion can create illusions and alter perception.

To explain exactly how this occurs, let me begin with the differences of perception that may occur without involving error or emotion. Suppose that the object of perception that we all are seeing (the object *per se*) is a black, circular, flat thing.[8] If it is a record, a piece of plastic, and something else as well, then according to Aristotle, those latter things are perceived *per accidens*, even though particular perceivers may not perceive it as those things and they may not, therefore, be "their object." Although with my knowledge of records what I perceive it as is a record, and with another's knowledge of the mysteries of Lil, what she or he perceives it as is the sacred God, and so on, still what is perceived *per accidens* is the record and the sacred God. While what is seen *per se* and even *per accidens* remains the same, the object *per accidens* that it is perceived as need not be the same for the devotee in Lil and myself. We can say "our objects" of perception are different.

So now we can see how different people seeing the same thing *per se*, may see different things *per accidens*. What we now need to understand is the case of misperception, and misperception through emotion.[9]

We have noted that the object of perception *per se* is not subject to misperception, while the object *per accidens* is. The sorts of error involved here include misperception of what the object of perception *per accidens* is (*DA* 418a15), and illusion (*Somn.* 460b19). In these cases, the object of perception *per accidens* that it is perceived as is not in fact the same as the object of perception *per accidens*. Given that emotion is held to be responsible for misperception, its means of influence is through the expectation and consequent putting together of a given object of perception. Let me illustrate these points.

Suppose we have two people. George is swept by fear; Harry is exceedingly calm and confident. Both hear a loud sound (object *per se*); George hears a gun firing (object *per accidens*); Harry hears the backfiring of a car (object *per accidens*). Suppose, in fact, a car did make the loud sound. Then we say that through his fear George is expecting (*dokein, Somn.* 460b6) fearful events to occur. The object *per se* can be taken for the firing of a gun; and, through the expectation, the loud sound is heard, although misheard, by being put together (*suntithemenōn, Somn.* 460b13) as a gun firing. The emotion involves certain expectations. In terms of those expectations what the object of perception *per accidens* is perceived as can be put together erroneously. Suppose now it was a gun firing. What we say of Harry is that he is not expecting anything untoward, that his confidence precludes any such thing. Hearing the loud sound (object *per se*), he puts it together differently—misperceives—and this is what he hears.

Turning to the example in *De Somniis*, we find that even where the resemblance is very faint, the coward is meant, through expectation, to put together an enemy that is not there (an object of perception *per accidens*). Turning to the examples of the *Nicomachean Ethics*, the servant hears a sound, is expecting something, and through the haste and warmth of the emotion puts it together accordingly, thereby misperceiving. Without further ado, the servant springs to action. Likewise, the dog hears a sound, is expecting some evil, and through the warmth and hastiness of the emotion puts together that the knock of a friend as that of an enemy. Without further ado, it springs to action.

Thus the distinction in *De Anima* helps to explain the suggestion of both *De Somniis* and the *Nicomachean Ethics*. Moreover, we can understand why Aristotle says in this latter work that the servant hears but does not hear an order (1149a31). For he or she hears the object *per se*, the sound, but through his or her emotion he or she is expecting something, and does not hear (does not put together) the object *per accidens*, the order issued.

Thus far, we can explain how Aristotle takes misperception to arise through emotion. That the emotion controlling us is seen to predispose us to see things in terms of it through expectation, is, I believe, a plausible suggestion on Aristotle's part: emotion is supposed to be part of our way of viewing the world. Our way of viewing the world is the way we put things together, and thus brings about an alteration of perception.

That the emotion controlling someone affects one's perception is a good part of the explanation of how a person is seduced to dissent from what is, for others, unambiguous. What something is perceived as (*per accidens*) differs for one moved by a particular emotion. The judgments based on this perception would be askew correspondingly.

Still this does not seem adequate to explain how, say, the lover gets all wrong what is plain to others, and never catches on. Of course, one should maintain that the lover constantly misconstrues, so long as the emotion is present. This must be part of the answer. But we should also recall the warmth and hastiness both of the dog and of the servant mentioned in the *Nicomachean Ethics*. That warmth and hastiness helped to explain that and how one mishears what one hears. In addition, it helps to explain why neither the dog nor the servant takes in all the relevant information. Rather, they spring to action. Remember, the wary dog hears but does not look to see, so immediate is its reaction. Likewise, we can say that lovers hear a little but through their emotion mishear, and spring to action (here, misjudge). In so doing the lover has not listened to all the evidence, fastening on to some only, and that misheard and misjudged. All the rest is judged in terms of it.

There can, therefore, be a variety of reasons why lovers seem able to misjudge even in light of what appears to be insurmountable evidence to the contrary. What they take in, they misconstrue. To the extent they continue to take in, they continue to misconstrue. Through the warmth and hastiness, and the expectation of emotion, they stop considering further evidence, and instead view the entire matter in terms of what they have already taken in and determined. This completes the fourth explanation of emotion altering judgments—though one should add that it may well be augmented by any of those methods discussed so far, the favor/disfavor method seeming very likely to be involved here.[10]

What spurred us on to search for a fourth explanation has been found: we have an explanation that does not rely on emotion having a specific aim or goal, and one that can account for the seduction of judgment although the evidence to the contrary is clear enough. Rather than relying on the end of the emotion, this explanation relies on the emotion having a certain expectation and a person's putting together what something is perceived as *per accidens* in light of this. This may be plausibly said of the hopeful person; indeed, it would seem plausible regarding all the emotions; and thus this explanation applies most generally.

5

Although the need to search for additional explanations has been met, this does not exhaust all the answers implicit in Aristotle for the ways in which emotion alters judgments. In the characterization of emotion that we began with (1378a20–23), we find that pleasure and pain play a key part. Pleasure and pain can provide us with a further, albeit very general, explanation of the effect of emotion upon judgment. According to *De Anima* (431a8–10), as something is painful or pleasant it is avoided or pursued. Thus the person experiencing a pleasant emotion (e.g., love) will be moved to focus on the matter more than one who is not in a state of pleasure. In contrast, the person experiencing a painful emotion (e.g., anger) will be moved to avoid the matter, unlike the person not in a state of pain. The greater attention upon the beloved provided by love's pleasure will make possible a deeper appreciation than could otherwise be had; the depleting of attention upon the one with whom one is angry, brought on by anger's distress, will make for less appreciation than would otherwise be had. Through attention or its opposite, one's judgments may be influenced. To this extent, things do not seem the same; and this is a fifth way in which emotion alters judgments.

Clearly this is a very general explanation, relating to emotions only insofar as they are pleasant or painful. Although the influence upon judgment is brought on by the pleasure or the pain of the emotion, the operation of that change is a result of attention or its lack. Moreover, it should be noted that other considerations may substantially alter the influence of attention and its lack. Greater attention needn't bring greater clarity; less attention needn't degrade judgment. In the case of love, for example, insofar as the previous explanations are also appropriate, the greater attention brought by love's pleasures may serve to further beguile rather than illuminate. Still, insofar as one feels pleasure or pain, one has a better or worse opportunity to understand. Insofar as one is so influenced, emotion alters judgment.

These different methods answer our question as to how well equipped Aristotle is to explain emotion's ability to alter judgment. He is well equipped. Doubtless, there can be other answers consistent with the Aristotelian framework, and some of these we can anticipate. (For example, we might expect an explanation parallel with the fourth, but having expectation and "putting together" alter judgment directly.) Nevertheless, it is these five that are implicit in Aristotle's works. Their complexity varies from the simplicity of the first and fifth to the intricacies of the fourth. All, I think, provide plausible solutions to the problem addressed. To this, it should be remembered that when we come to account for instances of emotions affecting judgment, often we shall find that more than one explanation is involved. They need not be separate. Still, the principles remain distinct. Thus we end with the following two kinds of changes of judgment involving emotion: (1) change of judgment as a consequence of emotion; (2) change of judgment as a constituent of emotion. The former has the following species: (a) connivance, (b) alteration through favor and disfavor, (c) alteration through perception, (d) alteration through pleasure and pain.

II

Having dealt with the first of our tasks, let us now consider the second aspect of Aristotle's characterization of emotion: pleasure and pain accompanying emotion. Some points may be readily stated. The definition of anger holds that it is with pain; contemplating, dwelling upon, and achieving its revenge is pleasant (*Rhet.*, 1378b1–5, 1370b29); those disposed to be angry are those in pain (1379a10–21, cf. *DA* 403a18–20). And one can go on to cite similar information regarding various *pathē*. But to do so would not go very far to explain what Aristotle means by pleasure and pain accompanying *ta pathē*.

What could Aristotle mean by saying that emotions are accompanied by pleasure and pain?[11] A number of interpretations are possible. In our terms, it might have the status of an observation of a frequent occurrence, much like "parents accompany their young children to new schools." There is no necessity here; it is an observation regarding two things that often concur. Alternatively, we could see Aristotle's claim as some kind of conceptual point.[12] If so, there are at least two ways this might go. "Accompanying" might suggest a link between two separate concepts, the word "accompanying" relating the two; or the point might be that the concept of emotion includes within it an accompanying pleasure or pain. Further there is a concern for the nature of that which accompanies. Is the pain, for example, that accompanies shame an instance of pain of the same kind that accompanies anger? Or is the pain peculiar to shame and of a different sort from that which accompanies anger?

The thought that emotion's accompaniment by pleasure and pain is like parents and young children need not delay us very long. After all, the point is not offered as an observation from certain occurrences. Instead, the claim is stated as though a point were being made about the concept of emotion. Moreover, when different emotions are set out, the accompaniment by pleasure and pain seems a part of the definition of these emotions rather than an observation about something separate that typically accompanies. Further, were the point one of simple concurrence, then we could expect the language to reflect an analogous discussion in Plato's *Philebus,* using "*meta*" only and not "*hepetai*" to make the point about *ta pathē*.[13]

If we are to understand Aristotle in terms of a conceptual point, there is an apparent anomaly that should be noted. When contrasting hatred and anger (*Rhet.* 1382a11–13), Aristotle goes out of his way to point out that hatred, unlike anger, has no pain. Since the implication is not that hatred is a pleasure, the point must be that hatred is without feeling, cold, accompanied by neither pleasure nor pain. Mind you, while this anomaly is certainly striking, it should not undermine our understanding of emotion being accompanied by pleasure and pain—even if hatred can only be understood as an exception.[14]

If "accompanying" introduces a conceptual link, what sort of link is it? Is it a link between two distinct concepts, one always attending the other (perhaps as do cause and effect), or is it that the concept of emotion includes within it pleasure and pain? Now, simply speaking of "accompanying" might suggest the former to us, so that, for example, when the definition of anger is given as a certain sort of longing, the pain could be understood as something necessarily accompanying this longing but itself distinct from the emotion. If true, this would mean that the pain was not part of the emotion, and would not be required in the definition of the emotion—though it would need be noted as a necessary accompaniment of the emotion. But since we find that the accompanying pain is placed within anger's definition, Aristotle means more than a necessary accompaniment; emotion includes the pleasure or pain. This conclusion is further confirmed when we observe that many of the emotions are defined as pains or disturbances (e.g., fear, shame). Thus Aristotle includes pleasure and pain within the concept of emotion when he speaks of "accompanying."[15]

The link between emotion and accompanying pleasure and pain is to be understood in terms of a conceptual claim. Further, pleasure and pain are part of the emotion. Now, we must ask whether the pain felt in, say, fear, is unique to fear, or is it interchangeable with the pain of shame? Do the relevant pains or pleasures differ only in number and intensity?

Before dealing with this question we should notice that even if the relevant pains or pleasures do not differ in kind, the absurdity would not follow that if, say, the judgment appropriate to fear was made and at the same time a pain arose (say, in the foot), one would then be afraid. This does not follow because the linking together of the elements in the definition is done in a way stronger than simple concurrence. This, I have argued, is part of the force of "accompany." Moreover, if we look at the definitions of the various emotions, consider fear, we find that the pain is not just conjoined with a particular judgment, but caused by that judgment. "Let fear be defined as a pain or troubled feeling caused by the impression of an imminent evil that causes destruction or pain" (*Rhet.* 1382a20–22, Freese's translation). Thus, for a variety of reasons, there is no possibility that such an absurdity could follow within the Aristotelian framework.

Having dismissed such a misunderstanding, let us turn to our alternatives: the pain or pleasure of an emotion being unique, or the pain or pleasure being different in number and intensity but never in kind. The definitions given in the *Rhetoric* are plausibly interpreted either way; and within that work I see no reason for confidence that Aristotle holds that there are kinds of pleasures and pains.[16] It may be tempting, then, to draw the modest conclusion: the pains and pleasures of different emotion types differ in number and intensity but not in kind. However, if we expand our horizons somewhat, I think we shall see the stronger position to be Aristotle's.

The *Nicomachean Ethics* provides reason to think the pleasure or pain is specific to a given emotion and not shared with other emotions.

> For this reason pleasures seem, too, to differ in kind. For things different in kind are, we think, completed by different things (we see this to be true both of natural objects and of things produced by art, e.g., animals, trees, a painting, a sculpture, a house, an implement); and, similarly, we think that activities differing in kind are completed by things differing in kind. Now the activities of thought differ from those of the senses, and both differ among themselves, in kind; so, therefore, do the pleasures that complete them. (1175a22–28, Ross's translation)

Given that Aristotle goes on to talk about the pleasures of flute playing as opposed to those of argument, and given that the pleasures of the different senses vary, it is reasonable to conclude, concerning emotions, that the pleasure of love differs in kind from that of joy. Likewise, it is reasonable to conclude that the pain of anger differs in kind from that of shame. Thus the pain or pleasure of emotions differ from one to another in number, intensity, and kind. This means that the proper reading of the definitions, again taking fear as our example, is the following: "Let fear be defined as a painful or troubled feeling caused by . . ." rather than "Let fear be defined as a painful or troubled feeling, caused by. . . ." The pleasure or pain that accompanies completes the emotion, rather than supervenes upon it.[17]

We can say the following about the accompaniment of emotion by pleasure and pain. The pleasure or pain is part of the concept of the emotion; neither is separable from the emotion. For each emotion-type there is a type of pleasure or pain peculiar to that emotion. They complete the emotion.[18]

With this observed, it must be recalled that the role of pleasure and pain in emotion is not exhausted by the "accompanying" relationship. As noted already, in addition to the pain or pleasure of the emotion, contemplating and achieving the aim of the emotion (where appropriate) is pleasant, the bodily precondition for the emotion may be pleasant or painful, and so on.

III

Concerning Aristotle's characterization of emotions, we have seen how emotions alter judgment, are an alteration of judgment, and what it means to say that emotions are accompanied by pleasure and pain. We now come to our third task. Throughout, we have spoken of *ta pathē* as the emotions. That is surely the right translation, given the examples Aristotle offers us. But does his notion match our own?

Implicit in Fortenbaugh is an answer to this question.[19] Fortenbaugh takes the concern here to be clearly that of the emotions because he believes Aristotle's characterization of *ta pathē* is implicitly qualified in terms of the *Philebus*'s "psychic attributes." Because of this, *ta pathē* are held to be quite distinct from desires such as hunger and thirst; and all doubts that by "*ta pathē*" Aristotle has grasped the emotions are dispelled. Although I find this conclusion agreeable, I do not think Fortenbaugh's argument is adequate. First, there seems to be no reason to be confident that Aristotle's characterization is so qualified: Aristotle never hints at this. Second, elsewhere Aristotle does offer a list of what are emotions and takes them to involve the body (*DA* 403a16–19). Thus the suggestion that *ta pathē* are distinct from desires because Aristotle thinks that *ta pathē* are "psychic" rather than "bodily" is not an accurate portrayal of Aristotle's position. Third, when it is recalled that Aristotle often does include bodily desire (*epithumia*) in with *ta pathē* (cf. note 1 of this essay), Fortenbaugh's proposal becomes more and more doubtful. Fourth, even if it were clear that the *Philebus*'s qualification was intended, and we did not have to worry about *epithumia* or Aristotle's claim of a bodily nature for various emotions, it still would not be evident that *ta pathē* are the emotions. For included in the *Philebus*'s psychic attributes are *pothos* (yearning) and *erōs* (sexual desire), 47e1–2. As is especially clear concerning sexual desire, these are often seen to be types of desire (see *Republic* 549c6–8, *Rhet.* 1385a24, *NE* 1118b8 ff.). Hence, even were Aristotle to be building upon Plato, it does not seem that this itself is to grasp the notion of emotion. Consequently, if Aristotle has grasped the notion, this is not to trace over old blueprints, but to redraw boundaries within the human soul.

My own position is that Aristotle is redrawing boundaries. Yet that he is doing so requires justification; how and why he is doing so requires explanation. To resolve these matters, we should begin by turning our attention back to the *Rhetoric*'s characterization of *ta pathē*, examining how the "accompaniment" of *hēdonē* and *lupē* sharpen and refine this notion.[20] This will lead us to consider other ways in which the *Rhetoric* hones *ta pathē*. Examining these matters should provide insight into what Aristotle understands by "*ta pathē*" here and elsewhere, how well it matches our own notion of emotion, and how it contrasts with Aristotle's notion of desire.

Let us begin with our concepts. Were we to try to set forth all the elements of our "inner life," we would wind up with an extensive list, including yearnings, moods, thoughts, wants, perceptions, pleasures, satisfactions, hankerings, and so forth. Obviously, a complete list would fill pages, but I think the following distinctions will serve here to mark off major areas that Aristotle is concerned with: (1) sensations, (2) desires, (3) emotions, (4) thoughts, (5) perceptions, (6) attitudes, (7) pleasures and pains. We shall examine the first six in light of the seventh. The object is to see what work the accompaniment of pleasure and pain accomplishes. This, I think, will provide some insight into Aristotle's notion of *ta pathē* with its accompaniment by *hēdonē* and *lupē*.

It seems to be the case that desires and emotions require pleasure and pain in a way sensations, attitudes, perceptions, and thoughts do not. Take thinking. As I think about how best to put my point, the process is neither pleasant nor painful; as I think about a vacation to France, the thought is pleasant. Thus while pleasure or pain may attend my thoughts, there is no necessity to it.[21] Sensation too may be pleasant or painful: the warming of the sun is pleasant; its burning is painful. But sensation need not be either pleasant or painful, just as the sensation of a gurgling stomach or a twitching eye is neither pleasant nor painful. Parallel considerations apply to perceptions and attitudes.[22] But emotions and desires (and here we are thinking of their occurrent manifestations) do not seem like this. My desire for a drink is something disturbing to me: its satisfaction is just that, a pleasure. And this would seem to be so for all desires. Of emotion, it seems that it must in some way involve pleasure or pain. Anger, shame, and sadness are themselves painful or distressing; love and joy are pleasant. The pleasure or pain of these is not just coincident, but necessary to the emotion or desire.

By speaking of what must involve pleasure and pain, we limit ourselves to emotions and desires. Turning to Aristotle, that is an interesting consequence. For, likewise, by speaking of the accompaniment of *hēdonē* and *lupē*, since that accompaniment is best understood in terms of a necessary and conceptual claim (see section II of this essay), Aristotle thereby limits himself to what we call emotions and desires. Moreover, all this seems to fit in with Aristotle's theorizing. That Aristotle does take pleasure and pain to do this work concerning emotions is clear both through his claim that *ta pathē* (which, at least, include the emotions) are accompanied by *hēdonē* and *lupē*, and through his definitions of various emotions as types of *hēdonē* and *lupē*. That he takes pleasure and pain to be central to desire (*orexis*), and its other face, aversion, we see in *De Anima*, 431a8–16: what is pleasant is pursued; what is painful is avoided. Again in the *Rhetoric*, 1385a23–25, we see that desire (*orexis*) is a discomfort seeking satisfaction.

But how far does this get us?

We are seeking to understand what sort of notion Aristotle develops with *ta pathē* in the *Rhetoric*'s characterization of them. We have looked at the accompaniment of *hēdonē* and *lupē*, finding that through this accompaniment we understand how a realm exhausted by emotions and desires is delimited. Yet the examples mentioned in the *Rhetoric*'s initial characterization of *ta pathē*, as well as the examples he goes on to discuss, concern emotions only, not desires. This suggests that in his *Rhetoric* Aristotle moves to a conception like that of emotion. Still, we remain puzzled on our own terms as well as on Aristotle's about the basis for the exclusion of desire.[23] Moreover, we can't discount the possibility that desire's exclusion from the *Rhetoric* is simply an omission on Aristotle's part. For it is worth recalling that lists of *ta pathē* in other works do include desire (e.g., *NE* 1105b21).

We need to investigate Aristotle's notion of desire.[24] Desire (*orexis*) is not some one, homogeneous, all-encompassing domain; rather it includes: (1) spiritedness, *thumos;* (2) wish, *boulēsis,* and (3) appetite, *epithumia* (*Motu* 700b22, *DA* 414b2, *EE* 1223a25–27). Because of this complexity, the differences between these must be considered. We need to discover how each is analyzed and then to reflect upon the exclusion or inclusion of each of these from the *Rhetoric*'s notion of *ta pathē*, doing so from the vantage of *ta pathē* as emotions.

Consider *thumos* (1). The characterization given to it is very much like that of anger, *orgē*. It too seems painful, while the prospect and achievement of its aim is a pleasant thing, revenge (*EE* 1229b31, *NE* 1116b23–1117a9). Indeed, *thumos* is offered as an example of a *pathos* in the *Rhetoric* (1378b4, 1379a4).

The fact and means of its inclusion is significant. "*Thumos*" here and elsewhere is used as another way of speaking about *orgē* (see *NE* 7.6). Since it is so understood, the inclusion of *thumos* in the *Rhetoric*'s discussion of *orgē* does not expand *ta pathē* beyond that of the emotions; rather the understanding of *thumos* is as an emotion. *Ta pathē* in the *Rhetoric* remain the emotions.

Next consider *boulēsis* (2). Aristotle is not tempted to include *boulēsis* as one of the *Rhetoric*'s *pathē;* and this exclusion is quite appropriate. Pleasure and pain do not seem to characterize the desire. Moreover, *boulēsis*'s first aim is *to on kalon* (*Met.* 1072a27, cf. *Rhet.* 1369a2). If it relates to pleasure and pain at all in terms of its aim, it does so incidentally (cf. *Top.* 146b3, 147a1–4, *Rhet.* 1381a1–4). Thus *boulēsis* does not satisfy the pleasure/pain test as emotions do, but, at most, as perception or thought does.[25] This is to say that *boulēsis* does not satisfy the *Rhetoric*'s first test for *ta pathē*. Hence this type of desire is not to be confused with emotion; and Aristotle has good reason to exclude *boulēsis* from his list of *ta pathē* in the *Rhetoric*, and elsewhere (*NE* 1105b21, *EE* 1220b12).

One might object that the argument argues too much. Shame, *aischunē*, like *boulēsis*, does not aim at pleasure or pain, yet remains a *pathos*. Thus my argument that *boulēsis* does not aim at pleasure or pain is not a reason for its exclusion as a *pathos*. However, the cases are importantly different. For while *boulēsis* only relates incidentally to pleasure or pain, shame is defined as a pain (*Rhet.* 1383b15). Thus this latter, but not the former, satisfies the pleasure/pain test; and *boulēsis* has rightfully been excluded as a *pathos*.

So far, so good. By reflecting on the nature of desire, we can see why two of its forms, *boulēsis* and *thumos*, create no difficulties for the hypothesis that in the *Rhetoric* Aristotle is developing a conception of the emotion, a conception that distinguishes emotion from desire. We have only *epithumia* (3) to contend with.

Since *epithumia* is not mentioned in the passage from the *Rhetoric* we are concerned with, nor discussed in the various studies of *ta pathē* in the *Rhetoric*, this hypothesis seems likely. However, we still have to find justification for the exclusion of *epithumia*. Moreover, since *epithumia* has been counted as a *pathos* elsewhere (*NE* 1105b21, *EE* 1220b12), we need an explanation of these differing claims.[26]

Epithumia (appetite or sensual appetite) is a desire for the pleasant (*Rhet.* 1370a17, *DA* 414a5–6, *Top.* 147a2); like anger and other painful emotions it is characterized as painful (*NE* 1119a4). *Epithumiai* include and are explained in terms of the desires for food, drink, and sex (*NE* 1118b8 ff., cf. *DA* 414b13).[27] As something itself unpleasant craving the pleasure of satisfying its lack, movement as a result of appetite is not very mysterious (*DA* 433a25, cf. *Rhet.* 1369b15, 1379a10–11). It is taken to be contrary to choice (*NE* 1111b16), a wild beast (*Polit.* 1287a31). Its operation occurs without involving reason: "But appetite leads without persuading, being devoid of reason" (*EE* 1224b2, Solomon's translation). We have here something well suited to causal analysis.

From this characterization, we can see that the exclusion of *epithumia* (unlike that of *boulēsis*) cannot be accounted for through failing to satisfy the pleasure/pain test. Moreover, there is no indication (as there was concerning *thumos*) that "*epithumia*" is or can be but another name for an emotion. What, then, accounts for its absence from the *Rhetoric*?

I suggest that what justifies this desire's exclusion is the *Rhetoric*'s other major characterization of *ta pathē*: emotions being the things on account of which the ones altered differ with respect to their judgments (*Rhet.* 1378a120–121). If I am right in saying that *epithumia* is excluded because it does not meet this demand, then the *Rhetoric* delimits something very like what we mean by emotions, provides for a justification of this, and advances beyond Plato's spirited realm. A fascinating and perceptive development. But one that requires some argument before we grant it. For although *epithumiai* do not seem to be emotions, and the *Rhetoric*'s exclusion of them as *pathē* seems to be a recognition of this, we cannot be sure that this is so until we see that that part of the characterization of *ta pathē* that speaks of altering judgments does properly exclude *epithumiai*.

I think that it does. There is no need for a difference in judgment between one who is thirsty and one who is hungry: each may hold all the same judgments, but the former seeks food while the latter seeks drink. Indeed, being hungry or thirsty does not require the holding of any particular judgments, or any judgments at all. Moreover, it is not itself a reasonable or unreasonable state. As Aristotle suggests, it is devoid of reason (*EE* 1224b2). However, as Aristotle recognizes, emotions are rather different from this. Those in a different emotional state do differ with respect to judgment; for example, whereas the envious will view another's good fortune as undeserved, the emulous will not. Being in an emotional state requires judgments, particular judgments (see section I). Moreover, an emotional state is itself reasonable (fear of a formidable enemy) or unreasonable (fear of a mouse).

Thus the two, epithumetic desire and emotion, do seem importantly different with regard to the role of judgments. It would seem, then, that Aristotle has noted the difference, distinguished the realms, and provided justification for this.

Still, one might doubt that what Aristotle has set forth is really adequate, even though right-headed. After all, is there not a sense in which an *epithumia* might bring about a change of judgments? For example, hunger's pang could make one so irritable that one comes to a very harsh view of someone who interferes with one's attempt to acquire food. Again, the alcoholic's thirst may be so strong that the person decides that wood alcohol is not so bad. However, it is not the hunger or the thirst that alters judgment. For, as we have seen, what these desires do is seek out their own satisfaction. Rather, the difference in judgment that may arise in such situations will arise through one's anger, irritation, despair, or reflections upon these matters. And Aristotle follows this up by noting that emotions often arise when desire is present.

> Men are angry when they are pained, because one who is pained aims at something; if then anyone directly opposes him in anything, as, for instance, prevents him from drinking when thirsty, or not directly, but seems to be doing just the same; and if anyone goes against him or refuses to assist him, or troubles him in any other way when he is in this frame of mind, he is angry with all such persons. Wherefore the sick, the necessitous [those at war], the love-sick, the thirsty, in a word, all who desire something and cannot obtain it, are prone to anger and easily excited. (*Rhet.* 1379a10–17, Freese's translation)

Any change of judgment here is only an incidental result of hunger or thirst, and quite remote from it. Epithumetic desire remains devoid of reason; it is not itself sufficient to alter judgments. The changes of judgments are to be explained by having been roused to emotion or reflection upon these matters.

Aristotle is right in thinking that emotions are quite different from these desires, *epithumiai;* and he is able to locate just what accounts for the difference. Like epithumetic desire, emotions too have an object, involve pleasure and pain, and through this latter are involved in pursuit and avoidance. However, in addition, emotions have a much more wide-ranging aim. Through expectation, they alter the way we put things together. Moreover, they require judgments, judgments subtle and complex in structure. And because of this, emotions are themselves alterations of judgments (anger views its object as having insulted one, *Rhet.* 1378a31), and alter judgments (hope leads to a better view of one's prospects, *Rhet.* 1378a1–4). In contrast, because *epithumia* has only the satisfaction of eating, drinking, and so on, what counts as satisfaction here is much more restricted, and will not involve changes of judgment. That Aristotle excludes *epithumia* from the list in the *Rhetoric* is justified; *epithumia* as an emotion does not belong.[28]

The thesis that Aristotle is delimiting a realm of emotion finds further confirmation. For not only does Aristotle recognize the difference between *epithumiai* and emotions, but also he utilizes this difference. *Epithumia*, we have seen, is not subject to rational principle (is not reasonable or unreasonable). Moreover, when strong and violent it can expel the power of calculation (*NE* 1119b5–15). Thus whereas the angry person may reason poorly in deciding to wreak a terrible vengeance, the person of unquenchable thirst *qua* in the grip of said thirst does not reason at all, but simply seeks the object of his or her desire.

This role for *epithumia* is utilized elsewhere. For example, in a discussion of incontinence Aristotle's position is not that the desire for the sweet alters the universality of one's opinion that forbids tasting. Rather, one follows one's desire to taste and loses sight of the opinion. Once more, desire seems to expel rather than alter reasoning (*NE* 1147a25–1147b17). All this is rather different from the way, say, hope brings about a favorable interpretation of what is ambiguous or envy views the good fortune of another as undeserved.

Yet another utilization of the difference between *epithumia* and emotion has to do with the obedience of emotion, but not *epithumia*, to reason. If emotions are the sorts of things that rationally alter our judgments, one can expect them to be open to reason. Similarly, if *epithumia* does not rationally alter judgments, one would not expect it to be open to reason. Aristotle appreciates this when he says:

> Therefore anger [*thumos*] obeys the argument in a sense, but appetite does not. It is therefore more disgraceful; for the man who is incontinent in respect of anger is in a sense conquered by argument, while the other is conquered by appetite and not by argument. (*NE* 1149b1–4, Ross's translation; cf. 1119b7)

This contrast is fairly drawn between *epithumia* and emotions in general. Thus while you might convince a person not to act on their *epithumia*, say, for food, you cannot talk that person out of feeling hungry. Hence we find Aristotle observing: "It is assumed that there is no gain in being persuaded not to be hot or in pain or hungry or the like, since we shall experience these feelings none the less" (*NE* 1113b27–30, Ross's translation). In contrast, not only might you convince a person not to act on their emotion, say, fear, but also you might talk the person out of it. This latter you might do by convincing them that one of their judgments whence their fear arose was wrong, or you might convince them that even though all is as judged, the object feared is not worth fearing. And by convincing the person you also move them.[29] The contrast between the two is that while we give grounds for emotions, we only give causes for thirst and other *epithumiai*. Thus the former, but not the latter, is, in this sense, conquered by argument. Thus it is the former, but not the latter, that Aristotle concerns himself with and explains the grounds upon which they are felt (*Rhet.* 1378a28).

In view of the interaction between the rational soul and desire, we must digress to notice that the contrast between epithumetic desire and emotion becomes more complicated in certain instances. Epithumetic desires, we have seen, are the sorts of things that get set in motion, halted, stemmed, suppressed, expelled, and so on. The causal chains for any particular desire can be quite diverse. Consider sexual desire. Gestures, clothing, movement, glances, pictures—all these may serve to "turn one on or off." A causal conception is in operation here in a clear-cut way. However, it may seem a little less clear-cut when we consider that reading certain passages from novels may have the same effect. For here it seems as though epithumetic desire is available to reason. And that may upset the contrast established. But if such cases are ones in which we want to say that epithumetic desire is said to be "available to reason," it is so in a way importantly different from the availability of the emotions. First, the case remains one of being turned on or off, of causation. Although reading the novel may dampen or arouse one's ardor, still one has been turned off or on, shocked or titillated. One has not been reasoned into anything or persuaded, in the way one may be moved to anger by being persuaded that someone has insulted you. So whereas emotion admits of rational persuasion, epithumetic desire still is not available to reason. The complication here has been that, as an animal capable of reason, the means of rousing epithumetic desires are that much richer, involving the rational soul, but still not in a way to be confused with emotion's involvement with the rational soul. Second, to the extent one still wants to say "No, my desire really has been rationally altered here," that we can quite happily accommodate by the operation of *boulēsis*, not *epithumia*. That is to say, in the example above, we have not only epithumetic desire in operation, but also rational desire. For that the desires are distinct has no implication about forced separability or lack of interplay among them. And it is possible that deliberative desire could enter into the picture here.[30] Thus the contrast between *epithumia* and emotion stands.[31]

Hence not only is the exclusion of *epithumia* and all desire from the list in the *Rhetoric* reasonable, but also the implications are appreciated and utilized elsewhere.

What I have just argued is that in the *Rhetoric* and elsewhere Aristotle shows a perceptive awareness of the differences of operation of epithumetic desire and emotion. Before that I argued that Aristotle's other sorts of desire (*thumos* and *boulēsis*) do not interfere with the suggestion that Aristotle is delimiting the realm of emotion in the *Rhetoric*. My conclusion is that the characterization of *ta pathē* in the *Rhetoric* distinguishes emotion from other elements of our inner life: the pleasure/pain test setting emotion and certain desires quite apart from the other elements, the alteration of judgment setting emotion quite apart from *epithumia*.[32] That the *Rhetoric* does not mention or expand upon the *pathos orexis* or *epithumia* is not an oversight or error, but a recognition that *epithumia* and *orexis* are not to be understood as emotions.[33]

Setting forth the notion of emotion is a sophisticated advance in the realm of philosophical psychology. However, at least one problem lingers. Why is *epithumia* here excluded from the list of *ta pathē*, while elsewhere included?

Developmental explanations are often employed in this sort of situation, arguing, for example, that here Aristotle abandons the Platonic psychology that mesmerized him elsewhere. However, we cannot be certain that the *Rhetoric* is Aristotle's last word in this area of psychology; and since Aristotle utilizes these distinctions at some points in his ethical works, but does not utilize them at other points (*NE* 1105b21, *EE* 1120b12), a developmental explanation cannot resolve this problem. We must search for some other sort of explanation. There are a number of possibilities.

The most radical explanation suggests that the picture of *ta pathē* that has emerged is wrong. In the *Rhetoric* Aristotle simply chose not to use *epithumia* as an example; and we have made a mountain from what is not even a molehill. But I suggest that too much has been gained; there is too much rigor, too much perceptiveness, too great an appreciation of the consequences by Aristotle for this explanation to be adopted.

A different explanation urges that sometimes Aristotle wrongly includes *epithumia* (*NE* 1105b21, *EE* 1220b12). There are the differences noted between *epithumia* and *ta pathē*; Aristotle is aware of them; yet his inclusion of *epithumia* in the lists of *ta pathē* in the ethical works is a lapse, a failure to appreciate fully and mark out adequately what he does elsewhere. Alternatively, one can suggest that Aristotle is driving at a slightly different point than our analysis of the *Rhetoric* suggests. What he really wants to do is to note a group of things that (*a*) relate to pleasure and pain, and (*b*) "in one way or another," however remotely, alter judgment. All *ta pathē*, including *epithumia*, do these. The absence of *epithumia* from the *Rhetoric* is just a failure to list and discuss fully. That we find very important differences between the one way and the other is interesting and important to us, but does not signify for Aristotle's analysis of *ta pathē*. He may be dividing the cake differently from us, but not therefore mistakenly.

These two approaches are not really that far apart. The latter tries to claim that Aristotle's conceptions when brought forth on his own terms are different from our own—although the approach admits that at certain points he does draw the contrasts as we do. The former views Aristotle in terms of distinctions we make (accusing him, in parallel and quite important passages in his ethical works, of failing to appreciate adequately what he at other times takes to be important). Neither of these ways of resolving the matter is as satisfactory as we might like. Both interpretations make Aristotle's analysis of *ta pathē* broken-backed and admit that he should have been aware of the broken nature. The former view's contention that in the ethical works Aristotle is guilty of a glaring error through his inclusion of *epithumia* as a *pathos* is unsatisfactory. Equally unsatisfactory is the latter view's contention that although Aristotle is aware that emotions as such alter judgments, while epithumetic desires do not, he nevertheless ignores this in the *Rhetoric* opting for an "in one way or another"—especially since *epithumia* is not listed or discussed there. Also difficult to believe in the latter interpretation is Aristotle's silence about his thesis that emotions but not *epithumiai* are altered by reason. In addition, this interpretation by supposing *epithumia* as a legitimate candidate for a *pathos* in the *Rhetoric* fails to appreciate that whereas the *pathē* Aristotle does mention and discuss do have a "with whom," *epithumia* does not. Thus neither of these explanations should be accepted. We need a different sort of approach.

The differences in scope given to *ta pathē* throughout Aristotle's work (see *DA* 403a1–7, 17–19; *Cat.* 9b9–10a10) might suggest that rather than trying to find a unified or developing (although broken-backed) theory of *ta pathē*, "*ta pathē*" in its different contexts varies with the purposes at hand in extension and intension. We shall focus on the relevant discussions in the *Rhetoric, Eudemian Ethics,* and *Nicomachean Ethics.* By so approaching the matter, I think we shall find a more satisfactory explanation—although not without its own difficulties.

We have seen that the two criteria present in the *Rhetoric* distinguish in an insightful way the emotions from the other elements of one's inner life. The examples Aristotle chooses, develops, and excludes bear this out. Turning to the lists of *ta pathē* in the ethical works, we find similar lists, although *epithumia* is included. Hence these are not lists of the emotions. But we should also notice that while we do find the pleasure/pain test, we do not find anything about altering judgments.[34] Consequently, the lists with their inclusion of *epithumia* match perfectly with the single pleasure/pain test. Viewed in this way, Aristotle seems to wield the two principles with subtle appreciation of their implications in the *Rhetoric*, the *Eudemian Ethics*, and the *Nicomachean Ethics*.

Well and good, we might think, but still it remains puzzling in its way. Why does Aristotle speak of *ta pathē* in these similar, but importantly different ways? Why not stick with one, preferably the most subtle?

These differences in intension and extension can be explained, I believe, by noticing the issues Aristotle is addressing at a given time. At the appropriate places in the ethical works, Aristotle is trying to discover where virtue lies. The alternatives he offers are: *pathē, dunameis, hexeis*. In light of these contrasts and the goals sought, it seems quite reasonable that *ta pathē* should include more than emotion. The distinction between epithumetic desire and emotion does not matter to this ongoing discussion. Whether *ta pathē* are subject to reason will not matter to the discovery that virtue is a *hexis*. Moreover, given that Aristotle wants to hold that virtue concerns the *pathē*, he means it to concern epithumetic desire as well as the emotions. For virtue concerns occurrent rumblings, which may lead us astray, whether they be rumblings subject to reason or not.[35] Hence Aristotle does not bother about the second criterion; and *epithumia* is rightly included. Here *ta pathē* resemble what Hume and others call "the passions." However, when Aristotle's purposes are different—when he is trying to offer a theory of those affections relevant to rhetorical purposes, when he is trying to avoid the Platonic tendency of seeing rhetoric as sophistical, and when, as in certain parts of the ethical works, he is trying to appreciate the differences between *epithumia* and anger—then the differences between things that do and do not influence judgment, are and are not influenced by judgment, are crucial. The *Rhetoric*'s interest in *ta pathē* has to do with persuasion and as a result Aristotle sharpens the notion to concern those things that do affect judgment. Thus Aristotle excludes *epithumia*, which does not similarly affect judgment. Moreover, this explains the introduction of his second criterion, a criterion not introduced elsewhere.[36]

Aristotle does not hold a broken-backed theory with all its awkwardness. Moreover, we appreciate how skillfully Aristotle uses the different senses of "*ta pathē*." Where he is concerned to speak of the role of judgments concerning affection, he adequately gives the notion of *ta pathē* as emotion. Where his interest is not so specific, he includes *epithumia* in with emotions, but there correctly excludes the judgment criterion. And where his concern, as in *De Anima*, is with any affection of the soul, he expands his list and properly drops the pleasure/pain criterion. In all these cases the theory is adequate, skillful, and is not subject to the above complaints.[37]

This completes our third task. If the arguments are right, the consequences are impressive. In the *Rhetoric* Aristotle develops a notion of emotion to which he turns elsewhere. As well as coming to this notion, he isolates those features that set emotion apart from other elements of the human soul. We have come to see what it means to say that *ta pathē* are accompanied by *hēdonē* and *lupē*, as well as how these help to refine the notion of emotion. We have come to see the ways in which *ta pathē* can alter judgment, as well as how this also helps to refine the notion of emotion. In addition, we have seen that Aristotle is quite able to call upon the notion of emotion when needed, and related notions when they are needed. By this ability to wield the features that distinguish these notions, by his sensitivity to the different notions and their place, we see an extremely subtle philosopher at work.

NOTES

This chapter is a substantially revised version of an essay of the same title published in *Phronesis* 27 (1982): 144–174.

I should like to thank Professor J. L. Ackrill, J. Barnes, D. Browning, L. Judson, P. Mitchell, and the Euthyphrones Discussion Group for their criticisms and suggestions. I should also like to thank A. Rorty for her helpful advice and for granting me the occasion to return to these matters to rethink them once more. Where I have not profited from the advice and opportunities given to me, the errors remain mine alone.

1. One might think that the concern is so obviously that of emotion that this question hardly bears investigation. Given the examples he offers, given that *ta pathē* are meant to be occurrent phenomena, given that "the emotions" is a reasonable translation of "*ta pathē*," Aristotle has surely grasped the notion of emotion here. However, we need to be a bit more cautious before drawing this conclusion. For there are more occurrent phenomena than emotions; and Aristotle often includes as a *pathos* *epithumia*, a type of desire that includes hunger and thirst (*NE* 1105b21, *EE* 1120b12). This, plus doubts that Plato ever clearly distinguishes emotion and desire, should lead us to consider the matter carefully. Should it turn out that Aristotle does develop the notion of emotion, he has redrawn psychic boundaries in a very insightful way.

2. In his stated definitions of pity and indignation an aim is not explicitly announced. Rather, it is part of the larger concept of these emotions. We find the same thing in envy and emulation. Part of the concept of envy involves preventing one's neighbor from possessing certain goods, while emulation strives to make oneself fit for such goods (*Rhet.* 1388a35–37). From these aims we can explain certain changes of judgment.

3. It is plausible that there will be certain cases in which there is no such discrepancy. Someone might lose track of what they did believe and so come to be persuaded by their own pronouncements.

4. In the examples imagined, I am taking it that the subject matter of pity or indignation, envy or pity is the same. But even so self-deception, inconsistent belief systems, and so on, may alter one such that in any given case the explanation

does not hold the influence it might otherwise. This will be so for many of the cases considered here. I shall comment upon this influence no further.

5. The alteration is a seduction unless one is simultaneously aware of the presence and workings of the disposition and desire. Such awareness is not typical, although it is certainly possible.

6. The term translated here as "anger" is "*thumos*," not "*orgē*." I assume that *thumos* is meant to be an emotion. This seems to accord with most translations and with the *Rhetoric*, and elsewhere, in which Aristotle happily switches from *thumos* to *orgē*. The apparent interchangeability between the two will be significant to a later stage of this argument.

7. If J. Cooper is right (in an unpublished paper entitled "Aristotle on the Ontology of the Senses"), then contrary to D. W. Hamlyn's translation of *De Anima* (Oxford, 1968), "*krinein*" means "distinguish," not "judge"; and the perceiving of both types of objects is, properly speaking, a matter of perception.

8. This is a variation of an example of Cooper's.

9. Concerning the plausibility of the thesis, modern theorists may be inclined to reject different types of objects of perception, speaking instead of differences in perception. However one chooses to characterize the difference, there is here an additional, distinct way in which emotion alters judgment.

10. Under the favor/disfavor case I include what is objectively ambiguous. In the case of misperception I have spoken of what is not itself ambiguous. An interesting case is one in which something is not itself ambiguous, but seems so due to carelessness or inattention. This sounds very much like the case of the hasty servant. When the carelessness concerns perception, it is. However, where something seems ambiguous through inattention in evaluation, then we have a second version of the favor/disfavor case: one version explicable by the ambiguity of the phenomena; the other explicable by ambiguity arising through inattention.

11. K. J. J. Hintikka, "On the Interpretation of *De Interpretatione* XII–XIII," *Time and Necessity* (Oxford, 1973), pp. 53–55, speaks of the meaning of "*hepesthai*." Unfortunately, his conclusions are meant to be restricted to that text, and will not help us here.

12. In drawing a contrast between an empirical observation and some sort of conceptual claim, I do not mean to suggest that this would be Aristotle's way of putting the contrast. I only mean to provide a rough but here useful way of illuminating Aristotle's claim.

13. The problems that arise in the *Philebus* through using "*meta*" to explain the place of pleasure and pain, and Aristotle's appreciation of this in his *Topics* with respect to the emotions are well illustrated by W. W. Fortenbaugh, "Aristotle's Rhetoric on Emotions" *Archiv für Geschichte der Philosophie* 52 (1970): 40–70, especially pp. 55–56.

14. How the claim about hatred is to be understood is an interesting matter. One attempt to explain this apparent anomaly would be to observe that hatred should take pleasure in the destruction of the hated. But even so, it would be explained by the fact that contemplating and achieving one's aim is pleasant (*Rhet.* 1370b29, 1378b1–5). It is no more a matter of hatred being a pleasure than the sweetness of anger's revenge is a matter of anger being a pleasure.

Perhaps part of the reason for this apparent anomaly is that the description of hatred in the *Rhetoric* is similar to what is elsewhere called a *hexis*. Since a *hexis* has more a dispositional than occurrent tone, the need to speak of pleasure or pain is that much weaker. But this is only partially satisfying. For hatred remains classed as a *pathos*.

The most plausible explanation of hatred's characterization is that Aristotle's way of thinking about these matters is often in terms of what is always or for the most part. Thus when making what we can best describe as a conceptual claim, Aristotle is happy to do so in a way that speaks of what is "for the most part." Thus Aristotle feels free to allow for emotions in which we are deadened. (For further discussion of this and its application to the *Eudemian Ethics'* discussion of *ta pathē* see M. Woods, *Aristotle's Eudemian Ethics* [Oxford, 1982], especially pp. 109–110, and my "*Eudemian Ethics* 1220b11–13," *Classical Quarterly* 34 [1984]: 135–138).

15. If this is right, then although we find Aristotle using "*meta*" in his definition of anger, the "*hepetai*" controls the "*meta*." The accompaniment of pleasure and pain does not suddenly become contingent here (see note 13 of this essay).

16. That being pained disposes one to emotion (*Rhet.* 1379a10–21), and that the point seems to be about pain in general, rather than a necessary matching between a certain sort of pain predisposing one and a corresponding emotion disposed to, might suggest that there are no kinds of pains and pleasures in emotion. However, that the pains that predispose one need not divide into kinds is no reason to doubt that the pain of the emotion does so divide. After all, the pain of anger is not the pain in one's tooth that has disposed one to anger.

17. Aristotle does not offer a full analysis of pain in the *Nicomachean Ethics*. But he often considers pleasure and pain in terms of health and disease. If pain is like disease, then it is a privation of pleasure; and as a divergence from a pleasant condition, separating pains into kinds becomes messy. More serious problems in applying the analysis of pain implicit in the *Nicomachean Ethics* to emotion occur insofar as a pleasure proper to each activity would imply that if we can speak of the activity of being angry or being ashamed, then that activity should be a pleasure. This is absurd and contrary to Aristotle's analysis of these emotions. Hence the analysis of pain in the *Nicomachean Ethics* seems unsuited in some respects to account for painful emotions.

The problem could be resolved by giving pain its own character (not simply a privation), and admitting that pains complete certain activities. Thus pain would as much complete anger as pleasure completes love. However, to the extent that the *Nicomachean Ethics* offers an account of pain, this is not it (but see note 21 of this essay).

18. It is not the case that the completion in the case of flute playing or argument is just like the completion in the case of the emotions. For while flute playing can occur without being completed, the emotions do not. Anger is not anger unless it is painful.

19. Fortenbaugh, "Aristotle's *Rhetoric* on Emotions," pp. 40–70.

20. To avoid confusion I will use Greek terms for Aristotle's concepts and English terms for modern concepts.

21. One might object that in view of Aristotle's analysis of *hēdonē* and *lupē* in the *Nicomachean Ethics*, this claim should not be made. For any unhindered activity should be pleasant, including thinking. Thus an attempt to see what is behind the notion of *ta pathē* in the *Rhetoric* is doomed if one continues in this way. However, we have already seen that some thoughts on pleasure and pain in the *Nicomachean Ethics* are out of step with the analysis in the *Rhetoric*. Thus I am not assuming Aristotle to be bound in every detail to the theory in the *Nicomachean Ethics*; I am allowing that in thinking out a different problem Aristotle might not depend upon or be loyal to some of his conclusions elsewhere. This may be to skate on rather thin ice, but it is not unusual for Aristotle to forgo theoretical consistency for observations closer to the truth. Moreover, there is evidence to suggest that some of the thoughts on pleasure and pain are different in the *Rhetoric*. Many of the emotions are defined as types of pain. It seems implausible that by this each emotion is meant to be a lack of something. A lack of what? Thus the disease model is inappropriate here. Pain seems to be understood as having a character of its own; and that is why it is sufficient for the definitions of the various emotions. Not every unhindered activity is pleasant. Elsewhere (*EE* 1220b13), Aristotle speaks of perceptible pleasure and pain. Here too the disease model is unlikely. Thus we might expect some unhindered activities to be pleasant, others to be painful, others still to be neither pleasant nor painful.

22. At one point in *De Anima* (413b23), Aristotle speaks of *aisthēsis*, including pleasure and pain (see *Sensu* 436a8–11). This does not disturb my thesis, since I take his point there to be that where we speak of *aisthēsis*, the possibility of pleasure or pain is introduced, and not that *aisthēsis* must be pleasant or painful; i.e., not that it must be accompanied by pleasure or pain. That this is the right way to interpret Aristotle is suggested by the erroneous nature of the alternative interpretation. The interpretation finds further confirmation in the fact that where Aristotle speaks of *ta pathē* and explicates this with "accompanying pleasure and pain," he does not introduce *aisthēsis* as an example (*Rhet.* 1378a20, *EE* 1220b12, *NE* 1105b21), whereas when *ta pathē* have been expanded and *aisthēsis* is included the claim of an accompaniment by *hēdonē* and *lupē* is dropped (*DA* 403a1–7).

23. That desire is not an emotion may need some argument. Its inclusion as an emotion is counterintuitive; and I shall advance arguments, one consequence of which is to distinguish emotion from desire.

24. Analyses of the desires different from the one to follow can be found in J. M. Cooper's "Some Remarks on Aristotle's Moral Psychology," *Southern Journal of Philosophy* 27 (suppl.) (1988): 25–47; M. C. Nussbaum's Aristotle's *De Motu Animalium* (Princeton, 1978), pp. 334–337.

25. Aristotle's earlier claim that desire is a discomfort seeking satisfaction is, effectively, modified in the case of *boulēsis*. This, in part, is an appreciation of the point that the intellectual desires do not run along the same lines of distress and pleasure in the way bodily desires do.

26. It is noteworthy that Fortenbaugh supposes that "*ta pathē*" in the passages from the *Nicomachean Ethics* and the *Eudemian Ethics* means "the emotions" (see "Aristotle and the Questionable Mean-Dispositions," *Transactions of the American Philological Association* 99 [1968]: 203–231, at p. 207). Here too the reference to

the "psychic attributes" from Plato's *Philebus* is thought to be implicit. Earlier, I suggested, concerning the *Rhetoric*, that this reference to the *Philebus* was both questionable and, if true, still does not provide us with the notion of emotion. Thus I argued that care is needed when claiming that the concern of the *Rhetoric* was that of emotions. These considerations apply to the passages from the two *Ethics* as well. More important, the inclusion of *epithumia* (which for Aristotle is to include desires such as hunger and thirst) in the two *Ethics* precludes the idea that here Aristotle is implicit referring to the *Philebus*'s "psychic attributes" and bars the claim that by "*ta pathē*" in the relevant passages from the two *Ethics* Aristotle means "the emotions." What it does mean, we shall discuss shortly.

It must be emphasized that this dispute about the two *Ethics* (and the *Rhetoric*) cannot be dismissed as "quibbling." For, as Fortenbaugh himself is keen to show, there is a world of difference for Aristotle between the operation and nature of shame or fear versus that of hunger or thirst. Where and why Aristotle includes or excludes these latter is significant.

27. I am not here concerned with comparing and contrasting each sort of desire. However, I would like to note one point of contrast between *epithumia* and *boulēsis*. While *epithumia* aims at the pleasure of food or drink, *boulēsis* may take pleasure in achieving its aim (*to on kalon*) but does not act for the sake of such pleasure (see *EE* 1235b19–24).

28. A quite different consideration for the distinction between *epithumia* and *ta pathē* arises when we consider one of the headings under which *ta pathē* is analyzed, the person with whom one typically feels the *pathos* (*Rhet.* 1378a24). *Ta pathē* seem to involve one with others; the person one loves, hates, is angry with, is ashamed before, and so on. *Epithumia* is not like this. Thirst is not bound up with others, but with the seeking of drink. So, similarly, hunger, and the desires of the senses. Erotic desire seems out of tune with this insofar as the object typically is another person. Short of withdrawing the point of contrast, one might urge that erotic desire can be satisfied without the existence of another, but *philia* cannot. Moreover, there need be no social involvement with another in the case of *erōs*, while there is with *philia*, *orgē*, and other emotions. Thus while *ta pathē* require others, *epithumia* does not.

29. This latter would be a matter of convincing a person to change his values. So, by converting to Buddhism one might lose one's fear of dying.

It is significant that emotions only "listen to argument to some extent" (*NE* 1149a25, cf. *Mem.* 453a25–30). The thesis is not so strong that the relevant change about the facts or values is or forces a change of emotion. Rather emotion is available to reason. Aristotle leaves room for what we call irrational emotions, be they so from lack of foundation in the first place (fear of a mouse) or loss of a foundation. Hence to convince is not necessarily to move. And in this we have a further contrast between *boulēsis* and *ta pathē*. In addition to failing to satisfy the pleasure/pain test, *boulēsis* does not just listen to some extent.

30. That *boulēsis* is available to reason is not in question. Its exclusion from the realm of emotion has been accounted for on other grounds. It is also worth emphasizing here that the attempt has not been to say that Aristotle's distinctions within desire match our own. Rather the attempt has been to say that Aristotle's

characterization of *ta pathē* excludes desire; and *ta pathē* matches our notion of emotion.

31. But is not there still a sense in which one can and does speak of having "reasonable appetites"? Yes, but this sense is the following: one's appetites are well brought up so that what they desire is in conformity with rational principle. Unlike rational principle or emotions, *epithumia* is not itself rational, but spoken of so only insofar as it conforms to *logos*. The truly virtuous have such *epithumiai;* the continent and incontinent do not. As a result, these latter have to control their *epithumiai*, although, as we have seen, sometimes *epithumia* will expel any reasoning present.

32. That part of *thumos*, if any, which is not to be seen as equivalent to *orgē* is excluded from the realm of emotion by this second test. Moreover, were one dissatisfied with the exclusion of *aisthēsis* (see note 22 of this essay) its exclusion from *ta pathē* is also supported by this latter test.

33. There are two spots in Aristotle that might present difficulties for this understanding of desire, and consequently the distinction between it and emotion. First, in the *Rhetoric* (1370a19–25) Aristotle distinguishes desire into rational and irrational desire, instead of the typical triad. The rational desires seem to be more sophisticated. Such desires do not present serious problems for my analysis. For although this is a different way of examining desire, it can be dealt with in much the same fashion I dealt with the sophistication within erotic desire, and the sense of "reasonable appetites" spoken of in note 31 of this essay. Second, a discussion of the soul in the *Nicomachean Ethics* 1.13 may seem to present problems. There Aristotle talks of *hormai*, impulses. These seem to be available to reason, yet they do not seem to be *boulēsis*. Still, this is not too troublesome. They are said to be reasonable and listen to reason as does the son to the father. Now, this seems to be a matter of a certain sort of habituation. If so, this is a "reasonable" appetite of the sort mentioned in note 31. Moreover, the discussion of *hormai* is unique and very difficult to square with the earlier discussion of the soul in chapter 9, as well as with the discussions in *De Anima*. So, at worst, this passage can be dealt with as a matter of Aristotle wandering from his normal path. Most important, Aristotle makes it clear that this discussion lacks precision (1102a22–32). That Aristotle himself does not take this way of dividing the soul too seriously means that we need not be bothered if it conflicts with more serious attempts to understand distinctions within the human soul (but see Cooper, "Some Remarks," who takes the work done here to be far more central than have I).

34. The absence of this criterion is further evidence that Aristotle is up to something very different in the *Nicomachean Ethics* and the *Eudemian Ethics* than he is in the *Rhetoric;* and that "*ta pathē*" in the ethical works cannot be "the emotions."

35. This is another reason why Fortenbaugh cannot be right in his understanding of "*ta pathē*" from the relevant passages in the *Nicomachean Ethics* (see his "Aristotle, Virtue and Emotion," *Arethusa* 2 [1969]: 163–185, especially note 24). Virtue is not just a preparation and control regarding emotions and actions, but also *epithumia*. The inclusion of these desires is more in the Aristotelian spirit. For, as we observed in note 31 of this essay, persons of perfect virtue have trained their desires so as to be moderate in them, while the continent are not moderate in

them, but have control over them. Indeed, Aristotle's whole picture of moral education has to do with the training of emotions and desires. Thus the inclusion of the control of one's desires seems to help create a better description of virtue's place in our moral life.

36. I shall not here deal with the passages from the *Categories* or *De Anima* in detail. They are interesting, but a full analysis would take us too far afield; and would not help us with the issues here. Let me only say that a similar approach to these passages will explain the use of "*ta pathē*" there. The general direction would seem to be the following. In *De Anima* the concern is whether attributes of the soul involve the body. "*Ta pathē*" is used to collect these attributes; and hence the list is much expanded from any so far examined (*DA* 403a1–7). A second list at 403a17–19 more closely resembles that of the *Rhetoric*. Perhaps it is taken to be more obvious that emotions concern the body than it is not emotions concern perception, thought, and other such attributes mentioned in the first list. But it must be said of both lists that the remarks are problem-initiating rather than problem-solving. Hence Aristotle uses a very nontechnical and nonrefined sense of "*ta pathē*." Indeed, he provides no criterion for them.

In the *Categories* a general interest in *ta pathē* brings Aristotle to speak of those of the soul. These seem to be occurrent rather than dispositional features; and their temporary nature is featured. Again, a rather nontechnical conception is in use. Aristotle is roughly mapping the area, rather than sharpening a philosophical tool with which to resolve a particular problem. As we have seen, matters are rather different in the *Rhetoric*. Further examination of these and other passages, particularly from the vantage of their metaphysical commitments, can be found in A. O. Rorty's "Aristotle on the Metaphysical Status of *Pathē*," *Review of Metaphysics* 38 (1984): 521–546.

37. Although this does solve our problems, I mentioned that this proposal has a difficulty. In the *Rhetoric* (1388b33), having completed his analysis of *ta pathē*, Aristotle reviews his progress. At this point he does include *epithumia* as a *pathos*. This runs contrary to Aristotle's development so far. Indeed, given Aristotle's understanding of *epithumia* (see earlier), this inclusion must be seen either as an uncareful moment or as undercutting all that Aristotle has achieved in his characterization and explanation of *ta pathē* in the *Rhetoric*. I would suggest that it be seen as an uncareful moment.

I should add that one alternative explanation of what Aristotle has done in the *Rhetoric* yet remains. Instead of seeing Aristotle as defining a notion of emotion that distinguishes emotion from desire, one might suggest that what Aristotle has done is to refine a subset within desire (*orexis*); the subset is emotion. Evidence for this view would include Aristotle's inclusion of *thumos* as one of the key notions of *orexis*, yet his willingness to understand "*thumos*" as apparently synonymous with "*orgē*." Evidence consistent with this includes the exclusion of *epithumia* as a *pathos*, and the inclusion of *orexis* within the definition of anger. What seems to count against this explanation is that Aristotle does not ever list *ta pathē* as a type of *orexis*. Moreover, many of the emotions are defined without reference to desire, and without reinterpretation as a desire. It seems as though we must wait for another thinker within the tradition of Aristotle—Aquinas—to offer an explicitly motivational analysis of emotion.

An Aristotelian Theory
of the Emotions

John M. Cooper

Aristotle's ethics and political theory are constructed round a closely knit family of psychological concepts: those of happiness (*eudaimonia*), virtue (*aretē*), practical wisdom (*phronēsis*), action (*praxis*), state or habit (*hexis*), desire (*orexis*), pleasure and pain (*hēdonē* and *lupē*), choice or decision (*prohairesis*)—and the emotions or passions (the *pathē*). In his ethical treatises Aristotle elaborates theoretical accounts of all the members of this family but two: desire and emotion—and since two of the three types of desire that he recognizes (appetites and spirited desires) are cross-classified by him as emotional states, the emotions are even more isolated in that anomalous position than that may make it sound. The most we get in any of the ethical treatises is an illustrative list, the longest of which (in *NE* 2.5) reads as follows: appetite, anger, fear, confidence, envy, joy, feelings of friendliness, hatred, yearning (that is, for an absent or lost person that one is attached to), eagerness to match another's accomplishments, and pity. Aristotle provides no general, analytical account of the emotions anywhere in any of the ethical writings. And we are in for disappointment if we look for this in his supposedly scientific account of psychological matters in the *De Anima*.

As is well known, Aristotle does however develop fairly detailed accounts of some eleven or twelve emotions—on a generous count, perhaps fifteen—in an unexpected place, the second book of the *Rhetoric*, his work on the art of public speaking. Can we turn there to find Aristotle's full theory of the emotions? Regrettably, an adequate answer must take account of a number of complexities—I will be elaborating some of these as I go along, and attempting to assess their significance. But, by way of preliminary orientation, let me give the short answer that I will be attempting to justify in the course of the essay. The discussion of the

Rhetoric's specifically limited set of emotions cannot be regarded as based upon or providing us with Aristotle's final, "scientific" theory (as we would be entitled to regard any comparable theory in the ethical works or the *De Anima*). Rather, what we find there is, from the point of view of Aristotle's mature ethical and psychological theory, a preliminary, purely dialectical investigation that clarifies the phenomena in question and prepares the way for a philosophically more ambitious overall theory, but does no more than that. However, as we go through the particular emotions that he discusses, we can see certain patterns emerging that, although not found in his discussion of each emotion, plainly could be made the basis for a comprehensive general theory, and one that is of considerable interest, both philosophically and historically. Having done the work on the selected emotions dealt with in the *Rhetoric,* Aristotle had achieved certain systematic insights that he could have used as the basis for a positive philosophical theory of the nature of emotions. But he never got around to doing that; at least as far as we know, he did not.

Before turning to Aristotle's accounts of the emotions in Book 2 of the *Rhetoric,* I need to say something about how the emotions fit into his overall project in that work.

At the beginning of *Rhetoric* Book 1 Aristotle argues that there are precisely three "technical" or artful ways that public speakers have of persuading their audiences. In the body of the work, including his discussion of the emotions, he aims to provide the information aspiring orators need in order to train themselves to wield these three instruments on the basis of real knowledge, and so lay claim to the possession of a true art of oratory. First, Aristotle says, public speakers need to appear to their hearers to be intelligent, good, and well-intentioned persons (that is, ones who have good character). Second, they need to induce in their audiences appropriately directed states of emotion that will influence their audiences' judgment on the matter under discussion in a way favorable to the orators and their cases. Third, they need to present reasons that the audience will find plausible and will cause them to judge as true whatever conclusions the orators are trying to promote (they need to *argue* well). It is mostly in connection with the first and especially the second of these objectives that Aristotle provides information about the emotions in Book 2. The orator needs to know how to represent himself to the audience as being moved by such emotions as will help to establish him as a good person in general, and well-intentioned toward the audience in particular; and he needs to know how to engender in them the emotions that will cause them to judge the matter as he wishes them to.

Throughout the *Rhetoric* Aristotle limits himself, in preparing and presenting his material on how to wield the three instruments of persuasion, to a dialectical survey of the relevant data from common sense and "reputable opinion" (in Greek, the *endoxa*) that bear on the matters he takes up. He does indeed say that rhetoric is something like an offshoot of both dialectic *and* ethics (or politics), but it is clear that by referring to ethics as one parent of rhetoric he does not intend to say that rhetoric borrows opinions from an accomplished philosophical theory of ethical matters. He says quite plainly, so far as the premises of an oratorical argument go, that opinions must be drawn from what is reputable and plausible, and not from the results of a special science, not even from the philosophical theory of politics or ethics (1.4.1359b2–18, with 1.2. 1358a21–26)—what here he actually calls political or ethical science (*epistēmē*). If rhetoric did that it would no longer be mere rhetoric, but would turn itself into the science or theory in question, actually establishing its conclusions, rather than merely getting people to believe them on grounds persuasive to them. And it seems that this restriction to *endoxa* applies across the board: in selecting the materials from which to represent his own character in a favorable light and in engendering in the audience helpful emotions, as well, the orator will depend upon a dialectical knowledge of reputable opinions about the emotions, and not a "scientific" knowledge derived from a fully justified philosophical theory of them. Accordingly, when Aristotle in Book 2 offers to the orator information about the emotions that he is to use in engendering or preventing emotions in his hearers, this is an exercise in dialectic. He is collecting and sorting through, for the aspiring orator's benefit, the established and reputable opinions about what the various relevant emotions are, and about various relevant points about them.

Where the instilling of emotions is concerned, it is easy to see, however, that the dialectical appeal to such opinions will be different from what it is in the case of the other two instruments of persuasion. A systematic, dialectical study of the various *endoxa*—the recognized and highly reputed opinions—about what is good and bad for communities, right and wrong, legal and illegal, worthy of praise and the reverse, is obviously a very good way of preparing oneself to construct arguments on these matters before a classical Greek audience, whether in a deliberative, judicial, or ceremonial context. These are precisely the opinions that the audience can be expected to regard highly themselves, and so to be swayed by, if the opinions can be marshaled in such a way as to support logically the point of view for which the orator is speaking, or at any rate to seem to the audience to do so (see 1356a35–36). Likewise, in attempting to represent himself to the judges as intelligent and perceptive about practical matters, and as a serious person of good general character, he needs to be guided by the recognized and reputed indicators of these characteristics. For, again, it is likely that his audience will be disposed to

regard a person as having good character if he displays just those indicators in his speech, and avoids displaying the contrary ones. Here what
matters is to know what one's hearers will think favors a certain conclusion
that one desires them to reach.[1]

When one comes to the orator's wielding of the remaining "way of
persuading," by inducing the appropriate emotional state of mind in his
audience, the story must necessarily be more complicated. For here it is
evidently not enough to know what the audience will think people are like
who are prone to become angry or afraid, or to feel pity, or to have
vindictive or friendly feelings, and so on. Nor is it enough to know toward
what sorts of persons the audience thinks that people typically feel these
feelings, or under what circumstances and occasions.[2] (These are the
three subtopics into which Aristotle divides his treatments of the emotions
in Book 2 [see 2.1.1378a23–28].) The orator's purpose is actually to make
his hearers feel in some of these ways, and prevent them from feeling in
other ways, toward specific persons on given occasions and circumstances
(toward his client in a judicial case, for example), and to use these feelings
to direct or influence their judgment. Plainly, whatever the grounds are
for proceeding dialectically here, it ought not to be simply because doing
so gives one the ability to influence the audience's opinions about who is
or isn't in a given state of feeling toward a given other person! If what
he needs to do is actually to make them angry, it hardly matters whether
they also think they are.

It seems clear that Aristotle's restriction of the orator to dialectical
knowledge of the emotions rests upon his general view that qualification
for expertise in oratory must rest only upon that kind of knowledge. But
from his own philosophical point of view what makes it acceptable to him
to restrict the orator in this way is that he himself believes that ethical
theory (what he calls here ethical or political science, which does aim at
establishing the facts about what the emotions really are, and so on), itself
starts from, and is responsible to, the very *endoxa* that dialectic and rhetoric
are specially directed to acquire effective control over. So, if in learning
about the various passions—their surrounding psychology, their objects
and occasions—the "artistic" orator turns to the recognized and reputable
opinions about these matters, and not somehow directly to the phenomena
themselves, he is at least behaving no differently from the way Aristotle's
full-fledged moral and political philosopher behaves, in beginning his own
investigations of these matters.[3] If what results is less than what Aristotle
thinks a fully independent philosophical theory might ideally be able to
achieve, he himself thinks there is good reason to accept the accounts he
will provide as approximately true. As we proceed we will see for ourselves
that what Aristotle offers his aspiring orators, and us modern readers too,

is well grounded in an appropriately thoughtful study of the emotions themselves, and not merely what people say about them.

As I have said, Aristotle distinguishes and devotes at least some direct attention to the defining characteristics of fifteen emotions. He gives separate, formal treatment to twelve, in the following order: feeling angry (*orgē*), feeling mildly (*praotēs*), feeling friendly (*philia*, i.e., *to philein*), feeling hatred (*misos*), feeling afraid (*phobos*), feeling confident in the face of danger (*tharrein*), feeling disgraced (*aischunē*), feeling kindly (*charin echein*), pity (*eleos*), righteous indignation (*nemesan*), envy (*phthonos*), and feeling eagerness to match the accomplishments of others (*zēlos*). Actually, it is not perfectly clear whether Aristotle means to say that *praotēs* (feeling mildly) is a state of feeling on its own, or only the absence of angry feelings when they would be expected or justified; his definition of *praünsis*, becoming calm or mild, explicitly makes it simply a settling down and quieting of anger (1380a8).[4] But I take this to be a lapse, and suppose he does mean to treat feeling mildly as a separate emotion. Two further feelings are named more or less incidentally and accorded briefer, but still not insubstantial treatment: schadenfreude (an accompaniment of envy [1386 b34–1387a3 and 1388a23–25]), and feeling disdainful, an accompaniment of eagerness to match others' accomplishments (1388b22–28). A third, unnamed feeling, which stands to righteous indignation as schadenfreude does to envy—it is pleasurable feeling at the punishment or other come-down of those who deserve it—also comes in for brief treatment (1386b25–33 and 1387b14–20).

In studying these chapters it is important to bear in mind that Aristotle means to discuss throughout states of *feeling*—passions or emotions, conditions in which one's mind or consciousness is affected, moved, or stirred up. This applies equally to *philia* and *charis* (feeling friendly and kindly) despite some awkwardness of expression, as it does to anger, fear, and the other more obvious cases of such feelings. I begin, then, with some remarks on Aristotle's discussions in 2.4 and 2.7 of these two feelings.

Awkwardly, Aristotle defines *charis* (what I am translating as "kindly feelings") in 2.7 in terms of action not feeling: it is "helping someone in need, not in return for anything[5] nor for the good of the one helping, but for that of the one helped." Formally, then, the person who "has *charis*" is the one who acts in this helping way; the definition apparently makes no reference to the emotion that might lead to such action. Or does it? Perhaps one should take Aristotle's reference to helping actions as indicating, elliptically, the emotion that leads to them (akin to friendly feelings, I suppose: a warm feeling of attachment to someone, with a desire to do that person good for her or his own sake). But of course what Aristotle should primarily be telling aspiring orators about is a feeling that they need either to engender in or remove from their audience's mind. And in what follows in 2.7 (1385a30–1385b11) he seems to limit himself to discussing the means of showing an audience that someone has shown *them charis* or failed to do so. Nevertheless, the connection to an emotion of the audience's is perhaps implicit even here, as is suggested at two places (1380a27 and 1380b32) in 2.3, where Aristotle says we don't (can't) get angry at people who are apparently mistreating us, if they have treated us excessively kindly in the past. His point is that, just as fear of someone conflicts with and prevents simultaneous anger at them (1380a31–33), so the emotion of kindly feeling (that results from one's recognizing kind treatment from a person in the past) conflicts with and prevents simultaneous anger against them for a present apparent insult or unjustified belittlement. So his point in talking in 2.7 about who has and who has not behaved kindly to the audience in the past is to provide the orator with a means of engendering, out of naturally arising gratitude, or preventing, feelings of kindness in the audience—for example, toward persons in court or toward the people of other cities whose petitions might be before an assembly or council for decision.

I turn now to 2.4, on friendly feelings and hatred. This chapter is anomalous in several ways. In every chapter except this one Aristotle overtly organizes his discussion in accordance with a tripartite pattern for discussing the emotions that he lays down at the end of 2.1 (1378a23–30). After giving his definition of the specific state of feeling, he goes on to discuss (not always in the same order) (*a*) what personal conditions or circumstances, especially what psychological conditions (what other feelings or beliefs, in general what frames of mind), make people apt to experience the feeling (*pōs echontes* or *diakeimenoi*), (*b*) what sorts of people they do or do not feel the feeling toward (*tisin* or *pros tinas*), and (*c*) what the occasions are of their having, or not having, the feeling for that kind of person (*epi poiois* or *dia poia*). His allegiance to this program is quite striking in each chapter, even where he understandably lumps together the discussion of the second and third points. We get this tripartite structure presented in every chapter, in virtually the same language each time.[6]

This language and this structure for the discussion are totally absent from the chapter on friendly feeling and hatred. It is true that the chapter begins with a promise first to define friendly feelings[7] and then to say who people feel that way (*tinas*) toward and why (*dia ti*). But there is no separate mention anywhere in the chapter of the very important first point, the frames of mind that tend to promote our feeling that way. And the language here (and subsequently in the chapter where he addresses the third point, the occasions of friendly feeling) is not paralleled in any of the other chapters (see *poiētika philias*, 1381b35, *poiētika echthras*, 1382a1–2). Finally, the whole discussion, although genuinely illuminating and insightful, has fewer signposts and is more of a miscellany than any other discussion in this part of the treatise.

As a consequence, we face special difficulties in interpreting what Aristotle says about these emotions in this chapter. I mentioned just now that he begins by giving a definition of friendly feelings, *to philein*. This is exactly as we should expect: in the *Nicomachean Ethics* (8.5.1157b28–29) he ranks friendly feeling (*philēsis*) as an emotion or feeling, in contrast to friendship (*philia*), which he says is a settled state involving decision. The definition itself in the *Rhetoric* is very close to the account given in the *Nicomachean Ethics* of goodwill (8.2.1155b31–32), which helps to make the connection that Aristotle promised at the beginning of Book 2 (*Rhet.* 2.1.1378a19–20) between the discussion of the emotions and instruction in how to present yourself in speaking as having the interests of your audience at heart (i.e., as he says, having goodwill for them).[8] The definition of *to philein* runs as follows: "Let us suppose having friendly feelings to be wishing someone what you think are good things, for his sake and not for your own, and being ready, as far as you can, to act accordingly."[9]

However, he goes on immediately[10] to speak instead of friendship, or rather what it is to be friends with someone—the established relationship in which two persons are disposed to feel friendly toward one another at appropriate times. This shift of focus continues virtually throughout the chapter, to such an extent that people sometimes take the chapter to be about not mere friendly feelings, but friendship itself. But that is a mistake. Aristotle's introduction into a discussion of friendly feelings of talk about friends and friendship is quite understandable, from two points of view. First of all, one purpose of the discussion is to provide an orator with material from which to represent himself in speaking as moved by genuine concern for his audience's interests, and he will succeed especially well in this endeavor if he can get them to think of him as actually a friend of theirs—someone who is habitually moved by such feelings in relation to them. Moreover, knowing who is ordinarily taken to be someone's friend could give an orator excellent means of getting an audience to feel friendly feelings toward himself or those for whom he may be a spokesman: describing someone as their friend is a likely way to induce the audience to respond with friendly feelings. We must, then, guard carefully against the mistake of thinking that Aristotle's advice to the orator is aimed at helping him to make his audience actually become his own or his client's friends, rather than merely to make them have friendly and well-disposed feelings. The latter task is difficult enough: if taken seriously the former would actually be impossible in the time available!

In introducing the topic of the emotions at the beginning of Book 2 Aristotle characterizes emotions generally as follows (1378a20–23): they are things "that change people so as to alter their judgments and are accompanied by *lupē* (conventionally translated "pain") and *hēdonē* (conventionally translated "pleasure")—for example anger, pity, fear, and the like, and their opposites." The association of the emotions with *lupē* and *hēdonē* occurs so standardly in Aristotle[11] that one is apt to accept it here, too, without much thought—as if he meant nothing more than that when we experience these things we always have a mild like or dislike for the way we are then feeling, and/or that we tend to experience some pleasures or pains in consequence of feeling an emotion. I think it will repay us, however, to stop and ask carefully what Aristotle can or does mean by this. To begin with, we should notice that six of the ten emotions for which he gives formal definitions are defined as instances of *lupē* (*lupē tis*): fear, the feeling of being disgraced, pity, righteous indignation, envy, and eagerness to match others' accomplishments are all defined this way. A seventh (anger) is defined as a certain desire accompanied by *lupē* (*meta lupēs*). So he makes *lupē* a central, essential feature of many of the emotions: it is even the genus of six of them. Curiously, he does not mention either *lupē* or *hēdonē* in his formal definitions of kindly and friendly feelings (which I quoted earlier); one would think the parallel with these other emotions would have led him to define them in terms of *hēdonē*. Nor does he explicitly mention pleasure in his definition of confidence in the face of danger (*to tharrein*)—although when he says that confidence essentially involves "the impression (*phantasia*) of what keeps us safe as being near, of what is fearsome as being non-existent or far off" (1383a17–18)[12] one might think that indicates that pleasure *is* essential to it. "The pleasant" is counted by him as one sort of apparent good, namely what impresses one as good quite independently of what one *thinks* is good,[13] and safety here would count as such an apparent good. And in discussing schadenfreude and the unnamed accompaniment of righteous indignation (to neither of which does he give a formal definition), he mentions pleasure (*chairein, hēdesthai*) in such a way as to suggest that he thinks it is their genus, just as the genus of envy and righteous indignation is said to be *lupē*.[14]

There is, then, ample evidence that Aristotle actually defines those emotions that he thinks involve *lupē* in terms of it, and weaker evidence that he is correspondingly inclined toward defining the emotions that involve pleasure in terms of *hēdonē*.[15] What does he intend here by *lupē* and *hēdonē*? Let us take *lupē* first. Elsewhere Aristotle uses the term (together with its verb) quite variously, to cover both bodily pain and all kinds and degrees of negative mental response and attitude, ranging from mild dislike to deep distress.[16] In nonphilosophical Greek *lupē* usually indicates a pretty strong state of feeling, some real distress, and it has a special application to people when they are grieving.[17] It is in something close to this ordinary usage that Aristotle uses the word in this context in the

Rhetoric. He speaks of pity, righteous indignation, and envy each as being a pain characterized by turmoil (*lupē tarachōdēs*, 1386b18–19; and see 1386b22–25), although he mentions only pain and not turmoil in their formal definitions (1385b13–16, 1386b8–10, 1387b22–24). And he actually defines both fear and the feeling of being disgraced as "pain and turmoil" (*lupē tis kai tarachē*, 1382a21, 1383b14) about something.[18] If, as I just did, one translates *lupē* here as "pain" one must understand this as meaning "distress," "feeling upset," something that in these more extreme instances can be accompanied and qualified by psychic turmoil. Aristotle's words for pleasure have a similarly various usage elsewhere, covering everything from some bodily sensations to mental attitudes varying from simple liking and gladness to elation and vivid enjoyment.[19] Given the contrast with feelings of distress about something brought about by the pairing of *hēdonē* and *lupē* in this context, it would seem reasonable, perhaps mandatory, to take *hēdonē* here as connoting some sort of positive mental excitement—the active relishing of something, and not merely being pleased or glad about it, or just liking it in some way or other.

So the terms *lupē* and *hēdonē* in Aristotle's definitions of the emotions, explicit or implied, serve much the same function that is covered in Stoic accounts by such picturesque terms as throbbing (*ptoia*), contraction and expansion (*sustolē* and *diachusis*), being uplifted and cast down (*eparsis* and *ptōsis*), depression (*tapeinōsis*), and gnawing (*dēxis*). *Lupē* and *hēdonē* indicate, with less descriptive ingenuity than the Stoics' terms do, the character of the emotions as psychic disturbances in which we are set psychically in movement, made to experience some strong affect.

Accordingly, the emotions as Aristotle represents them in *Rhetoric* Book 2 are feelings either of being distressed and upset about something, or of being excited about and relishing something. In both cases they are taken to be intrusive feelings, ones that occupy the mind and direct the attention (so that, as Aristotle says, they can "change people so as to alter their judgments"). Anger, fear, the feeling of being disgraced, pity, righteous indignation, envy, and the eagerness to match other people's accomplishments are feelings of distress at one or another apparent circumstance currently within one's attention that one takes to be a bad thing. Confidence in the face of danger, schadenfreude, and the unnamed accompaniment of indignation that gives a person pleasure at the punishment or other come-down of those meriting it, are all instances of relishing what impresses one as being a good thing.

It is worth emphasizing that in his discussion of each of these ten emotions, with the exception of the last two, Aristotle is quite firm and explicit that the emotion arises from one's having the impression or appearance (*phantasia*) that something good or bad has happened, is happening, or is about to happen. Indeed, for seven of them—anger, fear, the feeling of disgrace, pity, envy, righteous indignation, and the eagerness to match another's accomplishments—he includes this impression in the formal definition; and for confidence it is included in the nearest thing to a definition that he provides (1383a17–18, discussed earlier). Similarly, one finds references to such appearances also in his account of feeling mildly (1380a10 and 35), as one would expect if that is the emotion opposed to anger. The omission in the case of schadenfreude and the unnamed accompaniment of righteous indignation should not cause surprise, given the extreme brevity of his treatment of them; but we are entitled to infer a role for such impressions in the generation of these emotions from their relationship to envy and indignation respectively (as we also can for disdain from its relationship to "eagerness"): all these latter emotions are said to depend upon one's impressions of things. It seems likely that Aristotle is using *phantasia* here to indicate the sort of nonepistemic appearance to which he draws attention once in *De Anima* 3.3 (428b2–4), according to which something may appear to, or strike one, in some way (say, as being insulting or belittling) even if one knows there is no good reason for one to take it so. If so, Aristotle is alert to the crucial fact about the emotions, that one can experience them simply on the basis of how, despite what one knows or believes to be the case, things strike one—how things look to one when, for one reason or another, one is disposed to feel the emotion. It is not merely when you know or think that someone has mistreated you that you may become angry. Being unable to control an emotion is, partly, taking as a ground of it something that you know was not one at all.

Thus it is fairly clear that, for a majority of the emotions he deals with, Aristotle regards them as involving essentially a feeling of distress or pleasure caused by the way things currently in his or her attention strike the person in question. About hatred, and, as we have seen, friendly and kindly feelings, Aristotle is less forthcoming in identifying precisely what the feeling is, whether one of distress or of relishment. But on Aristotle's emerging general view one would expect friendly and kindly feelings, at least, to be cases of pleasurable excitement, just as confidence, schadenfreude, and the unnamed accompaniment of indignation are. Nor with hatred and friendly and kindly feelings does he make a point of including in his account a reference to things appearing in some particular way. That is partly because for these emotions he makes no allusion at all in the definition itself to the emotion's objects and occasions.[20] For it is because he does that in the other cases that he finds the opportunity to insert the reference to such appearances.

On Aristotle's view, what, however, is the nature of the affect involved in hatred? Here I confess myself puzzled. He does not say anything to link hatred positively to either pleasure or distress, and it does not seem plausible to identify it as essentially a feeling of pleasurable excitement of any kind (however much, like anger, it might involve pleasurable thoughts about what you will do to the one you feel that way toward if you get the chance). On the other hand, Aristotle denies that it involves being distressed at all (2.4.1382a13). So it is quite unclear how he envisages hatred as based in the one or the other sort of feeling, as his general conception of the emotions seems to require. He is led to say that it does not involve a feeling of distress as a consequence of his correct, and very interesting, observation (1382a8–12) that anger makes you want to subject the person you are angry at to pain (physical or mental), in return for the distress he or she has caused you in belittling or insulting you and so making you angry, whereas hatred makes you want the person hated to be badly off, even to cease existing (1382a15). He seems to think that because in hatred there is no special desire to inflict pain (to affect how the hated one feels), but only to ruin him (to affect how he is), hatred ought not to involve any underlying feeling of distress either. That does not, however, seem a good reason: Aristotle recognizes that the feelings of disgrace and eagerness to match others' accomplishments both involve a distressed state of mind, but neither aims at causing distress in another; nor, it seems, does either of these feelings (seem to Aristotle to) derive in any way from imagining distress as felt by another person, as perhaps pity does. And, of course, there is no danger of failing to keep anger and hatred distinct if both are based in feelings of distress; the same is true of envy and pity, for example, on Aristotle's account, and they are nonetheless kept perfectly distinct by other features of the two definitions. But perhaps in saying that hatred does not involve a distressed state of mind, as anger does, Aristotle is thinking of the impersonality of hatred: you can hate whole classes of people, not merely individuals, as he points out (1382a4–7), and you need not have been personally affected in any way by a person you nonetheless hate (1382a2–3). It might seem to Aristotle that distress must have some local or immediate external cause of a kind that would therefore be lacking in hatred. Hatred is, in any event, an especially complex emotion: it seems much more a settled state, although subject to increased or lessened intensity, than many of the other emotions are, and it seems that unlike many of them there is no plausible ground for thinking that other animals experience it. In fact, one might make the case that hatred rests upon a fully reasoned judgment, and not the mere appearance or impression, that the hated person is bad and detestable—so that it could seem to be an emotion of the reason itself, and not of the other parts of the soul as Aristotle conceives them.[21] So it may be to Aristotle's credit that he shows himself not comfortable imposing upon hatred his general account, according to which each emotion involves essentially either pleasurable excitement or a distressed state of mind.[22] Still, one remains puzzled.

I come now to some special features of Aristotle's treatment of anger. Aristotle defines anger as "a desire (orexis), accompanied by distress, for what appears to one to be punishment for what appears to one to be belittlement by people for whom it was not proper to belittle oneself or someone close to one."[23] Of the several definitions, or partial definitions, of anger that one finds elsewhere in his works, this is closest to that which, with slight variations, occurs several times in the Topics[24]—as suits the dialectical character of the definitions in the Rhetoric. Interestingly, anger is the only emotion he examines in these chapters that he defines formally as an instance of desire, that is orexis (which is Aristotle's usual word for desire in general)—although it is worth noting that, in contrasting hatred and anger, he says that hatred is a desire (ephesis) for what is bad (for the person hated) (1382a8). That friendly feeling is also an instance of desire is perhaps implicit in his definition of it as "wishing someone what you think are good things . . ." (1380b35–1381a1), since "wishing" is regularly treated by Aristotle as one of the three basic forms of desire. Presumably kindly feeling, too, involves a similar wish.[25] Both before beginning his detailed survey (at 2.1.1378a4) and immediately afterward (at 2.12.1388b33) Aristotle does indeed mention appetitive desire (epithumia) as itself being one of the emotions, but he does not devote a chapter or part of a chapter to it.[26] Appetite comes in for prominent and highly interesting discussion at two places in the treatment of other emotions, anger (1379a10–22)—we will have a look at this passage shortly—and kindly feelings (1385a22–30), but it is not subjected there or anywhere in this part of the work to analysis as an emotion all on its own. So anger really does stand out from the other emotions as Aristotle treats them here: only it is defined in part as an orexis (desire) for anything.

From what we have already seen, it is clear enough what makes anger not only a desire but an emotion, according to Aristotle. Because it is accompanied by lupē, anger is a distressful, agitated desire for revenge; the angry person is upset about having been treated with apparent disregard and belittlement. In other words, it is not a cool and "rational" desire, a desire judiciously considered, to inflict pain or other punishment. In Rhetoric 1.10.1369a1–4, Aristotle uses "anger" (orgē) itself as the name of one of the three types of desire that he there distinguishes (the other two being wish and appetite). That would imply that the type of desire to which anger belongs, according to the Rhetoric definition, was by its nature agitated and distressful. In other writings, however, Aristotle regularly distinguishes between anger and "spirited" desire (thumos), using the latter as the name for his second type of desire and treating anger as a special case of it, the case where the desire is extremely agitated and distressed.[27] It is perhaps understandable that in such a dialectical discussion as that provided by the *Rhetoric* such refinements are neglected. But when they are taken into account, anger on Aristotle's view turns out to be (*a*) an especially agitated and distressful instance of "spirited" desire, (*b*) aroused by and directed specifically at what strikes the angry person to have been inappropriate and unjustified belittlement of himself or someone close to him, (*c*) aiming at inflicting a compensating pain on the belittler—as a means of demonstrating that he is not an inferior and trivial person, but a person whose power to inflict pain in return shows that he must be respected and paid heed to. Thus, in his account of anger, Aristotle combines three distinct elements that are indeed found elsewhere in his discussion, but are nowhere else so clearly integrated: the angry person is in an agitated state of mind, caused by the way certain events or circumstances have struck him (whether or not he also believes that that is how they are), which is also a desire to respond in a well-motivated way to those events or circumstances as they appear to him.

As I mentioned above, anger has a special relationship, according to Aristotle, to the other type of nonrational desires, the appetites. The passage where he brings this out is worth quoting in full (1379a10–22):

> As for our own frame of mind: we become angry when we are distressed. For a person who is feeling distressed is bent on something. So if anyone blocks him directly or indirectly in whatever it may be, for example a thirsty man in his drink, or if anyone acts contrary to him or does not act to support him, or makes trouble for him when he is in this state of mind, he becomes angry at them all. Hence people who are ill, or poor, or in love, or thirsty—in general, experiencing some appetitive desire and not getting what they want—are prone to anger and easily stirred up, especially against those who belittle their present condition. Thus a sick man is made angry when belittled in regard to his illness, a poor man in regard to his poverty, a man fighting a war in regard to the war, a man in love in regard to his love, and so with the others. Each of these people is carried along to his own anger by the emotion he is already feeling.[28]

The upset feeling that belongs to anger in all these cases is an offshoot of the upset feeling the person has been experiencing in having some aroused, but unsatisfied, appetite. It is as if a preexistent energy, the appetite, gets redirected when blocked or obstructed, and becomes or gives rise to this new feeling of distress, the anger.

It is only in connection with anger, and only in this passage, that Aristotle devotes full attention to the ways in which different emotions interact so as to cause or prepare the ground for one another. As I have mentioned in passing, he does allude two or three times elsewhere to the opposite effect, the prevention of one emotion by the presence of another: for example, he says that people do not have friendly feelings for those of whom they are afraid (1381b33), that fear for oneself prevents feeling pity for another (1385b32–34), and that people feel disgraced when something apparently dishonorable about themselves comes to light before persons whom they esteem or admire (1384a26–29). But it is only here that he points toward any general theory of the underlying psychology of the emotions through which one might attempt to explain such phenomena as these, and work out other interactions among the different emotional states.

In other respects, too, the discussion of the emotions in the *Rhetoric* offers a less than fully comprehensive theory. Aristotle limits himself to just fifteen states of mind, ones selected so as to cover the range of emotions that the orator needs to know about in order to compose his public addresses with full effectiveness—whether by representing himself as motivated by them, or by finding means to arouse them in his audience and direct them suitably for the purposes of his discourse. So Aristotle neglects, as not relevant for this purpose, a number of emotions that a more general, independently conceived treatment of the emotions would presumably give prominence to. Thus grief, pride (of family, ownership, accomplishment), (erotic) love, joy, and yearning for an absent or lost loved one (Greek *pothos*) hardly come in for mention in the *Rhetoric* and are nowhere accorded independent treatment.[29] The same is true even of regret, which one would think would be of special importance for an ancient orator to know about, especially in judicial contexts. Furthermore, as we saw especially clearly in the case of anger, Aristotle seems to recognize three central elements as constituting the emotions—they are agitated, *affected* states of mind, arising from the ways events or conditions *strike* the one affected, which are at the same time *desires* for a specific range of reactive behaviors or other changes in the situation as it appears to her or him to be. However, he does not draw special attention to this common structure, and he does not accord equal attention to each of the three elements in the case of every emotion he discusses. Thus he may seem to neglect unduly the element of desire in his accounts of fear, confidence, pity, and the feeling of disgrace, and the second element, that of being struck by an impression that things are a certain way, is barely indicated in his accounts of friendly and kindly feelings and hatred. Similarly, we have seen that he denies that hatred involves feelings of distress, and that seems to imply that the first element, an affected state of mind, is absent from this emotion; and the corresponding pleasurable affect is no part of his definition of friendly and kindly feelings. So one cannot say more than that there seems to underlie Aristotle's discussions of the emotions in *Rhetoric* Book 2 an emerging general theory along these lines. Having done the dialectical work of assembling the data about these fifteen emotions in the *Rhetoric,* he might have gone on to address similarly the remaining major emotions, and advanced to the construction of a general, independent theory that would surely have held great interest. I hope I have been able to show that, nonetheless, his accounts of the emotions in the *Rhetoric* are richly suggestive, and rewarding from the point of view of the history of philosophy and of philosophy of mind and moral psychology too.

NOTES

This essay is a lightly edited version of my 1992–1993 S. V. Keeling Memorial Lecture, delivered at University College, London, in May 1993. The lecture, in turn, was based on my paper "Rhetoric, Dialectic, and the Passions," *Oxford Studies in Ancient Philosophy* 11 (1993): 175–198. The first version of that paper was prepared for delivery at an international Symposium on Philosophical Issues in Aristotle's *Rhetoric* sponsored by the Philosophical Society of Finland, Helsinki, August 1991. Subsequently I read revised versions at departmental colloquia at Dartmouth and Pomona colleges. I would like to thank the organizers of the Helsinki symposium, and especially Juha Sihvola, for their hospitality, and the other participants, both local and from abroad, for stimulating and helpful discussion of many interesting issues in the *Rhetoric,* including the ones treated in this essay. The essay as published owes a great deal to criticisms and suggestions made in discussion on all three of these occasions, but I am especially grateful to Alexander Nehamas for his detailed and perceptive written comments on the penultimate version. It was while I was a Fellow of the Center for Advanced Study in the Behavioral Sciences that I prepared the Keeling Lecture, and I am grateful to the center and to the Andrew W. Mellon Foundation, which provided financial support for my fellowship, for their assistance.

1. Here and throughout this discussion of *endoxa* I restrict my attention to the aims and practices of the individual Aristotelian artistic orator. His function is to do the best the circumstances permit to find things to say that his hearers will take as bases for believing whatever it is he is arguing for; his art does not consist in discovering the truth and attempting to persuade them of that. Two considerations should be borne in mind, however, lest my discussion give the impression that for Aristotle the art of rhetoric is completely value- and truth-neutral. First, as we will see more fully below, Aristotle thinks that the *endoxa* the orator appeals to in marshaling his argument and representing his character bear a strong positive relation to the truth—they somehow *reflect,* and so indicate, the truth. Second, his remarks at 1.1 (1355a20–24, 29–33) about the usefulness of the art of rhetoric indicate that, at least in judicial and deliberative oratory, where there are speakers on both sides, the joint function of the artistic orators who speak on any question is to help the hearers to reach the best, most truthful decision possible on the matter at hand. By listening to excellently prepared speeches on all sides of the question, a mass of people are placed in the best position such a mass can be in to decide correctly: they have before them all the relevant truth-indicators, each as favorably presented as possible.

2. See 2.1.1378a23–28, where Aristotle gives this threefold division of the material to be treated in preparing the orator for his task—except, of course, that there he says he will investigate how people *are* when they are angry, etc., not how any audience will think they are.

3. On this see J. M. Cooper, review of *The Fragility of Goodness*, by M. C. Nussbaum, *Philosophical Review* 97 (1988): 553–555, and "Ethical-Political Theory in Aristotle's *Rhetoric*," *Aristotle's Rhetoric: Philosophical Essays*, ed. D. J. Furley and A. Nehamas (Princeton, 1994), pp. 203–205.

4. By contrast, in his treatments of the other two "negation" feelings on his list, hatred and confidence, it seems fairly clear that he regards them as positive states of feeling on their own, not merely the absence of the feelings with which they are contrasted—friendly feelings and fear, respectively. But he gives no formal definition of *misos* at all, and the closest he comes to a definition for *tharsos* (1383a17–18) is partial at best, so we are left to draw this inference from his descriptions of the circumstances, etc., for these feelings. One should note, however, that at one place Aristotle equates those experiencing confidence simply with those who are *apatheis* under certain circumstances (1383a28): he means, of course, free of the *pathos* of fear, but this is certainly a careless remark at best if he thinks of confidence as one *among* the *pathē*, as it seems clear that, officially, he does.

5. That is, not so as to get anything in return: acting to return a favor already received is not being ruled out here, as E. M. Cope, *The Rhetoric of Aristotle, with a Commentary*, rev. and ed. J. E. Sandys (Cambridge, 1877), wrongly feared the language might suggest.

6. See 2.2.1379a9–10, 1379b27–28; 2.3.1380a5–7; 2.5.1382b27–29, 1383a14–15; 2.6.1383b12–13; 2.7.1385a16–17, 30–31; 2.8.1385b11–12, 1386a3–4, 16–17; 2.9.1387a5–8; 2.10.1387b21–24, 1388a23–24; 2.11.1388a29–30, 1388b24–27.

7. He writes: τὴν φιλίαν καὶ τὸ φιλεῖν ὁρισάμενοι λέγωμεν, 1380b34. I believe the *kai* here is likely to be epexegetic; that is, I think it likely that *philian* has the sense here that Aristotle gives to it at *NE* 2.5.1105b22 and *Top.* 4.5 126a12, where the contexts put it beyond doubt that it means not "friendship" (an established personal relationship, or a settled state of character of some sort) but an occurrent feeling, or type of feeling. In effect, *philia* substitutes in these contexts for *philēsis* as the noun for *to philein*. Hence in the first sentence of *Rhetoric* 2.4 Aristotle is not promising to give us two definitions, one of friendship and one of friendly feeling, but only the one definition, of friendly feeling, that he immediately provides. (This is the only formal definition, with the usual *estō*, anywhere in the chapter.) When he adds (1381a1–2) a statement about what makes someone a friend of someone else this is not a backward way of fulfilling a promise to define friendship, but the needed introduction of the notion of a friend—the sort of person who regularly experiences friendly feeling—on which so much of what follows is going to be based.

8. I take it that Aristotle's language at 1378a19–20 (περὶ δ' εὐνοίας καὶ φιλίας ἐν τοῖς περὶ τὰ πάθη λεκτέον), linking the two terms together in this way, indicates that we are to go to the chapter on friendly feeling to find out how to represent this aspect of our own characters. Alternatively, one might think he is directing us to the entire subsequent discussion—so that, for example, one might pick up pointers from 2.7 on kindly feelings and 2.8 on pity to use in presenting oneself

as "well-disposed" to the audience by making oneself appear to feel pity or kindness for them or theirs. In view of the special linkage at 1378a19–20 between *eunoia* and *philia*, however, I think this alternative interpretation is not likely to be correct.

9. The Greek for "wish" here is *boulesthai*. In Aristotle's technical philosophy of mind a "wish" is a rational kind of desire, one deriving from our capacity to reason about what is good or bad for us, whereas what he is talking about here is supposed to be a *pathos*, a nonrational feeling. (*Boulēsis* never appears in any of Aristotle's lists of *pathē*, in the *Rhetoric* or elsewhere—as both of the other two sorts of *orexis* do, at one place or another.) It is worth noting, also, that earlier in the *Rhetoric* (1.10.1369a1–4) Aristotle presents his division of desires into rational and nonrational, with "wish" serving as the name for the former kind, as grounded in *endoxa*. How can Aristotle think that friendly feeling is based in wishing and yet that it is a *pathos*, something essentially nonrational? Perhaps we should take his use of the word "wish" in some broader way in 2.4, one that permits it to cover at least some nonrational desirings; see 2.11.1389a8 where he seems to use "wishes" to refer in a general way to the desires of young people, which he characterizes before and afterward as appetitive, sharp but not persistent.

10. I do not believe R. Kassel, *Aristotelis Ars Rhetorica* (Berlin, 1976), is right to put 1381a1–2, *philos . . . antiphiloumenos* in brackets as a later addition, possibly by Aristotle himself, to the text. The δ' after *philos* is perfectly in order, as marking the additional remark about friends that this sentence introduces, and the sequence of thought runs a lot better with the sentence than without it.

11. See *NE* 2.5.1105b23; *EE* 2.2.1220b13–14 (with the potentially significant addition of *aisthētikē* before *hēdonē*); *MM* 1.7.1186a13–14. It appears that in some way Aristotle is following Plato in this: see *Philebus* 47e1–48a2, and what follows there (to 50e4).

12. Aristotle does not offer a formal definition of *to tharrein*. He only says that what it is can be gathered easily from the definition already provided of fear, of which it is the opposite (1383a14–15), and then adds this remark about the impression of what keeps us safe. Perhaps one is licensed to infer from this (mimicking the definition of fear) that confidence actually *is* ἡδονή τις ἐκ φαντασίας τῶν σωτηρίων ὡς ἐγγὺς ὄντων, τῶν δὲ φοβερῶν ὡς ἢ μὴ ὄντων ἢ πόρρω ὄντων. But Aristotle does not explicitly say this.

13. See *EE* 2.10.1227b3–4, 7.2.1235b25–29.

14. See *Rhet.* 1386b26–32, 1387a1–3.

15. I have been led in examining this evidence to suppose that the general association of the *pathē* with *lupē* and *hēdonē* announced at 1378a21–22 anticipates these definitions in terms of these two opposites. This does not preclude, as Aristotle makes explicit in the case of anger (see 1378b1–9), that in an emotion that was based in *lupē* there should be involved (*hepesthai*) also some pleasure; but these pleasures will be, as they are for anger, secondary ones, ones that depend upon special further features of the state of mind of the person feeling the emotion. These secondary pleasures are not part of the definition of the emotion. On anger, see further below.

16. For bodily pain, see for example *DA* 2.2.413b23 (the pain of worms), *EE* 3.1.1229a34–41 (the pains that can kill you), and *EE* 7.8.1241b9 (the pains of childbirth); for bodily pain plus physical disgust, *NE* 7.7.1150a9–10 (the pains of touch, and of taste); the dislike of doing sums or writing, *NE* 10.5.1175b17–20; the distress caused a proud man if he is not given some honor or if he is put under the rule of some unworthy person, *EE* 3.5.1232b12.

17. At *MM* 1.7.1186a16 we find *lupēthēnai* given alongside *orgisthēnai* and *eleēsai* as examples of emotions: there *lupēthēnai* presumably has the sense of "grieving," rather than generic "distress," so as to be coordinate with these other two emotions, which are of course quite specific ones.

18. Thus of the emotions based in *lupē* Aristotle omits to associate *tarachē* only with anger and eagerness to match the accomplishments of others (*zēlos*).

19. For bodily pleasures, i.e., pleasurable sensations, see *NE* 2.3.1104b5–6, 7.13.1153b33–34, and *EE* 1.4.1215b5; the pleasure of eating sweets in the theater, indulged especially when the play is bad, *NE* 10.5.1175b10–16; the refined pleasure in well-turned and becoming jokes taken and given by the tactful person, *NE* 4.1128a25–28; the wondrous pleasures philosophy is said to give, *NE* 10.7. 1177a25.

20. At 1381b12 one reads that "we hate people if we merely think (*hupolambanōmen*)" they are thoroughly wicked. This might be taken to assign a role in hatred for full belief where in the other emotions an impression is said to be sufficient. But that would probably be to place too much weight on a somewhat incidental remark.

21. To make this case one would want to take seriously Aristotle's reference (see note 20 of this essay) to belief in (not an appearance of) the wickedness of the hated person. Even if hatred is an "emotional" state of reason, however, that would provide no good grounds on which to deny that it involves distress or pleasure: on Aristotle's understanding of these latter phenomena they can be experienced in the having of reasoned thoughts, as readily as in nonrational sorts of activity.

22. In any event, the opinion that hatred does not involve a distressed state of mind appears a well-entrenched one with Aristotle. He repeats it, again by contrast with anger, in a very different context in *Polit.* 5.10.1312b33–34 (anger and hatred are, together with contempt, the leading causes of the overthrow of tyrannies). His description of hatred there makes one almost think he is talking about no emotion or passion at all, but a fully reasoned, dispassionate rejection and dislike. (I have benefited from discussion with Myles Burnyeat about the issues raised in this paragraph.)

23. 2.4.1378a31–33: I translate the text of Kassel (see note 10 of this essay), taking *tōn . . . mē prosēkontōn*, as he suggests (following the construction at 1379b12), to refer to the perpetrators of the insult. It is odd that Aristotle only specifies within this appended explanatory phrase that the objects of the insult are the person himself or someone close to him, but there seems no reasonable alternative to so taking the text, as transmitted.

It is surely evident that the two occurrences of forms of *phainesthai* here are to be taken as references to how the angry person takes things (how they strike him, how they appear to him to be), if only because of the parallel here to the similar, and unmistakable, references to such appearings that occur regularly also in the case of other emotions analyzed in this part of the *Rhetoric* (fear, 1382a21, etc.; confidence, 1383a17; *aischunē*, 1384a23, etc.; pity, 1385b13, etc.; righteous indignation, 1387a9; envy, 1387b11; *zēlos*, 1388a30; and see also 1380a10, on feeling mildly, the feeling opposed to anger). And note the free variation between *hupolēpsis oligōrias* and *phainomenē oligōria* in the texts of the *Topics* cited in note 24 of this essay. The badly mistaken tradition of translating the forms of *phainesthai* in the *Rhetoric*'s definition of anger by "conspicuous" or the like (one finds this both in W. R. Roberts's Oxford translation [*Rhetoric* (New York, 1954)] and in Dufour's in the Budé [*Rhétorique* (Paris, 1932)]) seems to go back to Cope-Sandys (ad loc.). I doubt if it would even have occurred to anyone to take the Greek so, if it were not for the (odd-looking) first occurrence of *phainomenēs* here with *timōrias:* it certainly does seem attractive to suppose that anger involves a desire for *conspicuous* punishment for the insult, and that rendering seems more appropriate to the facts about anger than "apparent" or "what one takes to be." But it does not do well for the belittlement itself: anger does not require a conspicuous lack of regard, just one that one notices or takes to be there. One may suspect the text, as L. Spengel (*Aristotelis Ars Rhetorica* [Leipzig, 1867]), followed by W. D. Ross in the OCT (*Aristotelis Ars Rhetorica* [Oxford, 1959]), did in over-boldly bracketing *phainomenēs*; but in any event there seems no doubt at all that, if Aristotle did write it, he meant by it not "conspicuous" but "apparent," "what impresses one as being."

24. See *Top.* 4.6.127b30–31, καὶ ἡ λύπη καὶ ἡ ὑπόληψις τοῦ ὀλιγωρίας ἐν τῷ τί ἐστι; 6.13.151a15–16, λύπη μεθ' ὑπολήψεως τοῦ ὀλιγωρεῖσθαι; 8.1.156a32–33, ἡ ὀργὴ ὄρεξις εἶναι τιμωρίας διὰ φαινομένην ὀλιγωρίαν. It is worth noting that in the first two of these definitions, but not the third, the angry person's view that he has been belittled is cast in terms of belief, an opinion rationally arrived at (*hupolēpsis*), rather than merely an impression or appearance. The *Rhetoric* seems more self-consciously decisive in favor of the latter type of definition, not only in the case of anger but in that of other emotions as well.

25. But, as we have seen, Aristotle's formal definition of friendly feeling speaks rather of what the person with this feeling is moved to do (to help someone in need) than the feeling itself and its characteristics. I have already mentioned (note 9) the difficulties Aristotle causes himself by defining friendly feeling, supposedly an emotion and so something nonrational, as based in a "wish."

26. In taking up anger and appetite as causes of potentially condemnable actions at 1.10.1369b14–16, he refers the reader forward to his discussion of the emotions in Book 2 to find out about anger, but goes on right there to speak about appetite (at the end of 2.10 and in 2.11). The omission of a discussion in Book 2 of appetite therefore seems to be have been well planned. The fact that in Book 1.10–11 he explains what *epithumia* is, by way of telling us what pleasure is and what gives pleasure to different people, may explain why he omits to discuss *epithumia* as a *pathos* in 2.2–11: in effect, he had already said in 1.10–11 what he thought needed to be said about it, and saw no need to go further. However, he nowhere gives or openly implies this explanation, so I put it forward only as a conjecture.

27. On *thumos* see, for example, *DA* 2.3.414b2 and *MM* 1.12.1187b37; for *orgē* as a special case of *thumos*-desire see *DA* 1.1.403a30 and *Top.* 8.1.156a32, with *Top.* 4.5.126a8–10 and 2.7.113b1.

28. I translate the text of Kassel (see note 10), omitting the bracketed words in 1379a13 but disregarding the brackets in 1379a15–18.

29. The last two emotions are among the ones Aristotle lists in *NE* 2.5. 1105b21–23.

Mixed Feelings in Aristotle's *Rhetoric*

Dorothea Frede

THE PROBLEM

Psychology, as it is usually understood nowadays, cannot be found in Aristotle's official work on "psychology," the *De Anima*. That treatise contains a study of the natural faculties of all living beings, of motion, perception, and also of thinking, the mental function special to human beings.[1] Students looking for enlightenment on questions about the human soul's motivating forces or its general emotional makeup will instead find themselves referred to either the Aristotelian ethics or the *Rhetoric* where this aspect of human nature is dealt with extensively. All would be well if the theories developed in those sources were in agreement, so that we could paste together a coherent picture of Aristotelian psychology; but alas, they are not, or at least not in some important respects.

One major discrepancy concerns the emotions, and that will be this essay's concern. In his *Rhetoric* Aristotle holds that most emotions (*pathē*) have a mixed nature, because they contain a mixture of pleasure and pain. He defines anger (*orgē*), for example, as a feeling of annoyance mixed with a portion of pleasure because it anticipates revenge (1378b2). Love is a kind of longing that contains the pleasure of either remembering or anticipating contact with the loved one, and fear contains a portion of hope for relief (1383a5). No such emphasis on their mixed nature is found in his treatment of the emotions in his ethics.[2] This discrepancy might, of course, be quite harmless; it might mean no more than that in real life human emotions are hardly ever pure in their content and direction. The inclusion of mixed emotions in the *Rhetoric* would then be due to this work's practical aspects. As law professors often remind their students, crystal-clear cases hardly ever occur in practice.

That there is more to the mixed nature of these feelings than that, however, is clear when we realize that the admixture of the opposite seems to form a part of the definition of these emotions. Aristotle can therefore not solely be concerned with empirical observations; rather his concern is with matters of principle, and matters of principle must never be taken lightly! What adds to the gravity of the case is that Aristotle is not the inventor of the theory that emotions are intrinsically mixed phenomena. He seems to have inherited it from Plato, who has much to say about mixed feelings in connection with his discussion of pleasure and pain in his late dialogue *Philebus*. Pleasure is defined there as the restoration of a disturbance of the natural equilibrium, while pain represents a process of disintegration, the disturbance that pleasure is the remedy for (*Philebus* 31d, 32a–b).[3] Thus Plato gives a kind of medical explanation of pleasure and pain, which he also extends to the explanation of the emotions. The reasons for his adopting such a revolutionary theory will be discussed shortly, after we have taken a closer look at the extent to which Plato influenced Aristotle in this respect. That his influence is indeed very profound comes to the fore when we realize that Aristotle in his *Rhetoric* does not just borrow certain features of Plato's description of the emotional states (which he then for some reason discards in his ethics), but seems to accept the *Philebus*'s basic conception of pleasure and pain as the supreme genera of the emotions. Although he is not very explicit about his reasons for, and the extent of, this borrowing, his definition of pleasure and pain (*Rhet.* 1369b32–1370a39) leaves little doubt about the Platonic origin of that theory.

The problem I propose to solve in this essay is the reason for Aristotle's accepting Plato's medical account of the emotions for his *Rhetoric*, while roundly rejecting this view as mistaken in his ethics, where he argues that pleasure is tied to perfect activities of the soul. Such a blatant disagreement about basic assumptions in his account of human motivation calls for an explanation. Discrepancies within the Aristotelian writings are notoriously a vexed subject. There are three standard explanations that are commonly offered. First, Aristotle may simply have changed his mind. He may have turned against Plato's conception of the emotions after he wrote the *Rhetoric*. Second, the discrepancy might be due to a different aspect of the question of what emotions are; what concerns him in his *Rhetoric* might be of minor importance in his ethics. Finally, when Aristotle seems to contradict himself, it might be because he is not professing his own doctrine, but expresses "common views" (*endoxa*), which he does not for the moment want to question.

Some scholars have indeed regarded the theory of the *Rhetoric* as an *endoxon*, on the ground that such a medical view agrees well with popular conceptions of diseases as disturbances of the natural balance of the body.[4] That is probably right, as far as most doctors' opinions on the nature of diseases are concerned. But although there are some indications that Empedocles maintained such a view of the nature of simple physical pleasures and pains,[5] no one before Plato seems to have extended this theory to include the emotions. It therefore cannot be assumed that it had become a piece of common folk-psychology. Not only that: it took Plato himself a long time to develop his mature view of pleasure as a restoration of a natural balance, and Socrates in the *Philebus* has great trouble making himself understood when he explains it to his interlocutor. In addition, rhetoricians are not supposed to make the emotions the central topic of successful public speeches, they are supposed to learn how to handle them. Aristotle must therefore be concerned with giving them a true account of their nature in his *Rhetoric* instead of commonly acceptable opinions.[6] So the *endoxon* theory won't fly.

The first of the three explanations mentioned above, namely that Aristotle simply changed his mind as he got away from his master Plato, seems to have a much better chance. Most scholars regard the *Rhetoric* as an early work, especially its first two books that are relevant here.[7] They were probably written while Plato was still alive and Aristotle taught at his school and must have served as his lecture notes. His theory of the emotions in the *Rhetoric* was, then, quite naturally a piece of Platonic heritage, which Aristotle discarded in his mature work on ethics. This explanation of a simple change of mind in Aristotle suffers from one major defect: it is too simple. This is not to deny that Aristotle was originally under Plato's influence and later changed his mind. What the simple explanation cannot explain, however, is the fact that Aristotle left his account in the *Rhetoric* unchanged. He notoriously doctored his texts throughout his life, made changes and additions, and the *Rhetoric* is no exception. Rudolf Kassel has marked many passages as later additions, not only by later editors but by Aristotle himself.[8] Nor can his continued faithfulness to Plato be explained away as a mere oversight on his part; the theory of pleasure and pain, as well as the discussion of the various emotions, does not play a marginal role in the *Rhetoric,* nor is the subject treated in a perfunctory way. It forms an important part of the discussion in the first book, and it is dealt with at quite an unusual length in the second.[9] It is therefore difficult to imagine that Aristotle did not notice that remnant of Platonism, once he had changed his mind and rejected Plato's conception of pleasure and pain as processes of disintegration and restoration. We therefore have to take a closer look at the two different conceptions of pleasure and pain in Aristotle and see whether there is a better explanation than chronology and development. But before we do that, we have to see what Plato's own view of the matter actually is.

PLATO'S CONCEPTION OF PLEASURE AND PAIN

As everyone familiar with Plato's work knows, pleasure was a lifelong problem for him. He seems to have changed his mind several times about the nature and value of this phenomenon. His earlier work contains rigorous condemnation of pleasure, as well as praise—at least this is so, if he was serious in the *Protagoras* about defining virtue as "the art of measuring pleasure and pain." I myself doubt very much that he meant it seriously, but he at least toyed with the idea. Yet at roughly the same time he strongly condemned pleasure as the number one tempter and disturber of the human soul. In the *Phaedo* he has nothing good to say about pleasure at all; the philosopher should have no part in it (69a ff.; 83b–d). And in the *Gorgias* he depicts the life of a pleasure-seeker as Sisyphean labor: it is like filling a leaky jar with a sieve (493b). In *Republic* Book 9 (583b–587a), however, he forges an uneasy truce with pleasure, by admitting special pleasures for the philosopher, which are infinitely superior to the common pleasures. But Plato cannot have long been satisfied with that solution. Even the most ardent admirer of philosophy will at best be amused by his "hedonic calculus," that the philosopher lives exactly 729 times more pleasantly than the tyrant (587e). Philosophy's delights may be unusually fine and long-lasting, but no one will insist on such an immense quantitative superiority. Seriously problematic in his account of pleasure itself is the fact that Plato mixes together two different concepts or metaphors. First he calls pleasure a motion: there is a motion from "down below" to an intermediary state, from pain to painlessness, which is not a real pleasure, and then there is a motion from the painless intermediary state to a "true above," a true delight.[10] He then supplements the metaphor of the upward motion by the metaphor of pleasure as a filling of a lack (585a–586b): true pleasures, like the philosopher's, are fillings with "really real" things. All other pleasures are illusory and should therefore be called "bastard-pleasures" (587b–c). What is unsatisfactory about this mixing of metaphors is that Plato avoids a clear pronouncement as to whether the specious pleasures are pleasures or not. This explains, then, why he later devoted an entire dialogue to the clarification of this issue. It seems to have taken Plato quite a while till he saw his way in that matter, if it is true that the *Philebus* is one of his latest works. There he presents us with a truly magisterial solution to the whole problem, a unified account of pleasure and pain that is free from all such flaws.

The novelty of his conception in the *Philebus* may not be apparent at first sight, because he retains the *Republic*'s notion that pleasures are processes and speaks of them as fillings of a lack. The crucial difference is that he now subsumes all pleasures (including the philosopher's) under one genus and treats them all as equally real, although not as equally good. This is the account that I called "medical" earlier, because it treats all pleasures as restorations of the natural harmonious state in body or soul. I will give only the briefest sketch as to the implications of Plato's unified theory of pleasure and pain, because he is not the topic of this essay.[11] What is new about this treatment of pleasure is that Plato can now use one concept for all pleasures, and, more important, that he can also explain what is wrong with them, without resorting to the old and implausible saw that pleasure is never more than a distraction, a disturbance, or a disease of the soul. His overall critique of pleasure now is not that it is illusory, but that pleasure is at best a "remedial good," because it is always the restoration of some disturbance or the filling of a lack. We would, of course, be better off if we had no need for replenishment or remedies at all, just as we would be better off if we needed no doctors. That he now treats it at least as a remedial good and as a necessity, shows that Plato has made his peace with certain aspects of human nature: we are always deficient in one way or another, and so some pleasures are necessary, and some are even good. Pleasures are acceptable when the deficiency is not painful but represents an unfelt lack, and when the object that fills us or restores the equilibrium is true and pure. Needless to say, the pleasure of learning (not of knowing!) is one of the true and good processes, but there are also other harmless pleasures like those of pure sense perception. Plato now holds that the best human life (since we are not gods and cannot live in perfect equilibrium) is a life mixed together from reason and pleasure.

The most interesting new feature in Plato's unified theory is that he can now justify the claim that some pleasures have an intelligible content, because they involve beliefs about states of affairs. There is nothing mysterious about this claim: we actually quite often refer to such pleasures or pains; for instance when we say "She is pleased because (she thinks that) she won the competition," or when we say "He is terribly upset thinking that he flunked the exam." Such "propositional attitudes" can be true or false, because the person can be mistaken: she actually may not have won, and he might not have failed. She may be falsely pleased, and he may be falsely pained.

The discovery that pleasures and pains are intentional states that are defined by what they are about represents an important innovation. For this "aboutness" of pleasure and pain allows Plato to claim that they can be true or false, as well as subject to moral evaluation. Take the case of people who can only enjoy a present when they know that it is expensive. What they really enjoy is not the thing, the gift itself. What they really enjoy is the presumed fact that this thing was expensive. If that turns out to be false, it ruins their fun. When they find out that the gift did not come from Bloomingdale's and did not cost $180, they will be upset, because all their pleasant assumptions have been false. But not only can such pleasures be false, they can also be judged morally wrong, if we think that people ought not to condition their pleasures in gifts by the price. There are, of course, worse kinds of pleasures than these, such as sadistic pleasures, and Plato can rightly claim that these are entertained by a vicious soul. There is something intrinsically wrong with the pleasure of people who enjoy watching someone drown. So our pleasures and pains conform to our moral conditions: "Tell me your pleasures and I will tell you who you are," as we might say. Such moral evaluations are possible, once the complexity of certain pleasures has been discovered and the view is given up that all pleasures are mere indistinct feelings that are caused by certain drives and cravings.[12]

The notion that certain pleasures and pains have propositional content also explains Plato's account of complex emotions like fear, anger, longing, mourning, jealousy, or malice (47c–50e).[13] This point is crucial for our purposes, because it represents the point of agreement between Plato and Aristotle's *Rhetoric:* mixed emotions are desires to remedy an injury or disturbance combined with the pleasant expectation of restoration. This needs specification: anger and wrath are pains at suffering an insult, but they always also contain the desire for—and the pleasant anticipation of—revenge,[14] as Plato argues, using the famous lines from Homer, that wrath embitters the soul of the best, but is at the same time sweeter than soft flowing honey (*Iliad* 18.108–110). Similarly, longing contains the expectation of meeting the beloved, lamentation that of consolation. Only where there is no hope for relief at all is there no pleasure mixed with the painful realization of loss, hurt, or deprivation. In such cases we would not speak of wrath, longing, or mourning, but of despair or utter resignation.

The bittersweetness of feeling is not confined to negative emotions, according to Plato; it can also be found in what would be taken to be sheer pleasures. He demonstrates this with an example that would seem at first highly implausible, namely with laughter in comedy. What kind of disturbance or pain could be involved in this most innocent of all pleasures? Plato regards our amusement when we see others making fools of themselves as a kind of schadenfreude, a pleasure that is laced with malice (*Philebus* 48a ff.). What justifies such a claim? He seems to go on the assumption that our laughter is not due to the intrinsic funniness of the situation, because we ourselves would not want to be in the other's shoes, let alone find it amusing. If we laugh at others, it must then be due to a hidden resentment toward them; if we were their true friends, we would not be amused but would rather feel upset by their foolishness. So comic laughter is a kind of relief for hidden (or not so hidden) ill will against others. Regardless of whether we find Plato's analysis of comic laughter entirely satisfactory, we must grant him that there is always some edge in our feelings about others when we laugh at them, as we can see from the fact that comic laughter at ourselves is something that comes with much practice, if at all. Self-laughter was no component in ancient comedy.

This summary shows how Plato's conception of pleasure and pain can account for many of our emotions: if we were in complete equilibrium, at ease with ourselves and the world, we would not enjoy many of the experiences we do in fact enjoy. We would have no need for such pleasures. We would neither enjoy comedy nor would we be entertained by tragedies. So regardless of possible objections to his analysis of the human emotions connected with comedy or tragedy, his explanation of our more complex emotions in terms of disturbance and restoration with a propositional content represents enormous progress, both from a psychological and from a philosophical point of view. We can see that Aristotle had good reasons for being intrigued by the possibilities of explaining the emotions on the basis of Plato's late theory.[15] For the notion that pleasures and pains can be complex mental processes with intentional objects allows him to fine-tune the definitions of these emotions. And that is precisely what Aristotle does in his depiction of the different emotional states in the *Rhetoric.*

PLEASURE, PAIN, AND THE EMOTIONS IN THE *RHETORIC*

That the emotions should receive so much attention in the *Rhetoric* comes as something of a surprise, because in its introduction Aristotle enjoins that proof, not an appeal to the emotions, ought to be the hallmark of rhetoric. He severely reproves his predecessors for totally missing the essence of rhetoric by focusing on the audience's emotions. To engage in such manipulation is speaking "outside the subject" and actually forbidden by law in well-run societies (1354a11–21). Why, then, does he himself soon afterward devote so much effort to them and treat them as a valuable part of the "means of proof" (*pistis,* 1356a1)? Is this merely a concession to the bad ways of the real world? "If the opponent does it, I have to be ready to do it too?" The fact that Aristotle deals with the emotions in connection with forensic speech, where the emotions are most likely to sway the audience by their feelings of sympathy and antipathy, while in politics the consideration of the expedient precludes much emotional manipulation (1354b31–1355a1), prima facie confirms this suspicion.

That these dark suspicions are groundless emerges when we look at the context in which Aristotle introduces the emotions in forensic rhetoric (1368b1 ff.).[16] He does not offer clever tricks to sway the audience through melodrama. The audience's emotions are in fact not mentioned in that connection; instead Aristotle first broaches the subject of the emotions when he tackles the question of why people break the laws. To make plausible that the accused did or did not commit an action or was justified in doing what he did, the orator has to know in what condition and for what reasons people commit injustice and against what kind of victim. So the motivations for crime have to be discussed, including the psychological dispositions that make people liable to commit such actions. In that sense reference to the *pathē* forms a legitimate part of forensic speech because it concerns the proof of guilt or innocence (1368b1–5).

This is not the only legitimate employment of the emotions as part of proofs in rhetoric, according to Aristotle. To influence the audience's emotions is also of great importance, because the listeners will judge differently if they are well- or ill-disposed toward the speaker and his case. They will therefore also have to be convinced of the speaker's good intentions (*eunoia*, 1378a8).[17] Jurors, for instance, will not be convinced of any cause, no matter how justified it is, if they see the matter in an adverse spirit, and if they regard as good or just what they should judge to be bad and unjust, or vice versa. So "working on the audience's feelings" (1377b28–31) is a legitimate part of oratory. Although it is not part of proof of the subject matter ("outside the demonstration," 1378a7), it is a legitimate part of speaking to the subject as long as it is not used as a mere camouflage for speaking "outside the subject matter." Studying the *pathē*, their nature and origin, is then a legitimate part of "technical" rhetoric, as Aristotle had announced earlier (1356a23–25). So much, in brief, on the question of why Aristotle devotes so much effort in his *Rhetoric* to the clarification of the nature of the emotions and to the question of what is involved in each of them, in spite of his initial disapproval.

The fact that there are these two different kinds of uses of the emotions in rhetoric has important consequences for the way in which Aristotle treats them. First of all, the difference in aspect explains a seeming repetitiousness in his discussion of the emotions. A brief survey in 1.11 is followed by a much more extensive discussion in Book 2. More important, the difference in aspect explains the substantial change in perspective and content: in forensic speech the emotions are used to explain the defendant's actions; when it comes to the audience's dispositions it is rather a matter of influencing their judgment.[18] The difference this makes in Aristotle's overall theory of the emotions can unfortunately not be fully discussed here, since it would presuppose a thorough review of the text. I am primarily concerned with the "forensic use" of the emotions, because that is where Plato's influence is most clearly recognizable. Because criminal action involves both emotive reaction and the motivation for actions through desire, the mixed nature of certain emotions naturally comes to the fore.

Aristotle broaches the subject by giving a survey of all human motivations: people do what they do knowingly and intentionally because they regard it either as useful or pleasant or to avoid what is detrimental or unpleasant. There are thus two different ultimate motivating forces: rational wish (*logistikē orexis*) that aims for what is useful or expedient, and nonrational desire (*alogos orexis*) that aims for pleasure and the avoidance of pain (1369a1–4).[19] *Pathos*, the term translated here as "emotion," comprises all the so-called nonrational desires, with the addition of anger. So when Aristotle refers to the emotions he speaks of states that involve all kinds of nonrational desires.[20] The angry person thirsts for revenge, the stingy one craves money, the coward does whatever it takes to avoid danger, the overly ambitious person is driven by the quest for honor.

This division, neat as it sounds at first, has its problems. First, we would like to know why rational desire (*boulēsis*) should be "unemotional," as it were. Why should we not also like and enjoy when we get what we approve of on rational grounds, or dislike something harmful? And why, then, does he speak of rational desire, if there is no emotional involvement? Second, why does Aristotle at first separate rational desire from nonrational desire (*epithumia*) for pleasure (1369a1–4), but later stipulate that some of the *epithumiai* are nonrational (*alogoi*), others are "with reason" (*meta logou*, 1370a18)? Does this not vitiate his whole dichotomy? Are there nonrational pleasures with reason?

The first question is easy to answer: Aristotle does not claim that our rational desires must be unemotional. His contention is merely that our rational predilections are determined exclusively by our conviction that the thing in question is beneficial, either to ourselves or to humankind in general. We might decide that to build a certain bridge is a good thing, without any feelings whatsoever. We then "want" that thing, because we have decided that it is a good thing. Every rational decision to act implies a rational desire in this sense, otherwise there would be no action at all. But that does not mean that I, as a member of the bridge committee, have to feel very warmly about bridges, love bridges, and so on. I want to have it built, because it is generally necessary and useful. The determining motive here is exclusively the rational calculation that something is to our advantage (1369b7–9), not any kind of feeling. Although there might be all sorts of feelings harbored by those who make such decisions, it is a rational decision as long as it is the rational wish (*boulēsis*) and not the feelings (*epithumia*) that determine them.[21]

The second question needs a more detailed discussion, because the nonrational desires "with reason" directly concern the emotions. To answer it we have to take a closer look at Aristotle's definition of pleasure and pain and at their relationship to desire and belief. "Let it be assumed by us (*hupokeisthō*) that pleasure is a certain movement of the soul (*kinēsis*), a sudden and perceptible settling down (*katastasis*) into its natural state, and pain the opposite" (1369b33–35). So all processes in the soul that restore our own nature are pleasant, and all that imply some destruction thereof are painful. It is clear that Aristotle at this point resorts to the Phileban "remedial" conception of pleasure (without mentioning his source or Plato's name) as the filling of a lack or settling of a disturbance and pain as the corresponding deficiency or disturbance.[22] It should also be clear why such disturbances and the desire for restoration are called nonrational. Although they do not happen without a cause, they are not matters of deliberation or choice, and because they just "happen" to the individual, the corresponding pleasant restorations are also nonrational. We experience desire satisfaction as pleasant without any rational considerations or calculations. What then allows for a distinction between nonrational and rational desires? The desires that are caused by the needs of the body, such as hunger, thirst, or the sexual desires, are entirely nonrational: they do not involve any reasoning (1370a20–25). Other desires arise on the basis of certain beliefs concerning what we need, even though they are not the result of rational choice (1370a19–20, 25–27).[23] Such desire-provoking beliefs account for a lot of human pleasures and pains: I may become inordinately hungry for money because I am persuaded that much money would be gratifying, especially if I see others reveling in it. Such persuasions are painful and their fulfillment pleasant qua need and qua fulfillment. I may begin to crave a Porsche, when I see my friends whisking by in flashy cars, or when I become convinced that I am not a proper person unless I do the same. For that reason, then, Aristotle says that "there are many things that we desire to see or acquire when we have heard them spoken of and are convinced that they are pleasant" (1370a25–27). Since the craving involves a kind of belief, it is *meta logou*, but insofar as it is not a matter of rational choice that I become disturbed about my lack of such a car, it is not based on rational calculation. I do not choose to be disturbed, nor do I choose to desire the fulfillment of my craving.[24]

If Aristotle is serious about adopting the Platonic account of pleasure and pain, does he regard all emotions as disturbances and restorations or a mixture of the two? He is, unfortunately, even less explicit than Plato about the details of his theory. He does not anywhere use the word "mixture," nor does he explicitly define desire as a pain mixed with the pleasure of anticipated relief. We can at best infer from the definition of pleasure as the restoration of the natural state that the preceding desire is or implies a disturbance. Furthermore, his explanation of the *pathē* as states that are accompanied (*hepetai*, 1378a19–20; cf. *akolouthei* at

1370a15–16)^{25} by pleasure and pain may suggest that there is only a looser connection between the emotions and concomitant feelings of pleasure and pain. On the other hand, not only does Aristotle define many of the emotions as pains or pleasures, as in the case of anger, fear, and their opposites, but he early on identifies the influence of the *pathē* as either pleasant or painful, as friendliness or hatred (1356a14–16). Thus his loose way of expressing the nature of *pathos* at the beginning of the second book as "involving pleasure and pain" seems to be due to his unwillingness to engage in a longer elucidation of the kind we find in Plato (*Philebus* 46d–47a). Although all emotions involve both disturbances and restorations, some are experienced as pleasures because the pleasant aspect is preponderant, others as pains because the painful aspect is more prominent. That Aristotle is indeed following Plato's model will be confirmed when we take a closer look at his treatment of the individual emotions. They can all be subsumed under pleasure or pain as their supreme genera, depending on whether the overall impression of this amalgam of feelings is pleasant or painful.^{26}

Since for Aristotle human nature includes all those traits that have become habitual, acquired tastes as we would say, there are many things we can feel deprived of, whose restitution we desire.^{27} This conception not only explains why we have so many different desires and needs; it confirms at the same time our surmise about why Aristotle calls them nonrational: once we have acquired certain dispositions, they are not up to rational choice. If I feel deprived of something, I do not choose to want it. And if I get it, I do not decide to be pleased. Pleasure automatically follows when we experience the fulfillment of our needs.^{28} Therefore no matter what someone may tell us, or what we may tell ourselves, we simply "have" these desires and are pained or pleased anyway. This does not preclude thinking from influencing our emotional states. We can talk ourselves into or out of feeling many needs and their alleged satisfactions and we are open to manipulation by others. In addition, we can be quite mistaken about what we think our satisfaction consists in. That is why Plato speaks about "false pleasures" (*Philebus* 36c–50e) and Aristotle about "seeming" pleasures (1369b23). We experience many pains because we believe that we are being deprived of something, and we experience many pleasures because we think that we are getting or will get what we need, and often these beliefs are quite mistaken, and thus we are wrongly displeased or pleased. In addition, these pleasures and displeasures may be appropriate or inappropriate. Because they may or may not be what a decent person ought to find desirable or undesirable, they are also subject to moral evaluation.^{29} So much, then, for the question of why Aristotle holds that there are pleasures that involve beliefs, even though they are based on *alogoi epithumiai*. It is not their content that is nonrational, but the occurrence of the positive or negative affection that makes the object of the desire appear attractive or repulsive.

All this shows why Aristotle holds that we have to know people's nature, including their acquired nature, if we want to know why they enjoy certain things and are pained by others. Rhetoricians therefore have to have insight into different personalities if they want to give plausible characterizations of the likely motivations that are due to different people's likes and dislikes. To characterize someone as an idler, for instance, we point out that the person is not used to making any kind of sustained effort. All exertion will be unnatural and painful, while amusement and playful pastimes are always welcome to this person (1370a9–16). The same applies to persons who acquire more obnoxious habitual natures that may lead them to criminal activities. They will have an inordinate craving for money or beauty or power and will be depicted accordingly by the rhetorician.

These brief indications summarize Aristotle's extensive discussion of what is involved in the emotions. They must suffice to show why many emotions have an intrinsically mixed nature (see 1370b15, in most desires pleasures are contained). It is not because we are waffling or ambiguous in our attitudes, as the ordinary sense of "mixed feelings" would suggest. Their mixed nature is due to the fact that emotional states are based on the recognition of a need and that they contain certain expectations of their assuagement. This is especially true in the case of emotions that result from another's hostile actions.[30] Anger is a kind of pain, because it is stirred by the belief that someone has done something nasty to me that I did not deserve. This pain about the "kick against my shin" would not be called "anger" if it did not include the desire for revenge and the notion that revenge might be within my reach. We do not get angry with those beyond our power, or only much less so (1370b13–15). Anger is thus a pain mixed with pleasure. The rage of Achilles is Aristotle's prime example, just as it was Plato's. Achilles does not feel only pain at being humiliated by Agamemnon. If he did, that state would not be called anger, at least not according to Aristotle. To be called "anger," it must at the same time contain the desire for retaliation and the hope of achieving it. And that is what the *Iliad* is all about. It is the song about Achilles' wrath *and* his revenge.

We see now why for Aristotle most desires, *epithumiai*, are pains that involve some pleasure. Distress implies not only the desire for relief but also, to some degree, the anticipation through memory or *phantasia* (1370a30) of a successful cure for what is bothering us:

> The lovesick always take pleasure in talking, writing, or composing verses about the beloved; for it seems to them that in all this recollection makes

the object of their affection perceptible. Love always begins in this manner, when men are happy not only in the presence of the beloved, but also in his absence when they recall him to mind. This is why, even when his absence is painful, there is a certain amount of pleasure in mourning and lamentation; the pain is due to his absence, but there is pleasure in remembering and, as it were, seeing him and recalling his actions and personality. (1370b19–28)

In a survey of the different emotions Aristotle shows what needs there are in each case and how they are satisfied by their corresponding pleasures.[31] He explains various desires for pleasure as the need for self-restoration or self-completion and shows how this motivates many human enterprises: Being honored and admired gives the person the imagination (*phantasia*) of possessing those qualities that adorn the good man. Humans love most things for the promises they contain, not because they represent some possession of theirs. For this reason people care for admiration or even flattery: a flatterer provides at least the illusion that we have admirable properties. We enjoy being loved because we have a need for being cherished (1371a18–20) and flattery gives us the illusion of greatness. One further example must suffice here to demonstrate the richness of Aristotle's analysis: he claims that we all (not only the belligerent and ambitious among us, but peace-loving people as well) love victory so much, because we have a natural need for superiority over others. This explains the enjoyment of all competitive games, including victory in litigation: we all desire to prove our superiority in some way. That is also why we don't really enjoy easy victories, because they do not prove much about us. So here too, the motive is the need of and hopes for self-perfection, whether we are right or wrong about what we conceive perfection to be.[32]

The picture of the nature of the emotions changes when Aristotle turns to the analysis of the audience's emotions that fills more than half of the *Rhetoric*'s second book. There is even a new kind of definition of the *pathē*. They are no longer tied to the concept of desire,[33] instead they are defined as that which cause people to change with respect to their judgment (*krisis*, 1378a19–20), while pleasure and pain are merely referred to as concomitants or constituents of these mind-altering means (ibid.). But if in the subsequent discussion of the individual emotions the question of a mixture of pleasure and pain is not raised again,[34] this does not necessarily signify that Aristotle has quietly dropped the "remedial" account of the emotions inherited from Plato. It shows only that the emphasis is no longer on desire but on judgment as the main constituent of the emotions. For as far as the audience is concerned, the question is not, or not immediately, what actions they may desire, but rather whether they are favorably or unfavorably disposed toward the case in question, and that depends on their judgment of the factors involved, who has done what to whom and for what reason. Thus Aristotle discusses positive and negative attitudes separately and focuses on the beliefs and social relations on which different emotive reactions are typically based. Since he usually starts with the negative emotion and often omits to describe their positive counterpart, we get only a dim view of pleasant emotions in the second book of the *Rhetoric*. But the very fact that Aristotle defines most negative emotions as kind of pains and/or disturbances (*lupē kai tarachē*) shows that he has not given up on the essentially Platonic conception of the *pathē*.[35]

There are, to be sure, some emotions that do not fit into this schema. Especially friendliness, hatred, and favor cannot be explained as disturbances and their abatements (2.4, 2.7), because no personal infringement is implied or presupposed. But this shows only that he regarded generic unity as less important than the need to accommodate all positive and negative attitudes that are important for the orator's practical purposes.[36] Such insouciance must have been facilitated for him by the fact, already commented on above, that now it is the audience's judgment that is at stake, rather than the desire for action that explained the motivation of the presumptive lawbreakers. Whether Aristotle overstrains the conception of the emotions when he makes them do double duty of explaining both the desiderative and the judgmental element in human attitudes is a difficult question that cannot be pursued here.

This all too brief summary must suffice to show that Aristotle has put Plato's insight that emotions have a content beyond the sheer feeling of elation or suffering to good use. For that reason a closer look at his "casebook" rewards all those who are curious about the fruitfulness of the "remedial" explanation of the emotions. His explanations in fact go far beyond the orator's immediate concerns with the emotional motivations and judgments. He confirms, among many other things, the *Poetics'* claim that enjoyment of artistic creativity is due to our innate love of learning (namely, the filling of a lack): we enjoy figuring out in drama who does what, and the poet must make it easy for us, but not too easy, to draw our own conclusions. In general, as Aristotle says, "it is pleasant to supply what is wanting," or rather "to finish off what is lacking" (1371b25).[37] Unfortunately, this is not the place for a further evaluation of the fruitfulness of his insights for our own understanding of the emotions. The Platonic-Aristotelian medical conception of the emotions as complex mixtures of pleasures and pains that involve beliefs and expectations explains, for instance, why we don't apply an ice bag when people are red-hot with anger, but appease them instead through reasoning with them. We will tell them, for instance, that the perpetrator did not mean to slight them, or that he is beneath their notice, or that it is in vain to seek redress. In short, we try to change the people's beliefs, rather than their temperature, because a change of belief will also change their feelings.

Such eulogies about the innovativeness of this theory may prompt the reader's perplexed question: what is so spectacular about this discovery concerning the emotions that Plato and Aristotle receive special credit for it? Haven't people tried to talk others out of—or into—certain feelings from the dawn of civilization? No doubt they have done that; the *Iliad* is full of attempts to talk Achilles out of his wrath. But that humankind has always known this in practice does not mean that they were aware of the principles of their actions, namely of the fact that the emotions are based on beliefs. If working out the principles that are known only implicitly is the philosopher's business Plato has done pioneer's work toward explaining the emotions, and Aristotle deserves credit for making it serviceable for the rhetorician's purposes. Rhetoricians must know these principles, they must be fully aware of their conditions, if they want to be successful in applying them in practice. Orators have to have all the ins and outs of the emotions at their fingertips.

PLEASURE, PAIN, AND THE EMOTIONS IN THE ETHICS

If this "remedial" theory of the emotions is so adaptable to all purposes, and if it possesses a high explanatory value, why then did Aristotle drop it in his ethics? "If it ain't broke, don't fix it." But Aristotle did fix it, and he must have had strong reasons for doing so. As I mentioned earlier, he not only drops the account, he rejects the Platonic conception of pleasure as a process of restoration or a filling of a lack in unmistakable terms in his *Nicomachean Ethics*.[38] We will have to pass over the detailed list of his various objections to the identification of pleasure with a *genesis* or *kinēsis*, because this would need a lengthy discussion of his criticism of—and of his fairness to—Plato. The main reason for his disagreement with the remedial account is that he now has a better candidate for what pleasure itself is: Pleasure is no longer connected with processes of restoration, but with activities. An activity, an *energeia*, is for Aristotle not a process that achieves some further end, it is an action that already contains its own end. It is complete in and by itself.

What Aristotle means when he speaks of "self-sufficient activities" is easy to comprehend even for readers not well versed in his ethics. We only have to reflect on some of the activities we like doing best, whether they consist of playing chess or tennis, climbing mountains, canoeing, doing math, playing the piano, or reading. Usually we do these things just for their own sake, not for some further reward or end; and usually we do them without the idea of "filling a lack" or "completing" or "bettering ourselves" by doing them. In fact we continue doing them and enjoying them, even when we already know how to do them perfectly. Many of our favorite activities are of that kind. The sheer experience of the activity is sufficient and pleasant in itself. On the basis of this new conception of activity (*energeia*), Aristotle now defines pleasure as the crowning result of a successful ("unimpeded") activity for which we have a natural inclination (*NE* 10.1174b23). The better the activity, the better the agent is fitted to it and disposed to carry it out, and the better the object of that activity, the more pleasant is it. When we are doing something really well, then pleasure supervenes "like the bloom of youth," as Aristotle adds in an unusual touch of poetic metaphor (1174b33).

Thus the development of the conception of *energeia* or *entelecheia,* as the active realization of full human potential, makes Plato's conception of pleasure as a filling of a lack obsolete. Pleasure, according to Aristotle's new conception, is no longer a remedy for a deficiency. It represents an integral part of human happiness itself, because happiness consists in being active. When I am active in a way that is most suitable to my nature, then I am happy—at least if I can live in this way for a sufficiently long time. When such an agreeable activity goes well, then I am also at the same time enjoying myself. Pleasure, according to this new conception, does not represent the ultimate aim in human life. Rather, the achievement of our ultimate good, the full active life, contains pleasure as its concomitant. Exercising our talents is therefore the most rewarding and at the same time the most pleasant activity we can engage in. In that way the pleasure we experience can serve as a litmus test of our happiness: if your long-term activities do not please you, then you are spending your life doing the wrong thing, and it is a clear sign that you are neither naturally nor habitually fit for it.

The pleasure or pain derived from performing an action serves as a litmus test in Aristotelian ethics in yet another, and even more important, sense. The moral state of that agent, his or her moral taste, is revealed by what a person enjoys or dislikes doing. Nothing is therefore as apt to prove a person's moral makeup as whether a corresponding action is enjoyed or disliked. Magnanimous persons do not only treat their friends with liberality, they enjoy doing so. Penny-pinchers, by contrast, reveal themselves as such even if they treat others on the same scale, because they cannot hide their pain or reluctance at the expense. Aristotle therefore regarded the acquisition of the right moral taste with the right pleasures and pains as the all-important principle of moral education. The maxim attributed earlier to Plato would apply to him too: "Tell me your pleasures and I will tell you who you are." The difference is that the Plato of the *Philebus* is speaking about a person's deficiencies that are cured by pleasant "fillings," while the Aristotle of the *Nicomachean Ethics* is speaking about actions performed and enjoyed.

We can now see why Aristotle's new conception of pleasure presupposes the rejection of the Platonic notion of pleasure. Pleasure is no longer a remedy, pleasure is a perfection.[39] The need to adjust the conception of pleasure to his mature conception of moral virtue and happiness may not have been his only motive for this change of mind, however. Aristotle also puts his finger on the most serious defect in Plato's theory, namely that perfect beings and perfect activities must be "joyless." Plato was quite aware of this consequence of his theory; in the *Philebus* he explicitly declares that the perfect state of undisturbed harmony does not contain any kind of pleasure: it is not fitting that the gods should experience either pleasure or pain (*Philebus* 33b). But it seems that this very claim left Aristotle unsatisfied. Many of us would agree with him, because there is definitely something odd about it; for it presupposes that whenever we enjoy something, we are thereby necessarily filling a lack. This may be a satisfactory explanation of some of our pleasures, but in other cases it would seem to beg the question to make such a claim. If I admire a piece of art, is this really a process of filling an unperceived lack? Once I am filled, can I not enjoy it anymore? Are all our pleasant activities merely "fillings" or "refillings," not something we can enjoy even though we have no "lacks"? Plato would, no doubt, assert the former, because he is quite conscious of the conditions of his theory of pleasure; that is why he regards it as only a secondary, a "remedial" good. Once he had settled for this conception, there is no room for pleasures of perfection. Even the philosopher only enjoys learning, not knowing, the truth (*Philebus* 51e–52b).

For Aristotle, by contrast, perfection is not limited to the gods. There are perfect activities, which consist in exercising our already perfected faculty for doing something. This is the gist of his conception of a perfect *energeia* or *entelecheia*, which he sharply distinguishes from processes that lead to an end, and which are imperfect by their very nature.[40] By contrast to Plato's gods, Aristotle's gods therefore enjoy themselves. The famous Unmoved Mover does enjoy his eternal thinking of thinking (1154b26; cf. *Met.* 12.1072b16). But human beings can also enjoy themselves perfectly, once they are mature individuals with fully developed faculties and talents. All this shows why Aristotle's new conception of pleasure is quite incompatible with the notion of pleasure as the filling of a lack: it does not admit of what we call "joi de vivre," the pleasure that Aristotle regards as part of human happiness as such (*NE* 1175a10–21).

THE PLATONISM OF THE *RHETORIC*

Given the importance of Aristotle's change of mind concerning the conception of pleasure and its role in ethics, it is all the more puzzling that

he left the old conception intact in his *Rhetoric*. His conception of pleasures as processes cannot be a mere relict of his early Platonizing period,
strangely overlooked in later revisions of his book.[41] If ever he took up
the *Rhetoric* again, he could not have failed to see that it contained the
Platonic theory he had criticized with such severity in his ethics. The only
remaining solution is that for some special reason the Platonic concept of
process-pleasures fits the concerns of the *Rhetoric* better than his own later
activity-pleasures.

Is there anything connected with the topic of rhetoric itself, a particular aspect, that explains his unusual conservatism? There is indeed an
explanation, but it is not limited to rhetoric and its demands in particular;
it rather concerns the emotions themselves. The fact of the matter is
simply that Aristotle's activity-pleasures cannot be used to explain most
emotions at all, because these attitudes are not tied to activities, or only
in a quite extended sense. Some rumination on pleasures and pains as
activities must suffice to reveal the problem. If I am angry because
someone has slighted me of whom I would rightly have expected better
treatment, I am not in pain because my activity of thinking about this
person is going badly. Nor is it painful because thinking about the insult
is against my nature. It is not an activity that I dislike and therefore do
badly, as I do when I have to play bridge all day long against my own
inclinations and find this activity "a pain in the neck." An insult pains me
because it is an infringement on my dignity, something done to me.[42] Nor
does the pleasure of anticipated revenge consist in "thinking well" about
it and without impediment. I may, of course, in addition enjoy picturing
in detail how I will dress this person down in front of everybody, but the
pleasure of revenge consists in the anticipated assuagement of my grief
by revenge, not in the further activity of "picturing it well."

We cannot go through the whole list of emotions, positive or negative,
to confirm the claim that Aristotle's activity conception is inappropriate
for the explanation of such pleasures and pains; a few examples must
suffice. If I watch my neighbor's good fortune with envy, this painful
feeling (mixed with the pleasure of secret hope that his fortune won't last)
does not come from my well- or ill-conducted activity of watching him.
When people take pleasure in rescuing friends in distress, they do not
usually enjoy the rescue as an activity—as a successful performance. Nor
do they enjoy the activity of thinking clearly and without impediment
what a nice activity this is. As Aristotle himself states in the *Rhetoric*, it is
rather the need for completion or satisfaction that makes it a desirable
and enjoyable thing to do.[43] Grudgingly watching my neighbor, being
afraid for a friend's life, are not activities, while doing math well or
playing a Beethoven quartet well are activities of the kind Aristotle has
in mind in the *Nicomachean Ethics*. Emotions are often caused by activi-

ties,[44] and lead to activities, but the emotion itself is not a concomitant of a well- (or ill-) performed natural activity. Plato's explanation of negative emotions as disturbances, and of pleasures as the corresponding restorations of the natural equilibrium certainly has its drawbacks, as we have seen, but it does better at explaining these emotions than Aristotle's later conception of activity-pleasures. This is not to dispute that Aristotle is right in maintaining the superiority of perfect pleasures over remedial pleasures as a concomitant of the happy life. He may well be right that an active life in accordance with our best dispositions and talents is at the same time a happy and a pleasant life. I only want to dispute the idea that his new theory of pleasure and pain covers all cases. The mixed emotions are among the cases where Aristotle's theory does not seem to work. This, then, must be the reason why he left his early account of the emotions untouched in the *Rhetoric*, even after he had changed his mind about the nature of pleasure in his ethics.

That Aristotle should focus so much on remedial emotions in his *Rhetoric* while he largely left them aside in his ethics is actually not surprising. When we search for motives in everyday concerns or try to influence others, we are usually concerned with some deficiency or at least with the assumption of a need. This is most prominent when it comes to explaining the actions of lawbreakers: there is the need for money on the side of the poor, the need for silly amusement on the side of the wealthy, the need for revenge on the side of the vengeful, the need for luxury on the side of the weak-willed, the need for escape on the side of the coward. People who suffer from such defects enjoy restorative pleasures—as they understand their own needs. If they cannot satisfy them by legal means, they do so by illegal actions. They are clearly not candidates for the enjoyment of such complete and unimpeded activities as doing math or philosophy, or of seeing beautiful sights.[45] But it is not just people with character flaws who are subject to emotions with an inherently mixed nature. We all are constantly subject to them, simply because there are always occasions in our lives for some infringement on our happiness, occasions for fear, anger, longing, mourning, and all the rest of the emotions that Aristotle so carefully describes in his *Rhetoric*. The pleasure they contain is therefore usually a remedial pleasure, namely the pleasure of getting rid of what bothers us. Most of the opportunities for oratorical skill are cases where something has been done to someone that calls for a remedy, as in court cases, or cases involving the needs of the community, as in political speeches. There is always a kind of relief or release involved. Thus the remedial pleasures quite naturally stand in the center of an orator's concerns.

The reason Aristotle can neglect these remedial pleasures in most of his ethics is that his concern there is with happiness and with the kind of pleasure that accompanies virtue. None of the "mixed feelings" forms an integral part of a virtuous act or of happiness in general. The happy persons who enjoy acting in accordance with their virtues and best talents are not full of jealousy, hatred, fear, or anger, although Aristotle would and did admit that even a happy life may have to cope with a fair amount of emotional stress and strain (*NE* 1100b22–1101a8). Nor, on the other hand, does Aristotle in the *Rhetoric* claim that it is particularly good or happy to undergo mixed emotions. Of many of them he clearly does not think that they are good at all; it is just not possible to live a life free of all anger, fear, jealousy, and enmity. It is precisely these "facts of life" the rhetorician has to handle and make use of. He will leave it to the philosopher to tell us how to enjoy the perfect pleasure of unimpeded activities in a perfect life. Hence divulging the "real nature of pleasure" in the light of the *Nicomachean Ethics* would have done nothing to enhance the orator's skill.[46] There is a division of labor between the *Rhetoric* and the *Nicomachean Ethics* concerning the nature of pleasure, in accordance with the different demands of each work.

But if division of labor was all that separates the account of pleasure in these two works, why did Aristotle not settle for a compromise solution, once he had developed the idea of activity-pleasures? Couldn't he have accommodated both process- and activity-pleasures and pointed out the difference in perspective concerning the pleasure of "doing" and the pleasure of "getting"? That he did not do so in the *Nicomachean Ethics,* even though he retained the process-pleasures in his account in the *Rhetoric,* seems incomprehensible, especially in view of the fact that the *Nicomachean Ethics* betrays his awareness of the existence of process-pleasures. A certain ambiguity about the conception of pleasure is implicit, it should here be added, throughout the *Nicomachean Ethics.* The "pleasures" that the multitude wants as the good clearly is not the pleasure of being active (1095b16), nor is the intemperate's penchant for bodily pleasure related to activity (1104b5, 1107b3–8).[47] The ordinary everyday pleasures that humans share with other animals are based on physical desire (*epithumia*), and involve the filling of a lack. Pain is called a disturbance and destruction (1108a2–1118b4).[48] Even in the passages that contain his defense of activity-pleasures Aristotle betrays his awareness of process-pleasures, as for instance when he censors Plato for taking eating and drinking as the model for all pleasures, apparently ignoring the fact that not all pleasures are like that (1173b13–16).

Why then did he not include the pleasures of restoration in his definition of pleasure and pain in the two central passages in Books 7 and 10 of the *Nicomachean Ethics*? Why, in other words, would he limit pleasures to perfect activities and deny that processes, as incomplete activities, can have their own, different kinds of pleasures? The same question can be raised regarding Plato: Could he not also have agreed to such a compromise, had he ever been able to see the usefulness of Aristotle's notion of activity? He did, after all, treat the theoretically possible third life of pure thought as an active life. So why not call it joyful? The reason why Plato could not have settled for such a compromise is not just that he probably was no longer around when Aristotle came up with the ingenious concept of *energeia*.[49] His whole project in the *Philebus* was designed to subsume all pleasures under one highest genus, in accordance with the demands of dialectic, the "gift of the gods" (*Philebus* 16c ff.). But obedience to the rules of dialectic was not his only reason for preserving the generic unity of pleasure and pain. He was aiming at a unified theory of pleasure to make them all compatible, comparable, and censurable. If he had granted activity-pleasures as a second genus, he would have once more been confronted with the decision as to which of the two genera of pleasures are the "real" pleasures and which contains only "bastard" pleasures. As long as pleasure must be defined by one supreme genus, it cannot straddle both process and completeness. The same principle seems to be at work in Aristotle's case. He, too, is moved by the need to preserve generic unity. This need exerts what in German is called *Systemzwang*, conformity to the system. Its consequence is that whatever does not have the same definition, cannot be called by the same name; hence one or the other kind of pleasure would be called "pleasure only homonymously," as Aristotle is wont to say. That he obeyed this *Systemzwang* is not a sign that Plato's shadow still dominated him, nor is it a sign of narrow-mindedness on his part. The need to search for generic unity haunted philosophers time and again, until Wittgenstein pointed out convincingly that we can well accommodate plurality because there are some perfectly well-formed concepts like "game," where there is no generic unity, no unifying definition, but at best a loose family resemblance.[50]

Given these latter-day insights, both the Platonic and the later Aristotelian accounts of pleasure suffer from the same defect: neither is sufficient to cover the whole range of phenomena that it supposedly explains. In principle, Aristotle at least could have known better. There are extenuating circumstances, of course. He may have been carried away by his enthusiasm for his new notion of activity-pleasures as the final touch of the happy life when he wrote the *Nicomachean Ethics*, so that he found process-pleasures a negligible nuisance.[51] That may well be what happened, but we should also not underestimate the force of the *Systemzwang* that worked on him just as it did on Plato. Philosophers want it tidy, and sometimes the complexity of the phenomena won't allow as much tidiness as they want. So Aristotle in his ethical writings neglects or even denies the entitlement of the process-pleasures to be called pleasures, while in the *Rhetoric* the *Systemzwang* works in the opposite direction. If pleasure is defined as a process, it cannot at the same time accommodate the conception of pleasure as a perfect activity.

What remains a puzzle, then, is Aristotle's more or less conscious decision not to make any revisions of the Platonic view in the *Rhetoric*. He may have decided to leave it intact as long as he did not see his way toward fixing the matter, in the hope that he could eventually find a solution at some later point of time that was never to come. Nor would such a decision be out of character for Aristotle, as all his friends and admirers will be able to confirm. If it is a sign of a truly great mind not to be excessively concerned with consistency, then Aristotle displays this kind of greatness of mind to a very high degree. The Philosopher, who falsely got the reputation of narrow-minded system-building, thereby impeding all progress in later centuries, comports himself with remarkable unconcern for tidiness. While he insisted on it in matters of principle, he was, fortunately, not nearly as neat in practice, and so he left standing what a narrower mind would have deleted. We owe him thanks for this, because it is from inconsistencies in great minds that we learn. In this case we can learn much from the *Rhetoric* about the emotions and their inherently mixed nature that is not properly worked out in the *Nicomachean Ethics*. We should therefore be grateful that Aristotle did not streamline his earlier account to make it conform to his later thought.

NOTES

1. At the beginning of *De Anima* (403a16–403b19) Aristotle introduces the emotions as motivating forces and indicates the problem of their psychophysical nature; he never gives a more detailed analysis, however.

2. There are just the barest hints at a mixed nature in the discussion of emotions in *NE* 3 (fear at 1115a7; anger as a pain mixed with pleasure of anticipated revenge at 1117a6–7 and 1126a13–25), but it is not taken up later in the discussion of the nature of pleasure and pain.

3. Pleasure and pain are the highest genera of all emotions in Plato's *Philebus*, because all positive states are regarded as pleasures, and all negative ones as pains or displeasures.

4. Cf. E. M. Cope, *An Introduction to Aristotle's Rhetoric* (London, 1867), p. 235; A. J. Festugière, *Aristote: Le Plaisir* (Paris, 1936), p. 624; I. Düring, *Aristoteles* (Heidelberg, 1966), pp. 118–121. J. C. B. Gosling and C. C. W. Taylor, *The Greeks on Pleasure* (Oxford, 1982), pp. 194–199. For a critical discussion and a "doxography" on this issue, cf. W. W. Fortenbaugh, "Aristotle's *Rhetoric* on Emotions," *Archiv für Geschichte der Philosophie* 52 (1970): 40–70.

5. On the prehistory of the physiological account and Empedocles, see Gosling and Taylor 1982, pp. 19–23.

6. *Endoxa* are clearly demarcated as such (cf. 1360b14–18); the manifold definitions of happiness "all agree that it is that." The same is true for the long

catalog of goods that reflects common standards. Aristotle's assertion that the definition of pleasure should be "neither unclear nor overly precise" (1369b31–33) does not show that he is concerned with an *endoxon,* but rather that he is not prepared to give any justification for it.

7. The discussion of style and arrangement in Book 3 is often regarded as a later addition.

8. All textual references in this essay are to R. Kassel, *Aristotelis Ars Rhetorica* (Berlin, 1976).

9. The text contains in fact many elements of Aristotle's mature ethics: that we deliberate about means, not ends (1362a17–20); virtue is defined as a *hexis;* his list of virtues exceeds the Platonic catalog of four virtues and agrees with *NE* (1362b12–13; see also 1366b1–3).

10. *Republic* 583a–584e recalls the way out of the Cave, and is very likely meant to recall that image; but this spelunkian groping does not answer the question as to the ontological status of physical and "emotional" pleasures.

11. For a more extensive discussion of the evolution of Plato's view on pleasure, see my article, "Disintegration and Restoration: Pleasure and Pain in Plato's *Philebus,*" *The Cambridge Companion to Plato,* ed. R. Kraut (Cambridge, 1992), pp. 425–463, and the introductory essay to *Plato: Philebus* (Indianapolis, 1993).

12. For a contemporary discussion of this issue, see B. A. O. Williams and E. Bedford, "Pleasure and Belief," *Proceedings of the Aristotelian Society* 33 (suppl.) (1959): 57–72, 73–92.

13. Plato does not use *pathos* as a generic term for the emotions but describes the psychological states as mixtures of pleasure and pain; the mixtures are called pleasure or pain respectively, if one or the other element is preponderant.

14. Desire, *epithumia,* is treated in the *Philebus* as pain with the wish for relief based on memory (34c–35d).

15. We will have to ignore here the use Plato makes of his own theory of the emotions in his *Laws* (644c ff.) and its influence on Aristotle. W. W. Fortenbaugh (*Aristotle on Emotion* [New York, 1975]) comments extensively on the development leading from later Platonic theory to the Aristotelian conception. He does not give sufficient credit to the subtlety of Plato's analysis in the *Philebus* (cf. 9–12), however, and ignores the question of the relationship between pleasure, pain, and the emotions because he concentrates on the propositional content of the emotions and their relationship to moral dispositions. He therefore does not discuss the change between the *Rhetoric* and the *Nicomachean Ethics.*

16. In order to avoid needless repetition Aristotle presents the material rather schematically: in his discussion of political speech he focuses on the question of expediency (*Rhet.* 1.6), in that of praise speech on virtue (1.9), and in forensic speech on the emotional aspect (1.10); this does not mean, however, that political speech is confined to the good in the sense of useful (*chrēsimon, sumpheron*), epideictic speech to the good in the sense of noble (*kalon*), forensic speech to the good in the sense of what is pleasant (*hēdu*).

17. The speaker therefore has also to establish his character, *ēthos;* but we will have to leave that aspect aside here.

18. I owe the insight into the importance of that distinction to Gisela Striker and her graduate students at Harvard, who discussed an earlier draft of this essay with me. This discussion made me realize that Aristotle's twofold approach has

important conceptual consequences that make him compromise the Platonic model. In addition, I have to acknowledge that Aristotle's treatment of the emotions in the *Topics* shows that his conception of the emotions presupposes an intensive discussion of that question within the Academy. The Phileban influence may therefore have been much more indirect than I make it sound.

19. We shall leave aside "habit" (*ethos*) as another motivating force of what is done intentionally (1369a1), for Aristotle will soon point out that acquired tastes are also geared toward seeking pleasure and avoiding pain (1369b6–9).

20. That *pathos* is the generic term for nonrational desire emerges when Aristotle sums up his discussion of the motivating forces by saying that everyone acts either from reason or emotion (1369a17–18: *dia logismon ē dia pathos*). That anger (*orgē*) is treated as a special kind of nonrational desire (1369a4) shows that he still presupposes the Platonic psychology with a tripartition of the soul (which Plato does not mention in the *Philebus*).

21. Not all rational desires are morally good, of course. The good I may want because of my calculations of my advantage may be very much to the detriment of others (see the *idion sumpheron*, 1354b9). So crime can be rationally, as well as emotionally, determined.

22. There has been some controversy whether Aristotle meant to give a proper definition or not, especially by those commentators who recognized the Platonic origin of this definition and its disagreement with Aristotle's concept of pleasure in his ethics (E. M. Cope, *The Rhetoric of Aristotle, with a Commentary*, rev. and ed. J. E. Sandys, 3 vols. [Cambridge, 1877], p. 200; Cope, *An Introduction to Aristotle's Rhetoric*, p. 235; W. M. A. Grimaldi, *Aristotle, Rhetoric I: A Commentary* [New York, 1980], pp. 243–246). But such attempts to downplay the importance of Aristotle's Platonizing terminology (both *kinēsis* and *katastasis* are terms used by Plato, see *Philebus* 34a, 42d, 46c) ignore the importance of this definition of pleasure for the subsequent discussion of the emotions, as well as the closeness between the Platonic and the Aristotelian conception of mixed emotions.

23. Kassel regards the whole passage with the insertion of rational desires as a later interpolation by Aristotle himself, supplemented by some later editor (1370a20–27). He may well be right, but this would show that Aristotle did not want to change his basic account of the emotions at a later time (cf. *NE* on nonrationality of the emotions, 1106a2–3.)

24. Aristotle presupposes the following schema of motivations for action:

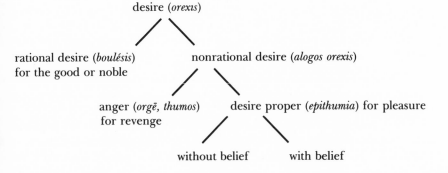

25. *Hepesthai* can signify a close connection such as that of implication or containment, as Aristotle's elucidations at 1363a27–32 show.

26. Pleasures are actually rarely mentioned, but cf. the pleasure at deserved good fortune (1386b25–1387a3) and schadenfreude as the counterpart of envy (1388a24–27).

27. The inclusion of a habitually acquired nature (*hexis*) represents Aristotle's one major departure from the Phileban conception of pleasure. For Plato there is a fixed natural equilibrium, while for Aristotle the natural state is a matter of habit, as well. This modification shows that Aristotle has adapted the Platonic remedial conception for his own purposes, so that its insertion is neither superficial nor merely conventional.

28. The difference between rational and passionate decisions is neatly described by Aristotle in his distinction between punishment and revenge (1369b11–15): punishment is done for the sake of another (i.e., the injured party), to make things right (which is a rational good). Revenge is a passionate action of the injured person, fulfilling the need to get even (which is a nonrational pleasure).

29. Although pleasure is the ultimate aim of those desires (1369b15), some pleasures and desires are *chrēsta*, because they involve "good opinions" (1369a18–24).

30. Because Aristotle regards the immediate impression of a wrong done (an *aisthēsis* or *phantasia*, 1370a27–35) as a condition for pain, he denies that such abstract aversions as hatred for an enemy or a vicious person involve pain. Plato would, no doubt, have claimed that all aversion is a disturbance of the equilibrium.

31. For a closer analysis of the emotions, their internal structure and their function for rhetorical purposes, see J. M. Cooper, "Rhetoric, Dialectic, and the Passions," *Oxford Studies in Ancient Philosophy* 11 (1993): 175–198. Cooper does not spend much time on the question of their mixed character, except that he recognizes that most emotions share the features of being based on distress or agitation and involve desire. He points out, very plausibly, that the selection of the emotions under discussion is mainly determined by the rhetorician's practical purposes; that is, that Aristotle focuses on those most likely to be relevant in public speaking.

32. Not all cases in Aristotle's text square altogether well with the notion that desire includes the anticipation of self-completion, and Kassel's surmise of later interpolations by Aristotle himself may well be right. But if he later added to the list (as indicated by awkward interruptions in the text and by needless repetitions) this only confirms that he saw no reason to discard the basic model of explaining the emotions, but rather deliberately upheld the view taken over from Plato.

33. Desire (*epithumia*) and the hope for its fulfillment is mentioned only once as the means to foster a favorable view, while lack of emotion or negative attitude instills the opposite attitude (1378a3–5).

34. The notable exception is anger, which is once again defined as a desire (*orexis meta lupēs*, 1378a30), with the pleasure of anticipated revenge as its natural concomitant.

35. Most negative emotions are defined as a pain and/or disturbance (fear, 1382a21–22; shame, 1383b13–15; pity, 1385b13–16; indignation, 1386b12 and

1387a9–10; envy, 1387b22–24; emulation, 1388a30–33). That pain implies desire is mentioned at 1379a13. That emotions are treated as *kinēseis* comes to the fore in the discussion of why people are *eukinetoi* (1379a26–29) and when appeasement of anger is called a *katastasis* at 1380a9.

36. As Striker pointed out to me, the fact that in *Top.* 125b28 ff. Aristotle denies that pain should be regarded as the genus of anger shows that the Platonic point of view was at least questioned in discussions in the Academy and that different approaches were tried out.

37. Aristotle's treatment of the emotions in the *Poetics* is too complex a subject to be discussed here. A good survey of the problematic and of the ample literature on this issue is contained in E. Belfiore, *Tragic Pleasures* (Princeton, 1992), especially pp. 226–253.

38. He does so in the two sections that deal with the conception of pleasure, 7.11–13 and 10.1–5. Both passages in the *Nicomachean Ethics* reject the "remedial" conception of pleasure as the mistake of someone who does not see that pleasure is an *energeia* (1153a16–17). How the two different sections are related to each other must be left aside here, as must be the treatment of pleasure in the part of the *Eudemian Ethics* that does not overlap with the *Nicomachean Ethics* and in the *Magna Moralia*. On this issue cf. Gosling and Taylor, *The Greeks on Pleasure*, Appendix B.

39. "Perfection" does not necessarily carry a positive sense. Although in discussing happiness Aristotle speaks only of pleasures of good persons, there are also bad or evil pleasures. So perfect rascals might enjoy perfectly detestable acts, once their moral dispositions are settled (whether they can do so consistently is another question). It is precisely on this point that Plato would disagree: according to his conception such pleasures are always the fillings of immense lacks, the sign of a diseased personality.

40. That is how *kinēsis* is defined: it is an incomplete activity, an *energeia atelēs*, because it does not have its end in itself and goes through various stages of different nature that each have their own ends (cf. *NE* 1174a19–1174b14 and *Phys.* 201b32; *Met.* 1048b30). On the distinction between change and activity in its application to pleasure, cf. Gosling and Taylor, *The Greeks on Pleasure*, pp. 300–317.

41. There are quite a few traces of later additions, for instance his references to the *Analytics* (*Rhet.* 1356b9, 13557a29, 1357b24) or to the *Politics* (1366a21–22), as well as to later historical events (cf. the reference to the "common peace" with Alexander after the death of King Philip in 336 at 1399b12–13). We have also seen earlier that Aristotle deviated from Plato's model by including habitual moral dispositions among the "natural" states that are attained by restorative pleasures.

42. In his ethics Aristotle neglects pain, apart from defining it as an impediment to successful activity (1175b17–24). That "activity badly done against one's own inclinations" does not cover all cases of pain or displeasure does not occur to him in the ethics. He does not realize that, for example, mourning the loss of a friend cannot be well accounted for in those terms, as a kind of ennui about something I have to do or undergo against my will and inclinations.

43. Some people, of course, enjoy it as a performance; but this is the reason

why we watch such actions with dismay: it is a travesty of the urge to help. Aristotle's depiction of actions "flowing from" the agent's personality therefore sometimes verges on self-satisfied philistinism: there is no real disturbance for the sake of others. On the other hand, Aristotle is very good at explaining that doing a good act with pain is not a sign of moral worth.

44. Emotions are often followed by actions; one may for instance wonder whether people can really be angry if they do not act on the opportunity to take revenge. But anger is not the emotion that accompanies or completes the activity of taking revenge, nor is it the emotion that accompanies or completes the suffering of unjust treatment. That all pleasures should be concomitants of intensive activities that are natural to their perpetrator (and all pains the concomitant of bad; that is, listless and unwillingly performed activities, 1175b16–24) is not plausible. Hopes and memories are not pleasant because I hope and remember "intensively and without disturbance," but because their object would fulfill a need of mine.

45. The concept of *energeia* is conspicuously absent from the *Rhetoric*. Apart from Book 3 (1410b36, 1411b28, 1412b32 where it has a different connotation), the concept occurs only twice in the *Rhetoric* (1361a24, 1378b10) but without any special prominence or emphasis. It is typically not employed when Aristotle speaks about the pleasure of doing what one is best suited for (1371b30).

46. The *Rhetoric*'s remedial account does not do so well for positive attitudes that do not obviously involve pain or disturbance, such as well-intendedness (*eunoia* or *charis*) and friendship (*philia*); but they are the only emotions that do not have at least a negative tint.

47. Aristotle's account for the physical pleasures and pains is highly awkward and unconvincing: he claims that the "fillings" are pleasant only incidentally, because in this case the part of the soul that is not impaired is active (1152b35–36, 1173b11–15). See also J. O. Urmson's comments on the confusion of physically pleasant sensations with activity-pleasures, "Aristotle on Pleasure," *Aristotle: A Collection of Critical Essays,* ed. J. Moravcsik (Garden City, 1967), pp. 323–333. J. Annas treats his wavering as a compromise with the common moralizing viewpoint, "Aristotle on Pleasure and Goodness," *Essays on Aristotle's Ethics,* ed. A. O. Rorty (Berkeley, 1980), pp. 285–299, especially p. 291.

48. The list of passages that presuppose the "filling" account must be kept short here. Pleasures and pains play an important role in the explanation of incontinence. The pleasures of the incontinent are clearly not regarded as the pleasures of a hyperactive person (1146b8 ff.). There is disturbance through *pathē* (1147a14–17); incontinence is due to influence of necessary pleasures or excess of others (cf. incontinence due to the desire for gain, honor, or the avoidance of pain, 1147b21–1148b14). In the only passage where Aristotle comments on the relation between the emotions (*pathē*) and pleasure and pain, he seems to rely on the same account as in the *Rhetoric* (*NE* 1105b19–23: pleasure and pain "accompany them").

49. It is not impossible that Plato did know of Aristotle's concept of *energeia,* because it is not only heavily emphasized in the earlier *EE* (1224b12, 1225a35,

1236b28, and 1249b6–8; cf. discussion of pleasure tied to activity, 1249a17–26), but also in the certainly very early *Protrepticus* (58, 15).

50. That Aristotle should have rather admitted different kinds of pleasures is suggested by W. F. R. Hardie, *Aristotle's Ethical Theory* (Oxford, 1980), p. 304. Other commentators are less explicit about this point, either because they shy away from attributing inconsistencies to Aristotle (see Grimaldi, *Aristotle: Rhetoric I*, p. 244) or because they regard the *Rhetoric*'s conception as essentially un-Aristotelian (cf. p. 2 n. 4), or because they have not taken sufficient stock of the problematic.

51. His disregard for the special problem with the *pathē* does not amount to gross negligence, since he focuses on activity as the constituent of human happiness right from the beginning in his *NE* (1.7 ff.). The pleasure taken in virtuous activities are more important in that connection than the affections through others (1100b12–22). See L. A. Kosman's observation that Aristotle loses sight of and interest in the emotions as his ethics progresses, "Being Properly Affected: Virtues and Feelings in Aristotle's Ethics," *Essays on Aristotle's Ethics*, ed. A. O. Rorty (Berkeley, 1980), pp. 103–116 ("their importance fades . . . ," p. 115).

Emotions in Context: Aristotle's Treatment of the Passions in the *Rhetoric* and His Moral Psychology

Gisela Striker

Aristotle's *Rhetoric* contains the most detailed and extensive treatment in the Aristotelian corpus of what the Greeks called the affections of the soul—the *pathē*, "passions" or "emotions."[1] This is a strange and remarkable fact, given the importance of emotional dispositions in Aristotle's theory of the moral virtues, and indeed in his moral psychology in general. The nonrational part of the soul whose virtues are the virtues of character (*NE* 1.13.1103a3–10) can be regarded as primarily the seat of the emotions. Hence one would expect to find a full account of the emotions either in the treatises on ethics or in *De Anima*; and indeed the first chapter of *De Anima* (403a29 ff.) seems to promise a proper scientific account of the subject. But it appears that Aristotle never got around to this task. In the absence of a systematic treatment of this part of his psychology, we may therefore turn to the *Rhetoric* to supplement what Aristotle says in other places.

However, evidence from this work must be treated with caution. Quite a few chapters in the *Rhetoric* are meant to provide the aspiring orator with materials for speeches on topics of general relevance—for example, the virtues for speeches of praise; human happiness or goods in general for giving advice; and so on. What Aristotle offers in these passages ought to be regarded as a collection of commonly acceptable theses that are likely to convince a not very educated audience, rather than as Aristotle's own considered views about the subject. Now the chapters about the emotions in Book 2 of the *Rhetoric* are supposed to tell the orator how to produce (or to avoid, as the case may be) emotions or emotional attitudes in his audience. This means that they should in principle be telling him the facts about psychology, not just what ordinary people might be inclined to believe. Yet what we find in these chapters does not look like a

treatise on psychology. Aristotle usually begins each chapter with a definition and then tries to derive from it the answers to the questions "from
what," "regarding whom," and "in what kind of state of mind" an emotion
will arise. He offers no general definition of what a *pathos* is, and he usually
does not try to argue for the correctness of his definitions. Most commentators have therefore concluded that the exposition in the *Rhetoric* is
an exercise in dialectic, based on "reputable opinions" (*endoxa*) rather
than scientific psychology.[2] But that would be odd, since these chapters
are supposed to tell the orator how to arouse or calm the passions, not
how to talk about them. What matters is not what people think about
emotion but what is in fact the case. John Cooper,[3] who notices the
difficulty, suggests an ingenious solution: perhaps Aristotle thought that
since rhetoric itself is not a science, and an orator may well be ignorant
of the principles of the scientific disciplines relevant either to his craft or
to the topics he discusses, an exposition of psychological matters written
for orators should not be based on the findings of scientific disciplines,
but proceed from plausible or respectable assumptions, as do the arguments of the orator himself. After all, such common or respectable views
also form the starting point of a serious philosophical investigation, and
they may be presumed to contain at least some truth, even if not clearly
expressed.

I do not find this consideration entirely persuasive. It seems to me that
there is a simpler, if somewhat trivial, solution to the puzzle. We should
accept, I think, the point that in order to arouse or to prevent emotions,
the orator should in principle know the truth about psychology, so far as
it may be available, and not just some plausible or popular views. But this
does not imply that he needs to be an expert psychologist himself. Much
like present-day lawyers or judges, he may be content with accepting the
results of scientific research without worrying about their theoretical
foundations or justifications—for example, judges and lawyers may
surely accept the expert opinions of engineers or architects regarding the
construction of a bridge without having to study engineering themselves.
So Aristotle's orator should rely upon the results of scientific psychology,
just as he is also supposed to rely upon the results of Aristotle's logical
investigations in *Prior Analytics* and *Posterior Analytics*. What we should
expect to find in the *Rhetoric* is not science or philosophical theory, but
theory-based results. This is what we do find where Aristotle refers to the
Topics or the *Analytics:* he will mention a theorem or result and then refer
the reader to the technical treatises for explanation or proof.[4] There are
no comparable references to a technical treatment of the emotions—for
the good reason, I take it, that Aristotle did not have a proper scientific
account, either his own or somebody else's. Aristotle seems to think
(1.10.1369b31–32) that what he needs for his purposes in the *Rhetoric* is

definitions, and those may again have to be adapted so as to be "neither unclear nor too precise."[5] The *Rhetoric* would obviously not be the place to develop a theory of the emotions, so Aristotle turns to the best available substitute: theories developed in the Academy, either by Plato or by Aristotle's fellow students, no doubt with some contributions from Aristotle himself. There is quite a bit of evidence in the *Topics* to show that various definitions of particular emotions were proposed and discussed in the Academy,[6] and Plato's *Philebus* contains something like a sketch of a more general theory in the section on "mixed" or "impure" pleasures (47c–50e), but it does not seem that the definitions Aristotle uses belong to an already established theory.[7] Now since philosophical views can also figure as premises in dialectical debates, Aristotle's definitions will not have more than the status of respectable assumptions, but I think we can be fairly confident that he chose those definitions or theses that he himself would have been inclined to accept. As a technical handbook for orators, the *Rhetoric* is neither an exercise in dialectical argument nor a piece of philosophical theorizing.

Given this kind of background, it is not surprising to find that Aristotle's treatment of the emotions in the *Rhetoric* does not proceed from a unified theoretical framework. As a matter of fact, I think that his brief discussion of emotions as motives, along with the long chapter on pleasure and "passionate desire"[8] (*epithumia*) in 1.10–11, is close to Plato's theories in the *Republic* and the *Philebus*, whereas the long section in 2.2–11 that deals with emotions as influencing judgment seems to go in a different direction—toward a theory that invites comparison with the Stoic one. I do not have the space here to substantiate these claims in detail, but I will try to indicate what I take to be the main differences between the two treatments of the emotions by a few examples. In the second part of the paper, I will turn to a brief comparison with the Stoics, which will inevitably take us out of the primarily psychological and morally neutral context of the *Rhetoric* and into moral psychology. I think that this comparison will also shed some light on the dispute between Stoics and Aristotelians about the relation between virtue and the emotions.

PASSIONS AS MOTIVES AND AS INFLUENCING JUDGMENT: BOOKS 1 AND 2 OF THE *RHETORIC*

The *pathē* come up in two different contexts in the *Rhetoric*: first, in the section on forensic speeches, they are mentioned as motives for wrongdoing, and one particularly important motive, *epithumia* or "passionate desire," is treated in 1.11—a long chapter about pleasure and what is pleasant. For anger, the other motive explicitly mentioned—and presumably for any other passions, such as jealousy, that might provide a motive for wrongdoing—the reader is referred to Book 2. This second, and main, treatment of the emotions considers them, in accordance with Aristotle's plan outlined in 1.2.1356a1–20, insofar as they have an influence on the attitudes and judgments of the listeners (2.1.1378a20 ff.). As is his custom in the *Rhetoric*, Aristotle avoids repetition by dealing with a subject only once, even if it should be considered from different perspectives.[9] So he does not pick up *epithumia* again in Book 2,[10] and he does not emphasize the role of the passions as motives for action in the longer section, leaving it to the reader to figure out how passionate desire may influence judgment (2.1.1378a4) or how envy or fear, for example, would lead to action. Apart from its prominence as a motive for wrongdoing, there may be yet another reason for the separate treatment of *epithumia* in Book 1, namely, that Book 2 focuses exclusively on emotions as relating to other people. Passionate desire or appetite may often be directed at other things that one would like to have rather than at persons, and so it might not fit very well into the schema that Aristotle uses in dealing with the other emotions. Be that as it may, Aristotle's division of labor between Books 1 and 2 has the interesting effect of separating, as it were, the desiderative from the cognitive aspects of emotion. I will come back to this point later on; let me first take a look at the two "theoretical frameworks" that seem to emerge from the different sections.

In 1.10.1368b32–1369a7, Aristotle introduces anger (*orgē*) and *epithumia* as two kinds of irrational desire (*alogos orexis*) on a list of seven possible "causes (*aitiai*) of action." One might at first find it odd that Aristotle mentions these two but not, say, the passions in general on a list that contains, as its other items, chance or accident (*tuchē*), nature, force or compulsion (*bia*), habit, and calculation or reasoning (*logismos*). But then one notices that *orgē* (anger) is used as a synonym of *thumos* (spirit), and *thumos* and *epithumia* (spirit and appetite) are of course the names of two of Plato's "parts of the soul" in the *Republic*. Since *thumos* as a synonym of *orgē* is normally used by Aristotle in a narrower sense than in Plato, where it is associated with a desire for honor, not primarily revenge, the two kinds of irrational desire still do not seem to be on the same level of generality—anger is a particular emotion, while "passionate desire," as 1.11 shows, seems to cover a number of different emotional states. However, at 1.10.1369a18, the expression *di' alogon orexin* (1369a2–3) is picked up by *dia pathos,* and so one might conclude that all the passions are supposed to be covered by "spirit and appetite," and that they are all to be seen as irrational desires. The Platonic psychology definitely seems to be in the background.

The same is true, I think, of the chapter on pleasure and the pleasant, which opens with a definition of pleasure as "a movement by which the soul as a whole is consciously brought into its normal state of being" (trans.

R. Roberts)—a definition patently borrowed from Plato's *Philebus* (31d ff.). Many commentators[11] have taken this as a sure indication that what Aristotle presents here cannot be his own view: after all, Plato's theory is explicitly rejected in Aristotle's official discussions of pleasure (*NE* 7 and 10). But this, I think, is a mist\ke. Pleasure is treated in the *Rhetoric* as the correlative of *epithumia*. "Whatever is passionately desired is pleasant, for *epithumia* is the desire for what is pleasant," says Aristotle (1.11.1370a16–18). By contrast, Aristotle's official theory in the *Ethics* makes real pleasure independent of *epithumia* and *lupē* (*NE* 7.12.1152b36). Nonetheless, in spite of Aristotle's official doctrine, pleasure as desire-fulfillment is not absent from the *Ethics* either. The pleasures involved in continence and weakness of will, or those adequately indulged by the temperate person, can hardly be taken as pleasures of Aristotle's preferred sort. Temperance is typically concerned with those "animal pleasures" (*NE* 2.10.1118a24–25) to do with food, drink, and sex; and we do not hear of cases of weakness of will that consist in playing the piano for an excessive amount of time, or neglecting one's children for the sake of solving yet another philosophical puzzle, although I would not object to seeing these as genuine cases of *akrasia*. Aristotle might have avoided some confusion in the *Ethics* if he had explicitly recognized at least two kinds of pleasure— desire-fulfillment on the one hand, and enjoyment of activity on the other. Instead, he decided to demote desire-fulfillment to the status of "accidental" pleasure (*kata sumbebēkos*, *NE* 7.12.1152b33–1153a2). In a discussion of motives for wrongdoing, however, the pleasures that correspond to passionate desire are clearly more relevant than the more refined activity-pleasures that take pride of place in the *Ethics*. So we do not have to invoke chronological considerations—such as the view that the *Rhetoric* is probably an early work—to argue that Aristotle's adoption of Plato's definition should be taken seriously.

The survey of pleasures seems to be indebted to the *Philebus* in yet another way: namely, in treating the emotions that fall under *epithumia*, such as, for example, erotic love, as involving both pleasure and pain. The parallels between Plato's suggestive sketch of an account of emotional states as mixtures of pleasure and pain (*Philebus* 47c–50e) and Aristotle's chapter on pleasure in the *Rhetoric* have been investigated in detail by Dorothea Frede,[12] to whom I am indebted for this point. To the extent that Aristotle is following Plato here, then, one might expect him to develop a view that treats emotions as "mixed feelings"—appetite (*epithumia*), as Aristotle casually says in *NE* 3.11.1119a4, goes with pain; on the other hand, the prospect of fulfillment will be pleasant. But as we will see, this is not what actually happens in Book 2. Already in 1.11, the fit between some of Aristotle's examples and the definition of pleasure as a conscious or perceptible return to the natural state is somewhat tenuous. When he speaks of the pleasure that comes from victory or from the impression that one is superior to others (*phantasia huperochēs*, 1370b33–34)—I suppose we might call this a kind of pride?—it is difficult to regard the desire to excel as a perceived lack or disturbance of the natural state, unless, of course, one takes it that being superior to others is everybody's natural condition. And while feeling inferior might count as distressing, leading to a desire to surpass or at least be even with one's peers or competitors, such feelings need not inevitably precede or accompany the pleasure of feeling superior: some people clearly enjoy competition and feel quite confident that they will succeed. Obviously, we might declare passionate desire to be always painful by definition, but these examples would seem to throw doubt upon such an assumption.

Whether or not Aristotle endorsed an account of the passions as mixed feelings at some point of his career, we cannot tell. However, he tends to use the phrase "accompanied by pain and (or) pleasure" (*hois hepetai lupē kai hēdonē*, 2.1.1378a21; *hois hepetai hēdonē ē lupē*, NE 3.1105b23; cp. *EE* 2.2.1220b13) to characterize the class of *pathē* in general, after giving a few examples, and this may be an indication that he started out from something like the Platonic account.

But the theoretical framework that seems to emerge from the longer treatment in Book 2 is different. For now, only three of the emotions are defined as forms of desire (anger, love or friendly feeling, and hate[13]), while no less than six out of ten are explicitly defined as forms of distress or pain (*lupē*). While some of the "painful" emotions may be associated with certain pleasures (e.g., fear with the hope of salvation), it seems clear that these pleasures are not seen as a necessary ingredient in "mixed feelings." More important, although most emotions classified as forms of distress will evidently lead to desires—such as the desire to escape an imminent danger, in the case of fear—those desires do not form a part of their definition. What serves as the defining feature—the *differentia specifica*, as it were—is in almost all cases an impression or appearance (*phantasia*)—that a terrible evil is near, that someone has suffered an undeserved misfortune, that one has been treated with disrespect, and so on—which causes the pain or disturbance. It is evident that Aristotle is deliberately using the term "impression" rather than, say, "belief" (*doxa*) in his definitions in order to make the point that these impressions are not to be confused with rational judgments. Emotions are caused by the way things appear to one unreflectively, and one may experience an emotion even if one realizes that the impression that triggered it is in fact mistaken.

An emotion is classified as a form of distress if the impression is negative—that something bad has happened or is about to happen—and one would expect that a positive impression, that something good has happened or is about to happen, should lead to the classification of the corresponding emotion as a form of delight or pleasure. This is not in fact the case for any of the explicitly discussed emotions in Book 2, although one might have thought that the "opposites" of anger, pity, and fear mentioned at the beginning (2.1.1378a20–23) would be the pleasant feelings contrasting with these forms of pain or distress. But most of the alleged "opposites" of the emotions treated in these chapters are not the emotional states that might correspond to the impression that some good thing has happened or will happen, but rather the state of mind corresponding to the absence of the specific distress. So calmness is opposed to anger, confidence (rather than relief) to fear, shamelessness (rather than, say, pride) to shame, while pity, rather than being opposed to something like taking pleasure in other people's good fortune, is opposed to two different forms of distress: righteous indignation (*nemesis*) and envy or jealousy (*phthonos*). The system of "opposites," as these examples already show, does not work very well. No doubt Aristotle introduces it because an orator may be out to prevent or restrain an emotion just as much as to provoke one, but it does not seem to be true that preventing or restraining a given emotion will automatically lead one to produce an opposite *emotion*. Another reason for the absence of pleasant emotions in Book 2 may lie in the fact that some of them show up, although not explicitly described as emotions, in the chapter on pleasures, 1.11. I have already mentioned the example of pride; others might be the feelings of lightheartedness and freedom from care (1370a14–15), or the pleasures of anticipation as well as relief (1370a32–1370b10).[14] The best candidate for a pleasant emotion in Book 2 might seem to be gratitude (*charin echein*, 1385a18), but here Aristotle works with a definition of *charis* (the favor for which gratitude would be felt) instead of describing or defining the actual emotion.[15]

It would be an exaggeration to say that Aristotle develops a systematic theoretical framework that classifies emotions as forms of pleasure or pain according to the positive or negative evaluative impressions that cause them, but he seems to be going in that direction, and at the same time moving away from the—possibly Platonic—view that treated the passions as irrational desires involving a mixture of pleasure and pain. If pleasure and pain are to serve as genera, then their species can hardly be treated as mixtures of both. This does not rule out mixed feelings, of course; but instead of describing each emotion as itself a mixture of pleasure and pain, one would now speak—quite plausibly—of mixtures of emotions: hope and fear, for example.

It seems to me to be no accident that this apparent change in theoretical outlook comes with the change of perspective from passions as motives for wrongdoing to passions as influences on judgment. An orator who seeks to produce a certain attitude in his audience need not, and in most cases does not, intend to get his listeners to proceed to immediate action. His aim is to make them see the case at hand in a certain way: to look favorably upon his client or upon the orator himself, or to take a negative view of his opponent. Which attitude they have will depend crucially, as Aristotle says, on the emotions they feel toward the persons involved in the case. And so his focus on judgment leads Aristotle to distinguish the emotion itself from the desire that may be caused by it. As I have already indicated, I take this to be a valid and important distinction. Even though nobody would wish to deny that emotions often lead to desires and hence motivate actions, most emotions are not only or not essentially desires or motives for action. Some emotions, such as pity and shame, can be present without leading to any specific desire at all, as when one feels pity for the hero of a tragedy or embarrassed about some foolish behavior of one's own. (I take it that the wish that things had turned out otherwise or that we had not behaved in such a stupid manner does not count as desire in the Aristotelian sense of *orexis*.) Fear will lead to a desire to escape the imminent danger, if that is possible, but it should still not be identified with that desire, for the desire may be there without the emotion, and perhaps a brave person will experience fear, but—if facing the danger is the courageous thing to do—still not even desire to run away. Finally, positive emotions like pride and relief would seem to be, or be based on, desire-fulfillments, not themselves desires.

I assume, then, that it makes sense to distinguish in principle between emotions and desires (notwithstanding the fact that a few emotions are indeed defined by Aristotle as desires, and that *epithumia* is, of course, a form of desire), and that the essential feature common to all the passions lies in the fact that they are caused by an evaluative impression or appearance.

To show how the *Rhetoric*'s account of the emotions fits into the moral psychology of Aristotle's *Ethics*, I turn now to a comparison with the Stoics, whose theory of the passions can in a way be seen as an elaboration of Aristotle's views, but who also arrived at diametrically opposed conclusions with regard to the relation of the emotions to moral virtue.

EMOTIONS IN MORAL PSYCHOLOGY: ARISTOTLE AND THE STOICS

Aristotle's discussions of the passions in the *Rhetoric* stay mainly on the level of straightforward psychology and away from moral evaluations, for the obvious reason that the orator has to be able to argue either side of a case. His purpose is to persuade and influence judgment, not to educate or, for that matter, to corrupt the audience. Hence Aristotle explains what will make people feel angry or embarrassed, grateful or jealous, rather than when or whether they ought to feel angry or grateful. The doctrine of the mean is conspicuously absent. For the Stoics, however, there could hardly have been such a thing as a morally neutral psychology of the emotions, since they considered emotions not as a normal and natural part of human experience but as disturbances or illnesses of the rational soul. Nonetheless, their account of the passions has much in common with Aristotle's, and in order to see how the theory adumbrated in Book 2 of the *Rhetoric* might have been developed into a systematic account of the emotions, including the positive ones and not limited to emotions relating to other people, it is instructive to take a look at the Stoic classification of the passions.[16] If we disregard for the moment the—admittedly crucial—difference between mere impression and full-fledged belief, we can see the Stoic schema as a plausible elaboration of Aristotle's sketch. What is common to all emotions is that they are based on (or, according to some sources, actually consist in) an evaluative belief. "Pleasure" and "pain" are used as generic terms for emotions due to the belief that something good or bad is present, while "passionate desire" (*epithumia*) and "fear" (*phobos*) are generic labels for emotions based on the belief that some good or bad thing is imminent or near.

The elevation of passionate desire and fear to the generic level, where Aristotle seemed to operate only with pleasure and pain, seems to me to be a plausible move, and one which alerts one to some peculiarities of Aristotle's less systematic treatment. We have already seen that the chapter on pleasure (1.11) seemed in fact to cover a number of different emotions under the headings of *epithumia* and *hēdonē*, and it is surely plausible to suggest that longing for one's beloved, for example, is different from the desire to win, just as the pleasure of seeing one's beloved is different from pleasure taken in victory. In the case of fear, it appears that Aristotle consciously opted for a rather narrow notion, linking fear exclusively with the prospect of great physical harm. He acknowledges elsewhere (*NE* 3.6.1115a10 ff.; cp. *EE* 3.1.1229a31–1229b22) that people are afraid of other things as well, such as embarrassment, and he occasionally uses what appears to be an already current definition of shame (*aidōs*) as "fear of disrepute" (*phobos adoxias, NE* 4.9.1128b12–13). But he may have preferred the narrower definition in order to keep fear as *the* emotion relevant to courage. Once again, I find the Stoic version plausible. Fear of physical destruction may be the most prominent case, but it still seems more accurate to describe other forms of anxiety as types of fear rather than simply as forms of distress.

The Stoic system, based as it is on types of evaluative belief, also shows up the distance between Plato's distinctions of types of motivation in the *Republic*, which seemed to underlie Aristotle's treatment of anger or "spirit" and passionate desire as motives, and a theory of the emotions taken by themselves. In the Stoic classification, all forms of passionate desire (including, notably, anger) are grouped together under *epithumia*. The other three kinds, by implication, should presumably not be understood as forms of desire, even though the general Stoic definition describes passion or emotion (*pathos*) as a kind of impulse (*hormē*). What is indicated by this term would seem to be rather a kind of concern, inclination or aversion as the case may be, that may, but need not, lead to immediate action. For the Stoics, as for Aristotle in a few passages, the emotions are primarily a kind of disturbance.

So far I have emphasized what I take to be striking similarities between the Aristotelian and the Stoic account of the emotions. But as is well known, Stoics and Aristotelians assigned very different places to the emotions in their respective moral psychologies. In terms of psychological theory, the decisive difference lies in the view the Stoics take of the impressions or beliefs that underlie the emotions. While Aristotle seems to regard emotion as a spontaneous and natural response to the way things appear to us,[17] the Stoics maintain that passion arises only when an impression is assented to and accepted as a truth. Because emotion is tied in this way to reason's ability to accept or reject an impression, the Stoics deny that young children are even capable of emotion. The evaluative responses and the desires of children are accounted for by a natural instinct for self-preservation and for concern for other human beings, which regulates their lives until reason can take over. In this psychological picture, the emotions seem to be superfluous: the action-guiding role they are said to have on the Aristotelian theory is filled first by natural instinct, then by reason. According to the Stoics, there is no need to postulate yet another natural capacity or source of motivation in the human soul in order to explain human behavior and action, including morally right action. If the emotions were natural, one would have to assume that they somehow contribute to the human good—but the Stoics insisted that far from being natural, the passions were a deplorably common aberration of reason,[18] an illness of the soul that arises from the error of ascribing real value or disvalue to the external objects that we are made to seek out or avoid by our instinctive inclinations and aversions.

Now it is true, of course, that on the Aristotelian theory, one and the same action or belief may be explained by reference to two or three different human capacities; and virtuous action in particular is explicitly said to require that reason and emotion be in agreement about the best way to act. But this is not because Aristotle gratuitously invokes two motives where one might be sufficient. It seems clear that Aristotle is not thinking in terms of theoretical economy. He is offering an account of what he takes to be observed facts, including the fact that normal human beings experience emotions; and he follows Plato in distinguishing emotions from both bodily urges and rational decisions or judgments. This seems to be the commonsensical line to take: given that emotions appear to be normal in the sense that every human being experiences them, Aristotle assumes that they are a part of our natural endowment and tries to make sense of them on the basis of that assumption.

The Stoic theory, on the other hand, seems to be motivated at least as much by moral as by psychological considerations. The Stoics apparently thought that both moral badness and human unhappiness have their origin in an excessive concern for things beyond a person's control—either passionate attachments to other people or strong desires and aversions toward those things that are relevant to self-preservation, and that humans as well as other animals will pursue or avoid under the guidance of their natural instincts. Human beings should indeed continue to follow the pattern of pursuit and avoidance set by nature, but a truly rational human being would eventually come to see that success in obtaining those things has no weight at all compared to the real goodness that is to be found in perfect rationality, as present in human virtue and in the divine order of the universe. A person who had reached this insight would attain both peace of mind and perfect moral virtue. What prevents most people from attaining this goal, according to the Stoics, is precisely their liability to passion—that is to say, their tendency to ascribe real goodness or badness to external things. Once reason has assented to the impression that one of the objects of our natural instinct is truly good, the effect, according to the Stoics, will be devastating. The erroneous belief will inevitably have an influence on subsequent impressions and judgments, and it will eventually lead to overwhelming and insatiable desires as well as inner turmoil caused by the frustration of those desires. If the passions are thus to be regarded as the source of all evils in human life, they can hardly be considered as part of nature's plan; and since, as we saw before, human action could in principle be accounted for in terms of reason and instinct alone, the Stoics felt justified in advocating the complete extirpation of the passions.

One might have some doubts about the Stoics' sweeping indictment of passion as the source of all the evils of human life, pointing out that cold-blooded crime seems to be at least as widespread, and arguably more horrifying, than the more spectacular variety of crimes of passion. It is not very plausible to suggest, for example, that the crimes of concentration camp doctors were motivated by an obsessive attachment to external goods of any sort. But in ancient times, defenders of the Aristotelian position seem to have focused rather on the claim that passion or emotion is unnatural and superfluous. Plutarch, for example, argues that the Stoic psychology is mistaken, as evidenced by the common phenomenon of inner conflicts between reason and emotion (*De Virtute Morali* 445a–447c), and that, furthermore, the moderate, allegedly unemotional impulses recognized as legitimate by the Stoics are really nothing but what Aristotelians would call a moderate degree of emotion (ibid. 449a–449b). The Stoics had convincing replies to both of these objections: they pointed out that "inner conflicts" can be construed as reason's wavering between different options rather than as a battle between opposed forces inside the soul, and that emotion is not needed to account for ordinary, everyday action. The debate between the advocates of Peripatetic *metriopatheia* (a moderate degree of emotion), on the one side, and of Stoic *apatheia* (freedom from emotion), on the other, as described by Plutarch, looks like something of a stalemate.[19] While the one side insists that emotion is natural and has to be accommodated even though it may occasionally lead to excess, the other side persists in its view that the passions, once admitted, will inexorably lead to disaster and should therefore be avoided. Both sides agree that virtue and right action must be explained in terms of reason's correct judgments and decisions. So long as the capacity to experience emotions is seen as just one more source of motivation that may either support or hinder reason, it seems unclear, at the least, why it should be needed for virtue, regardless of whether or not it can be avoided.

But once we realize that Aristotle, if not all of his later followers, distinguishes between the emotion as an affection of the soul caused by an evaluative impression and the desire, if any, that may arise from it—the cognitive and the motivational aspect of emotion—we can perhaps see more clearly what underlies his notorious thesis (*NE* 6.12.1144a29–1144b1) that moral virtue is required for the intellectual virtue of practical wisdom or intelligence (*phronēsis*). As the *Rhetoric* makes clear, emotions will have an influence on the way we see and judge other people and their actions as well as our own future prospects. Now if emotional dispositions are what underlies virtue of character, the influence of emotion on judgment cannot be regarded as merely distorting, a distraction, as it were, from rational thought. An orator's attempt to arouse or dispel emotions should also not be seen as mere manipulation, or as an attempt to produce conviction by illegitimate means.[20] If morally good people can be expected to have certain characteristic emotional responses, then the influence of emotion may sometimes be what is needed to see things in the right way. For example, it may be perfectly appropriate for a speaker to remind the people in the audience of services rendered to the community by his client, so as to make them feel grateful; and it may be equally legitimate to arouse pity for the victim of an undeserved misfortune. If the audience were impervious to such feelings, it might well arrive at an unfair or overly harsh verdict. Since emotion will have an influence on how we see and judge people and their actions, the right kind of emotional disposition may be what enables us to see things in the right moral perspective. If we had not been brought up to detest cruelty, for example, we might not even notice it as a bad thing and so would act cruelly or let cruelty pass without interfering. Again, if we had not learned to feel distress at the suffering or unfair treatment of others, we might overlook it or fail to be moved by compassion or indignation to try to prevent or alleviate suffering or to redress an injustice. What is at issue here is not the ability to figure out that cruelty or undeserved suffering are bad or undesirable in general. The Stoics would of course have insisted that their "wise man" was well aware of such things and would respond appropriately. The role of emotion as described by Aristotle seems rather to be that of directing one's attention to the practically or morally relevant features of a situation: "Fear makes people good at deliberation," as he puts it in *Rhetoric* 2.5.1383a6–7.

The person of practical wisdom, as Aristotle says in a famous passage (*NE* 6.12.1144a31–36), must start reasoning from the premise that such-and-such, whatever it may be, is "the end and the best." But unless she is a (morally) good person, this will not appear to her (*touto d' ei mē tōi agathōi, ou phainetai*). It seems to me significant that the verb translated as "appear" here is *phainesthai*—precisely the one that occurred (either as a verb or in its cognate noun *phantasia*) in the definitions of the emotions in Book 2 of the *Rhetoric*. Aristotle's concise remark can be understood in two ways, both of which may well be intended. First, a bad person might fail to notice what would be the best course of action in a given situation. For example, she might simply not perceive her neighbor as a person who has suffered an undeserved misfortune and who is therefore in need of help. Second, even if it were pointed out to her that help was required, she might not see that as the best course to take—it may not appear attractive to her, even if she ends up doing it. The first interpretation brings out the cognitive element; the second, the motivational role of emotional dispositions for moral character. It is the right kind of emotional disposition that enables the morally virtuous person to see or recognize what is the best in any situation. A bad person, by contrast, might be described as morally blind: not only will she fail to notice the relevant aspects of a situation but even if someone told her "what is best," she might fail to recognize it as the best. If this is correct, then the Aristotelians have a stronger argument to use against those who would rid us of our passions than just that emotions seem to be a natural phenomenon. They could claim that our capacity for emotional responses is what alerts us to morally important features of situations that we need to take into account in attempting to arrive at a rational judgment.

In the context of deliberation, an emotional response can be described as one that is in proportion to the good or evil perceived, and hence adequate, if the initial impression holds up under reflective scrutiny. Aristotle no doubt expects a virtuous person's emotions to be in line with "what the person of practical wisdom would determine" (*NE* 2.6.1107a1) because her spontaneous reactions will not be independent of her education, her previous experience, and the advice of others.[21] The fact that emotions are not the result of rational decision does not mean that they are mere reflexes—after all, Aristotle quite rightly distinguishes them from completely irrational appetites like hunger and thirst. Emotions are not based on reasoning, but, as Aristotle puts it, they (that is, the "part of soul" to which they belong) can be persuaded by reason (see *NE* 1.13.1102b25–1103a3). This means not only that we can sometimes be talked out of an emotion by arguments to show that our first impression was mistaken; it also means that our reason-based beliefs and convictions will make us disposed to be impressed in certain ways and to have the corresponding emotional responses. If Aristotle is right on this point, then the Stoic "argument from excess" loses much of its force. Aristotle would be the last to deny that passions can lead to excess—excess is, after all, what is essential to one sort of vice, like cowardice or greed. What Aristotle does deny is that emotion *must* lead to excess. Given Aristotle's view of the interaction between reasoning (both one's own and that of others) and emotion, I do not see why this should be regarded as unfounded optimism. It is true that Aristotle does not offer a recipe for avoiding the dangers of excess once and for all. But, as I have tried to show, he offers us some good reasons to think that in getting rid of the passions, we might lose more than we can hope to gain.

NOTES

In writing this paper, I have incurred debts to many people: first and foremost, to the graduate students in my spring 1994 seminar on Book 2 of the *Rhetoric;* to Dorothea Frede, for a lively and illuminating discussion of her own paper in that seminar; to the Discussion Club at Cornell, for a stimulating debate about a half-baked version of this paper; and to Mitzi Lee, Nancy Sherman, and John Cooper for helpful comments and criticism of the penultimate version.

1. I will use these two terms interchangeably in what follows. The point of using both is, I think, not just that they are both common translations of the same Greek word, but also that they seem to emphasize two different aspects of the subject. While "emotion" would seem preferable in an Aristotelian context, "pas-

sion" is more appropriate in the Stoic context. But it is important to realize that Aristotle and the Hellenistic philosophers were talking about the same thing.

2. See, however, W. W. Fortenbaugh, "Aristotle's *Rhetoric* on Emotions," *Archiv für Geschichte der Philosophie* 52 (1970): 40–70.

3. In his "Rhetoric, Dialectic, and the Passions," *Oxford Studies in Ancient Philosophy* 11 (1993): 178–184.

4. See, for example, 1.2.1356b9, 1356b12, 1357a30, 1357b22–25; 2.25.1403 a4–5, 1403a12.

5. This passage should be compared with *NE* 1.13.1102a23–26, where Aristotle says that the student of politics will have to study psychology as well, but only to the extent that it is needed for the purpose at hand: it might be tedious to go into greater detail. An example of a definition that would be "too precise" might be one that mentions the physiological side of an emotion as well as its formal account, such as the definition of anger discussed at *DA* 1.1.403a29 ff.

6. For discussions about the definition of particular emotions in the *Topics:* see, for example, on anger: 2.113a35–113b3, 4.125b28 ff., 4.126a6–12 (also mentions fear and shame), 127b27–32, 6.151a14–19, 8.156a32–33; on calmness or mildness (*praotēs*): 4.125b20–27; on indignation and envy: 2.109b35–110a4 (this should be compared with the lengthy disquisition about their opposition to pity at the beginning of *Rhetoric* 2.9).

7. Here I would disagree with Fortenbaugh (*Aristotle on Emotion* [New York, 1975]), who argues that Aristotle is working with a "bipartite" (human) psychology that replaces the Platonic "tripartite" theory in order to accommodate the emotions. Difficulties with the Platonic schema do surface in an interesting passage in the *Topics* (4.5.126a6–12), but I doubt that this is sufficient to speak of a new psychological theory. Plato's distinctions are clearly based on types of desire, while the distinction between the "reasoning part" and the part that can listen to or obey reason is based on the beliefs or judgments that can be attributed to the relevant "parts." One does not have to see these "divisions" as necessarily incompatible.

8. I avoid the usual translation of *epithumia* as "appetite" in this case, because Aristotle explicitly distinguishes belief-based desires from the purely irrational cravings like hunger and thirst, which have their origin in the body; see 1.11.1370a18–27.

9. The most striking example of this kind of economy is character as a "means of persuasion": instead of explaining how speakers may convince an audience of their moral wisdom and reliable character, Aristotle simply refers the reader back to his collection of common views about the virtues for speeches of praise or blame in 1.9, saying that "one would use the same things to establish one's own good character as one would for another person" (2.1.1378a16–19). He can hardly mean that the best way to present oneself as a morally good person consists in extolling one's own virtues, and so the reader is left with the task of adapting the materials given in 1.9 to a different purpose for which some further advice might well have been helpful. The chapters 10–11 in Book 1 probably also serve a double purpose: both to instruct the orator about likely causes of wrongdoing and to tell him what motives he may plausibly ascribe to wrongdoers.

10. Stephen Leighton ("Aristotle and the Emotions," *Phronesis* 27 [1982]: 162–165) argues that Aristotle probably intended to exclude *epithumia* from the realm of the passions because it is entirely irrational. But he overlooks the crucial passage in 1.11 in which Aristotle distinguishes between emotional *epithumiai* and bodily cravings, as well as the mention of *epithumia* as influencing judgment in 2.1.

11. See J. C. B. Gosling and C. C. W. Taylor, *The Greeks on Pleasure* (Oxford, 1982), pp. 194–199.

12. See her "Mixed Feelings in Aristotle's *Rhetoric*" in this volume.

13. The treatment of the last two is exceptional in several ways: *philia* (and presumably also, by implication, its opposite) is defined in terms of "wishing" (*boulesthai*), a verb that is elsewhere reserved for rational desire; and Aristotle seems to contrast hate with anger as being "without distress," unemotional rather than emotional, as it seems. It may be that the awkwardness arises simply from the fact that Aristotle is using definitions formulated for a different purpose. One way in which one might wish to set these two off from the rest would be to say that they seem to be emotional dispositions rather than occurrent emotions—*hexeis* rather than *kinēseis*, in Aristotle's terms. Still, whether or not a person is seen as a friend or an enemy will no doubt have an influence on the audience's emotional attitude, and so the treatment of these dispositions would seem to be appropriate in its place. But it is perhaps not surprising that friendship or goodwill and hate do not quite fit into the pattern used for the other emotions.

14. It is worth noting that chapter 1.11 already shows the characteristic use of *phainesthai* or *phantasia* to indicate the impression that causes an emotion; see 1370b8, b13, b33; 1371a9, a19, a23–24. A definition of *epithumia* parallel to that of *orgē* can perhaps be inferred from 1.10.1369b15–16 together with 1.11.1370a17–18: *orexis meta lupēs phainomenou hēdeos.*

15. Translators and commentators alike take chapter 2.7 to be dealing with "kindliness" or benevolence, the feelings of people who do favors to others, rather than the gratitude of those who see themselves as receiving a favor. But the Greek phrase *charin echein* normally means "to be grateful," and once we realize that this is the topic of the chapter, it is also clear that Aristotle is following his usual schema, dealing with people "toward whom," "on account of what," and "in what state of mind" gratitude is felt. (See Cooper, "Rhetoric, Dialectic, and the Passions," pp. 184–185, for the difficulties involved in reading the chapter in the usual way.) Aristotle presumably resorts to a definition of favor (*charis*) because no formal definition of gratitude (*charin echein*) was available. His advice about the "opposite" is clearly meant to show how one can persuade people that they have no reason to be grateful. Hence I propose to translate the opening sentences of 2.7 as follows: "To whom people feel grateful, on account of what, and in what state of mind, will be clear when we have defined favor. Let favor, then—that with regard to which the person who has received it is said to be grateful—be a service rendered to someone in need, not in return for something, but . . ."

16. For the general outline of the Stoic classification, see the testimonia in H. von Arnim, *Stoicorum Veterum Fragmenta* III (1903; reprint, Stuttgart, 1964), pp. 377–420. I have offered a more detailed account of the Stoic position in "Fol-

lowing Nature," *Oxford Studies in Ancient Philosophy* 9 (1991): 1–71, especially pp. 61 ff.

17. See *NE* 2.5.1105b19–1106a4 for the points that the capacity for emotion is natural and that emotions are involuntary.

18. The Stoics realized, of course, that it was paradoxical to maintain both that humans are made by nature to achieve perfect virtue and that just about every human being in fact turns out to be morally bad. It is not clear that they offered a convincing solution to the problem of the origin of evil. For some source materials on this question, see A. A. Long and D. N. Sedley, *The Hellenistic Philosophers* (Cambridge, 1987), vol 1, s. 65, pp. 410–423.

19. For a detailed discussion of this debate as presented in other ancient authors, see Martha Craven Nussbaum, *The Therapy of Desire* (Princeton, 1994), chaps. 10–12.

20. On the "appeal to emotion" as a legitimate part of the orator's performance, see Alan Brinton, "Pathos and the 'Appeal to Emotion': An Aristotelian Analysis," *History of Philosophy Quarterly* 5 (1988): 207–219.

21. For a fuller discussion of Aristotle's views on the education of the emotions, see Nancy Sherman, "The Role of Emotions in Aristotelian Virtue," *Proceedings of the Boston Area Colloquium in Ancient Philosophy* 9 (1993): 1–33.

Aristotle on Emotions
and Rational Persuasion

Martha Craven Nussbaum

I

Nikidion[1] is an emotional person. She loves her friends and feels joy in their presence, hope for their future. If one of them should die, she weeps and feels great grief. If someone should damage her, or someone dear to her, she gets angry; if someone should help her out, she feels gratitude. When others suffer terrible harms and wrongs, she feels pity for their suffering. And this means that she feels fear as well, since she perceives that she has similar vulnerabilities. She is not ashamed of these emotions. For the city in which she was raised endorses them, staging tragic festivals that encourage citizens to feel pity at the unjustified suffering of others, fear for their own similar possibilities. How will Aristotle deal with these aspects of her character?

In Aristotle's view, emotions are not blind animal forces, but intelligent and discriminating parts of the personality, closely related to beliefs of a certain sort, and therefore responsive to cognitive modification. He calls for cultivation of many emotions as valuable and necessary parts of virtuous agency. Nikidion's education here will not seek to extirpate the passions, although it will modify them; and it may even need to cultivate them further, should her dispositions in this regard prove deficient.

We will be in a better position to appreciate the significance of Aristotle's analysis if we sketch the view of the emotions shared by many ancient Greek theorists.

1. Emotions are forms of intentional awareness: that is (since no ancient term corresponds precisely to these terms), they are forms of awareness directed at or about an object, in which the object figures as it is seen from the creature's point of view. Anger, for example, is not, or not simply, a bodily reaction (such as a boiling of the blood). To give an adequate

account of it, one must mention the object to which it is directed, what it is about and for. And when we do this, we characterize the object as it is seen by the person experiencing the emotion, whether that view is correct or not: my anger depends upon the way I view you and what you have done, not on the way you really are or what you really have done.[2]

2. Emotions have a very intimate relationship to beliefs, and can be modified by a modification of belief. My anger, for example, requires a belief that I have been deliberately wronged by someone in a more than trivial way. Should I decide that this belief was false (that the alleged wrong did not in fact take place, or was not in fact a wrong, or was not done by the person in question, or was not done deliberately) my anger will be removed, or shift its target. At this point, positions diverge, some claiming that the belief in question is a necessary condition of the emotion, some claiming that it is a constituent part of the emotion, some that it is both necessary and sufficient for the emotion. The Stoics claim that the relation is one of identity: the emotion just is a certain sort of belief or judgment. The weakest thesis that seems to be accepted by any major Greek thinker, from Plato on, is the thesis that belief(s) of a certain sort are a necessary condition of the emotion in each case.[3]

3. All this being so, emotions may appropriately be assessed as rational or irrational, and also (independently) as true or false, depending on the character of the beliefs that are their basis or ground. Thus, rather than having a simple dichotomy between the emotional and the (normatively) rational,[4] we have a situation in which all emotions are to some degree "rational" in a descriptive sense—all are to some degree cognitive and based upon belief—and they may then be assessed, as beliefs are assessed, for their normative status.

Now, however, we shall turn to Aristotle, seeing how he develops this area of agreement and puts it to work in the analysis of specific emotions.

II

Even the bodily appetites—hunger, thirst, sexual desire—are seen by Aristotle as forms of intentional awareness, containing a view of their object. For he consistently describes appetite as for, directed at, "the apparent good." Appetite is one form of *orexis*, a "reaching out for" an object; and all the forms of *orexis* see their object in a certain way, supplying the active animal with a "premise of the good."[5] In other words, when a dog goes across the room to get some meat, its behavior is explained not by some hydraulic mechanism of desire driving it from behind, but as a response to the way it sees the object. Aristotle also holds that appetite—unlike, for example, the animal's digestive system—is responsive to reasoning and instruction (*NE* 1002b28–1103a1). He is talk-

ing about human appetite here, but he recognizes much continuity between humans and other animals, with respect to the capacity for acting
from a (modifiable) view of the good.

Where specifically human appetite is concerned, the case for intentionality and cognitive responsiveness is clearer still. Aristotle's account of
the virtue of moderation, which is concerned with the proper management of the bodily appetites (the appetites, he frequently says, that humans share with other animals), shows that he believes suppression is not
the only way to make appetite behave well. Indeed, suppression could
produce at best self-control, and not virtue. The virtue requires psychological balance (*sumphōnein*, 1119b15), so that the person does not char-
acteristically long for the wrong food and drink, at the wrong time, in the
wrong amount (1118b28–33). But this is achieved by an intelligent process of moral education, which teaches the child to make appropriate
distinctions, to take appropriate objects. The object of well-educated
appetite, he holds, is the "fine" (*kalon*, 1119b16).[6]

All types of desire are responsive to reasoning and teaching, then, to
some degree. But it is in connection with the emotions, rather than the
bodily appetites, that Aristotle develops the role of belief in desire most
clearly.[7] A number of texts in the ethical and psychological writings give
us help here, especially in determining the normative role of emotion
within the good human life. But it is above all in the *Rhetoric* that we find
Aristotle's detailed analysis of emotions such as anger, fear, pity, and
friendly love. Although much of the ethical material in the *Rhetoric* cannot
be used directly to reconstruct Aristotle's own ethical views—since it
provides the young orator not with Aristotle's considered view but with
popular views of ethical matters that would be likely to prevail in his
audience[8]—the material on emotion is not similarly circumscribed. For
Aristotle's project in these chapters is to enable the aspiring orator to
produce these emotions in an audience (*empoiein*, 1378a27). For this to
succeed, he needs to know what fear and anger really are, not just what
people think they are. If the popular view held that anger was a brutish
unreasoning bodily appetite, a fire in the heart, and the truth about anger
was that it was a complex cognitive disposition resting on beliefs of several
kinds, then it would be the latter view, not the former, that the orator
would need to know, since his aim is not to talk about anger but to produce
it. He does not need to know whether the things that usually make people
angry ought to do so, or whether their beliefs about what is fearful are
in fact true: that indeed is the business of the ethical writings, and we shall
turn to these in due course. But he needs to know what really produces
emotion; and it seems to be the underlying assumption of the whole
rhetorical enterprise that belief and argument are at the heart of the
matter. For the orator does not have the opportunity to work on people's

physiology, to give them drugs or light a fire under their hearts. If there is any hope of rhetoric's doing what Aristotle wants it to do, it had better be the case that emotions can in fact be created and taken away pretty reliably by discourse and argument. And this is what Aristotle now attempts to show. I shall focus on the cases of fear and pity. I shall begin from two important passages in the psychological works, and then turn to the detailed analyses in the *Rhetoric*.

Fundamental to Aristotle's analysis is a distinction between fear and fright or being startled. In two texts analyzing the building blocks of action,[9] he notes that a loud noise, or the appearance of enemy troops, may produce a startling effect, even on a brave person. The person's heart may leap from fright or startling, without its being the case that the person is really afraid (*DA* 432b30–31; cf. *Motu* 11). (The *De Motu Animalium* discussion adds a parallel example: sometimes the appearance of a beautiful person may produce sexual arousal, without its being the case that the person has sexual emotion of the sort that would really lead to action.) But if the person is only startled and not afraid, it is clear that he will not run away: as the *De Motu Animalium* argues, only a part of the body will be moved, and not the entire body. The *De Motu Animalium* analysis suggests that we see in such cases the effect of *phantasia*, or "appearing," without any concomitant *orexis*, reaching out, or desire.[10] (Emotion is a subclass of *orexis*.) The question must now be, What would have to be added to this being startled, in order to turn it into real fear?

The example resembles another one used by Aristotle in the sphere of perception, where he distinguishes simple *phantasia*, appearing, from belief or judgment.[11] The sun, he says, appears a foot wide: it has that look. But at the same time, we believe that it is larger than the inhabited world. Here we could expect a related consequence for action: if I have only the "appearance" that the sun is a foot wide, I won't be so likely to act on it. Here it is clear that the something that needs to be added, in order to turn the mere appearing into the usual sort of basis for human action,[12] would be an element of conviction or acceptance. It is in this that mere *phantasia* differs from belief. Although the contrast between *phantasia* and belief in Aristotle is sometimes depicted as one between nonpropositional and propositional cognitive attitudes, it is clear that this cannot be quite the right story for our case. For the *phantasia* of the sun as a foot wide involves, at the very least, combination or predication. It is a little hard to see where to draw the line between this and the "propositional." The real difference between *phantasia* and belief here seems to be just the difference that the Stoics will bring forward as the difference between *phantasia* and belief: in the former case, the sun strikes me as being a foot wide, but I don't commit myself to that, I don't accept or assent to it. In the latter case, I have a conviction, a view as to how things really are.

The very same contrast seems to be at work in our emotion examples. The loud noise strikes the brave man as something terrible, but, being a brave man, he doesn't accept that it is in fact terrible; he judges that it is not so terrible.[13] So he stands his ground. The ancient commentator Michael of Ephesus analyzes the De Motu Animalium's sexual case in a similar way, using the Stoic terminology of assent: the alluring object appears, and appears alluring: but, being a temperate man, the person in the example does not "assent to" the suggestion that this particular object is in fact alluring. He refuses it, and so we get just momentary arousal (an "involuntary erection," Michael writes), not emotion and not action. It seems, then, that Aristotle is agreeing with an analysis already suggested by Plato in Republic 2–3: in order to have emotions such as fear and grief, one must first have beliefs of a certain kind, beliefs that terrible things may befall beyond one's own control.

But we need to proceed cautiously: for the analysis of fear in the Rhetoric begins in an ambiguous manner. "Let fear be, then, a certain sort of pain and disturbance (tarachē) out of the appearance (phantasias) of an impending bad thing, either destructive or painful" (1382a21–23). And again, below, "It is necessary that those things are fearful that appear to have (phainetai echein) a great power to destroy or to harm in a way that leads to great pain" (1382a28–30). These passages might seem to connect fear with simple appearing, rather than with belief or judgment.[14] Then, if our analysis has been correct, fear would here be analyzed very differently, and connected with a mere impression as to how things are, rather than with a real conviction or commitment. Further pursuit of the question shows clearly, however, that no technical distinction between phantasia and believing is at issue in any of these analyses of emotion: phantasia is used, in the rare cases where it is used, simply as the verbal noun of phainesthai, "appear."[15] The passage contains no suggestion that phantasia is being distinguished from doxa, belief.[16] And indeed Aristotle feels free to use belief words such as dokein and oiesthai in connection with his analyses of emotions.[17] In other words, what is stressed is the fact that it is the way things are seen by the agent, not the fact of the matter, that is instrumental in getting emotions going. Intentionality, not absence of commitment, is the issue.

Aristotle has, in fact, a lot to say about the beliefs that are requisite for fear. The object of a person's fear must, he says, be an evil that seems capable of causing great pain and destruction, one that seems to be impending, and one that the person seems powerless to prevent. (Thus, he notes, we do not typically have throughout life an active fear of death, even though we know we shall die, since death usually seems far away; nor do we fear becoming stupid or unjust, presumably because we think this is within our power to prevent [1382a23].) What makes a person fearful is now given in a complex series of reflections, representing the sorts of judgments that might be involved in different cases of becoming afraid: for example, the thought that some other person has been insulted and is waiting for the opportunity to take revenge (1381a35–1381b4). In general, Aristotle continues, "since fear is with the expectation that one will suffer some destructive affect (*phthartikon pathos*), it is evident that nobody is afraid who thinks (*oiomenoi*) that he can suffer nothing" (1382b30–32). The belief is now out in the open, and is made a necessary condition of the emotion. Further, fear is said to be increased by the belief that the damage, if suffered, will be irreparable (1382b23), and that no assistance will be forthcoming. It is removed by the belief that (*nomizontes*) one has already suffered everything bad there is to suffer.

In short: fear, as described in this chapter, is a peculiarly human experience with a rich intentional awareness of its object, resting on beliefs and judgments of many sorts, both general and concrete. Phrases such as "They do not fear if . . ." and "the one who fears must . . ." indicate that these beliefs, or some of them, are necessary conditions of the fear. And, indeed, this suggestion also seems to be contained in the original definition, which uses the preposition *ek*, "out of": the distress and pain are not independent of the judgment, but result from it. Thus if the judgment changed, we could expect the feeling itself to change—as Aristotle himself insists, when he speaks of the conditions under which fear will be removed.

Let us now turn to pity. Pity is another painful emotion—*lupē tis*, a certain sort of pain. What sort of pain? "Pain at (*epi*) an appearing evil, destructive or painful, belonging to one who does not deserve to have it happen—the sort of evil that one might expect oneself to suffer, or some member of one's family" (1385b13–15). Three cognitive conditions for pity, suggested already in this opening definition, are unpacked in the analysis that follows. First, the person pitied must be thought to be undeserving (*anaxios*) of the misfortune. The word *anaxios* is given tremendous emphasis in the passage as a whole.[18] Aristotle remarks that the pitier must believe "that there are some good people; otherwise he will not pity, because he will think that everyone deserves the bad things that happen to them" (85b34–86a1). The (believed) goodness of the individual object of pity is also important: for it reinforces the belief that the suffering is undeserved (86b6–8). Such undeserved sufferings appeal to our sense of injustice (86b14–15).

Second, the person who pities must believe that he or she is vulnerable in similar ways. People who think that they are above suffering and have everything will not, he says, have pity. Aristotle is not at all friendly to this state of mind: twice he refers to it as *hubris* (85b21–22, 31). And third, the pitier must believe that the sufferings of the pitied are significant: they must have "size" (86a6–7; cf. the requirement for fear at 82a28–30). His list of the likely occasions for pity bears a close resemblance to his own list of significant impediments to good action in Book 1 of the *Nicomachean Ethics* (1099a33–1099b6). It includes death, bodily assault or ill-treatment, old age, illness, lack of food, lack of friends, having few friends, separation from one's friends, ugliness (which impedes friendship), weakness, being crippled, having your good expectations disappointed, having good things come too late, having no good things happen to you, having them happen but being unable to enjoy them (86a7–13).

Pity and fear are closely connected: what we pity when it happens to another, we fear lest it should happen to ourselves (86a27–28). The perception of one's own vulnerability is made, indeed, a part of the definition; so it follows from the logic of pity that the pitier will have self-directed fear as well (although not necessarily at the same time–for 86a22 notes that a good deal of self-directed fear can temporarily knock out pity). Most occasions for fear will also be occasions for pity, and indeed Aristotle asserts the other half of the biconditional at 1382b26–27; but in fact this is a slight overstatement, since some listed occasions for fear are occasions where one knows that one has done something wrong and fears (deserved) punishment; these will not be occasions for (other-directed) pity.

In short, these emotions have a rich cognitive structure. It is clear that they are not mindless surges of affect, but discerning ways of viewing objects; and beliefs of various types are their necessary conditions. But we can now say more. For we can see by looking at Aristotle's accounts that the beliefs must be regarded as constituent parts of what the emotion *is*. Fear and pity are both painful emotions. Nowhere in his analyses does Aristotle even attempt to individuate emotions by describing varieties of painful or (as the case may be) pleasant feeling. Emotions, instead, are individuated by reference to their characteristic beliefs. We cannot describe the pain that is peculiar to fear, or say how fear differs from grief or pity, without saying that it is pain at the thought of a certain sort of future event that is believed to be impending. But if the beliefs are an essential part of the definition of the emotion, then we have to say that their role is not merely that of external necessary condition. They must be seen as constituent parts of the emotion itself.

And we can go further. It is not as if the emotion has (in each case) two separate constituents, each necessary for the full emotion, but each available independently of the other. For Aristotle makes it clear that the feeling of pain or pleasure itself depends on the belief component, and will be removed by its removal. He uses two Greek prepositions, *ek* and *epi*, to describe the intimate relationship between belief and feeling: there is both a causal relationship (fear is pain and disturbance "out of"—*ek*—the thought of impending evils) and a relationship of intentionality or aboutness: pity is defined as "painful feeling directed at [*epi*] the appearance that someone is suffering . . ."). In fact, both relationships are present in both cases, clearly: for it is equally true that pity's pain is produced by the thought of another's suffering—Aristotle's rhetorical analysis relies on this—and also that fear is pain directed at the imagined future evil.[19]

Are the beliefs sufficient as well as necessary conditions for the full emotion? (Since they are clearly sufficient conditions for themselves, what we are asking here is whether they also are sufficient causes of the other constituent in the emotion, the feeling of pain or pleasure.) We do not get altogether clear information on this from the text. Throughout the chapters on emotion, we do find sentences of the form, "If they think X, then they will experience emotion Y"; this strongly suggests a sufficient condition view. In one case, Aristotle may even state the view: "It is necessary that people who think they are likely to suffer something should fear, and fear those people at whose hands they think they will suffer and those things they think they will suffer and at the time at which they think they will suffer" (1382b33–35). And in general, the whole point of telling the aspiring orator so much about the beliefs of emotional people is that he should have a reliable set of devices for stirring up these emotions. The orator, Aristotle writes, must know the targets and occasions of anger: "For if he should know one or two of these, but not all, he will be unable to produce anger (*empoiein*), and similarly with the other passions" (1378a24–28).

Our passage from the *De Anima* might have seemed to give a counter-example: the brave man has the same thought as the coward, but does not feel fear. We should, however, question whether the belief is actually the same. The brave man says to himself, "The enemy is approaching." He does not, I think, say to himself, "A terrible future evil is approaching, one capable of causing great pain and destruction." Or if he does say this, it seems reasonable to suppose that he will already be afraid. (Brave men, at least in the *Nicomachean Ethics*, do feel fear at the thought of death.) In short: if we get clear about exactly what the thought is—with all its evaluative elements—the alleged counterexamples are less weighty. We shall see that this is an important issue in the Stoic theory as well, where the evaluative content of the emotional person's judgment is salient. We can conclude, I think, that although evidence of a sufficient condition view is not clear, Aristotle has to believe that at least much or most of the time the belief does sufficiently cause the complex passion, or he could not take the pride he does in his rhetorical technique.

I have focused on these two emotions because they provide an especially clear illustration of the normative structure of Aristotelian emotion, and the connection of that structure to Aristotle's anti-Platonic views on luck. Anger is especially complex: for it has both a pleasant and a painful feeling component, these being associated with different, although closely related, sets of beliefs. It requires, on the one hand, the belief that one (or someone dear to one) has been slighted or wronged or insulted in some serious way, through someone else's voluntary action (1380a8); this, Aristotle insists, is a painful experience. (Once again, the pain is not a separate item directly caused by the world itself; it is caused by the belief that one has been slighted. If the belief is false, one will still feel that pain; and if one has been slighted without knowing it, one will not have it.) Once again, these beliefs are necessary constituents in the emotion. Aristotle makes it clear that if the angry person should discover that the alleged slight did not take place at all, or that it was not deliberately performed (80a8–10), or that it was not performed by the person one thought (78a34–78b1, 80b25–29), anger can be expected to go away. So too, if one judges that the item damaged by another is trivial rather than serious (*peri mikron,* 1379b35, and cf. 1379b31–32). But Aristotle holds that anger requires, as well, a wish for retaliation, the thought that it would be good for some punishment to come to the person who did the wrong—and the thought of this righting of the balance is pleasant (1378b1 ff.). The orator's whole effort—whether in inspiring anger or in calming angry people down (2.3)—is directed toward this complex cognitive structure.

The subject of love is a highly complex one in Aristotle's thought. The general rubric under which Aristotle analyzes love is that of *philia,* which, strictly speaking, is not an emotion at all, but a relationship with emotional components. But the fact that he analyzes it together with other emotions in the *Rhetoric* shows his recognition of the importance of those components. The relation itself requires mutual affection, mutual well-wishing, mutual benefiting for the other's own sake, and mutual awareness of all this. Both in the *Rhetoric* and the *Nicomachean Ethics,* the cognitive content of the emotions of *philia* is made overwhelmingly clear, since Aristotle informs us in detail that people who love one another do so on the basis of a certain conception or description of the object, and on the basis of their belief that the object has the feature or features in question—as well as their further beliefs that the object is well disposed to them, and so forth. It is perfectly clear that if any of these central beliefs turns out to be false, or becomes false, love will itself cease—unless it has in the meantime developed some other basis. (Thus a love based on a conception of the other person as pleasant to be with may, Aristotle holds, evolve over time into a love based on respect for good character.)[20] Erotic love is treated as a special case of *philia,* characterized by a special intensity. Usually it begins with a conception of the other party as pleasant; but it may mature into a *philia* that is based on character. Or if it begins asymmetrically, as a desire of one party for the other—so that it doesn't properly count as *philia* at all—it may, as the parties come to have more knowledge of one another, develop in the direction of greater mutuality, and come to be *philia.*[21] In any case, the description under which the parties perceive one another and the beliefs they have about one another are indispensable grounds of the emotion.

III

On further inspection, the beliefs involved in the central cases of emotion have one general feature in common, as Socrates and Plato already observed.[22] All, that is, involve the ascription of significant worth to items in the world outside of the agent, items that he or she does not fully control. Love, most obviously, is a profound attachment to another separate life,[23] which must remain as a separate center of movement and choice, not being engulfed or fused, in order for the relationship of love to be possible at all. And in the loves Aristotle values most highly, the participants view one another as good characters, therefore as fully independent choosers of the good; if one controlled the other, even to the extent that a parent does a child, the love would apparently be less good as love. But then, as Aristotle knows, it is perfectly possible for the relationship to be broken off—whether by death or separation or betrayal. So loves of a more than casual sort require a belief in one's own lack of self-sufficiency with respect to some of the most important things in life.

In pity and fear, there are related beliefs. For one who does not attach importance to things that can be harmed by the world will have nothing to fear—and so too, no reason to pity others when such things are damaged in their case. The listed occasions for pity—losses of friends and children, health problems, losses of opportunities, and so forth—all of these will give rise to pity only if those items are to some extent esteemed. Aristotle singles them out because he does esteem them (as we shall see); he does not say that one pities someone for losing a nail, or fears the destruction of a hairpin. In pity and fear, we acknowledge our vulnerability before the circumstances of life; we have those emotions, he makes plain, only if we really do think that life can do something to us, and that this something matters. Anger is closely related: for in anger we acknowledge our vulnerability before the actions of other people. Again, if we judge that the slight is trivial, we do not become angry.

As this suggests, the beliefs that ground the emotions are bound up with one another, in the sense that any deep attachment to uncontrolled things or persons in the world can provide the basis for any and all of the major emotions, given the appropriate changes in circumstance. Once one cares about a friend or family member, for example, one has, in addition to love itself, a basis for fear if that person is threatened, of grief if the person should die, of pity if she suffers undeservedly, of anger if someone else harms her. Love provides anger with a different kind of basis too: for as Aristotle notes, we expect those we love to treat us especially well, so if they do not, their slights seem all the more cutting, and we get angry at them more than at strangers (1379b2–4).

Believe now, with Socrates, that "a good man cannot be harmed" (*Apology* 41d, and cf. 30cd). Or believe, as the Socrates of Plato's *Republic* continues the argument, that "a good person is completely sufficient to himself for good living" (387–388). (This is so, according to Socrates, because virtue cannot be damaged by external contingencies, and virtue is sufficient for *eudaimonia*.)[24] If this is right, as the *Republic* goes on to argue, there will be no room for the emotions of pity, fear, and grief. For nothing that is not a lapse in virtue is worth taking very seriously; and a lapse in virtue, by definition under the person's own control, is an occasion for blame and reproach, not for pity. The things that are usually taken to be occasions for fear and pity—losses of loved ones, losses of fortune and political standing—are not really so: for "nothing among human things is worth much seriousness" (*Republic* 604b12–604c1). Tragic poetry, which displays such things as if they did have great significance, is to be dismissed from the city, for it "nourishes the element of pity in us, making it strong" (606b). Although Plato's guardians are permitted to retain a certain sort of anger—directed at the enemies of the city—it is obvious that most occasions for anger, too, are removed by the removal of vulnerability: the good person has no need for revenge, since the slights that others take to be harms and damages trouble him not at all.[25] And although love of a sort is present in the city of the virtuous, it is far from being the sort of love that tragedy depicts and that many people value. For it is based on the norm of virtuous self-sufficiency, and on the teaching that the good person "has least of all people any need for another person. . . . Least of all, then, is it to him a terrible thing to be deprived of a son or brother or . . . anything of that sort" (387d–387e).

Set over against the love and grief and pity of ordinary mortals is the ideal of the "wise and serene character, always consistent with itself" (604e). Plato remarks that it is difficult to represent such a figure in the theater, since audiences are used to more emotional volatility. Plato's dialogues, however, do represent such a figure: a Socrates who cares little for the prospect of his own death and who pursues his philosophical search regardless of his external circumstances. The *Phaedo* begins from a story that has all the ingredients of tragic emotion: its interlocutors remark that, accordingly, they expected to feel pity. But they did not, for Socrates' attitude to his impending death discouraged this response (58e, 59a). Xanthippe is sent away for her tears, Apollodorus sternly admonished for "womanish" behavior (60a, 117d). Socrates, by contrast, pursues the search for understanding without fear, resentment, or mourning.

What all this brings out is that emotions, while not "irrational" in the sense of being noncognitive, are based on a family of beliefs about the worth of externals that will be regarded as both false and irrational (in the normative sense) by a large segment of the philosophical tradition. This antitragic tradition will reach its fullest development in the Hellenistic schools, and especially in the Stoa.

IV

Unlike the Socrates of the *Republic,* Aristotle does not believe that the good person, the person of practical wisdom, is "sufficient unto himself" for *eudaimonia,* and therefore impervious to grief and fear. According to him, it is right to grieve at the death of a friend, since that is an acknowledgment of the importance of the tie and the person. As for fear: in *Nicomachean Ethics* Book 1, he makes room for the appropriateness of fear by insisting on the possibility of calamities so great that they can dislodge the person who was doing well from *eudaimonia* itself.[26] Later, in his account of proper courage, he makes this explicit, insisting that the courageous person will indeed feel fear and pain at the prospect of death, on account of the value that he rightly attaches to his own life. Defining fear in the same way as in the *Rhetoric* (1115a9), he insists that not all fears are appropriate. (For example, one might fear a mouse, and this is treated as something so absurd as to be pathological [1149a8].) On the other hand, "there are some things that one must fear, that it is noble to fear, and not to do so is shameful" (1115a12–13). As objects of proper fear he mentions disgrace, assault on or the killing of one's children or wife, and, above all, one's own death. The brave person fears death, but "in the appropriate way, and as reasoning instructs, he will stand his ground for the sake of the fine" (1115b11–13). In fact, Aristotle adds, a person will be "more pained at the prospect of death the more he has complete virtue and the more *eudaimōn* he is . . . for he will be aware that he is being deprived of the greatest goods, and this is painful" (1117b10–13). A person who is completely without fear does not strike Aristotle as virtuous (which would imply the possession of practical reason) but, rather, as unbalanced. "The person who is excessive in fearlessness has no name, but he would be a kind of mad or insensitive person, if he feared nothing, not earthquakes or waves, as they say about the Celts" (1115b24–27).

Pity is less frequently discussed in the ethical writings, since they focus on virtues one should cultivate within oneself more than on responses to the actions and fortunes of others. The discussion of reversals of fortune in *Nicomachean Ethics* Book 1, however, implies that Aristotle does recognize as legitimate a number of occasions for pity, the same group on which the *Rhetoric* focused in its account of that emotion. And in the discussion of voluntary and involuntary action, Aristotle speaks of pity in connection with actions that are involuntary on account of nonculpable ignorance—the sort of action he imputes to Oedipus in the *Poetics* (*NE* 1109b30–32, 1111a1–2).

In short, there are things in the world that it is right to care about: friends, family, one's own life and health, the worldly conditions of virtuous action. These can sometimes be damaged by events not under one's own control. For these reasons it is right to have some fear. The good person, rather than being a fearless person, is one who will have appropriate rather than inappropriate fears—*and* not be deterred by them from doing what is required and noble. The objects of fear are appropriate objects of pity when they happen to someone else. Education in proper fear and pity would consist in learning what the appropriate attachments are, and what damages one can reasonably expect in a variety of circumstances.

Anger is treated in a similar fashion. On the one hand, Aristotle clearly believes that many people get angry too much and for insufficient reasons. His choice of the name "mildness" (*praotēs*) for the appropriate virtuous disposition in this area reflects his conscious decision to pitch things rather toward the unangry than toward the angry end of the spectrum (1125b26–29). The virtuous person, he writes, gets angry only "in the manner that reason instructs, and at those people and for that length of time" (1125b35–1126a1). If anything, he errs in the direction of the deficiency—"for the mild person is not given to revenge, but is inclined to be forgiving [*sungnōmonikos*]" (1126a1–3). Reason, however, does tell this person that there are some very good reasons for getting angry, in connection with damages to things that it is really worth caring about:

> The deficiency, whether it should be called unangriness [*aorgēsia*], or whatever, is blamed. For those who do not get angry at the people at whom they should get angry seem dense, and also those who do not get angry in the manner they should and at the time and for the reasons they should. For they seem to be without perception or pain. And a person who is not angry

will not defend himself; but to allow oneself and one's loved ones to be trampled underfoot and to overlook it is slavish. (1126a3–8)

To be a slave, according to Aristotle's account, is to be at the disposal of another, the "living tool" of someone else's plan of life, lacking the integrity of one's own choice (*Polit.* 1.4). Aristotle is then saying here that, assuming one has made deep commitments to people and things that can be damaged by another, not to defend those commitments is to lose one's own integrity. Anger is said to be a necessary motivation for defending things that are beloved—presumably because anger is seen as an acknowledgment that the item damaged has importance, and without that acknowledgment one will have no reason to defend it. The belief in the item's importance, together with the belief that the slight or damage was voluntary, was held to be (usually) a sufficient condition for anger. So if anger is not on the scene, one would be led to the conclusion that some of the relevant beliefs are probably not on the scene. If the agent believes that there has been a damage and that it was voluntarily inflicted, but is not angry, then, if we follow Aristotle's account, we will have to conclude that the agent did not think the damage very important. It is this conceptual connection between anger and the acknowledgment of importance that explains why Aristotle holds it to be necessary for defensive action—not because it plays some mindless hydraulic role. The point is that if one does not have the beliefs that are sufficient for anger, it is hard to see why one would risk one's life, or even make painful effort, to defend the item in question. The mild person is not especially given to revenge, as Aristotle has said. But in the case of the deepest commitments, not to take some action seems to show a lack of "perception"; and if one has those practical perceptions, then one seems bound to be angry. Anger, in these cases, is a recognition of the truth.

Emotions, in Aristotle's view, are not always correct, any more than beliefs or actions are always correct. They need to be educated, and brought into harmony with a correct view of the good human life. But, so educated, they are not just essential as forces motivating to virtuous action, they are also, as I have suggested, recognitions of truth and value. And as such they are not just instruments of virtue, they are constituent parts of virtuous agency: virtue, as Aristotle says again and again, is a "mean disposition" (disposition to pursue the appropriate) "with regard to both passions and actions" (*NE* 1105b25–26, 1106b16–17, etc.). What this means is that even were the apparently correct action to be chosen without the appropriate motivating and reactive emotions, it would not count for Aristotle *as a virtuous action*: an action is virtuous only if it is done *in the way that* a virtuous person would do it. All of this is a part of the equipment of the person of practical wisdom, part of what practical rationality is. Rationality recognizes truth; the recognition of some ethical truths is impossible without emotion; indeed, certain emotions centrally involve such recognitions.

V

The person of practical wisdom, then, will approach a concrete situation ready to respond to it emotionally in the appropriate ways. What is appropriate is given by the general ethical theory, in the role it ascribes to external goods that can be damaged. This ethical theory is critical of much that Aristotle's society teaches. People often value too many of these external things, or value them too highly, or not enough. Thus they have too much emotion in connection with money, possessions, and reputation, sometimes not enough in connection with the things that are truly worthwhile. An important role for philosophical criticism is to insist on the central role of virtuous action, which can usually be controlled by one's own effort. But this control is not, and should not be, absolute. The emotions recognize worth outside oneself; in so doing, they frequently recognize the truth.

In Nikidion's education at the Lyceum, emotional experience can be expected to play a central role. If our account so far has been correct, a detached unemotional intellectual survey of all the true opinions seems impossible: in avoiding emotion, one avoids a part of the truth. In the process of sorting beliefs and intuitions, then, Nikidion and her fellow students will rely on their emotional responses and on their memory of emotional experience as guides to ethical truth. When confronted with a question such as, "Would a life without friends be complete or incomplete?" and "Is this a case of courageous action or not?" she will deliberate in an immersed way, consulting her fear and love and grief, along with other pertinent judgments. Her deliberation will for this reason be (according to her teacher) more and not less rational. And as Aristotle's view of moral development implies,[27] the same process of scrutiny will also refine the emotions, as it refines and educates all the involved elements of practical reason, making them more discriminating and responsive, better at confronting new situations in the future. Furthermore, the life Nikidion and her fellow students construct, as they work out a specification of their "target," will contain emotional experiences of certain types inside it, as valued elements in virtue. By relying on and further cultivating the emotions, they are trying, we might say, to keep themselves in health, and even to become healthier.

There seems, however, to be a tension in Aristotle's position. On the one hand, he describes the emotions as closely bound up with judgments, and therefore as capable of being modified by the modification of judgment. This picture implies not only that emotions can play a role in rational deliberation but also that they can be changed as beliefs of all sorts can be changed, by deliberation and argument. On the other hand, he makes a sharp distinction between character training and the philosophical study of ethics, on the grounds that emotions need to be balanced before the student can get anything much out of his philosophical arguments. Why, taking the view of emotion that he does, does he appear to insist on a separation between character training and philosophy? Why can't philosophical argument itself shape character? This question is of clear importance for philosophy's range and medical usefulness: for it was the demand for antecedent *paideia* that made the Lyceum an inhospitable place for the real-life (undisguised) Nikidion.

Why should Aristotle insist on a firm basis of good character before the application of philosophical medicine? Where does he think this basis comes from, and why does he think it different in kind from the other beliefs and judgments that are formed and modified by teaching?

First, in many passages where Aristotle discusses nonintellectual training and the need for discipline, he is probably thinking, above all, of the bodily appetites, which do have a substantial noncognitive component, although to some extent also they are responsive to reason. He does seem to believe that young people have difficulties of ethical inconstancy that come from their appetites, especially sexual appetite (see *Rhet.* 2.12.1389a3 ff.). For these desires, it appears that time to grow up is essential; without allowing for this, and also providing some early nonphilosophical training, we will never get people who are stable and undistractable enough for philosophy.

Second, Aristotle believes that the emotions, unlike many other beliefs, are formed above all in the family, in the child's earliest interactions with parents and other loved ones. The parent's love and the child's gratitude for the parent's love are fundamental to motivation and passion of all sorts in later life—as Aristotle argues against Plato. Here we see a reason why, while still holding a strongly cognitive picture of the emotions—love and gratitude are said to be based on certain perceptions and thoughts, whose absence in Plato's city is said to lead to an absence of care—Aristotle could think that philosophizing with adults can do little to change such basic patterns. Take someone raised in Plato's city, without a family, and it may be impossible in later life to instill the thoughts and attachments proper to the family. On the other hand, the early life in the family paves the way for future attachments to friends and city, in a manner that lies so deep in the personality that one might question how far philosophical examination can reach in altering those structures, even should they be judged to be defective.[28] It may be for this reason that in the *Nicomachean Ethics* Aristotle frequently refers to the emotions as "irrational"—

although, strictly speaking, his theories do not entitle him to use that word of them in either of its recognized senses: for they are (in his view) neither noncognitive nor (normatively) unjustified and false. They may, however, be more resistant to modification by teaching than other beliefs and judgments, on account of their history.[29] While depending on belief and judgment, the emotions may depend upon a type of belief and judgment that is less accessible to dialectical scrutiny than are most of the person's other beliefs.

VI

But Aristotle's insight suggests something more. It suggests that philosophy is not self-sufficient as a shaper of souls. Prior to her encounter with philosophy—prior to any encounter she could conceivably have with any conceivable philosophy—Nikidion has a material and institutional and relational life. And this life shapes her, for good or for ill. She is the child of her parents: their love and care, or the absence of it, shape her. She is the child of material circumstances of need or plenty: she is healthy or ill, hungry or full; and this, once again, shapes her—shapes not only her health, but her hopes, expectations, and fears, her capabilities for reasoning. She is the child of her city and its institutions: and these institutions shape her capacity for shame and self-esteem, for stinginess or generosity, for greediness or moderation. This shaping reaches deep into the soul, profoundly affecting what, even with philosophy, it can become.

And this creates another job for philosophy. This job is political. Philosophy can deal with students one by one, refining their capacities for the good life. But it can also, and perhaps more urgently, reflect about the material and social conditions of their lives, so as to design institutions that will allow people to be such that they can, if they wish, be further perfected in the philosophical way. Aristotle's students pursue not just their own *eudaimonia* but that of others: for they think about the design of political institutions, starting from the idea that the best political arrangement is the one "in accordance with which anyone whatsoever might do best and live a flourishing life" (*Polit.* 7.2; see previous discussion). Aristotle's critique of other political arrangements in *Politics* Book 7 devotes much attention to the conditions that shape emotions; so too does his own sketch for an ideal city in *Politics* Books 7 and 8.

In short: the apparent conservatism of Aristotle's dialectical education of Nikidion is only apparent. Radical change is excluded from the part of his educational scheme that deals with her as an individual. But that is not all that philosophy does. The individuals who do come to share in it partake in a task that is both radical and far-reaching: the design of a society in which money will not be valued as an end, in which honor will not be valued as an end, in which war and empire will not be valued as ends—a society in which the functioning of human individuals in accordance with their own choice and practical reason will be the ultimate end of institutions and choices. Granted that Nikidion must be a member of an elite in order to profit by the arguments Aristotle designed; still, the aim of her education is to make her capable of bringing the good life and the conditions that produce a good emotional character to her fellow citizens by politics.

NOTES

This essay is a shortened and lightly edited version of the chapter titled "Emotions and Ethical Health" in my *The Therapy of Desire: Theory and Practice in Hellenistic Ethics* (Princeton, 1994). Copyright © 1994 by Princeton University Press. Reprinted by permission.

1. Nikidion is a fictional pupil whose education in various philosophical schools is imagined throughout. The fact that Aristotle, unlike Plato and the major Hellenistic schools, did not teach women in his school is acknowledged in the prior discussion, and we imagine that Nikidion disguised herself as a man.

2. From this follows the possibility of directing emotions toward items that are not really there, whether absent or imagined. On the notion of "freedom of content" in the analysis of intentionality, and for an excellent overall treatment of the topic of intentionality in Aristotle's thought, see Caston 1992.

3. Posidonius's position on this question is unclear, and he comes closer than any other to a noncognitive view of emotion; but even he believes emotions can be modified by cognitive therapy.

4. I include this qualification since, in both ancient and modern discussions, the terms "rational" and "irrational" (and their Greek counterparts) are used, often confusingly, in both a descriptive sense (meaning, often, "cognitive" and "noncognitive") and also in a normative sense (meaning "conforming to [some] normative view of the right way to reason"). The Stoics will hold that all emotions are "rational" in the descriptive sense (all are judgments), but "irrational" in the normative sense (all are unjustifiable and false judgments). Galen tries to convict them of absurdity by pointing to this twofold use of the word *alogos,* but all he succeeds in showing is that there is a delicate terminological issue that needs attention.

5. See *De Motu Animalium* chapter 7; this whole issue is discussed in Nussbaum 1978, commentary and essay 4, and in Nussbaum 1986a, chapter 9. For recent defenses of this way of viewing Aristotelian desires, see Richardson 1992 and Charles 1984.

6. On the discriminating character of Aristotelian moral education generally, see Sherman 1989, Sorabji 1980; on the appetites and moderation, see Price 1989, Young 1988. Price makes an especially good case for the educability of sexual desire.

7. For an excellent account of this issue, see Leighton 1982; see also the earlier influential account in Fortenbaugh 1975. There are excellent accounts of

the cognitive structure of pity and fear in Halliwell 1986, and of anger in Aubenque 1957. See also Fillion-Lahille 1970.

8. Notice, however, that, given Aristotle's ethical methodology there is much continuity between the two.

9. *DA* 3.9, *Motu* chapter 11.

10. For this interpretation, see Nussbaum 1978.

11. *DA* 428b2–4; cf. *Insomn.* 460b19.

12. On Sorabji's (1993) account, Aristotle permits animals emotions, and these emotions are based on *phantasia* alone, without *pistis* (conviction based on persuasion). Sorabji points out that, although later Stoic-influenced commentators on Aristotle assimilated the distinction between *phantasia* and *pistis* or *doxa* to the distinction between mere appearing and appearing plus assent, Aristotle may have meant something subtly different: a distinction between an appearance plus a certain sort of unreflective assent and assent based on persuasion by argument. I agree that this would solve the problem of how Aristotle can grant emotions to animals without granting them belief (although we must remember that the evidence that he really does so is slight and largely in passages in which he is reporting popular views); on the other hand, I am not altogether convinced of this account of the distinction between *phantasia* and *doxa:* for there are many beliefs that Aristotle will call *doxai* that are not the result of persuasion by argument. In any case, the question is, I think, irrelevant to the interpretation of the *Rhetoric,* which appears innocent of these technical distinctions, and indeed of comparative biological thinking.

13. In this case, Aristotle does not raise the question whether the brave man feels some real fear; as we shall see, he later does raise it and, for certain cases, answers it in the affirmative.

14. So they have been interpreted by David Charles, in a fine paper delivered to the 1991 Helsinki conference on Aristotle's *Rhetoric.*

15. See for example *DA* 402b22–24, where the philosopher's project of speaking *kata tēn phantasian* about the attributes of soul is clearly the project of giving the best account he can, the one that makes the best sense of the evidence. It would be absurd to think of his project as that of producing an account "in accordance with" mere impressions, as opposed to conviction or belief. The verb *phainesthai* plus the infinitive means "seems to be such-and-such"; with the participle it means "is evidently such-and-such," and indicates a more confident sort of belief.

16. The distinction between *phantasia* and *doxa* seems to be introduced in one passage in Book 1 (1370a28) but is altogether absent from Book 2. In general, the account shows no awareness of the more technical psychological distinctions of the *De Anima.*

17. The words in question are *oiesthai, nomizein, logizesthai,* and *phainesthai* plus infinitive; also verbs of remembering and expecting. See 1385b17, 21, 22, 24, 32, 35; 1386a1–2, 26, 30–31. The word *phantasia* occurs only twice more in Book 2: once in the analysis of fear, once in that of shame (1383a17, 1384a23). When the noun does occur it is surrounded by occurrences of either *phainesthai* or other belief verbs; the definitions of anger, shame, pity, and spite all use forms of the verb.

18. Either it or its contrary (negated) occur at 85b14; 85b34–86a1; 86b7, 10, 12, 13. The judgment is repeated in the *Poetics: peri ton anaxion dustuchounta*, 1453a4, and *eleos men peri ton anaxion*, 1453a5. On the *Poetics'* treatment of these emotions, see Halliwell 1986, Nussbaum 1992.

19. See also 1378a20–23 where Aristotle defines passions as followed by pain and pleasure, as if the feeling were not even a proper part of the passion. The "followed" also gives some indication of the sufficient condition view: see subsequent discussion.

20. See the excellent treatment of these issues in Price 1989, chapter 4.

21. See Price 1989.

22. On Socrates on anger, see Vlastos 1991.

23. I leave to one side here the case of "self-love" (*philautia*), which is usually not treated as a case of genuine *philia*, and is given separate analysis.

24. See Vlastos 1991.

25. Thus Vlastos's 1991 claim that among Socrates' greatest achievements is to have transcended the morality of revenge needs some qualification: he transcends it, to be sure, but only by doing away, in the process, with the bases of love and pity as well. See Nussbaum 1991.

26. *NE* 1.11, especially 1101a9–14.

27. See Sherman 1989.

28. All this is analyzed extremely well, in much detail, in Sherman 1989.

29. For emotions as *aloga*, see for example *NE* 1102a28, 1102b29–34, 1111b1, 1168b20. Usually in such discussions the emotions are grouped together with appetitive desires. In *DA* 3.9, Aristotle is highly critical of the Platonic division of the soul into the *alogon* and the *logon echon*, which makes his uncritical use of it in the *Nicomachean Ethics* somewhat surprising.

REFERENCES

Aubenque, P. "La définition aristotélicienne de la colère." *Revue philosophique de France et de l'étranger* (1957): 300–317.

Caston, V. "Aristotle on Intentionality." Ph.D. diss., University of Texas at Austin, 1992.

Charles, D. *Aristotle's Philosophy of Action*. London, 1984.

Fillion-Lahille, J. "La colère chez Aristote." *Revue des etudes antiques* 72 (1970): 46–79.

Fortenbaugh, W. W. *Aristotle on Emotion*. London, 1975.

Halliwell, S. *Aristotle's Poetics*. Chapel Hill, 1986.

Leighton, S. R. "Aristotle and the Emotions." *Phronesis* 27 (1982): 144–174.

Nussbaum, M. *Aristotle's De Motu Animalium*. Princeton, 1978.

———. *The Fragility of Goodness: Luck and Ethics in Greek Tragedy and Philosophy*. Cambridge, 1986.

———. Review of Vlastos. *New Republic* (September 1991): 34–40.

———. "Tragedy and Self-Sufficiency: Plato and Aristotle on Fear and Pity." *Oxford Studies in Ancient Philosophy* 10 (1992): 107–159. A shorter version appears in *Essays on Aristotle's Poetics*, ed. A. O. Rorty (Princeton, 1992).

Price, A. W. *Love and Friendship in Plato and Aristotle.* Oxford, 1989.

Richardson, H. "Desire and the Good in *De Anima.*" In *Essays on Aristotle's De Anima,* ed. M. C. Nussbaum and A. O. Rorty. Oxford, 1992.

Sherman, N. *The Fabric of Character: Aristotle's Theory of Virtue.* Oxford, 1989.

Sorabji, R. "Aristotle on the Role of Intellect in Virtue." In *Essays on Aristotle's Ethics,* ed. A. O. Rorty. Berkeley, 1980.

————. *Man and Beast.* Ithaca, 1993.

Vlastos, G. *Socrates: Ironist and Moral Philosopher.* Cambridge, 1991.

Young, C. "Aristotle on Temperance." *Philosophical Review* 97 (1988): 521–542.

Between Rhetoric and Poetics

Paul Ricoeur

For Vianney Décarie and for Gérard Genette

RHETORIC AND POETICS

[Although our understanding of the art of rhetoric has its origins in Aristotle's analysis of the craft, we need to approach his account cautiously.] A simple examination of the table of contents of Aristotle's *Rhetoric* shows that we have received the theory of figures of speech from a discipline that is not merely defunct but amputated as well. For Aristotle, rhetoric covers three areas. A theory of argumentation (*inventio*, the 'invention' of arguments and proofs) constitutes the principal axis of rhetoric and at the same time provides the decisive link between rhetoric and demonstrative logic and therefore with philosophy (this theory of argumentation by itself takes up two-thirds of the treatise). Rhetoric also encompasses a theory of style (*elocutio*) and, finally, a theory of composition (*compositio*).

Compared to this, what the latest treatises on rhetoric offer us is a "restricted rhetoric,"[1] restricted first to a theory of style and then to the theory of tropes. The history of rhetoric is an ironic tale of diminishing returns. This is one of the causes of the death of rhetoric: in reducing itself thus to one of its parts, rhetoric simultaneously lost the nexus that bound it through dialectic to philosophy; and once this link was lost, rhetoric became an erratic and futile discipline. Rhetoric died when the penchant for classifying figures of speech completely supplanted the philosophical sensibility that animated the vast empire of rhetoric, held its parts together, and tied the whole to the *organon* and to first philosophy.

This sense of irremediable loss increases all the more if we remember that the broad Aristotelian program itself represented the rationalization (if not reduction) of a discipline that in Syracuse, its birthplace, endeavored to regulate all facets of public speech.[2] Because there was oratory [*éloquence*], public oratory, there was rhetoric. This remark implies a great deal. Originally, speech was a weapon, intended to influence people before the tribunal, in public assembly, or by eulogy and panegyric; a weapon called upon to gain victory in battles where the decision hung on the spoken word. Thus Nietzsche writes: "Oratory is republican." The old Sicilian definition "Rhetoric is the master of persuasion" (*peithous dēmiurgos*)[3] reminds us that rhetoric was added to natural eloquence as a "technique," but that this technique is rooted in a spontaneous creativity. Throughout all the didactic treatises written in Sicily, then in Greece after Gorgias established himself in Athens, rhetoric was this *technē* that made discourse conscious of itself and made persuasion a distinct goal to be achieved by means of a specific strategy.

Thus, before taxonomy of figures of speech, there was Aristotle's far more embracing rhetoric; but even before the latter, there was undisciplined common speech [*l'usage sauvage de la parole*] and the wish to harness its dangerous power by means of a special technique. Aristotle's rhetoric is already a domesticated discipline, solidly bound to philosophy by the theory of argumentation, from which rhetoric, in its decline, severed itself.

Greek rhetoric did not just have a singularly larger program than modern rhetoric; from its relation to philosophy, it derived all the ambiguities of its position. The properly dramatic character of rhetorical activity is explained well by the 'savage' roots of rhetoric. The Aristotelian corpus presents us with just one possible equilibrium between such extreme tensions, an equilibrium that corresponds to the situation of a discipline that is no longer simply a weapon in the public arena but is not yet a mere botany of figures of speech.

Rhetoric is without doubt as old as philosophy; it is said that Empedocles 'invented' it.[4] Thus, rhetoric is philosophy's oldest enemy and its oldest ally. "Its oldest enemy" because it is always possible for the art of 'saying it well' to lay aside all concern for 'speaking the truth.' The technique founded on knowledge of the factors that help to effect persuasion puts formidable power in the hands of anyone who masters it perfectly—the power to manipulate words apart from things, and to manipulate men by manipulating words. Perhaps we must recognize that the possibility of this split parallels the entire history of human discourse. Before becoming futile, rhetoric was dangerous. This is why Plato condemned it.[5] For him, rhetoric is to justice, the political virtue par excellence, what sophistry is to legislation; and these are, for the soul, what cooking in relation to medicine and cosmetics in relation to gymnastics are for the body—that is, arts of illusion and deception.[6] We must not lose sight of this condemnation of rhetoric, which sees it as belonging to the world of the lie, of the 'pseudo.' Metaphor will also have its enemies, who, giving it what one might call a 'cosmetic' as well as a 'culinary' interpretation, will look upon metaphor merely as simple decoration and as pure delectation. Every condemnation of metaphor as sophism shares in the condemnation of sophistry itself.

But philosophy was never in a position either to destroy rhetoric or to absorb it. Philosophy did not create the arenas—tribunal, political assembly, public contest—in which oratory holds sway, nor can philosophy undertake to suppress them. Philosophical discourse is itself just one discourse among others, and its claim to truth excludes it from the sphere of power. Thus, if it uses just the means that are properly its own, philosophy cannot break the ties between discourse and power.

One possibility remained open: to delimit the legitimate uses of forceful speech, to draw the line between use and abuse, and to establish philosophically the connections between the sphere of validity of rhetoric and that of philosophy. Aristotle's rhetoric constitutes the most brilliant of these attempts to institutionalize rhetoric from the point of view of philosophy.

The question that sets this project in motion is the following: what does it mean to persuade? What distinguishes persuasion from flattery, from seduction, from threat—that is to say, from the subtlest forms of violence? What does it mean, "to influence through discourse"? To pose these questions is to decide that one cannot transform the arts of discourse into techniques without submitting them to a radical philosophical reflection outlining the concept of "that which is persuasive" (*to phithanon*).[7]

A helpful solution was offered at this point by logic, one which, moreover, took up one of rhetoric's oldest intuitions. Since its beginnings, rhetoric had recognized in the term *to eikos*[8] (the probable) a title to which the public use of speech could lay claim. The kind of proof appropriate to oratory is not the necessary but the probable, because the human affairs over which tribunals and assemblies deliberate and decide are not subject to the sort of necessity, of intellectual constraint, that geometry and first philosophy demand. So, rather than denounce *doxa* (opinion) as inferior to *epistēmē* (science), philosophy can consider elaborating a theory of the probable, which would arm rhetoric against its characteristic abuses while separating it from sophistry and eristics. The great merit of Aristotle was in developing this link between the rhetorical concept of persuasion and the logical concept of the probable, and in constructing the whole edifice of a philosophy of rhetoric on this relationship.[9]

Thus, what we now read under the title of *Rhetoric* is the treatise containing the equilibrium between two opposed movements, one that inclines rhetoric to break away from philosophy, if not to replace it, and one that disposes philosophy to reinvent rhetoric as a system of second-order proofs. It is at this point, where the dangerous power of eloquence and the logic of probability meet, that we find a rhetoric that stands under the watchful eye of philosophy. It is this deep-seated conflict between reason and violence that the history of rhetoric has plunged into oblivion; emptied of its dynamism and drama, rhetoric is given over to playing with distinctions and classifications. The genius for taxonomy occupies the space deserted by the philosophy of rhetoric.

Hence, Greek rhetoric had not only a much broader program but also a problematic decidedly more dramatic than the modern theory of figures of speech. It did not, however, cover all the usages of speech. The technique of 'saying it well' remained a partial discipline, bounded not only from above by philosophy but laterally by other domains of discourse. One of the fields that remained outside rhetoric is poetics. This split between rhetoric and poetics is of particular interest to us, since for Aristotle metaphor belongs to both domains.

The duality of rhetoric and poetics reflects a duality in the use of speech as well as in the situations of speaking. We said that rhetoric originally was oratorical technique; its aim and that of oratory are identical, to know how to persuade. Now this function, however far-reaching, does not cover all the uses of speech. Poetics—the art of composing poems, principally tragic poems—as far as its function and its situation of speaking are concerned, does not depend on rhetoric, the art of defense, of deliberation, of blame, and of praise. Poetry is not oratory. Persuasion is not its aim; rather, it purges the feelings of pity and fear. Thus, poetry and oratory mark out two distinct universes of discourse. Metaphor, however, has a foot in each domain. With respect to structure, it can really consist in just one unique operation, the transfer of the meanings of words; but with respect to function, it follows the divergent destinies of oratory and tragedy. Metaphor will therefore have a unique structure but two functions: a rhetorical function and a poetic function.

This duality of function, which expresses the difference between the political world of eloquence and the poetic world of tragedy, represents a still more fundamental difference at the level of intention. This opposition has been concealed to a great extent for us, because rhetoric as we know it from the last modern treatises is amputated from its major part, the treatise on argumentation. Aristotle defines it as the art of inventing or finding proofs. Now poetry does not seek to prove anything at all: its project is mimetic; its aim (as will be elaborated later) is to compose an essential representation of human actions; its appropriate method is to speak the truth by means of fiction, fable, and tragic *muthos*. The triad of *poiēsis-mimēsis-katharsis*, which cannot possibly be confused with the triad *rhetoric-proof-persuasion*, characterizes the world of poetry in an exclusive manner.

Hence, it will be necessary to set the unique structure of metaphor first against the background of the mimetic arts, and then against that of the arts of persuasive proof. This duality of function and of intention is more radical than any distinction between poetry and prose; it constitutes the ultimate justification of this distinction.

THE INTERSECTION OF THE *POETICS* AND THE *RHETORIC:* 'EPIPHORA' OF THE NAME'

We will bracket provisionally the problems posed by the double insertion of metaphor in the *Poetics* and the *Rhetoric*. To do so is justified by the fact that the *Rhetoric*—whether it was composed or only revised after the *Poetics* was written[10]—adopts, pure and simple, the well-known definition of metaphor given in the *Poetics:*[11] "Metaphor consists in giving the thing a name that belongs to something else; the transference being either from genus to species, or from species to genus, or from species to species, or on grounds of analogy" (*Poet.* 1457b6–9).[12] Furthermore, in both works metaphor is placed under the same rubric of *lexis,* a word difficult to translate for reasons that will appear later;[13] for the present, I will say simply that the word has to do with the whole field of language expression. In fact, the difference between the two treatises turns on the poetic function of *lexis* on the one hand, and on its rhetorical function on the other, not on the position of metaphor among the elements of *lexis.* Thus, in each case *lexis* is the means by which metaphor is inserted, albeit in different ways, into the two treatises under consideration.

What is the nature of the link between metaphor and *lexis* in the *Poetics?* Aristotle begins by rejecting an analysis of *lexis* that would be organized according to 'modes of speech [*élocution*]' (*ta skhēmata tēs lexeōs*) and would link up with notions such as command, prayer, simple statement, threat, question, answer, and so on (1456b10). Hardly has this line of analysis been alluded to when it is interrupted by the remark: "Let us pass over this, then, as appertaining to another art, and not to that of poetry" (1456b19). This other 'art' can only be rhetoric. Then another analysis of *lexis* is introduced, one that no longer has to do with *skhēmata* but with *mērē* ('parts,' 'constituants') of diction: "Diction viewed as a whole is made up of the following parts: the Letter, . . . the Syllable, the Conjunction, the Article, the Noun, the Verb, the Case, and the Speech [*logos*]" (1456b20–21).

The difference between these two analyses is important for our purposes. The 'modes' of *élocution* are obviously facts of speech; in John Austin's terminology, these are the illocutionary forms of speech. On the other hand, the 'parts of diction' arise from a segmentation of discourse into units smaller than or as long as the sentence, divisions that today would arise from a properly linguistic analysis.

What is the result, for a theory of metaphor, of this change of level? Essentially, it is that the term common to the enumeration of parts of speech and to the definition of metaphor is the name or noun (*onoma*). Thus the destiny of metaphor is sealed for centuries to come: henceforth it is connected to poetry and rhetoric, not at the level of discourse, but at the level of a segment of discourse, the name or noun.

Let us turn now to the definition of metaphor cited above. I will draw particular attention to the following features:

The first characteristic is that metaphor is something that happens to the noun. As has been repeated since the introduction, in connecting metaphor to noun or word and not to discourse Aristotle establishes the orientation of the history of metaphor vis-à-vis poetics and rhetoric for several centuries. Aristotle's definition contains *in nuce* the theory of tropes, or figures of speech that focus on the word. Certainly, confining metaphor among word-focused figures of speech will give rise to an extreme refinement in taxonomy. It will, however, carry a high price: it becomes impossible to recognize a certain homogeneous functioning that (as Roman Jakobson will show) ignores the difference between word and discourse and operates at all the strategic levels of language—words, sentences, discourse, texts, styles.

The second characteristic is that metaphor is defined in terms of movement. The *epiphora* of a word is described as a sort of displacement, a movement "from . . . to . . ." This notion of *epiphora* enlightens at the same time as it puzzles us. It tells us that, far from designating just one figure of speech among others such as synecdoche and metonymy (this is how we find metaphor taxonomized in the later rhetoric), for Aristotle the word *metaphor* applies to every transposition of terms.[14] Indeed, its analysis paves the way for a global reflection concerning the figure as such. In the interests of a clearer glossary one might regret that the same term sometimes designates the genus (the phenomenon of transposition, that is, the figure as such) and sometimes a species (what later we will call the trope of resemblance). This equivocation is interesting in itself. Within it is hidden an interest distinct from the one that governs the taxonomies and culminates in the genus for classification, eventually becoming bogged down in the disaggregation of discourse. It is an interest in the transpositional movement as such, in processes more than in classes. We can formulate this interest as follows: what does it mean to transpose the meaning of words? This question could be set into the semantic interpretation proposed above. Indeed, to the extent that the notion of 'composite significant sound' simultaneously covers the domains of noun, of verb, and of locution (thus of the sentence), one could say that *epiphora* is a process that concerns the semantic kernel, not just of the noun and verb but of all meaningful linguistic entities, and that this process designates change of meaning as such. Let us keep in mind this extension of the theory of metaphor, supported by the homogeneous character of *epiphora,* beyond the limits imposed by the noun.

The counterpart of its indivisibility of meaning is the perplexity caused by *epiphora.* To explain metaphor, Aristotle creates a metaphor, one borrowed from the realm of movement; *phora,* as we know, is a kind of change, namely change with respect to location.[15] But we are anticipating the subsequent theory in saying that the word *metaphor* itself is metaphorical because it is borrowed from an order other than that of language. With the later theory we are supposing: (*a*) that metaphor is a borrowing; (*b*) that the borrowed meaning is opposed to the proper meaning, that is, to the meaning that 'really belongs' to a word by virtue of being its original meaning; (*c*) that one resorts to metaphor to fill a semantic void; and (*d*) that the borrowed word takes the place of the absent proper word where such exists. What follows will show that none of these diverse interpretations is implied by *epiphora* as it appears in Aristotle himself. At least, though, the vagueness of this metaphor about metaphor gives free scope to such interpretations. Any wish to avoid prejudging the theory of metaphor by calling metaphor an *epiphora* would be shattered quickly by the realization that it is impossible to talk about metaphor nonmetaphorically (in the sense implied by borrowing); in short, that the definition of metaphor returns on itself. Naturally, this warning applies to the subsequent pretension of rhetoric to the mastery and control of metaphor and of figures in general by means of classification—the word *figure* is itself obviously metaphorical. It takes in as well every philosophy that might wish to rid itself of metaphor in favor of nonmetaphorical concepts. There is no nonmetaphorical standpoint from which one could look upon metaphor, and all the other figures for that matter, as if they were a game played before one's eyes. In many respects, the continuation of this study will be a prolonged battle with this paradox.[16]

The third characteristic is that metaphor is the transposition of a name that Aristotle calls "alien" (*allotrios*), that is, "a name that belongs to something else" (1457b7), "the alien name" (1457b31). This term is opposed to 'ordinary,' 'current' (*kurion*), which is defined by Aristotle as "used by everybody," "in general use in a country" (1457b3). Metaphor accordingly is defined in terms of deviation (*para to kurion,* 1458a23; *para to eiōthos,* 1458b3); thus, as the enumeration quoted above indicates, the use of metaphor is close to the use of strange, ornamental, coined, lengthened, and shortened terms. In these characteristics of opposition or deviation and kinship are the seeds of important developments regarding rhetoric and metaphor:

(1) First, the choice of ordinary usage as point of reference foreshadows a general theory of 'deviations,' which becomes the criterion of stylistics for certain contemporary authors. This character of deviation is emphasized by other synonyms given by Aristotle for *allotrios:* "The perfection of Diction is for it to be at once clear and not mean. The clearest indeed is that made up of the ordinary words for things, but it is mean. . . . Diction becomes distinguished and non-prosaic by the use of unfamiliar terms [*xenikon*], i.e., strange words, metaphors, lengthened forms, and everything that deviates from the ordinary modes of speech [*para to kurion*]" (1458a18–23). In the same sense of deviation we have "escapes banality" (*exallatousa to idiōtikon*, 1458a21). Hence all the other usages (rare words, neologisms, and so on) that metaphor approximates are themselves also deviations in relation to ordinary usage.

(2) Besides the negative idea of deviation, the word *allotrios* implies a positive idea, that of a borrowing. Herein lies the specific difference between metaphor and all the other deviating usages. This particular meaning of *allotrios* derives not only from its opposition to *kurios* but also from its ties with *epiphora*. Thus, Ross translates, "Metaphor consists in giving the thing a name that belongs to something else" (1457b7). The displaced meaning comes from somewhere else; it is always possible to specify the metaphor's place of origin, or of borrowing.

(3) Must one say that ordinary usage has to be 'proper,' in the sense of primitive, original, native,[17] in order for there to be deviation and borrowing? It is but one step from the idea of ordinary usage to that of proper meaning, a step that leads to the eventually customary opposition between figurative and proper. Later rhetoric takes this step, but there is no evidence that Aristotle took it.[18] That a name belongs properly, that is to say essentially, to an idea is not implied necessarily by the idea of current meaning; this is perfectly compatible with a conventionalism like that of Nelson Goodman, which we will talk about in due course. The synonymy (referred to above) of "current" (*kurion*) and "usual" (*to eiōthos*), as also the proximity between "clarity" and "ordinary words" (1458a19), preserves the possibility of disconnecting the notion of ordinary usage from that of proper meaning.

(4) Another, contingent development of the notion of "alien" usage is represented by the idea of substitution. We will see later that an interaction theory is readily contrasted with the substitution theory by English-language authors. Now, the fact that the metaphorical term is borrowed from an alien domain does not imply that it substitutes for an ordinary word that one could have found in the same place. Nevertheless, it seems that Aristotle himself was confused on this point and thus provided grounds for the modern critiques of the rhetorical theory of metaphor.

The metaphorical word takes the place of a nonmetaphorical word that one could have used (on condition that it exists); so it is doubly alien, as a present but borrowed word and as substitute for an absent word. Although distinct, these two significations appear in constant association in rhetorical theory and in Aristotle himself. Thus, examples of the displacement of meaning quite often are treated as examples of substitution: Homer says of Ulysses that he performed "'ten thousand good deeds' . . . *in place of [anti]* . . . 'a large number'" (1457b12; emphasis added); similarly, if the cup is to Dionysus what the shield is to Ares, one could use the fourth term 'in place of' (*anti*) the second, and vice versa (1457b18). Does Aristotle mean that the presence of a borrowed metaphorical word is always linked to substitution for an absent, nonmetaphorical word? If so, the deviation involved would always be one of substitution, and metaphor would dwell under the sign of poetic license.[19]

Thus, the idea of substitution appears to be bound up firmly with that of borrowing; but the former does not proceed from the latter by necessity, since it admits of exceptions. On one occasion Aristotle cites the case in which no current word exists that could substitute for the metaphorical word. So, for example, the expression "sowing around a god-created flame" is analyzed according to the rules of metaphor of proportion (*B* is to *A* what *D* is to *C*)—the action of the sun is to its light what sowing is to grain (1457b25–30). But there is no name for the *B* term, at least in Greek. In this manner Aristotle points to one of metaphor's functions, which is to fill a semantic lacuna. This function supplements that of ornamentation in the later tradition. So, if Aristotle does not dwell on this point,[20] it is because he is interested here only in the analogy itself, and the absence of a word for one of the terms of the analogy, which could be supposed to jeopardize the analogy, he finds in fact does not prevent the analogy from functioning: "It may be that some of the terms thus related have no special name of their own, but for all that they will be metaphorically described in just the same way" (1457b25–26). Nevertheless, we can keep this exception in mind in anticipation of a modern critique of the idea of substitution.

In conclusion, the Aristotelian idea of *allotrios* tends to assimilate three distinct ideas: the idea of a deviation from ordinary usage; the idea of borrowing from an original domain; and the idea of substitution for an absent but available ordinary word. By contrast, the opposition between figurative and proper meaning, omnipresent in the later tradition, is not implied here. It is the idea of substitution that appears to bear the greatest consequences: for if the metaphorical term is really a substituted term, it carries no new information, since the absent term (if one exists) can be brought back in; and if there is no information conveyed, then metaphor has only an ornamental, decorative value. These two consequences of a purely substitutive theory characterize the treatment of metaphor in classical rhetoric. Rejection of these consequences will follow rejection of the concept of substitution; and this is itself tied up with a rejection of displacement or movement of names.

The fourth feature of this definition of metaphor is this: at the same time as the idea of *epiphora,* preserving the unity of metaphor's meaning, counterbalances the classificatory tendency that predominates in the later taxonomies, a typology of metaphor is outlined in the continuation of the definition. We are told that the transfer goes from genus to species, from species to genus, from species to species, or is made by analogy (or proportion). The outcome in subsequent rhetoric of the dismembering and counting out of the domain of *epiphora* as sketched here is that metaphor becomes nothing more than a figure related to the fourth type in Aristotle's list. It alone refers explicitly to resemblance—the fourth term in analogy is related to the third in the same way (*omoiōs ekhei,* 1457b20) as the second is related to the first; old age is related to life as evening is related to the day. We will reserve for later the question whether the idea of an identity or a similarity between the relationships exhausts the idea of resemblance, and whether the transfer from genus to species, etc., is not also grounded on resemblance. What interests us now is the relationship between this embryonic classification and the concept of transposition, which constitutes the unity of meaning of the genus "metaphor."

Two facts should be noted. First, transposition operates between logical poles. Metaphor occurs in an order already constituted in terms of genus and species, and in a game whose relation rules—subordination, coordination, proportionality or equality of relationships—are already given. Second, metaphor consists in a violation of this order and this game. In giving to a genus the name of a species, to the fourth term of the proportional relationship the name of the second term, and vice versa, one simultaneously recognizes and transgresses the logical structure of language (1457b12–20). The *anti,* discussed earlier, applies not just to the substitution of one word for another, but also to the jumbling of classification in cases that do not have to do only with making up for lexical poverty. Aristotle himself did not exploit this idea of a categorical transgression, which some modern authors compare to Gilbert Ryle's concept of 'category mistake.'[21] Doubtless this was because he was more interested, within the perspective of his *Poetics,* in the semantic gain attached to the transference of names than in the logical cost of the operation. The reverse side of the process, however, is at least as interesting to describe as the obverse. If pursued, the idea of categorical transgression holds not a few surprises in store.

I propose three interpretative hypotheses. First, in all metaphor one might consider not only the word alone or the name alone, whose meaning is displaced, but the pair of terms or relationships between which the transposition operates—from genus to species, from species to genus, from species to species, from the second to the fourth term (and vice versa) of a proportional relationship. This has far-reaching implications. As the English-language authors put it, it always takes two ideas to make a metaphor. If metaphor always involves a kind of mistake, if it involves taking one thing for another by a sort of calculated error, then metaphor is essentially a discursive phenomenon. To affect just one word, the metaphor has to disturb a whole network by means of an aberrant attribution. At the same time, the idea of categorical transgression allows us to fill out that of deviation, which seemed to be implied in the transposition process. "Deviation" appeared to belong to a purely lexical order, but now it is linked to a kind of deviance that threatens classification itself. What remains to be puzzled out is the relationship between the two sides of the phenomenon, between logical deviation and the production of meaning that Aristotle calls *epiphora*. This problem will be solved in a satisfactory manner only when the statement character of metaphor is fully recognized. The name-related aspects of metaphor can then become fully attached to a discursive structure. As we shall see later, Aristotle himself invites us to take this path when, in the *Rhetoric*, he takes up the obviously discursive metaphor of comparison (*eikōn*), or simile.

A second line of reflection seems to be suggested by the idea of categorical transgression, understood as a deviation in relation to a preexisting logical order, as a disordering in a scheme of classification. This transgression is interesting only because it creates meaning; as it is put in the *Rhetoric*, metaphor "conveys learning and knowledge through the medium of the *genus*" (1410b13). What is being suggested, then, is this: should we not say that metaphor destroys an order only to invent a new one; and that the category mistake is nothing but the complement of a logic of discovery? Max Black's integration of model and metaphor,[22] in other words of an epistemological concept and a poetic concept, allows us to exploit thoroughly this idea, which is completely opposed to any reduction of metaphor to a mere 'ornament.' Pushing this thought to the limit, one must say that metaphor bears information because it 'redescribes' reality. Thus, the category mistake is the deconstructive intermediary phase between description and redescription. However, this cannot be brought to light without prior recognition not only of the statement character of metaphor but also of its place within the orders of discourse and of the work.

A third, more venturesome hypothesis arises on the fringe of the second. If metaphor belongs to a heuristic of thought, could we not imagine that the process that disturbs and displaces a certain logical order, a certain conceptual hierarchy, a certain classification scheme, is the same as that from which all classification proceeds? Certainly, the only functioning of language we are aware of operates within an already constituted order; metaphor does not produce a new order except by creating rifts in an old order. Nevertheless, could we not imagine that the order itself is born in the same way that it changes? Is there not, in Hans-Georg Gadamer's terms,[23] a "metaphoric" at work at the origin of logical thought, at the root of all classification? This is a more far-reaching hypothesis than the others, which presuppose an already constituted language within which metaphor operates. Not only is the notion of deviation linked to this presupposition, but also the opposition between 'ordinary' language and 'strange' or 'rare' language, which Aristotle himself introduced, as well as, most definitely, the opposition introduced later between 'proper' and 'figurative.' The idea of an initial metaphorical impulse destroys these oppositions between proper and figurative, ordinary and strange, order and transgression. It suggests the idea that order itself proceeds from the metaphorical constitution of semantic fields, which themselves give rise to genus and species.

Does this hypothesis go beyond the boundaries of Aristotle's analysis? Yes, if one focuses on the explicit definition of metaphor as the *epiphora* of the name and if one's criterion of *epiphora* is the obvious opposition between ordinary usage and unusual usage. No, if one takes into account all that appears in Aristotle's own analysis outside of this explicit definition and this explicit criterion. One of Aristotle's observations (held in reserve until now) seems to justify the boldness of this rather extreme hypothesis: "It is a great thing, indeed, to make a proper use of the poetical forms, as also of compounds and strange words. But the greatest thing by far is to be a master of metaphor [literally: to be metaphorical, *to metaphorikon einai*]. It is the one thing that cannot be learnt from others; and it is also a sign of genius [*euphuias*], since a good metaphor [literally: to metaphorize well, *eu metapherein*] implies an intuitive perception of the similarity [*to to homoion theōrein*] in dissimilars" (*Poet.* 1459a3–8; see also *Rhet.* 1412a10).

Several things are notable in this text. (*a*) Metaphor becomes a verb, "metaphorize"; this brings to light the problem of usage (*khrēsthai*, 1459a5)—process prevails over result. (*b*) Next, the problem of use brings up that of 'appropriate use' (*prepontōs khrēsthai*). It is a question of "metaphorizing well," of "using in an appropriate way" the processes of *lexis*. The same strokes depict the user of this usage: he is the one called to this "greatest thing," to "be metaphorical"; he alone, unaided, can learn it or not learn it. (*c*) For—and this is precisely the point—to metaphorize well cannot be taught; it is a gift of genius, of nature (*euphuias to sēmeiōn estin*).

Are we not now back at the level of finding or inventing, of that heuristic that we said violates an order only to create another, that dismantles only to redescribe? All of modern creativity theory confirms that there are no rules for invention, no recipes for the concoction of good hypotheses, only rules for the validation of hypotheses.[24] (*d*) But still why can we not learn to 'be metaphorical.' Because to 'metaphorize well' is to 'see resemblance.' This phrasing may seem surprising. Up to this point resemblance has not been mentioned, except indirectly through the particular nature of the fourth sort of metaphor, that by analogy, which, as we have seen, is analyzed as an identity or similarity of two relations. But are we not forced to suppose resemblance at work in all four kinds of metaphor, as the positive principle of which "categorical transgression" is the negative side? Is it not necessary that genus and species be brought together in terms of similarity, for the name of either to be given to the other? Metaphor—or, better, to metaphorize, that is, the dynamic of metaphor—would rest, therefore, on the perception of resemblance. This brings us very close to our most extreme hypothesis, that the "metaphoric" that transgresses the categorical order also begets it. But that the finding or discovering peculiar to this fundamental metaphoric is that of resemblance calls for its own particular proof, which cannot be presented until much later.

AN ENIGMA: METAPHOR AND SIMILE (*EIKŌN*)

The *Rhetoric* presents an enigma of minor proportions. The *Poetics* contains nothing about simile or comparison; why then does *Rhetoric* 3.4 introduce a parallel between metaphor and comparison (*eikōn*),[25] when it claims to add nothing to the definition of metaphor given in the *Poetics*? This is a minor problem if one is dealing only with purely historical questions of priority and dependence within the Aristotelian corpus. On the other hand, it is extremely instructive for a study like this one, which is at pains to assemble all indications of an interpretation of metaphor in terms of discourse as against its explicit definition in terms of names and naming. Indeed, the essential feature of comparison is its discursive character. "Achilles sprang up like a lion." To make a comparison, one needs two terms that are both equally present in the discourse—"like a lion" is not a comparison by itself. Let us say (anticipating the terminology of I. A. Richards) that one needs a tenor (Achilles springs up) and a vehicle (like a lion).[26] We can discern the implicit presence of this discursive moment in the notion of *epiphora* (the transposition from one pole to another). It is as present in the categorical transference (giving the name of a species to the genus, etc.) as in the transfer by analogy (replacing the fourth term of a proportion with the second). The modern authors who say that to make a metaphor is to see two things in one are faithful to this feature, which simile brings to light and which the definition of metaphor as *epiphora* of the name could conceal. While it is true in a formal sense that metaphor is a deviation in relation to the ordinary use of words, from the dynamic point of view it proceeds from the encounter between the thing to be named and that foreign entity from which the name is borrowed. Simile makes explicit this mutual approach that underlies borrowing and deviation.

It may be objected that Aristotle's express purpose here is not to explain metaphor by means of simile, but simile by metaphor. And, true enough, in six spots Aristotle subordinates simile to metaphor.[27] The fact that later rhetorical tradition does not follow Aristotle here makes this point all the more remarkable.[28]

Several converging lines of argument serve to subordinate simile to metaphor. First, the realm of phenomena that come under simile is split up. One part, called *parabolē*, is connected to the theory of "proof," to which Book 1 of the *Rhetoric* is devoted. This consists in illustration through example, which can be historical or fictitious.[29] The other part, under the title *eikōn*, is attached to the theory of *lexis* and falls into the special domain of metaphor.

Let us further note that it is the special kinship between simile and the proportional metaphor that guarantees its place within the field of metaphor: "Successful similes also, as has been said above, are in a sense metaphors, since they always involve two relations [literally: they are said or made on the basis of two] like the proportional metaphor. Thus: a shield, we say, is the 'drinking-bowl of Ares,' and a bow is the 'chordless lyre'" (1412b34–1413a2). Indeed, the proportional metaphor comes to give the name of the second term to the fourth by elision from the complex comparison that holds not between the things themselves but between the relations of the two pairs of things. In this sense, the proportional metaphor is not as simple as might appear when, for example, we call Achilles a lion. Therefore, the simplicity of simile, when contrasted with a proportion between four terms, is not the simplicity of a word but that of a relation between two terms[30]—that very relation, in fact, that proportional metaphor results in: "The shield is the drinking-bowl of Ares." In this manner, the metaphor by analogy tends to become identified with the *eikōn;* so the supremacy of metaphor over the *eikōn*, if not reversed, is in any case 'modified' (ibid.). But it is because *eikōn* "always involves two relations"[31]—like metaphor by analogy—that the relation can be inverted so easily.

Lastly, the grammatical analysis of simile confirms its dependent status with regard to metaphor in general. They differ only by the presence or absence of a specific term of comparison: the particle like or as (*hōs*) in all the quotations in *Rhetoric* 3.4; in the example from Homer (whom Aristotle misquotes, incidentally), the verb (he compares) or adjective (similar) of comparison, and so on.[32] In Aristotle's eyes, the absence of some term of comparison in metaphor does not imply that metaphor is an abbreviated simile, as was claimed from Quintilian onward. Rather, simile is a metaphor developed further; the simile says "this is like that," whereas the metaphor says "this is that." Hence, to the extent that simile is a developed metaphor, all metaphor, not just proportional metaphor, is implicit comparison or simile.

Accordingly, the explicit subordination of simile to metaphor is possible only because the metaphor presents the polarity of the terms compared in an abridged form. "When the poet says of Achilles that he 'Leapt on the foe as a lion,' this is a simile; when he says of him 'the lion leapt,' it is a metaphor—here, since both are courageous, [Homer] has transferred to Achilles the name of 'lion'" (1406b20–23). Perhaps the best way to put it is that the element common to metaphor and simile is the assimilation that serves as foundation for the transfer of names. In other words, it is the apprehension of an identity within the difference between two terms. This apprehension of the genus by means of resemblance makes metaphor truly instructive: "When the poet calls old age 'a withered stalk,' he conveys a new idea [literally: he has produced a knowledge, *epoiēse mathēsin kai gnōsin*], a new fact, to us by means of the general notion [*dia tou genous*] of 'lost bloom' . . ." (1410b13–15). And herein lies metaphor's superiority over simile, that it is more elegant (*asteia*) (we will return later to metaphor's "virtue" of urbanity, of brilliance): "The simile, as has been said before, is a metaphor, differing from it only in the way it is put [*prothesei*]; and just because it is longer, it is less attractive. Besides, it does not say outright that this is that, and therefore the hearer is less interested [*dzetei*] in the idea. We see, then, that both speech and reasoning are lively in proportion as they make us seize a new idea promptly" (1410b17–21). Thus the chance to instruct and to provoke inquiry, contained in the abrupt subject-predicate confrontation, is lost by a too explicit comparison, which somehow dissipates that dynamism of comparison by including the comparative term. Beardsley's controversion theory[33] epitomizes the modern attempt to take the fullest possible advantage of this idea of semantic collision. And Aristotle saw that, underlying the *epiphora* of the alien name, a strange attribution operates: "this is that"—an attribution whose grounds simile makes clear only by displaying them in deliberate comparison.

Herein lies the interest of the confrontation between metaphor and simile. At the very moment that Aristotle subordinates simile to metaphor, he sees within metaphor this paradoxical attribution. In the same vein, consider a suggestion made in passing in the *Poetics* and then abandoned: "But a whole statement in such terms [deviations from ordinary modes of speech] will be either a riddle or a barbarism, a riddle, if made up of metaphors, a barbarism, if made up of strange words. The very nature indeed of a riddle is this, to describe a fact in an impossible combination of words (which cannot be done with the real names for things, but can be with their metaphorical substitutes)" (*Poet.* 1458a23–33). On the whole, then, this text tends to dissociate metaphor and enigma. But the problem would not even arise if they did not have a common feature, the common constitution that the *Rhetoric* always emphasizes under the heading of the "virtue" of elegance, brilliance, urbanity: "Liveliness is especially conveyed by metaphor, and by the further power of surprising the hearer; because the hearer expected something different, his acquisition of the new idea impresses him all the more. . . . Well-constructed riddles are attractive for the same reason; a new idea is conveyed, and there is metaphorical expression" (1412a18–24). We note once more the instructive and informative functions linked to a bringing together of terms that first surprises, then bewilders, and finally uncovers a relationship hidden beneath the paradox. But is not the proximity between enigma and metaphor founded completely on the odd name-giving, "this (is) that," that simile develops and depletes at the same time but that metaphor preserves by the brevity of its expression?[34] Deviation in the use of names proceeds from deviation in attribution itself—from what the Greeks call *para-doxa*, that is, a divergence from preexisting *doxa* (1412a26).[35] All this is a very clear lesson for the theoretician, but it remains an enigma to the historian.[36]

In conclusion, this close juxtaposition of metaphor and simile allows the question of *epiphora* to be taken up again. First, as simile, the transfer takes place between two terms; it is a fact of discourse before being a fact of name-giving. One could say of *epiphora*, too, that it is something involving two things or terms. Furthermore, the transfer rests on a perceived resemblance that simile makes explicit by means of its characteristic terms of comparison. The closeness of metaphor to simile brings to language the relationship that operates in metaphor without being articulated, and confirms that the inspired art of metaphor always consists in the apprehension of resemblances. We shall say that simile explicitly displays the moment of resemblance that operates implicitly in metaphor. The poet, as we read in the *Poetics*, is one who 'perceives similarity' (1459a8). "In philosophy also," adds the *Rhetoric*, "an acute mind will perceive resemblances in things far apart. Thus Archytas said that an arbitrator and an altar were the same, since the injured fly to both for refuge. Or you might say that an anchor and an overhead hook were the same, since both are in a way the same, only the one secures things from below and the other from above" (1412a10–15). To apprehend or perceive, to contemplate, to see similarity—such is metaphor's genius stroke, which marks the poet, naturally enough, but also the philosopher. And this is what remains to be discussed in a theory of metaphor that will conjoin poetics and ontology.

THE PLACE OF *LEXIS* IN RHETORIC

The definition of metaphor common to the *Poetics* and the *Rhetoric* and the very important variant introduced by the latter work have been established. The principal remaining task is to appreciate the difference in function that results from the different ways in which *lexis* is inserted in the *Rhetoric* and in the *Poetics*.

We begin with the *Rhetoric*, whose place in the Aristotelian corpus is easier to determine. As was noted at the beginning of this study, Greek rhetoric had an impressively larger scope and a conspicuously more articulated internal organization than rhetoric in its dying days. As the art of persuasion, the aim of which was the mastery of public speech, rhetoric covered the three fields of argumentation, composition, and style. The reduction of all of these to the third part, and of that to a simple taxonomy of figures of speech, doubtless explains why rhetoric lost its link to logic and to philosophy itself, and why it became the erratic and futile discipline that died during the last century. With Aristotle we see rhetoric in its better days; it constitutes a distinct sphere of philosophy, in that the order of the "persuasive" as such remains the object of a specific *technē*. Yet it is solidly bound to logic through the correlation between the concept of persuasion and that of the probable. In this way a philosophical rhetoric—that is, a rhetoric grounded in and watched over by philosophy itself—is constituted. Our subsequent task will be to display the intermediary links between the rhetorical theory of metaphor and such an enterprise.

Rhetoric's status as a distinct *technē* poses no great difficulties. Aristotle was careful to define what he calls *technē* in a classical text of his *Nicomachean Ethics*.[37] There are as many *technai* as there are creative activities. A *technē* is something more refined than a routine or an empirical practice and in spite of its focus on production, it contains a speculative element, namely a theoretical inquiry into the means applied to production. It is a method; and this feature brings it closer to theoretical knowledge than to routine. Now, is not such a project the ultimate stage of the technicization of discourse? Without doubt this is so; however, in Aristotle, the autonomy of *technē* is less important than its linkage with other disciplines of discourse, especially that of proof.

This linkage is assured by the connection between rhetoric and dialectic. With undeniable genius, Aristotle makes a statement right at the beginning of his work that keeps rhetoric under the sway of logic and, through logic, of philosophy as a whole: "Rhetoric is the counterpart [*antistrophos*] of Dialectic" (1354a1). Dialectic here refers to the general theory of argumentation as regards that which is probable.[38] So we now have the problem of rhetoric posed in terms of logic. Aristotle, we know, is proud to have invented that demonstrative argument or proof called the "syllogism." Now, to this corresponds the probable argument in dialectic called "enthymeme." Rhetoric is thus a technique of proof: "Only proofs have this character of technique" (1354a12). And because enthymemes are "the substance of rhetorical persuasion" (ibid.), rhetoric as a whole must be centered on the persuasive power attached to this kind of proof. A rhetoric dealing only with those methods likely to sway the judge's passions would not really be a rhetoric at all: "About the orator's proper modes of persuasion they have nothing to tell us; nothing, that is, about how to gain skill in enthymemes"; and a bit further, "Rhetorical study [*technē*] is concerned with the modes of persuasion. Persuasion is clearly a sort of demonstration. . . . The orator's demonstration is an enthymeme. . . . The enthymeme is a sort of syllogism" (1354b21–22, 1355a4–8).

This does not mean that there is no distinction between rhetoric and dialectic. Certainly rhetoric resembles dialectic in a number of ways: it deals with 'popular truths,' the accepted opinions of the majority of people;[39] it does not require special training, since anyone can discuss an argument, accuse another, and defend himself (*Rhet.* 1.1.1354a1–11). But in other ways they are different. First, rhetoric comes into play in concrete situations—the deliberations of a political assembly, judgment by a tribunal, public orations that praise and censure. These three sorts of situations that discourse takes place in define the three genres of rhetoric—deliberative, judicial, and epideictic. Whereas ancient rhetoric before Aristotle concentrated on the second (there the ways to influence a judge stand out), a rhetoric based on the art of argumentative proof will pay attention to all situations in which it is necessary to arrive at a judgment (*krisis, Rhet.* 1.1.12). This leads to a second point of divergence: such an art has to do with judgments regarding individual situations.

In addition, rhetoric cannot become absorbed in a purely 'argumentative' or logical discipline, because it is directed to 'the hearer' (1404a4). It cannot avoid taking into account the speaker's character and the mood of his audience. In short, rhetoric is a phenomenon of the intersubjective and dialogical dimension of the public use of speech. As a result, the consideration of emotions, of passions, of habits, and of beliefs is still within the competence of rhetoric, even if it must not infringe upon the priority of argument based on probability. So an argument that can properly be called rhetorical takes into account both the degree to which the matter under discussion seems to be true and the persuasive effectiveness it has, which depends on the quality of the speaker and listener.

This feature brings us to a final point. Rhetoric cannot become an empty and formal technique, because it is linked to what is contained in the most highly probable opinions, that is, what is admitted or endorsed by the majority of people. Now with this connection between rhetoric and noncritical subject matter goes the risk of turning rhetoric into a sort of popular science. This collusion with accepted ideas throws rhetoric into a scattered and dissipating pursuit of argument motifs or 'positions,' which amount to so many recipes to protect the speaker from being taken by surprise in debate[40]—a collusion, then, between *Rhetoric* and *Topics*, which was doubtless one of the causes of the former's death. Perhaps rhetoric finally died of an excess of formalism in the nineteenth century; paraodoxically, however, it was already doomed by its overburdening content—witness Book 2 of the *Rhetoric*, which abounds in what Kant would have called 'popular' psychology, 'popular' morality, 'popular' politics. This tendency of rhetoric to identify with a subscience of man poses a formidable question that could reflect back on rhetoric itself: does not the solidarity between rhetoric and topics, and beyond this, between rhetoric and a subscience of man, imply that the inclination to speak in parables, comparisons, proverbs, and metaphors arises from this same complex of rhetoric and the commonplace? We must keep this question in mind. But before heralding the death of rhetoric, this alliance at least assures it a cultural content. Rhetoric does not develop in some empty space of pure thought, but in the give and take of common opinion. So metaphors and proverbs also draw from the storehouse of popular wisdom—at least, those of them that are 'established.' This qualification is important, because it is this topology of discourse that gives the rhetorical treatment of *lexis* and metaphor a background and an aftertaste different from those of the *Poetics*.

All these distinctive features are reflected in the Aristotelian definition of rhetoric—"the faculty of observing in any given case the available means of persuasion" (1355b25, 1356a19–20). It is a theoretical discipline, but without determinate theme. Its measure is the (neutral) criterion of *pithanon*, of "the persuasive as such." This adjective transformed into a noun remains faithful to the primordial intention of rhetoric, namely persuasion, but it expresses rhetoric's movement toward a technique of arguments or proof. In this regard the relationship (lost in French and English) between *pithanon* and *pisteis* is very instructive. In Greek, *pisteis* (in the plural, i.e., 'proofs') marks the priority of objective argument over the intersubjective aims of the project of persuasion. And yet the initial notion of persuasion is not abolished; it is merely set aright. In particular, the orientation of argument to a listener—evidence that all discourse is addressed to someone—and its adherence to contents defined by the *Topics,* keep "the persuasive as such" from turning into a logic of probability. Thus, rhetoric will remain at most the *antistrophos* (counterpart) of dialectic, but will not dissolve into it.

It is now possible to sketch a truly rhetorical theory of *lexis,* and consequently of metaphor, since metaphor is one of its elements.

Let us note right away that the rhetorical and poetic functions of metaphor do not coincide: "The language [*lexis*] of prose is distinct from that of poetry" (1404a28).[41] Unfortunately, notes Aristotle, the theory of *lexis* is further ahead in poetry than in the field of public discourse.[42] He has to close the gap, if not fill a void. The task is not easy. We noted earlier that argumentation, style, and composition are the three parts of rhetoric. But since rhetoric really cannot be identified at all with the theory of style, which is just one of its parts, we might ask ourselves whether rhetoric does not have a privileged relationship with the 'discovery' (*eurēsis*) of arguments by the orator; that is, with the first part (of rhetoric). Was it not claimed that everything that does not concern proof is 'merely accessory' (1354a14, 1354b17)? And does not Book 3 confirm this privileged position in saying that "we ought in fairness to fight our case with no help beyond the bare facts: nothing, therefore, should matter except the proof of those facts" (1404a4–6)? So, it seems, it is only because of the 'defects of our hearers' that we need to linger over these external considerations (1404a8).

No one denies that the link is weak between *lexis* and the rest of the treatise, which is centered on argumentation. Nevertheless, we must not turn what is possibly just an accident in the composition of the treatise into an absence of logical connection between *pisteis* and *lexis.* "For it is not enough," says Aristotle, "to know *what* we ought to say; we must also say it *as* we ought; much help is thus afforded towards producing the right impression of a speech" (1403b15–18). It is the link between the way discourse appears and discourse itself that we must examine here, for in it germinates the future course of the idea of figure of speech. The "how" of discourse is distinct from the "what." Taking the same distinction up again later, Aristotle opposes "how . . . these facts [are] set out in language" to "the facts themselves" (*ta pragmata*) (1403b18–20). Now this 'appearance' is not external to discourse in the same way as is simple 'delivery' (*hupokrisis,* 1403b21–35), which has to do only with the way the voice is used, as in tragic plays (in the same way the *Poetics* distinguishes *lexis* from mere staging). Rather, one must search in the area of an 'appearance' more intimately connected to the dynamics of persuasion and to argument, which was said to be 'the stuff of proof.' In this case, *lexis* would rather be one kind of manifestation of thinking, linked to any kind of instruction (*didaskalia*): "The way in which a thing is said does affect its intelligibility [*pros to dēlōsai*]" (1404a9–10). When the proof itself is the only thing of importance, we do not bother about *lexis*; but as soon as the relationship to our hearer comes to the foreground, it is through our *lexis* that we teach.

So the theory of *lexis* seems bound to the thematic mainstream of the *Rhetoric* quite loosely, although not in as loose a manner as to that of the *Poetics*, which, as we shall see later, sums it up neatly as one 'part of the tragedy'; that is, of the poem. Now one might hypothesize that in poetry, the form or 'figure' and the meaning of a message are integrated to form a unity similar to that of a sculpture. But in oratorical delivery, the manner in which something is said retains an extrinsic and variable character. One might even venture to say that eloquence, or the public use of speech, involves precisely this tendency to dissociate style from proof. By the same token, the lack of consistency in the link between a treatise on argumentation and a treatise on style reveals something of the instability of rhetoric itself, torn apart by the internal contradiction within the very project of persuasion. Set between two limits exterior to it—logic and violence—rhetoric oscillates between its two constitutive poles—proof and persuasion. When persuasion frees itself from the concern for proof, it is carried away by the desire to seduce and to please; and style itself ceases to be the 'face [*figure*]' that expresses and reveals the body, and becomes an ornament, in the "cosmetic" sense the word. But this possibility was written into the origins of the rhetorical project, and moved within the very heart of Aristotle's treatise. To the degree that style is the external manifestation of discourse, it tends to separate the concern to 'please' from that of 'arguing.' It is doubtless because writing constitutes a second degree of exteriorization that the separation is particularly dangerous in this case: "Speeches of the written or literary kind owe more of their effect to their diction [*lexis*] than to their thought" (1404a18–19).

What, now, is the present status of the properly rhetorical features of metaphor? Do they throw any light on this manifestational function of *lexis*? Reversing the question, does *lexis* reflect in any way the internal contradictions of public speech?

Since rhetoric remains the art of 'saying things well,' its special features are those of good usage and are related to those of public discourse in general, and these last constitute what Aristotle calls the 'virtues' (the merits or 'excellences') of *lexis*. They guide what one might call the strategy of persuasion in public discourse. This idea of 'virtues of *lexis*' is so important that it provides the guiding thread for the analysis in Book 3 of the *Rhetoric*. Among these virtues, those that concern metaphor most directly are 'clarity' (3.2), 'warmth' (opposed to 'coldness,' 3.3), 'facility' (3.6), 'appropriateness' (3.7), and, above all, 'urbanity or elegance' (3.10).[43]

Clarity is obviously a touchstone for the use of metaphor. The expression that 'points out' (*dēloi*) something is clear. Now, it is the use of words in their ordinary fashion (*ta kuria*) that makes for clarity of style. In deviating[44] from ordinary usage, metaphor, together with all the other unusual expressions, also abandons clarity and makes 'the language appear more stately' (1404b9). In the eyes of ordinary citizens, it is as if they were confronted with a foreign (*xenen*) language (1404b10), for these variations and turns in language give discourse an out-of-the-ordinary air: "People like what strikes them, and are struck by what is out of the way" (1404b12). Actually, these remarks are more appropriate to poetry than to prose, where nobility and dignity befit only the more extraordinary subjects and personalities: "In prose passages they [effects that give an unfamiliar air] are far less often fitting because the subject matter is less exalted" (1404b14–15). Therefore, the ways in which poetic and rhetorical language operate are the same, but the latter is more subdued. Keeping this caveat in mind, one can say that "the chief merit of rhetorical discourse" is to give discourse an "unfamiliar" air, while not doing so in an obvious manner. Thus, rhetorical style combines clarity, embellishment, and the unusual, all in due proportion.

The interplay between distance and close kinship, to which I alluded earlier in connection with relationships of type in metaphorical transposition, contributes to this air of the 'unusual,' which finds itself set against the demand for clarity. It also gives rise to the enigmatic character of good metaphors (1405b3–5).[45]

The second quality or 'virtue' is treated negatively.[46] *Rhetoric* 3.3 deals with stylistic 'rigidity.' Among its causes it notes the inappropriate, even ludicrous, use of poetic metaphors in prose—style too grandiose or tragic, metaphors too far-fetched and thus obscure (as when Gorgias talks of "events that are green and full of sap") (1406b9–10). Prose must not be 'too much like poetry' (ibid.). What, then, shall be our criterion? Aristotle does not hesitate: "All these expressions fail . . . to carry the hearer with them" (*apithana*) (1406b14).[47]

The quality of 'appropriateness' (3.7) is another occasion for underlining the difference between prose and poetry. It is significant that this characteristic of the 'appropriateness' of style to its subject matter is called "proportion" (*to analagon*) by Aristotle. That which is appropriate for prose is not appropriate for poetry, because "poetry . . . is an inspired thing [*entheon*]" (1408b18).

But the most interesting remarks on the rhetorical use of metaphor are occasioned by reflections on the elegance and liveliness of expression (literally: urbane style, *asteion*, as opposed to popular or vulgar speech)

(*Rhet.* 3.10).[48] And it is in this context that Aristotle first speaks of the instructive value of metaphor. This quality really concerns the pleasure of understanding that follows surprise. For this is the function of metaphor, to instruct by suddenly combining elements that have not been put together before:

> We all naturally find it agreeable to get hold of new ideas easily: words express ideas, and therefore those words are the most agreeable that enable us to get hold of new ideas. Now strange words simply puzzle us; ordinary words convey only what we know already; it is from metaphor that we can best get hold of something fresh. When the poet calls old age "a withered stalk," he conveys a new idea, a new fact, to us by means of the general notion (*genous*) of "lost bloom." (1410b10–15)

Furthermore, Aristotle attributes the superiority of metaphor over simile to this same virtue of elegance. More concentrated and shorter than simile, metaphor astonishes and instructs rapidly. Here surprise, in conjunction with hiddenness, plays the decisive role.

To this same characteristic Aristotle attributes another feature of metaphor that has not appeared before, and that seems somewhat disconcerting at first glance. Metaphor, he says, "sets the scene before our eyes" (1410b33). In other words, it gives that concrete coloration—imagistic style, figurative style it is called now—to our grasp of genus, of underlying similarity. It is true that Aristotle does not use the word *eikōn* at all in the sense in which, since Charles Sanders Peirce, we speak of the iconic aspect of metaphor. But the idea that metaphor depicts the abstract in concrete terms is already present. How does Aristotle connect this power of "placing things before our eyes" to the feature of spiritedness, elegance, urbanity? By appealing to the characteristic of all metaphor, which is to point out or show, to 'make visible.' And this feature brings us to the heart of the problem of *lexis*, whose function, we said, is to 'make discourse appear to the senses.' "To place things before the eyes," then, is not an accessory function of metaphor, but the proper function of the figure of speech. Thus, the same metaphor can carry both the logical moment of proportionality and the sensible moment of figurativity. Aristotle enjoys combining these two seemingly contrasting moments: "Liveliness is got by using the proportional type of metaphor and by being graphic [literally: making your hearers see things]" (1411b21). This is true of all the examples listed in 3.10 (1411a25–1411b10). But, preeminently among all the others, the metaphor that displays the inanimate by means of the animate has this power of making relationships visible. One might be tempted to detect here some shameful traces of Platonism. Does not the invisible appear to us through the visible in virtue of the supposed resemblance of one to the other? Whatever the verdict on Platonism may be, if metaphysics is joined here to metaphor, it is truly Aristotle's meta-physics and not Plato's: "By 'making them see things' I mean using expressions that represent things as in a state of activity [*hosa energounta sēmainei*]" (1411b24–25). Showing inanimate things as animate is indeed not relating them to something invisible, but showing these things them-selves as if in act. Taking some remarkable expressions from Homer, Aristotle comments: "In all these examples the things have the effect of being active [*energounta phainetai*] because they are made into living be-ings" (1412a3). Now in all these examples the power of making things visible, alive, actual is inseparable from either a logical relation of pro-portion or a comparison (but as we already know, the backbone of simile with its two terms is the same as that of the four-termed analogy). Thus one and the same strategy of discourse puts into play the logical force of analogy and of comparison—the power to set things before the eyes, the power to speak of the inanimate as if alive, ultimately the capacity to signify active reality.

The objection might arise now that the frontier between prose and poetry has been erased. Is not Homer the author most frequently cited? And is it not said of Homer that "he represents everything as moving and living; and activity is movement" (1412a8)? Might metaphor not be a poetical process extended to prose?

This objection cannot be dealt with completely without returning to Aristotle's *Poetics*. Let us say provisionally that the difference lies not in the process but in the end that is envisaged. That is why figure-filled and enlivened presentation is treated in the same context as brevity, surprise, hiddenness, enigma, antithesis. Liveliness of speech serves the same pur-pose as all of these: persuasion of one's hearers. This purpose remains the distinguishing characteristic of rhetoric.

THE PLACE OF *LEXIS* IN POETICS

Let us take up the other side of the problem of the inclusion of metaphor in both rhetoric and poetry via the medium of *lexis*. What is poetic *lexis*? In the course of my reply, I will connect the definition of metaphor, common to both treatises, with the distinct function that the project of the *Poetics* gives it.

The definition of metaphor led us into a descent from *lexis* toward its elements, and among these, to the noun or name, which is transposed by metaphor. An inquiry into the function of metaphor now demands that we rise above the level of *lexis* toward its conditions or terms.

The most immediate term is the poem itself—here Aristotle considers the tragic poem specifically, or tragedy—seen as a whole: "There are six parts [*mērē*] consequently of every tragedy, as a whole [that is] of such or such quality, viz. a Fable or Plot (*muthos*), Characters (*ēthē*), Diction (*lexis*), Thought (*dianoia*), Spectacle (*opsis*), and Melody (*mēlopoia*)" (1450a7–9). The plot is "the combination [*sustasis*] of the incidents of the story" (1450a15). The character is what confers coherence upon action, by a sort of unique 'purpose' underlying the action (1450b7–9). The *lexis* is 'the composition of the verses' (1449b39). The thought is what a character says in arguing or justifying his actions (1450a7); thought is to action what rhetoric and politics are to discourse (1450b5–6). Hence the thought is the properly rhetorical aspect of the tragic poem (1456a34–36). Spectacle refers to the externally visible configuration (*cosmos*) (1449b33). Finally, melody is the "greatest of the pleasurable accessories of tragedy" 1450b17).

Staying now with the enumeration of the constituents of tragic poetry, we must, in order to understand the role of *lexis*, grasp how the relationships among all these elements are articulated. They form a network, as it were, in which everything centers on one dominant factor: the fable, the plot, the *muthos*. In fact, three factors together play an instrumental role: spectacle, melody, and *lexis* ("for these are, truly, the means used for imitation" [1449b33–34]). Two others, thought and character, are called the 'natural causes' of action (1450a1). Character gives action the coherence of purpose or valuation; and thought makes action coherent by arguing that its reasons are such-and-such. Everything links up within the factor called *muthos*, fable, plot. And here the sort of transposition of actions that Aristotle calls the imitation of nobler actions is achieved: "Now the action [that which was done] is represented in the play by the Fable or Plot" (1450a3). So there is no longer just a means-end or natural cause-effect relationship between *muthos* and tragedy, but a link at the level of essence. This is why, from the first lines of the treatise on, this inquiry is addressed to 'ways of composing plots' (1447a8). Thus, it is important for our purpose to have a keen sense of the proximity between the *muthos* of the tragic poem and the *lexis* of which metaphor is part.

The fundamental trait of *muthos* is its character of order, of organization, of arranging or grouping. This characteristic of order, in turn, enters into all the other factors: the arrangement of the spectacle, coherence of character, sequence of thoughts, and finally the ordering of the verses. Thus *muthos* is echoed in the discursive nature of action, character, and thought. Now it is essential that *lexis* also share in these traits of coherence—but how? Only once does Aristotle say that it originates *dia tēs onomasias hermēneian* (1450b15), which I should like to translate as language-istic interpretation [*l'interprétation langagière*], and which Ingram Bywater renders as "the expression of their thoughts in words."[49] Here there is no issue of prose versus poetry; this interpretation or expression, says Aristotle, "is practically the same thing with verse as with prose" (1450b16). This *hermēneia* or interpretation is by no means exhausted in what Aristotle has just termed *dianoia;* this latter, nevertheless, already contains all the rhetorical features that add to plot and character—and consequently it already belongs to the order of language (it is rhetorical like "everything [that is] to be effected [*paraskeuasthēnai*] by . . . language" [1456a37]). What this ordering in language still lacks is the coming into language, the fact of having been made manifest, of appearing in spoken words: "What, indeed, would be the good of the speaker, if things appeared in the required light even apart from anything he says?" (1456b8).[50] Drawing these three traits together—arrangement of the verses, interpretation by words, manifestation in language—we see the function of *lexis* taking shape as that which exteriorizes and makes explicit the internal order of *muthos*. We might even say that there is a relationship between the *muthos* of tragedy and its *lexis* like that between interior and exterior form. This, then, is how, within the tragic poem, *lexis* (of which metaphor is one part) is bonded to *muthos* and becomes, in turn, "one part" of tragedy.

Our investigation turns now to the relationship between the *muthos* of the tragic poem and the function of *mimēsis*. One must admit that very few modern critics speak favorably about the definition in terms of imitation that Aristotle gives for tragic and (secondarily) epic poetry. Most of them see in this concept the original sin of Aristotelian aesthetics, perhaps of all Greek aesthetics. Richard McKeon and, more recently, Leon Golden and O. B. Hardison have tried to clear up the misunderstandings obscuring the interpretation of the Aristotelian concept.[51] But perhaps our translators were hasty in choosing as the equivalent of the Greek *mimēsis* a term that we think we understand better than we really do. They chose "imitation," which turns out to be easily accused of a naturalistic tendency. It is only since the exclusively modern opposition between figurative and nonfigurative art that, ineluctably, we are really approaching the Greek *mimēsis*.[52] Furthermore, this development should not be mistaken for some desperate project of mustering those characteristics of *mimēsis* that distinguish it from a simple copy of nature.

Let us note, to begin with, that the concept of *mimēsis* is narrowed down remarkably in passing from Plato to Aristotle.[53] Its extension with Plato is boundless; it applies to all the arts, to realms of discourse, to institutions, to natural entities that are imitations of ideal models, and thus to the very principles of things. The dialectical method, understood in the broad sense as the procedure of dialogue, assigns determinations to the meaning of the word that are contextual for the most part, confronting the semanticist with a discouraging plethora of meanings. The only reliable guideline is the very general relationship between something that is and something that resembles, where the resemblance can be good or bad, real or apparent. The reference to ideal models merely allows the construction of a scale of resemblance, marking the degree to which this or that appearance approximates being. Thus, a painting could be described as "imitation of imitation."

Aristotle will have none of this. First of all, definition occurs at the beginning of scientific discourse, not as the outcome of dialectical usage. Words may have more than one meaning, but their use in science permits just one. And it is the division of the sciences that defines this normative usage. Consequently, one and only one literal meaning of *mimēsis* is allowed, that which delimits its use in the framework of the poetical sciences, as distinct from theoretical and practical sciences.[54] There is *mimēsis* only where there is a "making [*faire*]." So there could not be imitation in nature since, as opposed to making, the principle of its motion is internal. Moreover, there could not be imitation of ideas, since making is always production of an individual thing; speaking of *muthos* and its unity of composition, Aristotle remarks that "one imitation is always of one thing" (1451a30–35).

A possible objection is that the *Poetics* "uses" the concept of imitation but does not "define" it. This would be true if the only canonical definition were by means of *genus* and *differentia*. Now the *Poetics* defines imitation in a perfectly rigorous manner by enumerating its species (epic poetry, tragedy, comedy, dithyrambic poetry, compositions for flute and lyre), and then by relating this division into species to the division according to the 'means,' 'objects,' and 'modalities' of imitation. If one notes further that the "function" of imitation is to afford pleasure (we still have to learn what sort), one may hazard the interpretation[55] that imitation is defined in full by just this structure, which corresponds, point by point, to the distinction between material, formal, efficient, and final cause.

This nongeneric definition provides a fourfold structure so strong[56] that, in fact, it determines the distribution of the six 'parts' of tragedy. That is, three of them have to do with the object of imitation (*muthos, ēthos, dianoia*), two others concern the means (*melos, lexis*), and the last the manner (*opsis*). What is more, *katharsis*, although not a 'part' as such, can be linked to the fourth dimension of imitation, the 'function,' as the tragic variant of the pleasure associated with imitation. Accordingly, *katharsis* would be less dependent on the spectator's psychology than on the intelligible composition of the tragedy.[57] Imitation is thus a 'process,' the process of "forming each of the six parts of the tragedy,"[58] from plot through to spectacle.

We will concentrate, within this logical structure of imitation, on the two traits likely to interest our philosophy of the metaphor.

The first of these traits really belongs to the role of *muthos* in poetic creation. As I said above, this is what *mimēsis* is. More precisely, it is the "structure" of plot that constitutes *mimēsis*. Now this is quite a strange brand of imitation, which composes and constructs the very thing it imitates! Everything said about the 'whole and entire' character of myth, of the ordering of beginning, middle, and end, and in general of the unity and order of action (1451a28, 1451b23), helps distinguish imitation from all duplication of reality. We have also noted that, in various degrees, all the other constitutive elements of the tragic poem display the same character of composition, order, and unity. So, in different ways, they are all factors of *mimēsis*.

It is this function of ordering that allows us to say that poetry is "more philosophic . . . than history" (1451b5–6). History recounts what has happened, poetry what could have happened. History is based on the particular, poetry rises toward the universal: "By a universal statement I mean one as to what such or such a kind of man will probably or necessarily say or do" (1451b9). And through this universal 'kind' of man, the spectator "believes in the possible" (1451b16).[59] In this manner a tension is revealed at the very heart of *mimēsis*, between the submission to reality—to human action—and the creative action which is poetry as such: "It is evident from the above that the poet must be more the poet of his stories or plots than of his verses, inasmuch as he is a poet by virtue of the imitative element in his work, and it is actions that he imitates" (1451b27–29).

Further, it is this ordering function that explains why the pleasure that imitation gives us would be a variety of the pleasure that man finds in learning. What pleases us in the poem is the sort of clarification, of total transparency, that the tragic composition achieves.[60]

Therefore, it is only through a grave misinterpretation that the Aristotelian *mimēsis* can be confused with imitation in the sense of copy. If *mimēsis* involves an initial reference to reality, this reference signifies nothing other than the very rule of nature over all production. But the creative dimension is inseparable from this referential movement. *Mimēsis* is *poiēsis*, and *poiēsis* is *mimēsis*. A dominant theme in the present research, this paradox is of the utmost import; and it was anticipated by Aristotle's *mimēsis*, which holds together this closeness to human reality and the far-ranging flight of fable-making. This paradox cannot but concern the theory of metaphor. First, though, let us finish describing the concept of *mimēsis*.

The second trait of interest to this investigation is expressed in the following manner: in tragedy, as opposed to comedy, the imitation of human action is an imitation that magnifies, ennobles. This trait, even more than the preceding one, is the key to understanding the function of metaphor. Of comedy and tragedy Aristotle says that "the one would make its personages worse [*kheirous*], and the other better [*beltiones*], than the men of the present day" (1448a17–18). (This theme is repeated several times, see 1448b24–27, 1449a31–33, 1449b9.) Thus, *muthos* is not just a rearrangement of human action into a more coherent form, but a structuring that elevates this action; so *mimēsis* preserves and represents that which is human, not just in its essential features, but in a way that makes it greater and nobler. There is thus a double tension proper to *mimēsis*: on the one hand, the imitation is at once a portrayal of human reality and an original creation; on the other, it is faithful to things as they are and it depicts them as higher and greater than they are. With these two traits combined, we return to metaphor.

Relocated on the foundations provided by *mimēsis*, metaphor ceases to be arbitrary and trivial. If considered simply as a fact or element of language, it could be taken for a mere deviation in relation to ordinary usage, alongside the rare word, the newly coined, the lengthened, abbreviated, and altered. But the subordination of *lexis* to *muthos* already puts metaphor at the service of "saying," of "poetizing," which takes place no longer at the level of the word but at the level of the poem as a whole. Then the subordination of *muthos* to *mimēsis* gives the stylistic process a global aim, comparable to rhetoric's intention to persuade. Considered formally, metaphor as a deviation represents nothing but a difference in meaning. Related to the imitation of our actions at their best, it takes part in the double tension that characterizes this imitation: submission to reality and fabulous invention, unaltering representation and ennobling elevation. This double tension constitutes the referential function of metaphor in poetry. Abstracted from this referential function, metaphor plays itself out in substitution and dissipates itself in ornamentation; allowed to run free, it loses itself in language games.

Let us go further. Within the bounds of this second trait of *mimēsis*, is it not possible to apply a still more closely fitting relationship between the elevation of meaning proper to tragic imitation and operating in the poem taken as a whole, and the displacement of meaning proper to metaphor and taking place on the level of the word? Aristotle has a few remarks on the proper use of metaphor in poetry,[61] which are an exact counterpart of the expressions we assembled under the title of 'virtues' of metaphor in rhetoric. They tend toward a de-ontology of poetic language, which is not unlike the teleology of *mimēsis* itself.

What does Aristotle say on this point? "The perfection [virtue, *aretē*] of *lexis* is for it to be at once clear and not mean" (1458a18). What is meant here by clarity and meanness? A poetic composition that is at once clear and base is precisely one that employs only the most familiar vocabulary in its most common usage. Here, then, is the right place for deviation. Two strands meet here, the strange and the noble (*semnē*); and we cannot avoid pushing this connection further. If the "strange" and the "noble" meet in the "good metaphor," is it not because the nobility of such language befits the grandeur of the actions being depicted? Now I readily admit that this interpretation goes beyond Aristotle's intentions, but it is permissible in terms of his text and arose from my reading of it. In any case, if this interpretation is valid, we are forced to ask whether the secret of metaphor, as a displacement of meaning at the level of words, does not rest in the elevation of meaning at the level of *muthos*. And if this proposal is acceptable, then metaphor would not only be a deviation in relation to ordinary usage, but also, by means of this deviation, the privileged instrument in that upward motion of meaning promoted by *mimēsis*.

In this way we can discover a parallel between the elevation of meaning accomplished by *muthos* at the level of the poem and the elevation of meaning by metaphor at the level of the word—a parallelism that really should be extended to *katharsis*, which one could consider an elevation of feeling like that of action and of language. Considered from a functional point of view, imitation constitutes a unitary whole in which mythic elevation, displacement of language by metaphor, and the purging of feelings of fear and pity work side by side.

It will be objected, however, that no exegesis of *mimēsis* based on its connection to *muthos* can suppress the important fact that *mimēsis* is *mimēsis phuseōs*. For it is untrue that *mimēsis* is the final concept attained in the climb toward the primary concepts of the *Poetics*. It would appear that the expression 'imitation of nature' takes us out of the domain of the *Poetics* and into the *Metaphysics*.[62] Is the entire preceding analysis not subverted by restoring the connection between discursive creation and natural production? In the last analysis, does not linking the fullness of meaning to natural abundance render the deviation of metaphor useless and impossible?[63]

We will have to return, then, to the reference to nature, such a scandalous stumbling block in an aesthetics that nevertheless wishes to make room for *muthos* and metaphor.

If it is true that imitation functions in the Aristotelian system as the differentiating characteristic that distinguishes the fine and the useful arts from nature, it follows that the function of the expression 'imitation of nature' is as much to distinguish human making from natural production as to align them. The proposition that "Art imitates nature" (*Phys.* 2.2 194a21–22; *Meteor.* 4.3.381b6) introduces a discriminant as well as a connective element.[64] The precise meaning given by this thematic usage of the words cannot be outweighed by any simply operative usage, like that put into play by the different occurrences of the word *nature* or its cognates in the text of the *Poetics*.

It is because the aim of the expression 'imitation of nature' is to distinguish the poetic from the natural that the reference to nature does not appear at all as a restriction on the composition of the poem. The poem imitates human actions "either as they were or are, or as they are said or thought to be or to have been, or as they ought to be" (1460b7–11). An enormous range of possibilities is thus kept in play. On this basis one can understand how the same philosopher could have written "[The poet] is a poet by virtue of the imitative element in his work" (1451b28–29, 1447b1–5) and "The action [that which is done] is represented in the play by the Fable or Plot" (1450a4). It is also because nature leaves space for the "making" of imitation that human actions can be depicted as "better" or "worse," according to whether the work is tragedy or comedy. Reality remains a reference, without ever becoming a restriction. Therefore, the work of art can be judged on purely intrinsic criteria, without any interference (contra Plato) from moral or political considerations, and above all, without the burdensome ontological concern for fitting the appearance to the real. In renouncing that Platonic use of *mimēsis* that allowed even the things of nature to be taken as imitations of eternal models and allowed a painting to be called imitation of imitation, Aristotle undertakes not to use the concept of imitation of nature except within the limits of a science of poetic composition that has won its full autonomy. It is in the composition of the fable or plot that the reference to human action, which is in this case the nature being imitated, must become apparent.

In ending, I would like to venture a last argument that goes beyond the resources of a semantics applied to the words of a philosopher of the past, an argument that puts into play his meaning reactivated in a contemporary context and therefore arises from a hermeneutic. The argument concerns this very term *phusis*, the ultimate reference of *mimēsis*.

We believe that we understand *phusis* when we translate it by *nature*. But is not the word *nature* as far off the mark with respect to *phusis* as is the word *imitation* concerning *mimēsis*? Certainly Greek man was far less quick than we are to identify *phusis* with some inert "given." Perhaps it is because, for him, nature is itself living that *mimēsis* can be not enslaving and that compositional and creative imitation of nature can be possible. Is this not what the most enigmatic passage of the *Rhetoric* suggests? Metaphor, it relates, makes one see things because it "represents things as in a state of activity" (1411b24–25). The *Poetics* echoes that one may "speak in narrative" or present "personages as acting [*hōs prattontas*] and doing [*energountas*]" (1448a22, 28). Might there not be an underlying relationship between "signifying active reality" and speaking out *phusis*?

If this hypothesis is valid, it can be understood why no *Poetics* can truly ever have done either with *mimēsis* or with *phusis*. In the last analysis, the concept of *mimēsis* serves as an index of the discourse situation; it reminds us that no discourse ever suspends our belonging to a world. All *mimēsis*, even creative—nay, especially creative—*mimēsis*, takes place within the horizons of a being-in-the-world which it makes present to the precise extent that the *mimēsis* raises it to the level of *muthos*. The truth of imagination, poetry's power to make contact with being as such—this is what I personally see in Aristotle's *mimēsis*. *Lexis* is rooted in *mimēsis*, and through *mimēsis* metaphor's deviations from normal *lexis* belong to the great enterprise of "saying what is."

But *mimēsis* does not signify only that all discourse is of the world; it does not embody just the referential function of poetic discourse. Being *mimēsis phuseōs*, it connects this referential function to the revelation of the Real as Act. This is the function of the concept of *phusis* in the expression *mimēsis phuseōs*, to serve as an index for that dimension of reality that does not receive due account in the simple description of that-thing-over-there. To present men "as acting" and all things "as in act"—such could well be the ontological function of metaphorical discourse, in which every dormant potentiality of existence appears as blossoming forth, every latent capacity for action as actualized.

Lively expression is that which expresses existence as alive.

METAPHOR AND THE EQUIVOCALNESS OF BEING

The first counterexample opposing our hypothesis—that philosophical and poetic discourse are different—is provided by the type of speculation that Aristotle was the first to apply to the analogical unity of the multiple meanings of being. The question can be put this way: whenever philosophy tries to introduce an intermediate modality between univocity and equivocalness, is speculative discourse not forced to reproduce, on its own level, the semantic functioning of poetic discourse? If this were the case, speculative discourse would be brought about or induced in some way by poetic discourse. The very vocabulary used supports the hypothesis of an initial confusion of kinds. The word *analogy* seems to belong to both discourses. In poetics, analogy in the sense of 'proportion' is at the root of the fourth class of metaphor, which Aristotle termed metaphor 'by analogy' (or, in some translations, 'proportional' metaphor). To this day, some theorists do not hesitate to subsume metaphor and simile under the generic term of analogy, or to place the family of metaphor under this common heading. In philosophy, this same word is at the center of a certain discourse that claims its source in Aristotle and continues through the neo-Thomists.

I should like to show that, contrary to appearances, the intellectual labor that later crystallized in the concept of the analogy of being stems from an initial divergence between speculative and poetic discourse. I shall reserve for the second stage of the discussion the question whether it was possible to preserve this initial difference in the mixed forms to which discourse on God gave rise in philosophy and theology.

It is necessary therefore to begin at the greatest point of divergence between philosophy and poetry, the position established by Aristotle in the treatise on the *Categories* and in Books 3, 5, 6, and 11 of the *Metaphysics*.

The *Categories,* in which the term 'analogy' does not actually appear, produces a nonpoetic model of equivocalness and thus suggests the necessary conditions for a nonmetaphorical theory of analogy. Since Aristotle, through the neo-Platonists and the Arab and Christian medieval philosophers, down to Kant, Hegel, Renouvier, and Hamelin, this act of ordering that the *Categories* represents has remained the perennial signal task of speculative discourse. But the *Categories* raises its question of the connection between the meanings of being only because the *Metaphysics* poses the question that breaks with poetic discourse just as with ordinary discourse—what is being?

This question is entirely outside the bounds of all language games. For this reason, when the philosopher is confronted by the paradox that "being is said in several ways" and when, in order to rescue the diverse meanings of being from dispersal, he establishes between them a relation of reference to a first term that is neither the univocity of a genus nor the mere chance equivocalness of a simple word, the plurivocity that is thus brought to philosophical discourse is of a different order than the multiplicity of meaning produced by metaphorical utterance. It is a plurivocity of the same order as the very question that opened up the speculative field. The first term—*ousia*—places all the other terms in the realm of meaning outlined by the question: what is being? For the moment, it is of little importance whether these other terms are in a relation to the first term that could, justly or not, be called analogy. What is important is that a connection be identified among the multiple meanings of being, one which, although not proceeding from the division of a genus into species, nevertheless constitutes an order. This order is an order of categories, to the extent that it is the necessary condition for the ordered extension of the sphere of attribution. The regulated polysemy of being orders the apparently disordered polysemy of the predicative function as such. In the same way that categories other than substance can be 'predicated' of substance and thus add to the first meaning of being, so too, for every given being, the sphere of predication presents the same concentric structure extending progressively farther from a 'substantial' center, and the same expansion of meaning through the addition of determinations.

This ordered process has nothing in common with metaphor, not even with analogical metaphor. The ordered equivocalness of being and poetic equivocalness move on radically distinct levels. Philosophical discourse sets itself up as the vigilant watchman overseeing the ordered extensions of meaning; against this background, the unfettered extensions of meaning in poetic discourse spring free.

The lack of a common point of contact between the ordered equivocalness of being and poetic metaphor is attested to indirectly by the charge Aristotle leveled at Plato. Ordered equivocalness is to be substituted for Platonic participation, which is only metaphorical: "And to say that [the Forms] are patterns and the other things share in them is to use empty words and poetical metaphors" (*Met.* 1.9, 991a19–22). Thus philosophy must neither use metaphors nor speak poetically, not even when it deals with the equivocal meanings of being. But can it help doing what it must not do?

It has been argued that the Aristotelian treatise on the *Categories* forms a self-contained position only to the extent that it is supported by a concept of analogy that is itself compelled to draw its logical force from a domain other than the speculative order. But it can be shown that these objections prove at most that the *Categories* should be reworked, doubtless on a basis other than that of analogy; however, they do not prove that the semantic aim guiding the treatise is borrowed from a field other than the speculative.

First, one may object that the alleged categories of thought are only categories of language in disguise. This is the contention of E. Benveniste.[65] Beginning with the general claim that "linguistic form is not only the condition for transmissibility, but first of all the condition for the realization of thought" (1958, 56), the author attempts to demonstrate that Aristotle, "reasoning in the absolute, is simply identifying certain fundamental categories of the language in which he thought" (ibid., 57).[66]

The correlation established by Benveniste is irrefutable as long as one is considering only the passage from Aristotle's categories as enumerated by him to the categories of language. But what about the inverse path? For Benveniste, the entire table of the categories of thought is merely "transposed from categories of language" (1967, 61), "the conceptual projection of a given linguistic state" (ibid.). As for the notion of being, "which envelops everything," this concept 'reflects' (ibid.) the wealth of uses of the verb *to be*.

Evoking "the magnificent images of the poem of Parmenides as well as the dialectic of *The Sophist*" (ibid., 61), however, the linguist is forced to concede that "the language did not, of course, give direction to metaphysical definition of 'being'—each Greek thinker has his own—but it made it possible to set up 'being' as an objectifiable notion that philosophical thought could handle, analyze and define just as any other concept" (ibid., 62). And again: "All we wish to show here is that the linguistic structure of Greek predisposed the notion of 'being' to a philosophical vocation" (ibid., 63).

The problem is then to understand what principle of philosophical thought, applied to grammatical being, produces the series of meanings of the verb *to be*. Between what would be merely a list and what would be a deduction in the Kantian sense, there is room for an ordering, which in the post-Aristotelian tradition—and even in a few rare suggestions by Aristotle himself—came to be thought of as analogy.

Jules Vuillemin demonstrates in the second study of his work *De la logique à la théologie: Cinq études sur Aristote*[67] that the Aristotelian treatise on the *Categories* has a logical construction and that in grasping this, "one will perhaps find the thread of Aristotelian deduction, which up to now seems to have escaped analysis" (p. 77).

It is not without importance that the treatise on the *Categories* begins with a semantic distinction that, instead of marking a dichotomy, makes room for a third class. In addition to things that have only the name (*onoma*) in common but not the notion (*logos*), which Aristotle calls homonyms, and those that share both a common name and a notional identity—synonyms—there are also paronyms, that is, those things that derive their name from some other name, but differ from it in termination (*ptōsis*). Thus the grammarian derives his name from the word *grammar*, and the courageous man from the word *courage* (*Cat.* 1a12–15). Here for the first time an intermediate class is inserted between homonymous and synonymous items, and consequently between expressions that are merely equivocal and expressions that are absolutely univocal. The entire following analysis will attempt to widen the gap opened up by paronyms in the solid front of equivocalness and to lift the general ban on equivocalness laid by one of Aristotle's own theses, namely that "to mean more than one thing is to mean nothing at all."

There would be no point to this distinction, which still refers to things named and not directly to meanings, if it did not shed light on the formal organization of the table of categories. In fact, the decisive distinction, introduced in the second paragraph of the treatise, is the one that opposes and combines two senses of the copula *is:* namely, being-said-of (thus man, secondary substance, is said of Socrates, primary substance) and being-in (for example, musician, accident of the substance Socrates). This key distinction, around which the rest of the treatise is organized, makes the distinction between synonyms and paronyms functional: only the relation said-of allows synonymous attribution (the particular man is identically man).[68]

We said above that the two senses of the copula involved in the relations being-said-of and being-in are both opposed and combined. Indeed, by arranging these two features in a table noting absence and presence, one can derive four classes of substantives, two concrete (Socrates, man) and two abstract (a certain white, science). Aristotelian morphology is thus based on the intersection of two fundamental oppositions: the opposition of particular to general, which permits predication in the strict sense (being-said of) and that of concrete to abstract (which permits predication in the broad sense). The first opposition, understood in the realist sense, founds the irreducible obscurity of the copula, bound to the materiality of individual substances (with the exception of separate beings). The second opposition, understood in a conceptualist sense, replaces the alleged participation of Platonic ideas, which Aristotle denounced as simply metaphorical. The abstract is in the concrete potentially; its inherence too is tied to the obscure ground of individual substances.

How does analogy enter into this, if not explicitly (since the word is never mentioned), at least implicitly? Its avenue is this, that as the modalities of the copula become more varied, they progressively weaken the sense of the copula in the passage from primordial, essential predication—which alone is held to have a synonymous sense—toward derived, accidental predication.[69] A correlation suggests itself, therefore, between the distinction made in the *Categories* on the level of morphology and predication and the great passage of *Metaphysics* Book 3 on the reference of all categories to a first term, texts read by medieval thinkers within the framework of the analogy of being. This correlation is set forth in *Metaphysics* Book 6, the text par excellence on substance, which explicitly relates the various forms of predication—and hence the categories—to possible equivocation in regard to the first category, *ousia*.[70] But it is because "predication can be interpreted neither as the relation of element to set nor as the relation of part to whole" that it remains "an ultimate intuitive given, whose meaning moves from inherence to proportion and from proportion to proportionality."[71] It is this outcome that we shall consider later when we examine the passage from the analogy of proportion to the analogy of attribution, which is achieved explicitly only with medieval philosophers.

Before this, however, it is important to show that within the limits traced by the distinction made in paragraph 2 of the *Categories*, the subsequent series of categories is constructed soundly (in paragraphs 3 to 9 of this work) on the basis of a nonlinguistic model. The text 6.4, referred to earlier, offers a key: "For it must be either by an equivocation that we say [things] *are,* or by adding to and taking from the meaning of 'are.'" Substance, the primary category, is circumscribed by a set of criteria resulting from prolonged thought on the conditions of predication. A comparative study of the *Categories* and *Metaphysics* 6.3 renders no less than seven. Three are properly logical criteria of predication: as primary substance, it is not said-of and is not in; as secondary substance, it is the subject of synonymous and primordial attribution. Four are ontological criteria. Three of these are secondary—substance is a determined 'this,' it has no contrary, it does not involve degree. The last is essential: substance is capable of receiving contraries. On this foundation, the organization of Aristotle's *Categories* proceeds by weakening the criteria, as the deduction moves from that which resembles substance most to that which resembles it least.[72]

The entire problem of analogy (but not the word itself!) is contained *in nuce* in this derivation by means of diminishing criteria. Essence, taken as the first term in 6.4, is imparted by degrees to all the categories: "Essence will belong, just as 'what a thing is' does, primarily and in the simple sense to substance, and in a secondary way to the other categories also—not essence in the simple sense, but the essence of a quality or of a quantity" (*Met.* 6.4.1030a29–31; then follows the passage cited that opposes to mere homonymy the process of adding or subtracting various qualifications from being). This transcendental mode of predication can indeed be called paronym, by reason of its parallelism with *Categories* Book 1, and analogy, at least implicitly.[73] Analogy designates virtually this progressive weakening of the precision of the predicative function as one moves from primordial predication to derived predication and from essential predication to accidental predication (which is paronymous).[74]

What will later be termed analogy of attribution is precisely this relation of progressively extended derivation, which Aristotle bounds on one side by essential predication—which alone provides the exact or approximate forms of proportionality and for which, we shall see, Aristotle reserves the term 'analogy'—and on the other side by homonymy pure and simple or equivocity.

It was therefore of critical importance to show that the tripartite division—homonym, synonym, paronym—did indeed mark the opening of the treatise, thereby providing an introduction to the problem of analogy.[75]

Yet Aristotle does not call analogy what we have just termed a relation of progressively extended derivation. What is more, if the table of categories formed "by adding to and taking from the meaning of 'are'" does permit us to order the series of allegedly given terms, it does not show us why there must be other terms than the first nor why they are as they are. If we reread the canonical text of 3.2,[76] we see that the other categories are so termed with reference "to one central point [*pros hen*], one definite kind of thing [*kata mian phusin*]" (1003a33). But we do not see that the multiple meanings form a system. Aristotle may well declare that the lack of notional unity does not prevent there being a single science of the multiple senses of being. He may well affirm that terms that "are related to one common nature" give rise to a single science, for "even these in a sense have one common notion" (3.2.1003b14). For, in this case, "science deals chiefly with that which is primary, and on which the other things depend, and in virtue of which they get their names" (3.2.1003b16–18). These statements do not prevent this enigmatic relation of dependence from being merely alleged, nor what Aristotle offers as a solution from being perhaps just a problem hypostatized in the form of a reply.

It might perhaps be a wise step, at this point in our study, to ignore the medieval interpretation and draw all we can from the fact that Aristotle did not call this *ad unum* reference "analogy," in order to lay bare what is thought under this term. An 'aporetic' reading of Aristotle, like that proposed by Pierre Aubenque,[77] combined with the logical and mathematical reading of Vuillemin, permits us to isolate the operation by which medieval scholars, following a suggestion they found in other Aristotelian texts on analogy, tried to lessen the *aporia* of the "many meanings of being." From the perspective of my own inquiry into the heterogeneity of discourses in general and into the irreducibility of transcendental or speculative discourse to poetic discourse in particular, the aporetic interpretation applied to Aristotle's ontological discourse attests better than the medieval interpretation to the radical nature of the question, which for lack of a response is thus better exposed as a question.

Vuillemin has stated that primary attribution—that of a secondary substance to a primary substance—since it cannot be interpreted as the relation of element to set or as the relation of part to whole, is therefore "an ultimate intuitive given, the meaning of which moves from inherence to proportion and from proportion to proportionality" (1967, 229). It is thus the very opacity of primary attribution that suggests analogy. For Aubenque, it is the absence of a generic unity—the sole support of Aristotelian science—and the resulting impossibility of generating categories other than *ousia*, which prevent attributing any determined meaning to *ad unum* reference. Discourse on being is the site henceforth of an unending investigation. Ontology continues to be the 'sought after science.'

Whatever the status of the arguments that finally develop all the reasons, well known from Aristotle, for which being is not a genus, and adding as well those reasons of which Kant made us aware, which determine that the table of categories cannot form a system but remains in a state of 'rhapsody';[78] it nonetheless remains that the *aporia* in question, if indeed this is an *aporia,* results from an aim, a requirement, an exigency, the original character of which ought to be recognized. It is because ontology aims at a nongeneric science of being that even its failure is specifically its own. To develop the *aporia—diaporein—*as Aubenque wishes to do (1962, 221) is not to say nothing. For the effort that fails displays a particular structure, circumscribed by the very expression *pros ben, ad unum.* Something is required by the declaration even when it is put in the form of an *aporia:* "But everywhere science deals chiefly with that which is primary, and on which the other things depend, and in virtue of which they get their names" (*Met.* 3.2.1003b16). And a bit further: "Therefore, since there are many senses in which a thing is said to be one, these terms also will have many senses, but yet it belongs to one science to know them all; for a term belongs to different sciences not if it has different senses, but if it has no one meaning *and* its definitions cannot be referred to one central meaning" (*Met.* 3.2.1004a22–25). The search for this unity cannot be totally in vain for the very reason that the *pros ben* constitutes, 'in a certain sense,' one common notion, one definite kind of thing. If the science sought after were not structured in this way by the very form of the question, one could not even oppose, as Aubenque does, the reality of the failure to the 'ideal' of the investigation (1962, 240), or the actual analysis to the 'program.' The very disproportion between the analysis and its ideal attests to the semantic aim of this project, and it is on the basis of this aim that one could begin to look for something like a nongeneric unity of being.

In this respect, the rapprochement between ontology and dialectic, which the aporetic character of the doctrine of being seems to impose (Aubenque 1962, 251–302), cannot, in the author's own opinion, be pursued very far. Between dialectic and ontology, the 'difference in intention' (ibid., 301) is complete:

> Dialectic provides us with a universal technique of questioning, without concern for man's ability to answer; but man would not pose questions if he had no hope of answering them. . . . For this reason, the absence of prospective resolution required by the neutral character of the art of the dialectic is one thing; the actual incompletion of a project that by definition includes the very prospect of its accomplishment is something else again. (Ibid., 302)

One can pursue this point even further in an effort to understand the internal reasons why analogy presented itself as the solution to the central *aporia* of ontological discourse. If it is true, as Aubenque maintains, that this discourse receives its 'prospect,' its 'ideal,' and its 'program' from outside, namely, from the theology inherited from Plato, it becomes even more urgent for ontology to reply to this external appeal with its own resources.

I am all the more willing to delve into this problem of the encounter between theological and ontological discourse, which Aubenque opposes to the hypothesis of a simple chronological succession between two states of Aristotle's system (a hypothesis first presented, as we know, by Werner Jaeger), as I find in it a compelling illustration of my own thesis regarding the plurality of spheres of discourse and the fecundity of the intersection of their semantic aims.

Let us therefore grant that what feeds the problematic of unity are properly theological considerations applied to 'separate realities'—the supralunar astral order, unmoved mover, thought of thought. It becomes all the more urgent to know how ontology responds to this appeal. At the same time, the encounter, in Aristotle, between an ontological problem of unity coming from a dialogue with sophistry and a theological problem of separation coming from a dialogue with Platonism provides a sort of paradigmatic example of the attraction between different spheres of discourse.[79]

It is therefore of little consequence that Aubenque exaggerates the heterogeneity of theological and ontological discourse and that he over-dramatizes the encounter between an "impossible ontology," one lacking a conceivable unity among the categories, and a "useless theology" (ibid., 331) lacking a fixed relation between the God who reflects upon himself and the world he ignores. On the contrary, by transforming once again into an *aporia* Aristotle's thesis in *Metaphysics* 5.1 that the science of immovable substance is universal because it is primary, Aubenque makes problematical just what is at issue, namely the new semantic aim resulting from the encounter between the two orders of discourse.[80]

A new conceptual problem must be worked out, arising from the very interference between theology—even astral theology—which envisions not a hidden God, but a God presented as far away in astral contemplation, and our human discourse on being in the diversity of its categorial acceptations.[81]

Even if the conciliation proposed in 5.1—theology is "universal . . . because it is first"—is only the hypostasis of a problem in search of a solution, it remains that the denounced heterogeneity of ontological discourse on the multiple meanings of being and theological discourse on 'separate' being must not amount to total incommunicability between spheres of meaning. This would endanger the possibility of conceiving the interference required by the very thesis that aporetic ontology takes its perspective from unitary theology. I should even be tempted to see, in these arguments that tend to make this interference unintelligible at the very moment it is alleged, the profound reason that led Aristotle's successors, and perhaps even Aristotle himself, to appeal to analogy.

Let us consider these arguments. The divine, it is stated, being indivisible, cannot receive attribution and can give rise only to negations. In turn, the diversity of the significations of being can apply only to physical things, in which it is possible to distinguish substance, quality, quantity, and so on. In the final analysis, motion is the difference making the unity of being impossible in principle, and is the reason why the division into essence and accident applies to being. In short, it is because of motion that ontology is not a theology but a dialectic of division and finitude (Aubenque 1962, 442). Wherever something is in a state of becoming, predication is possible: predication is based on physical dissociation introduced by motion. But if this is the final word, how can one speak of an interference between ontology and theology? One can indeed criticize the failure of this endeavor. But this is not the question here. We have still to think through the very topic that Aristotle assigned himself, that of conceiving the horizontal unity of the meanings of being together with the vertical unity of beings.[82]

Now, Aristotle indicated the point where the two problematics intersect. It is *ousia*, the first category in attributive discourse and the sole sense of divine being.[83] Beyond this point, the two discourses separate, since nothing can be said concerning a being that is *ousia* alone, and since, in regard to beings that are *ousia* and something else also, the unity of meaning is dispersed. In any case, the divergence between the impossible discourse of ontology and the futile discourse of theology, the twinning of tautology and circumlocution, of empty universality and limited generalization—all proceed from a common center, *ousia*, which, in Aubenque's words, "will signify nothing other than the act of that which is, the completion of what is given in the fulfillment of presence, or, to use a word we have encountered before, *entelechy*" (1962, 406). Ontology may indeed be only the human substitute for a theology that remains impossible for us; *ousia* is still the crossroads where these avenues meet.

If the two discourses thus intersect at a point at once common to both and localizable in each of them, should not the 'sought after' science, drawing upon its own resources, respond to the proposal of unity made by the other discourse? Is it not from this internal necessity that the problem of analogy arises? The textual evidence in this regard is *Metaphysics* 11.5.1071a33–35. It says first that "the causes of all [things] are the same or analogous." Second, it states that the primacy of divine *ousia* underlies the categorial unity of being: "The causes of substances may be treated as causes of all things." The thesis remains unchanged even if one takes the as (*hōs*) in the weak sense of an as if.[84] In its third part, the text specifies (further, *eti*) that it is because the final cause is "first in respect of complete reality (*entelechy*)" that it is "the cause of all things."[85]

It is in this way that an aporetic reading of Aristotle highlights by contrast the doctrine of analogy, to the very extent that this reading began by bracketing it. Even if one finds this notion to be nothing but a problem hypostatized into a reply, it nevertheless designates the conceptual labor by which the human, the too human, discourse of ontology attempts to respond to the entreaty of another discourse, which is itself perhaps only a nondiscourse.

A question is in fact raised by the concept of reference *ad unum*. If there is no generic commonality among the many meanings of being, what can be the nature of the 'common notion' suggested by Aristotle in *Metaphysics* 3.2.1003b14? Can there exist a nongeneric commonality to rescue the discourse on being from its aporetic state?

The concept of analogy, evoked at least once in this context by Aristotle, intervenes at this point. The problem it raises here is the result of a second-order reflection on the *Categories*. It arises from the question of whether, and to what extent, reference to a first term is itself a conceivable relation. We have seen how this order of derivation can be produced by reflecting on the conditions of predication. We must now ask what sort of relation is generated in this way. Here the mathematical notion of analogy of proportion provides a means of comparison. Its origin guarantees its scientific status. By the same token, one can understand the approximation of the relation *ad unum* and proportional analogy as an effort to extend to the transcendental relation the benefit of the scientific character that belongs to the analogy of proportion.

I am all the more disposed to recognize the heterogeneous character of this rapprochement in that the earlier analysis of the points of interference of theological and ontological discourse has prepared us to pose the problem of analogy in terms of the intersection of discourses. Indeed, application of the concept of analogy to the series of meanings of being is itself also an instance of the intersection of spheres of discourse. And this intersection can be understood without reference to theological discourse, even if theological discourse will employ analogy later on in an effort to annex ontological discourse—at the price, however, of greatly altering this concept.

In Aristotle, certainly, the pure concept of analogy has nothing to do with the question of categories. It is due to a shift in meaning that weakens the original criteria that this concept is joined to the theory of categories and that a tangential relation in Aristotle is turned into a clear intersection in medieval philosophers.

It is this conceptual exercise more than its admittedly disappointing results that is of interest here. Contemporary logicians and philosophers may be justified in claiming that this effort has failed and that the theory of analogy is nothing but a pseudoscience. It can even be stated that this pseudoscientific character extends to the theological use of analogy as well, and that this in turn reflects upon the initial transcendental structure, enclosing onto-theology in a vicious circle. To my mind, this is not what is important. My express purpose is to show how, by entering the sphere of the problematic of being, analogy at once retains its own conceptual structure and receives a transcendental aspect from the field to which it is applied. Indeed, to the extent that it is marked by the domain in which it intervenes in its own distinct way, the concept of analogy assumes a transcendental function. By the same token, it never returns to poetry, but retains in regard to poetry the mark of the original divergence produced by the question, what is being? In what follows, we shall show that this inclination toward divergence is in no way weakened by the theological use of analogy. The rejection of metaphor as an improper analogy will attest to this.

It is not unimportant that the mathematical notion of analogy—far from being self-evident as a summary definition might lead one to believe (*A* is to *B* as *C* is to *D*)—crystallizes a prolonged exercise of thought. Its final definition expresses the solution to a paradox, namely how to "master the 'impossible relationships' between certain geometric dimensions and whole numbers, by reducing them indirectly to consideration of relations of wholes alone, or, more precisely, to inequalities of size."[86]

Could one not say that it is the conceptual labor incorporated in the definition, rather than its result, that was taken as a model for philosophical thought? Here again, extension from a radically nonpoetic pole occurs through the weakening of criteria.

The closest application is provided by the definition of distributive justice in the *Nicomachean Ethics* 5.3. The definition rests on the idea that this virtue implies four terms, two persons (equal or unequal) and two shares (advantages and disadvantages in the realms of honor or wealth); and that it establishes proportional equality in distribution between these four terms. But the application here of the idea of number, proposed by Aristotle,[87] concerns extension not of the idea of number to irrationals but of proportion to nonhomogeneous terms, provided that they can be said to be equal or unequal in some particular relation.

In biology, the same formal conception of proportion permits not only classification (by saying, for example, that flying is to wings as swimming is to fins), but also demonstration (e.g., if certain animals have lungs and others do not, the latter possess an organ that takes the place of a lung). By lending themselves to proportional relationships such as these, functions and organs provide the outline of a general biology (*Part. An.* 1.5).

The relation of analogy begins its migration toward the transcendental sphere when it is charged with expressing the identity of principles and elements that cut through the diversity of genera: thus, it is said, "as sight is in the body, so is reason in the soul, and so on in other cases" (*NE* 1.4.1096b28–29). Analogy still remains, formally, an equality of relations among four terms.[88]

The decisive step, the one that concerns us here, is taken in *Metaphysics* 11.4–5, where analogy is applied to the problem of the identity of principles and elements belonging to different categories.[89] Its formulation certainly still allows an equality or similarity of relations to appear; thus, one can write that privation is to form, on the level of elements, as cold is to heat in sensible bodies, as black is to white in qualities, as darkness is to light in relatives. In this respect, the transition from proportional analogy to reference *ad unum* is more than hinted at in a text from the *Metaphysics*,[90] to which medieval philosophers will return relentlessly. "Healthy," Aristotle notes, is said analogously of the cause of health, of a sign of health, and of the healthy subject. "Medical" is said analogously of the doctor, the scalpel, the operation, and the patient. Analogical extension is governed, then, by the order of the categories.

This formulation, however, cannot hide the fact that the analogy here concerns the categories, the very terms in which 'principles' (form, privation, and matter) come together through analogy. Not only is the number of these terms not specified by the relation itself, but the sense of the relation has changed. What is in question is the manner in which the terms themselves relate to one another, whereas the reference *ad unum* is limited to establishing dominance (the first term) and hierarchy (reference to the first term). This final weakening of the criteria results in a displacement from proportional analogy to the analogy of attribution.[91]

Modern logicians will be more sensitive than were medieval philosophers to the logical break that interrupts the extension of analogy as it moves from mathematics to metaphysics. To logicians, the unscientific features of analogy, taken in its final sense, add up to an argument against analogy.[92] The great text of *Metaphysics* 1.9.992b18–24 is turned against the philosopher and becomes the ultimate evidence of the unscientific character of metaphysics.[93]

Aristotle's failure, however, can have two meanings, between which a purely logical analysis cannot choose. According to the first, the transcendental project as such is stripped of all meaning; in line with the second, this project must be taken up again on some basis other than analogy and yet still remain faithful to the semantic aim that presided over the search for a nongeneric unity for the meanings of being. It is this interpretation that we have tried to develop here, by stressing in each instance the conceptual labor crystallized in the logical result. Because the "search" for a nongeneric bond of being remains a task for thought, even after Aristotle's failure, the problem of a "guide line" has continued to be raised down to modern philosophy. The reason the *Categories* has proved capable of continual consideration and reworking is that once the difference between the analogy of being and poetic metaphor was indeed thought.

In this respect, the first paragraph of the *Categories* remains highly significant. To say that there are not two classes of things to name—synonyms and homonyms—but three classes, with the insertion of paronyms, is to open up a new domain for philosophical discourse based on the existence of nonaccidental homonyms. From this point on, there is a continuous chain formed from the paronyms in paragraph 1 of the *Categories* to the reference *pros ben, ad unum* in *Metaphysics* 3.2 and 5.1. The new possibility of thought opened up in this way was that of a nonmetaphorical and properly transcendental resemblance among the primary significations of being. To say that this resemblance is unscientific settles nothing. It is more important to affirm that because it breaks with poetics, this purely transcendental resemblance even today attests, by its very failure, to the search that animated it—namely, the search for a relation that is still to be thought otherwise than by science, if thinking scientifically means thinking in terms of genus. But the primary task remains to master the difference between transcendental analogy and poetic resemblance. Based on this initial difference, the nongeneric bond of being can be—and without a doubt must be—thought according to a model that will no longer owe anything to analogy as such. But this step beyond analogy was possible only because analogy itself had been a step beyond metaphor. It will thus have proved decisive for thought that a segment of equivocalness was wrested once from poetry and incorporated into philosophical discourse, just at the time when philosophical discourse was forced to disengage itself from the sway of pure univocity.

NOTES

This essay is a shortened and edited version of Study 1 and section 1 of Study 8 from Paul Ricoeur, *The Rule of Metaphor: Multi-disciplinary Studies of the Creation of Meaning in Language,* trans. Robert Czerny, with Kathleen McLaughlin and John Costello, 9–43, 259–271. Copyright © 1977 by University of Toronto Press. Reprinted by permission of University of Toronto Press Incorporated.

    1. Genette 1970.
    2. Concerning the beginnings of rhetoric, see Cope 1867, vol. 1, pp. 1–4; Chaignet 1888, pp. 1–69; Navarre 1900; Barthes 1970, pp. 175–176; Kennedy 1963.

3. Socrates attributes this formula to Gorgias in the course of the dialogue that pits him against the Athenian master of rhetoric (*Gorgias* 453a). Its germ, however, was discovered by Corax, a student of Empedocles, and the first author (followed then by Tisias of Syracuse) of a didactic treatise (*technē*) on the oratorical arts. The expression itself conveys the idea of a governing and sovereign operation (Chaignet 1888, p. 5).

4. Diogenes Laeartius 8.57; "in the *Sophist* Aristotle reports that 'Empedocles was the first to discover (*eurein*) rhetoric'" (cited in Chaignet 1888, p. 3 n. 1).

5. The *Protagoras, Gorgias,* and *Phaedrus* lay out Plato's uncompromising condemnation of rhetoric: "But we won't disturb the rest of Tisias and Gorgias, who realized that probability deserves more respect than truth, who could make trifles seem important and important points trifles by the force of their language, who dressed up novelties as antiques and vice versa, found out how to argue concisely or at interminable length about anything and everything" (*Phaedrus* 267a–267b, trans. Hackforth; see also *Gorgias* 449a–458c). Finally, 'true' rhetoric is dialectic itself, i.e., philosophy (*Phaedrus* 271c).

6. "To be brief, then, I will express myself in the language of geometricians— for by now perhaps you may follow me. Sophistic is to legislation what beautification is to gymnastics, and rhetoric to justice what cookery is to medicine" (*Gorgias* 465b–465c, trans. W. D. Woodhead). The generic term for these simulations of art—cookery, cosmetics, rhetoric, sophistic—is "flattery" (*kolakeia*, ibid. 463b). The underlying argument of which this polemic presents the negative side, is that the mode of being called "health" in the order of the body has a counterpart in the order of the spirit. This homology of the two "therapies" regulates that of the two pairs of authentic arts, gymnastics and medicine on the one hand and justice and legislation on the other (ibid. 464c).

7. ". . . to discover the means of coming as near such success [in persuading] as the circumstances of each particular case allow" (*Rhet.* 1355b10); ". . . it is the function of one and the same art [rhetoric] to discern the real and the apparent means of persuasion, just as it is the function of dialectic to discern the real and the apparent syllogism" (1355b15); "Rhetoric may be defined as the faculty of observing in any given case the available means of persuasion" (1355b25); "But rhetoric we look upon as the power of observing the means of persuasion on almost any subject presented to us" (1355b32).

8. In the *Rhetoric* (2.24.1402a17–20), Aristotle credits Corax with inventing the rhetoric of the probable: "It is of this line of argument that Corax's *Art of Rhetoric* is composed. If the accused is not open to the charge—for instance if a weakling be tried for violent assault—the defence is that he was not likely to do such a thing." Nevertheless, Aristotle cites Corax in the context of "apparent enthymemes," or paralogisms. Plato before him had given the honor of fathering probabilistic argumentation to Tisias "or whoever it really was and whatever he is pleased to be called after [Corax, the crow?]" (*Phaedrus* 273c). Regarding the use of such *eikota* arguments in Corax and Tisias, see Chaignet 1888, pp. 6–7, and Dobson 1919, chapter 1, section 5.

9. The enthymeme, the 'rhetorical syllogism' (*Rhet.* 1356b5), and 'the example,' which belongs to the inductive order (1356b15), are frameworks for

arguments that "deal with what is in the main contingent" (1357a15). Now a contingency or a "probability is a thing that usually happens; not, however, as some definitions would suggest, anything whatever that usually happens, but only if it belongs to the class of the 'contingent' or the 'variable.' It bears the same relation to that in respect of which it is probable as the universal bears to the particular" (1357a34–35).

10. For the various hypotheses concerning the order of composition of the *Rhetoric* and the *Poetics,* see McCall 1969, pp. 29–35.

11. References to the actual wording of the *Poetics* are to be found in *Rhetoric* 3.2.1; 3.2.5: 3.2.7; 3.10.7. The development of *eikōn* in the *Rhetoric,* which has no counterpart in the *Poetics,* poses a separate problem.

12. Bywater, trans.

13. The problem of translating the Greek *lexis* has inspired a variety of solutions. Among French translators, Hatzfeld and Dufour (1899) employ "discours"; Hardy (1932) says "elocution"; and Dufour and Wartelle (1973) use "style" for *lexis* in *Rhetoric* 3. Among English translators, Ross (1949) says "diction," as does Bywater (1985); Cope (1877) says "style" and calls the *Aretai Lexeōs* the "various excellences of style." Lucas translates *lexis* by "style" (1967, p. 109), and says (1450b13): "*lexis* can often be rendered by *style,* but it covers the whole process of combining words into an intelligible sequence."

14. Lucas makes the following remark in *Aristotle's Poetics* (1968, p. 204): "*Metaphors:* the word is used in a wider sense than English 'metaphor,' which is mainly confined to the third and fourth of Aristotle's types." The generic notion of transposition is assumed by the use of the terms *metaphors* and *metapherein* in diverse contexts in Aristotle's work. For example the *Eudemian Ethics* makes use of species in place of an unnamed genus (1221b12–13), transfers a quality of one part of the soul to the entire soul (1224b25), and claims that we "metaphorize" in naming intemperance *akolasia* (1230b12–13). Note the parallel text in the *Nicomachean Ethics* 3.15 (1119a36–1119b3). Thus, metaphorical transposition serves to fill the gaps in common language.

15. *Phys.* 3.1.201a15; 5.2.226a32–226b1.

16. This paradox is the core of the argument of the article "White Mythology" by Jacques Derrida: "In every rhetorical definition of metaphor is implied not just a philosophical position, but a conceptual network within which philosophy as such is constituted. Each thread of the net in addition forms a turn of speech.... Thus the definiens presupposes the definiendum" (1955, p. 30). This recurring theme is particularly striking in Aristotle, whom Derrida explores at length (ibid., pp. 18 ff.): The theory of metaphor "seems to belong to the great unmoving chain of Aristotelian ontology, with his theory of the analogy of being, his logic, his epistemology, and more precisely with the basic organisation of his poetics and his rhetoric" (ibid., p. 36). I will mention here just some technical points concerning the interpretation of Aristotle: (1) The name is never so tightly bound to the being of things, in Aristotle, that things could not be named differently, or that one could not vary their names in the diverse ways enumerated under the heading of *lexis.* Of course, *Metaphysics* Book 3 asserts that "not to have one meaning is to have no meaning" (1006a30–1006b15). But this univocity does not

exclude the possibility of a word having more than one meaning; it prevents only, in Derrida's own words, "a spread which cannot be controlled" (1955, p. 49). Hence, a limited polysemy is permitted. (2) As for the analogy of being, this is strictly speaking a medieval doctrine, founded moreover on an interpretation of the relationship of the entire series of categories to its first term, substance (*ousia*). There is nothing to justify this short circuit between proportional metaphor and the analogy of being. (3) As we shall see later, there is no link between the notion of "current" (*kurion*) meaning and "proper" meaning, if by the latter one understands a primitive, original, indigenous meaning. (4) The ontology of metaphor which seems to suggest the definition of art in terms of *mimēsis* and its subordination to the concept of *phusis* is not necessarily 'metaphysical,' in the sense that Heidegger has given to this word. I will propose later an interpretation of the implicit ontology of Aristotle's *Poetics* that in no way employs the transition from the visible to the invisible.

17. Rostagni, it is true, translates *kurion* by *proprio* (*Index* 188 *ad proprio*); see 1457b3 (1928, p. 125).

18. This point is crucial for Derrida's interpretation. It constitutes one link in the demonstration of the close connection between the theory of metaphor and Aristotelian ontology. Even though the *kurion* of the *Poetics* and *Rhetoric* and the *idion* of the *Topics* do not coincide, Derrida says that "this whole 'metaphorology' seems to be sustained by the notion of the *idion*, though it does not occupy the forefront" (1955, p. 48). Now, a study of the *Topics* offers encouragement neither to the assimilation of *kurion* and *idion* nor especially to the interpretation of *idion* as being original, primitive, indigenous in the "metaphysical" sense. The manner in which the *Topics* deals with *idion* is based on considerations completely outside the theory of *lexis*, and foreign in particular to the theory of ordinary or unusual denominations. The "proper" (or "Property," trans. Pickard-Cambridge) is one of the four foundational notions that the tradition has called the "predicables," to distinguish them from the "predicaments," which are the categories (cf. Brunschwig 1967, introduction to the French translation of the *Topics*). It is with this in mind that the "proper" ("property") is distinguished from "accident," "genus," and "definition." Now what does this mean, that the "proper" should be a predicable? It means that every proposition (every concrete focus of reasoning) and every problem (every subject with which discourse is concerned) "indicates either a genus or a peculiarity or an accident" (101b17). In turn the peculiarity, or proper or property, is divided into two parts, one signifying "the essential of the essence" (Brunschwig's translation of *to ti ēn einai;* often called quiddity) and the other not signifying it. Now the first of these parts is called "definition" in the *Topics*, while the second in the "proper" ("Property") in its strict sense. Thus we have four predicables, "property or definition or genus or accident" (101b25). From these notions all propositions are formed, because every proposition must assign its predicate in terms of one of these predicables. Accordingly and henceforth, it appears that in setting the "proper" among the predicables, Aristotle situates it on a level distinct from that of denomination, to which alone belongs the opposition among ordinary words and metaphorical words, lengthened, abbreviated, and coined words, and so on. On the other hand, the "proper"

belongs to a logic of predication. This latter builds upon a double polarity: essential and nonessential, coextensive and noncoextensive. Definition is at once both essential and coextensive, while accident is neither essential nor coextensive. The proper is located midway between these two poles, as something which is not essential, but coextensive: "A 'property' is a predicate which does not indicate the essence of a thing, but yet belongs to that thing alone, and is predicated controvertibly of it" (102a18–19). Thus, to be capable of reading and writing is a property (is proper) with respect to being human. By contrast, to sleep is not proper to man, since this predicate can be applied to another subject and, conversely, cannot be substituted for the predicate "man" although nothing prevents it being implied that a given subject happens to be a man. Thus, the proper is somewhat less than the definition, but much more than an accident which may or may not belong to one and the same subject. Since it does not point to essence, I should say that the criterion retained for the proper is the commutability of subject and predicate, what Aristotle calls convertibility. As we see, no metaphysical abyss reveals itself here. It suffices that the predicate should be coextensive without being essential, according to the "crossed dichotomy" detailed above in the manner of Brunschwig. Furthermore, this criterion of coextensiveness finds its true function within argumentation itself: to show that a predicate is not coextensive is to refute a proposed definition. An appropriate method corresponds to this strategy, the topic of the proper, which applies to the good use of nondefinitional predicates that are neither generic nor accidental. Finally—and above all—the location of the theory of the proper within the *Topics* is enough to remind us that we are not here in a fundamental, or constitutive, order, but in the order of dialectic. "The formal objects" of dialectic, points out Brunschwig, are "the discourses about things and not the things themselves" (1967, p. 50); like "games based on a contract . . . each predicable corresponds to a particular type of contract" (ibid.). The partial topic of the "proper" is not exempt in this regard; it regulates the workings of discourse relative to the application of coextensive but nonessential predicates. Aristotle devotes Book 5 of the *Topics* to it; there we find the "proper" defined again, in 5.2 (129b1 ff.) and 5.4 (132a22–26). So Aristotle would only have had to make a "proper" meaning of this notion, in order to oppose the series of deviations of denomination to it; but he needed the notion of "current" meaning, which defines its use in denomination.

19. Concerning the vocabulary of substitution in Aristotle, see 1458b13–26: "To realize the difference one should take an epic verse and see how it reads when the normal words are introduced [*epithemenōn*]." He proceeds to use verb forms of 'substitution' four times in succession: *metatitheis, metathentos, metathēken, metatitheis* (1458b16, 20, 24, 26 respectively). Substitution works in both directions, from the current word to the rare or metaphorical, and from the latter to the former: "The same should be done with the strange word, the metaphor, and the rest; for one has only to put the ordinary words in their place to see the truth of what we are saying" (1458b18). But see the following note for the major exception, which occurs when metaphor names an "anonymous" genus.

20. We have already pointed to this use of metaphor as the transfer of naming in the case of an 'anonymous' genus, or of a thing that has no name. Examples

abound; see *Phys.* 5, the definition of growth and decay, the definition of *phora*. The problem is dealt with explicitly in the first chapter of the *Sophistical Refutations*, concerning ambiguity: "For names are finite and so is the sum-total of formulae (*logoi*), while things are infinite in number. Inevitably, then, the same formulae, and a single name, have a number of meanings" (165a10–13, trans. Pickard-Cambridge).

21. Ryle 1949, pp. 16 ff., 33, 77–79, 152, 168, 206.

22. Black 1962.

23. Gadamer 1960; on *metaphoric*, see pp. 71, 406 ff.

24. Hirsch 1967, pp. 169 ff.

25. McCall devotes a whole chapter to *eikōn* in Aristotle (1969, pp. 24–53). See also Cope 1867, pp. 290–292.

26. Richards 1934, 1937.

27. McCall 1969, p. 51, cites 3.4.1406a20, 1406b25–26, 1407a14–15; 3.10.1410b17–18; 3.11.1412b34–35, 1413a15–16.

28. Whereas Cope saw a perfect correspondence between the definition of simile as an 'extended metaphor' and the definition, coming from Cicero and Quintilian, of metaphor as a 'contracted simile' (1867, p. 290), McCall insists that the later tradition 'reverses' matters (1969, p. 51). The case of Quintilian (ibid., pp. 178–239) is particularly striking. He states: *in totum autem metaphora brevior est similitudo* ("on the whole metaphor is a shorter form of *similitudo*") (ibid., p. 230, from *De Institutione Oratoria Libri Duodecim* 8.6.8–9). McCall remarks that Quintilian has put the matter more strongly than if he had just said *brevior est quem similitudo*, or *brevior est similitudine*, expressions "which would put metaphor and *similitudo* on an equal footing" (ibid., p. 230). It is true that Le Guern disputes this interpretation (1973, p. 54 n. 1), invoking the Paris edition of 1527, which gives *brevior quam similitudo*. If this were so, "the classical explanation of metaphor would have its origin in a corruption of the text of Quintilian" (ibid.). The consistency of the post-Aristotelian tradition lends little credibility to this hypothesis.

29. As we saw earlier (note 9), *paradeigma* is distinct from *enthumēma* as a probable induction is from a probable deduction. There are two kinds of *paradeigma* or example, actual (or historical) parallels and invented parallels. The latter can be either 'illustrations' (*parabolē*) or 'fables' (*logoi*), such as Aesop's fables (*Rhet.* 2.20.1393a28–31). Ultimately, the heart of the opposition is between historical example, to which *paradeigma* reduces, and the illustrative parallel, which is the essence of *parabolē*. The unity of historical example and fictive comparison is purely epistemological, in that both are forms of persuasion or proof. On all this, see McCall 1969, pp. 24–29.

30. This adjective, *haploun* ('simple'), raises various problems of interpretation and also of translation. To call comparison simple, when one says on the other hand that it "speaks, or is made, on the basis of two," seems to be contradictory. Certainly one must agree that comparison, made up of only two terms and one relationship, is "simple" compared with proportional metaphor, which is composed of four terms and two relationships (see McCall's discussion of Cope's and Roberts's interpretations, 1969, pp. 46–47). For my part, I do not see any contradiction in calling simple the expression "a shield is a cup," from which the terms

"Ares" and "Dionysius" are absent. This does not prevent its being composed of two terms. By contrast, McCall uses the translation "involves two relations" (ibid., p. 45), the reason actually being its closeness to proportional metaphor. He refers to *Rhetoric* 3.4 (1407a15–18), which makes a point of the reversibility of proportional metaphor; if one can give the fourth term the name of the second, one must be able to do the opposite—for example, if the cup is the shield of Dionysius, it is quite appropriate to call the shield the cup of Ares.

31. Cope 1877 translates 3.10.11 as follows: "Similes . . . are composed of (or expressed in) two terms, just like the proportional metaphors" (p. 137). And he comments: "The difference between a *simile* and a metaphor is—besides the greater detail of the former, the simile being a metaphor *writ large*—that it always *distinctly expresses* the two terms that are being compared, bringing them into *apparent* contrast; the metaphor, on the other hand, *substituting* by *transfer* the one notion for the other of the two compared, identifies them as it were in one image, and expresses both in a *single* word, leaving the comparison between the object illustrated and the analogous notion which throws a new light upon it, to suggest itself from the manifest correspondence to the hearer" (ibid., pp. 137–138).

32. It is the same in 3.10.7: the example borrowed from Pericles contains the explicit marks of comparison (*houtōs . . . hōsper*); on the other hand, that taken from Leptines displays metaphor's brevity—"he would not have the Athenians let Greece 'lose one of her two eyes'" (1411a2–5). The examples of 3.11.12 and 3.11.13 are also to be considered from this point of view (1413a2–13). It is true that Aristotle's quotations are generally inexact. Among those that can be verified (*Republic* 5.469d–469e; 6.488a–488b; 10.601b), the first two contain neither the conjunction nor the verb nor the adjective of comparison ("Do you see any difference between . . . ?" "Conceive this sort of thing happening . . ."); only the third contains a term of comparison ('resemble'). The grammatical mark can vary, however, without affecting the general meaning of the comparison. This is noted by McCall, who speaks of an 'overall element of comparison' in connection with 'stylistic comparison' (1969, p. 36), as opposed to the illustrative comparison whose purpose is to prove.

33. Beardsley 1958.

34. A similar relationship underlies the suggested affinity between proverbs (*paroimiai*) and metaphors (1413a14–16). These are metaphors, it is suggested, that relate species to species. The proverb is, in effect, a comparison pursued between two orders of things (the man abused by the guest whom he has received into his house and the rabbit eating the crop of the peasant who brought him onto his land) (ibid.). The "like" of comparison can be omitted here just as in metaphor, and with the same result: the relationship is that much more striking to the extent that it is unexpected, even paradoxical and bewildering. This same paradox, which is connected to explicit or implicit comparison, is also the kernel of hyperbole, which is nothing but an exaggerated comparison that is developed in the face of obvious differences. Thus, Aristotle can say, "Successful hyperboles are also metaphors" (1413a19).

35. In this sense, 'new' metaphors (to use a name borrowed from Theodorus), which Aristotle likens to "paradoxical" metaphors, are not exceptions to a rule, but rather are metaphors par excellence.

36. Why does Aristotle say the *eikōn* is "of the nature of poetry" (1406b25) when the *Poetics* ignores it? (The sole mention of the word *eikōn* in the *Poetics* has nothing to do with comparison—1448b10, 15.) Is the opening not provided when the *Poetics* extols "the art of metaphorizing well" and links it to the ability to perceive similarities (1459a5–8)? All we can do is note this strange neglect: "the odd absence of *eikōn* from the *Poetics* must be left unresolved" (McCall 1969, p. 51).

37. "Now since architecture is an art and is essentially a reasoned state of capacity to make, and there is neither any art that is not such a state nor any such state that is not an art, *art* is identical with a state of capacity to make, involving a true course of reasoning. All art is concerned with coming into being, i.e., with contriving and considering how something may come into being which is capable of either being or not being, and whose origin is in the maker and not in the thing made; for art is concerned neither with things that are, or come into being, by necessity, nor with things that do so in accordance with nature (since these have their origin in themselves)" (*NE* 1140a6–16, trans. Ross).

38. It would be impossible to overemphasize the humbling—the "loss of prestige," says Brunschwig in his introduction to Aristotle's *Topics*—that dialectic suffers in passing from Plato's hands into those of Aristotle. Sovereign and synoptic science in Plato, it is only the theory of probabilistic argumentation with Aristotle (see Aubenque 1962, pp. 251–264; Gueroult 1963).

39. The *endoxa of Rhetoric* 1.11 (1355b17) are defined precisely in *Topics* 1.10 (104a8): "Now a dialectical proposition consists in asking something that is held [*endoxos*] by all men or by most men or by the philosophers, i.e., either by all, or by most, or by the most notable of these, provided it be not contrary to the general opinion; for a man would probably assent to the view of the philosophers, if it be not contrary to the opinions of most men" (trans. Pickard-Cambridge). The *endoxa* are ideas taken up into the 'center-play' [*jeu à deux*] that constitutes dialectical discussion (Brunschwig 1967, p. xxiii). This characteristic of propositions is the signature of dialectical syllogism, whose premises are 'assented to in reality' (ibid., p. xxiv), as opposed on the one hand to demonstrative syllogism, whose premises are intrinsically true, and on the other hand to "apparently endoxal" propositions, which make reasoning materially eristic.

40. Brunschwig relates the question of *topoi* to that of dialectical reasoning in the following way: "As a first approximation, the *topoi* can be described as rules, or if one prefers, as recipes for argumentation, arranged to supply effective tools to a very precisely laid out activity, that of dialectical discussion" (1967, p. ix). The author adds: "Closely bound up with the activity which they pretend to take from the level of blind practice and advance to that of methodic art, the *Topics*, the *vademecum* of the perfect dialectician, run the risk of appearing to be an art of winning at a game that no one plays any longer" (ibid., p. ix). But then, why speak of *topoi* to designate this "machinery for constructing premises on the basis of a given conclusion" (ibid., p. xxxix)? One can emphasize the fact that the *topoi* are scattered about, or the fact that each has an assembling function. On the one hand, stress can be put on the "non-systematic and seemingly headless [character] of logical thought" in the dialectical order (ibid., p. xiv), and on the closed nature of the isolated units located in this fashion. But one can also draw attention to the

fact, as does *Rhet.* 2.26 (1403a17), that each *topos* "embrac(es) a large number of particular kinds of enthymeme." This unifying function is exercised in succession by the topics of accident, genus, proper or property (Book 5), and definition.

41. Düring 1966 sees grounds in this opposition between prose and poetry for calling *Rhetoric* Book 3 "die Schrift 'von der Prosa'" (pp. 149 ff.). While mindful of the definition in the *Poetics* (1450b13), which identifies *lexis* with the verbal expression of thought, Düring notes that in the context of the *Rhetoric*, *lexis* tends to become more and more like "die literarische Kunstprose" (ibid., p. 150), yet without reducing to a theory of kinds of style (*charaktēres* or *genera dicendi*), which is a Hellenistic creation.

42. It is interesting to note the reasons for this superiority: "It was naturally the poets who first set the movement going; for words represent things, and they had also the human voice at their disposal, which of all our organs can best represent other things" (*Rhet.* 3.1.1404a20–22).

43. Cope 1867 observes that while the overall outline was already familiar in Aristotle's time, the division into four 'excellences'—purity, perspicuity, ornament, and propriety—"is not accurately made, nor the order regularly followed" (p. 279). Moreover, the line is broken frequently, by the study of similitude for instance, or by considerations that do not fit easily into an enumeration of the virtues of *lexis*, like the remarks concerning the 'form' of *lexis* (rhythm, free-running and periodic style, 3.8 and 3.9).

44. The verb that designates deviation—*exallattō, exallaxai*—comes up twice: "Such variation from what is usual" (1404b8) and "They depart from what is suitable, in the direction of excess" (1404b30). In each instance, an unusual usage is opposed to one that is customary and commonplace (*to de kurion kai to oikeion,* 1404b32) or suitable (*prepon,* 1404b30).

45. It is more difficult to relate to the theme of 'clarity' what is said immediately after in regard to the 'beauty' words should have: "The beauty, like the ugliness, of all words may, as Licymnius says, lie in their sound or in their meaning" (3.2.12.1405b6–7). And a bit further on: "The materials of metaphor must be beautiful to the ear, to the understanding, to the eye or some other physical sense" (3.2.12.1405b17–18). It seems that the function of pleasing prevails here over that of indirect signification. The polarity of clarity and beauty might reflect something of the tension at the heart of eloquence or style, which was spoken of earlier.

46. For Cope, this disquisition on errors of style or bad taste does not imply the introduction of a specific excellence or virtue that would be 'warmth' in style (1867, pp. 286–290).

47. The same argument—avoidance of what would be too poetic—is applied to metaphors intended as euphemisms, and in general to circumlocutions (3.6.4.1.1407b32–35).

48. Cope's commentary is particularly brilliant (1867, pp. 316–323).

49. Ross 1923 gives the same rendering; Lucas 1968 opts for "communication by means of words."

50. Hardy 1932 remarks, "The text and the meaning of this sentence are very much in doubt." The French translation—"car quelle serait l'oeuvre propre du personnage pariant, si sa pensée était manifeste et ne résultait pas de son lan-

gage"—is less clear than Bywater's (1985), which emphasizes that language in general, like the figure in particular (as mentioned earlier) functions as the manifesting, the "making-it-appear," of discourse. Hence, what 'thought' still lacks in order to become poem is the "appearing." In this regard, Derrida observes: "If there were no difference between *dianoia* and *lexis* there would be no room for tragedy. . . . The difference is not restricted to the possibility that a character may think one thing and say another. He exists and acts in the tragedy only on condition that he speak" (1955, p. 32).

51. McKeon 1936 and 1954, pp. 102–223; Golden and Hardison 1958.

52. In the second text cited in the preceding note, McKeon points to the *aesthetics of genius* as the source of the pejorative interpretation of *mimēsis*.

53. On all this see McKeon, to whom, in large part, the development of what follows is owed. He insists on the necessity of always re-creating the philosophical contexts in which a concept acquires meaning, and of relating every definition to the philosopher's own methodology.

54. McKeon writes: "Imitation functions in that system as the *differentia* by which the arts, useful and fine, are distinguished from nature" (1936, p. 131).

55. Golden and Hardison 1968, pp. 68–69, 79, 87, 93, 95–96, 115; and the epilogue, "On Aristotelian Imitation," pp. 281–296. Similarly, Else 1963 is justified in dwelling on the paradox of defining *poiēsis* as *mimēsis*. He notes, with reference to 1451b27–33: "What the poet makes, then, is not the actuality of events but their logical structure, their meaning" (1963, p. 321). It is in this manner that creating and initiating can coincide. In this way also, the feeling of terror itself can be caused by imitation (1453b8), in that the plot itself is the imitation (1963, pp. 410–411, 447–450).

56. It constitutes, according to Hardison (1963, p. 96), the 'first logical unit' of the *Poetics*. At the same time it adds to the significance of Aristotle's introductory remark, "Let us follow the natural order and begin with the primary facts" (1447a13).

57. Golden and Hardison 1963, p. 115. Hardison depends here on a Golden article, "Catharsis."

58. "Tragic imitation, then, can be understood as a six-part process that begins with plot" (Golden and Hardison 1963, p. 286).

59. Hardison goes so far as to say that the tragic poem "universalizes" history or nature (1963, pp. 291 ff.). History as such proffers nothing but the singular, nothing but undifferentiated individuals. Now the story is an intelligible interpretation of history, in a broad sense including or embracing a collection of single things. An action thus 'universalized' would obviously not be a copy.

60. The interpretation of tragic *katharsis* proposed by Golden acquires a certain measure of plausibility at this point, to the extent at least that the purification of pity and terror is mediated by the clarification effected by the intelligibility of the plot, spectacle, characters, and thought.

61. See the words "perfection" or "virtue" (*aretē*, 1458a18), "rule of moderation" (*metrion*, 1458b12), "improper" (*aprepōs*, 1458b14), "proper use" (*to harmottom*, 1458b15, and *prepontōs khrēsthai*, 1459a4).

62. It is worth noting the occurrences of the word *phusis* in the *Poetics*, as these constitute a network replete with allusion pointing beyond that work. *Mimēsis* is the first thing to be mentioned if one is to follow the natural order (1447a12): here, "nature" designates the division of knowledge according to the order of things, in virtue of which imitation is to be found in the orbit of the sciences of "making." The concept of *telos* occasions an indirect allusion to nature: "It is the action in it, i.e., its Fable or Plot, that is the end and purpose of tragedy" (1450a22). In a slightly less allusive fashion it is said that "the first essential [*arkhē*], the life and soul [*psukhē*], so to speak, of Tragedy is the Plot" (1450a38), whereas thought and character are the 'natural cause' of the actions (1450a1). As for imitation itself, it is linked to nature in that "imitation is natural [*sumphoton*] to man" (1448b5); moreover, man is distinct from the animals in that "he is the most imitative of creatures" (1448b7). It is nature again that among men distinguishes the most gifted artists (mastery of metaphor "is a sign of genius [*euphuis*]," 1459a7); indeed, poets take up comedy or tragedy as their own natures dictate (1449a15). Finally, among all the poetic genres, the development of tragedy, which is born in improvisation and is thus in continuity with nature, culminates at a certain point when it attains its natural form (1449a15). Furthermore, the characteristics of order, of completeness (*teleion*), of symmetry—in brief, everything that makes of a tragedy a perfect composition, something whole in itself—at the same time reveal "the limit . . . set by the actual nature of the thing" (1451a9). Thus the concept of nature, although not thematized as such in the *Poetics*, returns repeatedly as an operational concept.

63. For Derrida (1955, pp. 36–37), the tightly drawn agreement linking *mimēsis* and *phusis* constitutes one of the most penetrating indices of the dependence of metaphorology with respect to onto-theology. One could say that this partnership reveals the "gesture constitutive of metaphysics and of humanity" (1955, p. 37). The preceding note owes much to Derrida, in both its substance and its tone of analysis.

64. The formula "art imitates nature" pervades Aristotle's work. Décarie (1963) notes it already in the *Protrepticus*, where it contrasts with a Platonic formulation (*Laws* 10.888e–890d). "And nature's product always has an end and it is always constituted in view of a higher end than that of the product of art; for art imitates nature, not nature art" (1963, p. 23 n. 3). The formula does not serve here to distinguish, nor even to coordinate; it seeks to subordinate. But the context shows us why: the exhortation to philosophize, which is the object of the treatise, is based upon "the will of nature" (ibid.). It is necessary, therefore, to move from the teleology of art to an even higher teleology. In a different way. Aristotle's *Physics* (2.2.194a21–27) argues from what is seen in art to what must be demonstrated in the case of nature, namely, composition of form and of matter, and teleology. The argument reads as follows (trans. Hardie and Gaye): "*If* . . . art imitates nature . . . it would be the part of physics also to know nature in both its senses [form and matter]." And the text continues, "nature is the end or 'that for the sake of which'" (194a28). The same formula evidently could be read in the opposite sense and would thus distinguish art from nature on the grounds that art receives the characteristic of having an end from nature. This

is the very source of the autonomy of art: for it is not the things produced, there to be copied, which are imitable in nature, but production itself and its teleological order, which remains to be understood and which the plot may reconstruct. On imitation in Aristotle, see Aubenque 1962, pp. 487–508.

65. Benveniste 1966, pp. 55–64.

66. The first six categories refer to *nominal* forms: that is, the linguistic class of nouns; then, in the general class of adjectives, two types of adjectives designating quantity and quality; then the comparative, which is the "relative" form by reason of its function; then the denominations of place and time. The next four are all verbal categories: the active voice and the passive voice; then the category of mediative verbs (as distinct from active verbs); then that of the perfect as "being a certain state." (It should be noted that Benveniste's linguistic genius succeeds in interpreting these last two categories, which have embarrassed countless interpreters.) In this way, Aristotle thought he was defining the attributes of objects but he was really setting up linguistic entities (1966, p. 60).

67. The second study bears the very direct title "The System of Aristotle's *Categories* and Its Logical and Metaphysical Signification" (1967, pp. 44–125). I shall invert the order followed by Vuillemin in his work because my purpose is different from his: Vuillemin wants to show that analogy comes from a pseudoscience that links up with theology. This is why he moves directly to a discussion of analogy and its logical deficiency in the first study of his book. Since I want to show the split between philosophical and poetic discourse at the point where they appear to be closest, I go directly to the point where the split is widest: this is the point where Vuillemin does justice to the systematic construction of the Aristotelian treatise on the *Categories*.

68. Vuillemin 1967, p. 110.

69. "In the same way, Aristotle assumes the theory of analogy in the *Categories:* being is said in different ways, but these different acceptations are ordered in that they all derive, more or less directly, from a fundamental acceptation that is the attribution of a secondary substance to a primary substance" (1967, p. 226).

70. "For it must be either by an equivocation that we say [things] *are,* or by adding to and taking from the meaning of 'are' (in the way in which that which is not known may be said to be known)—the truth being that we use the word neither ambiguously nor in the same sense, but just as we apply the word *medical* by virtue of a *reference* to one and the same thing, not *meaning* one and the same thing, nor yet speaking ambiguously; for a patient and an operation and an instrument are called medical neither by an ambiguity nor with a single meaning, but with reference to a common end" (*Met.* 6.4.1030a31–1030b4). Décarie exhibits the connection between Book 6 and the outline of the multiple meanings of being in Book 4; he underlines that "the other categories derive their meaning from this primary being" (1961, p. 138). This pivotal semantic and ontological function of *ousis* is lost from sight somewhat in an aporetic interpretation of Aristotelian ontology.

71. Vuillemin 1967, p. 229. For Vuillemin, the pseudoscience into which Western philosophy has strayed begins here. According to him, analogy was erased from modern philosophy only when, in Russell, Wittgenstein, and Carnap,

a single, fundamental signification was attributed to the copula, namely, that an element belongs to a class. "At that moment, the notion of analogy disappeared and Metaphysics as a science was made possible" (ibid., p. 228). This, of course, assumes that the meaning of the verb *to be* is exhausted in this logical reduction—precisely what we deny in the present work.

72. "It is indeed this ontological description, superimposed on logical description, that can properly be considered the guiding thread of the deduction" (1967, p. 78). "Philosophical analysis must continually correct grammatical appearances and reverse the order of subordination that grammar implies. At the same time, it makes the guiding thread of the deduction apparent" (ibid., p. 86).

73. This is what Vuillemin does: "So, if there is no quiddity, in the primordial sense, with respect to a composite such as *white man*, there will be quiddity in a derivative sense. There will be predications by analogy, not in a synonymous but in a paronymous fashion; the predication is thus 'transcendental'" (1967, p. 63).

74. Vuillemin restores the fundamental breakdown by subdividing each of the two classes of essential and accidental predication into primordial and derivative, then each of the four classes obtained in this way in terms of the difference between primary substance and secondary substance. The table of a priori possibilities of predication is found in 1967, pp. 66–75.

75. Vuillemin recognizes this: "The theory of analogy, implicit in the theory of paronyms, allows us to consider under the same principle—although, we might say, in a progressively diminishing relation—the signification of the copula, the relation of subordination between secondary substances, and the relations of subordination between abstract particulars and abstract generalities on the one hand and between abstract generalities on the other" (1967, p. 111). We shall say nothing here regarding the fourth part of the *Categories* (paragraphs 10–15): Enumerating postpredicaments, Vuillemin observes, allows the series of categories to be placed within Aristotle's metaphysics; by introducing the rudiments of a theory of motion, the treatise sets out the distinction between three kinds of substance and the subordination of the universe to the third substance (God), and sketches "the unity of logic, physics and theology" (ibid.).

76. "So, too, there are many senses in which a thing is said to be, but all refer to one starting point: some things are said to be because they are substances, others because they are affections of substance, others because they are a process towards substance, or destructions or privations or qualities of substance, or productive or generative of substance, or of things which are relative to substance, or negations of one of these things or of substance itself" (*Met.* 3.2.1003b6–10). On this point, we refer to Décarie's excellent commentary, which stresses again the "common notion" role of *ousis*, thanks to which "a single science is entrusted with studying all beings as beings" (1961, p. 102).

77. Aubenque 1962.

78. Aubenque goes so far as to see in Aristotle a tragic character comparable to that of Pascal, who upheld "the impossibility of the necessary" (1962, p. 219 n. 2).

79. The text in question here is *Metaphysics* 1, where Aristotle applies his notion of reference to a first term no longer to the sequence of meanings of being

out to the very hierarchy of beings. Therefore, *ousia* is no longer the first of the categories; rather, divine *ousia* is supreme being. This reference to a first term, no longer on the level of meanings but on the level of beings, is supposed to serve as the basis for the very discourse on being. "For one might raise the question," Aristotle says, "whether first philosophy is universal, or deals with one genus, i.e., some one kind of being; for not even the mathematical sciences are all alike in this respect—geometry and astronomy deal with a certain particular kind of thing, while universal mathematics applies alike to all. We answer that if there is no substance other than those which are formed by nature, natural science will be the first science; but if there is an immovable substance, the science of this must be prior and must be first philosophy, and universal in this way, because it is first" (*Met.* 5.1.1026a23–30). Décarie's inquiry into "the object of metaphysics according to Aristotle" attests to the continuity of the link between ontology and theology throughout the entire Aristotelian corpus (concerning this passage from the *Met.*, see Décarie 1961, pp. 111–124).

80. Aubenque readily grants this: "The reality of *khōrismos* can be experienced less as an irremediable separation than as the invitation to overcome it. In short, between ontological investigation and contemplation of the divine, relations can and must exist that the word *separation* is not sufficient to express fully" (1962, p. 335).

81. See Aubenque's analysis of theological appendices in various places in *Metaphysics* 3 and of the physical preparation in 11.1–5 of the theological exposition in 11.6–10 (1962, pp. 393 ff.)

82. "The impossible ideal of a world whose unity would be restored . . . must remain, at the very heart of irremediable dispersion, the guiding principle of human investigation and action" (Aubenque 1962, p. 402). And a little further on: "The unity of discourse could never be given in itself; nor could it ever be 'sought,' moreover, if discourse were not directed by the ideal of a subsisting unity" (ibid., p. 403). Again, "if the divine does not exhibit the unity ontology seeks, it nonetheless guides ontology in its search" (ibid., p. 404). And finally, "it is the necessity of motion that, through the mediation of philosophical discourse, divides being against itself according to a plurality of meanings, the unity of which is still indefinitely sought after" (ibid., p. 438).

83. "*Ousia*," Aubenque says, "is one of the rare words that Aristotle employs to speak both of sub-lunary realities and of divine reality, without any indication that this common denomination is merely metaphorical or analogical" (1962, p. 405). This remark should be followed by a more decisive recognition of the unitive function that falls to the category of *ousia.*

84. Aristotle "can only have meant the following: human discourse must proceed as *if* the causes of essences were the causes of all things, as if the world were a well-ordered whole and not a rhapsodic series, as if all things could be traced back to the first among them, that is to essences, and to the first of the essences, as to their Principle" (Aubenque 1962, p. 407).

85. Ross understands this in the following way: "Except as regards the first cause, things in different genera have only analogically the same causes" (1923, p. 175).

86. Vuillemin 1967, p. 14. The author shows that the mathematical notion of analogy stems from the modification by Theaetetus of an earlier definition that applied only to rational numbers. It is through the operation of *alternating diminution*—which implies development *ad infinitum* (ibid., p. 13)—that the idea of number could be extended to irrationals by Greek mathematicians.

87. ". . . (proportion being not a property only of the kind of number which consists of abstract units, but of number in general (*holōs arithmou*]). For proportion is equality of ratios, and involves four terms at least . . ." (*NE* 1131a30–32).

88. It is at this point in the continuous extension of mathematical analogy and in the weakening of its criteria that the relation of proportionality rejoins the theory of metaphor, or at least its most "logical" aspect, proportional metaphor. But poetic discourse merely utilizes it, whereas philosophical discourse sets out its theory, placing it on a trajectory of meaning somewhere between mathematical proportion and reference *ad unum*.

89. "The causes and the principles of different things are in a sense different, but in a sense, if one speaks universally and analogically, they are the same for all" (*Met.* 11.4.1070a31–33). See also 11.5.1071a4 and 27, and, of course, the passage cited above (11.5.1071a33–37).

90. *Met.* 11.2.1003a34–1003b4; 3.4.1030a35–1030b3.

91. On this point, see Vuillemin 1967, p. 22.

92. Considering the terms of analogy themselves, he will observe that the common attribution of being to substance and to accident implicitly reduces judgments of relation to judgments of predication. Now, the true judgment of predication (if one puts aside essential definition) does not allow reciprocation. But above all, by placing substance at the head of metaphysics, philosophy designates a term for which no science exists, since substance is in every case a determined individual and science deals only with genera and species. For this reason, the order of things escapes the scientific order, which is abstract and does not treat substances in the primary sense. Considering in addition the relation of the other categories to substance, the logician can only repeat Aristotle's own admission: if science is generic and if the bond of being is not generic, then the analogical bond of being is not scientific. We must then recognize "the lack of scientific communicability among the genera of being" (Vuillemin 1967, p. 41).

93. "In general, if we search for the elements of existing things without distinguishing the many senses in which things are said to exist, we cannot find them, especially if the search for the elements of which things are made is conducted in this manner. For it is surely impossible to discover what 'acting' or 'being acted on,' or the 'straight' is made of, but if elements can be discovered at all, it is only the elements of substances; therefore either to seek the elements of all existing things or to think one has them is incorrect" (*Met.* 11.9.992b18–25).

REFERENCES

Aubenque, P. *Le Problème de l'êitre chez Aristote. Essai sur la problématique aristotélicienne.* Paris, 1962.

Austin, J. L. *How to Do Things with Words?* ed. J. O. Urmson. Oxford, 1962.

Barthes, R. "L'ancienne rhétorique, aide-mémoire." *Communications* 16 (1970): 172–229.

Beardsley, M. C. *Aesthetics.* New York, 1958.

Benveniste, E. *Problèmes de linguistique générale.* Vol. 1. Paris, 1966.

Black, M. *Models and Metaphors.* Ithaca, 1962.

Brunschwig, J., ed. *Topiques* [Livres I à IV]. Paris, 1967.

Bywater, I. *The Poetics.* In *The Complete Works of Aristotle,* ed. J. Barnes. Princeton, 1985.

Chaignet, A. E. *La Rhétorique et son histoire.* Paris, 1888.

Cope, E. M. *An Introduction to Aristotle's Rhetoric.* London, 1867.

———. *The Rhetoric of Aristotle, with a Commentary,* rev. and ed. J. E Sandys. 3 vols. Cambridge, 1877.

Décarie, V. *L'Objet de la métaphysique selon Aristote.* Montréal-Paris, 1961.

Derrida, J. "White Mythology." In *Margins of Philosophy,* trans. A. Bass. Chicago, 1982.

Dobson, J. F. *The Greek Orators.* New York, 1919.

Dufour, M. *Aristote. Rhétorique.* Paris, 1932.

Düring, I. *Aristoteles, Darstellung und Interpretation seines Denkens.* Heidelberg, 1966.

Else, G. F. *Aristotle's Poetics: The Argument.* Cambridge, 1963.

Gadamer, H.-G. *Wahrheit und Methode.* Tübingen, 1960.

Genette, G. "La rhétorique restreinte." *Communications* 16 (1970).

———. *Figures.* Vol. 1. Paris, 1966.

Golden, L. "Catharsis." *Transactions of the American Philosophical Association* 42 (1962).

Golden, L., and O. B. Hardison. *Aristotle's Poetics, a Translation and Commentary for Students of Literature.* Englewood Cliffs, N.J., 1958.

Goodman, N. *Languages of Art, an Approach to a Theory of Symbol.* Indianapolis, 1968.

Guéroult, M. "Logique, argumentation et histoire de la philosophie chez Aristote." In *Mélanges en hommage à Ch. Perelman: La Théorie de l'argumentation. Perspectives et applications.* Louvain-Paris, 1963.

Hardy, J., trans. *Poétique.* Paris, 1932.

Hatzfeld, A., and M. Dufour, trans. *La Poëtique d'Aristote.* Paris, 1899.

Hirsch, E. D. *Validity in Interpretation.* New Haven, 1967.

Jaeger, W. *Aristotle,* trans. R. R. Robinson. Oxford, 1934.

Jakobson, R. "Closing Statements: Linguistics and Poetics." In *Style in Language,* ed. T. A. Sebeok. New York, 1960.

Kennedy, G. A. *The Art of Persuasion in Greece.* Princeton, 1963.

Le Guern, M. *Sémantique de la métaphore et de la métonymie.* Paris, 1973.

Lucas, D. W. *Aristotle's Poetics.* Oxford, 1968.

McCall, M. *Ancient Rhetorical Theories of Simile and Comparison.* Cambridge, 1969.

McKeon, R. "Literary Criticism and the Concept of Imitation in Antiquity." *Modern Philology* 34 (1936): 1–5. Reprinted in R. S. Crane, ed., *Critics and Criticism: Essays on Method by a Group of the Chicago Critics* (Chicago, 1952).

————. "Imitation and Poetry." In *Thought Action and Passion*. Chicago, 1954.

Navarre, O. *Essai sur la rhétorique grecque avant Aristote*. Paris, 1900.

Peirce, C. S. *Collected Papers*. Cambridge, 1931–1958.

Quintilian. *De Institutione Oratoria Libri Duodecim*. Leipzig, 1798–1834.

Richards, I. A. *Coleridge on Imagination*. London, 1934.

————. *The Philosophy of Rhetoric*. Oxford, 1936.

Ross, W. D. *Aristotle*. London, 1923.

Rostagni, A. *La Poetica*. Torino, 1928.

Ryle, G. *The Concept of Mind*. London, 1949.

————. "The Theory of Meaning." In *British Philosophy in the Mid-Century*, ed. C. A. Mace. London, 1957.

Vuillemin, J. *De la logique à la théologie. Cinq études sur Aristote*. Paris, 1967.

Artifice and Persuasion: The Work of Metaphor in the *Rhetoric*

Richard Moran

What, indeed, would be the good of the speaker,
if things appeared in the required light
even apart from anything he says?
—POETICS 1456b8

The distinction between the literal and the metaphorical has never been a merely descriptive one. From its origins in ancient Greek thought, G. E. R. Lloyd reminds us that, as with the development of the category of myth as fiction, "the invention of the category of the metaphorical took place against a background of overt polemic" (Lloyd 1987, 172). And the philosophers engaged in this polemic left no doubt as to which side of the conceptual divide they were placing themselves on. Like the more recent invention of the category of the ideological, the concept of the metaphorical is originally devised for application to the discourse of others. It is itself a rhetorical weapon.

Traces of this polemic are discernible in some pre-Socratic debate, and Plato's writings are rich both in figurative invention and in condemnation of the seductive errors wrought by rhetorical tropes. But we do not find there the analysis of concepts answering to our distinction between the literal and the metaphorical, and it is not until Aristotle that metaphor per se becomes an explicit subject for philosophical reflection. Even Aristotle's conception of *metaphora* is not exactly coextensive with our contemporary "metaphor." The familiar root sense of *metaphora* is that of a transfer (*epiphora*) of a word or name from its home context to another one. But this definition is general enough to apply to many usages that would not ordinarily come under our contemporary understanding of metaphor. And indeed, for Aristotle, the "transfer from genus to species or from species to genus" (*Poet.* 1457b8) will be taken to include such phrases as "Odysseus did a thousand noble deeds" (since "a thousand" is a species of "many"), or saying that a thief has "taken" rather than "stolen" something (*Rhet.* 1405a27), and even the case of referring to something as "completely" destroyed, or to death as the end of life (*Met.* 1021b26–30). These are all *metaphora*. Whereas for us, usages of this sort would either be thought of as perfectly literal or at least as belonging to some other category than the metaphorical.

Nonetheless, the conceptual relation is close enough to make Aristotle's problems ours. Most contemporary philosophical discussions of metaphor have treated it as a problem in the philosophy of language, and much recent debate has centered on the question of whether or not there is such a thing as specifically "metaphorical meaning," and if so, how it is related to literal meaning. These are not Aristotle's problems, but the issues that concern him with respect to the *rhetorical* uses of metaphor are as much with us as ever. These center on such questions as: How does metaphor *persuade*, what qualities specific to it enable it to play such a role, and how do its workings compare with those of explicit, literal argument? To what extent is metaphor a legitimate vehicle of understanding, and to what extent does its rhetorical usefulness depend on a lack of understanding, on the part of the audience, about its functioning? Without presenting anything like a theory of how metaphor functions, Aristotle's discussion of metaphor in the *Rhetoric* points in certain directions for seeking answers to such questions which contemporary discussion would do well to follow up. This brief discussion can only aim to bring out a couple of such problems, and suggest ways in which they may be resolvable within the terms of Aristotle's text.

As the first philosopher to direct sustained theoretical attention to the specific workings of metaphor, Aristotle is famously ambivalent about its power and appropriateness in philosophy. He will sometimes charge other philosophers (e.g., Plato) with failing to provide genuine explanations, and instead dealing in "empty words and poetical metaphors,"[1] and he asserts categorically in the *Topics* (139b34) that "everything is unclear (*asaphes*) that is said by metaphor." His attitude is not always so dismissive, however, not even in philosophical contexts, and he often makes explicit mention of particular metaphorical transfers that are not only harmless, but are seen as actually instructive.[2] And in fact, when he comes to consider metaphor in the *Rhetoric* (1405a8) he claims for it the special virtue of being clear (*saphes*), ascribing to it the very quality (and "to a high degree") which he withheld from metaphor altogether in the *Topics*. Further, his account in the *Rhetoric* of what metaphor accomplishes would appear to give it a valuable place within the concerns of philosophy generally. "We learn above all from metaphors" (1410b12), he tells us, and his fondness for analyzing all metaphors as proportional figures makes him emphasize their role in teaching in particular the categorical relations between things (e.g., between genus and species). And indeed, he relates the operation of metaphor and philosophical understanding explicitly, when he says "Metaphor must be by transference from things that are related, but not obviously so, as it is a sign of sound intuition in a philosopher to see similarities between things that are far apart" (1412a10–13).

This sketch is not meant to suggest that all traces of ambivalence about metaphor are absent from the *Rhetoric* itself. Book 3 begins with a brief review of the development of the art of *lexis* or style, which includes some disparaging comparisons of the rhetorician with an actor (a favorite Platonic comparison), as well as the complaint that nowadays the actors have become more important than the poets whose lines they speak (1403b33). Metaphor is understood as one of the elements of *lexis;* but even though the last of the three books of the *Rhetoric* is devoted to the discussion of style and arrangement, Aristotle takes the fact of its importance to be mostly regrettable. In the context of civic discourse, he sees attention to style or delivery to be necessary only due to the corruption of political life (1403b34, 1404a5). In a better world, those in public debate would concern themselves only with the facts of the case, and seek to give neither pleasure nor offense.

Nonetheless, being pleasing (*hedu*) is one of the three primary virtues assigned to metaphor, the other two being lucidity (*saphes*), as mentioned, and strangeness (*xenikon*) (1405a8). Regarding strangeness, Aristotle begins his discussion by grouping together figurative language with unusual words and foreign borrowings. All of these may serve to elevate one's style, and lend an appearance of dignity (*semnos*) to the discourse (1404b9). At first, this may seem an odd assortment of verbal devices to group together; yet there is a good sense in which metaphor is indeed a borrowing, not from a foreign language, but from one region of a language to another. In metaphor the term is temporarily employed outside its home context, to which it continually returns. Foreignness is described here as a positive virtue of *lexis,* and not simply as something to be tolerated as an inevitable aspect of anything that could count as metaphor. Aristotle explicates this idea in a striking metaphor of his own.

> Men feel toward language as they feel toward strangers [*xenous*] and fellow citizens, and we must introduce an element of strangeness into our diction because people marvel at what is far away, and to marvel is pleasant. (1404b9–12)

Thus, metaphor is figured as having some of the qualities of the exotic and the fascinating; but at the same time we recognize that strangers do not have the same rights as our fellow citizens. They easily fall under suspicion, their loyalty is not to be trusted, and they can be expelled as soon as their services are no longer needed. Thus a kind of ambivalence colors even the description of the specific virtues of metaphor, before we come to consider its functioning.

How do the specific virtues ascribed to metaphor contribute to the general aim of the art of rhetoric? In providing an occasion for marveling, strangeness contributes to pleasure in a straightforward way. But that same quality may, of course, conflict with the third virtue of lucidity, and thus defeat the aims of the rhetorician. This tension among the virtues particular to metaphor is, however, considerably less problematic than a related one that follows immediately in Aristotle's discussion, and which suggests that clarity itself, at another level, may conflict with the goals of rhetoric. At the beginning of Book 1 we learn that "rhetoric may be defined as the faculty of observing in any given case the available means of persuasion" (1355b27). We now learn in Book 3 that attaining this very aim is interfered with by its being too obvious that this is what the speaker is seeking. This is especially so to the extent that skill or artifice in composition or delivery is manifest in the speech.

> One must not be obviously composing; one must seem to be speaking in a natural and unstudied manner, for what is natural is convincing (*pithanon*), what is studied (*peplasmenōs*) is not. People distrust rhetorical tricks just as they distrust adulterated wines. (1404b19–21)[3]

Thus, while it is a virtue of style in general, and metaphor in particular, to be clear or manifest, the aims of style and metaphor seem to require an absence of clarity about themselves, a concealment of their artfulness and their aims.[4] Perhaps it is meant to be obvious why such artifice in public speech is mistrusted. And perhaps it is especially advisable in a democracy for a public speaker to appear "to be speaking in a natural voice." For persuasiveness is not only a matter of what is said and how it is said, but also a matter of the trustworthiness of the character of the speaker. Indeed, early in Book 1 Aristotle says that "his character may almost be called the most effective means of persuasion he possesses" (1356a13). The audience must see the speaker not only as reliable in the sense of well informed, but also in the sense of being possessed of a good character, and not liable to seek to manipulate them.

However, this appeal to the character of the speaker assumes that we already know just what there is to be mistrusted in the use of highly "composed" or skillful diction (*lexis*). The appearance of artifice may indeed make the audience suspicious of the character of the speaker, and his speech will then lose in persuasiveness. But what is the basis of the suspicion of such artifice in the first place? This question is especially pressing in the context of Aristotle's discussion of metaphor since the primary focus of his account of what metaphor accomplishes is the "ease of learning" of various unobvious systems of relations (1410b10). It is not immediately apparent what there is to be suspicious of in that, and Aristotle will say little that is explicit about what there is in the "composed" character of metaphor that would need concealment.[5]

The kind of suspicion at issue here is specifically concerned with persuasion, and is therefore to be distinguished from other ways in which we in the audience may be "tricked," and may take pleasure in that very experience. The artifice involved in riddles or in wit also needs to be concealed, at least for a time, in order to function. A riddle may set up a certain expectation, only in order to defeat it; and whatever pleasure we take in this depends on our not seeing through the trick at once. (See the joke about the sandals and chilblains at 1412a30.) There is a kind of deception (*exapatan*) in this, and a pleasure taken in that very deception. But it is much less puzzling than the relation of pleasure and deception with respect to the art of rhetoric and metaphor, since such a riddle does not involve persuasion (*peithō*) about some matter.

In the context of persuasion this recommendation of concealing one's art also raises questions about the situation of the audience, and its understanding of itself. On the one hand, we marvel at what is strange in diction, and take pleasure in this marveling. On the other hand, we are said to mistrust the speaker to the extent that he does not conceal his intention to compose in such a way as to give us this pleasure. If a certain kind of speaker were of a sort that was seen to be simply untrustworthy or unreliable or ill-informed, it would make sense for us to simply avoid him, refuse him our ear. Were we to listen to him, we would be liable to be misled, and we have no desire simply to believe what is false.

But this is not what we in fact do with respect to the rhetorically skillful speaker. We recognize that his speech gives us pleasure, and not in virtue of being unreliable, but in at least two ways mentioned by Aristotle. First, as mentioned, his diction presents us with something strange and far off to marvel at (*to thaumaston*). And second, he provides us an occasion for learning something with ease [1410b10]. And both the marveling and the learning are said to be pleasant or sweet (*hedu*). We are of at least two minds about this pleasure, however, for awareness of the speaker's art and intent to provide that pleasure makes us less inclined to believe what he is telling us. Note that what Aristotle says is not simply that the *pleasure* will be lost, say, either through awkwardness or self-consciousness. What he says at 1404b20 is that if the speaker is obviously composing, then his speech will invite suspicion and fail to carry *conviction* (*pithanon*). Hence we in the audience know ourselves to be inclined to be moved to conviction in ways which we ourselves do not credit or find justified. We will come to believe things in ways that we would reject if we were to be made aware of them. And we will knowingly make ourselves available to those speakers and situations that put us in this position. We want the orator to move us, but in ways that require that he distract us from the fact that this is what he is doing.

It is as if we in the audience know ourselves to be *akratic* with respect to the gratifications of oratory. We know we will not in fact avoid the speeches of the skillful orator, because it is in part his business to provide pleasure, and we will make ourselves available to that pleasure. But the explanation of our double-mindedness cannot be that we want the pleasure without the risk of being persuaded of something unwarranted, for how would it help that for the speaker to *conceal* his art and his intent? In that case the risk would only be the greater, for being unknown to us.

As a final problem, concerning metaphor in particular, it is not clear that the actual concealing of the art and intention of the speaker is even initially consistent with the aim of speaking to an audience, intending to communicate something. For a metaphorical utterance must be known to be one if it is to be understood at all, or understood in the right way. If the audience does not realize that the speaker is speaking figuratively (i.e., nonliterally) they will not be moved by his speech, and they will not be convinced by what he says. They could only take him to be misapplying his words (for example, in referring to Achilles as a lion), and perhaps failing to make sense altogether. Neither the effects of pleasure nor persuasion will be attained unless the audience is quite aware that they are being addressed by a speaker who is deliberately employing some specifically composed figure of speech. So, in addition to the question of *why* the speaker should need to conceal his art, there is the question of *how* it could be possible for him to do so if he is not to produce mere confusion in his audience. And it will not clarify matters to say at this point that the speaker needs the audience to have *some* awareness of the fact that he is deliberately composing and speaking figuratively, but just not too *much* awareness.

As mentioned, Aristotle's insistence on the need for suppressing the appearance of artifice in figurative speech is particularly surprising in the light of what he says about what metaphor accomplishes. Throughout his remarks about the general function of metaphor he is quite generous in his praise.

> [H]uman nature delights in learning something with ease. Words express a meaning, and those words are the most pleasing which make us learn something. . . . We learn above all from metaphors. . . . We are attracted by those things which we understand as soon as they are said or very soon afterwards, even though we had no knowledge of them before, for then there is a learning process, or something very like it. (1410b9–25 passim)

To understand Aristotle's picture of the rhetorical functioning of metaphor, and the problematic role of the appearance of artifice, we need to start by looking more closely at the complex interrelations between pleasure and learning, and how they contribute to each other. For if we just consider them independently, it is clear enough that they are both good things, and then it is hard to see the necessity of anything hidden in a process involving them both. The suspicion of artifice, on the other hand, requires reference to a *prior* role for pleasure in bringing one to find persuasive something one would otherwise find unconvincing. As we have seen, the reception of metaphor leads to the perception of systems of resemblance, which, as a species of learning, is itself pleasurable. Everything at this stage may be fully manifest. But pleasure does not only *attend* the learning of something new, it can also play a prior contributory role in changing someone's mind, a role whose legitimacy will be open to question. This is not, however, because pleasure itself is presented as a *reason* for believing anything. The rhetorician is not striking a kind of bargain with his audience; as it were, trading pleasure for conviction. (That would involve a kind of self-deception that Aristotle nowhere suggests is part of rhetorical persuasion.) Rather, there is a prior role for pleasure in making one receptive to the speaker, relaxing one's suspicions, and imaginatively entering into a different viewpoint. As Aristotle puts it early in Book 1 of the *Rhetoric*, "Persuasion may come through the hearers, when the speech stirs their emotions. Our judgments when we are pleased and friendly are not the same as when we are pained and hostile" (1356a14–16).

There is pleasure, then, at both ends of the process of the rhetorical functioning of metaphor. It is a movement of the soul that makes one receptive, and thus facilitates other such movements, including patterns of attention and the entertaining of ideas. One begins to associate and explore the implications of certain comparisons in ways that one would not have otherwise done, but for the pleasure induced by the speaker. His speech has, for the time being, altered the contents and activity of one's mind. And since this grasping of ideas is itself pleasurable, we can expect such a process to have a certain momentum, as pleasure induces learning something new, which in turn, as pleasurable, induces further responsiveness and ideational activity. All of this the rhetorician is counting on, and seeking to channel in certain directions.

The artifice of metaphor contributes to each stage of this process. But it is not either the grasping of new ideas or the pleasure that attends it that breeds mistrust of the speaker. Rather, suspicion enters in when the obtrusive appearance of artifice raises the question of the speaker's designs upon us. Since we are aware that pleasure is disarming (and take the speaker also to be so aware), if he seems too manifestly intent on pleasing us, we will begin to question how he intends to exploit this disarmed state, and thus re-arm ourselves. Further, the speaker's overt desire to please highlights a questionable imbalance in the situation of speaker and audience. For as the desire to please becomes more transparent, this clashes more suspiciously with the fact that his communicative aim is *not* fully "mutual," between speaker and hearer, since his ultimate rhetorical intentions, and the function of his chosen metaphor within them, are only imperfectly understood by the audience. Following the speaker in figurative thought thus requires an extension of trust to take up the slack of mutuality; and the speaker who seeks our trust had best not call attention to just how deeply he will be drawing on it.

There is a further way for Aristotle in which the rhetorical effectiveness of metaphor relies on the apparent withdrawal from the scene of the speaker's assertive intention. This concerns the imagistic and quasi-experiential role he assigns to the reception of successful metaphor. Figurative language does not simply *tell* us that one thing is like another; rather, it functions in such a way as to *make us see* one thing as another, or in the light of another. Such a description of the workings of metaphor is, of course, itself metaphorical and not literal. It requires explication of its own. But it is in many ways *the* privileged metaphor for the functioning of metaphor, and it has its origins in Aristotle's insistence, throughout the *Rhetoric,* that the successful metaphor will "set things before the eyes" of the audience, and that this quasi-experiential effect will be crucial to both the convincingness and the emotional appeal of the speech. It is no exaggeration to say that the primary virtue of metaphor is for Aristotle the ability to set something vividly before the eyes of the audience (*pro ommaton poiein*) (1410b34).

There are several aspects to Aristotle's quasi-experiential aspect of metaphor which go beyond the mere having of a mental image.[6] He glosses the notion of *pro ommaton poiein* in 1.10 by saying that the speaker succeeds in this when he employs figures which project a sense of activity (*energeia*) (1411b27). The context in which Aristotle stresses the importance of activity aligns it with the related notions of productivity and movement (*kinēsis*), and he especially praises the figures in Homer that represent something inanimate as if alive (e.g., the arrow "eager to fly") (1411b34). Qualities such as eagerness and the like are not, of course, proper to everything that is alive, but only to sentient, primarily human, life. Thus the explication of *energeia* in metaphor is progressively refined from the representation of movement, to the representation of something alive, to the more specific trope of personification. In addition, the importance of the quality of aliveness in metaphor in 1.10 is implicitly counterposed to the previous discussion of the need to avoid frigidity (*psychra*) in one's style in 1.3 (see 1406a–b passim). The frigid metaphor fails to carry conviction (*apithana*), and the term *psychra* carries with it connotations not only of what is cold, but more specifically of what is dead, unreal, and ineffectual. Finally, Aristotle's gloss of *pro ommaton poiein* in terms of *energeia* explicitly relates this virtue of metaphor not only to what is imagistic, in motion, alive, and animated, but also to what is fully present and fully actualized. Thus the general discussion in 1.10 concludes: "The words should bring things before our eyes; they must give an impression of things happening in the present, not in the future. These three things should be aimed at: metaphor, antithesis, and vividness (or actuality) (*energeia*)" (1410b35).

Not surprisingly, then, there is a great deal packed into the single figure of *pro ommaton poiein*, as a metaphor for the functioning of effective metaphor. There are two issues in particular that an explication of these passages should clarify: first, what the specifically *rhetorical* advantage of these qualities is, and second, how the qualities of imagery and activity are presented as being related to each other. Paul Ricoeur's subtle reading of Aristotle on metaphor (reprinted in this volume) is one of the few contemporary discussions that gives due weight to the emphasis in the *Rhetoric* on setting something "before the eyes," and he discusses this in connection with the emphasis on the representation of things in action, things moving as if alive. But he understands the sense of activity exclusively as pertaining to that which is represented in the metaphor, and thus his reading of Aristotle here culminates in the speculation that "to present men 'as acting' and all things 'as in act'—such could well be the ontological function of metaphorical discourse, in which every dormant potentiality of existence appears as blossoming forth, every latent capacity for action as actualized" (p. 355). Whatever may be ultimately at stake in this language, in restricting the sense of "activity" to the side of what is represented, such an account neglects the fact that the insistence on *energeia* is presented by way of explaining what is *meant* by "setting before the eyes," and how it is achieved (1411b25). That is, *pro ommaton poiein* is recognized as itself a metaphorical expression and in need of elucidation, and the various senses of *energeia* are presented as explications referring to the same phenomenon that the original visual metaphor gestures toward. The idea is not simply that the thing to be set before the eyes of the audience should be something shown in action, but also that we only learn what is meant by the figurative expression "setting before the eyes" in this context by attending to the special requirement of activity both on the part of the responses of the audience as well as on the part of the metaphorical subject.

Before considering an interpretation of the connection between imagery and activity along these lines, it will be helpful first to consider the prior question of how something imagistic, rather than discursive, may further the aims of the rhetorician. Some light is shed on this question by another modern writer, always worth consulting on these matters. Echoing Aristotle's language of "setting before the eyes," Kenneth Burke describes the strategic importance of the shifting between ideas and images in the workings of rhetoric.

> There is a difference between an abstract term naming the "idea" of, say, security, and a concrete image designed to stand for this idea, and to "place it before our very eyes." For one thing, if the image employs the full resources of imagination, it will not represent merely one idea, but will contain a whole bundle of principles, even ones that would be mutually contradictory if reduced to their purely ideational equivalents. Ideationally, a speaker might have to go through much reasoning if he wanted to equate a certain measure with public security. But if he could translate it imaginally into terms of, say, the mother, he might profit not only from this one identification, but from many kindred principles or ideas which, when approached in this spirit, are associated with the mother-image.... Assume, for instance, that there are five major principles of appeal in a mother-image (security, affection, tradition, "naturalness," communion). Then assume an ideological argument identifying a cause in terms of security, but not explicitly pleading for it in terms of these four other principles. Now, if the speaker, in winding up his argument for his cause as an aid to security, translates it into a mother-image, might he not thereby get the "unearned increment" from the other four principles vibrant in this same image? (Burke 1969, 87)

First of all, what is *profit* and what is *earning* in this context? In simplest terms, the profit to the rhetorician is the gaining of the conviction of the audience about some matter. And this will be unearned to the extent that the speaker has not provided reasons for belief about this matter, and, indeed, may not even have raised that particular matter explicitly for consideration.

What is the rhetorical importance of the fact that the profit is *unearned* from the standpoint of reason giving? There are several aspects to this gain. One relatively superficial advantage is simply that the speaker is spared the trouble of arguing his case for each of the other four principles. This is a gain because he need not marshal his reasons, and, even more, because he may not have any such reasons in the first place. But it is not simply a matter of getting something for free. There is a more important gain from inexplicitness arising from the fact that it leaves the speaker free to disavow, at any later time, those implications or conclusions drawn from his image which he might later be obliged to defend or explain away. Burke suggests something of this when he mentions that certain elements of the image cluster may contradict each other. The speaker is not responsible for resolving any such contradictions, and may selectively exploit them as he sees fit. Explicit, literal speech carries with it the risks and responsibilities of being right or wrong, justified or unjustified, in what one asserts. It is with respect to what one has explicitly asserted that one can, or can most easily, be charged with having claimed something false, or spoken in ignorance, or having said something inconsistent with one's previous words. Whereas to the extent that, instead of making some explicit assertion, the speaker provides an image before the eyes of the audience, whose implications they are to work out for themselves, he may profit from such implications as are useful to him, while privately reserving the right to disown any which might later be charged against his account.

There is a further general advantage in addressing an audience through something "set before their eyes" rather than through literal, explicit assertion. In presenting his audience with an image for contemplation, the speaker appears to put them in the position of working out the meaning of a phenomenon rather than in the position of believing or disbelieving something they are being told. The imaginative activity on the part of the audience, as it moves among the five principles contained in the single image, may easily present itself to the mind as a process of *discovery*, something one is experiencing and working out for oneself, rather than as a matter of believing the report of some possibly unreliable or untrustworthy speaker. Hence, by employing such a figure, the speaker may hope to produce a sense of conviction on the part of his audience that does not appear to rely on his own credibility.

Suppose this provides the beginnings of an account of the rhetorical importance of the contrast between something imagistic (or quasi-experiential) and something more discursive and literal.[7] We would now need to see how in Aristotle these virtues of the imagistic are related to the virtues of activity and animation (*energeia*) in effective metaphor. At the beginning of 1.11, Aristotle defines what he means by "setting something before the eyes" of the audience, and how this is achieved, by reference to metaphors of activity and animation (1411b24–27). We saw that for Aristotle this connotes not merely movement, but primarily living activity, and indeed, the full-blown figure of personification. The rock of Sisyphus, the spears of the Trojans, no longer appear as inanimate objects, but now confront us as beings endowed with shamelessness, or as longing to feed on human flesh. The transformation is thus in the direction from mere thing to a sentient being confronting us, provoking a response from us. Hence the "activity" in question when something is figuratively "set before our eyes" is not on one side only. Rather, it is part of what Aristotle says he means when he speaks of something "set before the eyes" that the mind of the hearer is provoked, set into motion, and engaged imaginatively with the metaphor. *Energeia* is thus not only on the side of what is depicted, but what is depicted is specifically figured as a living thing demanding some set of responses from the audience, some mental activity of its own. The specifically imagistic quality of live metaphor only is so because of the responsive activity of the mind. (Here as elsewhere it is a mistake to think of mental imagery as the passive perception of an internal object, rather than as a particular imaginative activity.) The aim of *pro ommaton poiein* is to get one's audience to *do* various things, to imagine in a lively fashion that involves much associating, connecting, and emotional responding. By contrast, a frigid style is both lifeless in itself and fails to move us (see 1.3).

Such imaginative activity on the part of the audience contributes directly to the rhetorician's aim of persuasiveness. The "profit" of his speech will be "unearned" because, in part, it is the audience that is engaged in the productive labor of constructing and exploring various useful associative connections within the image. But the crucial advantage here is not simply the surplus value obtained by having others work for you, but rather the miraculous fact that shifting the imaginative labor onto the audience makes the ideas thereby produced infinitely *more* valuable rhetorically than they would be as products of the explicit assertions of the speaker.[8] They are the more valuable because the ideas derived from the image will be both more memorable and less subject to suspicion for having been worked out by the audience themselves. And this rhetorical advantage of something image-like set before the eyes dovetails nicely with the previous one involving the avoidance of the commitments of explicit assertion. Presenting a picture whose full meaning is yet to be worked out gains the speaker many of the advantages of assertion without all the costs of reason giving, commitment to logical consequences, and so on. And it is because the implications of the image are developed through the imaginative activity of the audience themselves that the ideas elicited will borrow some of the probative value of personal discoveries, rather than be subjected to the skepticism accorded to someone else's testimony. If there is any need to suppress the appearance of artifice here it is not because the audience is unaware that they are listening to a carefully composed speech, or that they are being addressed in deliberately contrived metaphors. But it may be that they need to be distracted from their own role in producing the conviction that the speaker is counting on; or rather, from the fact that, while conviction here may depend on the appearance of personal discovery, the direction taken by the mind remains under the guidance of the speaker's choice of figures. Aristotle's ambivalence about metaphor will then be explained by the fact that both its value as a vehicle of understanding and the dangers of its rhetorical abuse stem from the same features of its "live" imagistic power.[9]

NOTES

1. "And to say that they [Plato's Forms] are patterns and the other things share in them is to use empty words and poetical metaphors" (*Met.* 991a21, see also 1079b26).

2. See *Met.* 1015a11 on the transfer between nature and essence. See also *Met.* 1019b34 on potency or power in geometry, and *NE* 1167a10 on transferring (*metapheron*) the name friendship (*philia*) to benevolence (*eunoia*), as a kind of inactive friendship.

3. In ordinary contexts of action, *peplasmenos* refers to something done by artifice or pretense. A bit later in the text, Aristotle describes the operations of metaphor in even stronger terms suggestive of a kind of theft (*kekleptai*) (1404b24, 1405a30).

4. Longinus also claims that rhetorical figures will be most effective when their figurality is concealed, in chapter 17 of his treatise *On the Sublime*.

5. Other forms of artifice are also to be avoided in the interests of convincingness. At 1408b22 Aristotle says that prose should not be metrical, for the reason that "metrical prose is unconvincing (*apithanon*) because it betrays artifice (*peplasthai*)." Even if we agree with this point in the case of prose, this raises a question of how we are to account for the persuasiveness of poetry itself which is metrical and artificial, and is, of course, known by both speaker and audience to be so.

6. Indeed, in a different context Aristotle denies that imagination (*phantasia*) alone is productive of emotion: "When we believe (*doxasomen*) something to be fearful or threatening, emotion is immediately produced, and so too with what is encouraging; but when we merely imagine we remain as unaffected as persons who are looking at a painting of some dreadful or encouraging scene" (*DA* 427b21–24).

This claim about *phantasia* may be in conflict with several passages in the *Rhetoric*, which come prior to the discussion of metaphor (e.g., 1370a28, 1378b10, 1383a17), but I will not enter into that here. Significantly, *phantasia* in the sense of imagination does not appear to be an element in Aristotle's account of metaphor and the effect of "bringing before the eyes."

7. For some more on the rhetorical advantages of metaphor as *figure*, see Moran 1989.

8. In line with the economic metaphor, we should recall that the Greek term *energos* may also refer to productive land or capital.

9. In writing this paper I have benefited in various ways from conversation with Myles Burnyeat, Catherine Elgin, Alexander Nehamas, Ruth Padel, Laura Quinney, and Amélie Rorty, for which I'm very grateful.

REFERENCES

Barnes, J., ed. *The Complete Works of Aristotle: The Revised Oxford Translation.* Princeton, 1984.

Burke, K. *A Rhetoric of Motives.* Berkeley, 1969.

Bywater, I., trans. *The Poetics.* In *The Complete Works of Aristotle: The Revised Oxford Translation,* ed. J. Barnes, vol 2. Princeton, 1985.

Grube, G. M. A., trans. *On Poetry and Style.* Indianapolis, 1989.

Lloyd, G. E. R. *The Revolutions of Wisdom: Studies in the Claims and Practice of Ancient Greek Science.* Berkeley, 1987.

Moran, R. "Seeing and Believing: Metaphor, Image and Force." *Critical Inquiry* 16 (1989): 87–112.

Padel, R. *In and Out of the Mind: Greek Images of the Tragic Self.* Princeton, 1992.

———. "Metaphor: The Fifth-Century Absence?" Unpublished manuscript.

Roberts, W. R., trans. *Rhetoric.* New York, 1954.

Rhetorical Means of Persuasion

Christopher Carey

In the *Rhetoric* (1356a) Aristotle distinguishes three means of persuasion (*pisteis*) which can be produced by the rhetorician's art. The term used, *pistis*, although frequently translated "proof," is broader in its semantic range than the English word would suggest. Its use encompasses the related qualities of trust, trustworthiness, credence and credibility, and extends to objects and means used to secure trust or belief. This breadth of usage explains the disparate contents of Aristotle's list, and his inclusion of items that have no bearing on factual proof; he lists argument (as Aristotle puts it, "to demonstrate something or appear to demonstrate"), the character of the speaker, and the disposition created in the hearer. Aristotle considers the first of these to be the the proper task of rhetoric, the other two being additional effects necessitated by the nature of the audience. Certainly this item is different in kind from the others in that demonstration by argument addresses itself more or less directly to the issue to be decided, while the other two *pisteis* listed have only an indirect bearing at most on the issue. These indirect "proofs" do however play a major role in Attic oratory, and accordingly Aristotle feels compelled to accept and advise on their use. In this chapter I shall examine the range of effects sought by their deployment in the Attic orators, and the means used.

1

Pathos is defined broadly by Aristotle (*Rhet.* 1356a, 1377b) as "creating a certain disposition in the audience." Aristotle was not the first rhetorician to stress the importance of *pathos*. Emotional appeal formed a major component of the rhetorical handbooks circulating in his day (*Rhet.*

1354a). Gorgias in his *Helen* (9–10) lays great emphasis on the emotive power of the spoken word. Quintilian attests Prodicus's interest in emotional effect (*Institutio Oratoria* 3.1.12). Thrasymachus dealt with pity in a work called *Eleoi*, literally *Pities* (Plato, *Phaedrus* 267c; *Rhet.* 1404a). The treatment went beyond the contents of emotional appeal to embrace the acting skills necessary for effective delivery. The generation and removal of anger were also dealt with. In this as in many respects classical rhetoric is merely systematizing existing practice, for emotional appeal is the product neither of Athenian democracy nor sophistic teaching. Emotional appeal figures in the arsenal of the Homeric speaker, and is a pronounced feature in the political oratory of Solon and Alcaeus.[1] The speech of Sthenelaidas urging the Spartans to vote for war against Athens in Book 1 of Thucydides (1.86) is not noticeably lacking in emotional appeal; nor is his Spartan audience any less moved by this appeal than the democratic Athenian assembly that voted with Alcibiades for war on Syracuse in 415 (Thucydides 6.8–24). In the forensic process too, emotional appeal predates sophistic rhetoric. Hesiod's warnings to the nobles who will judge his suit with his brother Perses (*Works and Days* 202 ff., 248 ff.) are designed to intimidate as well as reform. Aeschylus's *Eumenides* (633 ff., 711 ff.) demonstrates that emotional appeal was well established in Athenian trials by the early 450s.

Common to all speakers is the basic need to secure the goodwill of the hearer.[2] The speaker will often use the *prooemium* to lay claim to qualities that the audience will respect,[3] or stress the disadvantages of his situation as a claim to sympathy. Thus the speaker of Demosthenes 54 says (§1):

> Since all my friends and relatives, whose advice I sought, though they stated that his actions rendered him liable to the procedure of summary arrest for muggers and the indictments for malicious assault (*hubris*), none the less advised and urged me not to take on a task beyond my abilities, nor to be seen bringing a complaint beyond my years for the injuries I suffered, I did just this and because of them I brought a private action, though I should have preferred most of all to put him on trial for his life.

The projection here of the modesty that the Athenians expected of the young makes a powerful initial demand for a sympathetic bearing. Likewise we find speakers stressing the magnitude of the danger facing them (Lysias 19.1), the extent of the wrong done to them (Demosthenes 45.1), their inexperience in speaking or their complete inexperience of the legal system (Antiphon 1.1; Isaeus 10.1; Demosthenes 41.2) as a claim for sympathy. An important component in the establishment of goodwill is the neutralization of any hostility against the speaker, a topic to which the theorists devoted a great deal of attention.[4] This hostility can arise from a number of sources. It may be generated by previous speakers. This is especially so in the case of a defendant in court, since the prosecutor as first speaker was in a position to create a prejudice against the defendant before the latter uttered a word (see especially Demosthenes 45.6). The hostility could also arise from the matter itself or the political climate. Demosthenes 57 was delivered during a court hearing by a man ejected from his deme under the general scrutiny of deme members authorized by the Demophilus decree of 346/5. It is clear from the proem that there was a general prejudice against the individuals ejected by the demes. The speaker is therefore obliged to plead at length for a fair hearing (1–6). The nature of the brief could also adversely affect audience reception. In forensic cases where the law allowed rewards for successful prosecutors it was necessary to establish at the outset that profit was not the motive (as [Demosthenes] 53.1 ff., 59.1 ff.), since this suspicion would inevitably arise in the jurors' minds. Equally, when bringing a serious charge in matters that did not affect the prosecutor directly, it was useful, given the instinctive public hostility toward meddlesomeness (*polypragmosyne*), to stress the public spirit (Lycurgus 1.3–6) or paradoxically the private hostility that motivated the action (Lysias 14.1 ff.; Demosthenes 22.1 ff.; [Demosthenes] 58.1 ff.; Aeschines 1.1–2). Prosecution of relatives inevitably excited hostility in a society that placed enormous weight on the solidarity of the family. In such cases it was important to quell the prejudice by stressing the importance of the issue or to transfer the hostility by presenting the resort to legal action as a course forced on oneself by the intransigence of the opponent (see Antiphon 1.1–4; Lysias 32.1; Isaeus 1.6; Demosthenes 39.1, 41.1–2; [Demosthenes] 48.1). Prejudice could also arise from the identity or circumstances of the speaker. One important factor singled out by Anaximenes is age (*Rhetorica ad Alexandrum* 1437a). Given the diffidence expected of youth, the jurors might feel that a youthful prosecutor was displaying precocious legal expertise or excessive ambition. This had to be countered by presenting recourse to law as forced upon one by the opponents or stressing the lack of supporters to undertake the burden of prosecution (Isaeus, fr. 6; [Demosthenes] 58.2–4).

The discussion of *eunoia* so far has concentrated on the opening, in accordance with the narrow approach of the classical handbooks (*Rhet.* 1415a; *Rhetorica ad Alexandrum* 1436b, 1441b) and the inescapable fact that the introduction of any speech must establish a bond between speaker and audience if the rest of the speech is to do its work. However, the bid for *eunoia* is not confined to the proem. We find attempts to counter prejudice directly in the proof section, as at Demosthenes 37.52–53:

> Well now, when anyone asks him: "And what case do you have in response to Nicobulus?" he says: "The Athenians hate money lenders. Nicobulus is unpopular; he walks fast and has a loud voice and carries a stick. All this," he says, "is in my favour." And he is not ashamed to say this, nor does he

think that his hearers understand that this is the reasoning of a sycophant, not a victim.

We may also compare Demosthenes 45.77 and Lysias 16.20. The positive bid for *eunoia* is equally at home in proof and in the narrative section. In both it may be achieved subtly through the personality projected by the speaker, which can be used to create or sustain the required bond of sympathy. (This is dealt with in the following section.)

Beyond the basic need for a hearing, the precise effects sought depend on the situation of the speaker. In forensic oratory this amounts in part to the role in court, prosecution or defense. Common to both is the need to arouse hostility against the opponent. However, this inevitably figures more prominently in the speech of the plaintiff, who must move the jurors first to convict and then (where appropriate) to impose the desired penalty. The appeal for anger is often (at least to the reader accustomed to modern legal hearings) surprisingly explicit, with the use of key words such as *orgē* (anger), *misein* (hate), *aganaktein* (resent). So for instance Lycurgus 1.134: "Yet when a man is hated and ejected even by those who have suffered no wrong, what should he suffer from you who have been treated in the most monstrous manner?" Commonly the audience is made to feel that they have been wronged personally. In the case of political trials this is easy enough, for by definition the defendant is accused of an offense against the city. But even in trials with no political dimension there is a consistent tendency to present the offense as an attack on values important to the city as a whole, and to induce the jurors to register the feelings they would have if they themselves were the victims, as at Demosthenes 54.42: "I urge you then, jurymen . . . just as each of you would hate the perpetrator if he himself were the victim, to register anger in the same way against Conon here, and not to regard as private any such offence of this sort which might perhaps happen to another too."

These examples of appeal to anger come from the proof section. But the narrative may contain such appeals in the form of explicit value judgments intermingled with the statement of the "facts" of the case in order to give the narrative a pronounced bias, as in the following extract from Aeschines (1.40):

> For this man, first of all, as soon as he was past boyhood, used to sit in the Piraeus at the medical establishment of Euthydicus, on the pretext of learning the trade but in reality because he had made a firm decision to sell himself, as the sequel showed. The names of all the merchants or other foreigners or citizens who had the use of Timarchus' body during that period I shall pass over, so that no one can accuse me of going into excessive detail about everything. But I shall confine my account to the people whose house he has lived in, disgracing his body and the city and earning money

by the very means for which the law forbids a man from political action or speech.

Anger may, however, be aroused less overtly by the manner of the presentation of the offense. The following account of the funeral of Lysias's brother Polemarchus is a particularly fine example (12.18–19):

> And when after his death he was taken forth from the prison for burial, though we owned three houses they would not even let him be carried out from one of them, but they hired a tent and laid him out. And though we had many robes they gave none for the burial in answer to our request, but one friend gave a robe, another a pillow, others various items for his funeral. And though they had six hundred shields belonging to us, though they had so much silver and gold, and bronze and jewellery and furniture and women's clothing, more than they ever expected to acquire, and a hundred and twenty slaves, of whom they took the best and gave the rest to the public exchequer, this is the extent their insatiable and petty greed reached and the demonstration they gave of their character: the gold ear-rings of Polemarchus' wife, which happened to be the ones she possessed when she first came to his house, Melobius took from her ears.

The brutality of the murderers is compounded by their pettiness in refusing even the resources for a basic funeral. Pity for the victims, hence anger against the perpetrators, is aroused by the humiliating need for a rich man's family to beg such trifling items from friends and by the contrast between the generosity of private citizens and the meanness of those in power. The climax is the petty greed of the perpetrators, effectively presented by the long list of confiscated goods, leading to the act of wrenching a pair of earrings from the widow's ears. Authorial judgment is explicitly present, but far more telling is the skillful use of detail. Examples from Lysias might be multiplied. But this effect is not confined to him. The following passage is taken from the prosecution of the ex-prostitute Neaira ([Demosthenes] 59.38):

> Stephanus spoke encouragement to her in Megara and inflated her confidence, saying that Phrynion would regret it if he laid hands on her; he would keep her as his wife and introduce the children she had at that time into his phratry as his own and give them citizenship; nobody in the world would harm her.

This account is designed to raise anger at the casual abuse of the solemn right of Athenian citizenship. It achieves its effect by the vivid presentation of male bravado designed to impress a mistress.

Another common approach is to generate prejudice against the opponent by means of matters tangential or irrelevant to the issue. This practice falls under the general heading of *diabole*. This word is derived from the verb *diaballein*, which means "to cause hostility between/against."

Aristotle (*Rhet.* 1415a) and Anaximenes (*Rhetorica ad Alexandrum* 1436b–1437b, 1441b–1442b, 1445a) associate the creation or removal of *diabole* with conclusion and introduction, respectively. But this element is at home in any part of the speech. In narrative one can deploy tangential material to create hostility. Thus the narrative in Pseudo-Demosthenes 53.4–18, which bases the decision to prosecute in a public action on grounds of personal enmity, in passing destroys the good character of the opponent by accusing him of a range of actions of which base ingratitude to a loyal friend is the least. Such allegations are particularly effective if repeated, for the effect, even without independent support, is to create the plausibility that comes from internal consistency, as in the repeated presentation of Stephanus as a sycophant in Pseudo-Demosthenes 59 or the repeated references to drunkenness in Lysias 3.5–9 and Demosthenes 54.3–6. The range of prejudices manipulated by speakers, in both narrative and proof, is very wide. We find allegations of luxury (Demosthenes 21.158, 36.45; Aeschines 1.42, 1.53, 95–100); sexual incontinence or deviation (Andocides 1.100, 1.124–127; Lysias 14.25, 14.26; Isaeus 8.44; Demosthenes 36.45; Aeschines 2.99); theft or violence (Isaeus 4.28, 8.41–42; Lysias 14.27; Demosthenes 57.65); political misconduct or (after 403) unsoundness (Lysias 18.19, 30.9–14; Isocrates 16.42–44; Demosthenes 21.202–204; Aeschines 1.106–115); lack of patriotism, evidenced in evasion of public taxes and duties (Isaeus 5.45; Demosthenes 21.154 ff., 54.44; [Demosthenes] 42.22; Aeschines 1.101); spurious citizenship or base or servile extraction (Lysias 30.2; Demosthenes 18.129–130, 21.149–150; [Demosthenes] 59.44); and of course sycophancy ([Demosthenes] 40.32, 58.6, 58.10–12, 59.41, 59.43, 59.68; Aeschines 1.1). Given the general hostility to professionalism in legal contexts, expertise in the law and oratorical skill are also charges to be hurled at adversaries (Isaeus 10.1; Demosthenes 21.189, 57.5; Lycurgus 1.31). Allegations of misconduct may concern associates and relatives (Lysias 13.67–68, 14.30, 14.35–40; [Demosthenes] 25.77). Moreover, since the litigant sought to benefit from the status of his witnesses and supporting speakers, his opponent's *diabole* might be extended to them (Lysias 30.34; Demosthenes 54.34 ff.; Aeschines 1.131, 1.181).

A related emotion triggered in particular by prosecutors is fear. Litigants insist that a judgment for the opponent will open the door to unbridled wrongdoing (Demosthenes 19.342 ff.; [Demosthenes] 59.112–113; Aeschines 1.192). We also find attempts to intimidate the jurors either by suggesting that the gods will take note of and action for a misjudgment, or that the jurors will disgrace or compromise themselves in the eyes of their loved ones, the city, or the rest of Greece. Lycurgus (1.146) warns the jury: "Rest assured, gentlemen, that each of you now while voting in secret will make his attitude clear to the gods";[5] the speaker of Pseudo-

Demosthenes 25.98 says: "Suppose then you leave the court, and the bystanders, both foreigners and citizens, watch you and look at each man as he passes and gauge the acquitters from their faces. What will you say, men of Athens, if you abandon the laws before you leave?"

The counterpart to the prosecutor's demand for anger is the plea for pity from the defense. Appeals for pity are not confined to the defendant. However, for the prosecutor they are largely a means to an end. Pity for the victims of the opponent's wrongdoing is stimulated in order to excite anger against the perpetrator. But it is the defendant who needs to move the jurors to gentler emotions. The crudest method, much criticized and satirized (see Aristophanes, *Wasps* 568 ff., 976 ff.; Plato, *Apology* 34c–d), but still effective (or considered effective) enough to remain a standard procedure, was to have one's family mount the stand, weeping and wailing, in order to bring home to the jurors the damage that conviction would inflict. The same effect might be sought with words, either with reference to the speaker himself (Lysias 4.20, 24.22 ff.; Isaeus 2.44; Demosthenes 57.70) or with reference to defenseless or infirm relatives entirely dependent on him (Lysias 7.41; [Demosthenes] 40.56).

An overlapping appeal is that for gratitude. The importance of gratitude was universally acknowledged, and it is common for litigants to remind the jury of benefactions bestowed on the city by self or family, including ancestors, in order to stake a claim, often explicit, to their gratitude (Lysias 3.47, 18.27, 20.30; Isaeus 4.27, 7.37–41; [Demosthenes] 50.64). And just as the litigant hopes to gain from the stature of his supporting speakers, so he hopes that some measure of the gratitude due for their benefactions will accrue to himself.

The discussion so far has largely concentrated on the law courts. But *pathos* as a means of persuasion is not confined to forensic oratory. It is also at home in deliberative oratory. It is important for the modern reader to bear in mind that the neat divisions in classical rhetoric are the product of schematization by theorists rather than oratorical practice. In addition to the inevitable overlaps between political and forensic oratory in a political system that relied on the law courts, there were in classical Athens significant similarities between the political and forensic processes. From the speeches in Thucydides it is clear that already in the fifth century political oratory concerned itself with many of the topics found in judicial oratory: expediency, justice, honor.[6] The mode of argument is the same. And the need to direct the emotional response of the jurors is the same. For the politician proposing alliance or intervention, attack or retaliation, is in part an advocate for or against friend or foe. He is moreover in direct competition for the hearers' favor no less than the litigant. The political process was highly competitive, and the speaker supporting any policy is almost by definition impinging on the interests of a political faction.

The similarity between forensic and political oratory becomes explicit on occasion, most notably in the speech that Thucydides attributes to Cleon in the debate on the fate of Mytilene in 427. Cleon seeks to excite hostility against the opposing speakers by alleging that they have been bribed, an example of *diabole*, as his opponent Diodotus notes (Thucydides 3.42; cf. 3.38, 3.40.1). Diodotus also complains that Cleon treats the debate as a trial of the Mytilenaeans, and Cleon makes explicit his desire to stimulate the Athenians to anger (Thucydides 3.44, 3.38.1, 3.40.7). This procedure is not peculiar to Cleon or the Athenians. The Corinthians at Sparta before the Peloponnesian War, when arguing for war against Athens, in effect appear as speakers for the prosecution, as the Athenian ambassadors note (Thucydides 1.68–71, 1.73). They accuse the Athenians of wrongdoing and explicitly appeal for Spartan anger. Demosthenes' anti-Macedonian policy inevitably involves an attempt to stimulate hostility against Philip (Demosthenes 2.6–10, 4.9–11, 4.37, 4.42, 6.6–20). Nor is Cleon unusual in attacking his political opponents as part of the deliberative process. Demosthenes' assault on the dominant faction in the *Third Olynthiac* is even more virulent (21–32).[7]

Another emotion equally at home in political contexts is fear. The Corinthian criticism of Athens at Sparta is designed to appeal to existing Spartan fear of Athenian expansion, just as Demosthenes seeks to arouse Athenian fear of Macedonian expansion. The reverse of this effect is confidence, noted by Aristotle (*Rhet.* 1378a) as an important factor in deliberations about the future. The clearest examples are the speech of the Corinthians before the outbreak of the Peloponnesian War in Book 1 of Thucydides, which is full of quite wild speculation about the prospects for success (1.121–122), and the speech of Alcibiades in support of the Sicilian expedition in Book 6, which is equally unrealistic (17.2–18.2).[8]

2

For Aristotle the use of *ēthos*, moral character, as a means of persuasion consists in creating through the speech a character (*Rhet.* 1377b) that will induce the required degree of trust on the part of the hearer. As with *pathos*, practical usage predates theory. Nestor's appeals to his age and experience in the *Iliad* (as at 1.260 ff.) constitute a claim to personal authority in military debate, just as Pindar's references to his poetic authority or relation to his patron (*Olympian* 1.111 ff., *Nemean* 7.61 ff.) constitute a claim to authority for his praise. In practice, *ēthos* and *pathos* are closely connected, for one effect of *ēthos*, as well as inducing a degree of trust, is also to produce a feeling of goodwill in the audience toward the speaker, so that the projection of the appropriate character achieves more subtly the effect sought by explicit appeals for a favorable hearing.[9]

Reference to civic virtue, which establishes overall good character, also involves an implicit appeal for gratitude. Moreover, one effect of *diabole* is to undermine the credibility of the opponent as well as inducing hostility, by suggesting that his way of life is such as to render statements from him unreliable.

Aristotle regards *ēthos* as more at home in deliberative oratory and *pathos* in forensic (*Rhet.* 1377b), according to a tendency toward schematization typical of the treatise and the writer. This view is reflected in the list of desired characteristics singled out by Aristotle as the province of *ēthos:* wisdom, virtue, and goodwill toward the audience. Certainly Aristotle is right to stress the significance of *ēthos* in deliberative oratory. The need to project a trustworthy character was especially important in the Athenian context of individual competition for influence. And the characteristics singled out can certainly be exemplified in surviving speeches. Virtue, for instance, is exemplified in the claim to honesty of Pericles in Thucydides 2.60 and Demosthenes at 5.12, goodwill toward the audience in the readiness to take the risk of telling the unpalatable truth at Demosthenes 3.21, 3.32 (cf. 4.51), or the high-minded devotion to the city's good at 8.1, 8.21–24 (cf. 16.1). Wisdom appears in various guises, as the bluff, straight-talking simplicity of Cleon in the Mytilenaean debate or of Demosthenes at 5.11, for instance, or the cool-headed calculation of Cleon's opponent Diodotus. Aristotle's list is incomplete, however, even for deliberative oratory, since other effects may be sought, as when the young Demosthenes diffidently apologizes for speaking first in a debate at 4.1, or when the same author modestly attributes part of his success in public deliberation to good fortune at 5.11.

Furthermore, *ēthos* was equally important in the law courts. In addition to the basic need to project a personality that invited belief, the Athenian tendency to view the trial as a detail in a broader canvas rather than an occurrence isolated from the rest of the life of litigants and city made appeal to activity beyond the courts inevitable. In such a context, the general conduct of an individual offers a useful means of determining the balance of probability in the individual instance. This implicit view was reinforced during the classical period by the increased reliance on argument from probability. *Ethos* may thus overlap implicitly with explicit argument. The simplest way to project the appropriate persona was to list explicitly the services one had bestowed on the city. The kind of services mentioned naturally depend on the status of the speaker. Unfailing performance of military service, scrupulous, generous, or enthusiastic payment of property taxes (*eisphorai*) or performance of public duties (*leitourgiai*), loyalty to the democracy during the period of the Thirty, tend to figure (see Lysias 13.77, 24.25; Isaeus 7.38–42; [Demosthenes] 34.38–39; Demosthenes 54.44).

Less blatant is the use of value judgments and general observations. By laying claim to certain beliefs that agree with accepted social values a speaker can with contrived inadvertence reveal something of his character. A wide range of effects may be sought. Patriotism and public-spiritedness are evident in the following remark from the first defense speech of Antiphon's *Second Tetralogy:* "I thought in training my son in skills which especially benefit society that some good would emerge for both of us; the result has been the reverse of my expectations" (3). The javelin throw that killed a fellow athlete is placed in the context of training for war, and both the boy who threw the javelin and his father are presented as contributing to the well-being of the state. Respect for the laws is exemplified in the opening words of Demosthenes 47: "I think the laws are quite right, jurymen" (cf. Antiphon 1.1, 5.75). The point the speaker goes on to make is quite specific to prosecutions for false witness. But the opening strikes exactly the right general note. Nobody ever alienated a Greek jury by praising the laws. Respect for parents is evidenced in the following passage ([Demosthenes] 40.12):

> [My father] urged me as soon as I reached eighteen to marry the daughter of Euphemus, because he wished to live to see children born from me. I for my part obeyed, jurymen, because I thought it my duty, both beforehand and when these men were causing him pain by suing him and making trouble, to do the opposite and give pleasure by doing everything which might gratify him.

Openness, manifested explicitly in a readiness to reveal things that one might be expected to conceal, or a promise to tell the whole story from the beginning, helps to establish trust (Lysias 1.5, 3.10; Demosthenes 39.1, 45.2). Simplicity, manifested in inexperience of public speaking and ignorance of the law courts (Antiphon 1.1, 5.1; Lysias 1.5, 12.4; Isaeus 8.5; Demosthenes 27.2), offers the promise of unadorned fact. A display of piety, expressed either (where the magnitude of the issue and the stature of the participants warrant, as at Demosthenes 18.1; Lycurgus 1.1) in prayers or in judgments on the alleged piety or impiety of others (Demosthenes 54.39–40; [Demosthenes] 59.72–78, 59.109, 59.116–117, 59.126), appeals to a very basic value. Particularly important in lawsuits is the quality of restraint. The speaker should in general avoid appearing weak. But in the context of a society that believed that the courts should be a last rather than a first resort, a readiness to tolerate a degree of discomfort or disadvantage rather than sue both establishes a commendable disposition and emphasizes the magnitude of the injuries suffered, so that again *ēthos* overlaps with argument. An explicit example is Pseudo-Demosthenes 56.14: "We agreed to this proposal, not because we were ignorant, jurymen, of our rights under the contract, but because we thought we should tolerate some degree of disadvantage and reach agreement and not give the appearance of fondness for litigation." Such restraint is especially commendable in the context of a family quarrel, as at Demosthenes 39.36: "Why are you so quarrelsome? Don't be. And don't be so hostile towards us. I'm not hostile towards you; for even now, just to make this clear to you, I'm speaking more for your good in insisting that we should not have the same name." Wisdom (or at least a capacity for reflection), given prominence by Aristotle, can be conveyed by the use of generalization (as at Demosthenes 57.27), although in general sententiousness is more at home in trials with a pronounced political flavor, or involving public figures. In such cases the scope for self-importance allows for appeal to the model of the jurors' ancestors or other political systems and for quotations from the poets,[10] all of which, apart from any overt message or emotional appeal, help to convey an impression of sagacity and moral weight. The elevated moral sentiments also help to create a bond of sympathy between the speaker and his audience.

For the projection of *ēthos* what is unsaid may be as important as what is said. The "rules" (in the limited sense of tacitly accepted norms) of decorum in an Athenian court were essentially the same as for everyday life. Although potentially a limiting factor where unsavory matters must be discussed, in practice this etiquette allowed a speaker credit for good moral character by refusing, implicitly or explicitly, to call a spade a spade. The most sustained example is the prosecution of Timarchus by Aeschines, the basis of which is an allegation that Timarchus has forfeited the right to participate in politics by prostituting himself. At no point does Aeschines make explicit what exactly Timarchus has done. He makes clear that Timarchus has allowed himself to be used sexually for money, but he is content to refer in roundabout ways to the activity involved. The result is a sustained presentation of the speaker as a man who will not stoop to describe vile behavior, and the effect is to create a rapport between speaker and audience and commensurate gulf between audience and opponent, an individual who stoops to do what decent men will not even say. The same sustained effect is created throughout Pseudo-Demosthenes 59. Much of the character assassination of the defendant Neaera relies on the undisputed fact that she was in her earlier days a prostitute. The speaker Apollodorus refers repeatedly to her sexual career, but always by means of periphrases. The silence may become explicit, as at Demosthenes 21.79 (cf. 54.9, 54.17; Aeschines 1.55): "And then in front of my sister, who was in the house then and still a girl, they said disgraceful things, the sort of things their sort would say (I could not be induced to repeat to you any of the things said then), and to my mother and me and all of us they uttered insults speakable and unspeakable."

In the passages considered so far the presentation of *ēthos* is explicit or nearly so. However, all the effects listed above can be achieved more subtly, as in the case of *pathos*, by the adroit presentation of the "facts" of the case. Here at least Aristotle shows an awareness, largely missing in his own treatise and (to judge by the bland generalizations about narrative quality that he attributes to his predecessor at *Rhet.* 1416b) largely lacking from contemporary and earlier rhetorical theory in general, of the potential of narrative as proof. He notes (*Rhet.* 1416a) in his brief discussion of narrative: "You may slip into your narrative such things as relate to your virtue, such as: 'I was constantly advising him, telling him what was right, not to abandon his children,' or your opponent's villainy: 'He answered me that wherever he himself was he would get other children.'" The advantages of this technique are that the exposition of character appears uncontrived and that the hearer draws the character by inference for himself. The resultant persona is therefore more plausible. The account of the dealings of Apollodorus with Nicostratus ([Demosthenes] 53.5 ff.), as well as revealing the latter's ingratitude, also testifies to the generosity of Apollodorus and his adherence to the time-honored ethic of supporting friends in need. The following passage ([Demosthenes] 47.38) for all its brevity is no less revealing: "I went into the house to make seizure of furniture; the door happened to be open when Theophemus came and he had still not gone in; and I had ascertained that he was not married." The last clause hints delicately at the complex of ideas regarding women in Greek society. It presents the speaker as a man who avoids any risk of disturbing the seclusion of decent women unrelated to him. He thus reveals himself as a man of decency and restraint even in the heat of a dispute.

There is another aspect to the use of character as a means of persuasion; that is dramatic characterization. In any legal hearing the listener will be on the alert for signs of dissimulation. In the Athenian context the tradition that the litigant represent himself, together with the scope for the use of bought material or expertise (from commonplaces to whole speeches), made the "fit" between speech and speaker a factor of some importance, at least to the extent that any obvious dissonance would jar. Here again, as so often, there is an overlap between *ēthos* and *pathos*, since the general disapproval of professionalism in the law courts would render the jurors sympathetic to a speaker who could present himself convincingly as an untutored novice attempting to present the unadorned truth in his own words.

It would appear that the potential of character in this theatrical sense was grasped only imperfectly by theoreticians. Aristotle touches briefly on this aspect of character in his discussion of "appropriateness"/"propriety" of style (*to prepon*)[11] at *Rhetoric* 1408a, where he says that the use of language appropriate to such external characteristics as age, sex, nationality, and to the way of life of the individual imparts *ēthos*. Here and at *Rhetoric* 1417a, where he advocates the inclusion in the narrative of details appropriate to "each *ēthos*" in order to make the narrative *ēthikos*, he has in mind not just moral character but also plausibility. What Aristotle has in mind is expressed more lucidly in chapter 15 of *Poetics*. "Secondly, characters must be fitting; for it is possible for a woman to be manly in character, but it is not fitting for her to be so manly or clever [sc. as a man]." The same section of *Poetics* includes another specification that is relevant to the courts, the requirement that character should be consistent (*homalos*). The absence of any hint of this quality in *Rhetoric* suggests that Aristotle has not thought through the implications for rhetorical theory of the notion of character as dramatic construct. And even in the discussion of propriety he does not go beyond the inclusion of detail.

Practitioners too were slow to grasp the potential of dramatic characterization. The verbal pyrotechnics of Gorgias and the ornate manner of Protagoras and Prodicus as presented by Plato and Xenophon (Plato, *Protagoras* 320d–322d; Xenophon, *Memorabilia* 2.2.34) would lend themselves badly to dramatic characterization since the style, while suitable perhaps to a political figure who has less need to conceal his training, could not plausibly be used by an ordinary man. The earliest of the logographers, Antiphon, although aware of the importance of moral character, appears to have had no conception of the potential of *ēthos* in the dramatic sense. The speakers in his *Tetralogies* all have a uniformity of manner that betrays the author's hand no less than that of the speakers in Thucydides. The same is true of the speeches written for real court cases. The speaker of Antiphon 5, Euxitheus, as a young man complains of the inadequacy of his speaking skills to present his case convincingly, but does so in a style heavily influenced by the Gorgianic love of balance and assonance (5.1). His successors, however, show an awareness that the manner of utterance should reflect the status and circumstances of the speaker. When writing for private individuals they generally avoid a style whose sophistication would jar with the client's claim to be an ordinary man. Speakers other than major political figures also avoid grandiose effects such as appeals to poets. And as a rule they do not lay claim to a greater degree of knowledge than that of the audience.

Only one writer, however, fully appreciated the potential of dramatic characterization, the speechwriter Lysias, who in several surviving speeches creates a vivid and consistent portrayal of the speaker. This does not amount to a detailed character portrayal. Too much detail would obtrude, and might actually impede the purpose of the speech by diverting attention from the "facts" and the speaker's arguments. Lysias simply selects one or two distinctive characteristics and by presenting these consistently creates the illusion of depth of characterization.

The first speech in the corpus, *On the Killing of Eratosthenes*, composed for a man accused of homicide, whose defense is that the killing was lawful since he caught Eratosthenes in adultery with his wife, presents us with a simple individual. The circumstantial narrative shows us a man who foolishly trusted his adulterous wife until his eyes were opened. It also tells of the hasty attempt on the night of the killing to put together a posse since the speaker was unprepared for what happened. One effect is to induce a feeling of sympathy for the speaker as a decent man whose trust has been abused. Another is to strengthen his "factual" case. Since, as we subsequently learn, the relatives of the dead man are alleging that he was the victim of a plot, the characterization is central to the defense case, for the personality that emerges from the narrative is too simple to be capable of the cunning attributed to him.

In the third speech, *Against Simon*, a defense against a charge of intentional wounding, we are presented at the outset with a retiring figure, a man of mature years acutely embarrassed to find himself in court because the case arose from a dispute between two rivals for the sexual favors of a young man. The detailed narrative then presents us with two contrasting portraits, the shameless and violent Simon who does not scruple to harass and assault the speaker and the boy, and the speaker, who repeatedly strives to avoid any trouble. The speaker's retiring disposition is germane to the charge against him, since the effect of the characterization is to suggest an individual who is incapable of behaving in the ostentatiously aggressive manner alleged.

Speech 16, written for a man who has been opposed at his scrutiny as member of the Boule on the grounds that he served in the cavalry under the Thirty, opens with an expression of confidence in his ability to satisfy even his enemies of his worth. After briefly answering the charge against him he proceeds to give an account of his way of life, which in both public and private spheres shows the same generosity toward others and attests his readiness to face danger on behalf of the city. Implicit in the claims of energy, courage, and generosity is a suggestion that the city will be deprived of important qualities if he is not allowed to serve it. Implicit in the frank self-praise is a suggestion of candor, which further implies an inability to deceive by concealing the past.

Lysias 7 presents us with an individual whose explicit claim to cleverness is supported by the thorough and astute array of arguments to demonstrate his innocence. He is charged with the removal of a sacred olive stump from his property, an act that he presents as reckless folly. The calculating personality projected by the speech appears incapable of such recklessness. Finally, in Lysias 24, composed for a cripple faced with the termination of his disability pension, we are presented with a cheeky, irreverent character who alternates between humor and pathos. The effect aimed for is in part the impression of a "rough diamond" speaking in his own words, in part an obfuscation of the factual case by emotional appeal and humor.[12]

As this survey indicates, Lysias uses dramatic characterization to secure two effects. The first, tactical, effect is a plausible "fit" between the alleged or discernible circumstances of the speaker and what he says so that the intervention of the professional speechwriter is concealed. The second effect is strategic. The characterization in all but one of the above cases is intended to confirm the speaker's version of his case by presenting an implied argument from probability; the implication, sometimes reinforced elsewhere in the speech by explicit argument, is that the character before the jury is incapable of behaving in the manner alleged. In the case of Lysias 24, the character still contributes to the refutation of the opponent's case, but only in a more general way by allowing the speaker to present his evasion of the allegations against him as the normal behavior of a naturally humorous disposition. Thus again the classical distinction between the different sections of the speech, while it is of value as a formal description, is inadequate as a description of purpose, for the narrative is capable of sustaining the burden of proof, and the method used, argument from the general (the evidence of character implicitly presented to the court) to the particular (the specific allegations) on the basis of probability, is the staple of argumentation from the birth of Greek rhetoric.

The only other Greek writer of the period to achieve comparable vividness of characterization is Demosthenes in the speech *Against Conon* (54), a speech that bears so strong a resemblance to Lysias 3 that one is inclined to suspect direct influence. In both speeches we have the same structural feature of the preliminary narrative (Lysias 3.5–10; Demosthenes 54.3–6), and in both one effect of the narrative is to present the speaker as a model of restraint. Since the opponent Conon intends to argue that what Ariston presents as a gratuitous assault was no more than a battle between rival gangs, and since he may well be arguing that Ariston was the instigator, it is as useful for Demosthenes as it is for Lysias to present his client as a model of *apragmosyne.*

There is a complementary aspect to dramatic characterization: that is, the presentation of the opponent. In the passage from *Rhetoric* 1416a cited earlier, Aristotle shows an awareness that use of narrative details to suggest the character of the opponent can be rhetorically effective, although it is not clear whether he would class this with *ēthos* or *pathos.* Something has already been said on this subject under the heading of *diabole* (see the preceding section). In its more developed forms, however, this technique belongs as much with *ēthos*, in that the presentation of character is being used not merely to secure an emotional effect but to create a consistent picture of the opponent that increases the plausibility of the allegations against him. The shameless and relentless Simon of Lysias 3, the greedy and petty Diogeiton of Lysias 32, Stephanus in Pseudo-Demosthenes 59, who sells his services for unscrupulous gain and engages in blackmail and false accusations, the arch-betrayer Alcibiades in Lysias 14, the violent and drunken Conon and his family in Demosthenes 54,[13] are all presented with a consistency and vividness that through intrinsic plausibility invite belief, irrespective of the degree of supporting evidence.

3

A persistent theme in this discussion has been the flexibility of oratorical practice of the classical period in comparison with rhetorical theory. Like other fourth-century writers Aristotle subdivides the speech and recognizes appropriate points in the speech for specific effects. Actual orators and logographers are less tidy; they tend to blur distinctions between these subdivisions, as far as deployment of *ēthos* and *pathos* are concerned. In particular, the narrative, especially but by no means exclusively in Lysias, proves to be far more flexible than classical rhetoricians supposed. From what we can gather, instructions for narrative tended to be simplistic and uniform; Aristotle at least shows an awareness that narrative can be varied, and that it can achieve more than one effect. Aristotle's threefold division of *pisteis* proved very influential with his successors, and deservedly so. There are however pronounced overlaps in effect between *ēthos* and *pathos*, just as there are overlaps in effect between different parts of the speech. And in the hands of a master, *ēthos*, in the sense of dramatic characterization, may fulfill the role of argument. Like all schemata, it is useful as a rough guide only.

NOTES

Reprinted with minor modifications from *Persuasion: Greek Rhetoric in Action,* ed. Ian Worthington (London, 1994), chapter 2. Copyright © 1994 by Routledge. Used by permission.

1. See Solon, fr. 4W (fear), Alcaeus, fr. 129V (anger), 130 (pity), 74 (fear).

2. Writers of the Roman period tend to confine *pathos* and equivalent terms to more powerful emotional effects. The goodwill of the audience on the other hand is treated under *ēthos* (character). See for example Cicero, *De Oratore* 2.27.225, and see in general R. Volkmann, *Die Rhetorik der Griechen und Römer in systematischer Übersicht* (Hildesheim, 1963), pp. 272 ff. However Aristotle in his

definition of *pathos* in oratory speaks in very general terms of creating a "disposition" (the verbs *diatithenai, diakeisthai*) and of emotions as "all those factors through which people undergo a change of attitude towards their decisions" (*Rhet.* 1378a), and he locates *eunoia* with *philia* among the emotions (*Rhet.* 1378a). This broader approach corresponds better with observable practice in the orators; since *eunoia* can be invited with reference to the situation as well as the personality projected by the speaker, it does not belong exclusively in the sphere of *ēthos*.

3. For the overlap between *pathos* and *ēthos* see the next section.

4. See Thrasymachus, *apud* Plato, *Phaedrus* 267d; *Rhet.* 1354a on his predecessors, and his own precepts *Rhet.* 1415a, 1416a–b, Anaximenes, *Rhetorica ad Alexandrum* 1436b–1437b and 1442a–b.

5. See Lysias 12.100 (the dead), [Demosthenes] 59.109 and 59.126.

6. See G. Kennedy, *Art of Persuasion in Ancient Greece* (Princeton, 1963), p. 204.

7. See also Thucydides 2.63.2–3, 6.12.2 and Lysias 34.1–2.

8. See Pericles at Thucydides 1.141.2–143.5, 2.62.1–2. Thucydides praises Pericles' ability to stimulate fear and confidence in the Assembly as necessary: 2.65.9.

9. For *ēthos* as a means of creating *eunoia* see note 2. For the overlap between *ēthos* and *pathos* see D. A. Russell, "Ethos in Oratory and Rhetoric," *Characterization and Individuality in Greek Literature,* ed. C. Pelling (Oxford, 1990), p. 212.

10. Demosthenes 18.289, 19.247, 19.255, 21.143–150; Aeschines 1.128–129, 1.143–152, 1.180–182; Lycurgus 1.98–100, 1.102–110, 1.111–123, and 1.128–129.

11. Dion. Hal. *Lysias* 9 likewise sees *to prepon* solely in terms of style.

12. For detailed discussion of the presentation of character in these speeches see S. Usher, "Individual Characterization in Lysias," *Eranos* 63 (1965): 99–119; C. Carey, "Structure and Strategy in Lysias XXIV," *Greece and Rome* 37 (1990): 44–51, and *Lysias: Selected Speeches* (Cambridge, 1989), pp. 10, 61–62, 89–90, and 116–117.

13. See Carey, *Lysias,* pp. 207 and 210 ff.; C. Carey and R. A. Reid, *Demosthenes: Selected Private Speeches* (Cambridge, 1985), pp. 78 and 82; and C. Carey, *Apollodoros Against Neaira: [Demosthenes] 59* (Warminster, 1992), p. 90.

The Composition and Influence of Aristotle's *Rhetoric*

George A. Kennedy

THE COMPOSITION OF THE *RHETORIC*

How and when the text of the *Rhetoric* developed into the form that we now read has been discussed by scholars without reaching complete agreement. Although most would perhaps admit that different parts of the work were originally written at different times, some would insist that the whole was rather thoroughly revised, presumably at a late date in Aristotle's career, and that it represents a unified view of its subject,[1] while others are more impressed by inconsistencies between various parts.[2] It can, of course, be argued that however it was composed, Aristotle left the treatise in substantially the form in which we have it and that it represents his thinking at one point in time, that it was read as a unity by students from ancient to modern times without serious difficulties, and that what is important is not how it evolved but how it can be understood as a theory of rhetoric. But this view does require the conscientious reader to exercise considerable ingenuity in interpreting some passages to mean something different from what they literally say. To a greater extent than most works of Aristotle, the *Rhetoric* shows signs of haste, for example, in the haphazard way the chapters on *pathos* and *ēthos* in Book 2 are integrated into the whole, in the inconsistent use of the term *topos*, and in the absence of examples in some passages in contrast to their abundance elsewhere.

Differences in approach to the *Rhetoric* seem to reflect different assumptions and different objectives on the part of readers. Some believe that it should be possible to make objective and true statements about politics, ethics, and rhetoric in the way that scientists seek to make objective and true statements about the physical world (although whether even the latter is possible is now sometimes called into doubt). Such a view is variously known as logocentrism or foundationalism. In dealing with

416

a text these readers seek the intent of the author, and in the case of Aristotle they regard the author as one who at all times knew exactly what he was doing and expressed his full intent. Others feel that the nature of human language introduces a factor that is always centrifugal, escaping the author's control and that meaning arises from context and from the reader. They welcome differences as opening an opportunity for ongoing dialogue. Aristotle's own view lay somewhere between these schools. Unlike Plato, he did not believe that there was such a thing as abstract truth about human values; but he also thought that progress could be made toward some consensus about the good life on the basis of probable argument through dialectic. In this sense, Aristotelianism is an open philosophical system, always subject to revision.

To a greater extent than his predecessors, Aristotle thought that knowledge grows and develops over time, that philosophy and scholarship is a collegial process in which assumptions are continually reexamined, and that there are numerous avenues that have not yet been opened up.[3] His students, Theophrastus in particular, carried on this work; and we continue to do so today. As Abraham Edel has emphasized, Aristotelian thought is a network of interreacting ideas, constantly in development.[4] There is a method common to all parts; and there are certain common assumptions, of which one of the most important is the concept of potentiality/actuality. Aristotle defines rhetoric as a potentiality (*dynamis*, 1.2.1); his treatise represents an attempt to visualize it when actualized in its fullest form, but he would doubtless agree that there is more in rhetoric (and in any other discipline) than is met with in his philosophy. It is an interesting mental exercise to try to enter into the evolution of his own thought. If one does so, it is possible to see in the text a kind of debate in Aristotle's mind between a more philosophical and a more pragmatic view of rhetoric (a continuation of what is found in Platonic dialogues) and possible also to enter into this debate in making one's own judgments about the nature, functions, and morality of rhetoric.

The outside dates for the development of the *Rhetoric* are from about 360 to about 334 B.C. In 360 Aristotle was a student in Plato's Academy and living in Athens, where rhetoric in its many forms enjoyed perhaps the greatest prestige and influence in its history. Plato's hostility to it could have whetted Aristotle's attempt to understand it better, an attempt probably made around 360 in the lost dialogue *Gryllus* and continued in his early teaching of rhetoric in the 350s. In 335, after an absence of twelve years, he returned to the hotbed of debate in Athens, having lived meanwhile in the courts of kings in Assos and Macedon and having reflected deeply on many aspects of life and society. There is no reasonable doubt that the *Rhetoric*, along with the *Poetics* and the *Constitution of the Athenians*, is one of his most Athenian works, primarily addressed to

Athenians; for only in Athens did rhetoric fully function in the way he describes, and it is from Athenian rhetoric that he draws the largest number of his practical illustrations. That he hoped eventually to return to Athens is probable, given its leadership in Greek intellectual life; and that the possibility of returning loomed large in his mind at least by 338, when Philip defeated the Athenians at Chaeronea, is also likely. That he hoped to have some practical influence on life in Athens and elsewhere seems clear from the passion evident throughout the *Nicomachean Ethics*. Although his revisions of the *Rhetoric* were never complete, the evidence supports the view that he worked on the treatise between 340 and 335 in anticipation of his return to Athens and the opening of a school there. The most compelling evidence is furnished by the historical allusions, of which the latest are to events in that period.

Dionysius of Halicarnassus, writing in the late first century B.C., devotes his *First Letter to Ammaeus* to answering an unnamed Peripatetic philosopher who had claimed that Demosthenes learned the art of rhetoric from Aristotle. Dionysius assumes that the Peripatetic meant that Demosthenes was familiar with the *Rhetoric* (whether by reading it or by hearing it delivered as a series of lectures is not said); and he also regards the treatise in three books as a single work, written all at one time. Living in Rome, Dionysius probably used the edition published by Andronicus, noted in the next section. Dionysius argues that the Peripatetic was mistaken (because when the *Rhetoric* was written, Demosthenes was already at the height of his career) and that the converse is true: Aristotle wrote the treatise on the basis of a comparative study of the works of Demosthenes and other orators. His evidence for the date of composition falls into two groups. The first are the cross-references in the *Rhetoric* to the *Topics, Analytics,* and *Methodics,* which he takes as showing that Aristotle had earlier written a number of his most substantial works and was therefore well along in his career. He does not consider the possibility that cross-references could have been added at a later date to otherwise completed passages. Second, Dionysius seeks to show on the basis of historical references in the treatise that it was written after all of Demosthenes' great public speeches of the period of the Olynthian War in 349–348 B.C., after Philip's breaking his alliance with Athens in 340–339 and even after *On the Crown,* delivered in 330. The latter argument, however, is unconvincing in that it requires an unsubstantiated identification of the trial of "Demosthenes and those who killed Nicanor" (2.23.3) with Demosthenes' defense of Ctesiphon in *On the Crown.*

It is probably prudent to separate attempts at dating Books 1–2 from the dating of Book 3, since these may have originally been separate works. The list of the writings in Diogenes Laertius, along with various other oddities, contains (5.24) an *Art of Rhetoric* in two books and a treatise *On*

Lexis, also in two books (style plus arrangement?). Perhaps more compelling, Books 1–2 not only do not anticipate but seem to forestall any consideration of style until the final transitional passage in 2.26.3. Possibly, Aristotle, in his final set of revisions, decided to link two works together to make a single treatise; possibly the linkage was made by the grammarian Tyrannio or by Andronicus of Rhodes.

In Books 1–2 the latest historical references seem to be to the embassy from Artaxerxes (2.20.3) and the trial of Philocrates (2.3.13) in 343, the death of Diopeithes in 342 or 341 (2.8.11), Philip's envoy to Thebes in 339 (2.23.6), Demades' comment about Demosthenes' policy (2.24.8, any time after 338), and finally the Common Peace (2.23.18, probably that imposed by Macedon on Greece in 336). It is worth noting that reference to events after 340 all occur in chapters 23–24 of Book 2—the discussion of topics, a section of the work that Aristotle introduces with the verb *parasēmainō* (2.22.17), indicating that it is a kind of supplement. This suggests that Aristotle may have integrated these chapters into the *Rhetoric* about 336 or 335. One implication is that the concept of the *topos* as applied to rhetoric is a relatively late addition to the treatise. In 1.2.21–22 Aristotle makes a sharp distinction between *idia* and *topoi* and throughout Books 1 and 2 continues to talk about *idia;* but in what may be a late addition in 1.15.19 he refers to the *idia* as *topoi,* and in 1.2.22 and 1.6.1 as *stoikheia,* which in 2.22.13 and 2.26.1 he says are the same as topics. From this we might conclude that Aristotle eventually came to the view, shared by most later rhetoricians, that what he had earlier called *idia* or *stoikheia* are a kind of topic, differing from common topics in being specific to a particular body of knowledge.

A general hypothesis of the composition of Books 1–2 might start with what John Rist calls the "early core" of the treatise,[5] 1.5–15, with numerous references to historical events before 350 and some philosophical concepts that Aristotle later abandoned. Some revision was subsequently given to these chapters, including perhaps the insertion of chapter 8 with its cross-reference to the *Politics.* The "early core" seems to require 1.3–4, or something like them, to define the species of rhetoric and introduce the discussion of deliberative oratory. The discussions of *pathos* in 2.2–11 and of *ēthos* in 2.12–17 apparently originated in a separate context and have been imperfectly integrated into the *Rhetoric* at a relatively late stage by occasional references to the needs of a speaker and a transition in 2.18; the beginning of 2.20 sounds as though it originally followed 1.5–15. The otherwise unneeded statement in 2.14.4 about the maturity of the mind at the age of forty-nine could be taken as a wry reference to the fact that Aristotle was that age when he wrote the passage, thus around 335 B.C. The concluding chapters of Book 2 (18–26) are the adaptation of Aristotle's dialectic to rhetoric, a product of the period 340–335 B.C. With this must go 1.2, the definition of rhetoric and its parts, which organizes the whole revision.

The dating of 1.1 is the most problematic. It seems difficult to associate it with a revision of the work that added 2.2–17, since it rejects concern with the matters discussed there. Although it is the most Platonic part of the work, it is difficult to connect it with Aristotle's earliest teaching of rhetoric if our sources are correct that that was of a general, practical sort.[6] Possibly it should be thought of as an introduction to rhetoric for his associates in the Academy at the time he was teaching a more general course to others. Possibly it resulted from his teaching of rhetoric to Alexander as an extension of instruction in dialectic and part of a general course in philosophy. He may have let it stand in the final version for his return to Athens because he liked this linkage, possibly because he liked the challenge to traditional teaching and thought it worthwhile for students in his new school to meet an extreme view of philosophical rhetoric at the outset, knowing that this would be modified as study continued.

Even if Book 3 was originally a separate work, its development seems to have been roughly parallel to that of Books 1–2. Walter Burkert pointed out that the reference to Theodorus in 3.2.4 sounds as though he was alive when it was written, putting it probably in the 350s.[7] That would mean that some of the material may go back to Aristotle's early teaching of rhetoric—logically enough if that teaching was indeed of a popular sort. This may include some of the discussion of diction in 3.2–12 and Aristotle's version of a traditional rhetorical handbook in 3.13–19, but some of the discussion has certainly been added later or revised. The latest historical references seem to be to the *Philippus* of Isocrates (e.g., 3.10.7, 3.11.2, and so on), published in 346 B.C., and other references to Isocrates in 3.17.10–11 could be taken to imply that he was still alive, putting them before his death in 338. Again, teaching Alexander may have drawn Aristotle's attention back to the matter of style. Two references to "Attic" or "Athenian" orators (3.11.16 and 3.17.10) may imply that Aristotle was not in Athens when he wrote these passages, putting them before 335. The final revision of Book 3 refers to, and somewhat expands, the discussion of metaphor in the *Poetics*, and Aristotle's interest in Athenian drama and in making a reply to Plato's view of imitation, although possibly awakened by teaching Alexander, seems better associated with a hoped-for return to Athens. It may well be that he arrived with the two works completed and that he inaugurated his school there with lectures on these two subjects of special interest to an Athenian audience. The text of the *Rhetoric* suggests that some revision was made hastily, perhaps in preparation for his return. We cannot be certain that in teaching rhetoric Aristotle read out the treatise we have; even if he did so he is likely to have expanded and commented on its contents as he went along or to have omitted some parts; and one hopes he responded to questions from the audience.

THE HISTORY OF THE TEXT AFTER ARISTOTLE

The geographer Strabo (13.1.54), an often well-informed writer of the late first century B.C., and the historian-philosopher Plutarch (*Sulla* 26.1–2), writing a hundred years later, are the major sources for the early history of the text of the works of Aristotle. They are in general agreement and probably drew on the same source. The tale they tell has not always been believed, but in the case of the *Rhetoric* it is consistent with the very limited knowledge of the treatise shown by Greek and Latin writers from the late fourth to middle of the first centuries B.C. The story goes as follows.

After Aristotle's death his library became the property of his most famous student, Theophrastus, who had succeeded him as head of the Peripatetic School. (Theophrastus wrote on several aspects of rhetoric; and although these works have not survived, they seem often to have been an extension of Aristotle's thinking. "Topics," enthymemes, delivery, and style were all treated by him, his treatise *On Lexis* being especially influential. In this work he seems to have reformulated Aristotle's discussion of the virtue of style in terms of diction and composition under four major headings: correctness, clarity, ornamentation, and propriety.[8] After Theophrastus's death [about 285 B.C.], some of Aristotle's still unpublished manuscripts probably remained in the Peripatetic School in Athens, and copies of some were probably made for research libraries, of which the most important was the great Library at Alexandria in Egypt; but there is no clear indication that the *Rhetoric* was among these books.) Aristotle's library was inherited from Theophrastus by the philosopher Neleus and taken to Scepsis in Asia Minor, where it fell into the hands of people who were not scholars. To prevent the books from being seized by agents for the library at Pergamum, these owners hid them and then forgot about them. Thus, the Peripatetics after Theophrastus did not have the original works of Aristotle, or at least not all of them. Subsequently, perhaps about 100 B.C., Aristotle's library, now in a damaged condition, was sold by the heirs of those who had hidden it to Apellicon of Teos, living in Athens. After Apellicon's death it was seized by the Roman general Sulla and sent to Rome, around 83 B.C. There the grammarian Tyrannio "arranged" the works and furnished copies to Andronicus of Rhodes, who "published" them and drew up lists of the works.

It has often been assumed that some editing was done by Tyrannio and Andronicus, and one possibility is the combining of Books 1–2 of the

Rhetoric with Book 3, including some of the transitional passages. The reference to Aristotle's *Lexis* in Demetrius (*On Style* 116) may imply that he regarded it as a separate work; and, as noted in the section before, Diogenes Laertius (5.24), writing much later, lists an *Art of Rhetoric* in two books, not three, as well as a work *On Lexis* in two books. Possibly, two traditions existed, one containing all three books, one containing only Books 1–2. The version known to Quintilian (2.17.14) had three books.

When Cicero wrote *On Invention* as a very young man and before the arrival of the library of Apellicon in Rome, he knew that Aristotle had written on the subject, he describes the work as providing aids and ornaments to the art (1.7), and he attributes to Aristotle the view that the duty (*officium*) of the orator was exercised in three *genera:* demonstrative, deliberative, and judicial. That, of course, is not quite what Aristotle says in 1.3, but it does indicate that the division of rhetoric into three species was traditionally, and rightly, associated with Aristotle. This may well represent an oral tradition that goes back to Aristotle's own students in the fourth century rather than a knowledge of the text in the intervening centuries.

Even if the *Rhetoric* were available to scholars between 300 and 100 B.C., new developments in rhetorical theory had rendered it obsolete as a school text. Hermagoras of Temnos, in the middle of the second century, had worked out stasis theory, a systematic way to determine the central question at issue in a speech. Aristotle shows some awareness of such matters in 1.13.9–10 and 3.15, 17 but failed to present a systematic theory, which by Cicero's time was the foundation of the study of rhetorical invention, and continued so throughout the Byzantine period. In the study of style, the Stoics had developed the theory of tropes and figures of speech, concepts unknown to Aristotle; and these two were major concerns of later rhetoricians. Aristotle's topical theory did remain a subject of interest, although modified by subsequent writers including Cicero, Quintilian, and Boethius.

When Cicero wrote *On the Orator* in 55 B.C., he clearly had some knowledge of the *Rhetoric*, probably from the edition of Tyrannio and Andronicus; and the discussion of invention in *On the Orator* 2.114–306 is considerably more Aristotelian than what is found in *On Invention* or in the other early Latin treatise, *Rhetoric for Herennius*. Cicero refers to the *Rhetoric* repeatedly and even makes his character Antonius claim to have read it in Athens in the late second century B.C. (2.160). Aristotelian influences include the role of logical proof, presentation of character, and emotional appeal (2.115), described later in *Orator* 69 as the three *officia* of the orator—to prove, to delight, and to move—and then associated with the three kinds of style: plain, middle, and grand. This represents an important and long influential restatement and extension of Aristotle's basic concepts in *Rhetoric* 1.2.

The Aristotelian works were reedited and extensively studied in later antiquity, beginning with Alexander of Aphrodisias around A.D. 200; but the *Rhetoric* was given very little attention. In the new organization of the corpus it was assigned to the *Organon*, following the *Topics* and preceding the *Poetics*. By implication, rhetoric was to be regarded as a logical tool, not as a practical or productive art. There are only occasional references to the treatise in writers of the Roman empire or early Middle Ages, but it did survive intact because of its Aristotelian authorship. Our earliest—and often best—manuscript is *Parisinus* 1741, written in the tenth century. It is a compilation of rhetorical treatises by Menander, Dionysius of Halicarnassus, and others, plus the *Rhetoric* and *Poetics;* there are two, rather short Greek commentaries on the *Rhetoric* written in the twelfth century, one attributed to a certain Stephanus, one anonymous.[9] The work was also known to Arabic scholars of Greek philosophy; and in the thirteenth century Hermannus Alemannus in Spain made a Latin translation of an Arabic commentary attributed to al-Farabi. Two Latin translations of the Greek text were then produced, introducing the *Rhetoric* to the Western Middle Ages. The first of these, the Old Translation, was perhaps the work of Bartholomew of Massina; and the second was by William of Moerbeke, urged on by Thomas Aquinas. Giles of Rome then wrote a Latin commentary; but (as this commentary indicates) what interested readers of the time was not the rhetorical theory (for which they kept to the Ciceronian tradition) but its political and moral teachings.[10]

In the fifteenth century George of Trebizond brought Aristotle's theory to the attention of Italian humanists and prepared a new Latin translation, which was the first printed version of the *Rhetoric* (about 1477). The complete Greek text was not printed with early editions of Aristotle's philosophical works and first appeared in 1508 in the Venice edition of the collected *Rhetores graeci,* published by Aldus Manutius. Thereafter, new editions of the Greek text began to appear, and new translations were made.[11] The first English version, a kind of outline summary, was the work of the political philosopher Thomas Hobbes, printed in London in 1637. Although the *Rhetoric* was much read in the later Renaissance and although important scholarship on the text and the fine commentary of E. M. Cope appeared in the nineteenth century, real appreciation of the significance of the treatise is a phenomenon of twentieth-century interest in speech communication and critical theory.

The division of the original *Rhetoric* into two or three books can be attributed to Aristotle himself, and presumably reflects the convenient length of a papyrus scroll in his time. The division into numbered chapters was first made by George of Trebizond in the fifteenth century as a convenience for teachers and readers and is generally logical, although some discussions are divided into separate chapters when the Greek suggests they should be read as continuous. The division of chapters into numbered sections originated in the Bipontine edition of J. T. Buhle (Zweibrucken, 1793) and is often erratic. The standard way to refer to specific passages in the Greek text is by use of page, column, and line numbers in the 1831 Berlin edition of the complete works of Aristotle as edited by Immanuel Bekker.

NOTES

From *On Rhetoric: A Theory of Civic Discourse,* trans. George A. Kennedy, pp. 301–309. Copyright © 1991 by George A. Kennedy. Reprinted (with minor changes) by permission of Oxford University Press, Inc.

1. See, for example, W. M. A. Grimaldi, *Studies in the Philosophy of Aristotle's Rhetoric* (Wiesbaden, 1972).

2. See, for example, F. Solmsen, *Die Entwicklung der Aristotelischen Logik und Rhetorik* (Berlin, 1929), and J. M. Rist, *The Mind of Aristotle: A Study in Philosophical Growth* (Toronto, 1989).

3. See, for example, *Soph. Ref.* 34 and *Rhet.* 3.1.

4. A. Edel, *Aristotle and His Philosophy* (Chapel Hill, N.C., 1982).

5. Rist, *The Mind of Aristotle,* pp. 85–86, 136–144.

6. The chief sources are Cicero, *On the Orator* 3.141, *Orator* 46; Philodemus, *On Rhetoric* 2:50–51 Sudhaus; Quintilian 3.1.14; Diogenes Laertius 5.3. See A.-H. Chroust, "Aristotle's Earliest Course of Lectures on Rhetoric," *L'Antiquité Classique* 33 (1964): 58–72. Chroust's article has been reprinted in *Aristotle: The Classical Heritage of Rhetoric,* ed. K. Erickson (Metuchen, N.J., 1974), pp. 22–36.

7. W. Burkert, "Aristoteles im Theater: Zur Datierung des 3. Buch der *Rhetorik* und der *Poetik,*" *Museum Helveticum* 32 (1975): 67–72.

8. See especially Cicero, *Orator* 79.

9. Texts in volume 15 of *Commentaria in Aristotelem Graeca,* ed. H. Rabe (Berlin, 1896). On Byzantine study of the *Rhetoric,* see T. Conley, "Aristotle's *Rhetoric* in Byzantium," *Rhetorica* 8 (1990): 29–44.

10. On Western medieval study of the *Rhetoric,* see J. J. Murphy, *Rhetoric in the Middle Ages* (Berkeley, 1974), pp. 89–101.

11. See P. D. Brandes, *A History of Aristotle's Rhetoric* (Metuchen, N.J., 1989).

SELECTED BIBLIOGRAPHY

This listing has been compiled from the bibliographies provided by contributors to this volume and from the excellent bibliographies in G. A. Kennedy, *Aristotle on Rhetoric* (Oxford, 1991), and in J. Barnes, M. Schofield, and R. Sorabji, eds., *Articles on Aristotle,* vol. 4 (London, 1979).

EDITIONS AND TRANSLATIONS

Ackrill, J. L., ed. and trans. *'Categories' and De Interpretatione.* Oxford, 1963.

Barnes, J., ed. *The Complete Works of Aristotle: The Revised Oxford Translation.* Princeton, 1984.

Bekker, I., ed. *Aristotelis Rhetorica et Poetica: ab Immanuele Bekkero tertium edite.* 2 vols. Berlin, 1859.

Bekker, I., and C. A. Brandis, eds. *Aristotelis Opera.* 5 vols. Berlin, 1831–1870.

Bonitz, H. *Index Aristotelicus.* Part of *Aristotelis Opera,* vol. 5, ed. I. Bekker. Berlin, 1870. Reprinted separately, Berlin: Akademie-Verlag, 1955.

Brunschwig, J., ed. *Topiques,* vol. 1 [Books I–IV]. Paris, 1967.

Bywater, I., trans. *The Poetics.* In *The Complete Works of Aristotle: The Revised Oxford Translation,* ed. J. Barnes. Princeton, 1985.

Cooper, L., trans. *The Rhetoric of Aristotle.* New York, 1932.

Cope, E. M. *The Rhetoric of Aristotle, with a Commentary,* rev. and ed. J. E. Sandys. 3 vols. Cambridge, 1877.

Dufour, M., ed. *Rhetorique Aristote.* 3 vols. Paris, 1932 and 1960–1973.

Forster, E. S., trans. *The Topics.* Cambridge, Mass., 1960. ~

Frede, D., trans. *Plato: Philebus.* Indianapolis, 1993.

Freese, J. H., trans. *Aristotle: The "Art" of Rhetoric.* London, 1926.

Gauthier, R. A., and J. Y. Jolif, eds. and trans. *L'Ethique à Nicomaque.* 2d ed. 4 vols. Louvain, 1970.

Grimaldi, W. M. A., ed. *Aristotle, Rhetoric I: A Commentary.* New York, 1980.

———. *Aristotle, Rhetoric II: A Commentary.* New York, 1988.

Jebb, R. *The Rhetoric of Aristotle*. Ed. J. E. Sandys. Cambridge, 1909.

Kassel, R., ed. *Aristotelis Ars Rhetorica*. Berlin, 1976.

Kennedy, G. A., ed. and trans. *On Rhetoric: A Theory of Civic Discourse*. Oxford, 1991.

Kirwan, C., ed. and trans. *Aristotle's Metaphysics: Books Gamma, Delta and Epsilon*. Oxford, 1971.

Lawson-Tancred, H. C., ed. and trans. *The Art of Rhetoric*. London, 1991.

Lord, C., trans. *The Politics*. Chicago, 1984.

Moraux, P. *Aristoteles Graecus*. New York, 1976.

Pacius, J. *Aristotelis Organon cum commentario analytico*. 2d ed. Frankfurt, 1597.

Pickard-Cambridge, W. A., trans. *"Topica"* and *"De Sophisticis Elenchis."* In *The Works of Aristotle*, vol. 1, ed. W. D. Ross. Oxford, 1928.

Rackham, H., trans. *The Athenian Constitution: The Eudemian Ethics: On Virtues and Vices*. London, 1952.

Roberts, W. R., trans. *Rhetoric*. New York, 1954.

Robin, L., ed. *Platon. Phaedre*. 4th ed. Paris, 1954.

Roemer, A., ed. *Aristotelis Ars Rhetorica: Cum Nova Codicis Ac et Vetustae Translationis Collatione*. Leipzig, 1885.

Ross, W. D., ed. *Prior and Posterior Analytics*. Oxford, 1949.

———. *Ars Rhetorica*. Oxford, 1959.

Schneider, B. *Aristotelis Latinus: Rhetorica*. Leiden, 1978.

Smith, R., trans. and ed. *Prior Analytics*. Indianapolis, 1989.

Spengel, L., ed. *Rhetores Graeci*. 3 vols. Leipzig, 1853–1856.

———. *Aristotelis Ars Rhetorica cum Adnotatione Leonardi Spengel*. 2 vols. Leipzig, 1867.

Stewart, J. A. *Notes on the Nicomachean Ethics of Aristotle*. 2 vols. Oxford, 1892.

Taylor, T., trans. *The Rhetoric, Poetics, and Nichomachean Ethics of Aristotle*. 2 vols. London, 1818.

Thompson, d'Arcy. *Historia Animalium*. Vol. 4 of *The Works of Aristotle*, eds. J. A. Smith and W. D. Ross. Oxford, 1910.

Tricot, J., ed. *Aristote. Organon. Vol. 6. Les Refutations sophistiques*. Paris, 1950.

Welldon, J. E. C., trans. *The Rhetoric of Aristotle*. London, 1886.

SECONDARY WORKS

Ackrill, J. L. "Aristotle on Eudaimonia." In *Essays on Aristotle's Ethics*, ed. A. O. Rorty. Berkeley, 1980.

Annas, J. "Aristotle on Pleasure and Goodness." In *Essays on Aristotle's Ethics*, ed. A. O. Rorty. Berkeley, 1980.

———. "Comments on Stephen Halliwell's 'Popular Morality, Philosophical Ethics and the *Rhetoric*.'" Symposium Aristotelicum, 1990.

———. "Aristotle on Memory and the Self." In *Essays on Aristotle's De Anima*, ed. M. C. Nussbaum and A. O. Rorty. Oxford, 1992.

Arnauld, A. *La Logique, ou l'art de penser*. Paris, 1858.

Arnhart, L. *Aristotle on Political Reasoning*. DeKalb, 1981.

Atherton, C. "Hand over Fist: The Failure of Stoic Rhetoric." *Classical Quarterly* 38 (1988): 392–427.

Aubenque, P. *Le probleme de l'etre chez Aristote*. Paris, 1962.

———. "*Logos* et *Pathos*." Symposium Aristotelicum, 1990.

Barnes, J. "Aristotle's Concept of Mind." In *Articles on Aristotle*, vol. 4, ed. J. Barnes, M. Schofield, and R. Sorabji. London, 1979.

———. "Aristotle and the Methods of Ethics." *Revue Internationale de Philosophie* 133–134 (1980): 490–511.

———. "Proof and the Syllogism." In *Aristotle on Science: The Posterior Analytics*, ed. E. Berti. Padova, 1981.

Barnes, J., M. Schofield, and R. Sorabji, eds. *Articles on Aristotle: Psychology and Aesthetics*. 4 vols. London, 1979.

Barwick, K. "Die Gliederung der Rhetorischen *techne* und die horazische Epistula ad Pisones." *Hermes* 57 (1922): 16–18.

Belfiore, E. *Tragic Pleasures*. Princeton, 1992.

Benoit, W. L. "Aristotle's Example: The Rhetorical Induction." *Quarterly Journal of Speech* 66 (1980): 182–192.

Berti, E. "Zenone di Elea inventore della dialettica?" *La Parola del Passato* 43 (1988): 1941.

Black's Law Dictionary. 3d ed. St. Paul, 1933.

Blundell, M. W. "*Ethos* and *Dianoia* Reconsidered." *Essays on Aristotle's Poetics*, ed. A. O. Rorty. Princeton, 1992.

Bolton, R. "The Epistemological Basis of Aristotelian Dialectic." In *Biologie, logique, et metaphysique chez Aristote*, ed. D. Devereux and P. Pellegrin. Paris, 1990.

Bonner, R. J. *Evidence in Athenian Courts*. Chicago, 1905.

———. *Lawyers and Litigants in Ancient Athens*. Chicago, 1927.

Bonner, R. J., and G. Smith. *The Administration of Justice from Homer to Aristotle*. 2 vols. Chicago, 1930.

Brandes, P. D. "The Composition and Preservation of Aristotle's *Rhetoric*." *Speech Monographs* 35 (1968): 482–491.

———. *A History of Aristotle's Rhetoric*. Metuchen, N.J., 1989.

Brandis, C. A. "Über Aristoteles' *Rhetorik* und die griechischen Ausleger derselben." *Philologus* 4 (1849): 1–47.

Brunschwig, J. "Introduction." In *Topiques*, vol. 1 [Books I–IV]. Paris, 1967.

———. "Aristotle on Arguments Without Winners or Losers." In *Wissenschaftskollege Jahrbuch 1984/1985*, ed. P. Wapnewski. Berlin, 1986.

———. "Remarques sur la communication de Robert Bolton." In *Biologie, logique et metaphysique chez Aristote*, ed. D. Devereux and P. Pellegrin. Paris, 1990.

———. "Rhétorique et dialectique, *Rhétorique et Topiques*." In *Aristotle's Rhetoric: Philosophical Essays*, ed. D. J. Furley and A. Nehamas. Princeton, 1994.

Brunschwig, J., and M. Nussbaum, eds. *Passions and Perceptions*. Cambridge, 1993.

Buckley, T. *Aristotle's Treatise on Rhetoric*. London, 1910.

Burkert, W. "Aristoteles im Theater: Zur Datierung des 3. Buch der *Rhetorik* und der *Poetik*." *Museum Helveticum* 32 (1975): 67–72.

Burnet, J., ed. *Aristotle: Ethics*. London, 1900.

Burnyeat, M. "The Origins of Non-deductive Inference." In *Science and Speculation: Studies in Hellenistic Theory and Practice*, ed. J. Barnes, J. Brunschwig, M. Burnyeat, and M. Schofield. Cambridge, 1982.

———. "Enthymeme: Aristotle on the Logic of Persuasion." In *Aristotle's Rhetoric: Philosophical Essays*, ed. D. J. Furley and A. Nehamas. Princeton, 1994.

Carawan, E. M. "*Erotesis:* Interrogation in the Courts of Fourth-Century Athens." *Greek, Roman and Byzantine Studies* 24 (1982): 209–226.

Carey, C. *Lysias: Selected Speeches*. Cambridge, 1989.

Cassin, Barbara, ed. *Le Plaisir de Parler*. Paris, 1986.

———. *Positions de la sophistique*. Paris, 1986.

Caveing, M. *Zenon d'Elee Prolegomenes aux doctrines du continu. Etude historique et critique des Fragments et Temoignages*. Paris, 1982.

Charles, D. *Aristotle's Philosophy of Action*. Ithaca, 1984.

———. "Fear: Imagination and Belief." Helsinki conference, 1991.

Chroust, A.-H. "Aristotle's Earliest Course of Lectures on Rhetoric." *L'Antiquite Classique* 33 (1964): 58–72.

Cohen, L. J. *The Probable and the Provable*. Oxford, 1977.

Cole, T. *The Origins of Rhetoric in Ancient Greece*. Baltimore, 1991.

Conley, T. "*Pathe* and *Pisteis:* Aristotle, *Rhet.* II 2–11." *Hermes* 110 (1982): 300–315.

———. "The Enthymeme in Perspective." *Quarterly Journal of Speech* 70 (1984): 168–187.

———. "Aristotle's *Rhetoric* in Byzantium." *Rhetorica* 8 (1990): 29–44.

———. *Rhetoric in the European Tradition*. New York, 1990.

Consigny, S. "Transparency and Displacement: Aristotle's Concept of Rhetorical Clarity." *Rhetoric Society Quarterly* 17 (1987): 413–419.

Cooper, J. M. "Emotions and Dialectic." Helsinki conference, 1991.

———. "Rhetoric, Dialectic, and the Passions." *Oxford Studies in Ancient Philosophy* 11 (1993): 175–198.

———. "Ethical-Political Theory in Aristotle's *Rhetoric*." In *Aristotle's Rhetoric: Philosophical Essays*, ed. D. J. Furley and A. Nehamas. Princeton, 1994.

Cope, E. M. *An Introduction to Aristotle's Rhetoric*. London, 1867.

Corbett, P. J. "Introduction." In *Aristotle's Rhetoric,* trans. W. R. Roberts. New York, 1984.

Crem, T. M. "The Definition of Rhetoric According to Aristotle." *Laval Theologique et Philosophique* 12 (1956): 233–250.

Cronin, J. F. *The Athenian Juror and His Oath*. Chicago, 1936.

Denyer, N. *Language, Thought and Falsehood in Ancient Greek Philosophy*. London, 1991.

De Romilly, J. *Magic and Rhetoric in Ancient Greece*. Cambridge, 1975.

Düring, I. *Aristotle in the Ancient Biographical Tradition*. Goteborg, 1957.

———. *Aristoteles. Darstellung und Interpretation seines Denkens*. Heidelberg, 1966.

———. "Aristotle's Use of Examples in the *Topics*." In *Aristotle on Dialectic*, ed. G. E. L. Owen. Oxford, 1968.

Engberg-Pedersen, T. *Aristotle's Theory of Moral Insight*. Oxford, 1983.

Erickson, K. V., ed. *Aristotle: The Classical Heritage of Rhetoric.* Metuchen, N.J., 1974.

Euben, J. P. *The Tragedy of Political Theory: The Road Not Taken.* Princeton, 1990.

Euben, J. P., J. Wallach, and J. Ober. *Athenian Political Thought and the Reconstitution of American Democracy.* Ithaca, 1994.

Festugière, A. J. *Aristote: Le Plaisir.* Paris, 1936.

Fortenbaugh, W. W. *Aristotle on Emotion: A Contribution to Philosophical Psychology, Rhetoric, Poetics, Politics, and Ethics.* New York, 1975.

———. "Aristotle's *Rhetoric* on Emotions." In *Articles on Aristotle,* vol. 4, ed. J. Barnes, M. Schofield, and R. Sorabji. London, 1979.

———. "Theophrastus on Delivery." *Rutgers University Studies* 2 (1985): 269–288.

———. "Aristotle's Platonic Attitude Toward Delivery." *Philosophy and Rhetoric* 19 (1986): 242–254.

———. "Cicero's Knowledge of the Rhetorical Treatises of Aristotle and Theophrastus." In *Cicero's Knowledge of the Peripatos,* ed. W. W. Fortenbaugh and P. Steinmetz. London, 1989.

Frede, D. "The Cognitive Role of *Phantasia* in Aristotle." In *Essays on Aristotle's De Anima,* ed. M. C. Nussbaum and A. O. Rorty. Oxford, 1991.

———. "Disintegration and Restoration: Pleasure and Pain in Plato's *Philebus.*" In *The Cambridge Companion to Plato,* ed. R. Kraut. Cambridge, 1992.

Furley, D. J., and A. Nehamas, eds. *Aristotle's Rhetoric: Philosophical Essays.* Princeton, 1994.

Gaines, R. N. "Aristotle's Rhetorical Rhetoric." *Philosophy and Rhetoric* 19 (1986): 194–200.

Gallop, D. "Animals in the Poetics." *Oxford Studies in Philosophy* 8 (1990): 145–171.

Garver, E. "Aristotle's *Rhetoric* as a Work of Philosophy." *Philosophy and Rhetoric* 19 (1986): 1–22.

———. "Making Discourse Ethical: The Lessons of Aristotle's *Rhetoric.*" *Proceedings of the Boston Area Colloquium in Ancient Philosophy* 5 (1991): 73–96.

———. "Aristotle's *Rhetoric* on Unintentionally Hitting the Principles of the Sciences." *Rhetorica* 6 (1988): 381–393.

Genette, G. *Figures of Literary Discourse.* Trans. Alan Sheridan. New York, 1982.

Gignon, O. "Aristoteles, *Topik* 3.1–3." In *Aristotle on Dialectic,* ed. G. E. L. Owen. Oxford, 1968.

Gosling, J. C. B., and C. C. W. Taylor. *The Greeks on Pleasure.* Oxford, 1982.

Grayeff, F. "The Problem of the Genesis of Aristotle's Text." *Phronesis* 1 (1956): 106–108.

Green, L. D. "Aristotelian Rhetoric, Dialectic, and the Traditions of *Antistrophos.*" *Rhetorica* 8 (1990): 5–27.

Grimaldi, W. M. H. "Rhetoric and the Philosophy of Aristotle." *Classical Journal* 8 (1958): 371–375.

————. "Studies in the Philosophy of Aristotle's Rhetoric." *Hermes* (Wiesbaden) 100 (1972): 115–135.

————. "Rhetoric and Truth. A Note on Aristotle, *Rhetoric* 1355a21–24." *Philosophy and Rhetoric* 11 (1978): 173–177.

————. "*Sēmeion, Tekmerion, Eikos* in Aristotle's *Rhetoric.*" *American Journal of Philosophy* 101 (1980): 383–398.

Griswold, C. "Commentary on Garver." *Proceedings of the Boston Area Colloquium in Ancient Philosophy* 5 (1991): 97–105.

Hacking, I. *The Emergence of Probability: A Philosophical Study of Early Ideas about Probability, Induction and Statistical Inference.* Cambridge, 1975.

Halliwell, S. "Style and Sense in Aristotle's *Rhetoric.*" *Review of International Philosophy* 47 (1993): 50–69.

————. "Popular Morality, Philosophical Ethics and the *Rhetoric.*" In *Aristotle's Rhetoric: Philosophical Essays,* ed. D. J. Furley and A. Nehamas. Princeton, 1994.

Hamilton, W. *Lectures on Logic,* ed. H. L. Mansel and J. Veitch. Edinburgh, 1860.

Hardie, W. F. R. *Aristotle's Ethical Theory.* 2d ed. Oxford, 1980.

Hauser, G. A. "The Example in Aristotle's *Rhetoric:* Bifurcation or Contradiction?" *Philosophy and Rhetoric* 1 (1968): 78–90.

————. "Aristotle's Example Revisited." *Philosophy and Rhetoric* 18 (1985): 171–180.

Havelock, E. A. *The Literate Revolution in Greece and Its Cultural Consequences.* Princeton, 1982.

Hellwig, A. *Untersuchungen zur Theorie der Rhetorik bei Platon und Aristoteles.* Gottingen, 1973.

Hempel, C. G. *Aspects of Scientific Explanation and Other Essays in the Philosophy of Science.* New York, 1965.

Hill, F. I. "The *Rhetoric* of Aristotle." In *A Synoptic History of Classical Rhetoric,* ed. J. Murphy. New York, 1976.

————. "The Amorality of Aristotle's *Rhetoric.*" *Greek, Roman, and Byzantine Studies* 22 (1981): 133–147.

Hovland, C. *Communication and Persuasion.* New Haven, Conn., 1953.

Irwin, T. H. "Aristotle's Concept of Morality." *Proceedings of the Boston Area Colloquium in Ancient Philosophy* 1 (1985): 115–143.

————. "Ways to First Principles." *Philosophical Topics* 15 (1987): 109–134.

————. *Aristotle's First Principles.* Oxford, 1988.

Jaeger, W. *Aristotle, Fundamentals of the History of His Development.* Trans. R. R. Robinson. Oxford, 1934.

Johnstone, C. L. "An Aristotelian Trilogy: Ethics, Rhetoric, and the Search for Moral Truth." *Philosophy and Rhetoric* 13 (1980): 1–24.

Kantelhardt, A. "De Aristotelis *Rhetoricis.*" Dissertation, Gottingen, 1911. Reprinted in *Rhetorika, Schriften zur aristotelischen und hellenistichen Rhetorik,* ed. R. Stark (Hildesheim, 1968).

Kassel, R. *Der Text der aristotelischen Rhetorik: Prolegomena zu einer kritischen Ausgabe.* Berlin, 1971.

Kennedy, G. "Review of W. D. Ross, ed., *Aristotelis Ars Rhetorica.*" *American Journal of Philology* 82 (1961): 201–205.

———. *The Art of Persuasion in Ancient Greece.* Princeton, 1963.

———. *Classical Rhetoric and Its Christian and Secular Tradition from Ancient to Modern Times.* Chapel Hill, N.C., 1980.

———, ed. *The Cambridge History of Literary Criticism: Vol. 1, Clasical Criticism.* Cambridge, 1989.

Keyt, D., and F. D. Miller. *A Companion to Aristotle's Politics.* Oxford, 1991.

Kneale, W. *Probability and Induction.* Oxford, 1946.

Knuuttila, S. "Remarks on Induction in Aristotle's Dialectic and Rhetoric." *Review of International Philosophy* 47 (1993): 78–88.

Kosman, L. A. "Being Properly Affected: Virtues and Feelings in Aristotle's Ethics." In *Essays on Aristotle's Ethics,* ed. A. O. Rorty. Berkeley, 1980.

Kroll, W. "Rhetorik." In Pauly-Wissowa-Kroll's *Realencyclopadie der classischen Altertumswissenschaft,* Supplement 7, 1940.

Labarriere, J.-L. "L'Orateur politique face a ses constraintes." In *Aristotle's Rhetoric: Philosophical Essays,* ed. D. J. Furley and A. Nehamas. Princeton, 1994.

Lear, J. *Aristotle, the Desire to Understand.* Cambridge, 1988.

Leighton, S. R. "Aristotle and the Emotions." *Phronesis* 27 (1982): 144–174.

Levin, S. R. "Aristotle's Theory of Metaphor." *Philosophy and Rhetoric* 15 (1982): 24–46.

Lienhard, J. T. "A Note on the Meaning of *Pistis* in Aristotle's *Rhetoric.*" *American Journal of Philology* 87 (1966): 446–454.

Lloyd, G. E. R. *Magic, Reason and Experience.* Cambridge, 1979.

———. "The Theories and Practices of Demonstration in Aristotle." *Proceedings of the Boston Area Colloquium in Ancient Philosophy* 6 (1990): 371–401.

Loraux, N. *The Invention of Athens: The Funeral Oration in the Classical City.* Trans. A. Sheridan. Cambridge, Mass., 1986.

Lord, C. "The Intention of Aristotle's *Rhetoric.*" *Hermes* 109 (1981): 326–339.

———. *Education and Culture in the Political Thought of Aristotle.* Ithaca, 1982.

———. "On the Early History of the Aristotelian Corpus." *American Journal of Philology* 107 (1986): 137–161.

MacDowell, D. M. *The Law in Classical Athens.* Ithaca, 1978.

MacKay, L. A. "Aristotle, *Rhetoric,* III, 16, 11 (1417b12–20)." *American Journal of Philology* 87 (1986): 446–454.

Madden, E. H. "The Enthymeme, Crossroads of Logic, Rhetoric and Metaphysics." *Philosophical Review* 61 (1952): 368–376.

———. "Aristotle's Treatment of Probability and Signs." *Philosophy of Science* 24 (1957): 167–172.

Matson, P. P., P. Rollinson, and M. Sousa, eds. *Readings from Classical Rhetoric.* Edwardsville, Ill., 1990.

Mayhew, R. A. "Aristotle's Criticism of Plato's *Republic*: A Philosophical Commentary on *Politics* II 1–5." Ph.D. dissertation, Georgetown University, 1991.

McBurney, J. H. "The Place of the Enthymeme in Rhetorical Theory." *Speech Monographs* 3 (1936): 49–74.

McCall, M. *Ancient Rhetorical Theories of Simile and Metaphor.* Cambridge, Mass., 1969.

McDowell, J. "Virtue and Reason." *Monist* 62 (1979): 331–350.

———. "The Role of *Eudaimonia* in Aristotle's Ethics." In *Essays on Aristotle's Ethics,* ed. A. O. Rorty. Berkeley, 1980.

Merlan, P. "Isocrates, Aristotle, and Alexander the Great." *Historia* 3 (1954): 68–69.

Meyer, M. "Toward an Anthropology of Rhetoric." In *From Metaphysics to Rhetoric,* ed. M. Meyer. Dordrecht, 1989.

Miller, C. R. "Aristotle's 'Special Topics' in Rhetorical Practice and Methodology." *Rhetoric Society Quarterly* 17 (1987): 61–70.

Moraux, P. "La joute dialectique d'apres le huitieme livre des *Topiques.*" In *Aristotle on Dialectic,* ed. G. E. L. Owen. Oxford, 1968.

Moravcsik, J. M. E., ed. *Aristotle: A Collection of Critical Essays.* Garden City, N.J., 1967.

Murphy, J. J., ed. *A Synoptic History of Classical Rhetoric.* New York, 1972.

Natali, C. "Aristote et les methodes d'enseignement de Gorgias." In *Positions de la Sophistique,* ed. B. Cassin. Paris, 1986.

———. "Paradeigma: The Problems of Human Acting and the Use of Examples in Some Greek Authors of the Fourth Century B.C." *Rhetoric Society Quarterly* 19 (1989): 141–152.

———. "Due modi di trattare le opinioni notevole. La nozione di felicità in Aristotle, *Retorica* I 5." *Methexis* 3 (1990): 51–63.

———. "Opinioni, verità, prassi in Aristotele e la recente rivalutazione della retorica." In *Dimonstrazione, argomentazione dialettica, e argomentazione retorica nel pensiero antico,* ed. A. M. Battegazzore. Genoa, 1993.

Nehamas, A. "Pity and Fear in the *Rhetoric* and the *Poetics.*" In *Essays on Aristotle's Poetics,* ed. A. O. Rorty. Princeton, 1992.

Nikolaides, A. G. "Aristotle's Treatment of the Concept of *Proates.*" *Hermes* [Wiesbaden] 110 (1982): 414–422.

Nussbaum, M. C. *Aristotle's De Motu Animalium,* Essays 4 and 5. Princeton, 1978.

———. *The Fragility of Goodness: Luck and Ethics in Greek Tragedy and Philosophy.* Cambridge, 1986.

Nussbaum, M. C., and A. O. Rorty, eds. *Essays on Aristotle's De Anima.* Oxford, 1992.

Oates, W. J. "Evidence from the *Rhetoric.*" In W. J. Oates, *Aristotle and the Problem of Value.* Princeton, 1963.

Ober, J. *Mass and Elite in Democratic Athens: Rhetoric, Ideology, and the Power of the People.* Princeton, 1989.

Organ, T. W. *An Index to Aristotle in English Translation.* Princeton, 1949.

Owen, G. E. L. *Logic, Science and Dialectic: Collected Papers in Greek Philosophy,* ed. M. C. Nussbaum. London, 1986.

———, ed. *Aristotle on Dialectic.* Oxford, 1968.

Palmer, G. P. *The Topoi of Aristotle's Rhetoric as Exemplified in the Orators.* Chicago, 1934.

Patzig, G. *Aristoteles Politik*. Gottingen, 1990.

Pearson, L. *Popular Ethics in Ancient Greece*. Stanford, 1962.

Pease, A. S. "Things Without Honor." *Classical Philology* 21 (1926): 27–42.

Pelling, C., ed. *Characterization and Individuality in Greek Literature*. Oxford, 1990.

Price, R. G. "On the Place of Validity." *Philosophy and Rhetoric* 25 (1992): 341–350.

Raphael, S. "Rhetoric, Dialectic and Syllogistic Argument: Aristotle's Position in *Rhetoric* I–II." *Phronesis* 19 (1974): 153–167.

Reeve, C. D. C. *Practices of Reason: Aristotle's Nicomachean Ethics*. Oxford: 1992.

Richardson, H. "Desire and the Good in *De Anima*." In *Essays on Aristotle's De Anima*, ed. M. C. Nussbaum and A. O. Rorty. Oxford, 1992.

Ricoeur, P. *The Rule of Metaphor*. Trans. R. Czerny, with K. McLaughlin and J. Costello. Toronto, 1977.

Rist, J. M. *The Mind of Aristotle: A Study in Philosophical Growth*. Toronto, 1989.

Roberts, W. Rhys. "Notes on Aristotle's *Rhetoric*." *American Journal of Philology* 45 (1924): 351–361.

Roemer, A. "Zur Kritik der Rhetorik des Aristoteles." *Rheinisches Museum für Philologie* 39 (1884): 491–510.

Rogers, K. "Aristotle's Conception of *To Kalon*." *Ancient Philosophy* 13 (1993): 355–371.

Rorty, A. O. "The Place of Pleasure in Aristotle's Ethics." *Mind* 83 (1974): 481–497.

———. "Akrasia and Pleasure: *NE* Book 7." In *Essays on Aristotle's Ethics*, ed. A. O. Rorty. Berkeley, 1980.

———. "Aristotle on the Metaphysical Status of *Pathē*." *Review of Metaphysics* 38 (1984): 521–546.

———, ed. *Essays on Aristotle's Ethics*. Berkeley, 1980.

———. *Essays on Aristotle's Poetics*. Princeton, 1992.

Rosenfield, L. W. "The Doctrine of the Mean in Aristotle's *Rhetoric*." *Theoria* 31 (1965): 191–198.

Rosenmeyer, T. G. "Gorgias, Aeschylus, and *Apate*." *American Journal of Philology* 76 (1955): 225–260.

Ross, W. D. "Introduction." In *The Student's Oxford Aristotle*, ed. W. D. Ross. 6 vols. Oxford, 1942.

———. *Aristotle*. New York, 1964.

Ryan, E. E. "Aristotle's *Rhetoric* and *Ethics* and the Ethos of Society." *Greek, Roman and Byzantine Studies* 13 (1972): 291–308.

———. *Aristotle's Theory of Rhetorical Argumentation*. Montreal, 1984.

Salkever, S. G. *Finding the Mean: Theory and Practice in Aristotelian Political Philosophy*. Princeton, 1990.

Salmon, W. *Logic*. Englewood Cliffs, N.J., 1963.

Sandys, J. E. "Introduction." *The Rhetoric of Aristotle*, trans. R. C. Jebb. Cambridge, 1909.

Schofield, M. "Aristotle on the Imagination." In *Essays on Aristotle's De Anima*, ed. M. C. Nussbaum and A. O. Rorty. Oxford, 1992.

Schroder, J. "Ar. *Rhet.* A2. 1356a35–b10, 1357ia22–b1." *Hermes* [Wiesbaden] 113 (1985): 172–182.

Schutrumpf, E. "Some Observations on the Introductory Chapter of Aristotle's *Rhetoric.*" In *Aristotle's Rhetoric: Philosophical Essays*, ed. D. J. Furley and A. Nehamas. Princeton, 1994.

Sichirollo, L. *Storicita della dialettica antica.* Vicenza, 1965.

Solmsen, F. *Die Entwicklung der aristotelischen Logik und Rhetorik.* Berlin, 1929.

———. "Aristotle and Cicero on the Orator's Playing upon the Feelings." *Classical Philology* 33 (1938): 390–404.

———. "The Aristotelian Tradition in Ancient Rhetoric." *American Journal of Philology* 62 (1941): 35–50, 169–190. Reprinted in *Aristotle: The Classical Heritage*, ed. K. V. Erickson (Metuchen, N.J., 1974).

———. "Introduction." In *Aristotle's Rhetoric and Poetics*, trans. W. Rhys Roberts. New York, 1954.

———. "Review of R. Kassel's *Aristotelis 'Ars Rhetorica.'* " *Classical Philology* 74 (1979): 68–72.

Spengel, L. *Über die Rhetorik des Aristoteles.* Munich, 1851.

Sprute, J. "Der Zweck der aristotelischen Rhetorik." In *Logik, Ethik, Theorie der Geisteswissenschaften, XI. Deutscher Kongress für Philosophie Gottingen*, ed. G. Patzig, E. Scheibe, and W. Wieland. Hamburg, 1977.

———. *Die Enthymemtheorie der aristotelischen Rhetorik.* Gottingen, 1982.

———. *Die Entwicklung der aristotelischen Logik and Rhetorik.* Gottingen, 1982.

Stanford, W. B. *Greek Metaphor.* Oxford, 1936.

Stark, R., ed. *Rhetorika, Schriften zur aristotelischen und hellenistichen Rhetorik.* Hildesheim, 1968.

Sullivan, D. L. "The Ethos of Epideictic Encounter." *Philosophy and Rhetoric* 26 (1993): 113–133.

Taylor, A. E. *Aristotle.* Rev. ed. New York, 1955.

Thurot, Ch. *Etudes sur Aristote: Politique, Dialectique, Rhetorique.* Paris, 1860.

Urmson, J. O. "Aristotle on Pleasure." In *Aristotle: A Collection of Critical Essays*, ed. J. M. E. Moravcsik. Garden City, N.J., 1967.

Vahlen, J. "Zur Kritik der Rhetorik des Aristoteles." *Reinisches Museum für Philologie* 9 (1854): 555–567. Reprinted in his *Gesammelte Philologische Schriften*, vol. 1 (Leipzig, 1911).

———. "*Rhetorik* und *Topik:* Ein Beitrag zu Aristoteles' Rhetorik." *Rheinisches Museum für Philologie* 22 (1867): 101–110. Reprinted in his *Gesammelte Philologische Schriften*, vol. 1 (Leipzig, 1911).

Vlastos, G. "The Socratic Elenchus." *Oxford Studies in Ancient Philosophy* 1 (1983): 27–58.

Wardy, R. *The Chain of Change: A Study of Aristotle's Physics VII.* Cambridge, 1990.

Wartelle, A. *Lexique de la Rhétorique d'Aristote.* Paris, 1982.

Wedin, M. *Mind and Imagination in Aristotle.* New Haven, Conn., 1988.

Wieland, W. "Aristoteles als Rhetoriker und die Exoterischen Schriften." *Hermes* [Wiesbaden] 86 (1968): 323–346.

Wiggins, D. "Deliberation and Practical Reason." In *Essays on Aristotle's Ethics,* ed. A. O. Rorty. Berkeley, 1980.

Wigmore, J. H. *A Students' Textbook of the Law of Evidence.* Brooklyn, 1935.

Wikramanayake, G. H. "A Note on the *Pisteis* in Aristotle's *Rhetoric.*" *American Journal of Philology* 82 (1961): 193–196.

Williams, B. A. O., and E. Bedford. "Pleasure and Belief." *Proceedings of the Aristotelian Society* 33 (suppl.) (1959): 57–92.

Wills, G. *Lincoln at Gettysburg.* New York, 1992.

Wisse, J. *Ethos and Pathos from Aristotle to Cicero.* Amsterdam, 1989.

Wörner, M. H. "Enthymeme—Eine Rückgriff auf Aristoteles in systematischer Absicht." In *Rhetorische Rechtstheorie,* ed. O. Ballweg and T. M. Seibert. Freiburg, 1982.

———. *Das Ethische in der Rhetorik des Aristoteles.* Freiburg, 1990.

Worthington, I., ed. *Persuasion: Greek Rhetoric in Action.* London, 1994.

Yates, F. *The Art of Memory.* London, 1966.

Zeller, E. *Aristotle and the Earlier Peripatetics.* Trans. B. F. Costelloe and J. H. Muirhead. New York, 1897.

Ziolkowskki, J. *Thucydides and the Traditions of Funeral Speeches in Athens.* Arno, 1981.

CONTRIBUTORS

Jacques Brunschwig is Professor Emeritus at the Université de Paris-I.

M. F. Burnyeat is Laurence Professor of Ancient Philosophy at the University of Cambridge and a Fellow of Robinson College.

Christopher Carey is Professor of Classics at Royal Holloway, University of London.

John M. Cooper is Professor of Philosophy at Princeton University.

Troels Engberg-Pedersen is Professor of the New Testament at the University of Copenhagen.

Dorothea Frede is Professor of Philosophy at the Universität Hamburg.

Stephen Halliwell is Professor of Greek at the University of St. Andrews, Scotland.

T. H. Irwin is Susan Linn Sage Professor of Philosophy at Cornell University.

George A. Kennedy is Paddison Professor of Classics, Emeritus, at the University of North Carolina at Chapel Hill and Visiting Professor of Speech Communication at Colorado State University.

Stephen R. Leighton is Associate Professor of Philosophy at the Queen's University, Kingston, Canada.

Richard Moran is Professor of Philosophy at Harvard University.

Martha Craven Nussbaum is Professor of Law and Ethics at the University of Chicago.

C. D. C. Reeve is Professor of Philosophy and Humanities at Reed College.

Paul Ricoeur is Professor Emeritus at the Collège de France.

Amélie Oksenberg Rorty is Professor of the Humanities and the History of Ideas at Brandeis University.

Gisela Striker is George Martin Lane Professor of Philosophy and of the Classics at Harvard University.

Robert Wardy is a Fellow of St. Catharine's College, University of Cambridge.

ACKNOWLEDGMENTS

The editor and the University of California Press are grateful to:

Mount Holyoke College for a Faculty Research Grant.
Scott Ruescher and Rita Bashaw for their help in constructing the bibliography.

Archivio Fotografico dei Musei Capitolini di Roma for permission to use Antonio Idini's photograph of a Hadrianic relief, "Orazione Funeraria per l'Imperatrice Sabina" (inv. 832), on the cover.

Ny Carlsberg Glyptotek for permission to use the photograph of a Roman copy of a statue of Demosthenes attributed to Polyeuktos (cat. no. 436a).

John M. Cooper for permission to reprint a revised version of his "Rhetoric, Dialectic, and the Passions," *Oxford Studies in Ancient Philosophy* 11 (1993): 175–198.
Harvard University Press and the Loeb Classical Library for permission to reprint selections from Demosthenes, "The Son of Teisias against Callicles, Regarding Damage to a Piece of Property," *Vol. 6: Private Orations L–LVIII*, trans. A. T. Murray (Cambridge, Mass., 1964), pp. 167–181, 187 (oration 56: 1–26, 35); and from Thucydides, *Vol. 2: History of the Peloponnesian War, Books III and IV*, trans. Charles Forster Smith, rev. ed. (Cambridge, Mass., 1930; rpt. 1988), pp. 57–85 (3.36–3.48).
Oxford University Press, Inc., for permission to reprint selections from George A. Kennedy's supplementary essays to Aristotle, *On Rhetoric: A Theory of Civic Discourse*, trans. George A. Kennedy (New York, 1991), pp. 299–309. Copyright © 1991 by George A. Kennedy.
Princeton University Press for permission to reprint selections from M. F. Burnyeat, "Enthymeme: Aristotle on the Logic of Persuasion," in *Aristotle's Rhetoric: Philosophical Essays*, ed. David J. Furley and Alexander Nehamas (Princeton, 1994), pp. 3–55; Stephen Halliwell, "Popular Morality, Philosophical Ethics, and the *Rhetoric*," in *Aristotle's Rhetoric: Philosophical Essays*, ed. David J. Furley and

Alexander Nehamas (Princeton, 1994), pp. 211–230; and Martha Craven Nussbaum, "Emotions and Ethical Health," *The Therapy of Desire: Theory and Practice in Hellenistic Ethics* (Princeton, 1994), chapter 3, pp. 79–101.

Review of Metaphysics and Jude P. Dougherty for permission to reprint selections from Amélie Oksenberg Rorty, "The Directions of Aristotle's *Rhetoric*," *Review of Metaphysics* 46 (1992): 63–95.

Routledge for permission to reprint Christopher Carey, "Rhetorical Means of Persuasion," in *Persuasion: Greek Rhetoric in Action,* ed. Ian Worthington (London, 1994), pp. 26–45.

University of Toronto Press Incorporated and Paul Ricoeur for permission to reprint selections from Paul Ricoeur, *The Rule of Metaphor: Multi-disciplinary Studies of the Creation of Meaning in Language,* trans. Robert Czerny, with Kathleen McLaughlin and John Costello (Toronto, 1977), 9–43, 259–271. Copyright © 1977 by University of Toronto Press.

University Press of America (Lanham, Maryland) and John J. Cleary for permission to reprint selections from Amélie Oksenberg Rorty, "The Psychology of Aristotle's *Rhetoric*," *Proceedings of the Boston Area Colloquium in Ancient Philosophy* 8 (1992): 39–79.

Van Gorcum and Robert Sharples for permission to reprint selections from Stephen Leighton, "Aristotle and the Emotions," *Phronesis* 27 (1982): 144–174.

ABBREVIATIONS FOR ARISTOTLE'S WORKS

Cael.	*De Caelo*
Cat.	*Categories*
DA	*De Anima*
EE	*Eudemian Ethics*
Gen. An.	*De Generatione Animalium*
Gen. Cor.	*De Generatione et Corruptione*
Insomn.	*De Insomniis*
Interp.	*De Interpretatione*
Mem.	*De Memoria et Reminiscentia*
Met.	*Metaphysics*
Meteor.	*Meteorology*
MM	*Magna Moralia*
Motu	*De Motu Animalium*
NE	*Nicomachean Ethics*
Org.	*Organon*
Part. An.	*De Partibus Animalium*
Parva	*Parva Naturalia*
Phys.	*Physics*
Poet.	*Poetics*
Polit.	*Politics*
Post. Anal.	*Posterior Analytics*
Pr. Anal.	*Prior Analytics*
Rhet.	*Rhetoric*
Sensu	*De Sensu et Sensibilibus*
Somn.	*De Somniis*
Somno	*De Somno et Vigilia*
Soph. El.	*De Sophistici Elenchi*
Soph. Re.	*Sophistical Refutations*
Top.	*Topics*

Designer: U.C. Press Staff
Text: 10/12 Baskerville
Display: Baskerville
Compositor/Printer/Binder: Braun-Brumfield, Inc.